THE RESURRECTION OF THE BODY

in Western Christianity, 200–1336

Lectures on the History of Religions
Sponsored by the American Council of Learned Societies, New Series
Number 15

THE RESURRECTION OF THE BODY
in Western Christianity, 200–1336

Caroline Walker Bynum

COLUMBIA UNIVERSITY PRESS   NEW YORK

A portion of the costs of publishing this book
has been borne by a Centennial gift from Erwin Glikes,
a Trustee of the Press from 1989 to 1994.

Columbia University Press gratefully acknowledges
a gift from the National Endowment for the Humanities
toward the costs of publishing this work.

COLUMBIA UNIVERSITY PRESS

NEW YORK   CHICHESTER, WEST SUSSEX

Copyright © 1995 Columbia University Press

Library of Congress Cataloging-in-Publication Data

Bynum, Caroline Walker.
    The Resurrection of the body in Western Christianity, 200–1336 /
Caroline Walker Bynum.
        p.   cm. — (Lectures on the history of religions ; new ser., no. 15)
    Includes bibliographical references and index.
    ISBN 0–231–08126–x (alk. paper) ISBN 0–231–08127–8 (pbk.)
    1. Resurrection—History of doctrines—Early church, ca. 30–600.
2. Resurrection—History of doctrines—Middle Ages, 600–1500.
3. Body, Human—Religious aspects—Christianity—History of
doctrines—Early church, ca. 30–600.   4. Body, Human—Religious
aspects—Christianity—History of doctrines—Middle Ages, 600–1500.
I. Title.   II. Series.
BT872.B96   1995
236'.8'09—dc20   94–17299
                                                              CIP

∞

Casebound editions of Columbia University Press books are printed on permanent
and durable acid-free paper.

Printed in the United States of America
C   10 9 8 7 6 5 4 3 2 1
P   10 9 8 7 6 5 4

This volume is the fifteenth to be published in the series of Lectures on the History of Religions for which the American Council of Learned Societies, through its Committee on the History of Religions, assumed responsibility in 1936.

Under the program the Committee from time to time enlists the services of scholars to lecture in colleges, universities, and seminaries on topics in need of expert elucidation. Subsequently, when possible and appropriate, the Committee arranges for the publication of the lectures. Other volumes in the series are Martin P. Nilsson, *Greek Popular Religion* (1940); Henri Frankfort, *Ancient Egyptian Religion* (1948); Wing-tsit Chan, *Religious Trends in Modern China* (1953); Joachim Wach, *The Comparative Study of Religions*, edited by Joseph M. Kitagawa (1958); R. M. Grant, *Gnosticism and Early Christianity* (1959); Robert Lawson Slater, *World Religions and World Community* (1963); Joseph M. Kitagawa, *Religion in Japanese History* (1966); Joseph L. Blau, *Modern Varieties of Judaism* (1966); Morton Smith, *Palestinian Parties and Politics That Shaped the Old Testament* (1971); Philip H. Ashby, *Modern Trends in Hinduism* (1974); Victor Turner and Edith Turner, *Image and Pilgrimage in Christian Culture* (1978); Annemarie Schimmel, *As Through a Veil: Mystical Poetry in Islam* (1982); Peter Brown, *The Body and Society: Men, Women, and Sexual Renunciation in Early Christianity* (1988); and W. H. McLeod, *The Sikhs: History, Religion, and Society* (1989).

Contents

Illustrations

Preface: Acknowledgments and Methodological Musings

This book began as a series of lectures under the auspices of the American Council of Learned Societies' Committee on the History of Religions. My idea was to treat several moments in the Western tradition in which the doctrine of bodily resurrection was debated, challenged, and redefined by Christian thinkers and to situate those debates in the context of changing attitudes toward bodies, living and dead. I wanted to focus not primarily on the formulation of doctrine but on the ways in which theologians and philosophers argued—on the specific images, examples, and analogies they employed to express their ideas. The opportunity to deliver these lectures was thus an occasion to explore and illustrate several concerns, both methodological and substantive. Although beginning with a tiny detail—with a few images used by a few writers to explain and embellish a notion of stunning oddness—I intended both to tackle large questions about the meaning of embodiment in the Western tradition and to assert my continuing confidence in the enterprise (sometimes today challenged or rejected) of attempting to read texts from the past in what we used to call "their own terms." The book that has grown from the original lectures is larger and more complex than they were. But it retains both the focus on certain moments of tension or debate in the Western tradition and a concentration on images in lived and literary context.

My study is in one sense rather old-fashioned intellectual history. It is because I am interested in ideas themselves that I have read widely in modern philosophy of mind and have occasionally explained ancient arguments with a technical precision derived from modern discussions of identity and of the mind/body problem. Moreover, I have sometimes used rather "internalist" explanations for changes in ideas, accepting the notion that new concepts may be elaborated in response to intellectual deficiencies in earlier concepts. Although I do much to situate the theology I study against the background of what preachers said about ill and dying bodies and what ordinary people did when they mourned for and buried their dead, I begin my study of each period by reading and ruminating on the ostensible and explicit topics of quite technical philosophical and theological writing.

In another sense, however, my study moves beyond old-style intellectual history, for it argues that the linguistic trappings of texts are often more telling than the explicit arguments, particularly for a period such as the Middle Ages, which placed a high value on conforming to positions formulated, even canonized as "authority," in a distant past. I assume that the technical arguments of philosophical and theological treatises frequently betray the problems they *cannot* solve—social and psychological as well as intellectual problems—in the limiting cases, examples, and metaphors they use and in the ways they distort or misread conventional tropes and images. I hope I never reduce an argument to its function or its social context, or treat theology as ideology. But I do think ideas are sometimes elaborated and sometimes betrayed (in the several senses of the word *betray*) in the specific metaphors that clothe them.

I therefore move into the social and religious context of theology and philosophy via the examples, limiting cases, and images used by polemicists and theologians. My understanding of what constitutes context is not determined by a modern theoretical position but by the language of ancient writers themselves. If I move to a consideration of gender or power, birth or burial, money or food in an effort to situate the debates I study, I do so because the authors I am reading slip into analogies drawn from these aspects of human experience, and slip into such images especially at points of tension, confusion, fallacy, self-contradiction, or absurdity. It is, of course, possible that I misread both the texts I study and my own motives, but it is important to the method I employ that I start with the text before me and follow *its* metaphorical connections rather than choosing a modern theoretical construct that predetermines what is the context for what. Much about the shape of the book that follows depends on my determination not to reject but to *add* to old-fashioned intellectual history by digging below its surface, via metaphors and examples, to a surrounding context.

The shape of this book derives also from its origin as a series of lectures. It retains traces of its original nature as essays, intended to tell an interconnected story yet to stand each as a separate study in the relation of theological image to social and religious practice. It did not begin as a survey of doctrinal development, and I have not revised it to bring it closer to any pretense of complete coverage. The book that follows is still a study of the debates of the years around 200, 400, 1100, 1200, 1270, and 1330; no one can be more keenly aware than I how much it loses by omitting the early Middle Ages in which materialist conceptions of bodily resurrection were elaborated in new ways and connected with new subtlety to both eucharistic theology and relic cult. Had I filled in the years between Augustine and Peter Lombard, however, I would never have finished.

Nonetheless, the book has departed from its original guise in one important respect. The medieval section is now much longer than the patristic one. While this is disappointing for reasons of symmetry, it is necessary and perhaps even fortunate in other respects. Resurrection belief was less central, yet more pervasive, in medieval theology than in early Christian writing. The twelfth century did not produce the treatises specifically on resurrection characteristic of the years around 200, and it is sometimes difficult to determine whether the doctrinal pronouncements of councils and bulls in 1180, 1215, 1277, and so forth, are mere repetitions of earlier legislation or passionate defenses against current threat. In considering the topic of bodily resurrection in the high Middle Ages, it is less obvious where to look than it is in the patristic period; yet many more kinds of evidence are available, including a large amount of iconographic material. I have ranged more widely in medieval than in early Christian evidence and have argued at greater length not only because, as a medieval specialist, I know the period better but also because it is in general less well known and less easily knowable.

One final point about the focus of my study must be stated explicitly. This book is not about eschatology or about soul but about body. It is not a survey of concepts of heaven and hell—a topic to which much recent scholarship has been devoted. Nor is it a study of millenarianism or of mysticism. Although I pay attention along the course of my story to changing ideas about soul, to the emergence of a new eschatological place—purgatory—and to fundamental shifts in concepts of time and self involved in stressing the moment of individual death rather than the end of the world or the return of a messiah to that world, my focus is on what we learn about ideas of embodiment through those discussions that treat it most frontally. I have looked at what theologians argued about bodily resurrection in order to understand what they thought about body.

This book thus provides a neglected chapter in the new history of the body that is being written by historians such as Peter Brown, Danielle Jacquart, Lynn Hunt, Thomas Laqueur, Roy Porter, Marie-Christine Pouchelle, and Claude Thomasset. Whereas these historians all treat body as a locus of sexuality, I argue that for most of Western history body was understood primarily as the locus of biological process. Christians clung to a very literal notion of resurrection despite repeated attempts by theologians and philosophers to spiritualize the idea. So important indeed was literal, material body that by the fourteenth century not only were spiritualized interpretations firmly rejected; soul itself was depicted as embodied. Body was emphasized in all its particularity and physicality both because of the enormous importance attached to proper burial and because of the need to preserve difference (including gender, social status, and personal experience) for all eternity. But the "other" encountered in body by preachers and theologians, storytellers, philosophers, and artists, was not finally the "other" of sex or gender, social position or ethnic group, belief or culture; it was death. To medieval theorists, fertility was also decay; the threat lodged in body was change itself. To make body essential to survival and to person, it was necessary to redeem not only the difference of particularity but also the difference of nonbeing.

It may seem almost perverse to focus on one of the partners in eschatology, body, rather than soul, while arguing that medieval Christianity is not fundamentally dualistic. Nonetheless it is only by studying eschatological concepts of the body that we see how imprecise is the boundary between spiritual and material in most Christian writing and how psychosomatic is the medieval understanding of self. Soul has been much studied in the past three hundred years, while body qua physicality has until recently been ignored. Yet, for medieval thinkers, body far more than soul raised technical philosophical questions about identity and personhood. It does so for us as well. I have studied body in the context of questions concerning burial, social hierarchy, gender, digestion, fertility, and selfhood because medieval texts themselves make these connections. It is a fascinating payoff of my study that a focus on the neglected eschatological component, body, should (as I explain in my introduction) bring us far closer than do considerations of soul to contemporary obsessions about identity and survival.

I am grateful to the History of Religions Committee of the American Council of Learned Societies, especially to Judith Berling and Frank Reynolds, for the invitation to deliver these lectures. I am also grateful to my audiences at the University of California at Berkeley, the University of Chicago, Harvard University, Oberlin College, and Sarah Lawrence College, for their perceptive questions and attentive listening. I thank especially Daniel Boyarin, Laura King, Thomas Laqueur, Don McQuade, and Anne Middleton at Berkeley; Wendy Doniger, Clark Gilpin, and Frank Reynolds at Chicago; Clarissa Atkinson, Thomas Bisson, Michael McCormick, and Catherine Mooney at Harvard; Marcia Colish, Jeffrey Hamburger, Paula Richman, and Grover Zinn at Oberlin; David Bernstein and Pauline Watts at Sarah Lawrence. Mary Beth Lamb was efficient and gracious in helping with arrangements at a time of transition and confusion for the series. My students Nora Berend, James Jonas Hamilton, Bruce Holsinger, Susan Kramer, Victoria Velsor and Anders Winroth provided cheerful and energetic research assistance. Librarians Beth Juhl and Michael Stoller guided me through the intricacies of the Columbia University Library.

The topic of this book is enormous; virtually every aspect of social, religious, intellectual, and political life for more than a thousand years is relevant to its exploration. If I have had both the time and the audacity to explore many of these aspects, it is because of my extraordinary good fortune in receiving grants from the John D. and Catherine T. MacArthur Foundation and the Getty Center for the History of Art and the Humanities. I am more grateful than I can express to these foundations and to the anonymous nominators and selectors whose confidence in me made it all possible. Their trust at first weighed heavily on me, but I hope they will feel that, in the end, what they gave me was not only opportunity but also intellectual courage. I owe a great deal to my colleagues at the University of Washington and Columbia University, who graciously rejoiced in my good fortune when they might well have envied or carped at it; I thank especially Wilton Fowler and Jere Bacharach at Washington and Jack Garraty at Columbia who arranged for me to take two and a half of my five MacArthur years free from teaching responsibilities.

So many friends and colleagues have contributed to the ideas explored here that I cannot thank them all. But I offer special gratitude to Ann Douglas, Emily Flint, Jean Howard, Martha Howell, Lynn Hunt, Natalie Kampen, Steven Marrone, Fred Paxton, Nancy Roelker, Guenther Roth, Wim Smit, Robert Somerville, Tracey Strasser, and Judith Van Herik. Roberta Bondi, Peter Brown, Patrick Geary, Rachel Jacoff, Edward Peters, and Katherine Tachau read the entire manuscript; Elaine Combs-Schilling, Giles Milhaven, and John Magee each read several chapters; much of what clarity the argument attains is owing to the trenchant criticism they offered from their very different perspectives.

I dedicate this book to my father Andrew Jackson Walker and to my daughter Antonia, who shares his surname, not only because each of them has helped me to think with new intensity about issues of identity but also because my love for them lies at the heart of my confidence that there is, in some sense, survival and even resurrection.

THE RESURRECTION OF THE BODY
in Western Christianity, 200–1336

Introduction: Seed Images, Ancient and Modern

 IN HER autobiographical fragment *Family Memories*, Dame Rebecca West tells the following story from her childhood in London in the years around 1900.

I remember so well that autumn afternoon when my father came into the garden down the steps from the French window, and found me busy at a flowerbed which I had cleared from the yellow hands of leaves cast by the chestnut trees.

"What are you digging up?" he asked in alarm. . . .

"I'm digging up conkers," I said.

"I doubt if there'll be any conkers in that flower bed," he objected. "Lettie and Winnie have been clearing them off each morning because of the spring flowers. Are you sure you're not digging up bulbs?"

"I'm sure they're conkers," I told him. "I buried them myself."

"Why did you do that?"

"I am God," I explained, "and they are people, and I made them die, and now I am resurrecting them."

"Oh, you are, are you?" said my father, and sat down on the iron steps and watched me, drawing on his pipe. Presently he asked, "But why did you make the people die if you meant to dig them up again? Why didn't you just leave them alone?"

To that I replied, "Well, that would have been all right for them. But it would have been no fun for me."[1]

The incident reveals much about the impish but religiously sensitive young Rebecca and about the Anglo-Irish father she adored. It also reflects one important constant in theological discussions of resurrection from the early church to the late twentieth century: the resurrection of the body is always connected to divine power.[2] Whatever else the doctrine of universal resurrection has been said to reveal, those who refer to it always use it to underline the extraordinary power necessary to create and recreate, to reward and punish, to bring life from death. But what actually interest me in this story are the conkers: horse chestnuts—so called from the children's game in which each player swings a chestnut on a string to try to break one held by his or her opponent. For horse chestnuts are seeds; if left in the ground, they will sprout. Yet to the young Rebecca they are inert. In this childish fantasy of playing God, the chestnut-people are buried and resurrected exactly the same, and they are "the same" in two senses of the word *same*—that is, "identical" and "similar." The child is certain she digs up the identical chestnut she earlier buried in a given spot in the ground; the chestnut, that is, continues numerically the same. It retains identity through spatiotemporal continuity. And the chestnut the little girl digs up looks sim-

---

1. Rebecca West, *Family Memories: An Autobiographical Journey*, edited and introduced by Faith Evans (New York: Viking, 1987), p. 207. The incident is also recounted in Victoria Glendinning, *Rebecca West: A Life* (New York: Fawcett Columbine, 1987), pp. 19–20; see pp. 39, 197, and 222–24 for West's sense of God as cruel and her rather Manichean cosmology.

2. See J. A. MacCulloch, "Eschatology," in *Encyclopaedia of Religions and Ethics*, ed. J. Hastings (New York: Scribner, 1914), vol. 5, pp. 373–91; A. Michel, "Résurrection des morts," in *Dictionnaire de théologie catholique*, ed. A. Vacant et al. (Paris: Letouzey et Ané, 1909–50) [hereafter *DTC*], vol. 13, pt. 2, cols. 2501–71; Jaroslav Pelikan, *The Shape of Death: Life, Death, and Immortality in the Early Fathers* (New York and Nashville: Abingdon Press, 1961); H. Cornélis, J. Guillet, Th. Camelot, and M. A. Genevois, *The Resurrection of the Body: Themes of Theology* (Notre Dame: Fides, 1964); H. M. McElwain, "Resurrection of the Dead, Theology of," in *New Catholic Encyclopedia* (New York: McGraw-Hill, 1967), vol. 12, pp. 419–27, especially p. 425; Milton McC. Gatch, *Death: Meaning and Mortality in Christian Thought and Contemporary Culture* (New York: Seabury Press, 1969); Joanne E. McWilliam Dewart, *Death and Resurrection*, (Wilmington, Delaware: Michael Glazier, 1986); Gisbert Greshake and Jacob Kremer, *Resurrectio mortuorum: Zum theologischen Verständnis der leiblichen Auferstehung* (Darmstadt: Wissenschaftliche Buchgesellschaft, 1986); Helmer Ringgren, "Resurrection," in *The Encyclopedia of Religion*, ed. Mircea Eliade (New York: MacMillan, 1987), vol. 12, pp. 344–50; and H. Crouzel and V. Grossi, "Resurrection of the Dead," in *Encyclopedia of the Early Church*, ed. A. Di Berardino, trans. Adrian Walford (New York: Oxford University Press, 1992), vol. 2, pp. 732–33.

ilar; it has not decayed or sprouted. To the eye at least, it is materially and formally the same conker as before; it has the same bits arranged in the same way.[3]

The seed is the oldest Christian metaphor for the resurrection of the body.[4] It is the dominant metaphor in that text which, more than any other, has determined discussion of resurrection: 1 Corinthians 15.[5] Yet to Paul the seed is not young Rebecca's conker: inert material, put into the earth and lifted out of it by divine will. The seed of 1 Corinthians 15 grows: as "bare" grain it dies in the ground, then quickens to new life in a new body. If it is "the same" at all, it is "the same" in the sense of numerical identity, not in the sense of similar appearance. Paul wrote:

> For by a man came death; and by a man the resurrection of the dead.
> And, as in Adam all shall die, so also in Christ all shall be made alive.
> But every one in his own order; the first-fruits, Christ; then they that are of Christ. . . .
> But some man will say: How do the dead rise again? Or with what manner of body shall they come?
> Senseless man, that which thou sowest is not quickened, except it die first.
> And that which thou sowest, thou sowest not the body that shall be; but bare grain, as of wheat. . . .
> But God giveth it a body as he will; and to every seed its proper body.
> All flesh is not the same flesh; but, one is the flesh of men, another of beasts, another of birds, another of fishes.

3. The precision I here introduce into discussions of identity derives from modern philosophical distinctions; for references, see my "Material Continuity, Personal Survival, and the Resurrection of the Body: A Scholastic Discussion in Its Medieval and Modern Contexts," in *Fragmentation and Redemption: Essays on Gender and the Human Body in Medieval Religion* (New York: Urzone Publishers, 1991), pp. 239–97. The question of how modern and medieval concepts relate now seems to me somewhat more complex than I argued in that essay, for (as I suggest in chapters 7 and 8 below) the most sophisticated fourteenth-century conceptions emphasize material continuity less than do either earlier discussions or modern ones. But the general argument I make in "Material Continuity"—that modern discussion, both popular and philosophical, tends to require embodiment for personhood and to reject Docetist and spiritualist positions—still stands. See below nn. 25–28.

4. For an overview of Biblical images, see Cornélis et al., *Resurrection*, pp. 101–22; C. Brown, "Resurrection," in *The New International Dictionary of New Testament Theology* (Exeter: Paternoster Press, 1978), vol. 3, pp. 259–309; Paul Gooch, "Resurrection," in *A Dictionary of Biblical Tradition in English Literature*, ed. David L. Jeffrey (Grand Rapids, Mich.: Eerdmans, 1992), pp. 662–65. For the image of the seed in the Koran and in rabbinic Judaism, see below, chap. 1, nn. 9, 130, and 132.

5. The Pauline text was often glossed with John 12.24; see Gooch, "Resurrection," p. 663.

And there are bodies celestial and bodies terrestrial. . . .

. . . For star differeth from star in glory.

So also is the resurrection of the dead. It is sown in corruption; it shall
rise in incorruption.

It is sown in dishonor: it shall rise in glory. It is sown in weakness: it
shall rise in power.

It is sown a natural body: it shall rise a spiritual body. . . .

Now this I say, brethren, that flesh and blood cannot possess the kingdom of God; neither shall corruption possess incorruption.

Behold I tell you a mystery. . . .

In a moment, in the twinkling of an eye, at the last trumpet; for the
trumpet shall sound and the dead shall rise again incorruptible; and
we shall be changed.

For this corruptible must put on incorruption; and this mortal must
put on immortality.

And, when this mortal hath put on immortality, then shall come to
pass the saying that is written: Death is swallowed up in victory.

(1 Cor. 15.21–54, Douay translation)

These verses are enigmatic, especially if considered in the context of
other Pauline writings. Romans 6–8, for example, seems to suggest that
our resurrection has already begun through baptism.[6] Resurrection is
thus the rebirth of embodied person, and it begins in this life. In contrast,
2 Corinthians 5.1–10 may be read as implying that we discard body when
we exchange our earthly clothing or tabernacle for habitation in heaven.[7]
Whatever it is that survives in paradise, it is not (according to this interpretation) either accompanied or reclothed by anything physical or
material.

Gospel accounts of Jesus's resurrection clearly imply the same range
of interpretation, from exaggeratedly physicalist to exaggeratedly spiritualist. They stress the materiality of Jesus's body, which ate boiled fish
and honeycomb and commanded Thomas the Doubter "Handle and see"
(Luke 24.39, 41–43). Yet they also underline the radical transformation
of the resurrected Christ, who passed through closed doors, was some-

6. This is also the viewpoint found in John 6 and 11.

7. On the relationship of the passages in 1 and 2 Corinthians, see C. F. D. Moule,
"St. Paul and Dualism: The Pauline Conception of Resurrection," *New Testament
Studies* 13 (1965–66): 106–23, and Paul Gooch, *Partial Knowledge: Philosophical
Studies in Paul* (Notre Dame: University of Notre Dame Press, 1987), pp. 81–83.

times not recognizable to his beloved disciples, and bade his friend Mary Magdalen "Touch me not!" (Luke 24.16–30, 31, 36, and 51; John 20.14, 19, and 21.4).[8] Moreover, in the Gospel of Luke at least, the two interpretations exist side by side, as if to complement each other.

Twentieth-century readings of 1 Corinthians 15 have complicated the issue further. Dominated by the great interpretive insight of the Swiss theologian Oscar Cullmann, who argued that early Christian ideas drew on the Jewish notion of the resurrection of the person rather than on a Greek notion of immortality of soul, most recent studies have understood 1 Corinthians 15 as referring to restoration and redemption of the person as a psychosomatic unity.[9] Some interpretation, both theological and philosophical, has gone so far as to take the position that Paul did not mean "body" at all, but rather "self" or "community" or even "disembodied person" (i.e., a kind of soul).[10] (The careful philological re-

8. On the discrepancies in the Gospel tradition, see Peter Carnley, *The Structure of Resurrection Belief* (Oxford: Clarendon Press, 1987), pp. 16–19.

9. Oscar Cullmann, *Christ and Time: The Primitive Christian Conception of Time and History*, trans. F. Filson, 3d ed. (London: SCM, 1962); idem, *Unsterblichkeit der Seele oder Auferstehung der Toten?* (Stuttgart: Kreuz, 1964); idem, "Immortality and Resurrection," in *Immortality and Resurrection*, ed. Krister Stendahl (New York, 1965), pp. 9–53; idem, "Immortality of the Soul or Resurrection of the Dead? The Witness of the New Testament," in *Immortality*, ed. Terence Penelhum (Belmont, Calif.: Wadsworth, 1973), pp. 53–84. Both of the recent monographs on Jewish notions of resurrection criticize Cullmann's interpretation as underestimating the diversity in Jewish thought; see George W. E. Nickelsburg Jr., *Resurrection, Immortality, and Eternal Life in Intertestamental Judaism* (Cambridge, Mass.: Harvard University Press, and London: Oxford University Press, 1972); Günter Stemberger, *Der Leib der Auferstehung: Studien zur Anthropologie und Eschatologie des palästinischen Judentums im neutestamentlichen Zeitalter (ca. 170 v. Chr.–100 n. Chr.)* (Rome: Biblical Institute Press, 1972); and chap. 1, n. 9 below. Some criticism of Cullmann seems to me rather beside the point, focusing as it does on whether texts have any traces of Greek body-soul terminology. What Cullmann draws attention to is the difference between seeing the human being as a person that dies (and then sleeps) until an end of time and seeing this being as a spirit (a nonmaterial and nondying element) housed in physicality. Put this way, one immediately sees that the Christian concept as it emerges by the high Middle Ages is neither.

10. Twentieth-century philosophy has generally rejected any sort of dualism; on this point, see John Perry, *A Dialogue on Personal Identity and Immortality* (Indianapolis: Hackett, 1978) and Sydney Shoemaker and Richard Swinburne, *Personal Identity* (Oxford: Blackwell, 1984). (For further discussion, see below n. 28, and "Material Continuity," in *Fragmentation and Redemption*, pp. 244–52 and pp. 398–400 nn. 22–43.) This rejection is both the background to Cullmann's reading of early Christian texts as referring to a unitary person and a factor in the widespread acceptance of his views. Following Cullmann, theologians in mid-century tended to accept that *soma* in Paul meant "person," not "body," (and was therefore related to the Hebrew notion of *nephesh* or "individual"); dualistic ideas in the church fathers were thus taken to be a later and alien importation from Greek philosophy. Building on

search of Robert Gundry, which establishes that Paul in fact uses *soma* [body] to refer to a morally neutral physical body and not just to person, makes this position largely untenable.)[11] But whatever the Pauline oxymoron "spiritual body" means, two points are clear. First, to Paul, the image of the seed is an image of radical transformation: the wheat that sprouts is different from the bare seed; and that bare seed itself, while lying in the earth, undergoes decay. Second, the image asserts (perhaps without any intention on its author's part) some kind of continuity, although it does not explicitly lodge identity in either a material or a formal principle. The sheaf of grain is not, in form, the same as the bare seed, nor is it clear that it is made of the same stuff. It acquires a new, a "spiritual" body. But something accounts for identity. It is *that which is sown* that quickens. If *we* do not rise, Christian preaching is in vain, says Paul; something must guarantee that the subject of resurrection is "us." But "flesh and blood cannot inherit the kingdom." Heaven is not merely a continuation of earth. Thus, when Paul says "the trumpet shall sound . . . and we shall be changed," he means, with all the force of our everyday assumptions, both "we" and "changed."

At no period has Christian treatment of resurrection entirely abandoned the Pauline metaphor of the seed. But the seed metaphor is not the major image in patristic and medieval discussions of eschatology. The resurrection of the body is also described by theologians as the flowering of a dry tree after winter, the donning of new clothes, the rebuilding of a temple, the hatching of an egg, the smelting out of ore from clay, the reforging of a statue that has been melted down, the growth of the fetus from a drop of semen, the return of the phoenix from its own ashes, the reassembling of broken potsherds, the vomiting up of bits of shipwrecked bodies by fishes that have consumed them. These are all complex images, and they by no means imply in every case the same set of philosophical or theological assumptions. The growth of seed or semen or an egg implies numerical identity through spatio-temporal continuity

---

this, theologians R. Bultmann and J. A. T. Robinson argued that the Pauline *soma* could be read as "community" (R. Bultmann, *Theology of the New Testament*, vol. 1 [New York: Scribner, 1951] and J. A. T. Robinson, *The Body: A Study in Pauline Theology* [London: SCM, 1952]). In *Partial Knowledge,* the philosopher P. Gooch has recently argued that Paul can be understood as referring to "disembodied persons." Cullmann himself, it is important to note, never suggested that the resurrected person might be immaterial; see above n. 9.

11. Robert H. Gundry, *Soma in Biblical Theology with Emphasis on Pauline Anthropology* (Cambridge: Cambridge University Press, 1976).

but not necessarily material continuity. The reforging of a statue seems to imply continuity of material but may only mean that exactly the same shape (i.e., continuity of form) accounts for identity. The image of smelted ore suggests that continuity of self is explained by continuation of the same material bits at the level of atoms or particles, whether or not what is reforged has the same form.

This book is intended to explore the plethora of ideas about resurrection in patristic and medieval literature—the metaphors, tropes, and arguments in which the ideas were garbed, their context and their consequences.[12] I assume, as I have done elsewhere in my work, that close analysis of specific images in the context of other images, of theological doctrine, and of religious and social practice, can guide us to the unspoken assumptions, especially the unspoken inconsistencies and conflicts, at the heart of people's experience of the world.[13] There is a risk, of course, in such an approach. The examples and limiting cases I take as significant *are*, in a sense, both trivial and quaint; my choice of them may thus seem arbitrary or, worse yet, calculated to shock. But I have not chosen them in order either to condescend toward medieval naiveté or to titillate modern curiosity. If I examine, for example, metaphors of cannibalism, debates about eaten embryos, or lyrical expressions of desire, it is because I find them revealing of the case being made by medieval authors. Indeed I argue that they are revealing exactly *because* they are offhand and oblique, for images often carry speculation or in-

12. My study is thus clearly related to the recent interest among medievalists in death and eschatology. But with the exception of a few, highly technical studies in German (see chap. 6, nn. 2 and 10 below), recent work has mostly concentrated on the experience of the soul or on the nature of the afterlife as a place. See Robert Hughes, *Heaven and Hell in Western Art* (New York: Stein and Day, 1968); Philippe Ariès, *Western Attitudes Toward Death: From the Middle Ages to the Present*, trans. Patricia Ranum (Baltimore: Johns Hopkins University Press, 1974); idem, *The Hour of Our Death*, trans. Helen Weaver (Oxford: Oxford University Press, 1981); Jacques Le Goff, *The Birth of Purgatory*, trans. Arthur Goldhammer (Chicago: University of Chicago Press, 1984); Colleen McDannell and Bernhard Lang, *Heaven: A History* (New Haven: Yale University Press, 1988); Piero Camporesi, *The Fear of Hell: Images of Damnation and Salvation in Early Modern Europe*, trans. Lucinda Byatt (University Park, Penn.: Pennsylvania State University Press, 1991). Alan Bernstein of the University of Arizona is at work on a fundamental study of patristic and medieval conceptions of hell.

13. This was especially the method I employed in *Jesus as Mother: Studies in the Spirituality of the High Middle Ages* (Berkeley: University of California Press, 1982). For more discussion of some of these methodological issues, see my "In Praise of Fragments: History in the Comic Mode," in *Fragmentation and Redemption*, pp. 11–26; and "Writing Body History: Some Historiographical and Autobiographical Observations," in *Disability Studies Quarterly* 12, no. 2 (Spring 1992): 14–17.

tuition or hunch far beyond what the technical terms at the disposal of medieval theorists—terms such as *eidos, substantia, persona*—can bear.

My starting point is thus a simple observation about a single image. Medieval treatments of eschatology, both scholastic and nonscholastic, to a large extent ignore or explicitly reject the seed metaphor of 1 Corinthians 15 and related analogies to organic growth. When they do use organic images, they (like the young Rebecca West) manipulate them in such a way as to emphasize material continuity and reassemblage. In twelfth- and thirteenth-century texts, the resurrected body is a jewel lifted from mire, a rebuilt temple, a vessel recast or reassembled after wanton destruction. If it is occasionally said to have "flowered" or "germinated," the kernel from which it arises is bones or dust, and the body that reappears is similar in structure and continuous in matter with the body laid down in the grave. Rare are the ideas of fertility, rebirth, and metamorphosis that in the ancient Mediterranean world clustered around the vernal equinox—ideas that surface still today in tales of the Easter bunny and rituals of dyeing eggs. The *locus classicus* and the source for medieval discussion—distinctions 43–50 of the fourth book of Peter Lombard's theological textbook known as the *Sentences*—addresses questions of the material reconstitution of the body such as might have been asked by those Corinthians who challenged Paul: "With what manner of body shall they come?"

Change is not ignored by twelfth-century discussion, nor is the glorified body of the blessed understood as just like an earthly body. But the emphasis is on an identity guaranteed by material and formal continuity, not on an opportunity for growth, escape, or rebirth. The graces given to the saved are added on to a body reconstituted from its previous bones and dust. Change is the enhancement of what is, not metamorphosis into what is not. By the early thirteenth century, the standard exegesis of 1 Corinthians 15.42–44 ignores altogether the image of the seed. "Sown a natural body . . . [raised] a spiritual body" is taken to refer to one of four gifts or dowries (*dotes*) bestowed on body, the bride, by her soul or bridegroom.

Peter Lombard's discussion, which set the terms in which medieval theorists treated eschatology, turns out upon further investigation to be a pastiche of borrowings. These borrowings come mostly from Augustine's *City of God* and *Enchiridion*, with bits from Gregory, Julian of Toledo, Jerome, Hugh of St. Victor, Honorius Augustodunensis, and the school of Anselm of Laon thrown in. The Augustinian passages are all lifted from Augustine's late works or from medieval compilations that themselves borrow from Augustine's late works. Nor are the passages "typical" of Augustine's eschatology, which sometimes uses naturalistic metaphors of germination or seasonal change to see resurrection as dynamic process or employs the statue image so as to suggest a reforging in which full material continuity is not required.

It thus seems as if, during the lengthy and complex patristic debates over resurrection (focused in the late second and early fifth centuries), images that imply material and structural continuity—i.e., continuity of particles and members—became more important. These images were mediated to the high Middle Ages in part through compilations made in the sixth to ninth centuries—a process of mediation fascinating in its own right but one I do not have time to explore in this book.[14] Such images, carrying a powerful and materialist understanding of the afterlife, were then borrowed by twelfth-century schoolmen to focus their discussion of resurrection.

Images of reforged pots, reconstructed ships, and rebuilt temples could not, however, be the only images of the redemption promised by Christ, for they implied a host of philosophical and religious problems. If my body is reassembled from its dust, which of the many possible bodies will return—the two-year-old, the young adult, the old woman of seventy? And why is the return of body, which is a locus of pain (as well as pleasure), desirable? What makes it morally or religiously significant? Why is the reconstitution of my toe or fingernail a reward for virtue? Material continuity cannot *account for* self; it cannot *be* salvation. Neither philosophically nor soteriologically does it seem enough to argue that a person survives and is redeemed if his or her physical particles survive. Nor, in view of the biological change we see around us, is it easy to hold that particles can survive until a far-off resurrection. Theories and images that suggest survival of the identical body (*idem*

14. I intend to return in a subsequent study to the concept of resurrection found in Gregory the Great and the Carolingian theologians. The intense materialism of their ideas must be set in the context of Western insistence on the special place of relics in devotion, on the Eucharist as literally the body of Christ, and on the incorruption of the Virgin's body in death and her perpetual virginity; see chapter 2, nn. 3, 179, below. My decision to jump over the early Middle Ages in this book—a decision necessitated originally by the five-lecture format—is, however, a defensible one. The texts utilized by twelfth-century theologians are those of late antiquity. Although the selection of excerpts these theologians drew on owes something to early medieval intervention, the move to exaggeratedly materialist images and concepts had occurred already in Tertullian and then again in Jerome and the late Augustine. It therefore seems acceptable to treat the forging of such notions in antiquity as background to a study of their use in the high Middle Ages.

in numero) as continuity of shape or structure, even as locus of spiritual response or desire, seem necessary as well.

Yet the two great theologians who forged elegant and philosophically defensible solutions to the problem of what accounts for personal identity, Origen (d. ca. 254) and Aquinas (d. 1274), found those solutions condemned exactly because they obviated the need for body's material continuity. Origen's understanding of the potential of the seed metaphor for expressing both radical change and a nonmaterial solution to the identity issue clearly contributed to the metaphor's decline in popularity. Aquinas's suggestion (elaborated by Peter of Auvergne, John Quidort of Paris, and Durand of St. Pourçain) that soul as substantial form accounts for identity—a theory that makes continuity of the fleshly stuff of body unnecessary—encountered deep opposition between the 1270s and 1300. From the second to the fourteenth centuries, doctrinal pronouncements, miracle stories, and popular preaching continued to insist on the resurrection of exactly the material bits that were laid in the tomb. When, for example, the German mystic Mechtild of Magdeburg (d. ca. 1282) received a vision of John the Evangelist in heaven, she saw a reclining crystal figure with utterly particularized brown eyebrows. But John, the beloved disciple, chosen for the special reward of bodily assumption, was still asleep. Mechtild says he was "buried." Certainly John was John, Jesus's special friend; he was in heaven, and to be in heaven is salvation. Yet, in Mechtild's treatment, it is as if body has ascended to heaven apart from soul. We can understand Mechtild's theologically somewhat questionable vision only against the background of practices and beliefs that made the stuff and structures of earthly body integral to glorified body, and glorified body integral to self.[15]

The condemnations of Aquinas were removed in 1325, and the bull *Benedictus Deus* of 1336 can be seen in a general sense as a victory for the position that emphasizes soul. By the early fourteenth century, it was possible—at least for logicians and theologians—to think of survival and identity of self without continuity of material particles. But hundreds of years of insistence on bodily resurrection had come to locate in "soul" much of our commonsense understanding of "body." Souls were gendered and ranked, bearing with them the marks of occupation, status, religious vocation, even martyrdom. Moreover, mystical and theological writing in the years around 1300 spoke repeatedly of body as a bride, whose absence in heaven distracted or "retarded" soul from full

15. See below, chapter 8, pp. 337–41, especially nn. 74–78.

joy in God. Although soul now seemed to carry not only the particularity of self but also the pattern of body, it needed body as a place to express that particularity and pattern. Even Dante (d. 1321), who made technically correct use of the Thomistic notion that soul accounts for identity, depicted his beloved Beatrice in the last cantos of the *Divine Comedy* not simply as soul. Dante the poet gave to his eponymous self a vision of the heavenly choir in their resurrection bodies even though his poetic encounter was set before the end of time.[16]

Thus, the basic conclusion of my study of resurrection is that a concern for material and structural continuity showed remarkable persistence even where it seemed almost to require philosophical incoherence, theological equivocation, or aesthetic offensiveness. This concern responded to and was reflected in pious practices of great oddness; without it, such late medieval curiosities as entrail caskets, finger reliquaries, and miracles of incorrupt cadavers are inexplicable. The materialism of this eschatology expressed not body-soul dualism but rather a sense of self as psychosomatic unity. The idea of person, bequeathed by the Middle Ages to the modern world, was not a concept of soul escaping body or soul using body; it was a concept of self in which physicality was integrally bound to sensation, emotion, reasoning, identity—and therefore finally to whatever one means by salvation. Despite its suspicion of flesh and lust, Western Christianity did not hate or discount the body.[17] Indeed, person was not person without body, and body was the carrier or the expression (although the two are not the same thing) of what we today call individuality.

Behind these complex ideas and images lay fear as well as fascination. The lability and friability of fleshly matter was avoided more than espoused. If both scientific and theological speculation struggled (in their different ways) to assert that identity can survive flux, such speculation over the long course of the centuries I explore was fueled more by horror

16. See below, chapter 7, pp. 298–305, and Bynum, "Faith Imagining the Self: Somatomorphic Soul and Resurrection Body in Dante's Divine Comedy," in *Imagining Faith: Festschrift for Richard Reinhold Niebuhr,* ed. Wayne Proudfoot and Sang Hyun Lee, forthcoming.

17. This is the point I have made in a very different way in *Holy Feast and Holy Fast: The Religious Significance of Food to Medieval Women* (Berkeley: University of California Press, 1987). It is worth repeating here what I say in the epilogue to that study. To take Western asceticism seriously is not to glorify it. But it makes no sense to see a deep concern with disciplining and experiencing the body and a tendency to express religious response in it as hostility toward or discounting of the somatic. Medieval Christianity is not dualistic in either a Gnostic, a Manichean, or a Cartesian sense.

at decay than by pleasure in fertility. Indeed fertility—biological process itself—was often taken as decay. I try, as I move through ancient and medieval texts, to place their language and concerns in the context of particular bodily practices, especially those concerning that paradigm of biological process: the cadaver. But the ultimate context for the tradition I study is not a particular historical moment but a *longue durée* of terror. Whatever ultimate glory medieval thinkers hoped for, however much they came to understand physicality and individuality as necessary components of self, they did so at the expense of freezing much of biological process and sublimating much of sensual desire.[18] We might wish it otherwise. But I would point out that the putrefaction medieval people both denied and transcended is a fact from which we are not yet, in the late twentieth century, released.[19]

Of the so-called world religions, only those that emerged in the Middle East or in the Mediterranean basin—rabbinic Judaism, Christianity, Islam, and Zoroastrianism—teach the resurrection of the body.[20] And,

18. To study medieval notions of body as fertility and decay—even to admit (as we must) that medieval theorists treated body far more frequently as locus of biological process than as locus of sensuality—is not to deny the importance of the topic of body qua sexuality so popular in recent scholarship. The fundamental works on this topic are now Peter Brown, *The Body and Society: Men, Women, and Sexual Renunciation in Early Christianity* (New York: Columbia University Press, 1988) and Danielle Jacquart and Claude Thomasset, *Sexuality and Medicine in the Middle Ages*, trans. Matthew Adamson (Princeton: Princeton University Press, 1988). On the subject of body history generally, see the excellent review article by Roy Porter, "History of the Body," in *New Perspectives on Historical Writing*, ed. Peter Burke (University Park, Penn.: Pennsylvania State University Press, 1991), pp. 206–32; and my "Bodily Miracles and the Resurrection of the Body in the High Middle Ages," in *Belief in History: Innovative Approaches to European and American Religion*, ed. Thomas Kselman (Notre Dame: University of Notre Dame Press, 1991), pp. 68–106, especially nn. 1–14.

19. It is important to remember that during the centuries I cover in this book rabbinic Judaism offered an alternative understanding of the self as embodied—one in which the paradigmatic physical self was emphasized more as fertile than as decaying; see Daniel Boyarin, *Carnal Israel* (Berkeley: University of California Press, forthcoming). It is also important to note that this acceptance of fertility, and thus in a certain sense of the female body, occurred in a deeply patriarchal context.

20. Ringgren, "Resurrection," pp. 344–50. On Zoroastrianism, see McDannell and Lang, *Heaven*, pp. 12–14. Historian of religion Wendy Doniger reminds me that Hinduism has many stories of the return, reassemblage, and revival of the body, frequently after it has been eaten and digested; see her *Dreams, Illusion, and Other Realities* (Chicago: University of Chicago Press, 1984), pp. 103–8 and 207ff. Pertinent also is the story of Trisanku's attempt to take his body with him to heaven in Valmiki, *The Ramayana of Valmiki: An Epic of Ancient India*, ed. Robert P. Goldman and trans. S. I. Pollock, vol. 1 (Princeton: Princeton University Press, 1984), bk. 1, chaps. 56–69, pp. 231–57, esp. pp. 232–38; and the story of the revival of a god and a human after

of these, Christianity has defended the idea that body is crucial to self in the most strident and extensive, the most philosophically and theologically confused (and rich) form. It is in the images through which resurrection doctrine has been debated, explored, and preached that we see most clearly the assumption that formal and material continuity is necessary for the survival of body and that the survival of body is necessary for self. It is also in the images that the costs of these assumptions are revealed. I hope this book will help us to understand the reasons why they developed and why they survived as they did.

The story I tell is thus a story of ideas about body, placed against the background of persecution and conflict, gender and hierarchy, and of norms and rituals for the care of the dead. But as I said in my preface, resurrection belief is only part of the full narrative of changing soteriological and eschatological hopes in the centuries between 200 and 1336. Since resurrection must also be understood against the background of changing assumptions about the afterlife, the soul, and the end of time, it will be useful to summarize these briefly here.

During the patristic period, millenarian expectation gradually abated. The bodily resurrection hoped for by Jews and Christians in the centuries just before and after the beginning of the Common Era was supposed to occur in a reconstituted universe—a "new heaven and new earth." The heroes and heroines of 2 Maccabees 7 and the Book of Daniel, like those of early patristic writers such as Papias and to some extent Irenaeus, were thought to sleep in *refrigerium* (repose or refreshment) until God should return to reign over an earthly kingdom. Such hopes had not disappeared by the fifth century, but few any longer expected the millenial age to come soon, and eschatological yearning was increasingly focused on heaven, to which soul might go while the bones still reposed underground. Oscar Cullmann seems to be right that early Christians, like their Jewish contemporaries, thought primarily of a unitary person, which slept in the dust between death and resurrection, whereas by late antiquity Christian theologians held soul to be immortal but defined body as that which falls and must therefore rise again.[21]

---

the former has been eaten by the latter; see Wendy Doniger O'Flaherty, ed., *Hindu Myths: A Source Book* (Harmondsworth: Penguin, 1975), pp. 282–89. The presence of such stories in a religion that teaches transmigration of souls is a complex phenomenon; it is not, of course, the same as a doctrine of the resurrection of the body at the end of time.

21. See above, n. 9, and below chap. 2, n. 9.

Although the doctrine of a physical return at the end of time was not discarded by mainstream Christians, hope concentrated increasingly on the soul's ascent to heaven. By the thirteenth century, soteriological expectation focused on a judgment seen to come at personal death. The individual's status for all eternity was determined at the moment when soul and body separated rather than at the last trumpet when they rejoined. Moreover, the emergence of the doctrine of purgatory—a third (and provisional) time and place to which the soul might go after death for cleansing and penance—lodged change or development in the afterlife, which had been the realm of stasis.

Thus, to put it a little simplistically, the awakened resurrection body *was,* to early Christians, the person; to later theologians it was a component (albeit an essential component) of the person. Early Christians expected the body to rise in a restored earthly paradise, whose arrival was imminent. Most late medieval Christians thought resurrection and the coming of the kingdom waited afar off in another space and time.[22] Images of physical resurrection were therefore images of a very different event in the first century and the fourteenth. Yet not only did the doctrine of resurrection hold continued importance during the high Middle Ages when increased emphasis on soul, purgatory, and the moment of personal death might seem to be diverting attention from it; I shall also argue below, in ways too complex to summarize here, that body was as important eschatologically at the end of the Middle Ages as in the second century, because it had, so to speak, somatized soul. Although this book is a study of bodily resurrection, soul will come into the story as well—especially in the thirteenth and fourteenth centuries when the doctrine of purgatory provides separated soul with a place in the afterlife all its own.

Both the literalist interpretation of resurrection popular in rabbinic Judaism and the early church and the somatized souls that populated late medieval tales of purgatory seem to modern tastes quite strange. Contemporary Christians tend to reject the more picturesque elements of conventional eschatology. Although opinion polls tell us that most Americans believe in heaven, it is clear that the resurrection of the body is a doctrine that causes acute embarrassment, even in mainstream Christianity.[23] Thoughts of "life after death" still conjure up for most

22. Richard Landes is at work on a study of medieval millenarianism that may alter our views.

23. James Bowman, review of Garry Wills, *Under God: Religion and American Politics* (New York: Simon and Schuster, 1990), in *The Times Literary Supplement,*

people some notion of a disembodied soul flying, rather forlornly, through pearly gates and golden streets. Preachers and theologians (especially Protestants) pride themselves on avoiding soul-body dualism, but pious talk at funerals is usually of the departed person surviving as a vague, benign spirit or as a thought in the memories of others.

Yet analysis of current philosophical discourse and of contemporary popular culture suggests that Americans, like medieval poets and theologians, consider any survival that really counts to entail survival of body. However much late-nineteenth and early-twentieth-century theology, psychology, philosophy, and theosophy studied out-of-the-body experiences and transmigration of souls as clues to survival and identity, today's movies and television shows—no less than academic philosophical discussions of person—consider obsessively the problem of embodiment.[24] Movies such as *Maxie, Chances Are, Robocop, Total Recall, Switch, Freejack,* and *Death Becomes Her* gross millions; their drama lies in the suggestion that "I" am not "I" unless my body, with all it implies (sex and sexual orientation, race, temperament, etc.), survives.[25]

March 29, 1991, p. 11; and Timothy C. Morgan, "The Mother of All Muddles," in *Christianity Today* (April 5, 1993), pp. 62–66, on the current debate within evangelical theology between Murray J. Harris and Norman Geisler on the resurrection body. And see McDannell and Lang, *Heaven,* pp. 307–52, on contemporary views of heaven. My interpretation of contemporary concerns differs from that of McDannell and Lang because they look at images of heaven in those who write explicitly about heaven whereas what strikes me is the concern for survival of body (whether qua person or qua component of person) wherever that survival is located spatially and temporally (that is, in heaven, in space, or here on earth, in future time, present time, or some alternative temporal dimension).

24. See Mark Silk, "The Limits of Faith," a review of Thomas Simmons, *The Unseen Shore: Memories of a Christian Science Childhood* (Boston: Beacon, 1991), in *The New York Times Book Review,* August 4, 1991, p. 14. On the Spiritualist movement in the early years of this century and its response to death, see David Cannadine, "War and Death, Grief and Mourning in Modern Britain," in *Mirrors of Mortality: Studies in the Social History of Death,* ed. Joachim Whaley (New York: St. Martin's Press, 1981), pp. 187–242, especially pp. 227–31 and 234.

25. Two particularly good examples from television are the September 25, 1987, episode of *Max Headroom,* "Deities," in which Christian ideas about resurrection of the body are parodied, and the May 25, 1991, episode of *Star Trek: The Next Generation,* "The Symbiant," in which the transfer of consciousness (represented as a physical creature similar to a clam) results in inextricable entanglement of body and consciousness. A number of other episodes of *Star Trek* and indeed the entire series *Quantum Leap* can be seen as exploring the problem of who the resulting person is when a consciousness body-hops. The ending of the film *Jesus of Montreal* makes the equation of resurrection (or bodily survival) and organ transplant absolutely explicit: the actor who plays Jesus brings sight to the blind, life to the dead, through the transplant of his eyes and heart. Even in a movie such as the gentle fantasy *Truly, Madly, Deeply* (in some ways a conventional ghost story), it is the physical presence of the lover who returns from the dead that causes the problem. These stories are very dif-

Medical sociologists, such as Fox and Swazey, must struggle to provide guidelines for organ transplants exactly because donors and recipients often assume that "self" is being transferred—an assumption on which much recent pulp fiction and journalism eagerly capitalizes.[26] The best of contemporary philosophy of mind tests its understanding of "self" in thought experiments no less odd than medieval considerations of risen umbilical cords and fingernails. As Nancy Struever has said, such philosophical discussions are "stuffed . . . with bizarre examples: there are split personalities, amoebalike fissions of the body, nuclear fusions of minds, brain transfusions—a monstrous zoo seems to be the proper arena of discovery."[27] These discussions tend to conclude that knowing, surviving, being, must be embodied.[28] Thus they struggle still with the difficulty of asserting joy, identity, and survival in the face of flux and putrefaction.

I do not intend to take my exploration of eschatology beyond the 1330s. I shall not trace visions of heaven beyond Dante's, understandings of identity beyond Durand's, theories of encounter with God beyond the controversy over the beatific vision and the yearnings of thirteenth-century women mystics. The images of dowries and jewels with

---

ferent from conventional tales of mediums summoning back spirits that have "crossed over." In such accounts the spirits reveal personality by their memories or by verbal quirks; body is not an issue.

This is not to suggest that all recent popular treatments of the survival question stress the necessity of body. The high-grossing movie *Ghost* uses a traditional ghost-story plot.

26. See Renée C. Fox and Judith P. Swazey, *The Courage to Fail: A Social View of Organ Transplants and Dialysis*, 2d ed. (Chicago: University of Chicago Press, 1974), pp. 27–32; and Bynum, *Fragmentation and Redemption*, pp. 244–52 and 397–400 nn. 18–43. For the emphasis in recent psychology on the "embodied-ness" of knowing, see George Lakoff, *Women, Fire, and Dangerous Things: What Categories Reveal about the Mind* (Chicago: University of Chicago Press, 1987) and Mark Johnson, *The Body in the Mind: The Bodily Basis of Meaning, Imagination, and Reason* (Chicago: University of Chicago Press, 1987).

27. Nancy Struever, "Philosophical Problems and Historical Solutions," in *At the Nexus of Philosophy and History*, ed. B. Danenhauer (Athens, Georgia: University of Georgia Press, 1987), p. 76. For a wonderful compendium of such thought experiments, see Douglas R. Hofstadter and Daniel C. Dennett, eds., *The Mind's I: Fantasies and Reflections on Self and Soul* (New York: Basic Books, 1981).

28. See Stuart F. Spicker, "Introduction," in *The Philosophy of the Body: Rejections of Cartesian Dualism*, ed. Spicker (Chicago: Quadrangle Books, 1970), pp. 3–23, a defense of the argument that body switching is logically impossible and that it is more correct than not to say that a person is his or her body. For a discussion of recent work in the philosophy of mind, see Jerry Fodor, "The Big Idea: Can There Be a Science of Mind?" *The Times Literary Supplement*, July 3, 1992, pp. 5–7, which argues that all current positions are materialist "for much the same reason that Churchill gave for being a democrat: the alternatives seem even worse."

which I conclude point forward toward great literary works, such as *The Pearl*, which I shall not treat. But one must stop somewhere. And the fourteenth century images with which I end are, of course, completely different (in their specific details if not in what they ultimately conjure up) from the images of space travel and mind transplant crucial to the present discussion of survival. Another set of essays would be necessary to take the story from the fourteenth to the early twentieth century. I merely suggest here that, whether or not it has always been the case in the modern centuries, it is certainly today true that considerations of self and survival take the body with impassioned seriousness. We face utterly different problems from the schoolmen and artists of the Middle Ages. Yet the deep anxiety we feel about artificial intelligence and organ transplants, about the proper care of cadavers, about the definition of death—an anxiety revealed in the images of bodily partition and reas-semblage that proliferate in our movies and pulp fiction—connects us more closely than most of us are aware to a long Western tradition of abstruse discussion of bodily resurrection.

Part One

THE PATRISTIC
BACKGROUND

One

Resurrection and Martyrdom: The Decades Around 200

 IN THE EARLY THIRD CENTURY, Tertullian of Carthage, the first great theologian to write in the Latin language, penned a polemical treatise on the resurrection of the flesh. Although his style is highly rhetorical and embellished—indeed even turgid and difficult—he speaks of last things explicitly as well as in images. Tertullian asserts:

> If God raises not men entire, He raises not the dead. For what dead man is entire. . . . What body is uninjured, when it is dead? . . . Thus our flesh shall remain even after the resurrection—so far indeed susceptible of suffering, as it is the flesh, and the same flesh too; but at the same time impassible, inasmuch as it has been liberated by the Lord.[1]

Such forceful and explicit arguments were necessary. At the end of the second century the resurrection of the body had become a major topic of controversy among Christians and between Christians and their pa-

1. For the full quotation see n. 88 below. A portion of this chapter was delivered as my presidential address at the meeting of the American Catholic Historical Association in San Francisco, on January 8, 1994. It will appear in a forthcoming issue of the *Catholic Historical Review* under the title "Images of Bodily Resurrection in the Theology of Late Antiquity."

gan critics. The idea and the images in which it was expressed had a long history.

It is not my intention in this book to give a complete survey of doctrine or metaphor, nor do I want to suggest theories about the origins of resurrection belief, which lie well before the decades of Jesus's earthly life. In the chapters that follow, I shall focus on various moments in Christian history when the idea of bodily resurrection—already introduced into theological discussion by the Pauline epistles—was debated, challenged, reaffirmed, and/or redefined. Nonetheless, I cannot begin my study of the late second century, which saw the first sustained explorations of the place of body in eschatology, without a brief consideration of the metaphors in which first- and second-century Christians spoke of resurrection. Although I shall focus in this chapter on the decades around 200—decades in which the analogies that became crucial for medieval theological discourse were first elaborated—I must discuss changes in images and assumptions that had crept into theology between the years in which Paul answered the Corinthians and those in which Tertullian faced, with very different arguments, both the intellectual threat of Gnosticism and the physical threat of martyrdom.

Early Metaphors for Resurrection: Fertility and Repetition

Some sort of return of the dead (at least the righteous dead) from Sheol was a staple of Jewish apocalyptic literature in the first centuries before and after the start of the Common Era.[2] The resurrection of Jesus was, for early Christians, both the central element in their teaching and an animating event for their mission. Resurrection of the dead, whether or not it was clearly connected to a millennial age and material recreation of the universe, thus seems to have been assumed by the sub-Apostolic Fathers, who mention it frequently.[3] Our earliest texts also suggest that

2. Arthur Marmorstein, *Studies in Jewish Theology*, ed. J. Rabbinowitz and M. S. Lew (London: Oxford University Press, 1950), pp. 145–61; Samuel G. F. Brandon, *The Judgement of the Dead: An Historical and Comparative Study of the Idea of a Post-Mortem Judgement in the Major Religions* (London: Weidenfeld and Nicolson, 1967), pp. 56–75; Nickelsburg, *Resurrection, Immortality*; Joseph Ntedika, *L'évocation de l'au-delà dans la prière pour les morts* (Louvain and Paris: Nauwelaerts, 1971), pp. 15–21; Stemberger, *Der Leib*; Shaye J. D. Cohen, *From the Maccabees to the Mishnah* (Philadelphia: Westminster, 1987), pp. 23, 89, 91–103, 220–24.

3. Angelo P. O'Hagan, *Material Re-Creation in the Apostolic Fathers* (Berlin: Akademie-Verlag, 1968); A. H. C. Van Eijk, " 'Only That Can Rise Which Has Previously Fallen': The History of a Formula," *Journal of Theological Studies*, n.s. 22 (1971): 517–

resurrection was sometimes spiritualized and that there was sometimes opposition to the idea, of the sort we find considered in 1 Corinthians 15.

As many scholars have noticed, the metaphors for resurrection in this early literature are naturalistic images that stress return or repetition: the cycle of the seasons, the flowering of trees and shrubs, the coming of dawn after darkness, the fertility of seeds, the return of the phoenix after five hundred years. The point of the metaphors is to emphasize God's power and the goodness of creation. If the Lord can bring spring after winter or cause the grape to grow from the vine, if he can create Adam from dust and cause the child to emerge from a drop of semen, surely he can bring back men and women who sleep in the grave.[4]

In these early texts, resurrection (which is, in some cases, the advent of an earthly paradise) is connected to the most extraordinary fertility. Papias, for example, says:

A time is coming when vineyards spring up, each having ten thousand vines . . . and every grape, when pressed, will yield twenty-five measures of wine. And when anyone of the saints takes hold of one of their clusters, another cluster will cry out: 'I am better. Take me. . . .' In like manner, a grain of wheat will grow ten thousand heads . . . and every grain will yield ten pounds of clean, pure flour; but the other fruit trees, too, as well as seeds and herbs, will bear in proportions suited to each kind; and all animals, feeding on these products of the earth, will become peaceable and friendly to each other, and be completely subject to man.[5]

The author of the fourth similitude of the text known as *The Shepherd of Hermas* explains that in the world to come the righteous will be like living trees that flower.[6] The Apocalypse of Peter, drawing explicitly on 1 Corinthians 15 as well as on Ezekiel 37.1–14, Revelation 20.13, and Enoch 61.5, says the righteous will reign in a region outside the earth,

---

29; Ton H. C. Van Eijk, *La résurrection des morts chez les Pères Apostoliques* (Paris: Beauchesne, 1974). The old article by H. B. Swete, "The Resurrection of the Flesh," *Journal of Theological Studies* 18 (1917): 135–41, is still useful.

4. In addition to the works cited in n. 3 above, see Dewart, *Death and Resurrection*; Michel, "Résurrection"; and R. M. Grant, "The Resurrection of the Body," *Journal of Religion* 28 (1948): 120–30 and 188–208.

5. The text, Papias Frag. 1.2–3, is close to 2 Baruch 29.5; it is quoted in O'Hagan, *Material Re-Creation*, p. 39.

6. Hermas, *Le Pasteur*, ed. and trans. Robert Joly, Sources chrétiennes [hereafter Sc] 53 (Paris: Éditions du Cerf, 1958), pp. 220–23; and see Van Eijk, *Résurrection des morts*, pp. 86–98.

where blossoms will never fade and fruit will abound. Beasts and fowl will give up all the flesh they have devoured, and God will do again what he did at creation—that is, join bone to joint, joint to sinew, and sinew to nerve, clothing all with flesh and skin and hair. The house of Israel will flower like the fig tree, and we shall live again and bear fruit, restored by the earth like the dry grain of wheat once entrusted to it.[7] The letter sent by Clement of Rome to the Christians at Corinth about 96 C.E. exhorts its readers to compare themselves to a tree or vine and uses a plethora of natural images for resurrection, especially the metaphor of the seed (which is explicitly said to die and decay in the earth before rising) and the analogy of the phoenix (which, in Clement's account, does not immolate itself but rather rises as a worm from its own decaying flesh).[8]

These texts of the late first and early second century depend in their resurrection imagery on Pauline metaphors of seeds and first fruits. But they do not mean at all what Paul means. By and large these images stress not the change from corruption to incorruption, or the difference between natural and spiritual, between the dry, dead seed and the flowering sheaf; rather, they make the world to come a grander and more abundant version of this world. Expressing enormous optimism about the goodness of creation, they draw such a close analogy between resurrection and natural change that they either make resurrection a process set in motion by the very nature of things, or they make *all* growth dependent on divine action.

Like 1 Corinthians, these texts suggest a kind of continuity but attribute it to no principle. Identity is not yet an explicit issue. As is true in some contemporary Jewish texts and in later rabbinic material as well, the natural metaphors mean that the whole person returns—

7. M. R. James, ed., *The Apocryphal New Testament* (Oxford: Clarendon Press, 1924; fifth impression with corrections 1953), pp. 508–21. For further discussion of the imagery of the Apocalypse of Peter, see below, p. 291. For a good general discussion of the genre of apocalypse, see Bernard McGinn, *The Presence of God: A History of Western Christian Mysticism*, vol. 1: *The Foundations of Western Mysticism* (New York: Crossroad, 1991), pp. 10–11. An exception to the extraordinarily organic images usual in early second-century material is the apocryphal "Acts of John," a Docetist text, which is basically an account of a series of resurrections from the dead (seen as an extension of healing). It uses images of breaking and reassembling stones and jewels to talk of restoration of the world. See M. R. James, ed., *Apocryphal New Testament*, Latin version, paragrs. 14–17, pp. 257–60.

8. Clement of Rome, *Epître aux Corinthiens*, ed. and trans. A. Jaubert, Sc 167 (Paris: Éditions du Cerf, 1971), chaps. 23–26 and 38, pp. 140–45 and 162–65. The letter shows a deep corporate sense; resurrection of the body here is in some sense a resurrection of community of the sort Gatch has emphasized in *Death: Meaning and Mortality*.

changed, perfected, pure, and fertile like a green tree, but still himself or herself.[9] Both Christian and Jewish texts reproduce and refute the carping of critics. They admit that we do not see cadavers rise up whole. But the answer they give to this objection is the answer of divine power: we cannot doubt that God raises the dead, for in his creation he does many wondrous things. Neither in philosophical argument nor in image is the question yet raised: What would account for the "me-ness" of the "me" that returns? If we look more closely at the use of the phoenix analogy in 1 Clement, we can see quite clearly that identity is not at stake. To later authors, the phoenix immolates itself and rises from the ashes the same bird, as the three children survived in the fiery furnace (Daniel 3.19–24, 91–94). To Clement, the bird dies; its flesh decays; a worm or larva is born from this putrefying flesh and feeds on it. Eventually the worm grows wings and flies to the altar of its triumph carrying the bones of the old bird, now stripped clean. Modern readers immediately worry that there appear to be two birds in this story; how therefore is it an analogy to resurrection? But Clement focused not on what ac-

9. In addition to the works cited in the introduction, n. 9, above, see George Foot Moore, *Judaism in the First Centuries of the Christian Era: The Age of Tannaim* (1927; reprint, Cambridge, Mass.: Harvard, 1966), vol. 2, pp. 287–392. Jewish texts of the first century of the Common Era displayed many different notions of resurrection and immortality, some predicated on a Greek soul-body dualism. See, for example, *The Biblical Antiquities of Philo*, trans. M. R. James (London: SPCK, 1917), bk. 3, chaps. 10, 51, 64, pp. 81–82, 217–18, 240; on problems with the text and its attribution see Stemberger, *Der Leib*, pp. 97–117. Basic texts on resurrection from the Babylonian Talmud (i.e., third to sixth century) retain naturalistic images, including burgeoning grain, for resurrection (although with a strong sense of material continuity rather than transformation). See Babylonian Talmud (Soncino edition), Kethuboth, 111b:

R. Hiyya b. Joseph said: A time will come when the just will break through the soil. . . . And they will blossom out of the city like grass of the earth (Ps. 72.16). . . . R. Hiyya b. Joseph said further: The just in the time to come will rise [apparelled] in their own clothes. This is deduced *a minori ad majus* from a grain of wheat. If a grain of wheat that is buried naked sprouts up with many coverings how much more so the just who are buried in their shrouds.

See also Babylonian Talmud, Sanhedrin, 91a–91b, which uses the grain analogy, the idea of the potter repairing his pot, the building analogy, and a parallel to the birth of a mouse from the earth (a kind of spontaneous generation), and says explicitly that we rise with our defects, which are then repaired. Somewhat later rabbinic material argues explicitly that bone is the element of material continuity and elaborates the embryological analogy for resurrection; Ezekiel 37 is used to suggest that God puts us back together in a process that parallels (or reverses the temporal order of) the way the fetus grows in the first instance. See Midrash Rabbah (3d ed. New York: Soncino Press, 1983): Leviticus Rabbah 18.1 (Zunz dates to mid-seventh century), Genesis Rabbah 28.3 (Zunz dates to sixth century), Ecclesiastes Rabbah (probably seventh century), 1.7.6–8, 3.2.1–2, 3.14.1–15, 5.8.5, 12.5.

Resurrection of the dead was one of the three core beliefs of rabbinic Judaism; see Cohen, *From Maccabees to Mishnah*, p. 220.

counts for the survival of the individual but on the return of phoenix from death and putrefaction. For him, individual, community, and generic nature fuse.[10]

By the end of the second century, however, things had changed. "Resurrection" was no longer simply a minor theme of discussion and apologetics; it became a major element in disputes among Christians and in Christian defenses against pagan attack. Entire treatises were devoted to the topic. Resurrection not of "the dead" or "the body" (*soma* or *corpus*) but of "the flesh" (*sarx* or *caro*) became a key element in the fight against Docetism (which treated Christ's body as in some sense unreal or metaphorical) and Gnosticism (which carried "realized eschatology" so far as to understand resurrection as spiritual and moral advance in this life and therefore as escape from body). The statements of belief for catechumens that appeared around 200 and soon after gave rise to various local creeds (one of which, the old Roman, became the so-called Apostles' Creed) required assent to the doctrine of *resurrectio carnis* not *mortuorum* or *corporum*.[11]

Scholars have tended to explain the acute concern for resurrection of a palpable, fleshly body as owing to several factors: first, the model of Jesus's own resurrection; second, the impact of millenarianism (which assumes reanimation, at least of the righteous); third, the conflict with Gnosticism (which saw flesh as evil and therefore Christ's body as in some sense unreal); fourth, Christian adoption of Hellenistic dualist anthropology (which assumes an opposition of soul and body and therefore forces the question "what survives?"); fifth, the emerging governmental structure of the third-century church (which was enhanced by the stress on difference or hierarchy entailed in the stress on body).[12] None of these arguments is wrong. But I would suggest that all except the fifth (to which I shall return in my next chapter) are to some extent tautological.[13] One cannot say that Christians taught literal, material, fleshly

10. See n. 8 above. On the phoenix myth, see Van Eijk, *Résurrection des morts*, pp. 53–55; O'Hagan, *Material Re-Creation*, p. 95.

11. See J. N. D. Kelly, *Early Christian Creeds*, 3d ed. (New York: David McKay, 1972). According to Crouzel and Grossi, "Resurrection," p. 732, the belief of the early creeds contains three components: first, resurrection will occur "on the last day" at Christ's second coming; second, everyone will rise; third, the body will be both identical and new.

12. See J. G. Davis, "Factors Leading to the Emergence of Belief in the Resurrection of the Flesh," *Journal of Theological Studies*, n.s. 23 (1972): 448–55; John G. Gager, "Body-Symbols and Social Reality: Resurrection, Incarnation, and Asceticism in Early Christianity," *Religion* 12, no. 4 (1982): 345–64.

13. The fifth argument, which has been made most clearly by Gager, "Body-Symbols," using the interpretations of Elaine Pagels in *The Gnostic Gospels*, is ultimately Durkheimian and functionalist. See below, chap. 2, pp. 109–113.

resurrection because Christ rose thus; there is a full range of interpretation of Jesus's resurrection in the Gospels and Paul, and if Christians chose eating the honeycomb rather than the *noli me tangere, that* choice requires explanation. One cannot argue that refutation of Gnosticism or Docetism required bodily resurrection, for the question is exactly: why *not* Docetism? Why did powerful voices among the Christians of the later second century reject more spiritual or gnostic interpretations of the resurrection body? A consideration of the images used for bodily resurrection may help us to understand more clearly what was at stake.

The Second Century: Organic Metaphors and Material Continuity

Careful study of the images used in major treatises on resurrection from the years around 200 reveals that the seed metaphor continues but in a sense almost antithetical to Paul's. It often now expresses a rather crude material continuity. Such continuity, sometimes understood as the continuity of particles or atoms, is both a defense against and an articulation of the threat of decay, which is understood as absorption or digestion. Nutrition (eating or being eaten—especially cannibalism) is the basic image of positive change and the basic threat to identity. The context of such images, indicated explicitly by the texts themselves, is persecution and an attendant concern for the cadavers of the martyred. Ignatius of Antioch, writing about 110 on his way to execution, already expresses much that is at the heart of such assumptions. Unconcerned in any technical sense with material continuity, Ignatius sees fragmentation and digestion by the beasts as the ultimate threat and thus as that over which resurrection is the ultimate victory—so much so that his endangered body becomes the eucharist and, as Van Eijk has argued, his martyrdom *is* resurrection.[14] Desiring complete destruction so that his followers will not be endangered by the need to bury his remains, Ignatius nonetheless says he will rise "with" or "by" his chains, which are, he says, "pearls"—an odd phrase, which seems to mean that whatever it is that rises, Ignatius's suffering is never to be lost because it is *who he is.*[15] He writes:

14. Van Eijk, *Résurrection des morts,* pp. 99–126; see also Virginia Corwin, *St. Ignatius and Christianity in Antioch* (New Haven: Yale University Press, 1960), pp. 171–72. For a sensitive argument that Ignatius's response is "mystical" in a broad meaning of the term, see McGinn, *Foundations of Mysticism,* p. 101.

15. Van Eijk, *Résurrection des morts,* pp. 122–23.

Let me be the food of wild beasts through whom it is possible to attain God; I am the wheat of God, and I am ground by the teeth of wild beasts that I may be found pure bread; instead, entice the wild beasts that they may become my tomb and leave behind no part of my body that when I fall asleep, I may burden no one.

. . . Fire and cross, and packs of wild beasts, the wrenching of bones, the mangling of limbs, the grinding of my whole body, evil punishments of the devil—let these come upon me, only that I may attain Jesus Christ.[16]

By the later part of the second century, the concerns Ignatius expresses here are couched in much more crudely literal language.

Two of the earliest second century treatises on the resurrection—Justin Martyr's and Athenagoras's—have been labeled apocryphal by some scholars partly because of the presence in them of certain technical scientific arguments (such as the chain consumption argument) that concentrate on material continuity and are sometimes thought to be later.[17] I accept these treatises, both because they are accepted in some recent scholarly considerations and because my study of metaphors establishes that the technical arguments at stake are compatible precisely

16. Ignatius, *Epistle to the Romans*, in Ignatius of Antioch and Polycarp of Smyrna, *Lettres: Martyre de Polycarpe*, ed. and trans. P. T. Camelot, Sc 10, 3d ed. (Paris: Éditions du Cerf, 1958), pp. 130–33; William R. Schoedel, trans., *Ignatius of Antioch: A Commentary on the Letters . . .*, ed. H. Koester et al. (Philadelphia: Fortress Press, 1985), pp. 175 and 178. The textual tradition of Ignatius is very complicated, but the letter to the Romans is accepted as genuine; see J. Ruis-Camps, *The Four Authentic Letters of Ignatius, the Martyr* (Rome: Pontificium Institutum Orientalium Studiorum, 1980); and Schoedel, *Ignatius*. These words are later quoted by Irenaeus, *Adversus haereses*, bk. 5, chap. 28, parag. 4; see Irenaeus of Lyons, *Contre les hérésies*, bk. 5, ed. and trans. Adelin Rousseau, Sc 152–153 (Paris: Éditions du Cerf, 1969), vol. 2, pp. 360–63, and Schoedel, *Ignatius*, p. 1 n. 2.

17. On Athenagoras, see R. M. Grant, "Athenagoras or Pseudo-Athenagoras," *Harvard Theological Review* 47 (1954): 121–29; Athenagoras, *Legatio and De Resurrectione*, ed. and trans. William R. Schoedel (Oxford: Clarendon Press, 1972), pp. xxv–xxxii; L. W. Barnard, "Athenagoras: *De Resurrectione*: The Background and Theology of a Second Century Treatise on the Resurrection," *Studia Theologica* 30 (1976): 1–42; idem, "The Authenticity of Athenagoras' *De Resurrectione*," *Studia patristica* 15 (1984): 39–49; Miroslav Marcovich, "On the Text of Athenagoras, *De Resurrectione*," *Vigiliae Christianae: A Review of Early Christian Life and Language* 33 (1979): 375–82; Crouzel and Grossi, "Resurrection," p. 732; and P. Nautin, "Athenagoras," in *Encyclopedia of the Early Church*, vol. 1, p. 95. On the authenticity of Justin Martyr's treatise, see Pierre Prigent, *Justin et l'Ancien Testament: L'Argumentation scriptuaire du traité de Justin contre toutes les hérésies comme source principale du Dialogue avec Trypho et de la Première Apologie* (Paris: Librairie Lecoffre, 1964), pp. 28–67 passim. The best treatments of the whole debate over chain consumption and cannibalism are Grant, "The Resurrection of the Body," pp. 120–30 and 188–208; and Barnard, "Athenagoras: Background."

in their materialism with contemporary treatises known to be authentic. With the exception of some fragments recently attributed to one "Josipos" and the *Epistle to Rheginos* (both of which see resurrection as largely spiritual), the major discussions of the resurrected body from the second half of the second century use predominantly organic metaphors but express through them material continuity.[18]

The Acts of Paul (from about 160), which explicitly understands resurrection both as victory over persecution and as an extension of—if you will, an extreme case of—healing, rejects the idea that resurrection can be generational continuity. Paul's opponents suggest that we "rise" in our children. But Paul (in the so-called Third Letter to the Corinthians, inserted here) objects: resurrection is of *all* of our particular flesh; it carries with it our identity.[19] We are seeds, which are cast into the earth bare and rot and then rise again with bodies. But we also rise as Jonah did from the whale, without a single hair or eyelash lost (the reference to Luke 21.18 is clear), and the flesh that rises bears the specific marks of our suffering as Christ's bore his wounds.[20] Similarly Justin Martyr, writing before 165, uses predominantly organic metaphors, which stress the glories of growth and the power of God to effect it.[21] To Justin, we are mud or seeds or semen; we must be healed and purified as we progress toward God. Thus the bodies we receive back in resurrection are formally complete (i.e., they possess all their organs); their defects are repaired.[22] Although Justin at times displays an almost Pau-

18. See the fragment formerly attributed to Hippolytus, in Pierre Nautin, *Hippolyte et Josipe: Contribution à l'histoire de la littérature chrétienne du troisième siècle* (Paris: Éditions du Cerf, 1947), text on pp. 108–27; and see P. Nautin, "Hippolytus," in *Encyclopedia of the Early Church*, vol. 1, pp. 383–85. On the *Epistle to Rheginos*, see W. C. Van Unnik, "The Newly Discovered Gnostic 'Epistle to Rheginos' on the Resurrection," *Journal of Ecclesiastical History* 15 (1964): 141–52 and 153–67; Malcolm Lee Peel, *The Epistle to Rheginos: A Valentinian Letter on the Resurrection: Introduction, Translation, Analysis, and Exposition* (London: SCM Press, 1969); and Elaine Pagels, "The Mystery of the Resurrection," *Journal of Biblical Literature* 93 (1974): 276–88.

19. Acts of Paul, Coptic MS version, parags. 14, 39, in M. R. James, ed., *The Apocryphal New Testament*, pp. 275 and 280.

20. "Third Corinthians," especially parags. 5 and 24–35, in James ed., *The Apocryphal New Testament*, pp. 288–92.

21. Prigent, *Justin*, argues that Justin's treatise may be part of his *Syntagma* against heresy, cut off and circulated separately, or it may be a rewriting of the relevant section by Justin himself. Justin's *Dialogue with Trypho*, chap. 80, would support the second suggestion; see the *Dialogue*, chap. 80, in *Justini Philosophi et Martyris Opera*, vol. 1, pts. 1 and 2, ed. J. K. T. Otto (Wiesbaden: M. Sändig, 1876; reprint 1969), pp. 287–93.

22. Justin Martyr, *I Apology*, chaps. 18–21, 51–52, and 66, in *Justini Opera*, ed. Otto, vol. 1, pt. 1, pp. 56–69, 136–43, 180–83; *Dialogue with Trypho*, chaps. 80–81 and 107 in ibid., pt. 2, pp. 286–97 and 382–85; and *On Resurrection*, in *Justini Opera*,

line sense of change, stressing that God must transform corruption into incorruption,[23] he also shows a concern for formal and material continuity and confronts directly the identity issue, asserting that what dies and what rises must be the same.[24] He points out that even the pagan philosophers believe the body decays only into indestructible bits, which can be reassembled.[25] And when he explains how God collects again our decomposed members, his images become inorganic ones. God reassembles or recasts us as a statue is reforged or as a jeweler, making a mosaic, puts the stones back together again.[26]

Theophilus of Antioch and Athenagoras, writing between 180 and 200, move closer toward understanding survival as material continuity and employ arguments taken from the science of their day to support this.[27] Theophilus explains resurrection in mechanical, inorganic metaphors as the remolding of a vessel so that flaws are removed.[28] When he deploys the standard set of organic metaphors, found in 1 Clement, he changes them so as to convey a sense that a material element persists; in his account, true biological change becomes inexplicable.[29] Theophilus admits that a seed in the earth rots away before it rises as a sheaf of wheat and that trees produce fruit out of what is invisible, but then he goes on to explain that this is like seeds surviving in bird droppings so that plants appear to rise where none were sown—a surprising (and, to

vol. 2, ed. Otto, 3d ed. (Jena: Fischer, 1879), pp. 210–49. And see Prigent, *Justin*, pp. 35–40. Unlike Justin's other writings, the *Dialogue with Trypho* has strong millenarian overtones.

23. See especially *I Apology*, chaps. 19 and 52, pp. 60–63 and 138–43; and *On Resurrection*, chaps. 4 and 10, pp. 222–23 and 244–49.

24. *On Resurrection*, chap. 4, pp. 222–23. Ibid., chap. 3, pp. 216–23, stresses (as does Jerome later) that all organs will rise, but they will not necessarily be used in heaven.

25. *On Resurrection*, chap. 6, pp. 228–33.

26. Ibid. Justin's pupil Tatian, whose work has been seen as Encratite and/or Gnostic, gives similar arguments. Tatian says that even if we are consumed by fire, annihilated in the water, torn to pieces by wild beasts, or vaporized, we are still "stored up" in God's treasury (Tatian, *Oratio ad Graecos and Fragments*, ed. and trans. Molly Whittaker [Oxford: Clarendon Press, 1982], chap. 6, p. 11). Tatian holds that the soul is dissolved at death along with the body; resurrection therefore will be of both.

27. Grant, "Resurrection," pp. 188–199; Barnard, "Athenagoras: Background," pp. 6–12; idem, "Authenticity," pp. 46–49.

28. Theophilus of Antioch, *Ad Autolycum*, bk. 2, chap. 26, ed. and trans. by Robert M. Grant (Oxford: Clarendon Press, 1970), pp. 68–69. And see R. M. Grant, "Theophilus of Antioch to Autolycus," *Harvard Theological Review* 40, no. 4 (1947): 227–56.

29. Theophilus, *Ad Autolycum*, bk. 1, chaps. 8 and 13, pp. 10–13 and 16–19. Theophilus also, however, makes use of organic metaphors in a way reminiscent of 1 Clement; see bk. 2, chaps. 14 and 15, pp. 48–53.

us, distasteful) analogy that stresses the continuity of a particular bit rather than the mystery of development.[30] Moreover he also says that resurrection is like the recovery of an invalid from sickness. The sick man's flesh disappears, and we know not where it has gone; he recovers and grows fat, and we cannot tell whence comes the new flesh. We say it comes from meat and drink changed into blood, but how can such change occur? It is really the work of God. The argument is so bizarre that one distinguished modern scholar has simply dismissed it as "confused."[31] But we need to note that it not only protects a constant core as the body that rises; it also protects that core against change via digestion as natural process—that is, against destruction by eating or being eaten. Because recovery from illness is a miracle, the invalid's new flesh does not come from food but from God. Thus it appears to be significant both that Theophilus associates resurrection and incorruption with God's care for the bones of the dead (a hard, material element of continuity)[32] and that cannibalism (digestion of human flesh by another human) is a crucial issue to him. Theophilus sees cannibalism as the most heinous charge leveled against Christians, and the most heinous act performed by pagans.[33]

In their discussions of resurrection, both Theophilus and Justin Martyr respond to the attacks of pagan critics, who find the idea not only ludicrous but also revolting. Who would want to recover his body? asked the pagan Celsus. Corpses are revolting—worse than dung.[34] These pagan attacks clearly found an echo in ordinary Christian congregations. Although an early third-century text warned Christians against what it saw as Jewish notions of corpse pollution,[35] two late second-century apologists, Tatian and Aristides, agreed that decaying matter was disgusting, even polluting.[36] By the time of Athenagoras's treatise on the

30. *Ad Autolycum*, bk. 1, chap. 13, pp. 16–19.
31. Grant, "Theophilus," pp. 229–34.
32. Theophilus, *Ad Autolycum*, bk. 2, chap. 38, pp. 96–99.
33. Theophilus, *Ad Autolycum*, bk. 3, chaps. 4–5 and 15, pp. 102–5 and 118–21.
34. See Grant, "Resurrection," pp. 188–99.
35. See Arthur Vööbus, trans., *The Didascalia Apostolorum in Syriac*, Corpus scriptorum christianorum orientalium [hereafter CSCO], 402, Scriptures Syri 176 (Louvain: Corpus SCO, 1979), vol. 1, pt. 2, pp. 242–47. The Syriac text is made from a Greek original of the third, possibly the early third, century.
36. For Tatian, see *Oratio*, chaps. 16–18, 20, and 25, pp. 33–39, 41, 47–49; and above n. 26. For Aristides, see Apology, chaps. 4–5 and 12, in R. Harris, ed., *The Apology of Aristides* (Haverford, Penn.: reprinted from Texts and Studies: Contributions to Biblical and Patristic Literature, Cambridge: Cambridge University Press, 1891), pp. 38–39 and 45–46. Aristides tackles explicitly the argument that earth is good because fertile; he argues rather that it is defiled both by excrement and by

resurrection in the closing years of the second century, the very choice of images seems to protect "body" from any suggestion that it might rot or even experience absorption, either above or in the earth. Athenagoras distrusts organic process. He struggles to establish, through scientific (basically Galenic) arguments, that body can be broken and reassembled precisely because it does *not*, through biological mechanisms, absorb anything else.[37]

To Athenagoras, the issue of identity is crucial.[38] In chapter 25 of the *De resurrectione* he argues that the human being cannot be said to exist when body is scattered and dissolved, even if soul survives. So "man" must be forged anew. But it will not be the same man unless the same body is restored to the same soul: such restoration is resurrection.[39] Resurrection must involve change, says Athenagoras. Indeed resurrection *is* change; judgment is not the basic reason for resurrection because not all are judged but all rise.[40] We have grown from soft seeds into bones and sinews, and we will decay again into the materials we came from.[41] Therefore, for dead and dissolved bodies to rise, they must be changed into incorruptible bodies; otherwise they would merely dissolve again.[42] But Athenagoras mentions the growth and decay of seeds and semen only to argue against such processes as paradigms of resurrection. Resurrection is the reassemblage of parts. God "can reunite fragments" that have been entirely "resolved . . . into their constituents." And he can do this because he knows what nature must be reconstituted and he knows where the particles are. Even if the body has been divided up among many animals who have eaten and digested it and "united [it] with their bodies," and even if these animals have then decayed or been eaten, God can still find the human bits to reassemble.[43]

corpses. He, however, praises the concern of both Christians and Jews for burying the dead (chaps. 14–15, pp. 48–50). In his text, ambivalence about natural process is thus very clear. On Aristides, see Johannes Quasten, *Patrology*, vol. 1: *The Beginnings of Patristic Literature* (Utrecht and Antwerp: Spectrum Publishers, and Westminster, Maryland: Newman Press, 1950), p. 171f., and P. Siniscalco, "Aristides," in *Encyclopedia of the Early Church*, vol. 1, pp. 72–73.

37. Barnard, "Athenagoras: Background," pp. 11–16; and idem, "Authenticity."
38. Barnard, "Athenagoras: Background," pp. 14–23.
39. Athenagoras, *De resurrectione*, in *Legatio and De Resurrectione*, ed. and trans. Schoedel, chap. 25, parag. 2, pp. 146–47.
40. Ibid., chaps. 12 and 14, pp. 114–19 and 120–23.
41. Ibid., chap. 17, pp. 128–31. It is important to note how much change Athenagoras admits here. He argues that the form of man is not inscribed on the seed or on the elements into which the cadaver dissolves; cf. the discussion of Origen and Gregory of Nyssa in chapter 2 below.
42. Ibid., chap. 15, pp. 122–27.
43. Ibid., chaps. 2–11, 25, pp. 90–113 and 146–49.

This is the famous chain consumption argument that becomes increasingly important in the third century. And Athenagoras understands it in its full complexity. For the problem is not really the attacks of carrion beasts or of worms in the grave: the problem is digestion and cannibalism. If meat and drink do not merely pass through us but become us, there will be too much matter for God to reassemble; on the other hand, if people really eat other people, even God may have trouble sorting out the particles. Athenagoras handles the problem by asserting, in chapters 5–7, that most food and drink pass through our bodies without really becoming them. God has designated certain foods as suitable for each species, and only those can be absorbed. Athenagoras then moves on, in chapter 8, to the astonishing argument that it is impossible for human flesh to absorb human flesh. He even asserts that we can find empirical verification for this in the fact that cannibals lose weight and waste away.[44]

Although some scholars have seen Athenagoras's earlier treatise, the *Plea* or *Legatio*, as springing from a fundamentally different set of philosophical assumptions, the work—at least on this issue—adumbrates exactly the same argument. Defending Christians against charges of cannibalism, Athenagoras argues, as did Theophilus, that pagans are the real cannibals. He calls them "fish," for fish were understood in ancient natural philosophy to be both promiscuous and cannibalistic.[45] Christians cannot be cannibals, asserts Athenagoras, for how can someone who believes in resurrection "offer himself as a tomb" to "bury within himself" those who will rise again?[46] Thus Athenagoras assumes that even the eaten dead must rise. But by assimilating stomach and grave and identifying cannibalism as the fundamental threat to identity,[47] he makes resurrection more a victory over physiological process than a fulfillment of it.

44. Ibid., chaps. 5–8, pp. 98–109. For pagan arguments that cannibalism is impossible, see Grant, "Resurrection," p. 196 n. 109.

45. Athenagoras, *Legatio*, trans. Schoedel, chap. 34, parag. 3, pp. 82–83, and Athenagoras, *Embassy for Christians and Resurrection of the Dead*, trans. Crehan (Westminster, Maryland: Newman Press, 1956), p. 166 n. 298. For an example of ancient opinion, see Hesiod, *Works and Days*, l. 277, in *Hesiod: The Homeric Hymns and Homerica*, trans. H. G. Evelyn-White, Loeb Classical Library (London: Heinemann, 1914), p. 22.

46. Athenagoras, *Legatio*, chaps. 12–13 and 35–37, pp. 24–29 and 82–87.

47. Ibid., p. 85: "What man who believes in a resurrection would offer himself as a tomb for bodies destined to arise? For it is impossible at one and the same time to believe that our bodies will arise and then eat them as though they will not arise, or to think that the earth will yield up its dead and then suppose that those whom a man had buried within himself will not reclaim their bodies."

Irenaeus and Tertullian: The Paradox of Continuity and Change

Scholars have always viewed the three great treatments of resurrection from the years around 200—Irenaeus's *Adversus Haereses*, Tertullian's *De resurrectione carnis*, and Minucius Felix's *Octavius*—as deeply "materialist," as driven by a powerful need to assert the palpable, fleshly quality of the body that will be rewarded or punished at the end of time. And it is true that all three of these authors sometimes employ metaphors that suggest, as did those of Athenagoras and Theophilus, that the resurrection body is exactly the same material body we occupy on earth, that is, that material continuity accounts for identity. Irenaeus, for example—without addressing the chain consumption argument or associating continuity with the survival of particles or bits—nonetheless discusses the identity question and lodges identity squarely in continuity of matter. He asserts that what falls must rise,[48] and draws analogies to the three children in the fiery furnace and Jonah in the whale.[49] He explains that, in the process of grafting, substance lasts although quality changes, and in healing, the withered and the healthy hand is the same hand. Indeed he treats resurrection as a special case of bodily restoration and underlines human materiality by stressing that the missing eye Christ repaired with a paste of dust was created from that dust.[50] Minucius Felix also explicitly addresses the identity issue. The pagan interlocutor in his dialogue asks the Christian: with what body do you rise? It cannot be the *same* body, for your former body has dissolved and anything now put together will be new.[51] Minucius's Christian spokesperson replies, drawing on many of the assumptions of the pagan position, that bodies *can* rise the same because things are not "lost to God." Whether dust or ashes, moisture or smoke, bodies perdure; their "elements remain in the keeping of God"—that is, their basic bits survive and await re-

48. See Van Eijk, " 'Only That Can Rise Which Has Previously Fallen.' "

49. Irenaeus, *Adv. haer.*, bk. 5, chaps. 5 and 12, in *Contre les hérésies*, bk. 5, ed. Rousseau, vol. 2, pp. 60–73 and 140–63. Irenaeus's complete treatise survives only in a rather literal Latin translation; Syriac and Greek fragments survive, and an Armenian translation of books 4 and 5; see A. Orbe, "Irenaeus," in *Encyclopedia of the Early Church*, vol. 1, pp. 413–16. See also Godehard Joppich, *Salus carnis: Eine Untersuchung in der Theologie des hl. Irenaeus von Lyon* (Münsterschwarzach: Vier-Türme-Verlag, 1965), pp. 56–78.

50. Irenaeus, *Adv. haer.*, bk. 5, chaps. 9–12, vol. 2, pp. 106–63.

51. Minucius Felix, *Octavius*, chaps. 5 and 11, in *Tertullian and Minucius Felix*, trans. T. R. Glover and G. H. Rendall, Loeb Classical Library (Cambridge, Mass.: Harvard University Press, 1931; reprint, 1977), pp. 320–27 and 340–45.

assemblage at the end of time.[52] Even when he uses images of natural cycles, such as the seasons, Minucius Felix stresses a material substratum. The body in the tomb is, he says, like a tree in winter, which is dry but will later put out shoots. Minucius uses natural analogies to justify the idea that the specific material components of the body subsist after death. Just as there are volcanoes and lightning bolts that burn without consuming, so bodies can perdure through the conflagration that ends the world; they can even survive eternally in the fires of hell. In these arguments, the words for destruction are "eating," "consuming," "digesting" (nutrire, consumare, pascere); what the risen body triumphs over even in hell (if eternal punishment can be called a triumph) is feeding or being consumed by fire.[53]

Tertullian also, as is well known, sees resurrection as reassemblage of bits.[54] In fact, Tertullian—following Stoic metaphysics—holds that all reality is corporeal. Even soul is composed of very fine material particles.[55] Reassemblage of bits therefore in some sense accounts for identity. As Irenaeus says, it is what falls that must rise. Tertullian is the first to use the etymological argument that cadaver is named from cadendo.[56] The whole person must be rewarded or punished, he asserts,

52. Ibid., trans. Rendall, chaps. 14–40, especially chap. 34, p. 421. "Corpus omne sive arescit in pulverem sive in umorem solvitur vel in cinerem comprimitur vel in nidorem tenuatur, subducitur nobis, sed deo elementorum custodia reservatur" (p. 420).

53. Ibid., chaps. 34–35, pp. 416–23, esp. pp. 418 and 422.

54. For a general discussion, see Ernest Evans, "Introduction," to Tertullian's Treatise on the Resurrection, ed. E. Evans (London: SPCK, 1960), pp. ix–xxxv; and Francine Jo Cardman, "Tertullian on the Resurrection," (Ph.D. diss., Yale University, 1974). On the rhetorical structure of the treatise, see R. Sider, "Structure and Design in the De resurrectione mortuorum of Tertullian," Vigiliae Christianae 23 (1969): 177–96. On the dating of Tertullian's works, see Timothy David Barnes, Tertullian: A Historical and Literary Study, 2d ed. (Oxford: Clarendon Press, 1985), pp. 30–56; Jean-Claude Fredouille, Tertullien et la conversion de la culture antique (Paris: Études augustiniennes, 1972), pp. 487–88; and Cardman, "Tertullian," pp. vi–vii, 202–31. For bibliography on Tertullian and recent critical editions of his works, see Gösta Claesson, Index Tertullianeus (Paris: Études augustiniennes, 1974–75); the Chronica Tertullianea published annually by Revue des études augustiniennes (Paris); R. D. Sider, "Approaches to Tertullian: A Study of Recent Scholarship," Second Century 2 (1982): 228–60; and P. Siniscalco, "Tertullian," in Encyclopedia of the Early Church, vol. 2, pp. 818–21.

55. Tertullian, De resurrectione mortuorum, ed. J. G. P. Borleffs, chap. 17, in Tertulliani Opera, pt. 2: Opera Montanistica, Corpus christianorum: Series latina [hereafter CCL] (Turnhout: Brepols, 1954), pp. 941–42. Tertullian asserts that soul is, however, indissoluble; it is not divided into particles at death; De anima, ed. J. H. Waszink, chap. 51, in Opera, pt. 2, pp. 857–58.

56. Tertullian, De res., chap. 18, pp. 942–44. He attributes the etymological argument to heretics; see Van Eijk, " 'Only That Can Rise Which Has Previously Fallen,' " p. 520–21.

because it was the whole person (soul and body intermingled) that sinned or behaved with virtue. But only body can rise, for only body is cast down; soul is immortal. Bodies therefore do not vanish; bones and teeth last and are "germs" that will "sprout" in resurrection. Jonah was not digested in the whale. Not even the clothes of the three children were burned in the furnace.[57] In an odd excursus (which David Satran has recently related to ancient medical lore and Jewish exegesis), Tertullian even argues that when the children of Israel wandered forty years in the desert, their shoes and clothes did not wear out, nor did their hair or fingernails grow.[58] If God can thus suspend natural laws in order to preserve shoe leather and garments, how much more can he preserve flesh or the particles thereof for resurrection? Although Tertullian uses all the naturalistic images (popular since 1 Clement) that suggest repetition rather than continuity,[59] he also stresses resurrection as regurgitation of undigested bits and employs materialistic images of the body as a mended pot, a rebuilt temple, or clothing donned anew. He understands that the need to affirm identity through a change as stunning and paradoxical as the change to changelessness is a philosophical challenge so deep as to necessitate a rejection of the standard Aristotelian definition: "a thing that has changed ceases to be what it is and becomes something else." Rather, Tertullian argues, "to be changed is to exist in a different form"; exactly the flesh that sinned must be rewarded.[60] Blessedness or damnation can only be added "like a garment" to the identical material body that earned these just deserts.[61]

Sometimes, to Tertullian, identity lodges more in structure than in matter. He argues that in the resurrection all of our organs are retained. Defects are healed, mutilations undone.

Now, if the death of the whole person is rescinded by its resurrection, what must we say of the death of a part of him? If we are changed for

57. Tertullian, *De res.*, chaps. 42, 43, 53, 58, pp. 976–79, 998–1000, 1006–7. See also his *Apologeticum*, ed. E. Dekkers, chap. 48, in *Tertulliani Opera*, pt. 1: *Opera catholica*, CCL (1954), pp. 165–68 (written at least twelve years earlier).

58. *De res.*, chap. 58, pp. 1006–7. See David Satran, "Fingernails and Hair: Anatomy and Exegesis in Tertullian," *Journal of Theological Studies*, n.s. 40 (1989): 116–20. On Tertullian's use of Jewish exegesis, see also J. Massingferd Ford, "Was Montanism a Jewish-Christian Heresy?" *Journal of Ecclesiastical History* 17, no. 2 (1966): 145–58.

59. Naturalistic images: *De res.*, chaps. 11–12, pp. 933–35; regurgitation images: *De res.*, chap. 32, pp. 961–63; materialistic images: *De res.*, chaps. 40–44, pp. 973–81.

60. *De res.*, chap. 55, pp. 1001–3; and see Cardman, "Tertullian," p. 118. Elsewhere in his works, Tertullian uses this definition.

61. *De res.*, chaps. 41–42, pp. 975–78.

glory, how much more for integrity? Any loss sustained by our bodies is an accident to them, but their entirety [*integritas*] is their natural property. . . . To nature, not to injury, are we restored.[62]

Thus we rise "whole" (*integer*), like a damaged and repaired ship whose parts are restored though some of the planks are new. Indeed the functions of the risen organs may change or disappear, but no part will be destroyed.[63] Mouths will no longer eat, nor will genitals copulate in heaven; eating and procreation are aspects of the biological change that is part of corruption. But some of these organs will have new uses. Mouths, for example, will sing praises to God. Even the genitals are good, argues Tertullian, because the cleansing of urination and menstruation is good in this life.[64] Such organs will have no function in the resurrection, but they will survive for the sake of beauty. We will not chew in heaven, but we will have teeth, because we would look funny without them.

Everything intrinsic to what we are must reappear in the resurrected body, asserts Tertullian, clearly locating particularity in body. Christians believe they receive back "the self-same bodies in which they died" (*corpora eadem . . . in quibus discesserunt*), for it is these details (i.e., of age, size, manner, etc.) that make bodies who they are.[65] In his treatise on women's dress, Tertullian even argues that if cosmetics and jewels were essential to women they would rise from the dead—an argument echoed by Cyprian fifty years later when he exhorts women not to wear face powder in this life lest God fail to recognize them when they appear without it in the resurrection.[66] In his two works on marriage, Tertullian asserts that although there will be no marrying in

62. *De res.*, chap. 57, pp. 1004–5; Holmes, trans., "On the Resurrection of the Flesh," in *The Ante-Nicene Fathers*, ed. A. Roberts and J. Donaldson, vol. 3 (1885; reprint, Grand Rapids, Mich.: Eerdmans, 1986), pp. 589–90.

63. *De res.*, chaps. 59–62, pp. 1007–11.

64. *De res.*, chap. 61, pp. 1009–10. This passage makes clear how much more complex Tertullian's ideas are than the charge of misogyny (so often made against him) allows. See F. Forrester Church, "Sex and Salvation in Tertullian," *Harvard Theological Review* 68, no. 2 (1975): 83–101.

65. Tertullian, *De anima*, chaps. 31 and 56, pp. 828–29 and 863–65; quotation from chap. 56, p. 864, lines 38–41. See also *De res.*, chaps. 55–63, pp. 1001–12.

66. Tertullian, *De cultu feminarum*, ed. A. Kroymann, bk. 2, chap. 7, in *Opera*, pt. 1, p. 361. Tertullian's basic argument is that women as well as men must be prepared for martyrdom; the body in which discipline, suffering, and death happen is the same body that will be lifted to heaven. Cyprian, *De habitu virginum*, chap. 17, in Cyprian, *Opera omnia*, ed. William Hartel, Corpus scriptorum ecclesiasticorum latinorum [hereafter CSEL] 3, pts. 1 and 2 (Vienna: C. Gerold, 1868), p. 199.

heaven (Matthew 22.23–32), we will rise male and female, and we will recognize those to whom we have been bound.[67]

Of the three authors I have just considered, only Minucius Felix, who draws on standard pagan cosmological notions, sees the resurrected body merely as the reassemblage of bits or parts. Both Irenaeus and Tertullian—with the daring inconsistency of genius—join to an extravagantly materialistic notion of the resurrection body an emphasis on radical change that retains overtones of Paul. Indeed, in contrast to Athenagoras or Minucius Felix, whose metaphors identify body with subsisting particles and suggest that organic change threatens identity, Irenaeus's so-called materialistic view of the body is often expressed in metaphors of fertility and biological transformation. Repeatedly Irenaeus uses the Pauline seed but stresses, as Paul did not, the putrefaction it undergoes in the earth. It rots and withers and decomposes.[68] The emphasis is especially interesting when we note, as R. M. Grant has done, that ancient writers such as Theophrastus did understand that what happens to seeds in soil is more complex than simply death or rot. Moreover the early second-century Apocalypse of Peter, in its use of the Pauline seed, stresses that grain is sown dry.[69] To Irenaeus, however, our body putrefies like a grain of wheat. Made from mud or slime, we return to slime again. Even the flesh of the saints is torn and devoured by beasts, ground into dust, chewed and digested by the stomach of the earth.[70] The paradigmatic body is the cadaver; flesh *is* that which undergoes fundamental organic change. The sprouting of the resurrected seed into the sheaf of wheat is a victory not so much over sin, or even over death, as over putrefaction.[71]

67. *Ad uxorem*, ed. A. Kroymann, bk. 1, chap. 1, parags. 4–6, in *Opera*, pt. 1, pp. 373–74; *De monogamia*, ed. E. Dekkers, chap. 10, parag. 6, in *Opera*, pt. 2, p. 1243. In *De pallio* (which may be a late work of Tertullian's Montanist period or an early work from just after his conversion), Tertullian connects ostentation with gender confusion and cross-dressing; upset because sumptuous dressing can efface the difference between a matron and a brothel keeper here on earth, Tertullian suggests that we need to keep the marks of particularity in heaven in order to maintain there such differences of rank. See *De pallio*, ed. A. Gerlo, chaps. 3–4, in *Opera*, pt. 2, pp. 738–46.

68. Irenaeus, *Adv. haer.*, bk. 5, chap. 2, parags. 2–3; chap. 7, parag. 2; chap. 10, parag. 2; chap. 28, parag. 4; chaps. 33–34; ed. Rousseau, vol. 2, pp. 30–41, 88–93, 126–33, 360–63, 404–37.

69. R. M. Grant, "Resurrection," p. 193. See also Richard Broxton Onians, *The Origins of European Thought About the Body, the Mind, the Soul, the World, Time, and Fate: New Interpretations of Greek, Roman, and Kindred Evidence . . .*, 2d ed. (Cambridge: Cambridge University Press, 1954), pp. 263–70 and 287–90.

70. Irenaeus, *Adv. haer.*, bk. 5, chaps. 14–16 and 28; ed. Rousseau, vol. 2, pp. 182–221 and 346–63.

71. J. Pelikan comes close to the point I am making here when he says that, to Irenaeus, the problem to which Christ must provide a solution is not sin but death; see *Shape of Death*, pp. 101–20.

How can they affirm that the flesh is incapable of receiving . . . life eternal, which [flesh] is nourished from the body and blood of the Lord, and is a member of Him?—even as the blessed Paul declares in his Epistle to the Ephesians, that "we are members of His body, of His flesh, and of His bones" (Eph. 5.30). He does not speak these words of some spiritual and invisible man, for a spirit has not bones nor flesh (cf. Luke 24.39); but [he refers to] that dispensation [by which the Lord became] an actual man, consisting of flesh, and nerves, and bones,—that [flesh] which is nourished by the cup which is His blood, and receives increase from the bread which is His body. And just as a cutting from the vine planted in the ground fructifies in its season, or as a corn of wheat falling into the earth and becoming decomposed (cf. John 12.24), rises with manifold increase . . . and then . . . becomes the Eucharist . . . ; so also our bodies, being nourished by it, and deposited in the earth, and suffering decomposition there, shall rise at their appointed time, the Word of God granting them resurrection.[72]

Irenaeus thus suggests that the proof of our final incorruption lies in our eating of God. The very "truth" of our flesh is "increased and nourished" in the Eucharist (*verum hominem quae ex carnibus . . . consistit, quae de calice . . . nutritur, et de pane quod est corpus ejus augetur*). We drink blood in the cup; blood can come only from flesh and veins; we know that our flesh is capable of surviving digestion exactly because we are able to digest the flesh of Christ. The fact that we are what we eat—that we become Christ by consuming Christ, but Christ can never be consumed—guarantees that our consumption by beasts or fire or by the gaping maw of the grave is *not* destruction. Death (rot, decomposition) can be a moment of fertility, which sprouts and flowers and gives birth to incorruption.[73] Because eating God is a transcendent cannibalism that does not consume or destroy, we can be confident that the heretics who would spiritualize the flesh are wrong. Flesh, defined as that which changes, is capable of the change to changelessness.

72. Irenaeus, *Adv. haer.*, bk. 5, chap. 2, paragr. 3; ed. Rousseau, pp. 34–41; trans. A. Robertson and J. Donaldson, in *Ante-Nicene Fathers*, vol. 1 (1885; reprint, Grand Rapids, Mich.: Eerdmans, 1981), p. 528.

73. At the end of book 5, Irenaeus's vision of the coming kingdom is of full material recreation, ablaze with fertility. The dead will rise to an earth of abundant food, in which animals will no longer eat animals. Thus the resurrection will bring a world in which consumption is filling and sustaining, not destructive; the problem of incorporation (how can one take in, or be taken into, without being destroyed?) is finally solved in the "new heaven and new earth."

Tertullian also—for all his stress on reconstitution both of a core of material particles and of a bodily structure—sees resurrection as radical transformation. Donning a "new garment" (i.e., adding something to a core) may be his favorite metaphor for gaining incorruption,[74] but he also uses the Pauline seed metaphor to stress how great is the change that comes to the flesh in glory.[75] Indeed, in many of the works of Tertullian's middle period, change (understood basically as rot or digestion) is the fundamental challenge or scandal, the attainment of changelessness the final victory. Paradoxically, however, it is exactly the metaphor of change or growth that must be used to speak of the transition to incorruption.

Tertullian, like Irenaeus, sees the earthly body as that which changes—especially that which eats, procreates, and rots. Adam's sin was gluttony, says Tertullian.[76] Even if God had not enjoined fasting, we would know from Adam's story how necessary it is. Food is poison, the primordial cause of death. It threatens what we are.[77] Thus those who fast prepare themselves not only for prison and the arena but also for the resurrection.[78] Slenderer flesh will go more easily through the nar-

---

74. *De res.*, chaps. 27, 42, 55, pp. 956–57, 976–78, 981–82.

75. *De res.*, chaps. 52–53, pp. 976–79. For a very positive and elaborate metaphor of growth, flowering, and fruition, see Tertullian, *De virginibus velandis*, ed. E. Dekkers, chap. 1, in *Opera*, pt. 2, pp. 1209–10, a discussion of the advance of creation toward the gospel.

76. *De ieiunio adversus psychicos*, ed. A. Reifferscheid and G. Wissowa, chap. 3, in *Opera*, pt. 2, pp. 1259–60; *Scorpiace*, ed. A. Reifferscheid and G. Wissowa, chap. 5, in *Opera*, pt. 2, pp. 1076–79.

77. *De ieiunio*, chap. 3, pp. 1259–60. Eating was a basic metaphor of incorporation; much of the discussion of food in the ancient world suggests either that the food we eat destroys us or that we destroy the food we eat. Christians struggled to find ways of using images of consumption, digestion, cannibalism, etc., to express an incorporation that does not destroy, that leaves the self separate from God yet saved by him. It is striking that, in the *Scorpiace*, chap. 7, pp, 1081–82, where Tertullian defends God against the charge that he wants human sacrifice because he allows the martyrdoms, the word for "sacrifice" or "destroy" is "eat" or "devour." If God really wants martyrdom, says Tertullian, we must count happy the man whom God has eaten (*et non beatum amplius reputasset quem deus comedisset*) (p. 1082, lines 10–11). The martyrs are not really devoured, of course, because they will rise again. *De res.*, chap. 32, pp. 961–62, equates resurrection with regurgitation: "Sed idcirco nominantur bestiae et pisces in redibitionem carnis et sanguinis, quo magis exprimatur resurrectio etiam deuoratorum corporum, cum de ipsis deuoratoribus exactio edicitur" (p. 962, lines 8–11). On the connection of eating-metaphors with ancient notions of death, especially as regards Tertullian, see Victor Saxer, *Morts, martyrs, reliques en Afrique chrétienne aux premiers siècles: Le Témoignages de Tertullien, Cyprien, et Augustin à la lumière de l'archéologie africaine* (Paris: Édition Beauchesne, 1980), pp. 44–46.

78. *De ieiunio*, chap. 12, p. 1270; *Ad martyras*, ed. E. Dekkers, chaps. 2 and 3, in *Opera*, pt. 1, pp. 3–6. See the interesting discussion of how the early martyrs used fasting to "train" for prison and execution in Maureen Tilley, "The Ascetic Body and

row gate of heaven; lighter flesh will rise more quickly; drier flesh will experience less putrefaction in the tomb.[79] "An over-fed Christian will be much more necessary to bears and lions . . . than to God."[80] Asceticism, to Tertullian, prepares us for glory by moving our flesh away from mutability and toward the incorruptibility and impassibility of heaven. Fasting and sexual abstinence make us like the children of Israel who achieved on earth such changelessness that even their nails and hair avoided growth, as their clothes avoided deterioration.

To Tertullian, as to Irenaeus, the paradigmatic earthly body is the corpse, and the ultimate indignity suffered by corpses is digestion. Tertullian fulminates against pagan gladiatorial combat as heinous assault on the beauty of bodies created by God; yet he emphasizes that all bodies come eventually to the ugliness and destruction of the grave.[81] Whether gently laid to rest in the tomb or torn and twisted—eaten by the "bellies of beasts," the "crops of birds," and the "guts of fishes"—we are all cadavers; we all end up in "time's own gullet."[82] Thus the final victory must be the eating that does not consume, the decay that does not devour, the change that transmutes only to changelessness. The fact that we eat God in the Eucharist and are truly fed on his flesh and blood is a paradoxical redemption of that most horrible of consumptions: cannibalism.[83] And to Tertullian cannibalism is not merely a metaphor for

---

the (Un)Making of the World of the Martyr" (Paper delivered at the AAR meeting, November 1990), p. 11.

79. De ieiunio, chap. 17, pp. 1276–77; see also chap. 12, pp. 1270–71. In this late work (probably from after 213), Tertullian implies that drier flesh will last longer in the tomb and suggests that this is a good thing. In the slightly earlier De anima (probably from 208–212), Tertullian stresses that what happens in the tomb does not matter; see chaps. 51–57, pp. 857–67.

80. De ieiunio, chap. 17, pp. 1276–77. To Tertullian, asceticism is martyrdom (see De ieiunio, chap. 12) and martyrdom is resurrection (Scorpiace, chaps. 12–13, pp. 1092–96). He even argues that to pagans, gladiatorial combat is "qualem potest praestare saeculum, de fama aeternitatem, de memoria resurrectionem" (Scorpiace, chap. 6, pp. 1079–81, esp. p. 1079, lines 24–26); how much more therefore should Christians eagerly welcome the true resurrection?

81. De spectaculis, ed. E. Dekkers, chaps. 12, 19, 21–23, in Opera, pt. 1, pp. 238–39, 244–47; and De anima, chaps. 51–52, pp. 857–59.

82. De res., c. 4, pp. 925–26. Tertullian asks whether the wise man can believe that something can return whole from corruption, ". . . in solidum de casso, in plenum de inanito, in aliquid omnino de nihilo, et utique redhibentibus eam ignibus et undis et aluis ferarum et rumis alitum et lactibus piscium et ipsorum temporum propria gula?" (p. 925, lines 13–17).

83. De res., chap. 8, pp. 931–32. See also Tertullian, Ad nationes, ed. J. G. P. Borleffs, bk. 1, chap. 2, in Opera, pt. 1, pp. 12–13, for charges of cannibalism against pagans; Apologeticum, chap. 48, pp. 165–68, where Tertullian reports that some pagans abstain from meat because it might be a relative reincarnated; and De pallio,

threat to identity. In a passage Aline Rousselle has made much of, Tertullian charges that pagans commit it when they eat the bodies of beasts from the arena who have in turn eaten the Christian martyrs.[84]

Tertullian stresses, explicitly and paradoxically, that the seed of 1 Corinthians 15 is a guarantee of identity exactly in its radical change. What decays and rises is the grain, but if there is to be rising, there must be transformation. The body is "demolished, dismembered, dissolved" in the ground; like Lazarus, it putrefies and stinks, for it lies more than three days in the grave.[85] Because it is so vile and vulnerable—torn by execution perhaps and certainly sullied by the uncleanness of nutrition and copulation—flesh must be transmuted in order to rise as a bride, shining like the angels.[86] Thus to Tertullian, the Transfiguration is inextricably tied to the resurrection. Our bodies will be not only raised but also glorified, like Stephen who appeared as an angel at his stoning or Moses and Elias who shone with a foretaste of glory when they appeared with Christ on the mountain.[87]

> But that you may not suppose that it is merely those bodies which are consigned to the tombs whose resurrection is foretold, you have it declared in Scripture: "And I will command the fishes of the sea and they shall cast up the bones which they have devoured. . . ."(Enoch 61.5) You will ask, Will then the fishes and other animals and carnivorous birds be raised again in order that they may vomit up what they have consumed . . . ? Certainly not. But the beasts and fishes are mentioned . . . in relation to the restoration of flesh and blood, in order the more emphatically to express the resurrection of such bodies as have even been devoured. . . .
>
> If God raises not men entire, He raises not the dead. For what dead man is entire, although he dies entire? Who is without hurt, that is

---

chap. 5, pp. 746–50, where he tells the story of a pagan who dined indirectly on his slaves by first feeding them to fish, which he then cooked. Minucius Felix (*Octavius,* chap. 30, pp. 191–92) makes a similar charge of cannibalism against pagans. Eusebius reports that one Attalus, while being burned, accused his persecutors of "eating men," something Christians would never do (*The Ecclesiastical History,* bk. 5, chap. 1, trans. Kirsopp Lake, Loeb Classical Library [London and Cambridge, Mass.: Heinemann and Harvard University Press, 1926; reprint, 1980], vol. 1, pp. 431–33). And see n. 132 below.

84. Aline Rousselle, *Porneia: On Desire and the Body in Antiquity,* trans. Felicia Pheasant (Oxford: Blackwell, 1988), pp. 118–19, discussing Tertullian, *Apologeticum,* chaps. 8–9 and 50, and *Ad nationes,* bk. 1, chap. 10, as evidence of (at least indirect) human sacrifice.

85. *De res.,* chap. 53, pp. 998–1000, esp. p. 998, line 6.

86. *De res.,* chaps. 62–63, pp. 1010–12.

87. *De res.,* chap. 55, pp. 1001–3.

without life? What body is uninjured, when it is dead, when it is cold, when it is ghastly, when it is stiff, when it is a corpse? . . . Thus, for a dead man to be raised again, amounts to nothing short of his being restored to his entire condition. . . . God is quite able to remake what He once made. . . . Thus our flesh shall remain even after the resurrection—so far indeed susceptible of suffering, as it is the flesh, and the same flesh too; but at the same time impassible, inasmuch as it has been liberated by the Lord for the very end and purpose of being no longer capable of enduring suffering.[88]

Scholars have criticized Tertullian for rhetorical and theological excess and most of all for inconsistency—for stressing resurrection as a prelude to punishment while relating it to the grace provided by Christ's rising, for glorifying flesh and creation while indulging in a castigation of woman that sounds misogynist and a castigation of body that sounds dualist.[89] But surely these inconsistencies—however offensively or incoherently expressed—are exactly the point. What must rise is the site of our rottenness. It is corruption that puts on incorruption. *Caro salutis est cardo:* the flesh is the pivot of salvation.[90]

Martyrdom

Historians used to assert that the doctrine of the resurrection of the flesh was established in polemical treatises from the late second century as part of the contest with Gnosticism.[91] We now know, however, that the question of the nature of the resurrected body continued to come up in important ways for hundreds of years and (as we shall see) did not always entail the same issues. Nonetheless, a careful look at the images and arguments of writings from around 200 helps us to understand what was fundamentally at stake in the earliest debates.[92] The specific adjectives, analogies, and examples used in treatises on resurrection suggest that the palpable, vulnerable, corruptible body Christ redeems and raises was quintessentially the mutilated cadaver of the martyr. Writers such as

88. Tertullian, *De res.,* chaps. 32 and 57, pp. 961–62 and 1004–5; trans. Holmes, *The Ante-Nicene Fathers,* pp. 567–68 and 590. I quoted a part of this second passage at n. 1; it is interesting to see how much more complex and rhetorical Tertullian's emphasis on "wholeness" seems after extended analysis.

89. For example, Cardman, "Tertullian."

90. *De res.,* chap. 8, p. 931, lines 6–7.

91. Van Unnik, " 'Epistle to Rheginos,' " pp. 141–52 and 153–67; Davis, "Factors," pp. 448–55; Gager, "Body-Symbols," p. 345; Kelly, *Creeds,* pp. 163–66.

92. On the method I employ here, of moving from text to context via image, see above, "Preface," pp. xvi–xvii.

Ignatius of Antioch, Justin, Irenaeus, Tertullian, and Minucius Felix had a quite specific death in mind—the voluntary, sacrificial death they both feared and yearned for—when they spoke of literal, physical resurrection as victory over it. The paradox of change and continuity that character-izes theological and hagiographical descriptions of the risen body seems to originate in the facts of martyrdom.

Recent scholarship has been inclined to downplay the numbers of Christian martyrs and to underline parallels between the expressionism and exhibitionism of pagan games and Christian executions.[93] And it is certainly true that both Christian fears of persecution and Christian pride in the endurance and courage of their cobelievers led to exagger-ated accounts of the numbers who died and of the extravagant nature of their suffering. Indeed, Christian apologists and historians paid tribute to the bravery of pagan gladiators in order to argue that Christians sur-passed it and suffered in a far worthier cause. Nonetheless, after a lull in the days of Trajan (d. 117) and Hadrian (d. 138), Christians—called by their opponents a "third race"—experienced periodic persecution.[94] Tales of the martyrdom of Polycarp at Smyrna in the 160s and of the executions at Lyons in circa 177 circulated in the years around 200 and strengthened both fear and determination. Some of our earliest discus-sions of resurrection were penned by Christians who led their commu-nities during waves of repression or themselves suffered torture. Neither research that minimizes the numbers of martyrs nor interpretation that draws parallels between pagan and Christian behaviors should be used to suggest that fear of martyrdom was an insignificant motive in shaping Christian mentality. Apologists such as Tertullian, Irenaeus, and Justin (himself "the Martyr") spoke of resurrection as God's gift to all bodies

93. See G. E. M. de Ste. Croix, "Aspects of the 'Great' Persecution," *Harvard The-ological Review* 47 (1954): 75–113; Charles Saumagne, "A Persécution de Dèce en Afrique d'après la correspondance de S. Cyprien," *Byzantion* 32 (1962): 1–29; Aline Rousselle, *Porneia*, pp. 108–40; W. Rordorf, V. Saxer, N. Duval, and F. Bisconti, "Martyr-Martyrdom," in *Encyclopedia of the Early Church*, vol. 1, pp. 531–36; David Potter, "Martyrdom as Spectacle" (Unpublished paper); and Carlin Barton, "The Sa-cramentum of the Gladiator" (Paper delivered at the meeting of the American Society of Church History, December 28, 1989). These last two articles take rather different approaches to the parallels between gladiatorial combat and martyrdom. See now also Carlin Barton, *The Sorrows of the Ancient Romans: The Gladiator and the Monster* (Princeton: Princeton University Press, 1992). Peter Brown, *Power and Persuasion in Late Antiquity: Towards a Christian Empire* (Madison, Wisc.: University of Wiscon-sin Press, 1992), chap. 2, argues that the courage of the martyr can be understood as analogous to that of the philosopher.

94. R. A. Markus, *Christianity in the Roman World* (London: Thames and Hudson, 1974), p. 24.

but especially to those that experienced suffering and partition in prison or the arena. Their images of stasis, hardening, and reassemblage in heaven gave to mortal flesh the promise of victory over what martyrs, and those who admired them, feared most: excruciating pain in the moment of dying and dishonor to the cadaver after death. Thus we should not find it surprising that early exhortations to martyrdom both express in graphic (even exalted) prose the suffering entailed and offer hope of resurrection as a protection against it.[95] Nor should we be surprised that early treatises on resurrection stress God's promise of a body both transformed and "the same," both impassible and identical with the flesh of earth.

Martyred flesh had to be capable of impassibility and transfiguration; suffering and rot could not be the final answer. If flesh could put on, even in this life, a foretaste of incorruption, martyrdom might be bearable. Those who watched and feared execution, yet exhorted themselves and others toward it, clung to the belief that (as Tertullian said) "the leg feels no pain in its tendons when the soul is in heaven."[96] "The bites of wild beasts" could be "glories to young heroes" in part because the body, disciplined by asceticism, had already "sent on to heaven" the "succulence of its blood."[97] Our oldest account of a martyrdom asserts that the fire "felt cold" to those who, under torture, fixed their thoughts on Christ.[98] Later martyr stories are filled with examples of saints who do

95. I agree with Carlin Barton (see n. 93 above) that Christian apologists cultivated and proselytized for the expressionism of suffering. They spoke of martyrs as scaling pinnacles of pain. At the same time I argue that they held out to potential martyrs the promise of an "anesthesia of glory" against pain. Such tendencies may appear to be contradictory. But both are present in the texts. Their combination is found in other cultural moments in which torture and execution play a crucial role. See, for example, the discussion of the Aztecs in Georges Bataille, *The Accursed Share: An Essay on General Economy*, trans. R. Hurley, vol. 1 (New York: Zone Books, 1988), pp. 45–61.

96. *Ad martyras*, chap. 2, p. 5, lines 6–7. The *Ad martyras* dates from ca. 197.

97. *De anima*, chap. 58, pp. 867–69; *De ieiunio*, chap. 12, pp. 1270–71. The passage in *De anima* also emphasizes a disjunction between body and soul, suggesting that the soul can avoid feeling the pain to which the body is subjected if it concentrates on heaven. Along similar lines, Maureen Tilley has pointed out that the letters of Cyprian provide advice to future martyrs about how to avoid terror and pain by imagining the instruments of torture as means of uniting with Christ's passion; see Cyprian, Letters 76, chap. 2, and 77, chap. 3, *Opera*, ed. Hartel, CSEL 3, pt. 2, pp. 829–30 and 835, and Tilley, "The Ascetic Body," p. 17.

98. *Martyrdom of Polycarp*, chap. 2, in Ignatius and Polycarp, *Lettres*, ed. Camelot, pp. 244–45; see Quasten, *Patrology*, vol. 1, pp. 76–79; and Helmut Koester, *Introduction to the New Testament*, vol. 2: *History and Literature of Early Christianity* (Philadelphia: Fortress Press, and Berlin and New York: de Gruyter, 1982), pp. 306–8. André Grabar has argued, picking up on the argument of K. Holl, that martyrs were called

not even notice the most exquisite and extraordinary cruelties.[99] Death for the faith was a necessary and palpable concern in writing and behavior during the late second century; hence it is not surprising that the impassibility of the risen body was stressed as a reward for such sacrifice or that the terror of execution was allayed by the suggestion that a sort of anesthesia of glory might spill over from the promised resurrection into the ravaged flesh of the arena, making its experience bearable. Cyprian, who in life exhorted, comforted, and advised future martyrs, supposedly appeared after his death to the martyr Flavian, saying: "It is another flesh that suffers when the soul is in heaven. The body does not feel [the death blow] at all when the mind is entirely absorbed in God."[100]

But the context of martyrdom, within which so much early theological writing emerged, made continuity of body important also. Irenaeus and Tertullian avoided any suggestion that the attainment of impassibility or glory entailed a loss of the particular self that offered up its own death for Christ. Identity was a crucial issue. As Tertullian said, all death (even the gentlest) is violent; all corpses (even the most respectfully buried) rot.[101] Resurrection guarantees that it is *these very corpses* that achieve salvation.[102] The promise that *we* will rise again makes it possible for heroes and ordinary Christians to face, for those they love and revere as well as for themselves, the humiliation of death and the horror of putrefaction.

---

witnesses because at the moment of their execution they had direct contact with God; see Grabar, *Martyrium: Recherches sur le culte des reliques et l'art chrétien antique* (Paris: Collège de France, 1946), vol. 1, p. 28. Eusebius, *The Ecclesiastical History*, bk. 5, chap. 1, pp. 433–35, also suggests that God keeps the martyrs from feeling pain.

99. Tilley, "The Ascetic Body," p. 14. See also eadem, "Scripture as an Element of Social Control: Two Martyr Stories of Christian North Africa," *Harvard Theological Review* 83, no. 4 (1990): 383–97.

100. *The Passion of Montanus and Lucius*, chap. 21, in Herbert A. Musurillo, *The Acts of the Christian Martyrs* (Oxford: Clarendon Press, 1972), p. 235; see Tilley, "The Ascetic Body," p. 17.

101. It is worth noting here that our oldest extant Christian prayer over a corpse stresses the contrast between an incorruptible God and creatures who must be lifted from change into changelessness: "God, you who have the power of life and death, God of the spirits and lord of all flesh . . . you who change and transform and transfigure your creatures, as is right and proper, being yourself alone incorruptible, unalterable, and eternal, we beseech you for the repose and rest of this your servant. . . .: refresh her soul and spirit in green pastures . . . and raise up the body in the day which you have ordained." See Frederick S. Paxton, *Christianizing Death: The Creation of a Ritual Process in Early Medieval Europe* (Ithaca and London: Cornell University Press, 1990), p. 22, who sees the prayer as Jewish in character.

102. *De anima*, chap. 51–52, pp. 857–59.

A fourth-century Syriac text, the *Didascalia of the Apostles*, which is based on an early third-century Greek original, argues: because we Christians believe in resurrection, we cannot excuse ourselves from martyrdom.[103] Whether thrown into the depths of the sea or scattered like chaff by the wind, we are still in the world, enclosed in the hand of God, and not a hair of our head shall perish (Luke 21.18). Christ made himself a body from the Virgin and raised himself from the dead; so he will raise all that is laid down, as he multiplied loaves and fishes or created an eye from clay and spittle.[104] Nothing can make the body unclean—neither nocturnal emissions of semen, nor menstruation and childbearing, nor even the putrefaction of the tomb. We Christians do not abominate a dead man because we know he will live again. Assembling in cemeteries, we offer up on the graves themselves the Eucharist, which is—this author asserts—not only Christ's body but also the likeness of our bodies in heaven.[105] What is striking in this text is not only the connection between resurrection and martyrdom but also the understanding of ultimate threat as the scattering and/or dissolution of the martyr's corpse.

To place the doctrine of bodily resurrection in the context of martyrdom is not to make a novel argument. Historians have long recognized that belief in resurrection tends to emerge in response to persecution; for the persecuted want to claim that those who die for their faith will be rewarded in another life with the good fortune they have clearly in some sense been denied in this one.[106] Yet posed as a rather crude form of compensation theory, the argument does not seem to work especially well for Christian teaching. Much as Tertullian, for example, stresses reward and punishment in his theology of resurrection, he does not men-

103. *Didascalia Apostolorum*, chap. 19, ed. and trans. Vööbus, vol. 2, pp. 167–75. It is worth underlining that this text is permeated both by a very strong sense of community created by the adversity of persecution and by an intense need to enforce hierarchy (husbands over wives, bishops over the people, etc.); see especially chaps. 1–12.

104. *Didascalia Apostolorum*, chap. 20, pp. 175–83. The passage also mentions Aaron's rod and the seed of 1 Corinthians 15.

105. *Didascalia Apostolorum*, chap. 26, pp. 223–47. The passages cited in nn. 103–5 are also found in the Latin *Apostolic Constitutions*, based on the Greek original and made (probably) between 375 and 400; see Vööbus, "Introduction," vol. 1, pp. 27*–28*.

106. See, for example, Gooch, "Resurrection," in *Dictionary of Biblical Tradition*; G. A. Barton and Kaufmann Kohler, "Resurrection," in *The Jewish Encyclopedia*, ed. Isidore Singer et al., vol. 10 (New York and London: Funk and Wagnalls, 1905), pp. 382–85; Frank Bottomley, *Attitudes to the Body in Western Christendom* (London: Lebus Books, 1979), p. 52.

tion resurrection in his early exhortations to martyrdom. There his argument is based on the parallel between Christian and pagan gladiators. The connection he draws is between faith and courage, not between faith and reward. If pagans can die for worldly glory, he argues, surely Christians can die for God.[107] He never quite says: God will reward the martyrs with resurrection and punish their persecutors, although he draws a singularly unlovely analogy between hell and the tortures of the arena[108] and speaks much of asceticism as a kind of martyrdom that prepares for resurrection.[109] When Tertullian does treat resurrection or immortality as reward (as, for example, when he discusses Revelation 6.9 or refers to Perpetua's vision of paradise peopled only by martyrs), the context is the question of burial. Like the author of the *Didascalia of the Apostles,* Tertullian associates dissolution in the arena with dissolution in the grave and finally with the dissolution of biological process itself.

Tertullian is concerned to refute those who think delay in burial injures the soul or that persons who die prematurely or violently or receive no burial, will wander the earth as ghosts or demons. He devotes much scorn to the pagan idea that souls survive in properly prepared corpses and carefully explains that Christian opposition to cremation has nothing to do with a need to preserve cadavers. Christians prefer to treat corpses gently out of respect, he says, but death is absolute. Resurrection is promised to all bodies, no matter how they died or how they are buried.[110] The horror that resurrection overcomes is finally not so much torture or execution as the dishonor of being treated as a common criminal after death.

Thus it appears that Lionel Rothkrug is right when he gives a more profound version of the compensation argument, suggesting that to Jews of the Maccabean period and to early Christians resurrection was a substitute for the burial owed to the pious.[111] When studied carefully, both Christian story and Christian polemic can be seen to make the connec-

---

107. See *Ad martyras* (from 197) and *De Corona militis* (from 208 or 211). *Ad martyras,* chap. 3, pp. 5–6, does mention attaining an incorruptible crown, and the *Scorpiace* (probably 211–12), chap. 6, pp. 1079–81, argues that a special "mansion" in heaven is a reward for martyrdom. But Tertullian's major argument is to compare pagan and Christian self-sacrifice.

108. *De spectaculis* (from between 198 and 206), chap. 30, pp. 210–12.

109. *De ieiunio,* chap. 12, pp. 1270–71; *De pallio,* chap. 6, p. 750.

110. *De anima,* chaps. 51–58, pp. 857–69.

111. Lionel Rothkrug, "German Holiness and Western Sanctity in Medieval and Modern History," *Historical Reflections/Réflexions historiques* 15, no. 1 (1988): 215–29.

tion between resurrection and proper burial absolutely explicit. For example, the fourth-century church historian Eusebius, incorporating into his history what we believe to be an authentic account of the martyrdom at Lyons in circa 177, reports that the Romans scattered and burned the bodies of the executed in order to dash Christian hopes of resurrection. Whether the account is correct in the motives it imputes, the fact that it imputes them suggests both horror at corpse violation and the possibility that some would interpret such violation as jeopardizing literal resurrection. Indeed in his treatise *Octavius*, Minucius Felix argues explicitly against the assumptions attributed to the Romans in Eusebius's account. Violating corpses is ineffectual, says Minucius; divine power can renew even pulverized dust. Thus resurrection is the ultimate victory, for it brings together the scattered bits of the church's heroes and heroines, providing for them the quiet sepulchre their executioners might prohibit and prevent.[112]

Minucius's reassurances suggest that Christians did worry passionately about the bodies of the martyrs. Other writings offer the same suggestion. As we have seen (p. 28 above), Ignatius of Antioch prayed to be totally devoured so that his followers would not be endangered by their desire to care for and reverence his remains.[113] Cyprian, writing in the middle of the third century, stressed burying the dead, especially the martyrs, as an act of charity.[114] Looking back from the early fourth century, Eusebius reported that the Romans had to post guards to prevent Christians from stealing the ashes or bones of the martyrs in order to bury them.[115] Although there is no evidence that the Romans reg-

---

112. Eusebius, *The Ecclesiastical History*, bk. 5, chap. 1, pp. 435–37. Book 8, chap. 7, pp. 270–73, makes it clear that denial of burial is an insult. Throughout book 5, chap. 1, book 8, chaps. 7–12, and book 10, chap. 8, Eusebius displays considerable fascination with the details of torture. In his *History*, bk. 5, chaps. 1–4, he incorporates a letter in the name of the Christians of Lyons and Vienne (probably written by Irenaeus himself shortly after the persecution of 177) describing the martyrs of Lyons; see P. Nautin, "Letter of the Church of Lyons and Vienne," in *Encyclopedia of the Early Church*, vol. 1, pp. 483–84. And see Minucius Felix, *Octavius*, chaps. 11, 34, 37–38; pp. 340–45, 416–21, and 426–35; on this passage see Arthur Darby Nock, "Cremation and Burial in the Roman Empire," *Harvard Theological Review* 25, no. 4 (1932): 334.

113. See above nn. 14 and 16.

114. Saxer, *Morts, martyrs, reliques*, p. 88.

115. Eusebius, *Ecclesiastical History*, bk. 5, chap. 1, vol. 1, pp. 435–37. The Acts of Carpus, Papylus, and Agathonice, chap. 47, (from the 160s) reports that the Christians secretly took up and guarded the remains; see *Some Authentic Acts of the Early Martyrs*, trans. E. C. E. Owen (London: SPCK, 1927), pp. 42–46, especially p. 46, and Quasten, *Patrology*, vol. 1, p. 183. For stories of early Christians caring for remains, see Nicole Hermann-Mascard, *Les Reliques des saints: Formation coutumière d'un*

ularly denied Christian adherents access to the bodies of the executed,[116] the early martyr stories clearly reflect a Christian fear that
the authorities want to insult cadavers and prevent burial.[117] The account of Polycarp's martyrdom, for example, asserts that Romans, Jews,
and the devil burnt the body in order to prevent Christians from re-
covering the sacred flesh that had remained unconsumed on the pyre
of execution.

The author of the Passion of Polycarp did not, however, leave the
victory to the persecutors. Focusing on the body, he told a story with a
different outcome and moral. Hard as it had been for the executioners
to bring death to the Christian hero, they had—so the author tells us—
finally succeeded. Polycarp had expired although his body remained. But
when the forces of evil attacked the body itself, they were without suc-
cess. Polycarp's flesh lasted unchanged, "not like flesh that burns, but
like bread that bakes, or gold and silver glowing in a furnace."[118] The
images are exactly those we find in theological treatises about resurrection, but here the martyr becomes while still on earth the hard and
beautiful minerals or undigested bread all our bodies will finally become
at the end of time.

Writers such as Tertullian, Minucius Felix, the author of the *Didascalia,* and the church historian Eusebius all connected resurrection and
martyrdom, both in image and in explicit argument. But the connection
had implications beyond the deaths of heroes. The very images used—
images of reforged vessels and rebuilt ships, of gold and jewels tempered
in the furnace, or of objects undigested in the bellies of fishes—suggest
that what God promised to those willing to die in his service was victory
not so much over the moment of execution as over putrefaction itself.
Resurrection was finally not so much the triumph of martyrs over pain
and humiliation as the triumph of martyrs' bodies over fragmentation,
scattering, and the loss of a final resting place. And the resurrection
promised especially to heroes and heroines was offered to all Christians

---

droit (Paris: Édition Klincksieck, 1975), pp. 23–26, and Alfred C. Rush, *Death and
Burial in Christian Antiquity* (Washington, D.C.: Catholic University of America,
1941), passim, especially pp. 122, 205–6.

116. See Henri Leclercq, "Martyr," *Dictionnaire d'archéologie chrétienne et de
liturgie,* ed. F. Cabrol and H. Leclercq [hereafter *DACL*], vol. 10 (Paris: Letouzey et
Ané, 1932), col. 2433.

117. See above, n. 112; Leclercq, "Martyr," cols. 2425–40.

118. *Martyrdom of Polycarp,* chaps. 15, 17, and 18, in Ignatius and Polycarp,
Lettres, ed. Camelot, pp. 262–65, 266–69; quoted passage at p. 264. The prayer put in
Polycarp's mouth refers to sharing "the cup" with Christ and to rising in body and
soul (ibid., p. 262).

as well. Hence the broader context within which the doctrine of the resurrection of the flesh should be located appears to be the vast subject of attitudes toward and practices concerning the bodies of the ordinary dead.

Burial Practices

It is no more novel to connect burial practice and resurrection than it is to connect resurrection and martyrdom. But once again I do not mean by this argument quite what previous scholars have meant.

It is well known that the second and third centuries saw basic changes in Roman burial practices, and twentieth-century scholarship has debated the relationship of these to Christian doctrine (albeit with remarkably inconclusive results).[119] Older theories held that the change from cremation back to the earlier practice of inhumation—a change that began about the time of Trajan (d. 117)—was a result in part of Christian opposition to cremation. When scholars had to admit that the chronology of developments made this idea totally untenable, they fell back on the partially tautological argument that the change in practice was a change in fashion, with no ideational underpinning.[120]

This claim is, in one sense, quite plausible. There is much recent, cross-cultural work in both anthropology and history that suggests that we can never find a causal relationship between doctrine and burial practice. Scholars have not, to my knowledge, been able to adduce a single case where a change in eschatology dictates precise changes in death rituals or where changing practice immediately entails a new theory of the afterlife.[121] This observation should not, however, lead us to argue

119. Franz Cumont, *After Life in Roman Paganism* (New Haven: Yale University Press, 1922); Henri Leclercq, "Incineration," *DACL*, vol. 7, pt. 1 (1926), cols. 502–8; Nock, "Cremation and Burial"; Rush, *Death and Burial in Christian Antiquity*; Onians, *Origins*; J. M. C. Toynbee, *Death and Burial in the Roman World* (Ithaca: Cornell University Press, 1971); Jean-Marie Mathieu, "Horreur du cadavre et philosophie dans le monde romain: Le cas de la patristique grecque du IVe siècle," in *La Mort, les morts, et l'au-delà dans le monde romain* (Caen: Centre de Publications de l'Université de Caen, 1987), pp. 311–20.

120. Nock, "Cremation and Burial," and Toynbee, *Death and Burial*.

121. See Paul-Albert Fevrier, "La mort chrétienne," in *Segni e riti nella chiesa altomedievale occidentale* (Spoleto: Presio la sede del Centro, 1987), vol. 2, pp. 881–942; Bailey Young, "Paganisme, christianisation, et rites funéraires merovingiens," *Archéologie médiévale* 7 (1977): 5–81; and Paxton, *Christianizing Death*, pp. 3–4. On the general point, see P. Reinecke, "Reihengräber und Friedhöfe der Kirchen," *Germania* 9, fasc. 2 (1952): 103–7; Edward James, "Merovingian Cemetery Studies and Some Implications for Anglo-Saxon England," in *Anglo-Saxon Cemeteries, 1979: The*

that belief expresses merely the desire to identify with a privileged class or to conform to prevailing fashion.[122] Nor should we conclude that the content of belief is arbitrary. Whatever causes the convictions that bring comfort to people in their deepest existential horrors, these convictions must be expressed in language drawn from and relevant to everyday experience. The specific images in which Christian theologians and polemicists spoke of resurrection thus seem to me to have everything to do with Mediterranean funerary practice, both with its privileging of hard, dry remains (bones or ashes) and with its treatment of corpse and grave as "that which eats."[123]

In general it is clear that both cremation and inhumation were efforts to mask, and therefore in some ways to deny, putrefaction.[124] Jews traditionally practiced ossilegium and/or inhumation, privileging bones as body.[125] Romans moved from inhumation to cremation and back to inhumation. But cremation was never, in the Roman world, antithetical to inhumation; rather it was a version of it. Ashes were frequently buried in sarcophagi, and a finger (the os resectum) was cut off before cremation to be buried with the ashes. Infants who had not yet developed milk teeth could not be cremated—perhaps because there was a question whether they would leave mineral remains for burial.[126] The increased popularity of inhumation in the later second and third centuries expressed, as both A. D. Nock and J. Toynbee have pointed out, a growing

---

Fourth Anglo-Saxon Symposium at Oxford, ed. P. Rahtz, T. Dickinson, and L. Watts (Oxford: B. A. R., 1980), p. 40; Elizabeth A. R. Brown, "Authority, the Family, and the Dead in Late Medieval France," *French Historical Studies* 16, no. 4 (1990): 803–32; Patricia Ebrey, "Cremation in Sung China," *American Historical Review* 95, no. 2 (1990): 406–28; and the works on Jewish ossilegium cited in n. 135 below. For the difficulties of identifying a collective mentality in antiquity, see Michel Vovelle, "Les attitudes devant la mort: Problèmes de méthode, approches, et lectures différentes," *Annales: Économies, sociétés, civilisations* 31 (1976): 120–32.

122. Nock may be correct that people moved to inhumation because it was an upper-class practice; he has not, however, explained why the upper classes preferred it. It will not do to adduce its expense (a sort of argument from conspicuous consumption) since cremated ashes could be treated in equally expensive ways—and were.

123. For pioneering work on the relationship between, on the one hand, the rituals and images used by the living and, on the other, the state of the deceased, see Robert Hertz, "A Contribution to the Study of the Collective Representation of Death," in his *Death and the Right Hand*, trans. R. and C. Needham (Glencoe, Illinois: Free Press, 1960), pp. 27–86, first published in *Année sociologique* 10 (1907).

124. In addition to the works cited in n. 119 above, see Louis-Vincent Thomas, *Le cadavre: De la biologie à l'anthropologie* (Brussels: Éditions Complexe, 1980).

125. See below n. 135.

126. See Onians, *Origins*, p. 267; Toynbee, *Death and Burial*, pp. 48ff.; Rush, *Death and Burial*, pp. 241–44; E. Valton, "Crémation," in *DTC*, vol. 3, pt. 2 (1938), col. 2316.

concern to treat cadavers gently and to minimize images of violence in the afterlife, however conceived.[127] Burying was seen as less traumatic than burning. But both were understood to produce hard mineral remains, which were placed under the earth, not scattered over it.

This desire for quiet sepulchre was in part a response to the rampant sadism of animal shows and public executions and to the growing moral outrage they generated.[128] Concern for a peaceful end was also expressed in the traditional practice of funerary banquets, celebrated on tombs and understood as feeding and pacifying the dead.[129] Indeed the Greek and Roman dead were fed in more direct ways as well; food was left on tombs, libations were poured there, and tubes were sometimes placed in graves directly over the mouths of corpses.[130] Stories circulated of the dead (especially those who died violently or were not properly buried) roaming abroad in search of food and drink. Both Jews and Romans spoke of the grave—and of extrapolations from it, such as Sheol or Hades—as devouring the departed.[131] Hence corpses were seen as eating and as "being eaten by" the earth. Early Christian polemicists occasionally spoke not only of beasts and pagans eating Christians in the arena but even of graves "eating" the dead and of soul "being buried in" or "eaten by" body when a child is conceived.[132]

127. As Paxton points out (*Christianizing Death*, p. 20), funerary rituals protected both the living from the dead and the dead from demons.

128. See Potter, "Martyrdom as Spectacle"; Barton, "Sacramentum"; and eadem, *Sorrows of the Romans*. On violence and pain in this period, see Jacques Paul, in *L'église et la culture en occident, ixe–xiie siècles* (Paris: Presses Universitaires de France, 1986), vol. 2, pp. 674–83; Michel Rouche, "The Early Middle Ages in the West," in *A History of Private Life*, vol. 1: *From Pagan Rome to Byzantium*, ed. Paul Veyne, trans. Arthur Goldhammer (Cambridge, Mass.: Harvard University Press, 1987), pp. 485–517; and Peter Brown, *Power and Persuasion*, chap. 2, and chap. 3 at nn. 100–3. And see n. 132 below.

129. See Nock, "Cremation and Burial," and Toynbee, *Death and Burial*. On funerary meals, see Saxer, *Morts, martyrs, reliques*, pp. 123–49, and Joan M. Petersen, *The Dialogues of Gregory the Great in Their Late Antique Cultural Background* (Toronto: Pontifical Institute of Mediaeval Studies, 1984), p. 142.

130. Cumont, *After Life in Roman Paganism*, pp. 44–56.

131. In many different layers of the Old Testament, the grave or the underworld or even Yahweh are spoken of as "eating" the dead; see Nicolas J. Tromp, *Primitive Conceptions of Death and the Nether World in the Old Testament* (Rome: Pontifical Biblical Institute, 1969), pp. 8, 21–32, 107, 172, 191–95, 212.

132. See above nn. 47 (Athenagoras sees cannibalism as making oneself a "tomb" for others), 77 (Tertullian sees God as "devouring" the martyrs), 103 through 105 (the *Didascalia* connects celebration of the Eucharist on the grave with not only survival but also redemption of bodiliness), and below chapter 2, n. 121 (Jerome fears transmigration of souls as a kind of chain consumption). And see Ariès, *Hour of Our Death*, p. 58 and passim. The curious polemic of Arnobius (*Adversus nationes*, ed. A. Reifferscheid, CSEL 4 [Vienna: C. Gerold, 1875]), which argues that God must bestow

Early Christianity, rabbinic Judaism, and the Koran all speak of the body that rises as bones or a seed.[133] Christian exegesis, like rabbinic, came to read the dry bones of Ezekiel 37.1–14 as referring not to the nation of Israel but to individuals.[134] The early rabbis taught that the person would rise when the "nut" of the spinal column was watered or fed by the dew of resurrection and that the bones of the just would roll through special underground tunnels to be reassembled in Jerusalem at the sound of the last trumpet—ideas that clearly reflect the Jewish practice of ossilegium and reburial in the Holy Land.[135] Without a home-

---

immortality on the soul as well as resurrection on the body, voices violent rejection of embodiment. See bk. 2, chaps. 39–43, pp. 79–82, which questions whether God could have sent souls into bodies to "be buried in the germs of men, spring from the womb, . . . keep up the silliest wailings, draw the breasts in sucking, besmear and bedaub themselves with their own filth, . . . to lie, to cheat, to deceive. . . .," and details the horrors of the arena as special proof of human depravity. Arnobius says spectators at the animal shows delight in blood and dismemberment, and "grind with their teeth and give to their utterly insatiable maw" pieces of animals who have eaten humans (trans. H. Bryce, in *Ante-Nicene Fathers*, vol. 6 [reprint, Eerdmans, 1978], pp. 449 and 450). In bk. 2, chap. 37, Arnobius speaks of the embodiment of souls as a process of going to earthly places, "tenebrosis ut corporibus inuolutae inter pituitas et sanguinem degerent, inter stercoris hos utres et saccati obscenissimas serias umoris. . . ." (CSEL 4, pp. 77–78). Arnobius's pupil, Lactantius, who also has a strong sense of body-soul dualism, gives a truly horrific description of the brutality of the arena; see *Institutes*, bk. 6, chaps. 20, in Lactantius, *Opera omnia*, ed. Samuel Brandt, CSEL 19 and 27, pt. 2 (Prague: Tempsky, 1890; reprint, Johnson, 1965), pp. 555–62.

133. Koran, Surah 56.60–61. See Onians, *Origins*, pp. 287–89, and Ringgren, "Resurrection," p. 349.

134. See n. 9 above.

135. Babylonian Talmud (Soncino ed.), Kethuboth, 111a–111b, in which a discussion of bones rolling through cavities to reach Jerusalem for resurrection is followed not only by the sprouting wheat analogy to explain our rising but also by extravagant descriptions of fertility in the afterlife that parallel those of Papias (enormous kernels of grain, grapes, etc.). For the use of Ecclesiastes 12.5 ("the almond shall blossom") to refer to the "nut" of the spinal column growing into the person at the resurrection, see Midrash: Rabbah (3d ed., New York: Soncino, 1983), Leviticus Rabbah 18.1; Genesis Rabbah 28.3. On some of these passages, see Moore, *Judaism*, vol. 2, pp. 377–87. See also Dov Zlotnick, trans., *The Tractate "Mourning" (Semahot)* (New Haven: Yale University Press, 1966), especially chaps. 2, 8, 9, 12, and 13, pp. 35–36, 57–60, 71–72, 80–85, which clearly reflects concern about corpse mortification and scattering and connects this to the practice of ossilegium and return of the bones to Palestine (the text may be mid-eighth century, but it may be much earlier).

On Jewish ossilegium, see Joseph A. Callaway, "Burials in Ancient Palestine: From the Stone Age to Abraham," *The Biblical Archaeologist* 26, no. 3 (1963): 74–91; Eric M. Meyers, "Secondary Burials in Palestine," *The Biblical Archaeologist* 33, no. 1 (1970): 2–29; idem, *Jewish Ossuaries: Reburial and Rebirth* (Rome: Biblical Institute Press, 1971); Pau Figueras, *Decorated Jewish Ossuaries* (Leiden: Brill, 1983). These works make it clear that very different understandings of person and of death and resurrection could attach to the bones; they seem, however, to agree that ossilegium land—a clear sense of holy place to focus eschatological dreams—Christians projected into heaven their hope of reassemblage and sprouting. But their basic images retained the notion that the person in some sense survives in hard, material particles, no matter how finely ground or how widely scattered. The grave will not consume us. It cannot be irrelevant to such imagery that the funerary practices of Romans and Jews—both cremation and inhumation—focused on the production of hard remains (ashes and bones) or that both groups found the idea of scattering these abhorrent and increasingly emphasized gentle burial.

Nor can it be irrelevant that both practice and polemic in the Mediterranean world closely connected ideas of eating and ideas of sepulchre.[136] Christians first opposed then adopted the Roman funerary meal. By the fourth century, the Eucharist was celebrated in graveyards, and the practice continued at least until the fifth century, despite some episcopal opposition.[137] The custom of placing the bodies of the martyrs in altars meant that the mass came to be celebrated over the "blood of the martyrs," even in churches.[138]

Moreover, cannibalism—the consumption in which survival of body is most deeply threatened—was a charge pagans leveled against Christians and Christians against pagans. Polemicists for both positions assumed that cannibalism is the ultimate barbarism, the ultimate horror.[139] To eat (if it were really possible) would be to destroy—and to take over— the power of the consumed.[140] Surely the odd assurances of Theophilus and Athenagoras that this cannot happen suggest their fear that it can.

---

was compatible with a notion of the human being as a unitary individual (nephesh) even in death; see Meyers, *Jewish Ossuaries*, pp. 89 and 92.

136. On the prominence of metaphors of consumption in the Greco-Roman world, see Wilfred Parsons, "Lest Men, Like Fishes . . .," *Traditio* 3 (1940): 380–88, and Bruce Dickins, "Addendum to 'Lest Men, Like Fishes . . .,'" *Traditio* 6 (1948): 356–7. See also Maggie Kilgour, *From Communism to Cannibalism: An Anatomy of Metaphors of Incorporation* (Princeton: Princeton University Press, 1990), pp. 20–62, a suggestive analysis that nonetheless misses much of the immediate context of the works it considers. The same is true of Camporesi, *The Fear of Hell*, which underlines the connection of eucharistic theology and ideas of the afterlife for a much later period. For an analysis of funerary meals, and funerary rituals generally, as ritual processes of separation and incorporation, see Paxton, *Christianizing Death*, pp. 5–9, 32–33, and the works cited there.

137. Saxer, *Morts, martyrs, reliques*, pp. 123–49.

138. Grabar, *Martyrium*, vol. 1, p. 35

139. See above nn. 33, 83, 84, and 132, and Grant, "Resurrection," p. 197ff.

140. On cannibalism as a way of taking over the power of the consumed (with the concomitant idea that torturing the one who is finally eaten increases his power), see Peggy Reeves Sanday, *Divine Hunger: Cannibalism as a Cultural System* (Cambridge:

Such fears may indeed provide a deeper link than has previously been noticed between early eucharistic theology and the doctrine of the resurrection.[141] Eucharist, like resurrection, was a victory over the grave. Tertullian and Irenaeus expressed in paradox what Athenagoras expressed in (questionable) science: even if executioners feed our bodies to the beasts and then serve those beasts up on banquet tables, we are not truly eaten. To rise with all our organs and pieces intact is a victory over digestion—not only the digestion threatened by torturers and cannibals but most of all that proffered by natural process itself. Small wonder then that the funerary Eucharist, at first condemned as a continuation of pagan piety, came to be seen as a palpable assurance that our flesh unites with the undigested and indigestible flesh of Christ in heaven. The Eucharist is a guarantee that the risen body we shall all become cannot be consumed.

Christianity spread among peoples for whom bodily change was theoretically inexplicable and to whom corpses were horrifying. For Romans and Jews (although in different ways), the cadaver that lay rotting in the grave was in some sense the locus of person; its putrefaction was both terrifying and polluting.[142] Moreover, decay was merely the final permutation in a body that was forever changing (eating, growing, giving birth, sickening, aging), and the more Christian apologists adopted the natural philosophy available in the ancient world, the less explicable such flux seemed.[143]

Change was the ontological scandal to ancient philosophers. Their basic effort was to fix identity in a world where (as Tertullian understood Aristotle to say) change meant ceasing to be one thing and becoming another. With such a notion of change, bodily process was fundamen-

---

Cambridge University Press, 1986) pp. 83–122 and passim; and my *Holy Feast and Holy Fast*, pp. 30, 319 n. 75, and p. 412 n. 77.

141. For a fine statement of the importance of early, literalist, eucharistic theology (from a point of view different from mine), see A. H. C. Van Eijk, "The Gospel of Philip and Clement of Alexandria: Gnostic and Ecclesiastical Theology on the Resurrection and the Eucharist," *Vigiliae Christianae* 25 (1971): 94–120.

142. See above, nn. 47, 119, 124, 129, and 132. The Jewish philosopher Philo said: "The body is wicked and a plotter against the soul, and is always a corpse and a dead thing. . . . Each of us does nothing but carry a corpse about, since the soul lifts up and bears without effort the body which is in itself a corpse." See E. R. Goodenough, "Philo on Immortality," *Harvard Theological Review* 39 (1946): 97.

143. See Grant, "Resurrection," pp. 120–30 and 188–208; Henry Chadwick, "Origen, Celsus, and the Resurrection of the Body," *Harvard Theological Review* 41 (1948): 83–102; Barnard, "Athenagoras: Background," pp. 8–12; Alain Le Boulluec, "De la croissance selon les stoiciens à la résurrection selon Origène," *Revue des études grecques* 88 (1975): 143–55; Ariès, *Hour of Death*, p. 95 and passim.

tally mysterious: upon close examination, either the process or the body tended to disappear.[144] If digestion, for example, was real transformation, the body was not an entity at all but merely a place or a moment through which food passed on its way to excrement or rot. If, on the other hand, the body as entity survived, real absorption of food seemed not to occur. One could hypothesize that particles of flesh or blood moved farther apart to make room for particles of bread or beef to come in between, but how could a particle of, for example, cow *become* Socrates?[145]

Second-century apologists such as Theophilus of Antioch and Athenagoras answered these arguments by the (to modern taste) unsatisfactory expedient of denying true material change. Irenaeus and Tertullian tried to sublimate the contradiction into paradox by asserting the power of God.[146] But biological process remained a threat to identity. Resurrection therefore had to replace process with stasis, to bring matter (changeable by definition) to changelessness. It had to restore body qua body, while transforming it to permanence and impassibility. The promise of spiritual body or immutable physicality remained an oxymoron.

That oxymoron went back to 1 Corinthians 15.44: "sown a natural body, raised a spiritual body." But, as we have seen, both the Pauline concept and the seed metaphor that expressed it came, by the early third century, to reflect concerns foreign to Paul. The seed that rises again as a sheaf of wheat came to express both the idea that material continuity guarantees identity and the notion that salvation is victory over partition, rot, decay—over change itself.

The transformation of the Pauline seed metaphor occurred against the background of other changes in ideas. By the early third century, polemicists for the resurrection of the flesh assumed a dualist anthropology that saw the human being as a union of soul and body; they also

144. Aristotle, of course, understood that digestion and growth threatened the persistence of the corporeal subject. In *De generatione et corruptione (1.5* [320a–322a], trans. E. S. Forster, *Aristotle: On Sophistical Refutations . . .*, Loeb Classical Library [Cambridge, Mass.: Harvard University Press, 1955], pp. 204–21) he tried to systematize change so that augmentation and diminution did not affect the body, which was thus understood to endure. Various Stoic thinkers, picking up on this, tried to maintain some kind of persisting substance. See Le Boulluec, "De la croissance . . .," p. 147. My point here is not to assess how successful the ancient efforts were philosophically but to indicate that the issue continued to be a problem.

145. See below chapter 3 at n. 60, and the passage from Aristotle's *De gen.* cited in n. 144 above.

146. Gedaliahu G. Stroumsa, "*Caro salutis cardo:* Shaping the Person in Early Christian Thought," *History of Religions* 30, no. 1 (1990): 35, makes the important point that pivotal concerns tend to appear early in a tradition but are often elaborated only slowly.

assumed that soul was in some sense immortal although several of them held, as had some authors of Jewish apocalyptic literature, that immortality is a gift from God, not an inherent characteristic of soul.[147] Nonetheless neither body-soul dualism nor the assumption of immortality solved the problem of survival of self. A theory of bodily return was, to these thinkers, essential. What polemicists for physical resurrection urged against both pagans and other Christians was a literal, materialist understanding of body that seemed to some philosophically untenable and theologically unnecessary. I have argued here that close attention to the metaphors in which this understanding is expressed tells us a good deal about what body really meant in the polemics of the years around 200.

Changes in resurrection metaphors to stress rot and rupture, followed by regurgitation and impassibility, suggest that the body that rises is quintessentially the martyr's body, in danger not just from pain and mutilation but also from scattering, dishonor, even cannibalism, after death. Resurrection is victory over partition and putrefaction; it is both the anesthesia of glory and the reunion of particles of self. Resurrection guarantees not only the justice denied to the living; it guarantees the rest and reassemblage—the burial—denied to the dead. The early third-century understanding of body seems thus to owe a good deal to the context of persecution. It owes something as well to slow shifts and deep continuities in attitudes toward the cadaver, and toward biological process, in the Mediterranean world of the third century.

By 400, the persecutions had been over for almost a century, and few could remember a time when wealthy and prominent pagan citizens had cremated their dead. When controversy over the resurrection of the flesh erupted again, as we shall see in my next chapter, new issues were at stake and a new context was reflected. But the deep—and deeply inconsistent—conception of identity as material continuity, characteristic of thinkers as different as Athenagoras and Irenaeus, lasted on in the disputes of the late fourth and early fifth centuries and set the agenda for medieval theology.

147. This was the position taken by both Arnobius and Lactantius; see n. 132 above.

Two

Resurrection, Relic Cult, and Asceticism: The Debates of 400 and Their Background

The Legacy of the Second Century

 IN THE YEARS AROUND 200, Irenaeus of Lyons (writing in Greek) and Tertullian of Carthage (writing in Latin) defended a literal, materialistic understanding of general resurrection against those who argued for a spiritual understanding of the risen body. The particles of our flesh—nourished and supported in this life by a eucharistic bread that was literally the flesh of Christ—would be reassembled by God at the end of time in such a way that no detail of bodily structure was lost, neither genitals, nor intestines, nor eyelashes, nor toes. Although only the flesh of the virtuous would don the garment of glory, all flesh would rise to receive its just deserts. Indeed the torn and twisted bodies of the martyrs might—at the very moment of execution—begin to shine with the splendid impassibility of the Transfiguration. Tertullian and Irenaeus drew on a host of images to express their conviction that exactly the flesh that is digested in the arena or the grave is transmuted to unchanging glory at the resurrection.

Nonetheless a paradox remained. Body is flux and frustration, a locus of pain and process. If it becomes impassible and incorruptible, how is it still body? If it remains body, how is its resurrection either possible or desirable?[1] To put it very simply: if there is change, how can there be

1. For the argument that the real attack on resurrection came not from Gnostic spiritualizing but from pagan notions of body and matter as ludicrous and disgusting, see Barnard, "Athenagoras: Background," pp. 8–12.

continuity and hence identity? If there is continuity, how will there be change and hence glory? Or to rephrase the issue in the images second-century apologists used far more frequently than technical philosophical argument: if we rise as a sheaf of wheat sprouts up from a seed buried in the earth, in what sense is the sheaf (new in its matter and in its structure) the same as and therefore a redemption of the seed? If we rise as a statue, which has been broken or melted down and then reassembled or reforged by the artist who first made it, how similar will the new statue be to the old in either material or design and why is such similarity salvation? Despite the conceptual and rhetorical power of writers such as Tertullian and Irenaeus, a problem remained.

We are often told that the doctrine of bodily resurrection did not become a major topic of controversy again until the irascible Jerome (egged on by Epiphanius) flailed out at the Origenists in the last years of the fourth century.[2] But theological writing between 200 and 400 makes it clear that the idea of resurrection continued to generate puzzlement, confusion, and incredulity in Christianity's pagan opponents as well as among the faithful.[3] Theologians such as Hilary of Poitiers, Cyril of Jerusalem, or Gregory of Nyssa not only summarized and repeatedly refuted pagan attacks; they also expressed exasperation at the "silly questions" and "sterile fears" of ordinary believers.[4] Duval may be right that Jerome lifted his references to the queries of Christians (like so much

---

2. Dewart, *Death and Resurrection,* and Van Unnik "Epistle to Rheginos," p. 143. And see chapter 1, n. 91 above. For Elizabeth Clark's argument that the late fourth-century debate moves rapidly away from the issue of resurrection, see below at n. 117.

3. At the end of the sixth century, Gregory the Great still found people who rejected or doubted the doctrine. In his answer, he underlined the question of identity, pointing out that I am not "I" if I rise in an aerial body. See *Morals on Job,* bk. 14, chaps. 55–58, *Patrologiae cursus completus: Series latina,* ed. J.-P. Migne [hereafter PL], 75 (Paris: Migne, 1849), cols. 1075–79. Gregory asserts that God can sort out one kind of digested flesh from another and one kind of dust from another. See *Homilies on Ezekiel,* bk. 2, homily 8, paragrs. 6–10, PL 76 (Paris, 1849), cols. 1030–34. Gregory devotes much attention to the seed metaphor, interpreting it so as to make it account for identity by material continuity; he also lays much stress on dissolution into particles or elements (which themselves survive) and stresses reassemblage of these particles at resurrection. He is fond of the metaphor of the pot and stresses its hardening in glory. See n. 112 below.

4. Hilary of Poitiers, *Sur Matthieu,* chap. 5, paragr. 8, trans. and ed. Jean Doignon, Sc 254 and 258 (Paris: Éditions du Cerf, 1978 and 1979), vol. 1, pp. 157–59. Cyril of Jerusalem, Catechetical Lectures, lecture 4, paragrs. 30–31, lecture 18, paragrs 2–18, in *Patrologiae cursus completus: Series graeca,* ed. J.-P. Migne [hereafter PG], 33 (Paris: Migne, 1857), cols. 491–94 and 1019–40. Much of Gregory of Nyssa's *On the Soul and the Resurrection* is devoted to answering objections. For his awareness that some of these are the same as those Paul met from the Corinthians, see Gregory, *De anima et resurrectione,* PG 46 (Paris, 1858), cols. 151–54.

else) from Tertullian,[5] but the major exponents of bodily resurrection throughout the period—Methodius, Basil, Gregory of Nyssa, Ephraim the Syriac, Macarius Magnes, Ambrose, Augustine—clearly reflect real discussion with worried believers who continued to raise the sort of objections Paul and Clement had met from the first-century inhabitants of Corinth.[6] Body is worse than dung, asserted the pagan Celsus (quoting Heraclitus); it is "a disgusting vessel of urine" and "bag of shit," said the Christian apologist Arnobius.[7] It is perpetual mutation, explained the theologian Basil. It can be the food of fish or carrion beasts or even of human beings, said Cyril of Jerusalem and Macarius (quoting pagan objections); how then will it be reassembled? Who would want it back, asked Ambrose; it is only a wretched prison for the soul, which aches to escape from pain.[8]

5. Yves-Marie Duval, "Tertullien contre Origène sur la résurrection de la chair dans le Contra Johannem Hierosolymitanum, 23–36 de saint Jerome," Revue des études augustiniennes 17, nos. 3–4 (1971): 227–78, especially p. 245. See also Henri Marrou, "La résurrection . . . et les apologists," Lumière et vie 3 (1952): 83–92, on use by later thinkers of objections considered by earlier apologists.

6. Basil, In psalmos: In ps. XLIV, paragr. 1, and In ps. CXIV, paragr. 5, PG 29 (Paris, 1857), cols. 387–88 and 491–92, says perpetual bodily mutation is a problem; see Michel, "Résurrection," col. 2534. Macarius Magnes [or of Magnesia] in his Apocriticus (which may be from around 400) gives the objections of pagan philosophy (which may be those of Porphyry); see C. Blondel, ed., Macarii Magnetis quae supersunt ex inedito codice (Paris: Édition Klincksieck, 1876) and T. W. Crafer, trans., The Apocriticus of Macarius Magnes (London: SPCK, 1919), whose translation reorders the work. On problems in dating and attributing this text see Johannes Quasten, Patrology, vol. 3: The Golden Age of Greek Patristic Literature from the Council of Nicaea to the Council of Chalcedon (Utrecht, Antwerp, and Westminster, Maryland: Spectrum and Newman Press, 1960), pp. 486–88. On whether or not the borrowings are from Porphyry, see T. D. Barnes, "Porphyry Against the Christians," Journal of Theological Studies n.s. 24 (1973): 424–42, especially pp. 424–30, and R. Goulet, "Porphyre et Macaire de Magnésie," Studia patristica 15 (1984): 448–52, both of whom argue that the objections are not to be understood as direct quotations from Porphyry. Macarius admits (bk. 4, chap. 30, ed. Blondel, p. 220; trans. Crafer, p. 155) that the doctrine of the resurrection is a difficulty. Ambrose, De excessu fratris Satyri libri duo, bk. 2, chaps. 102, 114, 121, PL 16 (Paris, 1880), cols. 1403, 1407–9, and in Otto Faller, ed., CSEL 73 (Vienna: Hölder-Pichler-Tempsky, 1955), pp. 305–6, 314, 317–18, warns against asking foolish and detailed questions about the resurrection and the resurrection body. On Methodius, Ephraim, and Augustine, see below.

7. For Origen, quoting Celsus, quoting Heraclitus, see Origen, Contra Celsum, bk. 5, chap. 24, PG 11 (Paris, 1857), cols. 1217–18; and trans. Henry Chadwick, Contra Celsum (reprint with corrections, Cambridge: Cambridge University Press, 1979), p. 282. For similar worry about decay, see Aphrahat, Demonstration 8, paragrs. 1–3, cited in n. 49 below. On Arnobius, see Adversus nationes, ed. A. Reifferscheid, CSEL 4, bk. 2, chap. 37, pp. 77–78; and chapter 1, n. 132, above. Macarius Magnes, Apocriticus, bk. 4, chap. 24, ed. Blondel, p. 205; trans. Crafer, p. 154, gives as a pagan objection the argument that God cannot do what is impossible, irrational, or evil; therefore he will not stand by and watch the beautiful heavens melt while restoring the "rotten and corrupt" bodies of human beings.

8. See nn. 4 and 6 above and Ambrose, De excessu Satyri, bk. 2, chap. 20, PL 16, cols. 1377–78, and CSEL 73, p. 260. On the theme of body as prison (also trap and

It is important for us to be clear that such discussions and concerns lasted throughout the third and fourth centuries. The fundamental contradiction between identity and change was not solved by any of the great fourth-century exponents of bodily resurrection—neither by Hilary of Poitiers, nor by Gregory of Nyssa, nor by Ephraim the Syriac, nor even by Augustine. Each—in rhetoric and metaphor, and sometimes (but not often) in logical argument—simply clung to both sides of the paradox. There must be something that rises; there is no *resurrection* without identity.[9] We know we are body; therefore body must rise. But there must be process and transformation as well, because the risen body must be radically changed. Unless something can change and still be the same thing, there can be no rising to glory of the corpse that has gone down into the grave. The enigmatic figure Macarius Magnes, for example, gives a vivid picture of the entire creation, groaning forever in flux. He associates decay, consumption, and fertility, even asserting that cannibalism is not horrible, for the child in the womb eats its mother in order to live. Yet Macarius also asserts the permanence of body fragments.[10] Resurrected flesh is simply smelted out by God like bits of gold or silver from clay.

> If then the power of fire is so strong . . . that it preserves the essence
> of each undestroyed, even though the gold has fallen into countless
> cavities and is dissolved into endless fragments and scattered into mire

---

tomb) of the soul, see Pierre Courcelle, *Connais-toi toi-même: De Socrate à saint Bernard* (Paris: Études augustiniennes, 1975), vol. 2, pp. 345–414.

9. See Van Eijk, " 'Only That Can Rise Which Has Previously Fallen.' " John of Damascus sums up the argument; his formulation becomes the *locus classicus* for scholastic authors of the high Middle Ages (*De fide orthodoxa*, bk. 4, chap. 27, PG 94 [Paris, 1860], cols. 1219–28, esp. col. 1219).

10. Macarius's summary of the pagan objections to resurrection is a powerful statement of the understanding of natural process as perpetual flux (see *Apocriticus*, bk. 4, chap. 24 [objection] and chap. 30 [answer], ed. Blondel, pp. 204–5 and 220–227; trans. Crafer, p. 153–63). Macarius's position on the cannibalism issue is complex. In discussing pagan objections to John 6.54 ("Unless you eat the flesh of the Son of Man . . ."), he meets the argument that cannibalism is bestial by asserting that it is "not strange and horrible" at all, for the fetus eats its mother in order to grow, and the child drinks her blood in nursing (bk. 3, chaps. 15, 16, 23, and 24, ed. Blondel, pp. 94–96 and 103–10; trans. Crafer, pp. 78–87). Repeatedly he draws an analogy between Christ's body and the earth and the products of the earth, assimilating all these to fertility. He thus suggests that bodies are really eaten by earth or worms or beasts; consumption and incorporation are not, to Macarius, charged with quite the horror they seem to stimulate in other fourth-century writers. Nonetheless, he also holds that bits are regurgitated for reassemblage (see bk. 4, chaps. 24 and 30, cited above). This would, of course, suggest (as does the possibly contemporary argument of Augustine) that on some level digestion does not really digest.

or clay, in heaps of earth or of dung; what are we to say about Him who ordained the nature of the fire? . . . Would he not have the power without even effort to change man . . . who is contained in matter of various kinds, and to set before Him safe and sound those who have . . . been eaten by wild beasts or birds, those who have been dissolved into fine dust . . . ? Will He be found to be less effective than the fire?[11]

Gregory of Nyssa holds that we rise like angels, without age or sex. But he also argues that we are reconstituted from exactly the same particles we were in life, although it is difficult to see how God can use such a large number of bits or why he will do so to create such a radically different body.[12]

Thus the contradiction between continuity and transfiguration was not resolved; the technical question of how identity survives through process was not answered; specific quibbles about exactly which bits will be reassembled were not met. I stress this because answers were available. In the first half of the third century, one of the greatest theologians of the ancient world, Origen of Alexandria, gave a highly satisfactory answer to the problem of identity, and he gave it in Pauline language. Employing in new ways the seed and garment metaphors popular since the second century, Origen accounted for identity through dynamic process and built radical change into resurrection.[13]

Origen and Methodius: The Seed versus the Statue

There is, of course, room for disagreement about what Origen actually said and what he meant.[14] His treatise on the resurrection has been lost, and some of the relevant passages in his other works survive only in

11. *Apocriticus*, bk. 4, chap. 30, ed. Blondel, pp. 223–24; trans. Crafer, p. 159.
12. On Gregory, see below, pp. 81–86. Gregory's position has been much debated; see Jean Danielou, "La résurrection des corps chez Gregoire de Nysse," *Vigiliae Christianae* 7, no. 3 (1953): 154–70; Gerhart B. Ladner, "The Philosophical Anthropology of Saint Gregory of Nyssa," *Dumbarton Oaks Papers* 12 (1958): 61–94; T. J. Dennis, "Gregory on the Resurrection of the Body," in *The Easter Sermons of Gregory of Nyssa: Translation and Commentary*, ed. A. Spira and C. Klock (Cambridge, Mass.: Philadelphia Patristic Foundation, 1981), pp. 55–80; Dewart, *Death and Resurrection*, pp. 147–56. For bibliography on Gregory, see Margarete Altenburger and Friedhelm Mann, eds., *Bibliographie zu Gregor von Nyssa: Editionen, Übersetzungen, und Literatur* (Leiden: Brill, 1988).
13. These were the basic Pauline metaphors of 1 Corinthians 15 and 2 Corinthians 5 and had been crucial to debate over the resurrection since Tertullian.
14. See, for example, Dewart, *Death and Resurrection*, pp. 121–22.

Latin translations that revise him in directions his fourth-century editor Rufinus considered to be more orthodox. Nonetheless, I am convinced by the recent work of Henri Crouzel and Jon Dechow that Origen saw himself as treading a middle way between, on the one hand, Jews, millenarian Christians, and pagans who (he thought) understood bodily resurrection as the reanimation of dead flesh and, on the other hand, Gnostics and Hellenists who (he thought) denied any kind of ultimate reality either to resurrection or to body.[15] Using the seed metaphor from 1 Corinthians 15, the reference to our angelic life in heaven from Matthew 22.29–33, and the suggestion in 2 Corinthians 5.4 that we are tents or tabernacles that must take on a covering of incorruption, Origen argued that we will have a body in heaven but a spiritual and luminous one. In his commentary on Psalm 1 (a passage that all his recent interpreters believe to be our best indication of his ideas), Origen says:

> Because each body is held together by [virtue of] a nature that assimilates into itself from without certain things for nourishment and, corresponding to the things added, excretes other things . . . , the material substratum is never the same. For this reason, river is not a bad name for the body since, strictly speaking, the initial substratum in our bodies is perhaps not the same for even two days.
>
> Yet the real Paul or Peter, so to speak, is always the same—[and] not merely in [the] soul, whose substance neither flows through us nor has anything ever added [to it]—even if the nature of the body is in a state of flux, because the form (*eidos*) characterizing the body is the same, just as the features constituting the corporeal quality of Peter and Paul remain the same. According to this quality, not only scars from childhood remain on the bodies but also certain other peculiarities, [like] skin blemishes and similar things.[16]

15. The bibliography on Origen is immense; see Henri Crouzel, *Bibliographie critique d'Origène* (The Hague: Steenbrugge, 1971), and supplement (1982); and idem, "The Literature on Origen, 1970–88," *Theological Studies* 49 (1988): 499–516. I have been particularly influenced by Chadwick, "Origen, Celsus, and Resurrection"; Henri Crouzel, "Les critiques adressées par Methode et ses contemporains à la doctrine origenienne du corps réssuscité," *Gregorianum* 53 (1972): 679–716; idem, "La doctrine origenienne du corps réssuscité," *Bullétin de littérature ecclésiastique* 31 (1980): 175–200 and 241–66; idem, *Origen: The Life and Thought of the First Great Theologian,* trans. A. S. Worrall (San Francisco: Harper and Row, 1989); Jon F. Dechow, *Dogma and Mysticism in Early Christianity: Epiphanius of Cyprus and the Legacy of Origen* (Macon, Georgia: Mercer University Press, 1988); Peter Brown, *Body and Society,* pp. 160–77; Elizabeth A. Clark, "New Perspectives on the Origenist Controversy: Human Embodiment and Ascetic Strategies," *Church History* 59 (1990): 145–62.

16. Origen, Fragment on Psalm 1.5, in Methodius, *De resurrectione,* bk. 1, chaps. 22–23, in *Methodius,* ed. Nathanael Bonwetsch, Die griechischen christlichen Schriftsteller der ersten drei Jahrhunderte [hereafter GCS], 27 (Leipzig: Hinrichs,

Origen here accepts the antique concept of the body as flux, expressed particularly in his day in the Galenic version of humoral theory. This fluctuating mass of matter cannot rise, he argues; it is not even the same from one day to the next.[17] And even if the bits of flesh present at the moment of death could survive, why would God arbitrarily decide to reanimate those bits as opposed to all the others that have flowed through the body between childhood and old age?

But, says Origen, there *is* a body; it survives from the moment of conception until death, taking on different qualities and adaptable to different circumstances yet recognizably itself.[18] This body is not soul, for soul—exactly because it is not material—never changes.[19] Rather body, as Origen understands it, changes in life; therefore it certainly changes after death.[20] He writes:

> And just as we would . . . need to have gills and other endowment[s] of fish if it were necessary for us to live underwater in the sea, so those who are going to inherit [the] kingdom of heaven and be in superior places must have spiritual bodies. The previous form does not disappear, even if its transition to the more glorious [state] occurs, just as the form of Jesus, Moses and Elijah in the Transfiguration was not [a] different [one] than what it had been.
>
> Moreover . . . "it is sown a psychic body, it is raised a spiritual body" (1 Cor. 15.44). . . . [A]lthough the form is saved, we are going to put away nearly [every] earthly quality in the resurrection . . . [for] "flesh and blood cannot inherit [the] kingdom . . ." (1 Cor. 15.50). Similarly, for the saint there will indeed be [a body] preserved by him who once endued the flesh with form, but [there will] no longer [be] flesh;

1917), pp. 244–48, and Epiphanius, *Haereses*, bk. 2, tom. 1, haeres. 64, paragrs. 14–15, PG 41 (Paris, 1858), cols. 1089–92; trans. Dechow, in *Dogma and Mysticism*, pp. 373–74.

17. On Christian use of Galen, see Barnard, "Athenagoras: Background," pp. 6–18. On the Stoic idea of the body as flux, see Le Boulluec, "De la croissance . . .," pp. 152–53; on the importance of natural philosophical ideas about flux as background to discussion of resurrection, see Grant, "Resurrection," and Chadwick, "Origen, Celsus, and Resurrection," pp. 86–91.

18. For Origen's explicit attention to the problem of identity, see *De principiis*, bk. 2, chap. 10, paragr. 1, and bk. 3, chap. 6; ed. Paul Kötschau, *Origenes Werke*, vol. 5, GCS, pp. 172–74 and 270–91. 1 Corinthians 15.35–38 was central to the concern for identity; see Crouzel, "Les critiques," p. 680.

19. That is, in the sense of corruption. Souls, of course, progress or regress morally. See Crouzel, "Les critiques," p. 689.

20. The final goal, however, is changelessness—that is, the transition to a "spiritual body" that cannot become a corpse. See *Dialogue with Heraclides*, ed. and trans. Jean Scherer, *Entretien d'Origène avec Heraclide*, Sc 67 (Paris: Éditions du Cerf, 1960), pp. 66–69.

yet the very thing which was once being characterized in the flesh will be characterized in the spiritual body.[21]

This is not the thirteenth-century Thomistic use of hylomorphism, which (as we shall see in my sixth chapter) lodges identity in Aristotelian form or soul and thereby produces both an ingenious solution and some complex problems in accounting for continuity of body between this life, the grave, and the life of heaven.[22] Rather Origen's body is, as Crouzel has argued, a substratum whose identity is guaranteed by a corporeal *eidos*. This *eidos* is a combination of Platonic form, or plan, with Stoic seminal reason (an internal principle of growth or development).[23] A pattern that organizes the flux of matter and yet has its own inherent capacity for growth, it is (although I introduce the modern analogy with extreme hesitation) a bit like a genetic code.[24]

Origen thus solved the problem of identity more successfully than any other thinker of Christian antiquity. And it is important to see what the solution accomplished. By accounting for the permanence of a body through material flux but attributing to that body its own dynamism, Origen's theory recognized that both the natural world and the human person really change. Growth now belonged to a self; process was fully real and could be fully good. The Pauline seed metaphor could therefore refer to fertility rather than to decay;[25] natural changes, such as the development of a fetus or the flowering of a fig tree—both images Origen used—became unambiguously appropriate to describe the journey toward heaven.[26] Yet the heaven to which our selves will go was understood as very far from earth, and the body, whose identity was guaranteed, became at the same time more fluid and potential, indeterminate and changeable.

Origen indeed vacillated on how far the transformation of the body

21. Origen, Fragment on Psalm 1.5; trans. by Dechow, *Dogma and Mysticism*, pp. 374–75; see above n. 16. See also *De principiis*, bk. 2, chap. 10, paragr. 2, pp. 174–75, and n. 25 below.

22. Origen's body is not Aquinas's soul as substantial form, nor is it the *forma corporeitatis* of Bonaventure or Henry of Ghent. (It allows for more change than the latter.) It is closer to Aquinas's second matter. But it is not that either, because it identifies *logos* with material substance. See Crouzel, "La doctrine origenienne," p. 247, and below chapter 6, pp. 256–61.

23. Crouzel, "La doctrine origenienne." See also idem, *Origen*.

24. There is always a danger in modern analogies, because they may attribute more clarity and consistency to ancient thinkers than they actually achieved.

25. See *De principiis*, bk. 2, chap. 10, paragr. 3, pp. 175–76; and *Contra Celsum*, bk. 5, chaps. 18, 19, 23; bk. 7, chap. 32; PG 11, cols. 1205–10, 1215–18, and 1465–68; and trans. Chadwick, pp. 277–79, 281–82, and 420–21.

26. On these images, see Crouzel, "La doctrine origenienne," pp. 247–49, quoting Origen on 1 Corinthians and on Matthew.

would go.[27] In his commentary on Matthew (which survives in the original Greek), he suggested that the resurrection bodies of the blessed will become "like the bodies of angels, ethereal and of a shining light"[28]— an idea that led the Second Council of Constantinople in the middle of the sixth century to condemn him for teaching that we will rise as spheres.[29] He argued that our resurrection bodies will be without age or sex, for certainly we will not grow or excrete or copulate in heaven; he even suggested that we will lose all memory of the relationships of earth.[30] Origen understood the body to carry through the flux and process of life the scars of its experiences; yet it is unclear whether those scars (or even the remembrance of those scars) are lifted into paradise.[31]

To Origen, the body that survives and rises is not the pot or statue or ship of Tertullian; it is not the dry bones of Ezekiel 37 or the dust of Genesis 3.7 and 2.19. It is not reassembled with all its parts or planks or organs intact; nor is it called again, as tiny decaying particles, from the stomach of the earth or the depths of the sea. It is clear therefore that Origen's theory of the body could answer the problem of chain consumption or cannibalism.[32] It could account for our survival not only

27. In his letter to Avitus, Jerome translated Origen as asserting that the resurrection body is intermediate; we will finally therefore achieve incorporeality. It is not certain that Origen taught this, although some of his followers in the late fourth century unquestionably did. See Crouzel, "La doctrine origenienne," pp. 260–61. The problem passage above all is De principiis, bk. 2, chap. 10, pp. 172–83.

28. Commentary on Matthew, ed. E. Benz and E. Klostermann, Origenes Werke, vol. 10, GCS (Leipzig: Hinrichs, 1935), bk. 17, chaps. 29–30, pp. 667–71; see also De principiis, bk. 2, chap. 10, paragr. 8, pp. 181–83, and Crouzel, "La doctrine origenienne," p. 189.

29. On whether Origen taught that the resurrection body was a sphere, see Chadwick, "Origen, Celsus, and Resurrection," pp. 94–102; A. Festugière, "De la doctrine 'Origèniste' du corps glorieux sphéroïde," Revue des sciences philosophiques et théologiques 43 (1959): 81–86; and J. Bauer, "Corpora orbiculata," Zeitschrift für katholische Theologie 82 (1960): 333–41. The passage often thought to have suggested the idea is On Prayer, chap. 31 (see PG 11 [Paris, 1857], cols. 551b and 552b).

30. Commentary on Matthew, ed. Benz and Klostermann, pp. 669–72; De principiis, bk. 2, chap. 10, paragr. 8, and chap. 11, pp. 181–92; Crouzel, "La doctrine origenienne," pp. 195–99. Clement of Alexandria also said sexual difference would disappear. Such phrases are always ambiguous; they can mean either freedom from sexual desire or bodily change. See Dewart, Death and Resurrection, pp. 120–21, and below at n. 57.

31. The point of Origen's denial of sexual difference in heaven is clearly that we should begin to be sexless here on earth by practicing continence. According to Jerome (In Epistolam ad Ephesios Libri tres, bk. 3, chap. 5, paragr. 28, PL 26 [Paris, 1884], col. 566–67), Origen argued that since we will one day be like angels—i.e., without sex— we should begin now to be what is promised. For a discussion of whether the stories of Origen's own self-castration that circulated in antiquity are reliable, see Dechow, Dogma and Mysticism, pp. 128–35, and Peter Brown, Body and Society, pp. 167–69.

32. See Crouzel, "Les critiques," pp. 679–80; and Chadwick, "Origen, Celsus, and Resurrection," pp. 85–90.

from birth to old age (with all that digesting and excreting in between) but also into the glory of the end of time. But it seemed to sacrifice integrity of bodily structure for the sake of transformation; it seemed to surrender material continuity for the sake of identity.

Origen's heady sense of the potency and dynamism of body remained enormously attractive, particularly to Eastern theologians, over the next 150 years. Some (such as Gregory of Nyssa) spoke with positive disdain about the survival of certain of our organs in heaven but used startlingly naturalistic images for the resurrection. Nonetheless, something very deep in third- and fourth-century assumptions was unwilling to jettison material continuity in return for philosophical consistency.[33] Identity, it appears, was not finally the question, for *that* question Origen could answer. The question was physicality: how will every particle of our bodies be saved? When Methodius of Olympus launched a massive attack on Origen's theory in the later third century, even the way in which he misunderstood the position he refuted indicates how far Origen's corporeal *eidos* was, for him, an answer to the wrong issue. As always, the metaphors used for resurrection themselves constitute an argument for what it entails. Methodius's rejection of Origen's theory is a rejection of the image of the burgeoning seed in favor of that of the reconstructed statue or temple.

We know little about Methodius.[34] His treatise *Aglaophon or Concerning the Resurrection*, although the source of Epiphanius's understanding of Origen and therefore enormously influential in the late fourth century, survives in its entirety only in an awkwardly literal, ninth-century Slavonic translation, accessible to most scholars only in Bonwetsch's German version.[35] A portion of this treatise survives in Greek in Photius's analysis of it.[36] The *Aglaophon* is a dialogue between

33. By the end of the fourth century, bodily integrity was for many thinkers so closely connected with material continuity as to be inseparable from it; see below, on Jerome.

34. On Methodius, see E. Amann, "Méthode d'Olympe," *DTC*, vol. 10, cols. 1606–14; Crouzel, "Les critiques"; Dechow, *Dogma and Mysticism*. Amann, op. cit., col. 1611, says: "Avec toutes ses insuffisances et même tous ses défauts, l'*Aglaophon* reste le traité le plus considérable et le plus digne d'étude que l'antiquité chrétienne nous ait laissé sur la résurrection."

35. See Nathanael Bonwetsch, *Methodius von Olympus*, vol. 1, *Schriften* (Erlangen and Leipzig: A. Deichert, 1891) for a German translation of the entire Slavonic corpus; idem, *Methodius*, GCS 27 (1917) gives the Greek text with a German translation of the Slavonic where the Greek is missing. The so-called Apocalypse of Methodius is an apocryphal text of perhaps the late seventh century.

36. See Bonwetsch, *Methodius (1917)*, pp. ix–xvii and xix–xxviii, and Amann, "Méthode," col. 1607. For a brief summary of the *Aglaophon*, see ibid., cols. 1610–11.

four interlocutors, two of whom (Aglaophon and Proclus) represent an Origenist position, both empirically and philosophically argued, and two of whom (Memianius and Methodius) refute this position with natural philosophy, with metaphysics, and with Scripture. Although the anti-Origenists of the 370s to 390s took the arguments of both Aglaophon and Proclus to represent Origen's thought, it is clear that Methodius misrepresents Origen in, among other things, Aglaophon's gloss of the much-disputed passage from Genesis 3.21 concerning the "tunics of skin" with which God clothed Adam and Eve, and in Proclus's interpretation of Christ's Transfiguration as equivalent to resurrection.[37] But Methodius's treatise is, in itself, a fascinating indication of what bothered a number of theologians about Origen's dynamic sense of body. On every level, from physiological to ontological, Methodius feared change. Indeed, so afraid was he of the threat to integrity as well as to material continuity that he interpreted Origen's *eidos* as external appearance or shape (that is, as a waterskin into and out of which matter flows), used against it the argument (with which Origen would have agreed entirely) that appearance in fact changes, and himself asserted an extravagantly materialistic position (similar to that of Athenagoras) in which every particle of the body subsists throughout life, never nourished or excreted or in any way invaded or altered.[38]

Methodius's fear of change manifested itself both in the (inappropriate) metaphors he chose to gloss Origen and in the metaphors he himself preferred and rejected. So wary was he of lodging activity in matter itself that in his treatise on virginity, the *Symposium*—his only work that survives in its entirety in the original Greek—he gives an account of reproduction designed to attribute all growth to God's "creative power." Generation is, he says, like a large house with a sculptor hidden inside. Men poke clay through holes in the house, but God goes around inside it, from hole to hole, and shapes the lumps into statues. It is as if change can only be good (i.e., be understood as fertility rather than decay) when it is totally effected by God.[39] The argument recurs in the *Aglaophon* in Methodius's suggestion that semen is analogous to a corpse, i.e., both need God's power in order to grow into a body.[40]

37. See Crouzel, "Les critiques," passim, especially pp. 693 and 697, and Dechow, *Dogma and Mysticism*, pp. 349–90.

38. Crouzel, "Les critiques."

39. Methodius, *Symposium* (or *Convivium Decem Virginum*), oratio 2, chaps. 4–6, PG 18 (Paris, 1857), cols. 51–58.

40. *De resurrectione*, bk. 2, chap. 20, ed. Bonwetsch (1917), pp. 372–74; (1891 ed.), pp. 234–36.

Throughout Methodius's work on resurrection, the same anxiety about change, as a threat both to integrity and to material continuity, is reflected in a persistent choice of organic metaphors for what is to be avoided, inorganic metaphors for what is to be saved. Not only does he reject Origen's use of the Pauline seed metaphor, both outright and by misinterpretation (i.e., by taking the *eidos* as external skin that cannot be both seed and sheaf); he also makes reassemblage the solution to flux.[41] Thus one of his major images for the body is a stone temple within which the tree of sin is growing. In death, the temple falls; the tree is rooted out. Then in resurrection the exact stones are reconstructed in the exact shape that subsisted before.[42] What grows and changes here is sinister, needing to be curtailed or destroyed; that which is salvageable is that—and only that—which persists unchanged.

Sometimes Methodius's two anti-Origenist interlocutors seem to concentrate on bodily integrity (the survival of organs) to the point of ignoring matter. In book 3, the image of a recast statue is used in such a way as to suggest that what counts is a restored and perfect shape, with all organs present and no mutilation or defect permitted. Recasting the statue is explicitly preferred to patching it up; the concern is for differentiated parts or organs, not for bits of matter. Memianius, the anti-Origenist interlocutor to whom most of the natural philosophical issues are delegated, is responding here to what Methodius thinks to be Origen's opinion that we will lack teeth in heaven.[43] Nonetheless, the discussion circles back to an emphasis on material continuity. Memianius argues:

If any bronze-artist has destroyed an image made of bronze and wishes to make another out of gold in place of the destroyed one . . . , anyone would say that it could be similar to the first one, but not that the first image had been itself renewed. Therefore when a spiritual body is resurrected in the old body's place, so, according to this [Origenist] opinion, neither is the form nor the element resurrected; it is not the deceased body but another, similar to it.[44]

41. *De resurrectione*, bk. 2, chaps. 24–30 and bk. 3, chaps. 16–7, ed. Bonwetsch (1917), pp. 381–88 and 398–400; (1891 ed.), pp. 240–49 and 258–62.
42. *De resurrectione*, bk. 1, chap. 41, ed. Bonwetsch (1917), pp. 285–87; (1891 ed.), pp. 138–40.
43. *De resurrectione*, bk. 3, chaps. 3–8, ed. Bonwetsch (1917), pp. 390–401; (1891 ed.), pp. 251–63.
44. Ibid., bk. 3, chap. 6, ed. Bonwetsch (1917), p. 398.

The implication is clearly that both material continuity and complete bodily integrity are necessary for resurrection. This leaves, of course, the familiar problem of identity: how can fluctuating flesh remain "the same"?

With what one modern authority has called "lamentable" results, Methodius entered into the discussion of natural process that engaged Athenagoras and Macarius as well as Origen.[45] Through the character of Memianius, he denies that digestion really occurs. Trees do not eat the earth, he argues, for if they did there would be holes around their roots.[46] In contrast to plants, bodies do in some sense process food, as Aristotle explains; but nutriment replaces only body fluids not bones, sinews, or flesh. It flows through the body like water through a canal. Blood, sweat, and menstrual fluid let off by the body are superfluities, not substance.[47] Even scars are simply the closing of old flesh over a gap or absence; there can be no such thing as new flesh.[48] Thus Methodius takes identity to lie in material continuity, aware that he does so by simply denying empirical evidence of organic change. Yet the very fact that the largest portion of his treatise is devoted to explaining away physiological process *as process* suggests that what truly concerns him is preservation of matter per se, not of matter as locus of identity. His question is not "how does tree continue as tree?" but "how does a tree particle avoid transformation into an earth particle?"

Aphrahat, Ephraim, and Cyril of Jerusalem: Immutable Particles in Process

Few writers in the century between Methodius and Jerome followed either Origen or Methodius very closely. In general, writers in Greek and Syriac—and certain Latin writers as well (for example, Ambrose and Hilary of Poitiers)—kept something of Origen's sense of change and fluidity although a few (such as Evagrius) jettisoned any claim that the body

45. Ibid., bk. 2, chaps. 9–14, ed. Bonwetsch (1917), pp. 346–60; (1891 ed.), pp. 208–22. And see Amann, "Méthode," col. 1611: "La critique des arguments scientifiques est d'une pauvreté lamentable . . . et les concepts physiologiques . . . sont littéralement enfantins."

46. *De resurrectione*, bk. 2, chap. 9, ed. Bonwetsch (1917) pp. 345–49; (1891 ed.), pp. 208–11.

47. *De resurrectione*, bk. 2, chaps. 11–13, ed. Bonwetsch (1917), pp. 353–57; (1891 ed.), pp. 215–21.

48. *De resurrectione*, bk. 2, chap. 13, ed. Bonwetsch, (1917), p. 358; (1891 ed.), p. 220.

is resurrected, and most retained an inconsistent emphasis on the survival of material bits or particles. These writers made wide-ranging use of dynamic images drawn from the earth itself. They evidenced thereby a deep concern with mutability and process, which could either threaten existence (by utterly destroying that which changes) or redeem the universe (by transmuting that which changes into changelessness). In either case, change to them was real, and often it was creative and good—fertility rather than, or in addition to, decay. Their natural images were not of cycles of return and repetition (as in, for example, the first letter of Clement) but of genuine growth. Heaven was far from earth, and the resurrected body, albeit a locus of particularity, of what makes us ourselves, did not need to be fully like the body we have here. Although they almost all insisted on a material continuity that their most advanced scientific knowledge held to be impossible, these theologians do not really seem to have worried a great deal about identity. They could therefore see matter as pregnant with potential for otherness. Thus they deepened, rather than refuting or rejecting, the paradox set forth by Tertullian and Irenaeus, for they insisted that the body that is redeemed in resurrection is a locus of pullulating putrefaction.

In contrast, Latin writers from the late fourth and early fifth centuries avoided dynamic metaphors. They pulled heaven and earth closer together, freezing each so that there was little process or development. Change was simply a scattering of static bits (the dust of Genesis 3.19) that could be restored by reassemblage. The resurrected body might be agile and beautiful, as was Christ's body after his resurrection, but such glory was laid down over it rather like a varnish that fixed its parts and particles in place. Body was not the Pauline seed, bursting under its own internal power into the bloom of heaven. For these Latin writers (especially Jerome and the later Augustine), the traditional inorganic images of reforged statues, recast vessels, rebuilt temples, or tents with new tent-cloths conveyed an emphasis not so much on identity as on material continuity and bodily integrity.

I cannot treat every major writer who addressed the issue of resurrection between 300 and 400. But before I turn to the new direction set by Jerome and Augustine in the early fifth century, I want to illustrate the variety of ways in which fourth-century authors retained something of Origen's sense of flux and transformation despite an emphasis on material continuity. I begin with two Syriac writers, Aphrahat and Ephraim, whose treatises, sermons, and hymns show an intense preoccupation with organic process.

To Aphrahat, the body that rises is the seed of 1 Corinthians; it is also a corpse.[49] Aphrahat stresses that bodies really decay,[50] but some locus of fertility remains in the earth, to flower when the trumpet sounds. Earth "eats" the dead, says Aphrahat; the worm "devours" them.[51] Yet earth is made by God "teeming" with life. To Aphrahat, the creation of Genesis 1.20–25 is what we would call spontaneous generation. Thus if earth can produce what "was not cast into it"—if it can give birth "in virginity" before seeds are sown in it—surely it can give up again that which is buried.[52]

There will always be people who cavil thus: "How do the dead rise again? Or with what manner of body shall they come?" (1 Cor. 15.35) For see how the body is decomposed and corrupted. And as time runs on, even the bones are reduced to dust and are unrecognizable.

If you enter a tomb in which a hundred dead bodies have been buried, you will find there not even a handful of dust.

. . . [So some say:] "If, of these hundred dead, nothing remains after a time . . . , surely the dead must be clothed with a new body when they revive. But it will surely be a celestial body that will clothe them, for where could a body come from, since there is nothing in the grave."

One who thinks thus is, however, foolish and ignorant. When the dead went away, they were something, and when they had been gone a long time, they became nothing. When the time of the resurrection comes, this nothing will become something according to its former condition, and a transformation will be added to its condition. . . .

Be convinced of this, you foolish one. Each seed will receive its own body. Have you ever sowed wheat and reaped barley? Have you ever planted a vine and produced figs? No. . . . So the body that is laid in earth, that very body shall rise again.

49. Aphrahat, *Aphraate le Sage Persan: Les Exposés*, trans. M.-J. Pierre, Sc 349 and 359 (Paris: Éditions du Cerf, 1988 and 1989), vol. 1, Demonstration 8, paragrs. 1–6 and 15, pp. 441–48 and 460–61; and *Aphraatis Sapientis Persae Demonstrationes*, ed. J. Parisot, Patrologia syriaca, ed. R. Graffin, pt. 1, vols. 1 and 2 (Paris: Firmin-Didot, 1894 and 1907), 1.1, cols. 361–72 and 387–92. On Aphrahat, see Robert Murray, *Symbols of Church and Kingdom: A Study in Early Syriac Tradition* (Cambridge: Cambridge University Press, 1975), p. 29 and passim; Sebastian Brock, *Syriac Perspectives in Late Antiquity* (London: Variorum, 1984); and idem, *Studies in Syriac Christianity: History, Literature, and Theology* (London: Variorum, 1992).

50. Aphrahat, Demonstration 22, paragr. 6, in Parisot ed., 1.1, cols. 999–1004.

51. Demonstration 22, paragrs. 4 and 6, in Parisot ed., 1.1, cols. 995–1004.

52. *Les Exposés*, ed. Pierre, Demonstration 8, paragr. 6, vol. 1, p. 447; and in Parisot ed., 1.1, cols. 371–72.

For it is with the body as with a seed: when it falls into the earth, it putrefies and rots; and it is from this putrefaction that it sprouts, burgeons, and gives forth fruit.

Just as ploughed land that is not sown with seed does not give fruit, even if it drinks much rain, so it is with the grave in which no dead are buried: no person shall come forth from it at the quickening of the dead, no matter how loudly the trumpet shall sound.[53]

In Aphrahat's interpretation, the seed metaphor expresses a greater insistence on identity and continuity than it did in Paul's and a greater attention to putrefaction.[54] Nonetheless Aphrahat also sees resurrection as fertility, the redemption of process. In his gloss of Ezekiel 37, for example, the reclothing of dry bones at the end of time is described as the growth of an embryo rather than as the instantaneous leaping together of disassembled components.[55]

There is even a suggestion of earlier millenarian ideas in Aphrahat's description of heaven. The righteous shall all come to judgment, he says, although not all will have the same reward.[56] But all bodies will be light and beautiful there, and we shall have no anger or lasciviousness but shall love each other with an "abundant love." "Male shall not be distinguished from female." The old will not die nor the young grow old. There will be beautiful trees "with fruit which never fails," and "of their taste no soul shall ever grow weary." It is not, of course, clear how literally all this is meant.[57] But even if it is metaphorical, we should note that the use of eating as an image for blessedness and heavenly life finds

53. *Les Exposés,* ed. Pierre, Demonstration 8, paragrs. 1–3, vol. 1, pp. 441–44; and in Parisot ed., 1.1, cols. 361–66.

54. There is also a stress on material continuity and it is associated with martyrdom. Aphrahat's Demonstration 21, "on persecution," paragrs. 8–9 and 22–23, discusses the three children in the fiery furnace and the seven brothers of 2 Maccabees as martyrs; Parisot ed., 1.1, cols. 951–58 and 985–90.

55. *Les Exposés,* ed. Pierre, Demonstration 8, paragr. 12, vol. 1, pp. 457–58; and in Parisot ed., 1.1, cols. 383–86. Paragrs. 7–10, pp. 448–56 (and Parisot ed., 1.1, cols. 371–82), stress bones as that from which the resurrected body will come and are very close to contemporary rabbinic discussion; see above, chapter 1, n. 135. For the same idea in Ephraim, see Edmund Beck, ed., *Des heiligen Ephraem des Syrers Carmina Nisibena,* CSCO, 218, 219, 240, 241, Scriptores Syri, 92, 93, 102, 103 (Louvain: Corpus SCO, 1961–63), vol. 241.103, hymn 65, pp. 91–92.

56. Demonstration 22, paragr. 19, in Parisot ed., 1.1, cols. 1029–32.

57. Demonstration 22, paragrs. 12–15, in Parisot ed., 1.1, cols. 1013–24. Aphrahat stresses that there will be "no female, nor generation, nor use of concupiscence . . . no want, nor any deficiency, . . . nor ending" (paragr. 13, col. 1015–16). All will be "sons of the Father" (paragr. 12, col. 1015–16). Whether this means that women will rise physiologically male would seem to depend on whether female sex is seen as a deficiency.

its complement in Aphrahat's continued use of digestion as a metaphor for decay and death. Although Aphrahat discards procreation and (possibly) sexual difference in heaven, he retains (perhaps not completely allegorically) another pleasurable process (tasting) and other differentiated organs (teeth and palates).

To Aphrahat's slightly later Syriac contemporary, Ephraim, the association of digestion with decay and of regurgitation with salvation became more explicit. Ephraim repeatedly described Sheol or the grave as "devouring."[58] Yet he also spoke of the earth regurgitating its dead and described animals, birds, and fish bringing pieces of human bodies for reassemblage at the moment of Judgment.

> Death will be overcome by trembling, and will vomit up all it has eaten, so that no dead will be left who is not brought to that place of judgment. And the dust of the earth will be commanded to separate itself from the dust of the dead; not the tiniest particle of that dust will remain behind; it will come before the Judge. All whom the sea has drunk, whom the wild animals have eaten, whom the birds have ripped asunder, whom the fire has burnt, all these will awaken and arise and come forth at the twinkling of an eye.[59]

Prominent among Ephraim's images for the risen body are Jonah, spewed up whole from the whale, and the reference in Matthew 17.27 to money found in the mouths of fishes.[60]

58. Ephraim, *Carmina Nisibena*, ed. Beck, vol. 241.103, hymn 55, chaps. 14–18, p. 70.

59. *Des Heiligen Ephraem des Syrers Sermones III*, ed. Edmund Beck, CSCO, 320–21, Scriptores Syri, 138–39 (Louvain: Corpus SCO, 1972), sermon 1, lines 502–15, vol. 321.139, p. 13. There is a great deal of debate in art historical work over whether Ephraim's sermons (the attribution of which is itself in doubt in some cases) are the source of the tenth- and eleventh-century iconographic program of the Byzantine Last Judgment, which depicts the regurgitation of parts. See Georg Voss, *Das jüngste Gericht in der bildenden Kunst des frühen Mittelalters: Eine kunstgeschichtliche Untersuchung* (Leipzig: E. A. Seemann, 1884), pp. 64–75; Otto Gillen, *Ikonographische Studien zum Hortus Deliciarum der Herrad von Landsberg* (Berlin: Deutscher Kunstverlag, 1931), p. 19; Beat Brenk, *Tradition und Neuerung in der christlichen Kunst des ersten Jahrtausends: Studien zur Geschichte des Weltgerichtsbildes* (Vienna: Böhlau, 1966), pp. 90–91, and chapter 4, nn. 104 and 106–8 below. A number of the elements of the program are clearly mentioned in the five sermons on "last things" edited in Beck's volume. The motif of fish, beasts, and birds giving up dismembered parts (and indeed the implication that the idea is scriptural) is not original with Ephraim, however; see above, chapter 1, n. 88.

60. Ephraim also used the widow's mite, the lost drachma, and the three children in the fiery furnace. See *Carmina Nisibena*, ed. Beck, vol. 241.103, hymn 46, pp. 43–47.

These images were intended to underline material continuity.[61] And Ephraim frequently went even further in stressing the restoration of every lost bit. For example, in the Nisibean hymns, he associated the miracle of the loaves and fishes with resurrection, arguing that if Christ had the apostles take care in this case to gather up every particle, so much the more would he collect every one of our bones at the end of time.[62] Moreover, Ephraim made ingenious use of the story of Peter's ear from Luke 22.51 to stress the restoration of every organ.

> For, if the divine one bent down and took the ear that was cut off from Simon and thrown away, and attached it again so that nothing was lost, how much more will he then at the resurrection search for every bit so that nothing of their dust remains behind. And as in the fiery furnace not a hair of their head perished (Luke 21.18), so he makes known the care he will practice at the resurrection.[63]

There is nonetheless nothing mechanistic or dualistic about Ephraim's conception of body. Body is sometimes a garment (an additional "something") that "we" take up or lay down. But it is far more often a seed, not the discarded husk heretics hold it to be but a kernel from which flowers a new stalk and ear. Although Ephraim sometimes speaks of body and soul as two constituent parts of the self, he often speaks as if body *is* person or self. We are laid in the earth only to sprout again, still our "self," in glory.[64]

To Ephraim, we will all rise as adults.

61. Hermann Möllers questions whether Ephraim has an idea of material continuity, arguing that he places survival more in "personhood" than in physical stuff (*Jenseitsglaube und Totenkult im altchristlichen Syrien, nach den Schriften unter dem Namen Afrems des Syrers* [Marburg: Nolte, 1965], p. 73). This seems to me essentially correct although if one pays close attention to Ephraim's own arguments and metaphors, there is clearly in them also a concern with the survival of physical bits. See Ephraim, *Commentaire de l'Evangile Concordant ou Diatessaron: Traduit du syriaque et de l'armenien*, trans. Louis Leloir, Sc 121 (Paris: Éditions du Cerf, 1966), chap. 8, paragr. 11, pp. 164–65.

62. *Carmina Nisibena*, ed. Beck, vol. 241.103, hymn 46, chaps. 10–11, pp. 45–46.
63. Ibid., chap. 9, p. 45.
64. Compare *Des heiligen Ephraem des Syrers Hymnen de Fide*, ed. Edmund Beck, CSCO, 154–55, Scriptores Syri, 73–74 (Louvain: L. Durbecq, 1955), vol. 155.74, hymn 73, p. 193, with *Des heiligen Ephraem des Syrers Hymnen contra Haereses*, ed. Edmund Beck, CSCO, 169–70, Scriptores Syri, 76–77 (Louvain: L. Durbecq, 1957), vol. 170.77, hymn 52, chaps. 9–13, p. 180. And see *Commentaire de l'Evangile concordant*, trans. Leloir, chap. 8, paragrs. 6–12, pp. 161–65.

One who dies in the womb of his mother and never comes to life, will be quickened at the moment [of resurrection] by [Christ] who quickens the dead; he will then be brought forth as an adult. If a woman dies while pregnant, and the child in her womb dies with her, that child will at the resurrection grow up and know its mother; and she will know her child.[65]

So we will, in heaven, lose our childishness but not our parents. Ephraim indeed appears to argue that we will retain our religious statuses and even the marks of experience. Body expresses what is important about self. Identifying the attainments of the new ascetic movement with the earlier sufferings of the martyrs, Ephraim emphasized that risen flesh reflects who we are and what we deserve. The martyrs will rise with gifts in their hands and the marks of tortures still on their bodies.

For the works of each will be to him a garment that he bears on his body. So one will wear the clothing of fasts and watching, prayers and humility, another the mantel of belief and the crown of chastity. The members of one will be stamped with the traces of iron teeth, the rack, and beatings. Another will bear on her shoulder a brand or carry severed members. . . . So the saints will stand bearing their works with them . . . and by them you too [will stand] who have cared for them. For many will appear there clad in the garment of penitence, which they have practiced.[66]

For all his emphasis on reassemblage, Ephraim's imagery is closer to Origen's than to Methodius's. His most powerful and complex metaphors are of process and change.[67] Indeed his conception of growth to-

65. *Sermones III*, ed. Beck, vol. 321.139, sermon 1, lines 517–24, p. 14. The passage clearly implies that the "defect" of being unborn will be erased by growth but that other distinctive marks will remain; otherwise the child and mother would not recognize each other. The sermon continues the theme of difference of gifts in lines 555–74, p. 15.

66. *Sermones III*, ed. Beck, vol. 321.139, sermon 2, lines 360–93, p. 28. Ephraim is describing martyrs and ascetics at the moment of the Second Coming. Their bodies will be clarified and glorified after Judgment.

67. Möllers (*Jenseitsglaube*, pp. 73–74) argues that Ephraim, like Aphrahat, sees resurrection as occurring in two stages: first the bodily stuff rises, then it is clothed with glory for heaven. This is correct, but if one looks at the metaphors Ephraim uses, the process is more dynamic and complex. On Ephraim's intense interest (and that of other Syriac writers) in postlapsarian procreation and domination of the earth, see Jeremy Cohen, "*Be Fertile and Increase, Fill the Earth and Master It*": The Ancient

ward resurrection is so optimistic that he sees cadavers themselves as fertile.[68] The body that rises is the Pauline seed, the egg of a grasshopper, a fetus in the womb.[69] The dead body "gives birth" to worms, says Ephraim; it "teems with living beings"; it even breeds in Sheol. How much more then will it "give birth," a barren womb miraculously made fertile, when God calls it to life?[70] In famine (asserts Ephraim), mothers may be driven to the horror of eating their own children. Yet Sheol does not digest her own; she vomits them up and learns "to fast."[71] In one of the most extraordinary images of the entire patristic discussion, Ephraim describes resurrection as incubation and hatching. Eggs, as he understands them, are born twice, first as dead matter, then as living.[72] He writes:

> And when the bird hatches her eggs, motionless dead bodies, her love shelters them; her wings embrace them; she forms voice and life in their lifelessness; the liquidness of the egg takes on beautiful form; and she awakens out of the shell the buried ones. Just so the graves will be split open by the rousing voice [of the Last Judgment].[73]

The image of Jesus as mother hen found in Matthew 23.37 takes on startling new intensity here. For all the technical differences Ephraim (like Aphrahat) would admit to exist between creation, generation, and resurrection, a sense of teeming stuff seems to lurk behind his natural images. Whether in the womb, in the stomach, or in the grave, flesh—like matter itself—seems always both dead and alive, decaying and fertile, inanimate and pregnant with potential. Only a heretic or a fool would see the egg in its nest or the corpse in its grave as really dead; the mother bird and the wise Christian know otherwise.[74]

---

and Medieval Career of a Biblical Text (Ithaca and London: Cornell University Press, 1989), p. 229.

68. Carmina Nisibena, ed. Beck, vol. 241.103, hymn 49, chaps. 4 and 8, pp. 54–55. He also sees fetuses as buried in wombs; ibid., hymn 65, chaps. 16–19, p. 92.

69. Carmina Nisibena, ed. Beck, vol. 241.103, hymn 46, chaps. 14–17, pp. 46–47; hymn 49, chaps. 4, 10, 14, pp. 55–56; and Hymnen contra Haereses, vol. 170.77, hymn 52, chaps. 4–13, pp. 179–80.

70. Carmina Nisibena, ed. Beck, vol. 241.103, hymn 49, chaps. 1–2 and 8, pp. 54–56; and hymn 37, chaps. 1–10, pp. 11–13.

71. Ibid., hymn 67, chap. 7, p. 95.

72. Ibid., hymn 46, chaps. 14–17, pp. 46–47; and see also Hymnen contra Haereses, ed. Beck, hymn 52, chaps. 4–13, pp. 179–80, where the seed of grain with its pod and the chick with its egg become almost the same image.

73. Carmina Nisibena, ed. Beck, vol. 241.103, hymn 46, chap. 16, p. 47.

74. Hymnen contra Haereses, vol. 170.77, hymn 52, chap. 12, p. 180.

The fourth-century Greek writer Cyril of Jerusalem, like his Latin-speaking contemporary Hilary of Poitiers, is somewhat more conventional in his use of resurrection imagery than the Syriac authors Aphrahat and Ephraim, but he too combines organic images of extreme change with a stress on material continuity.[75] Cyril, like Hilary, makes extensive use of the Pauline seed metaphor: "Cannot He, who brought what was not into being, raise up again that already in existence which has decayed? Will He who raises up the corn for us when it dies, year by year, have difficulty in raising up us, for whose sake the corn has been raised?"[76] Cyril employs the images of natural cycles popular since 1 Clement, but because he understands that they imply reanimation or mere repetition, he glosses them with an emphasis on transformation. Dormice revive after hibernation, he says, and flies and bees sometimes rise again after being drowned in water. But resurrection comes not after quiescence but after decay, and what rises is different from what died. Bees are born from worms, chickens from eggs, a phoenix from larva, which itself grows from rotted flesh; humans come from "weak, formless, simple elements" and then grow from undifferentiated fetuses into shipwrights or architects, soldiers or kings. So we will rise changed. We will be strong not weak, incorruptible not corruptible, and we will need no food to eat or stairs to walk on. Cyril even adds (a charming touch) that we will shine like iron in fire or glowworms on a summer night.[77]

75. See Hilary, *Tractatus super Psalmos*, PL 9 (Turnhout, 1857), In Ps. 1, chaps. 13–19, cols. 258–61, esp. 259a. Hilary stresses that the ungodly are ground to dust particles but not annihilated; they continue to exist as particles so they can be punished. Following Tertullian, Hilary argues that they do not lose existence but merely change state. In commenting on Matthew, however, Hilary explains resurrection with the metaphor of a growing plant (*Sur Matthieu*, bk. 5, paragr. 11, vol. 1, pp. 159–160). The metaphor is Origenist in its sense of internal process; nonetheless it sounds almost Methodian in stressing that no alien material is taken in. And Hilary also argues that we have "eternal materiality" (ibid., paragrs. 8 and 12, pp. 157–61). It is customary to stress that Hilary moved from "materialism" to "spiritualism" in his conceptualizing of the resurrection; see J. Quasten and A. di Berardino, *Patrology*, vol. 4: *The Golden Age of Latin Patristic Literature . . .*, trans. Placid Solari (1986), p. 33. My analysis suggests that it was common for elements of both to coexist in fourth-century thinkers. I find more continuity between Hilary's earlier and later works than the above generalization would admit and therefore more internal inconsistency in each work.

76. Cyril of Jerusalem, Catechetical Lectures, lecture 4, paragr. 30, PG 33, cols. 491–94; trans. Leo P. McCauley in *The Works of Saint Cyril of Jerusalem*, vol. 1 (Washington: Catholic University of America Press, 1969), p. 134. See also lecture 18, cols. 1017–60.

77. Lecture 18, paragrs. 5–21, cols. 1021–42. To say that we will rise changed does not mean that we will rise equal or indistinguishable; see especially paragr. 9, cols. 1027–28.

Yet Cyril, again like Hilary of Poitiers, is more concerned than were the Syriac writers with the permanence of bits, that is, with material continuity. He even pulls the seed metaphor completely out of shape, using it to underline the perdurance of particles, not the internal dynamic of growth. God holds us all in the palm of his hand like a mixture of seeds, writes Cyril; if a farmer can sort through such a variety of kernels, how much more can God sort out seeds? Instead of standing for the person who will flower into a new body at the resurrection, the seed kernel here stands for a piece of body, which must be matched to its other bits and reassembled at the end of time.[78]

Cyril makes it quite clear that his concern for bits is a concern for the fate of cadavers, especially holy cadavers. His reassurance that God holds us all like seeds in the palm of his hand follows a vivid and painful description of bodies torn apart and ground to dust by wild beasts or devoured by carrion birds who might scatter the parts as far away as India or the land of the Goths.[79] He even insists that we condemn grave robbers because exactly the body they violate is going to rise again.[80] He explains that the Old Testament story of the corpse that rose from the dead when cast into the grave with the prophet Elisha (4 Kings 13.21) should encourage us to believe not only that we will rise but also that a power lies in the bodies of the just even when their souls are not present. If handkerchiefs and aprons that have touched the saints can cure disease, surely we should believe that holy bodies themselves can raise the dead.[81]

Moreover, we must care for our bodies now, says Cyril, because exactly the flesh that dies will rise again. Banishing all wantonness and ornament, it should begin to walk on earth, as it will walk hereafter, with the Virgin-born Lord.[82] The Eucharist is the food for these pilgrim bodies, journeying to heaven. For Cyril as for Tertullian and Irenaeus 150 years earlier, eating God causes us to bear within our members, while still on earth, the incorruptible body we will be after the trumpet sounds. Through digesting God, we become indigestible to death.[83] There is thus throughout Cyril's writing an attention to physicality, to

---

78. Lecture 18, paragr. 3, col. 1019–22. Cyril also uses the statue metaphor; see ibid., paragr. 6, col. 1021–24.

79. Ibid., paragr. 2, cols. 1019–20.

80. Ibid., paragr. 5, cols. 1021–22.

81. Ibid., paragr. 16, cols. 1035–38.

82. Lecture 12, paragr. 34, cols. 767–70.

83. Mystagogical Lectures, lecture 22, paragr. 3, PG 33, cols. 1099–100.

the perdurance of bodily bits, that accompanies (somewhat incongruously) the extravagant metaphors of growth and transformation characteristic of much of the fourth-century understanding of resurrection.

Gregory of Nyssa: Survival, Flux, and the Fear of Decay

My final example of the persistence throughout the fourth century of an Origenist sense of the changeability of body—indeed my final example of the Greek tradition before I turn to the theology of the Latin Middle Ages and its background in the early fifth century—is Gregory of Nyssa. Scholarship on Gregory's treatment of resurrection disagrees so passionately about how Origenist—and how inconsistent—he is that I think we must accept that he is, philosophically speaking, profoundly inconsistent.[84] In places, Gregory understood Origen as Methodius represented him and attacked the idea of the corporeal *eidos* as external form or shape, using against it Origen's own exposition of the reality of flux. In other places, Gregory himself used a kind of *eidos* of the body to explain resurrection. And this *eidos* was sometimes Methodian—a seal or tag for bits of matter to protect them, as it were, from invasion or decay—but at other times it was Origenist—an internal principle that not only itself changed but also allowed the penetration and transformation of matter. Thus Gregory seems to have used Origen's own arguments against Methodius's misrepresentation of Origen, but he used a Methodian insistence on material continuity against what Origen really said.

The radical incongruity of Gregory's positions (which may have become more Origenist late in life but are not, even in his early writings, consistent) shows up particularly in his images.[85] When he emphasizes the perdurance of particles, he writes of the body as globules of mercury, which spring quivering into an indistinguishable mass at the resurrection.[86] Like Macarius, he sees God smelting out bits of body from surrounding clay.[87] He uses the familiar image of the potter collecting

84. See Ladner, "Philosophical Anthropology," pp. 61–94, especially p. 91 n. 149 on Cherniss's earlier criticisms of Gregory; Danielou, "La résurrection des corps," pp. 154–70; n. 12 above and n. 85 below.

85. T. J. Dennis has argued that Gregory's earliest position almost denied bodily resurrection and saw death as a kind of Platonic release of the soul; see Dennis, "Gregory on the Resurrection." By the time of the *De opificio*, however, Gregory was arguing for bodily resurrection.

86. Gregory, *De hominis opificio*, chap. 27, PG 44 (Paris, 1863), cols. 227c–228c.

87. Gregory, *De anima et resurrectione*, PG 46 (Paris, 1858), cols. 47–48.

sherds of broken pot.[88] Even when he explains that there is a form of the body that marks the soul so that soul knows how to summon back what it needs at resurrection, he says (and the analogy does not quite work to make his point) that pieces of the body are like herd animals. They join the herd in the morning, at the call of the shepherd, but in the evening they each know which barn to turn into as they are driven home.[89] This odd image shows how profoundly Gregory needs to combine perdurance of pieces (the animals remain themselves) with an internal dynamism in matter (it is the animals who turn homeward, not the barnyard that exerts the pull).

Other images emphasize body as external form or, alternatively, internal dynamic pattern. When Gregory treats body as if it were Methodius's misunderstanding of Origen's *eidos*, he calls it a leaky bottle, into which material must constantly flow. Or it is a pot with lead (i.e., sin) inside, which must be broken and reforged, without the lead, at the resurrection.[90] But Gregory also speaks of body as the seed of 1 Corinthians 15, retaining all the dynamism of the Pauline image as used by Origen. This body grows from within, taking in food that stimulates a process it carries in and of itself. It is not bits, for bits constantly change. It is not the external arrangement of the bits, for that too changes. Gregory stresses repeatedly that we will have neither genitals nor intestines in heaven. It is rather an in-itself-developing program or seal that shapes matter from within. Body is a stream, constantly in motion; like the seed, it rots and changes, but the new stalk comes from the rot that precedes it.[91]

There is no way to tidy Gregory into consistency. Nor should we see his version of the paradox of resurrection as a simple continuation of

88. Gregory, *De anima et res.*, PG 46, cols. 45–46; *Oratio catechetica magna*, chap. 8, PG 45 (Paris, 1863), cols. 33–38; esp. col. 35b–36b, where Gregory says we are like a pot that must be dissolved in order to rid itself of stain and defect before being reformed in resurrection.

89. Gregory, *De opificio*, chap. 27, PG 44, cols. 225b–226b.

90. Gregory, *Oratio catechetica magna*, chaps. 8 and 37, cols. 33–40 and 93–98; see above n. 88. The Great Catechism is from shortly after 380.

91. *De opificio*, chaps. 25 and 29, PG 44, cols. 215d–218a and 233–40; *De anima et res.*, PG 46, cols. 153–60. See esp. ibid., cols. 155b–c, 156b–c, where Gregory argues (as did Origen) that the body is by definition that which is constantly in flux. Gregory extrapolates from this idea to argue in the *Treatise on the Dead*, PG 46, cols. 521–22, that living is therefore a process of dying: "Quod ad subjectam materiam pertinet, homo non est idem hodie, qui heri fuit. Aliquid enim ex eo momentis singulis moritur, et fetet, et corrumpitur, et abjicitur. . . . Quamobrem, ut Paulus ait, quotidie morimur: [1 Cor. 15.31] quippe qui non idem semper manemus in ipso corporis domicilio, sed accessione decessioneque continua alii ex alio reddimur, et in novum assidue corpus immutamur."

the paradox explored by Tertullian and Irenaeus. Clinging as stubbornly as they did to the stuff of the body and insisting more stridently on the marking of its particles, Gregory nonetheless saw a far greater distance between heaven and earth than did the polemicists of the early third century. To Gregory, the body created in Eden ate (although not as we eat); it would have procreated (although not as we procreate),[92] but in heaven, the body will have no organs of generation or nutrition, no gender or age or passibility.[93] Scholars have often suggested that Gregory's inconsistency—an inconsistency echoed, as we have seen, in most fourth-century treatments of resurrection—is a reflection of the conflict of vast intellectual systems in the ancient world (for example, Platonism versus Christianity or spiritualism versus materialism).[94] But it seems to me that we will understand better why Gregory saw resurrection as such a contradictory combination of change and continuity if we consider exactly what body he had in mind when he wrote. Tertullian's emphasis on reassemblage of exactly the flesh that suffered sprang from his assumption that the paradigmatic body was the body of the martyr. So Gregory's concern for the survival of bits, marked with their experience yet transformed into an otherness far from earthly life, expressed the fact that for him the paradigmatic body was that of the holy ascetic— and not just any holy ascetic. Much of Gregory's discussion of resurrection is a discussion of the body of his sister Macrina.

Gregory discussed eschatology in many places in his work (including the *Treatise on the Creation of Man*, the *Catechetical Discourses*, a sermon on resurrection, and the *Treatise on the Dead*), but two of the major treatments have to do very directly with Macrina. The treatise *On the Soul and Resurrection*, written early in 380, soon after her death, is presented as a dialogue in which the dying Macrina comforts Gregory in his grief for her and for their recently deceased brother Basil. The *Life of Macrina*, written between the end of 380 and 383, shows the actual hopes and fears stimulated in Gregory by a very special cadaver.

92. *De opificio*, chap. 17, PG 44, cols. 187–92; chap. 18, cols. 195b–196b; chaps. 19–20, cols. 195–202. See also Jeremy Cohen, *"Be Fertile,"* p. 258.

93. Gregory elaborates this most fully in his late work, the *Treatise on the Dead*, PG 46, cols. 531–34, and see Danielou, "La résurrection," pp. 160–70. See also *De opificio*, PG 44, chaps. 18–21, cols. 191–204, and *De anima et res.*, PG 46, cols. 105–60, where Gregory shows concern both to affirm the resurrection of the identical atoms that die and to argue that all impurity and brutishness (including growth, eating, elimination, disease, and death) is sloughed off by the resurrected body (cols. 149a–150a). Being fat or thin, or any other characteristic that comes from flux or growth, has (says Gregory) nothing to do with the resurrection life (ibid.)

94. See above nn. 75 and 85.

As Jean-Marie Mathieu has recently demonstrated, Gregory, like other writers of the mid-fourth century, felt horror at decay.[95] "Mortal remains [except those of the martyrs] are to most people an object of disgust," he wrote, "and no one passes near a tomb with pleasure; if despite all our care, we find an open grave and cast our eyes on the horror of the body that lies therein, we are filled with disgust and groan loudly that human nature should come to this."[96] When the grave of his parents was opened to receive Macrina's body, he panicked. Horrified (as Basil and Gregory Nazianzus were also) at the prospect of disturbing a putre-fying corpse or of mingling bones from several bodies, Gregory sexual-ized what he feared by describing it with a reference from Leviticus that actually concerns incest ("The nakedness of thy father, or the nakedness of thy mother shalt thou not uncover"): "How, I ask myself, will I be spared . . . condemnation if I look at the common shame of human na-ture in the bodies of my parents, which are certainly decomposed, dis-integrated, and transformed into an appearance unformed, hideous, and repulsive?"[97] Behind Gregory's hope of resurrection lies a desperate de-sire that neither his parents nor his siblings will really decay, whatever appears to happen to their flesh. When he discusses the parable of Laz-arus and the rich man (frequently problematic for patristic exegetes), it is very important to him to explain that a soul between death and res-urrection can still have a finger *in potentia*—that Lazarus's finger still "exists" while decomposed.[98]

But if decay can be transcended, this must be accomplished by the particular Macrina or Basil who began to transcend it in life. To Gregory (as to Origen, Aphrahat, and Ephraim), the body of the ascetic begins already on earth to live the life beyond procreation and nutrition it will have in heaven. Here on earth we have many needs, writes Gregory; we are seduced by material things, buried (as it were) under the rubble of an earthquake.[99] But we must begin the journey toward the purity of heaven, shaking off uncleanness.

95. Jean-Marie Mathieu, "Horreur du cadavre," pp. 311–20.
96. *Oratio laudatoria martyris Theodori*, PG 46, col. 737c–d, 738c–d; see Gregory of Nyssa, *Vie de sainte Macrine*, ed. and trans. Pierre Maraval, Sc 178 (Paris: Éditions Du Cerf, 1971), p. 255 n. 2.
97. Ibid., pp. 254–55; and see pp. 86–88 and nn. 1–2. For examples of Gregory's horror at decay, see *De opificio*, chap. 25, PG 44, cols. 219–22, on the raising of Laz-arus—a discussion which describes in detail how revolting the corpse is—and *De anima et res.*, PG 46, cols. 13–14.
98. *De opificio*, chap. 27, PG 44, cols. 225–26.
99. *De anima et res.*, PG 46, cols. 97c–98c.

If there be in you any clinging to this body . . . let not this, either, make you despair. You will behold this bodily envelopment, which is now dissolved in death, woven again out of the same atoms, not indeed into this organization with its gross and heavy texture, but with its threads worked up into something more subtle and ethereal.[100]

The opening of the *Life of Macrina* shows Gregory's inconsistency not only about the distance a body must travel before resurrection in heaven but also about the extent to which bodily transformation begins here. Macrina, he writes, should not even be styled a woman, "for I do not know whether it is right to describe in terms of nature one who was raised so far above her nature." But he also says she began her ascetic commitment by resolving to remain "espoused" to a fiancé who had died, claiming he was "only absent on a journey, not dead."[101] Thus, in Gregory's account, the living Macrina is already beyond femaleness because she has reached the heights of human virtue, but she is also faithful to a suitor who clearly remains not only male but also betrothed to her—whose death is, "thanks to the hope of the resurrection," only an appearance. The resurrection body, which begins to be rewoven while still on earth, sheds much of what seems specific to its selfhood here, but Gregory, like Origen, is not fully consistent about exactly what is shed—either on earth or in heaven.

Gregory's deep confusion about the shape and substance of the body that rises reflects not only his conviction that ascetic accomplishment must be apparent in heaven; it also reflects his confidence that Macrina and Basil are relics, just like the relics of the forty martyrs their mother collected to lodge in the chapel where the family was subsequently buried.[102] Gregory tells us that while on his way to visit his dying sister, he dreamt of a martyr's relics, from which came a "blinding light," and he subsequently understood that Macrina was the relics, "mortal and unsightly remains," transfigured "with immortality and grace."[103] But such relics—if they are to perform the cures Gregory believes and recounts—must carry beyond the grave the power of the living saint; they must lift up (not erase) the experience they have borne in life. Gregory tells

100. Ibid., cols. 107a–108a; trans. William Moore and H. A. Wilson, *Nicene and Post-Nicene Fathers*, 2d series, vol. 5 (1892; reprint, Grand Rapids, Mich.: Eerdmans, 1979), p. 453.
101. *Vie de Macrine*, ed. Maraval, pp. 140–41 and 154–57.
102. Ibid., pp. 77–78.
103. Ibid., pp. 192–93, 200–1, and 218–25.

of a cancer on Macrina's breast, which she would not show to a doctor because of modesty, but both she and her mother prayed, and she made an ointment of mud and her own tears, and the tumor disappeared, leaving only a tiny scar. At Macrina's funeral, she was so beautiful her sisters had to cover her shining brilliance with a dark robe, but the scar remained, in death as it had been in life, "a memorial of the divine intervention, the result and the occasion of perpetual turning toward God through the action of grace."[104] The body of Macrina—miraculously healed and made immortal and yet marked by its own particular experience—seems to be what Gregory has in mind when he writes of resurrection as the reassemblage of "the identical atoms" we had on earth "in the same order as before" and yet insists that "there must be change."[105] The resurrected body is both the ascetic who becomes a relic while still alive and the relic that continues after death the changelessness acquired through asceticism.

Jerome and the Origenist Controversy: The Issue of Bodily Integrity

If relic cult and the ascetic movement of the fourth century are the context of Gregory of Nyssa's Origenist sense of body as changing and changed between earth and heaven, they are also the context for the vituperative attack against Origen and his followers launched in the 370s by Epiphanius and taken up twenty years later by Jerome. Jerome's ferocious polemic against bishop John of Jerusalem, penned in 397, arose from matters of ecclesiastical politics and personal ambition as well as from long-standing theological questions.[106] The doctrine of bodily resurrection was by no means the only issue at stake. But a major portion of the apparently unfinished philippic (chapters 23–36) addressed it, and exactly that portion had considerable influence later in the Middle Ages.[107]

104. Ibid., pp. 242–47.
105. *De anima et res.*, PG 46, cols. 135–54; see esp. col. 137c–138c, where Gregory insists that the body is a "calamity"; unless it is freed from brutishness and illness, we could not want it returned.
106. See John P. O'Connell, *The Eschatology of Saint Jerome* (Mundelein, Illinois: Seminary of St. Mary of the Lake, 1948); Duval, "Tertullien contre Origène . . . dans . . . saint Jerome," pp. 227–78; J. N. D. Kelly, *Jerome* (New York: Harper and Row, 1975), especially pp. 195–296; Peter Brown, *Power and Persuasion*, p. 138; E. Clark, "New Perspectives on the Origenist Controversy"; and eadem, *The Origenist Controversy: The Cultural Construction of an Early Christian Debate* (Princeton: Princeton University Press, 1992).
107. Duval, "Tertullien contre Origène," p. 278 n. 221.

Jerome attacked bishop John as an Origenist who merely pretended to adhere to the resurrection of the body but would not admit, when challenged, that the *corpus* that rises is true *caro* (flesh).

Jerome wrote:

I shall explain briefly the teaching of Origen concerning the resurrection (for you will not be able to understand the power of the antidote, unless you examine the poisons). Pay careful attention . . . [for] nine times asserting the resurrection of the body [*corpus*], he does not even once insert the resurrection of the flesh [*caro*]. . . . Origen says in many places, and especially in his fourth book on the resurrection, his exposition of Psalm 1, and his *Stromatiis*, that there is a double error in the church, ours and that of the heretics. [He says] we would be simple-minded and flesh-loving to say that these bones and this blood and flesh—that is, face and members and the whole complex of the body—will rise again in the last day, that is, that we will walk with feet, work with hands, . . . and digest food with stomachs. . . . Those who believe this tell us [he says] that we will then [in the resurrection] produce feces, give forth humors, take wives, and produce children. For why are there genitals, if not for marrying? Why are there teeth, if not for crushing food? . . . For when the soul by the command of God renounces the cold and mortal body, all things go back little by little to their matrices or original substances, flesh falls back to earth, breath mixes in air, moisture reverts to the abyss, heat flies up to ether. . . . Wine and milk mixed together do not perish, but you cannot separate again what is fused; so the substance of flesh and blood does not perish in its original matter, yet it cannot return to its former composite nor can they be again the same whole that they were before. . . .

[Yet, Origen concludes,] we confess the resurrection of the body in another way [*alia ratione*], the resurrection of those who have been placed in the grave and have decayed into ashes, Paul as Paul, Peter as Peter, individuals as individuals, for it cannot be that souls sin in one body and are punished in another. . . . Who, hearing this, would think [Origen] denies the resurrection of the flesh? He says that a specific reason [*ratio quaedam*] is placed by the artifice of God in individual seeds, which reason holds the future materials in the kernel from the beginning. . . . And as the size of the tree and the trunk, branches, fruit, and foliage are not seen in the seed but are however in the reason of the seed . . . so in the reason of human bodies certain ancient principles remain which will rise. When the day of Judgment comes . . . the seeds will stir at once and the dead will germinate [*germinabunt*] . . . but they will not be restored in the same flesh or in the forms they had before. . . .

You, [heretic,] say "body" and do not mean "flesh" at the same time, [for you wish to deceive] the ears of the ignorant. Believe me, your silence is not simple. For "flesh" has one definition, and "body" another. . . .

Job said: "And I shall be surrounded again with my skin and in my flesh I shall see God" (Job 19.26). . . . Does it not seem to you, then, that Job writes against Origen and for the truth of the flesh in which he sustained torments? For it grieves him that the suffering is in vain if another rises spiritually when this flesh has been carnally tortured. . . . If he is not to rise in his own sex and with the same members that were thrown on the dung heap, if the same eyes are not opened for seeing God by which he then saw worms, where therefore will Job be? You take away the things in which Job consists and give me empty words concerning resurrection; for how, if you want to restore a ship after shipwreck, do you deny a single part [*singula*] of which the ship is constituted?[108]

Jerome's attack on John did not engage Origen's true position or even accurately represent Jerome's own previous opinion about Origen.[109] Jerome was egged on by Epiphanius, who criticized Origen on the basis of Methodius's misrepresentation of his ideas. Moreover, as Duval has shown, a good deal of Jerome's polemic was borrowed from Tertullian's attack on the Gnostics and Docetists, and in some cases the passages from Tertullian, although used in rhetorically effective ways, were quite mangled as theology.[110] But if we ignore for a moment Jerome's response to and use of earlier thinkers and take his heated writing from the decade 395 to 405 as his own theology of the body, we find that the images on which I have been focusing in this book have undergone at his hands some very interesting changes in emphasis.

108. Jerome, *Contra Joannem Hierosolymitanum*, chaps. 25–30; PL 23 (Paris, 1845), cols. 375–82; 2d ed. (Paris, 1863), cols. 392–99.

109. In an early work, Jerome adopts Origen's opinion about loss of sexual difference in heaven; *In Epistolam ad Ephesios*, bk. 3, chap. 5, paragr. 28, PL 26 (1884), col. 566–67. See Elizabeth A. Clark, "The Place of Jerome's Commentary on Ephesians in the Origenist Controversy," *Vigiliae Christianae* 41 (1987): 154–71. Defending himself for the ambiguity of his stance on Origen, Jerome suggests in letter 84 that Origen's life and martyrdom for Christ excuse much (Letter 84, paragrs. 7–9, in Jerome Labourt, ed. and trans., *Saint Jerome: Lettres* [Paris: "Les Belles Lettres," 1949–63], vol. 4, pp. 132–35; and PL 22 [Paris, 1845], cols. 748–51).

110. Duval, "Tertullien contre Origène."

Jerome's favorite metaphors for resurrection were metaphors of reassemblage, such as the image of the ship in the passage I just quoted (an example, incidentally, of a garbled borrowing from Tertullian).[111] Using the shattered pot of Jeremiah 18.4, which is recast by the potter, Jerome repeatedly emphasized two aspects of reassemblage: first, the vessel is remade without defect—that is, without any part missing; second, it is cooked hard to make it more resistant to corruption.[112] Thus Jerome's stress was not so much on material continuity as on integrity, not so much on the salvaging of every particle absorbed by the earth as on the reconstitution and hardening of the bodily vessel so that every organ is intact and eternally protected from amputation. Moreover, Jerome explicitly rejected the seed metaphor from 1 Corinthians 15 because it expressed too much change between earth and heaven.[113] Paul's suggestion in verse 53 that immutability and immortality are "put on" (*induere*) was accepted and used to speak of glory as a garment (*indumentum* or *vestimentum*) donned by exactly the body we had before;[114] but Jerome expended considerable energy explaining that the seed of verses 35–44, which dissolves in the earth and draws to itself neighboring matter in order to rise in glorious foliage unlike the planted germ, is an inadequate image of the resurrection. The rare passage where Jerome does admit that we are seeds refers to conception not resurrection and to souls not bodies, and even there his language sounds oddly like the passage from Rebecca West I discussed in my introduction. God plants the soul in the uterus of the mother as seeds are sown in soil, but this God is a potter or bricklayer, and the seeds are inert objects without internal dynamic principles of their own. It is a curiously static notion of both seeds and embryonic development.[115]

It thus seems clear, as O'Connell has argued in his study of Jerome's eschatology, that Jerome assumes material continuity.[116] But what really

111. Ibid., p. 243.

112. Jerome, letter 84, paragr. 9, ed. Labourt, vol. 4 (1954), p. 136, and PL 22 (Paris, 1842), col. 750d; *Apologie contre Rufin*, bk. 1, paragr. 25, ed. P. Lardet, Sc 303 (Paris: Éditions du Cerf, 1983), pp. 71–72; *Contra Joannem*, chap. 33, PL 23, col. 385; and see Duval, "Tertullien contre Origène," p. 257. For a similar emphasis in Gregory the Great on the hardening of the body in resurrection, see Carole Straw, *Gregory the Great: Perfection in Imperfection* (Berkeley: University of California Press, 1988), pp. 54, 154, and 237.

113. Jerome, *Contra Joannem*, chaps. 23–26, PL 23 (Paris, 1883), cols. 390–95.

114. Ibid., chap. 29, col. 381.

115. Ibid., chap. 22, cols. 372–73.

116. O'Connell, *Eschatology of Jerome*, pp. 54–59, and Duval, "Tertullien contre Origène," p. 247. O'Connell considers the one passage in Jerome that might be taken to mean that the "same" body could arise constituted of different matter and concludes that it probably means merely that matter can be added by God to infant bodies

concerns him is integrity. Whereas fourth-century writers on resurrection in general clung to a non-Origenist emphasis on continuity of particles but still saw the body as greatly transformable and transformed in the journey to heaven, Jerome opposes the implication that sheaf is different from seed not because it threatens matter but because it permits organs and personal characteristics to disappear.

Elizabeth Clark, who has written brilliantly about the Origenist controversy of the 390s, has argued that attention moved fairly quickly away from the doctrine of resurrection and toward concern over procreation, sexuality, and sexual difference. Building on the ideas of Peter Brown, she suggests that Jerome, Theophilus of Alexandria, and the other anti-Origenists wanted to defend a kind of gender and class essentialism—that is, to elevate to the courts of heaven the differences between male and female, married and chaste, leader and follower, that were found naturally on earth and, in certain ways, enhanced within the monastic movement.[117] Her insight is a helpful one. Writing both against John of Jerusalem and against his old friend Rufinus, Jerome devoted much emphasis to the resurrection of our genitals (although he was also concerned about teeth and intestines).[118] In letter 84, written in 398, he included a misogynistic excursus in his defense of the resurrection of every organ:

> Neither the rich language of Cicero nor the burning eloquence of Demosthenes is sufficient for my anger against the fraudulent claims of those heretics who confess the resurrection in words but in their hearts deny it. Weak women take pleasure in [the heretical teaching that we will rise without sex], seizing their breasts, patting their stomachs, palpitating their loins, thighs, and smooth chins and declaiming: "What use is it to us if this fragile body shall be resurrected? We shall be like

---

that must rise adult. The discussion strengthens my conclusion that the basic issue in this period was less identity than material continuity and bodily integrity (see O'Connell, p. 58; and letter 108, paragrs. 23–25, ed. Labourt, vol. 5, pp. 190–94, PL 23, cols. 900–2). For the source of much of this interpretative concern with the identity issue, see Louis Billot, *Quaestiones de Novissimis*, 8th ed. (Rome: Pontificia Universitas Gregoriana, 1946), pp. 149–63.

117. See the works cited in n. 106 above, and Elizabeth Clark, review of Peter Brown, *Body and Society*, in *Journal of Religion* 70 (1990): 432–36.

118. *Contra Joannem*, chaps. 25–35, PL 23, cols. 392–405; *Contre Rufin*, bk. 2, chaps. 5–6, 11–12, pp. 109–11 and 133–35; letter 84, ed. Labourt, vol. 4, pp. 125–39 and letter 108, chaps. 23–25, vol. 5, pp. 190–96, PL 22, cols. 743–52 and 878–906. And see Peter Brown, *Body and Society*, pp. 382–84.

angels and have an angelic nature." From this one sees that they disdain to be raised in flesh and bones as Christ himself was raised.[119]

Jerome was concerned about sexuality as well as sexual difference. It is as if our genitals must be present in heaven, so that our victory over them—and our reward for this victory—can continue for all eternity. In his attack on Rufinus in 401, he states explicitly that amputation of members in the resurrection would mean we would all come to equality of condition; the virgin would then be equal to the prostitute.[120] Clark is clearly right that Jerome is concerned to maintain gender inequality and social hierarchy in heaven; she has also convincingly demonstrated that other issues at stake between Origenists and anti-Origenists involved anxiety about reproduction and sexual difference.

Nonetheless, it seems to me that Jerome feared more than a loss of differentiation in heaven. He feared fluidity and possibility because he feared absorption and decay. In short, what Jerome feared was change itself. In letter 124 to Avitus, he expressed outrage at the idea that we might not receive back the differentiated bodies we prepared and earned in life, but he situated this outrage in the context of a fear that we might fall all the way out of human bodies into those of animals or fish.[121] This reference to the transmigration of souls is not a fair criticism of Origen, but it clearly shows that, to Jerome, such transmigration is a kind of chain consumption. And the risk of falling into or being eaten by lower creatures endangers more than social hierarchy.

It may be that Jerome's controversy with the Origenists moved fairly rapidly beyond the issue of resurrection and that it engaged hierarchy and sexuality in a number of other ways, but it is also true that Jerome tended to circle back to resurrection. For example, he chose to bring it up in two letters written in 404. In letter 119, a discussion of 1 Corinthians 15.51, he underlined his anxiety about the decay of the cadaver;[122] in letter 108, an encomium on Paula addressed to her daughter, he dis-

119. Letter 84, chap. 6, ed. Labourt, vol. 4, p. 131, PL 22, col. 748.
120. *Contre Rufin*, bk. 2, chaps. 11–12, pp. 133–35.
121. Letter 124, chap. 4, ed. Labourt, vol. 7, pp. 98–99, PL 22, cols. 1062–63.
122. Letter 119, chap. 5, ed. Labourt, vol. 6, p. 99, PL 22, cols. 968–70. Jerome here quotes Didymus distinguishing immortality from incorruptibility. Everything mortal is corruptible, but not everything corruptible is mortal. Bodies deprived of souls are corruptible but not mortal; they cannot "die" for they are not alive. Drawing this distinction makes decay a separate problem from death and resurrection a triumph over both. Thus resurrection is clearly stated to be a solution to putrefaction.

cussed resurrection at length and stressed the gastrointestinal system almost as much as the genitals.[123]

Moreover, in the same year in which his beloved Paula died, Jerome waded into a controversy in Gaul over relics. Although he did not explicitly relate this debate with Vigilantius to his polemic against the Origenists about eschatology, he nonetheless focused his passionate rhetoric on denying the implication that holy cadavers are merely, and permanently, vile dust.[124] Vigilantius sees bodies as polluting, says Jerome; he laughs at the martyrs; he doubts their miracles; he denigrates asceticism by devaluing the bodies in which it is practiced;[125] he denies that the saints can be both in the tomb and with God. But:

> Are we sacrilegious when we enter the churches of the apostles? Was the emperor Constantius I sacrilegious who translated the relics of Andrew, Luke and Timothy to Constantinople? . . . Are bishops all to be adjudged sacrilegious, even idiotic, when they carry a vile object and dissolved ashes in . . . vessels of gold? Are the people of all the churches foolish who run to the holy relics and receive them with joy as if they discerned there a living and present prophet? . . . For you assert that the souls of the apostles and martyrs sit together either in Abraham's bosom or in the place of refreshment [*refrigerium*] or under the altar of God, and cannot be present away from their tombs and wherever they wish to be. For they are of senatorial dignity, not buried loathsomely among homicides. . . . Do you make laws for God? You chain up the apostles, so that they are held in custody until the day of Judgment and cannot be with their Lord, concerning whom it is written: "they follow the Lamb whithersoever he goes" (Rev. 14.4). If the Lamb is everywhere, those who are with the Lamb should be believed to be everywhere. When the devil and demons go about all over the earth, how can the martyrs, after the pouring out of their blood, be left waiting, shut up under the altar and unable to go out from thence? . . .

123. Letter 108, chaps. 23–27, ed. Labourt, vol. 5, pp. 190–96, PL 22, cols. 900–4. Chapters 27–28, pp. 196–97, make it clear that the doctrine of resurrection is a comfort to Jerome in his grief at the loss of a friend.

124. *Contra Vigilantium*, PL 23, cols. 353–68. And see also letter 109, ed. Labourt, vol. 5, pp. 202–6, PL 22, cols. 906–9.

125. It is significant that Jerome opposes Vigilantius both on relics and on asceticism. To Jerome, the body is valuable because it is where salvation happens. Thus disciplining it during life and honoring it after death are not contradictory (as they would be if asceticism were a sort of Platonic denial of the body) but complementary. See below, n. 135.

The saints are not called dead but sleeping. . . . Hence Lazarus who was to rise is asserted to have been sleeping (John 11.11).[126]

We however refuse cult and adoration not only to the relics of the martyrs but also to the sun and moon, the angels and archangels . . . and to every name that is named in the present world and in the world to come, lest we serve the creation more than its creator. . . . But we honor the relics of the martyrs that we may honor him whose martyrs they are. . . . Are the relics of Peter and Paul unclean? Is the body of Moses unclean, that body which according to Hebrew truth was buried by the Lord himself? . . . If it is not permissible to honor the relics of the martyrs, why do we read: "Precious in the eyes of the Lord is the death of his saints"? If their bones pollute what they touch, how did the dead Elias raise a dead man; how did that body which, according to Vigilantius, is impure give life [to a corpse]? . . . Then all the troops of the Israelite army and all the people of God were impure, because they bore through the desert the bodies of Joseph and the patriarchs and carried to the Holy Land these "unclean" ashes. . . . I repeat: are the relics of the martyrs impure? Then the apostles merit punishment for having, in funeral cortege, gone before the "unclean" body of Stephen and organized a great mourning in which our sorrow was changed into joy.[127]

It is important to see that Jerome does not defend relics here by asserting that they will rise although his contemporaries Victricius of Rouen and Augustine do connect relic cult and resurrection. Jerome admits that he himself fears corpses and needs reassurance that the martyrs are with them as well as in heaven.[128] The specter of decay lurks around the edges of this discussion.[129] Like sex, it fascinates Jerome precisely because it repels him. But decay and mutability are finally what

126. *Contra Vigilantium*, PL 23, cols. 358–60.
127. Letter 109, chaps. 1–2, vol. 5, pp. 202–5, PL 22, cols. 906–8.
128. *Contra Vigilantium*, PL 23, chap. 10, col. 363.
129. As an old man, Jerome described visits to the catacombs he and companions had made on Sunday afternoons when he was young (see *In Hiezechielem libri XIV*, bk. 12, commentary on 40.5–13, in *Opera:* pt. 1: *Opera exegetica*, vol. 4, ed. F. Gloria, CCL 75 [Turnhout: Brepols, 1964], pp. 556–57). He found the visits dismaying but fascinating. His account is evidence that Christians were visiting the catacombs even before pope Damasus had them cleaned and restored (see Kelly, *Jerome*, pp. 22–23, and A. D. Booth, "The Chronology of Jerome's Early Years," *Phoenix* 25 [1981]: 237–59, especially p. 257 n. 65).

Jerome denies. His charge against Vigilantius is that Vigilantius believes body to be vile and changeable. Denigrating the special bodies of the martyrs, Vigilantius accepts ordinary earthly bodies here below. Such a position seems to Jerome totally backward: rather, earthly bodies should be elevated toward heaven through fasting and chastity while alive so that they can be revered in the tomb once they are dead.[130] These bodies will rise on Judgment Day exactly the same as they have been on earth. Sherds of broken vessels, they will be put together again, just as they were before, and hardened by God to the immutability that is eternal glory.

In the years shortly after 200 Irenaeus and Tertullian had used images of sprouting wheat and reforged statues to express the paradoxical conviction that the body that rises is both profoundly the same and profoundly changed. Jerome, writing in 404, winnows the imagery and mutes the paradox. His masterful rhetoric moves earth closer to heaven, but it also moves heaven closer to earth. In his discussion of relics, the dead body becomes in a sense less dead; its putrefaction is denied. In his polemic for asceticism, the living body becomes less fertile and friable, less involved in nutrition, generation, process, and aging; it becomes, in a sense, less alive. Thus the earthly body, whether alive or dead, moves toward heaven while still on earth. In this it is like the body of the martyr at the moment of execution, and Jerome does not fail to point out that the body of the ascetic here below experiences both a continuation of the agony of martyrdom and a foretaste of the angelic life of heaven. But that resurrected body, similar down to its earlobes and fingernails to the body of this life, seems to provide a mirror of earth, not an alternative to it.

Augustine and the Reassembled Statue: The Background to the Middle Ages

Jerome's polemics against John of Jerusalem and Vigilantius were echoed and quoted in discussions of resurrection for the next eight hundred or nine hundred years. But the texts that fundamentally shaped the me-

130. See Letter 84, chap. 9, ed. Labourt, vol. 5, p. 135, PL 22, cols. 750–51, where Jerome asserts: "I do not despise the flesh in which Christ was born and resurrected. . . . I do not despise the clay which, converted after baking into a vessel without defect, reigns in heaven. . . . I love chaste flesh, virginal and fasting; I love of the flesh not the works but the substance; I love a flesh that knows it is going to be judged; I love that flesh which is, for Christ, at the hour of martyrdom, broken, torn to pieces and burned."

dieval discussion were the works—especially the later works—of Jerome's contemporary Augustine of Hippo. Complex though Augustine's own position may have been—influenced as it was by his Neoplatonic training, by certain emphases of the Cappadocian fathers, and by his deeply felt need to affirm the goodness of creation against the Manicheans[131]—it was his rather straightforward theory of resurrection set forth in the *City of God* (especially book 22), the *Enchiridion* (especially chapter 23) and the *De cura pro mortuis gerenda* that provided the questions and answers fundamental to the entire course of scholastic debate in the high Middle Ages.[132]

Although Augustine's emphases were different from Jerome's—chiefly in laying greater stress on change between the body of earth and the body of heaven—their view was essentially the same: resurrection is restoration both of bodily material and of bodily wholeness or integrity, with incorruption (which includes—for the blessed—beauty, weightlessness, and impassibility) added on. For all his valuing of the body as, in some sense, the conveyor of individuality as well as of hierarchy, for all his interest in process and his creative use (not dissimilar to Origen's) of Stoic seminal reasons to explain it[133]—Augustine rejects

131. See Paula Fredriksen, "Beyond the Body/Soul Dichotomy: Augustine on Paul against the Manichees and the Pelagians," *Recherches augustiniennes* 23 (1988): 87–114. See also H. Marrou and A.-M. Bonnardière, "Le dogme de la résurrection des corps et la théologie des valeurs humaines selon l'enseignement de saint Augustin," *Revue des études augustiniennes* 12, nos. 1–2 (1966): 111–36. I see Augustine's view of body and creation as less optimistic, more fraught, than do these interpretations, although I agree with them in placing the ultimate power of Augustine's position in its determination to redeem all of the natural world. See also Margaret R. Miles, *Augustine on the Body* (Missoula, Montana: Scholars Press, 1979); G. Watson, "St. Augustine, the Platonists, and the Resurrection Body: Augustine's Use of a Fragment from Porphyry," *Irish Theological Quarterly* 50 (1983/84): 222–32; and Gerard O'Daly, *Augustine's Philosophy of Mind* (Berkeley: University of California Press, 1987), pp. 70–79. For bibliographies of studies on Augustine, see A. Trapè, "Augustine of Hippo," in *Encyclopedia of the Early Church*, vol. 1, pp. 100–1.

132. It has been customary for scholars to stress that Augustine moved from an earlier position, emphasizing the difference of our angelic body from our earthly one, to a later, more materialistic position: see, for example, R. M. Grant, "Resurrection," p. 207; Dewart, *Death and Resurrection*, pp. 164–88; and John A. Mourant, *Augustine on Immortality* (Villanova, Penn.: Augustinian Institute, Villanova University, 1969). This is certainly correct. The early, more Platonic Augustine stresses the "spiritual body" of 1 Corinthians 15; the later Augustine stresses the "flesh and blood" body emphasized by Tertullian and Jerome. What I suggest here is that underlying this difference is a fear of natural change that made both positions—that of the spiritual resurrection body and that of the material resurrection body—a redemption and solution. It also made both positions somewhat inconsistent internally.

133. See, for example, Augustine, *The Literal Meaning of Genesis*, ed. John Hammond Taylor (New York and Ramsey, New Jersey: Newman Press, 1982), bk. 5, chaps. 4–5, 18, 20–23, pp. 150–53, 168, 171–76; PL 34 (Paris, 1841), cols. 325–27, 334, 335–38.

the Pauline seed metaphor with its attendant implication that body is fluid, dynamic, potential, open to infinite development. His metaphors for resurrection are metaphors of reassembled statues or vessels or buildings,[134] and he stresses (as did Tertullian and Jerome) that all particles return even if not necessarily to the same organ or part.[135] Indeed, when Augustine looks at change, he sees decay, so much so that he sometimes equates resurrection with escape from process. In sermon 155, he actually says: "Take away death [i.e., in this context, corruption or decay] and body is good."[136] If Adam and Eve had remained obedient in Eden, they would have come via process (i.e., eating—in this case, eating from the Tree of Life) to immortality; but once sin entered, process (especially eating) could result only in decay. God's grace and wisdom, however, make our gain greater than our loss, for after death, which is only a moment in the putrefaction that continues between birth and judgment,

134. See Marrou and Bonnardière, "Le dogme de la résurrection," pp. 116–17, which gives references to the parallel use of the statue metaphor in John Chrysostom.

135. Some interpreters have used this as evidence that Augustine did not maintain full material continuity; see Michel, "Résurrection," col. 2542. This interpretation seems to me a somewhat misguided attempt to make Augustine focus more on the issue of identity than he actually did. Augustine's view in the *City of God* and the *Enchiridion* was certainly as "materialistic" as the views of earlier thinkers, such as Tertullian, and Augustine never used his idea that the matter does not have to go to the same place as a way of allowing God to get rid of some of the matter (see *Enchiridion*, chap. 23, paragrs. 89–90, ed. E. Evans, *Aurelii Augustini Opera*, pt. 13, vol. 2, CCL 46 [Turnhout: Brepols, 1969], p. 97). His concern was to retain what was there at creation, not to make the self lie in something nonmaterial, such as shape or form. See n. 116 above, for the same issue in Jerome.

Dewart (*Death and Resurrection*, pp. 164–88) argues that Augustine is closer to Origen than to Methodius because he concentrates on intellectual, rather than physical, vision of God in heaven (see *De civitate Dei*, bk. 22, chap. 29, in B. Dombart and A. Kalb, eds., *Aurelii Augustini Opera*, pt. 14, CCL 47–48 [Turnhout: Brepols, 1955], vol. 2, pp. 856–62). Given Augustine's intense interest in the retaining of organs in heaven (an interest at least as powerful as Tertullian's), this seems to me a misplacing of emphasis. Certainly, compared to their immediate precursors the Cappadocians, Augustine and Jerome are far more "materialistic" in their interpretation of resurrection.

136. Sermon 155, in Augustine, *Sermones*, PL 38–39 (Paris, 1841), vol. 38, cols. 840–49, quoted passage at 849. The context is, significantly, Luke 21.18 ("Not a hair . . ."), Romans 7.24 ("Who shall deliver me from the body of this death?"), and 1 Corinthians 15.44 and 53. So escape from death and material continuity are linked. Augustine argues that delivery from the body of death is not delivery from body but from death. He says: "Detrahatur mors . . . inimica, et erit mihi in aeternum caro mea amica." See also *Enchiridion*, chap. 32, paragr. 91, CCL 46, p. 98, where Augustine says that the body's substance will be flesh in the resurrection; it will not, however, suffer corruption. And see A. Challet, "Corps glorieux," *DTC*, vol. 3 (1938), cols. 1896–97. The remark of Mourant, in *Augustine on Immortality*, p. 24, to the effect that Augustine, in such teaching, gives new importance to the body ignores the similarity of his position to much earlier thinking.

we can rise to incorruption. Once risen, we will truly escape change. We will have not only the *posse non mori* and *posse non commutari* of Eden but the *non posse mori, non posse mutari*, of heaven.[137] Augustine's early sermons may use organic, naturalistic images for many changes, including (occasionally) resurrection, but the texts of his middle and old age—the texts that set the course of Western discussion—expressed a profound fear of development and process. Whereas Syriac and Greek writing of the decades before Augustine shared this fear of putrefaction but sublimated process into redemption, the Augustine of the *City of God* and the *Enchiridion* saw salvation as the crystalline hardness not only of stasis but of the impossibility of non-stasis.[138]

The passages in Augustine that set the agenda for medieval discussion considered in even greater detail than had Tertullian or Jerome questions about exactly what details of the earthly body reappear in heaven. Will aborted fetuses rise? Will Siamese twins be two people or one in the resurrection? Will we all be the same sex in heaven? the same height and weight? the same age? Will we have to eat? Will we be able to eat? Will deformities and mutilations appear in heaven? Will nail and hair clippings all return to the body to which they originally belonged? Will

137. *Literal Meaning of Genesis*, ed. Taylor, bk. 6, chaps. 7–25, bk. 8, chaps. 3–5, vol. 1, pp. 182–205 and vol. 2, pp. 36–41, PL 34, cols. 342–54 and 374–77; *De civitate Dei*, bk. 13, 20–23, CCL 48, pp. 403–8; sermons 361–62, in *Sermones*, PL 39, cols. 1599–1634, and Mourant, *Augustine on Immortality*, appendix, pp. 50–126.

138. This is not to forget that the Augustinian notion of desire—particularly of the desire of soul for body—became in the late thirteenth and early fourteenth centuries a major source of a dynamic vision of heaven. See *Literal Commentary on Genesis*, bk. 12, chap. 35, trans. Taylor, vol. 2, pp. 228–29, PL 34, col. 483:

> Quia inest ei naturalis quidam appetitus corpus administrandi; quo appetitu retardatur quodammodo ne tota intentione perget in illud summum coelum, quamdiu non subest corpus, cujus administratione appetitus ille conquiescat. Porro autem si tale sit corpus, cujus sit difficilis et gravis administratio, sicut haec caro quae corrumpitur, et aggravat animam, de propagine transgressionis existens, multo magis avertitur mens ab illa visione summi coeli: unde necessario abripienda erat ab ejusdem carnis sensibus. . . . Proinde cum hoc corpus jam non animale, sed . . . spirituale receperit Angelis coaequata, perfectum habebit naturae suae modum, obediens et imperans, vivificata et vivificans, tam ineffabilis facilitate, ut sit ei gloriae quod sarcinae fuit.

It took centuries for this part of Augustine's ideas to come to prominence. It also took centuries for the "retarding," distracting desire he speaks of to become, for his commentators, something like what we mean by love. See below, pp. 132 and 252–53. For a perceptive discussion of how Augustine's eschatology looks forward to an end of time and to heaven rather than back toward a Golden Age and restoration (as did the Greek Fathers), see Kassius Hallinger, "The Spiritual Life of Cluny in the Early Days," in *Cluniac Monasticism in the Central Middle Ages*, ed. Noreen Hunt (London: Macmillan, 1971), pp. 37–38.

men have beards in their resurrected bodies? Will we "see" in heaven only when our eyes are open? Will we rise with all our internal organs as well as our external ones?[139]

These questions were not all equally important to Augustine. Some were posed merely as examples of the silliness of pagans or of credulous Christians.[140] Others were answered in different ways in different texts. (Augustine was consistent in holding that we rise with gender;[141] he was uncertain about our age at resurrection although he suggested in one passage that we will all rise aged thirty;[142] he was inconsistent about whether or not we return with the shape—i.e., height and weight—we had on earth.[143]) Still other questions adumbrated, without fully addressing, deep philosophical issues. For example, Augustine was not completely consistent about whether the martyrs rise with scars indicating their tortures, but in at least one passage (*City of God*, book 22, chapter 19) he equated such scars with personal experience or history and thereby suggested that body is in some way a necessary conveyor of personhood or self.[144]

139. The crucial passages are *Enchiridion*, chaps. 23–29, CCL 46, pp. 95–110; *De civitate Dei*, bks. 13, 19–22, CCL 48, pp. 385–414 and 657–758.

140. For Augustine's own references to contemporary discussion, see *Enarrationes in Psalmos*, In Ps. 88, vers. 5, PL 37 (Paris, 1841), cols. 1122–23, and ed. E. Dekkers and J. Fraipont, in *Aurelii Augustini Opera*, pt. 10, vol. 2, CCL 39 (Turnhout: Brepols, 1956), pp. 1222–23; *Enchiridion*, chap. 23, paragr. 84, p. 95; *De civitate Dei*, bk. 22, chaps. 12–20, pp. 831–41; sermon 361, chaps. 1–6, in PL 39, cols. 1599–1605, and Mourant, pp. 50–56.

141. *De civitate Dei*, bk. 22, chaps. 17–18, pp. 835–37; sermon 243, PL 38 (Paris, 1841), cols. 1145–47. Although Augustine discusses repeatedly the need for defects to be repaired, he never considers female genitals defective. Indeed, he asserts that the reference in Ephesians 4.10–16 to the "perfect man" includes women (*De civitate Dei*, p. 841).

142. *De civitate Dei*, bk. 22, chap. 15, p. 834. Augustine says he is uncertain whether the scriptural reference to "the age of the fullness of Christ" means that we all rise the same age, but (he asserts) the "wisest men" fix the age of the bloom of youth at thirty. Duval ("Tertullian contre Origène," p. 269) points out that the age of Christ at his resurrection was taken as a model for us all. The tradition of thirty as the age of peak human development was, however, older than Christianity. See below chapter 3, n. 15.

143. Compare *De civitate Dei*, bk. 22, chap. 15, p. 834, with *Enchiridion*, chap. 23, paragrs. 89–90, p. 97.

144. *De civitate Dei*, pp. 841–42. See Marrou and Bonnardière, "Le dogme de la résurrection," p. 129, citing P. L. Landsberg, who has argued that Augustine was the first to see the importance of this for the issue of individuality. The suggestion is implicit in Augustine's position, but one should not make too much of it; Augustine did not set himself the task of solving the problems of identity and/or individuation.

Jewish discussion of resurrection from about the same period holds explicitly that we rise with our defects, which are then repaired by God; see Babylonian Talmud (Soncino ed.), Sanhedrin, 91a–91b. In contrast, Augustine held that the blessed rise

What is most striking in such discussions is Augustine's insistence on keeping minute details of the heavenly body close to the earthly one, while adding (a crucial addition of course!) stasis.[145] Luke 21.18 ("Not a hair of your head . . .") caused trouble, as it did for other patristic exegetes, because hair was known to grow quickly and its exuberance was associated with wildness, with lack of cultivation and control.[146] Hence Augustine suggested in one passage that Luke 21.18 might refer to the number of hairs (rather than to their material particles).[147] His use of the statue analogy, which states that the material need not return to the part from which it originally came, can also be taken—as some modern commentators have taken it—to mitigate the necessity for material continuity.[148] But in general Augustine required material continuity as well as integrity or wholeness and shared with Ephraim and other fourth-century thinkers a tendency to use biblical passages that appear in fact to refer to intact individuals as if they described the re-collection of bodily bits. Sermon 127, for example, elaborates John 5.28 (which speaks of "those that are in the grave") as referring to scattered bones and ashes as well as corpses;[149] sermon 173 understands the parable of the lost sheep as a description of the collection of dispersed limbs.[150]

Emphasizing again and again how beautiful the blessed will be in heaven and defining beauty with a Neoplatonic emphasis on structure and harmony,[151] Augustine nonetheless assumes in many places that what is in fact the case here below is beautiful. Men will have beards in heaven because they must rise as handsome as possible; even the genitals will rise the same.[152] Augustine asserts explicitly that there will be

---

with defects repaired; we do not know, however—and we should not inquire—whether the damned rise with defects repaired or unrepaired.

145. See *Tractatus* 49, paragr. 10, *In Joannis Evangelium*, PL 35 (Paris, 1845), col. 1751–52.

146. See Satran, "Fingernails and Hair."

147. *De civitate Dei*, bk. 22, chap. 19, CCL 48, pp. 837–39; but cf. *Enchiridion*, chap. 23, paragrs. 89–90, CCL 46, p. 97, which stresses that no matter is lost.

148. See above nn. 135 and 147.

149. Sermon 127, chap. 10, paragr. 14, PL 38, cols. 712–17. It is important that Augustine comments that such scattered bodies are yet *Deo integra*. "Quomodo expressit carne mortuos? qui sunt in monumentis [John 5.28], quorum jacent sepulta cadavera, quorum favillae tectae sunt, quorum ossa dispersa sunt, quorum caro jam non est, et tamen Deo integra est. Veniet hora . . . omne quod periit, imo perisse putatur, restituetur. Si enim Deus fecit hominem qui non erat, non potest reparare quod erat?"

150. Sermon 173, chap. 2, paragr. 2, PL 38, col. 938.

151. See *De civitate Dei*, bk. 22, chap. 24, CCL 48, pp. 846–52; Fredriksen, "Beyond Body/Soul Dichotomy"; and Dewart, *Death and Resurrection*, pp. 164–88.

152. Sermon 243, PL 38, cols. 1143–47. See also sermon 155, in PL 38, cols. 840–49, and *De civitate Dei*, bk. 22, chap. 19, CCL 46, pp. 837–39.

rank and hierarchy in heaven.[153] Women and men will rise with their respective sexes, because there is sexual difference here below and virtue is achieved (and rewarded) in the context of what is possible for each particular individual. He assures us, however, that—although God certainly created women inferior—he did not have to create women in order to create inferiority. There are varying degrees of excellence even within the masculine gender.[154]

Although it is not quite clear to me what Augustine thought about the internal organs, he is certain they will rise.[155] Since nothing will be hidden in heaven but all will manifest its glory, it seems at least possible that he thinks the virtuous will be transparent, enjoying the sight of each others' harmoniously arranged livers and intestines in paradise. It is particularly suggestive that Augustine's consideration of the resurrection of inner organs occurs not only in the context of ridiculing the infantile obsessions of the credulous but also in a serious discussion (sermon 243) of the *noli me tangere*, a passage used by other patristic exegetes to underline how distant our spiritual body will be from earth.[156]

Augustine's various discussions of the weightlessness, beauty, impassibility, and incorruption we will gain in heaven form the background to the doctrine of the dowries of the glorified body developed in the high Middle Ages. His repeated emphasis on the yearning of the separated soul for body (an idea he himself traces to Platonic roots but is aware of inverting for Christian purposes) becomes an important com-

---

153. Sermon 132, chap. 3, paragr. 3, in PL 38, col. 736.

Quanto vos meliores, qui quod erunt homines post resurrectionem, hoc vos incipitis esse ante mortem? Servate gradus vestros: servat enim vobis Deus honores vestros. Comparata est resurrectio mortuorum stellis in coelo constitutis. *Stella enim ab stella differt in gloria,* ut Apostolus dicit: *sic et resurrectio mortuorum* [1 Cor.15.41–42]. Aliter enim ibi lucebit virginitas, aliter ibi lucebit castitas conjugalis, aliter ibi lucebit sancta viduitas. Diversa lucebunt: sed omnes ibi erunt. Splendor dispar, coelum commune.

It is important to note that the context is a discussion of proper conduct in marriage; Augustine asserts that men are stronger but that women often surpass them in virtue.

154. See *Literal Meaning of Genesis,* trans. Taylor, bk. 9, chap. 5, vol. 2, p. 75, PL 34 (Turnhout, 1886), col. 396. The central point of Augustine's discussion here is that man would have been a better companion for man; therefore woman was created for childbearing.

155. Sermon 243, PL 38, cols. 1143–46; and, for a similar argument, see *De civitate Dei,* bk. 22, chap. 24, CCL 48, pp. 846–52. Augustine's statement in sermon 243 that we will not be like statues, with only an exterior, parallels Origen's in *On Prayer,* 31.3; see above, n. 29.

156. Cf. *De civitate Dei,* bk. 22, chap. 12, CCL 48, pp. 831–33.

ponent of the medieval notion of flesh as essential to personhood.[157] There is in Augustine a real stress on body as necessary and beautiful in the resurrection, on the *non posse mori* of the end of time as a victory over earth that would never have come without the *felix culpa* of Adam and the incarnation and resurrection of God. But Augustine does not speak of this victory in metaphors of flowering plants, happy and nurturing bodies, fragrant or pregnant or fertile earth. Rather, fascinated though he is by germination, his accounts of natural process invariably gravitate toward the problem of rot. Although he does not say so explicitly, he seems unable to imagine a case of growth or change that is not in some way a deterioration or loss of identity. Only miraculous growth (for example, the miracle of the loaves and fishes) seems to him fully good.[158] As he says in book 4, chapter 3, of his *De Trinitate:* "The body— that is, the 'outer man'—is such that the longer life lasts, the more it is corrupted, whether through age, or sickness, or various afflictions, until it comes at last to the goal that is called by everyone death."[159] Bodies, to Augustine, are not seeds but inert or (even worse) rotting earth—the dust of Genesis 3.19.[160]

A distrust of organic images runs throughout Augustine's work. In chapter 1, book 22, of the *City of God,* he rejects the greening tree as a metaphor for resurrection because it has only the appearance of perpetuity. In chapter 24 he asserts that fecundity is good, seeds do sprout, but he seems to feel it necessary to insist (almost as Methodius did) that it is really God who effects the growth.[161] In book 3, chapters 14–17, of the *Literal Commentary on Genesis,* his discussion slips quite oddly from a consideration of creation as a kind of spontaneous generation to an articulation of horror at the possibility that beasts might eat human corpses.[162] In sermon 361 (from 410–411), one of his most important

157. See the passage quoted in n. 138 above. See also *De civitate Dei,* bk. 13, chap. 20, pp. 403–4. On Augustine's understanding of the desire of the soul for God, see McGinn, *Foundations of Mysticism,* pp. 310 and 329–33.

158. Sermon 130, in PL 38, cols. 725–28.

159. *De Trinitate,* bk. 4, chap. 3, ed. W. J. Mountain and F. Gloria, *Aurelii Augustini Opera,* pt. 16, CCL 50 and 50A (Turnhout: Brepols, 1968), vol. 1, p. 165, lines 17–21.

160. See sermon 242, chaps. 3–5, paragrs. 4–7, PL 38, cols. 1140–41; the context is a discussion of the problem presented by the "natural place" of the elements; how can a body made of earth be in the sky after resurrection? See also *De civitate Dei,* bk. 20, chap. 20, pp. 733–36.

161. *De civitate Dei,* bk. 22, chaps. 1 and 24, pp. 699–700 and 744–47.

162. *Literal Meaning of Genesis,* trans. Taylor, bk. 3, chaps. 14–17, vol. 1, pp. 89–92: the discussion moves from creation to the food chain and then from beasts eating cadavers to the promise of Luke 21.18. See also ibid., bk. 5, chap. 4, paragrs. 9–11, vol.

treatments of resurrection, he uses the seed of 1 Corinthians 15 and asserts that there is renewal in the earth. But he immediately associates fertility with rot, moves to a discussion of garbage and dung, and states that when we open graves, we find putrefying flesh and fall into despair. Insofar as he returns at all in this sermon to the seed and the hope of resurrection, it serves only as a guarantee that something subsists, not as a promise of change. Sermon 362 explicitly equates body with flux, suggests that the need to eat is the proof of our destructive mutability, and asserts that all dynamism must disappear in heaven if we are to be redeemed.[163] Throughout his writings, Augustine repeatedly equates living with eating;[164] yet he sees redemption as triumph over digestion and nutrition. Our goal is to be nourished into nonconsumption.

> *We know that when he shall appear, we shall be like him, for we shall see him as he is* [1 John 3.2]. Behold [you shall] understand what you will be nourished on and how you will [then] receive what nourishes you by eating. [And you shall understand it] thus: that what is eaten [then] is not diminished, but whoever eats it is supported in life. For now food maintains us by eating, but the food that is eaten is diminished. When however we begin to feed on justice, to eat wisdom, to taste that immortal food, we will be supported in life and the food will not be diminished. For the eye knows how to feed on light without diminishing the light. . . . When a wonderful food is praised to you on which you are going to dine, you prepare your stomach; God is praised to you, prepare your heart.[165]

For Augustine, there was no easy escape from the horrors of consumption and putrefaction. Not for him the solution of Athenagoras or

---

1, pp. 150–53, which seems to evidence a fear of "the seeds in things." Augustine discusses at great length whether God creates earth from which come trees which produce seeds, or whether he creates earth with seeds in it from which the trees come. It seems to be important to him to argue, from Genesis 1.11, that the first alternative is the correct one. Thus Augustine adduces Scripture against the notion of seeds in things—i.e., against a view of the world that makes spontaneous generation the paradigm.

163. For sermons 361 and 362, see PL 39, cols. 1599–1634, and Mourant, *Augustine on Immortality*, appendix, pp. 50–126.

164. See *Enchiridion*, chap. 23, paragr. 106, pp. 106–7, and sermon 264, PL 38, cols. 1212–18.

165. Sermon 127, chap. 5, paragr. 6, in PL 38, cols. 709. The elaboration in sermon 127 is, of course, allegorical, but the idea of being nourished into noneating is a theme underlying much of Augustine's discussion of the Eucharist and of the Garden of Eden. In *City of God* (bk. 13, chaps. 20–22, pp. 403–4) for example, he argues that after the resurrection we will not have to eat in order to not-decay.

Justin Martyr, of Methodius, or of his own contemporary Zeno of Verona—the denial, that is, that decay really dissolves, that digestion really consumes.[166] Augustine held that cannibalism is the most difficult objection of all to resurrection, but he absolutely refused to deny that nutrition and excretion really process flesh.[167]

Nonetheless Augustine insisted that resurrection is the reassemblage of bits. His lovely and psychologically perceptive treatise on the care of the dead reassured people that concern for cadavers is a natural and pious human instinct but that we need not fear: no destruction, digestion, or dissolution can really destroy the body.[168] Augustine repeatedly asserted that God would reforge or recast or re-collect in heaven (or in hell) the bits that constituted the person in life.[169]

> For if some one, famishing for want and pressed with hunger, use human flesh as food—an extremity not unknown, as both ancient history and the unhappy experience of our own days have taught us—can it be contended, with any show of reason, that all the flesh eaten has been evacuated, and that none of it has been assimilated to the substance of the eater, though the very emaciation which existed before, and has now disappeared, sufficiently indicates what large deficiencies have been filled up with this food? But . . . all the flesh which hunger has consumed finds its way into the air by evaporation, whence . . . God Almighty can recall it. That flesh, therefore, shall be restored to the man in whom it first became human flesh. For it must be looked upon as borrowed by the other person, and, like a pecuniary loan, must

166. See Zeno, *Tractatus,* bk. 1, tractate 16: *De resurrectione,* PL 11, cols. 371–86, esp. 385; and Michel, "Résurrection," *DTC,* vol 13, col. 2540. Commenting on 1 Corinthians 15, Zeno says: "Unde dubium non est in corporibus nostris, dum mortis lege seminantur, non substantiam, non imaginem, sed illud tantum quod inutile est, discuti, quod teritur, demutari, sicut scriptum est . . . corruptivum hoc induere incorruptionem. . . ." And see above, nn. 10 and 11, for a discussion of Macarius, who may come close to Augustine in both affirming and denying that digestion really digests.

167. *De civitate Dei,* bk. 22, chaps. 20–23, pp. 839–46. Augustine asserts in chapter 22 that cannibalism is the ultimate depravity.

168. *De cura pro mortuis gerenda,* PL 40 (Paris, 1841), cols. 591–610; and sermons 122 and 123, PL 38, cols. 680–86. And see *De civitate Dei,* bk. 19, chap. 12, pp. 675–78, where Augustine both expresses horror at putrefaction and chain consumption and asserts that the process is peaceful and harmonious. The moldering body is "assimilated to the elements of the world, and particle by particle enters into peace with them" (p. 689).

169. It is worth noting that in both *De civitate Dei* and the *Enchiridion* Augustine is quite concerned with the torments of hell, which he sometimes equates with the grave. But it is very important to him to insist that even bodies in hell are reassembled so that their torture can be perpetual; see *De civitate Dei,* bk. 19.

be returned to the lender. His own flesh, however, which he lost by famine, shall be restored to him by Him who can recover even what has evaporated. And though it had been absolutely annihilated, so that no part of its substance remained in any secret spot of nature, the Almighty could restore it by such means as He saw fit. For this sentence, uttered by the Truth, "Not a hair of your head shall perish" [Luke 21.18], forbids us to suppose that, though no hair of a man's head can perish, yet the large portions of his flesh eaten and consumed by the famishing [cannibals] can perish.[170]

Relic Cult

Between Tertullian and Augustine lay the ideas of Origen, which might have solved the technical problem of identity and established the Pauline seed as the image of resurrection. But they did not do so. Instead, for all the complex, organic, and in certain ways Origenist images of fourth-century theology, the discussions of the period between 395 and 430 established for the medieval West a very different image of resurrection. Jerome and Augustine returned to Tertullian's idea of the reassemblage of bits, adding to it a new emphasis on the beauty of wholeness and on a hardening of the body against change.

As I have already suggested in discussing Gregory of Nyssa with his more extravagant notions of growth between earth and heaven, relic cult was an important context for the early fifth-century understanding of the resurrected body. Even Gregory, who clung to an Origenist sense that we will shed the specificities of earth (such as sex or age) as we develop toward heaven, often seems to have had relics in mind when he discussed resurrection. Thus, he found it hard to relinquish the hope that every particle would be saved and in some way marked by having been the particular body it was here below. Jerome coupled an attack on disrespect for asceticism with a defense of relics as the noble places where virtue is achieved. Augustine—as a number of recent scholars have established—not only came in his last years to an enormous respect for relics and a belief in the miracles they performed but also made them the context for discussing resurrection as the reassemblage of every bodily bit.[171]

170. *De civitate Dei*, bk. 22, chap. 20, pp. 839–41; trans. M. Dods et al., *The City of God* (New York: Random House, 1950), p. 844.

171. Peter Brown, *Augustine of Hippo* (Berkeley: University of California Press, 1967), pp. 408–18; Saxer, *Morts, martyrs, reliques*, pp. 238–58; and Petersen, *Dialogues of Gregory the Great*, pp. 91–95. The last book of the *De civitate Dei* joins a

In 415 relics of the martyr Stephen—whose discovery played an important part in the council of Diospolis—were brought to the West by Augustine's friend Orosius and began to work miracles. In the winter of 424–25 (just as Augustine was finishing the *De cura pro mortuis gerenda*, a year after he had finished the *Enchiridion* and two years before he wrote book 22 of the *City of God*), the relics came to Hippo. As a young man in Milan, Augustine had been uninterested in relics, and the council of 401 held under his influence had tried to limit the practice of moving the dust of the saints. But by 422–23 Augustine had been convinced by accounts of the cures and visions at Uzalis and Carthage; he now ordered Stephen's miracles at Hippo to be recorded.[172] It is interesting to note that resurrections from the dead are significantly more frequent in the collection made under Augustine's supervision than in other miracle books of the period.[173]

The discomfort Augustine felt with natural process as akin to decay was manifest throughout his life; his early sermons agree with the *De cura pro mortuis gerenda* (and indeed with the writings of Tertullian and Irenaeus 200 years before) in expressing concern for pious burial yet confidence that (whatever horrors God permits to happen to the cadaver) we will all rise. But the emphasis on integrity—wholeness—in resurrection, like the repeated considerations of exactly how the bits return, occurred in Augustine's late writings. He jettisoned organic images for the change from earthly to resurrection body at the same time he discarded his suspicion of relics and their miracles. His concern in the *Enchiridion* and the *City of God* for the salvation of bits seems to express not only his pastoral obligation to answer the queries of the faithful but also his own increasing tendency to have relics in mind when thinking about bodies that would rise from the dead. As Victor Saxer has brilliantly explained, the dead were materialized by being divided up and distributed; the more the martyr's parts were spread throughout the

---

discussion of resurrection to a discussion of miracles performed by relics. Augustine scholars, especially De Vooght and Courcelle, have paid much attention to Augustine's change of mind on relics; see Pierre Courcelle, *Recherches sur les 'Confessions' de saint Augustin*, 2d ed. (Paris: E. de Bracard, 1968), pp. 139–53; D.-P. De Vooght, "Les miracles dans la vie de saint Augustin," *Revue de théologie ancienne et médiévale* 11 (1939): 5–16; and Saxer, *Morts, martyrs, reliques*, pp. 240–44. Courcelle has shown that between 390 and 400 Augustine was little inclined to accept miracles, but after 400 he begins to speak of miracles at tombs, and by 422–23 he accepts visions.

172. Peter Brown, *Augustine*, pp. 414–15; Saxer, *Morts, martyrs, reliques*, pp. 165–71 and 239–81.

173. Saxer, *Morts, martyrs, reliques*, p. 262.

Mediterranean world, the more he or she came to be seen as housed within the fragment.[174] Augustine's stress on the return of every segment or part of the broken statue when God reforges it at the end of time was surely related to the wonder-working presence in his own community of parts of the first martyr, parts that seemed in no religious sense defective, corrupt, or incomplete. If a mere fragment of Stephen cured the sick and raised the dead, it could not be less than the whole martyr. And if this tiny bit was already whole in Hippo, how can we think that any piece will be missing when the trumpet sounds?

The later part of the fourth century was an important period for the development of relic cult. Imperial legislation and Christian sermons against moving bodies into the city, dividing, or selling them, attest that such things were in fact happening and causing intense anxiety.[175] Scholars used to claim that Eastern and Western attitudes differed in this period, with Western theology and practice more horrified by and resistant to partition and translation. Recent work rightly de-emphasizes the difference.[176] Nonetheless it is perhaps significant that the text that delineates most clearly the growing tendency to stress wholeness as the characteristic of relics—and to relate such wholeness to resurrection—comes from the West. It is a celebration of the arrival of relics in Rouen,

---

174. Saxer, *Morts, martyrs, reliques,* passim, and especially pp. 311ff., and Grabar, *Martyrium,* vol. 1, pp. 40–42. On the intense concern in the period of persecutions to reassemble the bodies of the martyrs for burial, see Leclercq, "Martyr," *DALC,* vol. 10, cols. 2359–2512, especially cols. 2435–57, and Hermann-Mascard, *Les Reliques des saints,* pp. 23–26. Persecution, of course, divided bodies and often made it necessary to move them for burial. Christians responded to the dissonance thus created both by asserting resurrection to *be* reassemblage and by asserting the part to *be* the whole.

On the increasing tendency to speak of the saint as resident both in the grave and in heaven, see Sabine MacCormack, "Loca Sancta: The Organization of Sacred Topography in Late Antiquity," in *The Blessings of Pilgrimage,* ed. Robert Ousterhout (Urbana and Chicago: University of Illinois Press, 1990), p. 7, and Thomas Head, *Hagiography and the Cult of the Saints: The Diocese of Orleans, 800–1200* (Cambridge: Cambridge University Press, 1990).

On burial near as a way of protecting the corpse, see Yvette Duval, *Auprès des saints corps et âme: L'inhumation "ad sanctos" dans la chrétienté d'Orient et d'Occident du IIIe au VIIe siècle* (Paris: Études augustiniennes, 1988), pp. 194–201.

175. Saxer, *Morts, martyrs, reliques;* Peter Brown, *The Cult of the Saints: Its Rise and Function in Latin Christianity* (Chicago: University of Chicago Press, 1981); P. Séjourné, "Reliques," *DTC,* vol. 13, pt. 2, cols. 2330–65; Patrick J. Geary, *Furta Sacra: Thefts of Relics in the Central Middle Ages* (Princeton: Princeton University Press, 1978); Hermann-Mascard, *Les Reliques des saints;* Ariès, *The Hour of Our Death;* Leclercq, "Martyr"; and Grabar, *Martyrium.*

176. See works cited above in nn. 174 and 75 and Petersen, *Dialogues of Gregory the Great,* pp. 141–50.

written about 396 by Victricius, who had just received a second ship-
ment of holy body parts from Ambrose.[177] Victricius retains at least a
hint of the organic imagery used earlier in the fourth century to describe
resurrection. He sees relics as "first fruits" and says that they will
"flower" in heaven. Nonetheless his major image is of holy bodies as
the temples or buildings where the martyrs reside; they are "jewels,"
hard and whole. What Victricius fears is any suggestion that in receiving
such a gift he has contributed to mutilating or disempowering the saints.
He insists that the healings they perform do not drain them any more
than shining dims the sun. Blood is sealed in them; they never change.
Shimmering reflections of eternity, they are complete in every particle.

> Let no one, deceived by vulgar error, think that the truth of the whole
> of their bodily passion is not contained in these fragments. . . . We
> proclaim, with all our faith and authority, that there is nothing in
> these relics that is not complete. For where healing power is present
> the members are complete.
>
> . . . The Passion of the saints is the imitation of Christ, and Christ
> is God. Therefore, no division is to be inserted in fullness, but in that
> division which is visible to the eye the truth of the whole is to be
> adored. . . .
>
> I touch remnants but I affirm that in these relics perfect grace and
> virtue are contained. . . . He who cures lives. He who lives is present
> in his relics. . . .
>
> . . . It is toward these jewels that we should set the sails of our souls;
> there is nothing fragile in them, nothing that decreases, nothing which
> can feel the passage of time. . . . The blood which the fire of the Holy
> Spirit still seals in their bodies and in these relics shows that they are
> extraordinary signs of eternity.[178]

For several hundred years after Victricius, Western discussions of resurrection would occur mostly in the context of relic cult.[179] The domi-

177. Victricius of Rouen, *De laude sanctorum,* ed. Jacob Mulders, CCL 64 (Turnhout: Brepols, 1985), pp. 69–93; portions translated by J. N. Hillgarth in *The Conversion of Western Europe, 350–750* (Englewood Cliffs: Prentice-Hall, 1969), pp. 22–27.

178. Victricius, *De laude,* chaps. 9–12, CCL 64, pp. 83–90, trans. Hillgarth, pp. 24–
26 (chapter numbers differ in the translated version). For a continuation of this motif,
see the texts cited by Arnold Angenendt, "Der 'ganze' und 'unverweste' Leib: Eine
Leitidee der Reliquienverehrung bei Gregor von Tours und Beda Venerabilis," in ed.
Hubert Mordek, *Aus Archiven und Bibliotheken: Festschrift für Raymund Kottje
zum 65. Geburtstag* (Frankfurt: Peter Lang, 1992), pp. 33–50.

179. See nn. 3 and 112 above on Gregory the Great. One of the most extensive and
interesting texts to discuss resurrection in the context of relic cult is Braulio of Sar-

nant images would be metaphors of reassembling or hardening. Such images implied that decay was not really decay; parts were merely dispersed; even if swallowed, digested, made into alien flesh, excreted, or rotted, they did not finally become anything else. Increasingly, the hope of Christians lay in the promise that scattered bones and dust, marked in some way for their own bodies, would be reunited. It also lay in the conviction that every part, like every morsel of Christ's body eaten at the altar, *was* a whole. If a martyr was present in every minute bit of his dust, if he cured the sick and raised the dead, then both decay and partition could be overcome. The final change to stasis would come only at the end of time, but the jewellike hardness of the relic (whether it was to the eye of the beholder a part or a whole) could move the tired bodies of ordinary believers a little way toward the resurrection while still on earth.

Asceticism, the Church, and the World

In the later fourth century, relic cult and the doctrine of bodily resurrection were complementary ways of emphasizing the triumph of integrity over partition, of stasis and incorruption over decay.[180] Yet there are other ways of expressing victory over moral and physical putrefaction, and even the ascetics who strove to begin their victory while in this life differed in tactics and teaching. For example, some followers of Origen,

---

agossa, letter 42, in *Iberian Fathers*, vol. 2, *Fathers of the Church*, vol. 63, trans. Claude W. Barrow (Washington, D.C.: Catholic University of America Press, 1969), pp. 88–95. Writing in 649–50, Braulio responds to a query about whether all of Christ's blood rose at the resurrection. His interlocutor worries that, if it did, the supposed relics of Christ's blood venerated in churches are false. Braulio uses Augustine to argue that superfluous blood need not rise; therefore, the supposed blood on a column seen by St. Jerome is perhaps genuine. But Braulio urges his correspondent not to worry about such matters; he should place his faith in the blood of the Eucharist, which is surely Christ's. Braulio feels it important to underline that we do receive back our blood in our resurrection, and he uses Luke 21.18 to stress that "the Lord remembers and includes the smallest and most remote of our limbs when he speaks of the hair" (p. 91). Braulio clearly has a notion of a core of material that accounts for identity in resurrection. On Braulio, see Charles H. Lynch, *Saint Braulio, Bishop of Saragossa (631–651): His Life and Writings* (Washington, D.C.: Catholic University of America, 1938), especially pp. 94–109. For liturgical texts from the early Middle Ages that stress material continuity, see Michel, "Résurrection," col. 2545.

180. See also the suggestive remarks of Peter Brown in *Body and Society*, pp. 222–24, 293–94, 382–84, and especially pp. 440–43; and Robin Lane Fox, *Pagans and Christians* (New York: Knopf, 1987), pp. 445–48.

such as Evagrius, rejected entirely the notion that the body is maintained in resurrection.[181] Others, such as Gregory of Nyssa or Hilary of Poitiers, saw the fluid, dynamic body of 1 Corinthians 15 as winning out over the pull of corruption by leaving behind much of the specificity of the flesh we inhabit here on earth. Why then did some fierce ascetics, such as Jerome and, in his own way, Augustine, strain so to lift every organ and particle into the crystalline hardness of heaven? Why did propaganda for the monastic movement sometimes insist (as did Athanasius in his *Life of Anthony*) that *"this* body" shall rise, or argue (as did John Climacus) that we become incorruptible already in this life if we keep ourselves pure and glorify God?[182] Why bring heaven so close to earth? With this final question I return to an interpretative issue I raised in my first chapter and to much of the most creative scholarship done in the last ten years on late antiquity.

Using a model borrowed from Durkheimian anthropology and mediated through feminism, Elaine Pagels, John Gager, and Elizabeth Clark have recently argued that both the triumphant, institutional church of the fourth century and the branch of the ascetic movement that opposed Gnosticism, Platonism, and Origenism, projected into eschatology their newly achieved ecclesiastical and ascetic hierarchies.[183] This interpretation recognizes that figures such as Augustine and Jerome were profoundly uneasy with the culture of upper-class pagans; nonetheless, it sees them rejecting and inverting worldly distinctions of class and gender only to inscribe another version in an ascetic or ecclesiastical hier-

181. See the works by Elizabeth Clark cited in nn. 15, 106, and 117 above.

182. Athanasius, *The Life of Anthony*, chap. 92, trans. Robert C. Gregg, in *The Life of Anthony and the Letter to Marcellinus* (New York: Paulist Press, 1980), p. 97. John Climacus, *The Ladder of Divine Ascent*, chap. 15, in PG 88 (Paris, 1860), col. 892d–893a; trans. C. Luibheid and N. Russell (New York: Paulist Press, 1982), p. 179: "such a man [i.e., one of astonishing chastity] has already risen to immortality before the general resurrection." See also Anthony, Letter 1, in *The Letters of Anthony the Great*, trans. D. J. Chitty (Oxford: SLG Press, 1977), p. 5, where he says that the pure body here on earth receives "a portion of that spiritual body which it is to assume in the resurrection of the just." For a brilliant and evocative discussion of this, see Peter Brown, *Body and Society*, pp. 222–40.

183. Elaine Pagels, *The Gnostic Gospels* (New York: Random House, 1979); eadem, *Adam, Eve, and the Serpent* (New York: Random House, 1988); John Gager, "Body-Symbols"; and E. Clark, "New Perspectives on the Origenist Controversy." To summarize such complex argumentation in a single sentence is, of course, unfair. Gager, drawing on Pagels, speaks more of Christianity in general, Clark of asceticism. But the arguments of all three work essentially the same way. A very helpful discussion of asceticism is Robert Markus, *The End of Ancient Christianity* (Cambridge: Cambridge University Press, 1990), esp. pp. 199–211.

archy on earth that carries over, in its every detail, into heaven. John Gager, drawing on Mary Douglas, has indeed argued that conceptions of the body always reflect conceptions of society. He suggests that notions of the earthly body as transformable and the heavenly body as spiritual are expressions of rebellion against the world as it is, while notions of resurrection as involving both material continuity and bodily integrity undergird the power of ecclesiastical or moral hierarchy. The material- istic reading of resurrection is thus interpreted as a way of perpetuating sexual, social, and religious difference for eternity.

The argument is a problematic one. Applied to the details of historical change and to specific theological texts, it does not really work. It cannot explain, for example, why the powerful bishop Ambrose should have such a dynamic, open-ended, and spiritual conception of the resurrec- tion body whereas Jerome, who for all his authoritarian personality was in many ways a rebel, projects almost every bodily distinction and func- tion into heaven.[184] Nor does it take sufficient account of what was the greatest fear to late fourth- and early fifth-century elites: fear of absorp- tion by an invading other whom they called the barbarians.[185]

But in a general way, the argument is palpably accurate. Augustine and Jerome tell us that the doctrine of the resurrection is basically a doctrine of punishment and reward. It maintains hierarchy—not secular hierarchy but ecclesiastical and moral hierarchy—in heaven. Virgin and prostitute will not be equal, even if both repent; in God's house there are many mansions. What is lifted to heaven is what is earned on earth by a specific human person. Ascetic attainments, projected thus into heaven, become an undergirding of perpetual inequality, although we must not forget how profoundly asceticism, whether Origenist or anti- Origenist, rejected the gender and class inequalities of secular society. (Jerome wanted every molecule of Paula rewarded and understood those molecules to be unchangeably female, but Paula's superiority came from

184. Ambrose, *De excessu Satyri*, bk. 2, chaps. 53–70, PL 16 (Paris, 1880), cols. 1386–93, and in CSEL 73, pp. 276–88, and nn. 6 and 8 above. See also Ambrose, *De Isaac*, chap. 79, PL 14 (Paris, 1845), cols. 532–34, and in CSEL 32, pt. 1, ed. C. Schenkl (Vienna, 1896), pp. 698–700. Ambrose has a very Platonic notion of the self as a soul trapped in a body; his understanding of bodily resurrection stresses change and flow- ering; his images are astonishingly organic for the fourth-century West. For a few general comments on Ambrose's notion of bodily resurrection, see Frederick Holmes Dudden, *The Life and Times of St. Ambrose* (Oxford: Clarendon Press, 1935), vol. 2, pp. 665–68, and McGinn, *Foundations of Mysticism*, p. 272.

185. This fear was implicated in Christian uses of the cannibalism motif. As Mag- gie Kilgour has recently shown, "being eaten" was a fundamental image in classical literature for "being absorbed by a foreign culture—what we call 'going native.' " *From Communion to Cannibalism*, p. 23.

rebellion—with Jerome's help!—against the model of the privileged Roman matron.)[186]

With the partial exception of Jerome, however, the most materialistic of fourth- and fifth-century writers on bodily resurrection do not focus on maintaining distinctions owing to gender, sexual restraint, charismatic ability, or moral achievement.[187] The fate of fingernails and hair clippings, of aborted fetuses, and of the gastrointestinal system command greater attention. It is chain consumption in its most frightening form—cannibalism—that is taken to be the ultimate threat, the empirical fact that must be overcome. Eucharist is central to salvation because by digesting it we become indigestible to natural process.[188] In the theological literature of late antiquity, the fear that our self will perish is not expressed in elaborate metaphors (or natural philosophical discussions) of hermaphrodites, cross-dressing, gender transgression, sexual intercourse, and so forth, but rather in metaphors (and in technical treatments) of digestion and nutrition.[189] Athenagoras and Methodius insisted that human flesh could not be digested; Tertullian and Augustine insisted it could be. But all agreed that God could triumph over that which eats human beings—whether it be the whale that swallowed Jonah, the grave that eats the properly buried, or the desperate cannibal mother who devours her baby (a recurring image of depravity in late antique literature).[190] Both Augustine and Gregory of Nyssa devote more

186. See Anne Yarborough, "Christianization in the Fourth Century: Roman Women," *Church History* 45, no. 2 (1976): 1–17. Some of Yarborough's conclusions have recently been questioned, on the basis of evidence from inscriptions, by Michele R. Salzman, "Aristocratic Women: Conductors of Christianity in the Fourth Century," *Helios* 16, no. 2 (1989): 207–20.

187. Maintaining sexual difference in heaven in order to maintain his triumph over sexuality was clearly a special concern of Jerome's. When Augustine connects difference in heaven with difference on earth, he manages to imply both that difference lasts and that its moral import may be reversed—e.g., weak women may gain more merit than strong men. See above, nn. 118 through 120 and n. 153.

188. See the discussion of Ignatius, Irenaeus, and Tertullian in chapter 1 above; and Augustine, *Confessions*, bk. 7, chap. 10, ed. L. Verheijen, *Sancti Augustini Opera*, vol. 13, pt. 1, CCL 27 (Turnhout: Brepols, 1981), pp. 103–4.

189. We do occasionally find patristic discussions in which gender or sexuality function as images for social transgression and confusion; see above, chapter 1, nn. 67 and 103. Kilgour, *From Communion to Cannibalism*, p. 7, argues that in this period sexual intercourse is a "less totalizing but still bodily image for incorporation."

190. Augustine, *De civitate Dei*, bk. 22, c. 22, p. 844; see above nn. 169, 170, 172, and 175. Jerome, letter 127, paragr. 12, ed. and trans. Labourt, vol. 7, pp. 146–47, and PL 22, col. 1094, refers to cannibalism as part of the horror of the barbarian invasions. On the cannibalism libel, hurled back and forth between pagans and Christians, see above, chapter 1, nn. 44, 77, 83, 84, 132, 136, and 140. And compare the discussion of Macarius in nn. 10 and 11 of this chapter. Ambrose, *De excessu Satyri*, bk. 2, chap.

attention to the question of how Adam and Eve in paradise would have grown through eating into an immortality that made eating unnecessary, than they do to the topic of sex in Eden that so interests modern scholars. The situation of the triumphant and hierarchical church of the years around 400 is unquestionably reflected in its technical theological discussions of bodily resurrection. But I would suggest that the frenetic concern to forge an eschatology that retains every organ and particle in heaven reflects more than a need to support the authority of hard-working ascetics and bishops, more even than a defense of elite culture against the invading barbarians.

As several recent commentators have noticed, the literature of late antiquity throbs with fear of being fragmented, absorbed, and digested by an other that is natural process itself.[191] Second-century apologists had projected fertility into the millennium and even into heaven. Tertullian had written in glorious rhetoric of the beauties of creation although he too feared cannibalism. But by the time of Gregory of Nyssa and Augustine, procreation and nutrition—ways in which the world renews itself—were increasingly assimilated to putrefaction and death. The extraordinary bodily discipline of the ascetic movement, in both its Origenist and anti-Origenist branches, was directed toward making the body static and incorruptible. Change itself was the problem.

Yet, the theology of late antiquity rejected what were, philosophically speaking, the best solutions available. Instead of admitting flux, of allowing otherness, of lodging self in some sort of internally coherent and dynamic pattern (as did Origen), the majority of patristic theologians focused increasingly on material bits. They were willing to sacrifice philosophical coherence for the oxymoron of incorruptible matter. Jettisoning the glorious images of the natural world used by the sub-Apostolic writers and retained, in combination with darker images of decay, by the Greek and Syriac writers of the mid-fourth century, they

---

58, CSEL 73, pp. 280–81, says pagans worry about corpses that are eaten. The tendency of one culture to charge another, alien culture with cannibalism is so widespread that anthropologists have questioned whether cannibalism actually occurs; for varying views, see Marvin Harris, *Good to Eat: Riddles of Food and Culture* (New York: Simon and Schuster, 1985); W. Arens, *The Man-Eating Myth: Anthropology and Anthropophagy* (New York: Oxford, 1979); Peggy Reeves Sanday, *Divine Hunger*.

191. Three recent studies that suggest this (although in very different ways) are Mathieu, "Horreur du cadavre"; Piero Camporesi, *The Incorruptible Flesh: Bodily Mutation and Mortification in Religion and Folklore*, trans. T. Croft-Murray and H. Elsom (Cambridge: Cambridge University Press, 1988); and Kilgour, *From Communion to Cannibalism*.

were determined nonetheless to redeem the physical and material—to lift up to God its every fragment, particle, and atom.

The doctrine of bodily resurrection was not, then, a displaced discussion of power or of status, of sensuality, gender, or sex, of cultural encounter and otherness; it was a discussion—exactly as its proponents said it was—of death. And death was horrible, not because it was an event that ended consciousness, but because it was part of oozing, disgusting, uncontrollable biological process. Such process, beginning at conception and continuing in the grave, threatened identity itself. As Origen said, "river is not a bad name for the body"; yet in the topos known since Heraclitus, "you cannot step into the same river twice."[192] How then (asked ancient authors) do we survive the rushing stream of death within us? How can we be and remain ourselves? Jerome, Augustine, and Victricius of Rouen answered that question by asserting God's power to freeze every moment and sustain every particle of the flux that is "us." Resurrection made decay incorruptible. To ask why people in late antiquity had the stubborn courage to face the putrefaction that joins death to life is to ask for causal explanation at a level no modern theory addresses.[193] But to ask what that courage confronted, it is enough to read the texts themselves and follow their images as well as their arguments.

The extraordinary materialism of early fifth-century eschatology set the course of discussion for hundreds of years. It became the basis for the renewal of theological consideration of the body in the twelfth century. By the time of works such as Hugh of St. Victor's treatise on the sacraments, the textbook of Peter Lombard, and Herrad of Hohenbourg's *Hortus deliciarum*, the Pauline seed was almost forgotten; theological focus was squarely on the preservation of organs and bits. Augustine's *City of God* and *Enchiridion* (mediated through the compilations of Julian of Toledo and others) had become authoritative on the issue of judgment and resurrection. Even more than at the time of Gregory of Nyssa and Jerome, the paradigmatic body was the body of the saint, purified in life by denying those natural processes (especially nutrition and procreation) that threaten stability and glorified in death by becoming a jewel-

192. See n. 16 above on Origen, and Heraclitus, *On the Universe*, fragment 41, trans. W. H. S. Jones (Cambridge, Massachusetts: Harvard University Press, 1979), p. 483. See also fragment 78: "When is death not within ourselves? . . . Living and dead are the same, and so are awake and asleep, young and old" (trans. Jones, p. 495).

193. Even the Freud of *Civilization and Its Discontents* provides not so much an answer to this question as an alternative description of the courage.

like relic that miraculously protects the living against the decay of illness and death. Many of the most colorful miracles of the high Middle Ages can be explained and understood only in the context of this theology of resurrection inherited from the years around 400.

It is to the theology of the early twelfth century—the high point of Western materialist assumptions about the body—that I shall turn in my next chapter.

PLATE I. In this late twelfth-century miniature, painted under the direction of the learned abbess Herrad of Hohenbourg, Christ's salvific death on the cross is associated both with the establishment of church and eucharist and with the resurrection of the dead. The figure below the cross is Adam, progenitor and exemplar of all persons, whom popular legend held to be buried at Golgotha. The miniaturist associates the still-quite-dead Adam with the saints mentioned in Matthew 27.52, who awaken at the moment of the crucifixion. Herrad, *Hortus deliciarum*, fol. 150r (from a nineteenth-century tracing, made from the now-destroyed manuscript).

PLATE 2. Illustrating the Last Judgment with themes drawn from Byzantine iconography, this miniature depicts the moment of resurrection as one in which whole bodies (labeled in the inscription "the bones of the dead") rise from coffins while birds, beasts, and fish regurgitate parts for reassemblage. The saved are depicted here, and in an accompanying miniature, not as an indistinguishable mass of humanity, but in groups, the members of which are garbed and labeled so as to signal their particular religious statuses. *Hortus deliciarum*, fol. 251r (from a tracing).

PLATE 3. Recapitulating and reversing the regurgitation motif in fol. 251r, this elaborate depiction of the damned locates punishments of cooking, eating, and bodily partition in the lowest levels of hell. Below the reprobate boiled in cauldrons, Satan holding anti-Christ sits on a throne that eats sinners and rolls their decapitated heads under its feet. *Hortus deliciarum*, fol. 255r.

PLATE 4. This miniature, painted under the direction of Hildegard of
Bingen about 1165 to accompany one of the final visions of her *Scivias*,
shows in the lower left-hand corner the bones that rise again at the sound
of the last trumpet. Although the text of the vision speaks of the blessed
wafted up to heaven, the miniature itself seems to show detached heads of
both saved and damned rolled together in preparation for resurrection. The
motion from bottom to top in the miniature is thus from confusion to
order, part to whole. Hildegard, *Scivias*, book 3, vision 12, plate 33;
Wiesbaden, Hessische Landesbibliothek, MS 1, fol. 224r (made from a
colored photograph; manuscript lost since 1945).

PLATE 5. In Giotto's monumental depiction of the Last Judgment in
the Arena chapel at Padua (ca. 1305–10), the General Resurrection is
only a subordinate element and the motif of bodily partition has
disappeared. At the bottom left, the dead rise intact and fully enfleshed.
On the right, eating is a prominent motif among the tortures of hell,
but the body parts so noticeable in earlier depictions are absent.

DETAIL OF PLATE 5. In a tiny scene at the bottom of Giotto's great painting, the dead climb naked from the bare earth and from sarcophagi when the trumpet sounds. Above these small figures, the blessed, clothed in the garments of glory, enter into paradise.

PLATE 6. The eleventh-century mosaic on the west wall of the cathedral at Torcello, near Venice, is the best-known Western example of Byzantine Last Judgment iconography. The triumph of whole over part is illustrated here not only in the two ovals of the middle register but also in the structure of the entire composition. In the top zone, the blessed rise whole from the tomb, while below them the saints in paradise shimmer in glory. At the bottom right, Satan sits on a throne that devours sinners while vengeful angels prod separated heads, marked with the regalia of various secular and religious statuses. Below this, the damned appear as naked bodies and torsoes, and even further below, we find worm-eaten skulls, severed heads, and body parts. Thus, despite the orthodox doctrine that all rise intact for judgment, the damned are shown in a state of fragmentation that is a symbolic expression of their sins.

DETAIL OF PLATE 6. In the left portion of the middle register of the Torcello Last Judgment, birds and beasts regurgitate body parts for resurrection. Just above, several of the dead awaken, still in their shrouds. In the right-hand oval, fish vomit up the dead. The eye of the viewer is carried from the bones and body fragments in hell (lower right), upward past the depictions of regurgitation (middle register), to the resurrection of the blessed, intact, in the presence of Christ. The mosaic is a powerful depiction of the idea that salvation is wholeness, hell is decay and partition, redemption is regurgitation and reassemblage.

PLATE 7. This eleventh-century Greek gospel adds to the account of Judgment in Matthew 25.31–46 a visual gloss that has no parallel in the text. Although the gospel author speaks of the Son of Man on the throne of glory judging the nations of the earth, the miniature depicts body fragments in the lowest chambers of hell, above which Satan rides a voracious beast. To his left, fish regurgitate body parts, while above him the dead rise from sarcophagi and beasts vomit up torsoes and limbs. Crowning the miniature, Christ in glory sits with the elect. MS BN Gr. 74, fol. 51v.

PLATE 8. In this drawing of the crucifixion, from about fifty years before the similar depiction in the *Hortus deliciarum* (see plate 1), the dead who rise below the cross are Adam, Lazarus, and the saints of Matthew 27.52. MS Lat. qu. 198, Staatsbibliothek zu Berlin-Preussischer Kulturbesitz, fol. 320v (ca. 1132).

PLATE 9. In many twelfth- and thirteenth-century depictions of the crucifixion, Adam buried beneath the cross becomes a skeleton, a skull, or a heap of bones. MS 4, Hamburg, Stadtbibliothek, In scrinio 85, fol. 15a (twelfth century).

PLATE 10. This eighth-century Anglo-Saxon ivory, now in the Victoria and Albert Museum, depicts resurrected bodies at various stages of resuscitation. Some lie inert, fully wrapped in grave clothes; others struggle out of their shrouds. On the left a sitting figure receives his soul as a dove flying in at the mouth. In the bottom right-hand corner, the damned are swallowed by the mouth of hell.

PLATE 11. This illustration of Revelation 20.4 shows those who will not rise at the first resurrection as shrouded bodies in various stages of decay. Those who do rise point to the mark of Christ's favor on their foreheads or hands; even they, however, appear babylike, with rounded, undifferentiated bodies, which seem only at that moment to have acquired flesh. MS Douce 180, Bodleian Library, Oxford, p. 86 (ca. 1260–75).

PLATE 12. In this fine twelfth-century miniature of an angel locking
the souls of the damned into hell, the artist plays with and underlines
the notion of hell as a mouth by placing tiny mouths at its corners and
apex. Winchester Psalter, British Lib. MS 1846 Cott. Nero, c. 4, fol. 39
(ca. 1150–60).

PLATE 13. In another twelfth-century English psalter, Christ harrows hell by forcing the cross into Leviathan's mouth. The image parallels the words of the contemporary monastic author, Peter of Celle, who wrote that penitence and prayer, grasped like "the horns of the cross," can force hell to vomit up souls from its belly or shatter the molars in the mouth of death. MS Douce 293, Bodleian Library, Oxford, fol. 14r (ca. 1170–83).

PLATE 14. Throughout the Middle Ages, the resurrection of Christ, and the promise of resurrection to all humankind, were associated with the story of Jonah, swallowed and regurgitated intact by the whale. In this historiated initial S, the whale vomits up an undigested Jonah while above reigns a serene and majestic Christ. MS Clm 3900, fol. 82 (from about 1250).

PLATE 15 (whole and detail). The tympanum of the west portal of the church of Saint Faith at Conques (ca. 1135) shows, in the bottom register, the dead rising from coffins just above a small Christ, who welcomes the blessed through the door of paradise. Opposite these blessed, a hideous mouth pokes through the door of hell and swallows the reprobate into a space populated by twisted and tormented bodies. In the larger composition, the association of devouring and disorder with hell (on the right), wholeness and order with paradise (on the left) is clear.

PLATE 16 (detail of lower wall). In Greece, the Balkans, and Russia, motifs of swallowing and regurgitation continued down into modern times to be used to depict Last Judgment and General Resurrection. In this detail from the sixteenth-century refectory fresco at Lavra on Mt. Athos, hell or Leviathan swallows a beast that, in turn, swallows the damned.

PLATE 16 (detail of upper wall). Above and to the right of Leviathan, a veritable menagerie of creatures vomits up limbs and torsoes for reassemblage. Next to the trumpeting angel can be seen a bird, a beast, and a reptile presenting resurrected parts. It is hard not to wonder how the monks who took their meals before this gigantic fresco understood the use of eating as an image of destruction and dissolution, regurgitation as an image of salvation.

PLATE 17. In this thirteenth-century miniature from Bamberg-Eichstätt, salvation is clearly represented as triumph over fragmentation and decay. A corpse rises in its shroud, disentangles itself, and receives the garment of salvation, while other corpses receive their missing parts from the beasts who have devoured them. MS 1903 (olim 1833), Stiftsbibliothek, Melk, fol. 109v (ca. 1255).

PLATE 18. This initial from a Würzburg psalter, contemporary with the Bamberg-Eichstätt psalter reproduced in the previous plate, shows bodies rising from large sarcophagi at the sound of the last trumpet. One of the men is missing his arm below the elbow, and a doglike creature offers the severed member for reattachment. Close examination reveals that the original form of the initial showed the arm whole. MS Cim 15, fol. 204r.

PLATE 19. In the later Middle Ages, reliquaries came increasingly to underline the nature of the body parts contained within. The sheathing of gold and jewels suggested, however, that the bones inside possessed already something of the incorruptibility of heaven. This thirteenth-century silver arm reliquary with cabochon crystals sheaths the bone fragment with precious metal and gems.

PLATE 20. Although earlier than the container in the previous plate, this twelfth-century reliquary from the cathedral at Osnabrück provides an even more elaborate covering for the body part contained within. The opening at the back, which gives a partial glimpse of the wrapped relic, is a later addition.

PLATE 21. In the thirteenth century, the practice emerged of displaying relics in ostensoria or monstrances, such as this fourteenth-century example from Cologne. These containers, used interchangeably for displaying relics or the eucharistic host, sheathed the body of the saint or of Christ in the crystalline permanence of heaven while at the same time revealing that it was of the stuff of earth.

PLATE 22. The reliquary of Thomas Becket, made between 1173 and 1180 probably by a Rhenish goldsmith in England, is in the traditional casket or box form, with a gabled lid that suggests a roof. Such houselike containers deny the fragmentary nature of the relics housed inside, and even suggest that the parts are gathered into a whole, as believers are incorporated into the body of Christ, the church. In this case, however, the simulated ruby on the lid has been constructed of clear glass and foil to signal the nature of the relic contained within—the precious blood of the martyred bishop.

PLATE 23. By the thirteenth century, both text and sculpture sometimes conflated relic and resurrection, implying that the body at the end of time would be exactly the incorrupt particles that reposed in the grave. The left doorway of the west portal of Notre Dame cathedral at Amiens, made in the 1230s, depicts scenes from the life of the local saint, Firmin. The central scene in the middle register depicts the *inventio,* or discovery, of the saint's incorrupt body in such a way that the saint appears to be rising from the tomb.

PLATE 24. The earliest depictions of the afterlife known to be influenced by Dante's *Divine Comedy* show only heaven and hell, not purgatory. The monumental wall painting at the Campo Santo in Pisa from about 1330, now attributed to Buffalmacco, shows judgment and resurrection at the left, while, on the right, the wicked are tortured in the recognizable circles of Dante's hell. The presence of a judging Christ, avenging angels, and bodies rising from the earth makes it clear that the human figures shown here in full particularity of status and moral condition are embodied persons, not souls.

PLATE 25. Wall paintings from about 1357 in the Strozzi chapel of Santa Maria Novella in Florence, now attributed to Nardo di Cione, show Dante's heaven and hell. In the depiction of paradise, the ranks of the blessed, with angels interspersed among them, swell upward toward the thrones of the queen and king of heaven. The presence of angels blowing the last trumpet suggests that the human figures are resurrected persons, not the souls inhabiting aerial bodies about whom Dante wrote in his *Comedy*.

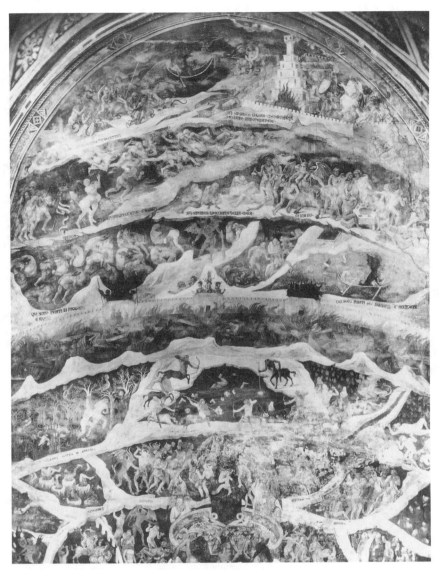

PLATE 26. In the Strozzi chapel depiction of Dante's hell, details of the *Inferno* are clearly recognizable. Satan devours the very worst of the damned in the lowest circle.

PLATE 27. The great tympanum of the west portal at St. Peter's church in Poitiers, from the 1130s, is typical of twelfth- and thirteenth-century scenes of General Resurrection and Final Judgment. In the lowest register, the dead rise intact and beautiful; just above this, they are divided forever into the blessed, who throng through the gate of paradise, and the damned, driven or pulled in chains toward the devouring mouth of hell.

PLATE 28. In this magnificent miniature, probably from the second quarter of the thirteenth century, demons fling the damned into the mouth of hell, while just above this, the saved, clearly differentiated anatomically into men, women, and children, contemplate a Christ in majesty at the very moment of their escape from the watery deep and the mouth of Leviathan. Trinity College Apocalypse, R.16.2, fol. 25r.

PLATE 29. The *Visions of Tondal*, written in south Germany in the mid-twelfth century by an Irish monk named Mark, was by far the most influential tale of a journey to the otherworld written before Dante's *Divine Comedy*, yet it was illustrated, so far as we know, only once. In this miniature from the later fifteenth century, we see the "valley of the homicides" depicted as a pot, in which a "great multitude of damned souls . . . were burned and roasted . . . then liquified and strained through the burning lid like a sauce strained through a canvas sieve." Getty MS 30, fol. 13v (from the 1470s, attributed to Simon Marmion of Valenciennes).

PLATE 31. In this detail from the ceiling mosaic in the Baptistry at Florence (probably from the second half of the thirteenth century), the conflation of digestion and damnation is clear. Satan's devouring throne is almost reduced to a pair of biting snakes, while from his ears spring two more snakelike heads that chew sinners. The man eaten by the left throne-head is also bitten by lizards; to his right another figure has been almost completely swallowed by a toad. Below the right throne-head, a figure lapped by flames appears as a disembodied head.

PLATE 30. A second miniature from the fifteenth-century illustrated manuscript of the *Visions of Tondal* shows the avaricious devoured by the beast Acheron. In the text, Tondal's soul, dragged into the jaws of Acheron by fiends, is mauled there by the biting of lions, dogs, serpents, and "other horrible beasts he could not recognize." Getty MS 30, fol. 17.

PLATE 32. In this fifteenth-century illustration of hell, from the Book of Hours of Catherine of Cleves, the artist underlines the threat of being swallowed and digested by placing mouths inside mouths. The Pierpont Morgan Library M. 945, fol. 168v.

PLATE 33. (Detail) On the central tympanum of the west portal of St. Stephen's church at Bourges (ca. 1240), the dead rise from their sarcophagi clearly male and female. All except prelates are naked, but social status is indicated by headgear. Above them, the souls of the just are seen reposing in Abraham's bosom, represented as a large napkin.

PLATE 34. When late medieval artists depicted the saints outside a
narrative context, they often showed them carrying their own body parts.
These severed limbs and mutilated fragments are more, however, than
mere attributes—i.e., aids to the identification of the saint. They are also
testimony to the power of God, who reassembles in resurrection the
bodies of those who die for the faith, but does not erase, even in the glory
of heaven, the marks (or aurioles) of their special courage. In this initial L
from a fourteenth-century manuscript, for example, the martyred Lucy
appears serene and beautiful, with her eyes both in their normal position
on her face and in the dish she carries. Modena, Biblioteca Estense Lat. MS
1023, fol. 17v.

PLATE 35. This thirteenth-century miniature shows executioners cutting off the breasts of St. Agatha in the third frame. In the fourth, her soul—a small naked figure, its hands crossed in prayer—escapes toward heaven, but the naked corpse is shown with its breasts intact. Paris MS Bibliothèque nationale, Nouv. acq. Fr. 23686, fol. 247v (ca. 1270–80).

purmenable gloire ou nos ttub puissient uenir pur la
haute pitie z pur lapitite misencorde ure seigneur qui
uit z regne pur toutes secces des secces amez. Cigme
ce lpisson saint quentin legloneus martyr

oir al qui ont sens z discretion.
doiuent uolentiers oir les pa
roles des uies des sauit martyrs
pozce que les conr alalaunge
nostre seigneur z alagloire
et pozce uos uoil greconimen
aer a dire. lauie mon seig
noz sauit quentin leglo
rieus martyr z sapinssion pur unes puroles.

Uoent que diocliaens z maximiens estoient en
peroz a rome souffoient al qui crestien estoient
apele grann persecutions pz lafoi ure seignoz z guz tor
menz pz auoir le regne purmenable upluloz enestorent
mis enchartres z empzisons oscures ou il estoient tant
quil mozoient pzlagrant destresce quil souffroient. Li
autre estoient tant uatu dematont z deueretres que li

PLATE 36. Another miniature in the manuscript seen in plate 35
shows St. Quentin being beheaded by soldiers in the fourth frame. In
the fifth, we see soldiers throwing his body into the Somme, but it
appears to be reassembled under its shroud. Three folios later, in an O
initial (not shown), Eusebia discovers Quentin's body, which is clearly
intact. Paris MS Bibliothèque nationale, Nouv. acq. Fr. 23686, fol. 100v.

Part Two

THE TWELFTH
CENTURY

Three

Reassemblage and Regurgitation: Ideas of Bodily Resurrection in Early Scholasticism

Herrad of Hohenbourg: An Introduction to Twelfth-Century Art and Theology

 TOWARD THE END of the twelfth century (probably between 1175 and 1185), Herrad, the learned abbess of Hohenbourg, presided over the compilation of a massive encyclopedia or summa, called the *Hortus deliciarum*, which told the story of salvation from the Creation, through the Incarnation and life of Christ, to the end of time.[1] This encyclopedia, produced on enormous vellum folios and illustrated with hundreds of pictures that were not only elaborately colored but also labeled with detailed inscriptions, was not, as far as we know, copied; it had little influence in the later Middle Ages. It was destroyed when the library of Strasbourg was burned in 1870 and has only recently been reconstructed in a facsimile edition based on nineteenth-century tracings, which reduce its glory to a series of misleading, cartoonlike sketches.[2] None-

1. Herrad of Hohenbourg, *Hortus deliciarum*, ed. Rosalie Green et al., *Commentary* (London and Leiden: Warburg Institute/University of London and Brill, 1979), p. 25. See also Herrad, *Hortus deliciarum: Recueil de cinquante planches . . . avec texte d'introduction historique, littéraire, et archéologique, suivi du catalogue complet des 344 miniatures et du commentaire iconographique des cinquante planches*, ed. Joseph Walter (Strasbourg: Le Roux, 1952); Otto Gillen, *Ikonographische Studien zum Hortus deliciarum*; and Gérard Cames, *Allégories et symboles dans l'Hortus deliciarum* (Leiden: Brill, 1971).

2. Herrad, *Hortus*, ed. Green, *Commentary*, p. 18; J. Rott, "L'Ancienne bibliothèque de Strasbourg, détruite en 1870: Les catalogues qui en subsistent," *Refugium*

theless the *Hortus deliciarum* can provide a starting point for my consideration of twelfth-century ideas of bodily resurrection because it graphically demonstrates, in both its miniatures and its text, their extreme materialism and literalism.[3]

Herrad's lengthy passages on judgment and resurrection—borrowed either directly from Augustine's *Enchiridion* or from Honorius Augustodunensis and Peter Lombard, who themselves borrowed from Augustine or from compilations based on him—discuss the physical state of the resurrected (their sex, size, color, age, etc.) and the details of their reassemblage or revivification. Much is made of the questions concerning aborted fetuses and pared fingernails that Augustine considered but also warned against as diverting curiosity from nobler matters. The chain consumption argument is elaborated with all the enthusiasm shown by opponents of bodily resurrection in the early church, although it is cheerfully refuted again and again with the assurance from Luke 21.18: "But a hair of your head shall not perish."[4]

Accompanying these lengthy discussions are two illustrations of the general resurrection, each as part of a larger composition. The first associates Christ's crucifixion with the creation of the church and the resurrection of the dead: below the cross are three sarcophagi, containing three figures who are alert and revivified (although one is still entangled in a shroud) and the quite dead skeleton of Adam (see plate 1).[5] The second is a Last Judgment, whose overall composition is unclear from the surviving tracings. Resurrection here is depicted both as enfleshed figures rising from tombs when an angel sounds the final trumpet and as bodily parts regurgitated by animals, birds, and fish, while another

---

animae bibliotheca: Mélanges offerts à Albert Kolb (Wiesbaden: Guido Pressler, 1969), pp. 426–42; idem, "Source et grandes lignes de l'histoire des bibliothèques publiques de Strasbourg détruites en 1870," *Cahiers alsaciens d'archéologie, d'art, et d'histoire* 15 (1971): 145–80; and Bynum, *Fragmentation and Redemption*, pp. 12–13.

3. On the literalism of medieval ideas of resurrection, see T. S. R. Boase, *Death in the Middle Ages: Mortality, Judgment, and Remembrance* (New York: McGraw-Hill, 1972), pp. 19–59.

4. Herrad of Hohenbourg, *Hortus deliciarum*, chaps. 850–52, 855, 887, 1090, ed. R. Green et al., *Reconstruction* (London and Leiden: Warburg Institute/University of London and Brill, 1979), pp. 423–35, 447, and 481.

5. Herrad, *Hortus*, fol. 150r, *Reconstruction*, plate 93, drawing 212, p. 267; see also *Commentary*, p. 173. The reviving figures are certainly meant to represent the saints mentioned in Matthew 27.52, which is inscribed on the picture; see ibid., p. 174. The coffin containing the single figure may also be intended to signify Lazarus. See below, chapter 4, n. 113. See also Herrad of Landsberg, *Hortus deliciarum (Garden of Delights)*, ed. and trans. A. D. Caratzas, commentary by A. Straub and G. Keller (New Rochelle: Caratzas Brothers, 1977), pp. 150–53.

angel rolls up the sky (see plate 2).[6] The choirs of blessed who appear before God for their reward stand not as an indistinguishable mass of humanity but attired (and labeled) with the specific characteristics of their religious statuses.[7] Inscriptions stress the wholeness and individuality of even those who rise in fragments. Below the naked figures emerging from sarcophagi, we read: "The bones of the dead will breathe anew [*resuscitabunt denuo*], and in their flesh they will see the Lord." An inscription above the regurgitated parts informs us:

> The bodies and members of people once devoured [*olim devorata*] by beasts, birds and fish are brought forth by God's command [*nutu Dei repraesentantur*], because the members of the saints will rise incorrupt as if of whole humanity, and not only via beasts as is depicted here [*ut ex integra humana massa resurgant incorrupta membra sanctorum, que non tantum per bestias*], and they will be presented at God's command.[8]

Moreover, salvation as regurgitation, reassemblage, and reclothing is matched by damnation as nudity, eternal digestion, and partition. In yet a third miniature, the bottom layer of a very unpleasant hell shows Satan holding Antichrist and sitting on a monstrous throne that eats and crushes sinners (see plate 3).[9] The most unfortunate of the damned are here depicted as detached skulls ground under cruel claws and as body pieces grasped in swallowing mouths—the visual recapitulation and opposite of the regurgitated parts found in the resurrection miniature.

As we shall see, the iconography of the *Hortus deliciarum* is no more original than the image of the reassembled pot or statue that Herrad borrowed from Honorius and Peter Lombard, who, in turn, borrowed it directly or indirectly from Augustine. The iconographic tradition appropriated by Herrad or her artist-collaborators was, however, Eastern and Greek rather than Western.[10] This appropriation, from the East, of a visual tradition that stresses salvation as reassemblage and the combina-

6. Herrad, *Hortus*, fol. 251r, *Reconstruction*, plate 141, drawings 326 and 327, p. 427. See also Caratzas, Straub, and Keller, ed., *Hortus*, pp. 224–31.

7. Ibid., drawing 325, p. 427.

8. For the inscription, see Herrad, *Hortus*, fol. 150, *Reconstruction*, plate 93, drawing 211, p. 267, and Caratzas, Straub, and Keller, ed., *Hortus*, p. 224 n. 2.

9. Herrad, *Hortus*, fol. 255r, *Reconstruction*, plate 146, drawing 338, p. 439. Satan holding Antichrist is parallel to Abraham holding souls in his bosom: fol. 263v, plate 152, drawing 344, p. 460. This parallel is generally present in Byzantine Last Judgment iconography. See also Caratzas, Straub, and Keller, ed., *Hortus*, pp. 234–35 and 242–43.

10. See below, chapter 4, pp. 188–97.

tion of such iconography with a Western textual tradition of extreme literalism, is striking—and all the more so because a very different treatment of resurrection *was* available in the West. Indeed Honorius Augustodunensis, the source of much of Herrad's discussion, himself also wrote of resurrection in a highly Origenist vein, using very different metaphors and concepts from those he bequeathed to Herrad. In Honorius's *Clavis physicae,* an abridgment of John Scotus Erigena's *De divisione naturae* that treats last things in a spiritualized fashion, we find both the organic metaphors of sprouting seeds and flowers familiar from 1 Corinthians 15 and the notion of transformation of the resurrected self beyond bodily particularities, such as size or sex, that is in the patristic period usually associated with the Pauline image. But the Origenist/ Erigenist aspect of Honorius was condemned, probably in his own day and certainly later on. The choices made by Herrad and her collaborators were those made generally in twelfth-century theology, iconography, spiritual writing, and popular story. In her text, as in most other twelfth-century treatments, the resurrected body is a jewel or a translucent glass, a shining garment, a rebuilt temple, or a statue reforged from its original material; dead and living are described as dust—assembled by God on the sixth day of creation, scattered in the long wait between death and the end of time, collected or swept together again by divine power when the judgment comes. In such accounts, the corporeal component of the self is stressed, and its identity (i.e., its survival through time) is equated with continuity of both matter and members.

In view of what historians of science, of art, of education, and of religious reform have told us about the twelfth-century enthusiasm for organic nature as metaphor—an enthusiasm seen perhaps most clearly in the proliferation of contemporary characterizations of the age as a "flowering" or "rebirth"—it is surprising to note such caution in eschatology.[11] Why did the age that supposedly re-discovered nature, "man," and "the individual" prefer to lift to heaven the details of earthly physicality, rejecting metaphors of process and open-ended development? What bothered twelfth-century theologians about images of the germination or flowering or re-nascence of the body at the end of time? In search of answers to these questions, I turn in this, my third chapter, to an exploration of the language in which scholastic writers spoke of resurrection. In chapter 4, I proceed to a consideration of the resurrection

11. Gerhart Ladner, "Terms and Ideas of Renewal," in *Renaissance and Renewal in the Twelfth Century,* ed. Robert L. Benson and Giles Constable (Cambridge, Mass.: Harvard University Press, 1982), pp. 1–33.

images found in spiritual writing and in iconography. In chapter 5, I treat the context of all these images (scholastic, monastic, and iconographic) in pious practice. I thus treat the revival of eschatological discussion in the twelfth century in the same way I treated debates of the second and fourth centuries: by moving from specific tropes, examples, and arguments to religious and social behavior, in particular the care of the dead.

A Scholastic Consensus: The Reassemblage and Dowering of the Body

Resurrection was one among many theological topics discussed in the schools of the early and mid-twelfth century. The discussion was mostly pieced together from passages in Augustine's late writings or from florilegia—such as Julian of Toledo's—made from Augustine's works. [12] Although, as we shall see, there was probably more disagreement on eschatological issues than most scholars have realized, scholastic writing showed an underlying predilection for metaphors of reassemblage and immutability to describe the resurrected and glorified body. To illustrate this, I shall begin with the work that became by the late twelfth-century the *locus classicus* for discussion of the resurrection: distinctions 43–50 of the fourth book of Peter Lombard's *Sentences*.[13]

Although almost pictorial in its vividness, the Lombard's treatment of eschatology is neither original nor coherent. It follows roughly the events of the end of time, from the trumpet blast to the glory of the

12. See Nikolaus Wicki, "Das 'Prognosticon futuri saeculi' Julians von Toledo als Quellenwerk der Sentenzen des Petrus Lombardus," *Divus Thomas* 31 (1953): 349–60; J. N. Hillgarth, "El Prognosticon futuri saeculi de San Julián de Toledo," *Analecta sacra Tarraconensia* 30 (1957): 5–61; idem, "Julian of Toledo in the Middle Ages," *Journal of the Warburg and Courtauld Institutes* 21 (1958): 7–26.

13. Peter Lombard, *Sententiae in IV libris distinctae*, ed. Collegium S. Bonaventurae (Grottaferrata: Collegium S. Bonaventurae ad Claras Aquas, 1971–81), vol. 2 (3d ed.), pp. 510–60. Nikolaus Wicki characterizes Peter Lombard's *Four Books of Sentences* as the first synthesis of eschatological sentences, but one that is lacking in cogency (*Die Lehre von der himmlischen Seligkeit in der mittelalterlichen Scholastik von Petrus Lombardus bis Thomas von Aquin* [Freiburg: Universitätsverlag, 1954] [hereafter Wicki, *Seligkeit*], p. 11). On the Lombard's sources, see ibid., pp. 12–14. For a useful and clear discussion of how Peter Lombard's *Sentences* became a textbook in the universities, see M.-D. Chenu, *Toward Understanding St. Thomas*, trans. A.-M. Landry and D. Hughes (Chicago: Henry Regnery, 1964), pp. 267ff. For detailed information both on the Lombard's sources and on parallel discussions in his scholastic contemporaries, see the notes to the Grottaferrata edition. F. M. Henquinet points out that the Lombard does not connect eschatology with the event of Christ's resurrection—an omission that thirteenth-century commentators would feel it necessary to fill ("Les questions inédites de Alexandre de Hales sur les fins dernières," *Recherches de théologie ancienne et médiévale* 10 [1938]: 56–59).

blessed before the throne of God, but if this is the principle of organization (and it is the only discernible one), a number of topics are treated out of order or considered, dropped, and considered again almost at random. What is striking, however, is the way in which the discussion gives pride of place to questions of the material reassemblage or reconstitution of the body.[14] Beginning with the admonition (borrowed from Augustine) that not all questions can be answered, Peter Lombard devotes distinction 43 to a discussion of whether those alive when the trumpet sounds must die before being raised. In distinction 44, he turns to such questions as the following: what age, height, and sex will we have in the resurrected body?[15] Will all matter that has passed through the body at any point be resurrected? Must bits of matter return to the particular members (for example, fingernails or hair) where they once resided? Will the bodies of the damned as well as the saved rise with their defects repaired? Are aborted fetuses resurrected? How can the bodies of the damned burn without being consumed? Will demons (although incorporeal) suffer from corporeal fire in hell? Distinction 45, after considering where souls reside between death and resurrection and asserting (without explaining) that the blessed will experience an increase of joy in bodily resurrection, turns to a lengthy consideration of the usefulness of prayers for the dead. Distinctions 46 and 47 explore in detail God's justice, especially the punishment of the damned. Distinctions 48 and 49 discuss specific questions concerning what we might call the topography and demography of blessedness: where exactly will Christ descend as judge? Of what quality will light be after the Last Judgment? Will all the elect shine with the same glory, see with the same clarity, and rejoice with the same joy? Distinction 50 returns to details of the condition of the damned and, after considering the question of how the finger

14. Marcia Colish, in her forthcoming book on Peter Lombard, argues that he shows what we might call pedagogical or didactic coherence—that is, a consistent tendency to work out moderate positions that reconcile earlier divergent opinions. See n. 16 below.

15. Lombard, *Sentences*, bk. 4, d. 43, c.7, and d. 44, chaps. 1–2, vol. 2, pp. 515–18. The Lombard explains that "to rise incorruptible" means to rise "without diminution of members." He then uses Ephesians 4.13 to assert that all will have the same age but not the same stature. Each person will receive the stature he had (or would have had) in youth. All will rise at the age to which Christ had come, which was, Augustine says, "about thirty"; for "thirty-two years and three months was Christ's age when he died and rose." Scripture does not say *vir* to indicate that all will rise male but to indicate that all will rise perfect.

The Lombard seems here to follow Julian of Toledo, who adapts Augustine's *Enchiridion*. The same material appears in Hugh of St. Victor's *De sacramentis*, bk. 2, pt. 17, chaps. 13–20; PL 176 (Paris, 1854), cols. 601–6. Note that Hugh says that "learned men" define "youth" as being achieved at about age thirty; after that, the process of decay sets in (col. 605B).

of Lazarus (Luke 16.22–26) could touch the tongue of the rich man when both (having died) were without body, repeats Augustine's warning that certain answers cannot be discovered.

As even such brief summary makes clear, the Last Judgment is primarily, to the Lombard, a matter of punishment and reward of exactly the same material stuff that constituted the body during life.[16] Thus it is not surprising that his basic image of the resurrected body is of particles or bits re-collected into a whole; even defects are seen—not as decay or old age flowering into youth and health—but as gaps to be filled in or as surpluses of material to be excised. As he writes in distinction 44, chapter 3, article 2, (borrowed in large part from Augustine's *Enchiridion*):

> Nor will anything perish of the substance of which the flesh of man is created but the natural substance of the body will be reintegrated by the collection of all the particles [*particulae*] that were dispersed before. And the bodies of the saints will rise without any defect, shining like the sun, all deformities they had here being cut off [*praecisis cunctis deformitatibus*].[17]

The extended metaphor used to explain resurrection is the case of a statue that is destroyed, or melted down, and reforged from the same material in such a way that the particles do not necessarily return to the same portion (or member) of the statue but are all incorporated into the remade whole (d. 44, chaps. 1–2).[18] When forced to consider images of sowing and growth by the apparent contradiction in 1 Corinthians 15 between resurrection in "the twinkling of an eye" and the necessity that all, like seeds, must die before quickening, the Lombard's exegesis simply equates "being sown" with "dying" and continues to describe resurrection as the reassemblage of "the dust of old cadavers" (d. 43, chap. 6, art. 2).[19]

16. In her forthcoming book, Colish argues that the Lombard takes a middle position in twelfth-century debates over eschatology between those (such as Honorius) who are curious about materialist details and those who wish to hold back from such speculation. She sees much of the materialist curiosity as emanating from Augustine and reads the Lombard's position as an implicit criticism of this. Although her interpretation is different from mine, it is not completely incompatible since my argument concerns not so much the extent of the Lombard's curiosity as his interpretation of the body as physical. Colish agrees that there is an anti-Origenist thrust in Peter and in much other early twelfth-century interpretation.

17. Lombard, *Sentences*, vol. 2, p. 519.

18. Ibid., pp. 516–17, borrowed from Augustine, *Enchiridion*, chap. 89.

19. Lombard, *Sentences*, vol. 2, p. 514, borrowed from Augustine, *De civitate Dei*, bk. 20, chap. 20.

Throughout this discussion, Peter's fundamental concern is to avoid both dissolution and deformity: the "same matter that becomes a cadaver when the soul departs" must be restored—but to a perfect body, one "without corruption or burden or difficulty."[20] Thus God will, if necessary, return particles of hair or nails to other members or make up defects; "for [He] takes care lest anything indecent occur."[21] It is at least as important to Peter Lombard that the reforged statue have no missing members (and no members of indecent size) as it is that all particles be used in its reconstitution.[22]

Although eschatology is tacked onto the end of Lombard's *Sentences* almost as an afterthought, the doctrine of the resurrection of the body has considerable importance in the textbook, for it figures in crucial ways in discussions of other than eschatological issues. Described as clothing that is put on and off, as a temple, a burden, an object of desire, or as dust or clay,[23] the resurrected body is considered both in connection with Christ's sojourn during the *triduum* and his resurrection and in connection with God's creating and sustaining of humankind in the Garden of Eden. To the modern reader's astonishment, the major conceptual problem Peter Lombard treats in these contexts is the problem of growth and nutrition. How can all humankind descend from the drops of Adam's semen—indeed how can any embryo grow into a child or any child into an adult—without taking in so much food that it becomes roast pig or bread instead of human nature? If we eat and grow and excrete for a lifetime, cutting our hair and fingernails and spilling our blood, how can God bring back all our particles when the trumpet blows? If food adds nothing to human substance, how do we grow? And why did God provide the tree of life in the Garden of Eden to sustain

20. Lombard, *Sentences*, bk. 4, d. 44, chap. 2, art. 2, vol. 2, p. 518 (borrowed from Augustine, *Enchiridion*, chap. 89), and chap. 3, art. 1, p. 518 (borrowed from *Enchiridion*, chap. 91).

21. Bk. 4, d. 44, chap. 2, art. 3, vol. 2, p. 518.

22. See n. 15 above. Peter Lombard sees resurrection as retaining differences of sex, height, and probably weight, but eliminating differences of age. A number of factors appear to be at work. There was an ancient tradition concerning the perfect age, but apparently no traditional "perfect stature." Technical concerns are clearly also involved; individual height is retained because if we all rose with Christ's height some would lose matter; individual age is not retained because both youth and senility can be seen as defects of matter. Theologians were comfortable with the addition of matter but unhappy with eliminating it unless the excrescence were clearly a deformity (as in the case of a second head). This is perhaps related to the discomfort with decay and diminution that is one of the major points of my discussion here. I return below to reasons behind the retention of biological sex.

23. Peter Lombard does sometimes speak of flesh as flowering; see, for example, bk. 3, d. 18, chap. 1, art. 5 (borrowing from Psalm 27.7), vol. 2, p. 112.

us?[24] If food *does* add to human substance, how can we avoid becoming what we eat? How, in cases of cannibalism or attacks by wild animals, can we remain ourselves when digested by others? What will happen to superfluity when we rise?

In considering these matters, the Lombard struggles to hold incompatible positions simultaneously. He asserts both, on the one hand, that growth really occurs (sometimes via food and sometimes without it), and on the other hand, that a perfect and material core of human nature for each one of us descends from Adam, continues throughout life, and rises at the end of time. He also maintains (with Augustine and Hugh of St. Victor) that the need to eat and to grow are not defects of human nature; indeed, eating from the tree of life in Eden would over time have produced immortality. But *feeling* the need to eat (i.e., hunger) *is* a defect, and, of course, there will be no eating or growing in heaven.

We find these opinions in book II, distinction 30, chapter 14, where Peter considers how all humankind can be in Adam when "there were not even so many atoms [*atomi*] as the number of men descended from him:"

> It can be answered that, materially and causally not formally, everything is said to have been in the first man which is naturally in human bodies; and it descends from the first parent by the law of propagation; in itself it is enlarged and multiplied with no substance from the exterior going over into it; and the same will rise in the future. Indeed it has help from foods but foods are not converted into human substance.[25]

Continuing the discussion in chapter 15, Peter quotes Matthew 15.17 as proof that we are not what we eat ("whatsoever entereth into the mouth goeth into the belly and is cast out into the privy") and then argues backward in time from the miraculous formation of a full human body for each individual at the resurrection to the possibility of human procreation and embryological expansion without the addition of alien substance.

24. The discussion comes from Augustine's *Literal Commentary on Genesis*, see above, chapter 2, nn. 137 and 162. In Augustine's discussion as well, the prominence of digestion is striking and not explained, at least to a modern reader, by the scriptural passage being glossed. The idea of eating one's way into a state where nutrition is not needed seems to reflect a deep need to transcend the physiological process of digestion.

25. Bk. 2, d. 30, chap. 14, art. 2, vol. 1, p. 504.

A boy who dies immediately after being born will be resurrected in that stature which he would have had if he had lived to the age of thirty, impeded by no defect of body. From whence therefore would that substance, which was small in birth, be so big in resurrection, unless of itself in itself it multiplied? From which it appears that even if he had lived, the substance would not have come from another source but it would have augmented itself, just as the rib [of Adam] from which woman was made and as the loaves of the gospel story [were multiplied].[26]

In such argumentation, the organic processes of nutrition and growth are treated as threatening to the nature of things.

Peter Lombard had at hand, of course, in Augustine's notion of seminal reasons, a model of growth in which the essential nature of something is maintained. And he sometimes made use of the idea that there is an unfolding pattern within a seed or particle of matter.[27] But even in the Augustinian idea of a seed, there were questions that disturbed Peter and his contemporaries. How was the unfolding induced? How far might it go? If development was impelled by food, then the essence of the thing seemed threatened. Might it not *become* food or unfold into something so dissimilar it was no longer itself? If development was not impelled by food, then the empirical evidence that connects eating and growth is denied. Divine power must then be invoked as an efficient cause in a startlingly large number of cases—as Hugh of St. Victor recognized in the *De sacramentis*, when he asserted that even ordinary growth is a miracle.[28] In short, behind much of the Lombard's discussion of creation and resurrection lies both an inability to understand by what mechanism something can grow and change and an inability to accept that, if it does grow and change, it can still be the same thing. Given such inadequate models for change, growth must be seen as the replication of exactly similar particles; resurrection must involve the reassemblage in exactly similar form of the identical pieces first gathered together to form the body.[29]

---

26. Vol. 1, pp. 504–5.

27. For example, bk. 2, d. 18, chap. 5, vol. 1, pp. 418–19.

28. Hugh, *De sacramentis*, bk. 1, pt. 6, chap. 37; PL 176, cols. 285–88; and see the translation by Roy J. Deferrari, *Hugh of St. Victor On the Sacraments of the Christian Faith (De Sacramentis)* (Cambridge, Mass.: The Mediaeval Academy of America, 1951), pp. 118–20. The position also meant that Augustine's opinion that food actually produces growth was rejected.

29. And see Hugh, *De sacramentis*, bk. 2, pt. 17, chaps. 14–15; PL 176, cols. 602–4; trans. Deferrari, pp. 458–60.

Peter Lombard's discussion of the Garden of Eden, of Christ's resurrection, and of last things is mostly borrowed from Augustine, Gregory, Jerome, Bede, and Julian of Toledo—mediated through early twelfth-century summae and sentence collections, chiefly those of Honorius Augustodunensis, Hugh of St. Victor, and the cluster of scholastics gathered around Anselm of Laon and William of Champeaux. Both in their choice of metaphors and in the course of their argumentation, these early-twelfth-century texts, like the Lombard's *Sentences*, treat the body as particles, all of which must continue so that they may finally be reassembled into a whole; organic growth—understood to be in some sense necessary because living entities in fact increase in size—is inexplicable and disturbing change and thus a challenge to identity.

Several of the sentences collected in the *Liber Pancrisis*, for example, discuss whether food is changed into body.[30] One fragment, which has been attributed to Anselm of Laon, clearly finds digestion an interesting topic and (quoting Matthew 15.17) details where exactly in the body the four parts of food go before they are excreted. But Anselm concludes, using a striking inorganic image, that the body does not rise with any increment gained from food:

> Thus is solved the [problem] of [the cannibal] who, from infancy, is fed with human flesh. For in the resurrection he will have that natural body of his own [i.e., what was in his first substance] and the others by whose flesh he has been fed will rise in the bodies that were naturally theirs.
>
> It is not irrational [to say this], because just as fire is fed by the food of pieces of wood but the wood is not however changed into the nature of fire, so the body is fed by the nourishment of food but this [food] is not converted into body.[31]

Indeed to this scholastic author, the particles of body remain in some way marked for their soul:

> After the dissolution of soul and body, there remain certain connections [*nexus*] which make them one person. We call it a *nexus* because

30. The *Liber Pancrisis* is a late twelfth-century compilation, probably by Peter Comestor, of early *sententiae* and *quaestiones*; see Odon Lottin, "Pour une édition critique du *Liber Pancrisis*," *Recherches de théologie ancienne et médiévale* 13 (1946): 185–201.

31. Odon Lottin, *Psychologie et morale aux XIIe et XIIIe siècles*, vol. 5: *Problèmes d'histoire littéraire: L'école d'Anselme de Laon et de Guillaume de Champeaux* (Gembloux: J. Duculot, 1959), no. 36, pp. 35–36. And see idem, *Psychologie et morale*, vol. 4, *Problèmes de morale*, pt. 1, pp. 15–58.

the soul of Peter has more concern and desire for [*plus respicit et exsp-ectat*] the body of Peter than it does for the body of Paul; according to this connection his soul and body [i.e., Peter's] are called one person [*persona una*].[32]

Hunger, eating, and wasting are central issues in many early sentence collections. One sentence fragment argues that Christ is superior to Adam not only because he does not have to die but also because he does not have to eat. Another uses the resurrection text from Luke 21.18 to argue explicitly that "substance does not perish" and bodies are not really "wasted from hunger" because God restores all flesh.[33] A set of anonymous questions *De novissimis* gives, as the major argument *against* resurrection, the impossibility of reassembling dust or halting organic process. It concludes that even Christ (who did not decay in the tomb) and those who are alive at the Judgment Day must, in "the twin-kling of an eye," put aside "whatever they have from exterior food." But once the extraneous is put aside, not a hair of our heads will perish; we will be put back together like a reforged statue.[34] A similar, anonymous set of sentences found in a Bamberg manuscript (*Bamberg Can 10*) cites Matthew 15.17, Augustine, and Bede on the problem of growth, dis-cusses the healing of the martyrs' wounds into visible but shining scars in the resurrection, and draws a detailed analogy to a wax statue.[35]

32. Ibid., vol. 5, no. 91, p. 78. The argument is essentially that of Gregory of Nyssa.

33. Sentences attributed to the school of Anselm of Laon in ibid., no. 347, p. 265, and no. 499, p. 321; see also no. 500, pp. 321–22.

34. Ibid., nos. 496–98, pp. 319–21. And see the rather similar but more sophisti-cated argument in the *De resurrectione* (Clm 14 508, fol. 62vb–63vb) of Peter of Capua (d. 1242), edited in Richard Heinzmann, *Die Unsterblichkeit der Seele und die Au-ferstehung des Leibes: Eine problemgeschichtliche Untersuchung der frühscholas-tischen Sentenzen- und Summenliteratur von Anselm von Laon bis Wilhelm von Auxerre* [hereafter Heinzmann, *Unsterblichkeit*], Beiträge zur Geschichte der Phi-losophie und Theologie des Mittelalters [hereafter BGPTM]: Texte und Untersuch-ungen 40.3 (Münster: Aschendorff, 1965), pp. 202–7. Peter says, at lines 9–12 and 18–22:

> Praeterea cibi convertuntur in veritatem humanae naturae, ergo et cibi resur-gent. Et ita non tantum carnem humanam sed etiam brutorum animalium car-nem tenemur credere resurrecturam. Respondeo: quidquid est de veritate hu-manae naturae resurget quidem. . . . Cibi autem non convertuntur in veritatem humanae naturae licet forte convertantur in carnem humanam quia aliqua caro est in homine quae non est de veritate humanae naturae, fovetur tamen eis et multiplicatur humana natura, nec sine illa posset subsistere. Sicut caro parvuli fovetur aqua quae tamen numquam transit in carnem parvuli.

Similar arguments were made earlier by Robert Pullus, Robert of Melun, Peter of Poitiers, and Simon of Tournai; see Heinzmann, *Unsterblichkeit*, pp. 145–225.

35. Lottin, *Psychologie*, vol. 5, no. 530, pp. 393–400.

Even outside the schools of the continent, the dominant metaphors in compilations concerning eschatology were ones of reassemblage and regurgitation. For example, a Middle Irish text from the late eleventh or early twelfth century that draws on Julian of Toledo says the dead will be "smelted and purified by the fire of Doom," then "[re]cast into a form more beautiful."

> Those that have been dissolved . . . , who have been devoured by wild beasts and dispersed in different places, will arise according to the counsel of the Lord, who will gather them and renew them, out of the place that He desires. . . . [I]t is [likely] in this case that they will arise there where they have been devoured and dispersed, for that is what is counted as their tomb.[36]

Neither the seed image of 1 Corinthians 15, nor the second-century argument that natural cycles of diurnal and seasonal change foreshadow the resurrection, disappear entirely from twelfth-century discussion. For example, Marbod, bishop of Rennes (d. 1123) gives a brief compendium of patristic opinion in his poem *De resurrectione corporum*. He speaks of the sun rising from burial under the earth (*sub tellure sepultus*), compares our resurrection to that of grasses clothed again after the nakedness of winter, and at least hints at an analogy to embryological growth by speaking of flesh and skin and bone rising from the grave.[37] Hugh of St. Victor in his *De sacramentis*, book II, part 17, chapter 13, uses similar metaphors of cycles and burgeonings and growth.[38] The so-called Munich summa (which is related to the *Summa sententiarum* and to Hugh's *De sacramentis*) says that the growth of a resurrected body from a dead child is like the multiplication of loaves in the gospel, the growth of Eve from the rib, or the emergence of a sheaf of grain from its seed.[39] Nonetheless Marbod's basic synonym for the cadaver is earth (*tellus*), ashes (*cinis*), cinders (*favilla*). His understanding of our seed-bodies is that found in the passage from Rebecca West with which I began this

36. Selections from the Book of the Dun Cow, pp. 34a–37b, ed. Whitley Stokes, in "Tidings of the Resurrection," *Revue celtique* 25 (1904): 232–59, esp. 234–41, and see n. 40 below. Note the similarity to the passage from Hugh of St. Victor cited in n. 43.

37. Marbod of Rennes, *Liber decem capitulorum*, chaps. 9 and 10 (on "the good death" and "the resurrection of bodies"), PL 171, cols. 1712–17. On Marbod, see Réginald Grégoire, "Marbode," in *Dictionnaire de spiritualité, ascétique, et mystique, doctrine et histoire*, ed. M. Viller et al. (Paris: Beauchesne, 1932ff.), vol. 10, col. 241–44.

38. *De sacramentis*, PL 176, cols. 601–2; trans. Deferrari, p. 457.

39. Lottin, *Psychologie*, vol. 5, pp. 374–75.

book: we are sown in furrows and pop up again revivified. The body that rises is the body that was buried—the same although not now dissolvable (*idem sed non resolubile corpus*).[40] Similarly, the point of the discussion in the Munich summa is not change of nature but continuity of matter. The whole body at the resurrection will be made up of little bits of itself—not a hair lost but not a single cell of roast pig added either![41] As Hugh of St. Victor put it, decay is dissolution into tiny particles; but "what falls must rise [i.e., be constituted] again."[42]

Earthly material from which the flesh of mortals is created does not perish before God, but into whatever dust or ashes it is resolved, into whatever breath or breezes it disperses, into whatever substance of other things or elements themselves it is converted, into the food and flesh of whatever animals or men it withdraws and is changed, to that human soul which animated it in the beginning so that it was made man and grew, at the moment of time it will return. . . .

For if a man, an artificer, can produce a statue, which for some reason he had made deformed, and render it very beautiful, so that nothing of the substance but only the deformity perish, and . . . can so scatter and mix all [the material] that he does not cause deformity or diminish quantity, what must we think about the Omnipotent?[43]

40. An Anglo-Norman poem (probably from the mid-thirteenth century) that gives a very free translation of the *Prognosticon* of Julian of Toledo (see n. 12 above) makes similar use of the dossier of patristic natural analogies. See P. Meyer, "Fragment du Dialogue entre l'évêque saint Julien et son disciple," *Romania: Recueil Trimestriel . . .* 36 (1907): 502–15; text on pp. 506–15. Verses 480–500 argue that if God can make trees to green and grain to produce fruit a thousandfold, he can certainly reassemble the flesh that has been destroyed. Verses 368–71 insist: it is our flesh and no other that returns. Verses 386–89 repeat that God makes and unmakes; if he can form (*fourmer*) earth into body and make (*mettre*) body into earth, so he can certainly "remettre" "la cher a terre." Verses 504–40 repeat the chain consumption argument in a form transmitted from Gregory the Great through Julian of Toledo; the point is that God can sort out what is man and what is beast even if a lion eats a wolf, who has eaten a man, and the lion dies and decays into dust. See also F. J. Tanquerey, "Originalité du Dialogue entre saint Julien et son disciple," *Mélanges de philologie et d'histoire offerts à M. Antoine Thomas par ses élèves et ses amis* (Paris: Librairie ancienne Honoré Champion, 1927), pp. 437–43.

41. See above n. 39. See also the fascinating discussion in the anonymous summa in Cod. Vat. lat. 10754, fol. 47ra–48rb, edited in Heinzmann, *Unsterblichkeit*, pp. 209–13, especially pp. 209–10, lines 8–68, which uses Augustine's image of the statue to lead into a discussion of whether hair is "of the truth of human nature," and p. 211, lines 69–85, to question whether human flesh, if eaten, is converted into animal flesh. And see below n. 56.

42. *De sacramentis*, bk. 2, pt. 17, chap. 13; PL 176, cols. 601–2; trans. Deferrari, p. 457.

43. *De sacramentis*, bk. 2, pt. 17, chaps. 14 and 16; PL 176, cols. 602–3 and 604; trans. Deferrari, pp. 459 and 460.

When Hugh quotes 1 Corinthians 15 verse 44 ("sown natural, raised spiritual . . .") or verse 50 ("flesh and blood shall not inherit . . ."), he does so to emphasize continuity and identity, not transformation: "Now insofar as pertains to substance, even then [i.e., in heaven] there will be flesh."[44] Thus the distance or dichotomy that is underlined by 1 Corinthians 15.44 is not a metaphor for growth or process; what is suggested is that exactly the same body we have here below will be endowed in heaven with certain additions that make further change impossible. If the healthy body is lighter and more agile than the sick one (says Hugh), can we not understand that God will make our earthly bodies subtle and swift enough to rise to heaven?[45] Indeed, so concerned is Hugh with the permanence of the corporeal after the end of time that he devotes considerable attention to explaining how the fires of hell can devour the risen bodies of the damned without either the fire or the flesh it tortures being consumed.[46] Although Peter Lombard is more interested in the psychological pain of infernal torture than in the worm and fire, he too stresses the incorruptibility—and thus the perpetual torture-ability—of the risen bodies of the damned.[47]

Hugh's suggestion that gifts of unchangeability are added to the glorified body, as delights are added to the blessed soul, builds on the idea (expressed earlier by Eadmer and Anselm of Canterbury) that God will give seven benefits to the risen bodies of the elect: beauty, swiftness, strength, liberty, health, pleasure, and everlasting life.[48] Similar notions

44. *De sacramentis*, chap. 17; col. 604; trans. Deferrari, p. 460; passage borrowed from Augustine.

45. *De sacramentis*, bk. 2, pt. 17, chap. 21; cols. 606–07; trans. Deferrari, p. 463.

46. *De sacramentis*, bk. 2, pt. 16, chap. 5; cols. 587–92; trans. Deferrari, p. 441–46; borrowed from Gregory the Great and Augustine.

47. Claude Carozzi sees a difference in emphasis between the Lombard and Hugh ("Structure et fonction de la vision de Tnugdal," in *Faire Croire: Modalités de la diffusion et de la réception des messages religieux du XIIe au XVe siècle: Table Ronde organisée par l'École française de Rome, en collaboration avec l'Institut d'histoire médiévale de l'Université de Padoue [Rome, 22–23 juin 1979]* [Palais Farnese, Rome: École française de Rome, 1981], pp. 223–34). And it appears to be true that Peter Lombard sees the tortures of hell more in psychological terms whereas Hugh details the physical tortures at considerable length: *De sacramentis*, bk. 2, pt. 16, chaps. 4–5, PL 176, cols. 586–93, and pt. 18, cols. 1–15, cols. 609–13. Hugh's account is, however, somewhat inconsistent, and both thinkers see the bodies of the damned as material. Both also follow Augustine in refusing to decide whether these bodies are restored without defect (see Lombard, *Sentences*, bk. 4, d. 44, chap. 4, vol. 2, p. 519; Hugh, *De sacramentis*, bk. 2, pt. 17, chap. 20, PL 176, cols. 605–6).

48. Eadmer of Canterbury, *Liber de beatitudine coelestis patriae*, PL 159, cols. 587–606, and Anselm, *Proslogion*, chap. 25, in *S. Anselmo d'Aosta: Il Proslogion, le Orazioni, e le Meditazioni*, ed. F. S. Schmitt and trans. G. Sandri (Padua: CEDAM, 1959), pp. 128–30. In light of the points I make in chapter 6 below, it is important to note that Anselm here uses 1 Corinthians 15.44.

are found in Honorius Augustodunensis's *Elucidarium* and in distinctions 44 and 49 of book 4 of the Lombard's *Sentences*. By the early thirteenth century, this idea becomes the doctrine of the four dowries (impassibility, subtlety or penetrability, agility, and clarity or beauty) with which the beatified soul endows the body it receives back at the end of time.[49] The contrast between earth and heaven suggested by the idea of the *dotes* is one of change and changelessness. What blessedness adds to matter is stasis. Despite hints that the departed soul craves its body in order to enjoy the full *voluptas* of the celestial kingdom,[50] the final victory—to Peter Lombard and Hugh of St. Victor as also to Jerome more than seven hundred years before—is neither the development of a refined sensibility nor the replacement of matter by spirit. It is rather the restoring of exactly the body we have here below in such a way that its particles can nevermore suffer dissolution, its instability nevermore divert the soul from its reward. As Peter Lombard said (borrowing from Augustine):

> There is no doubt that the human mind, rapt away from corporeal senses and having shed its flesh after death, is not able to see the incommutable substance as the holy angels see it, either from some more hidden cause or because there is present in it a certain natural desire to administer the body [*appetitus corpus administrandi*], by which desire it is retarded [*retardatur*] so that it does not continue uninterruptedly to the highest heaven until that desire is stilled [*conquiescat*]. For if the [living] body is such a burden because its governance is difficult and serious, by so much more is the mind diverted from vision of the highest heaven when the flesh is corrupted. Consequently when it receives not an animal but a spiritual body [1 Cor. 15.44], equal to the angels, it will have the perfect expression [*modum*] of its nature, obedient and ruling, vivified and vivifying, with such ineffable ease that what was to it a prison will be to it a glory.[51]

Although called "spiritual not animal," the resurrected body is to Peter Lombard both materially and formally the body we possess on earth. Its

49. A. Challet, "Corps glorieux," *DTC*, vol. 3 (1938), cols. 1879–1906, and Wicki, *Seligkeit*, pp. 202–37 and 280–97.

50. Anselm, *Proslogion*, chap. 25, ed. Schmitt and Sandri, *S. Anselmo*, pp. 128–30; Lombard, *Sentences*, bk. 4, d. 50, chap. 1, p. 553.

51. Lombard, *Sentences*, bk. 4, d. 49, chap. 4, art. 3, vol. 2, p. 553 (borrowed from Augustine, *Literal Commentary on Genesis*, bk. 12, chap. 35, PL 34, col. 483). See above, chap. 2, n. 138.

rising is victory over all instability, not merely that of digestion and partition, but that of desire as well.[52]

By the later twelfth century, theologians such as Magister Martin, Praepositinus, and William of Auxerre explored issues of eating, change, identity, and resurrection with much greater philosophical sophistication than did the early school texts of Honorius, Anselm, Hugh, and Peter Lombard. The basic questions concerning the resurrected human body were two. First, what is the core that will rise, the *veritas humanae naturae*? Second, is the resurrection natural or supernatural?[53]

In the context of these discussions, organic metaphors for resurrection were not just bypassed but explicitly rejected as inadequate accounts both of identity and of divine power. For example, the author of the little summa *Breves dies hominis*, edited by Heinzmann, argued that resurrection is not natural; thus organic metaphors are inappropriate for it. Bodies are not seeds, he explained; they do not sprout by an internal law of development. When the gospel speaks of seeds falling into the earth and dying in order to grow, this is an image for the soul's rise from sin. Where corpses are concerned, natural fertility is defective, even repulsive. We read in Ecclesiasticus that cadavers give birth to beasts and worms, but such birthing comes from a defect of nature; the power of nature would be for like to give rise to like. Thus the generation of cadavers is not generation but de-generation; it is, however, all the body can do without the power of God. Carefully underlining the conventional position that the *veritas humanae naturae* does not include what comes from food, the author of this little eschatological summa thus prefers to speak of the risen body as a golden image reforged by God or as ashes and bones collected from hidden places for reassemblage.[54]

Later in the century, another anonymous treatise on the resurrection insisted that resurrection is not natural. A seed may give rise to a seed, but man is not a phoenix; man is dust. According to nature, man can only decay and give rise to decay, as a putrefying tree gives birth to flies.[55] In such discussion, organic analogies are rejected not only because they

52. Thus Peter Lombard and Hugh of St. Victor tend to treat the vision of God as completion rather than yearning. For the very different treatment this idea receives from the mystics, see below chapter 8.

53. See Heinzmann, *Unsterblichkeit*, and Hermann J. Weber, *Die Lehre von der Auferstehung der Toten in den Haupttraktaten der scholastischen Theologie von Alexander von Hales zu Duns Skotus* (Freiburg: Herder, 1973) [hereafter Weber, *Auferstehung*].

54. Heinzmann, *Unsterblichkeit*, pp. 187–96. See Ecclesiasticus 10.11, 19.3.

55. Cod. lat. Bibl. Univ. Erlangen 260, fol. 74rb–vb, edited in Heinzmann, *Unsterblichkeit*, pp. 221–23, especially pp. 221–22, lines 36–50.

detract from divine power but also because the birth of one thing from another involves such change (and sometimes repulsive change) that two individuals seem involved rather than one individual in two conditions. The appearance of a worm from slime is not a *re*surrection.

Thus, reforged statues or pots, resumed clothing, and rebuilt temples were acceptable images for resurrection in a way seeds were not. The reuniting of bits into their previous shape seemed to express the recreation of the same thing that had existed before. But as the image of the reforged statue was given further consideration, it too came to present problems. Scholastic discussion agreed with Augustine that it was necessary only for the statue to be reforged from its original material in its original form, not that each particle occupy the same place. To Augustine, such a position seemed to take care both of the issue of divine power (surely a statue does not reforge itself or naturally regenerate its parts) and of the issue of identity (surely it is the same statue if it has the same shape and the same material). Augustine was more interested in explaining the perfection of the resurrected body, restored without lack or superfluity, than in accounting for identity; thus he suggested that bits of fingernails might well become toes in the resurrection. By the later twelfth century, however, scholastic theologians were quite puzzled about whether a statue reforged from the same material but distributed in different places was the same statue. An anonymous summa (Cod. Vat. lat. 10754) from mid-century debated the question of the returning particles of dust and concluded:

> [Thus] no member of my body will be what it was just before and so I will have another body.
>
> But this is false, as Job attests: [for] "in my flesh I shall see my God" (Job 19.26). Therefore we say, with Augustine and Job, that it will be the same body because it will be made from the same matter and it is only accidental whether that matter makes a hand or a foot. And we are not cheating in this conclusion. . . . It is better to be a simple catholic than a facile heretic.[56]

Indeed, by the turn of the century, William of Auxerre, who organized and handed down much of early scholastic discussion, argued that resurrection cannot be natural because nature cannot solve the identity problem. Job says we rise the same, but nature cannot remake the same

---

56. Cod. Vat. lat. 10754, edited in Heinzmann, *Unsterblichkeit*, p. 210, lines 52–59. Note that the statue in this text has been not just melted down but pulverized!

body; it can generate only similar bodies through the multiplication of individual cases. God, however, raises the exact ashes that lie in the earth: the resurrected body of Paul is made from Paul's ashes, not Peter's. These ashes are, moreover, Paul's *veritas humanae naturae,* containing every element necessary for perfection but not a superfluous particle, and this core of human nature, although formed from food, rises as flesh not as food.[57]

As schoolmen of the mid-thirteenth century were to stress, such discussion leaves a number of philosophical, physiological, and theological questions unsolved. In fact, so unsatisfactory did it seem that by the early fourteenth century debate shifted away from issues of material continuity and body. Partly because of the developing doctrine of purgatory, partly because of increasing insistence that the beatific vision could be received before the Last Judgment, partly because of the adoption by at least some theologians of a fully Aristotelian idea of form, eschatological discussion in 1300 tended to focus on soul, although material continuity as a component of bodily resurrection was not discarded.[58] But in the twelfth century, scholastic accounts of last things emphasized body. Six aspects of their highly problematic conclusions are worth underlining.

First, theologians generally agreed that body is necessary for personhood. Although certain early thinkers such as Hugh of St. Victor and Robert of Melun used Platonic concepts that made the soul the person, schoolmen after mid-century usually understood "person" as a composite of body and soul.[59] According to this definition, a self is not a soul using a body but a psychosomatic entity, to which body is integral. The philosophical challenge was not therefore to state the necessity of body;

57. Heinzmann, *Unsterblichkeit,* pp. 239–45, especially p. 243 n. 11.

58. See below chapters 6 and 7.

59. Heinzmann, *Unsterblichkeit.* The burden of Heinzmann's argument is to show the emergence in the twelfth century with Gilbert de la Porrée of a more Aristotelian conception of person over against the Platonic definition of man as soul found, for example, in Hugh of St. Victor and Robert of Melun. This argument is, however, to some extent misleading. Although technical definitions may have shifted from Platonic to Aristotelian, thinkers such as Hugh and Bernard of Clairvaux actually treated the human being as an entity composed of body and soul (see chapter 4 below and Weber, *Auferstehung,* pp. 123ff.). So indeed did the Fathers. Among patristic treatises on the resurrection, I find only Ambrose's *De excessu Satyri,* bk. 2, chap. 20, adhering to a strictly Platonic definition; see above chapter 2, n. 8. For recent revisionist opinion about Augustine's anthropology, see Miles, *Augustine on the Body;* Peter Brown, *Body and Society;* Joyce Salisbury, "The Latin Doctors of the Church on Sexuality," *Journal of Medieval History* 12 (1986): 279–89; Fredriksen, "Beyond the Body/Soul Dichotomy"; and Stroumsa, *"Caro Salutis Cardo."*

it was rather to state what body is that it can return after death and what it adds to person that separated soul lacks. In other words, the challenge was to explain philosophically and theologically why body is necessary, not merely to assert that it is so by defining person as a composite.

Second, scholastic accounts assume that body is flesh. What returns at the Last Judgment is a material, fleshly, human body. Although the gifts of impassibility, agility, and clarity might make that body far more beautiful than it was on earth, scholastic authors stressed that it rises with all its matter and members.

Third, there was great anxiety to account for the identity of the original and the resurrected body. No matter how important soul might be in accounting for person, thinkers assumed that continuity of material and of shape or structure was necessary for identity. Unless the same particles returned in the same structure, body was not the same; if body was not the same, person was not the same.

Fourth, since death was the fragmenting of the physical body into dust or particles, resurrection was return of exactly these physical particles. Thus resurrection was reassemblage. Issues of part and whole were important components of issues of identity.

Fifth, organic processes, especially those, such as eating, in which one substance disappeared into another, were both mysterious and threatening. Such processes were mysterious because there was no adequate scientific model available to account for organic change, and Joan Cadden's recent research has taught us that the recovery of Aristotle's work on nutrition and generation did not solve any problems in this regard.[60] The processes were threatening because much of the change in the natural world (e.g., aging, decay) was negative and because even positive change (such as pregnancy or germination) seemed clearly to divide one instance from another or to replace one individual with another rather than to guarantee continuity. Because natural process could not produce—or even account for—identity, resurrection had to be victory not merely over fragmentation but over biological change itself.

Sixth, the resurrected body was structurally as well as materially identical with the body of earth. Thus, resurrection resulted in immortality, not equality. Although all defects were repaired in rising (even the defect of babyhood or senility), the virtuous would not all shine with

60. Joan Cadden, "The Medieval Philosophy and Biology of Growth: Albertus Magnus, Thomas Aquinas, Albert of Saxony, and Marsilius of Inghen on Book I, chap. V of Aristotle's *De Generatione et Corruptione*, with Translated Texts of Albertus Magnus and Thomas Aquinas" (Ph.D. diss., Indiana University, 1971).

the same glory. Never losing its sex or size or the scars of its suffering, the body that returned was a conveyor of status and experience; it was rewarded for its *particular* sacrifices and achievements.[61] As Hugh of St. Victor put it: "Nor is it of consequence that . . . individuals coming to life again have different statures, because they [were] so when living." "This is in the plan of the Creator, that the peculiarity and likeness [to God] of each [person] be preserved in his own image . . . ," for there will be "in the bodies of those rising again . . . a reasonable *in*equality, just as there is among voices which combine in song."[62]

Honorius Augustodunensis and John Scotus Erigena: An Alternative Tradition?

The metaphors of reforged statues, of temples and garments, used in scholastic discussions of eschatology were not mere embellishments. They served as limiting cases in technical philosophical argument. Indeed, as the complex quotations concerning Augustine's recast statue indicate, they sometimes became the subject of a writer's investigation. I have thus suggested that they may show us the fundamental materialism of twelfth-century philosophical assumptions more clearly than the explicit (and confused) statements about "substance" and "flesh" we find in the texts.

Yet the account I have given here of a scholastic consensus on issues of resurrection and identity could be questioned. We have recently learned to see scholastic discussion more as pragmatic (and hence inconsistent) response to a host of pressing questions about daily living than as abstract philosophical solution to ontological queries.[63] More-

61. Thus not only is there a great gulf fixed between the damned and the elect, there are also great differences among the rank and file within the two groups. For twelfth-century examples of an emphasis on different gifts even in heaven, see Wicki, *Seligkeit*, pp. 238–55. The pseudo-Augustinian text *In dispari claritate erit par gaudium* (PL 45, col. 1892) was crucial. In a fascinating new study, Philippe Buc shows that there was debate about whether inequality in heaven was simply moral or a matter of worldly status as well; see Philippe Buc, *L'Ambiguité du livre: Prince, pouvoir, et peuple dans les commentaires de la Bible* (Paris: Beauchesne, 1993), chapter 2.

62. *De sacramentis*, bk. 2, pt. 17, chap. 15; PL 176, col. 603; trans. Deferrari, pp. 459–60 (emphasis mine). And see *De sacramentis*, bk. 2, pt. 18, chaps. 5–10 and 20; PL 176, cols. 610–11 and 616–17; trans. Deferrari, pp. 467–68 and 474–75, which stresses difference in rewards among the souls in heaven.

63. See Chenu, *Toward Understanding St. Thomas*; Valerie I. J. Flint, "The 'School of Laon': A Reconsideration," in *Ideas in the Medieval West: Texts and Their Contexts* (London: Variorum Reprints, 1988).

over, we must also confront arguments by French scholars, especially Claude Carozzi, that the early twelfth century saw fierce debate over the nature of the person after death.[64]

Responding to Jacques Le Goff's groundbreaking work on purgatory, Carozzi has argued that there were in the early twelfth century two "diametrically opposed" positions on the afterlife. The first was a literalizing position found in Hugh of St. Victor's *De sacramentis*, Bernard of Clairvaux's sermon 42 *De diversis*,[65] William of St. Thierry's *Treatise on the Nature of Body and Soul*, and the Irish "Vision (or Visions) of Tondal." The second or spiritualizing stance was found in Honorius Augustodunensis's *Elucidarium*, Guibert of Nogent's *De pignoribus*, and to some extent in Peter Lombard's *Sentences*.[66] According to Carozzi, the literalist position tended to make the soul corporeal even before the Last Judgment and won out in the large number of medieval accounts of people returning to earth after death with vivid stories of the tortures of hell and purgatory or the delights of heaven. The spiritualizing position, based on ideas derived from John Scotus, surfaced around 1100 but survived only very partially in the notion that damnation and salvation are, respectively, the absence and presence of God.

There are problems with accepting Carozzi's argument as stated. Given the *sic et non* structure of scholastic texts, it is very difficult to tell how much controversy there was in the early twelfth century either over the literal nature of heaven and hell or over the nature of the separated soul or over the corporeality of the resurrected body (and these are not, of course, the same issue).[67] It is true that Peter Lombard and

64. Carozzi, "Structure et fonction de la vision de Tnugdal." Carozzi differs from Le Goff in certain ways; see Le Goff, *Birth of Purgatory*, p. 389 n. 2, and appendix 4, p. 370.

65. Although its authenticity has been questioned, the sermon is probably genuine; see *Sancti Bernardi Opera*, ed. J. Leclercq, H. M. Rochais, and C. H. Talbot (Rome: Editiones Cistercienses, 1957–77), vol. 6, pt. 1, pp. 255–61; H.-M. Rochais, "Enquête sur les sermons divers et les sentences de saint Bernard," *Analecta sancti ordinis cisterciensis* 18 (1962): 16–17; idem, "Saint Bernard est-il l'auteur des sermons 40, 41, et 42 'De diversis'?" *Revue bénédictine* 72 (1962): 324–45; and Le Goff, *Birth of Purgatory*, pp. 160–65.

66. Honorius's *Elucidarium* is probably from before 1099–1102, his *Clavis physicae* from before 1123/33; William's *Treatise on the Body and Soul* dates from the 1120s; Guibert's *De pignoribus* is from about 1125; the relevant portion of Hugh's *De sacramentis* was written between 1135 and 1140; Peter Lombard's *Sentences* is from 1148–52; the "Visions of Tondal" is from 1149; Otto of Freising's *Two Cities*, composed between 1143 and 1146, is extant in a revised version dated 1157.

67. Carozzi tends to confuse or conflate these separate elements of eschatology, even where his medieval authors do not. For example, some of the treatments he cites as corporealizing the soul after death (especially those of Bernard of Clairvaux and

Hugh of St. Victor, Honorius Augustodunensis and Otto of Freising, each quote incompatible views on these matters. Moreover, each refers to disagreement ("some say . . . others say . . ."), and it is significant that in Honorius's *Elucidarium* and Otto's *Two Cities*—neither of which is a school text—these issues are almost the only ones treated as matters on which there is a significant difference of opinion.[68] But was there really controversy, rather than simply confusion, over eschatology? Those early twelfth-century passages that quote conflicting authorities on last things are often borrowed *in toto* from Augustine or Julian of Toledo or John Scotus (just as Jerome's references to contemporary debate were in fact often lifted from Tertullian). And what are we to make of the fact that those figures, such as Guibert, Honorius, and Otto, who not only at times spiritualize heaven and hell but also take an almost Origenist stance, speak of the resurrected body in extremely materialist terms as well? The greatest contradictions in the early twelfth century are not between writers but within writers.

William of St. Thierry) are merely reflections or direct quotations of Augustine's assertion that the separated soul yearns for the body it will receive in resurrection (see above n. 51); they are therefore in no sense incompatible with notions of purgation after death as psychological and spiritual experience. There was certainly confusion in the twelfth century, as attention began to focus on a purging stage for the soul between death and Last Judgment, but the idea that the soul yearns for the body does not mean (any more than it did for Augustine, from whom the twelfth century borrowed discussion of these matters) that the soul was corporealized before resurrection or the body spiritualized afterward. I do, however, argue below—in agreement with Carozzi, Zaleski, and Morgan—that the increased attention to (and particularization of) a somatomorphic soul in otherworld-journey and vision literature tended to corporealize the soul. I also agree that the notion of soul's yearning for body grew stronger in the later Middle Ages; this development tended to underline person as psychosomatic unity.

68. Yves Lefevre notes that Honorius only twice gives alternative opinions (bk. 1, q. 161, and bk. 3, q. 80) (see *L'Elucidarium et les lucidaires: Contribution, par l'histoire d'un texte, à l'histoire des croyances religieuses en France au moyen âge* [Paris: Boccard, 1954], p. 206). Both relate to resurrection: the first concerns whether Christ was in hell for the full three days between his death and Resurrection; the second concerns whether we all rise at age thirty and of the same stature. Otto of Freising in his *Chronica sive historia de duabus civitatibus* (ed. Adolf Hofmeister, Scriptores rerum Germanicarum in usum scholarum ex Monumentis Germaniae Historicis separatim editi [Hannover and Leipzig: Hahn, 1912], bk. 8, chaps. 18–27, pp. 416–36) gives contrasting opinions about how literal torture is in hell and about the meaning of 1 Corinthians 15. Much of this is borrowed from Honorius and does not therefore indicate that the debate continued in Otto's day. A similar problem of interpretation arises, for example, in Helinand of Froidmont, *Les Vers de la mort*, ed. F. Wulff and E. Walberg (Paris: Librairie de Firmin Didot, 1905), pp. 31–33, verses 34–36, where the poet comments that those who think there is no afterlife argue that we should live like pigs and enjoy ourselves here on earth. The verses do not necessarily mean that anyone articulated a fully skeptical position in the twelfth century.

Guibert of Nogent, for example, fulminates against the claims of the monks of St. Médard to possess Christ's tooth, finds deeply offensive the idea that the body of the Virgin might have decayed in death, and insists shrilly that the body we eat in the Eucharist is whole in every fragment. He argues that our resurrection is threatened unless every particle of Christ rose from the tomb. Yet Guibert completely allegorizes heaven and hell as ecstasy and loss.[69]

Honorius's *Elucidarium*, from which Herrad of Hohenbourg borrowed some of her most materialist passages, argues that those eaten by animals will be restored "from the same matter" so that not a hair of their heads perishes;[70] those born with two heads will rise with two bodies as well; those aborted in the womb before quickening will return to the father and mother from whom the matter of the seed came. Honorius explains that the blessed will rise naked and unembarrassed, translucent like beautiful glass (*ut splendidum vitrum perlucida*) but colored with the particular colors appropriate to their different religious statuses. He asserts that individuality will last in heaven, for an eye cannot be a foot or a man a woman; Peter, who can never again be a virgin, will have virginity in John.[71] Yet the same Honorius who here insists on individuality and materiality in the resurrection also insists (in a short text discovered and published by Endres) that "after the final resurrection of all people, the bodies both of the good and of the evil will

69. Guibert of Nogent, *De pignoribus sanctorum*, especially bks. 1 and 4, PL 156 (Paris, 1853), col. 611–30 and 666–80. For Guibert's concern with the bodily assumption of the Virgin, see bk. 1, chap. 3, cols. 623–24; for the argument that there are no bodily pains in hell nor are there corporeal glories in heaven, see bk. 4, chaps. 4 and 7, cols. 673–75 and 677. On Guibert, see John F. Benton, "Introduction," in *Self and Society in Medieval France: The Memoirs of Abbot Guibert of Nogent*, ed. John F. Benton and trans. C. C. S. Bland (New York: Harper Torchbook, 1970), intro., pp. 26–31; Klaus Guth, *Guibert von Nogent und die hochmittelalterliche Kritik an der Reliquienverehrung*, Studien und Mitteilungen zur Geschichte des Benediktiner-Ordens und seiner Zweige, Supplement 21 (Augsburg: Winfried, 1970); Marie-Danielle Mireux, "Guibert de Nogent et la critique du culte des reliques," in *La Piété populaire au moyen âge*, Actes du 99e Congrès National des Sociétés Savantes Besançon 1954: Section de philologie et d'histoire jusqu'à 1610, vol. 1 (Paris: Bibliothèque Nationale, 1977), pp. 293–301; and Bynum, "Bodily Miracles," pp. 77–78 and 99–100.

70. *Elucidarium*, ed. Lefevre, bk. 3, q. 45, p. 456. On Honorius, see Joseph A. Endres, *Honorius Augustodunensis: Beitrag zur Geschichte des geistigen Lebens im 12. Jahrhundert* (Kempten and Munich: Jos. Koesel, 1906); Eva Matthews Sanford, "Honorius: Presbyter and Scholasticus," *Speculum* 23 (1948): 397–425; and Flint, *Ideas in the West*, chaps. 5, 6, 7, 8, and 12.

71. *Elucidarium*, ed. Lefevre, bk. 3, qq. 104–6 and 116–18, pp. 467–69 and 472–74. Honorius even suggests that there will be sweet smells, lovely tastes, etc., in heaven.

be spiritual, and nothing thereafter will be corporeal, for God will be all in all as light is in air or iron in fire."[72] In the *Clavis physicae*, he uses images of natural growth to stress the transformation of the resurrected body into spirit, ridicules those who think bodies rise with sex or age or stature, and rejects the idea that there will be any difference in glory among those present in heaven.[73]

Even Otto of Freising, whose *Two Cities* achieves a remarkable synthesis of divergent traditions, argues that the Last Judgment occurs on earth and restores exactly the heavy, earthly, particular bodies we have here; but he holds as well that blessedness in heaven is a spiritual vision:

> For we must not suppose that souls, after they have been stripped from the body, or after they have taken up spiritual bodies and are not inferior to the angelic spirits in purity and rank, find delight in external things as men do in this life. Accordingly, whenever Holy Scripture says that their spirits are refreshed and affected by flowering and verdant meadows, by pleasant places, by the singing of birds, by fragrant things (such as cinnamon and balsam), such expressions should, it is clear, be interpreted spiritually rather than carnally.[74]

The examples of Guibert, Honorius, and Otto suggest that it is not quite right to see a controversy with carefully delineated positions in the early twelfth century. Rather there was deep confusion (often within the ideas of individual thinkers) over how materially to take a number of different components of eschatology: soul, resurrected body, the place of purgation, heaven and hell. Nonetheless, if we focus on treatments of resurrection, it does appear that Carozzi—and earlier scholars such as Endres—are right to see a curious survival of Origenist, spiritualizing views in certain texts. Although it is not clear how well those who initially repeated it understood it, there was an alternative tradition. This tradition went back to the great Carolingian philosopher, John Scotus Erigena.

72. Endres, *Honorius*, pp. 152–53; and see Honorius, *Clavis physicae*, ed. Paolo Lucentini (Rome: Edizioni di Storia e Letteratura, 1974), chaps. 301–8, pp. 243–61.

73. Honorius, *Clavis physicae*, ed. Lucentini, chaps. 271–73, pp. 218–22; see also chaps. 480, 481, and 487, not edited by Lucentini but (he indicates) borrowed literally from John Scotus Erigena; see Lucentini, ed., *Clavis physicae*, appendix, p. 286.

74. This presumably refers to the saints after the resurrection; Otto of Freising, *Historia de duabus civitatibus*, bk. 8, chap. 33, p. 451; trans. Charles Christopher Mierow, *The Two Cities: A Chronicle of Universal History to the Year 1146 A.D.* (New York: Columbia University Press, 1928), p. 508. Otto does hold a resurrected body to be necessary; see my discussion below, chapter 4, pp. 180–86.

On the issue of the resurrection of the body, the *De divisione naturae* of the ninth-century Irish philosopher and theologian John Scotus seems to realize the full brilliance of the Origenist position that is in its complexity of detail irretrievably lost to us with the loss of Origen's texts. By the time he began the *De divisione naturae* in 862, John Scotus Erigena had already elaborated some of Augustine's ideas in a distinctly Neoplatonic way. At the request of the Carolingian ruler, he had translated the Pseudo-Dionysius and other major works of Greek theology—Gregory of Nyssa, Maximus the Confessor, and Epiphanius—works that made the terms of the Origenist position clear whether or not they sympathized fully with it.[75] Erigena's view of the cosmos, derived from Pseudo-Dionysius and Gregory of Nyssa, is profoundly monistic: body is the final spilling forth or expression of a reality that emanates from God and will ultimately return. Produced by the coming together of the elements, which are an ontological level above it and therefore not material, our material, fleshly body is accidents or qualities not substance. Where John does speak of body as substance (*ousia*), he means an underlying pattern (like Origen's *eidos*) not a corporeal body, a collection of particles.[76] Erigena is aware that his position is Greek rather than Latin, and he states repeatedly that there is much disagreement over eschatology, although he insists that among Western thinkers Ambrose at least agrees with him.[77]

75. Maïeul Cappuyns, *Jean Scot Érigène: Sa vie, son oeuvre, sa pensée* (Brussels: Culture et civilisation, 1964), p. 189. On Erigena, see also Henry Bett, *Johannes Scotus Erigena: A Study in Medieval Philosophy* (Cambridge: Cambridge University Press, 1925); John J. O'Meara, *Eriugena* (Oxford: Clarendon Press, 1988); I. P. Sheldon-Williams, "A Bibliography of the Works of Johannes Scottus Eriugena," *The Journal of Ecclesiastical History* 10, no. 2 (1960): 198–224; and M. Brennan, *A Bibliography of Publications in the Field of Eriugenian Studies, 1800–1975* (Spoleto: Centro italiano di studi sull'altro medievo, 1977). Erigena's spiritualist ideas of body of course have their own context, which I cannot treat here. Carolingian spirituality had in general a very materialist concept of the body; see above, "Introduction," n. 14.

76. John Scotus Eriugena [or Erigena], *Periphyseon (De divisione naturae)*, ed. I. P. Sheldon-Williams with Ludwig Bieler, Scriptores Latini Hiberniae 7, 9, 11 (Dublin: The Dublin Institute for Advanced Studies, 1978–83), bk. 1, vol. 1, pp. 113–23, 143–57 (PL 122 [Paris, 1853], cols. 475C–480A and 489B–495B); and see John the Scot, *Periphyseon: On the Division of Nature*, trans. Myra Uhlfelder with Jean A. Potter (Indianapolis: Bobbs-Merrill, 1976), pp. 44–49 and 60–66. See also Sheldon-Williams' summary of John's argument, in *Periphyseon*, trans. Sheldon-Williams, vol. 3, pp. 8–22.

77. *Periphyseon*, bk. 5, chap. 8, PL 122, cols. 876C and 878D; see trans. Uhlfelder and Potter, bk. 5, p. 288. See also bk. 5, chap. 37, PL 122, col. 987B; trans. I. P. Sheldon-Williams and John J. O'Meara, *Eriugena: Periphyseon (The Division of Nature)* (Montreal and Washington, D.C.: Bellarmin and Dumbarton Oaks, 1987), p. 672.

What is striking, for my interests, is the fact that John Scotus elaborates, as did Origen, naturalistic imagery for the resurrection, making full use of Clementine cyclical metaphors and of the Pauline seed. The resurrection of the phoenix from ashes or the beetle from dung, the gradual unfolding of seeds in things, the turn of the seasons from winter to spring, all become analogies for a return to God that is transformation.[78] In direct contrast to Western patristic arguments (both in their original context and in their use by twelfth-century schoolmen), Erigena treats the continuing growth of fingernails and hair as a promise and symbol of resurrection, not as a problem for material reassemblage.[79] He uses Galatians 3.28 ("neither male nor female") to argue that Christ rose without biological sex, and so shall we.[80] John 14.2 ("in my Father's house are many mansions") and Ephesians 4.13 ("till we all come . . . unto the measure of the stature of the fullness of Christ"), used in the Western tradition to guarantee the survival of difference in heaven, become arguments that all spiritual bodies will be the same. For, asserts Erigena, all bodies will become spiritual bodies and all spiritual bodies souls, as moisture becomes steam or the seed the sheaf.[81] The image of the potter and the recast pot, so popular in patristic and twelfth-century scholastic texts, is explicitly rejected; in that passage, says Erigena, Paul "is not discussing bodily resurrection."[82] But Erigena again and again uses 1 Corinthians 15 to explain that "animal" is not "spiritual," to stress that we are a self that flowers into an other that is inherent in the original pattern, and to underline that all bodies rise as spirit.[83] In one of his most radical passages, John says:

---

78. *Periphyseon*, bk. 4, PL 122, cols. 800–15; see trans. Uhlfelder and Potter, pp. 263–65; bk. 5, PL 122, cols. 871–85, 899–907, and 952–55, see trans. Uhlfelder and Potter, pp. 282–91, 302–6, 323–25.

79. *Periphyseon*, bk. 5, chap. 23, PL 122, col. 900A–B; see trans. Uhlfelder and Potter, p. 303: "God has made in us symbols of resurrection in our two sets of ten nails, providing evidence about our hope. But also by the crown of the head, our hair. . . . For what seems in us dead body, i.e., hair daily cut and nails, grow again and symbolize the hope of resurrection." John is here giving (by quoting Epiphanius) what he understands to be the Greek arguments for resurrection as natural; he says this is a position he has since discarded.

80. *Periphyseon*, bk. 5, chap. 20, PL 122, cols. 892–94; see trans. Uhlfelder and Potter, pp. 295–96; see also, cols. 898–99, trans. Uhlfelder and Potter, p. 298.

81. *Periphyseon*, bk. 5, chaps. 36 and 38, PL 122, cols. 982C and 994C; see trans. Uhlfelder and Potter, pp. 339 and 342.

82. *Periphyseon*, bk. 5, chap. 37, PL 122, col. 985C; trans. Sheldon-Williams and O'Meara, p. 670.

83. *Periphyseon*, bk. 4, chaps. 5–6 and chaps. 12–15, PL 122, cols. 760–62 and 800–12, and see trans. Uhlfelder and Potter, pp. 229–31 and 263–65; bk. 5, chaps. 13, 23,

It is more tolerable indeed to those who think carnally to believe that earthly bodies will be changed into heavenly bodies than to believe in the annihilation of all corporeality. And I think the Apostle was speaking in the same mode of condescension [to the carnally minded] when he said of the resurrection of the earthly body: "It is sown an animal body, it shall be raised a spiritual body." For this was as if he said: The earthly and animal body, which is sown in the ground and undergoes the dissolution of corruption, shall rise up a spiritual and heavenly body; that is to say briefly, . . . it will change from earthly into heavenly, from corporeal into spiritual, but it will still however be body. From heaviness it will be changed into subtlety . . . as smoke is changed into flame. For whoever studies the writings of St. Ambrose or Gregory the Theologian, or his commentator Maximus, will discover that it is not a matter of a change from earthly into heavenly body, but a complete passing into pure spirit, and not into that which is called ether, but into that which is called mind [intellectus]. Ambrose indeed said that after resurrection, body and soul and mind are one. . . . And Gregory likewise said that at the time of resurrection, body shall be changed into soul, soul into mind, mind into God, so that God will be all in all, as air is changed into light. . . .

For they should not be listened to who say that after the future resurrection human bodies will shine in splendor in such a way that each will receive brightness to correspond to the merit of his earthly life whether good or bad; on the contrary . . . all human bodies will share the same glory and power in the same future, spiritually and immortally and eternally. . . . For the glory of the righteous will consist not in brightness of body, but in purity of contemplation, in which they shall see God face to face; nor shall the dishonor of the impious lie in ugliness of members but rather in deprivation of the vision of God.[84]

I cannot here deal with the full complexity of Erigena's position, and I deliberately avoid the question of his pantheism, to which most scholarly discussion of him has been directed.[85] But several points should be

---

and 36, PL 122, cols. 883–85, 899–907 and 978–83, and trans. Uhlfelder and Potter, pp. 290, 305, and 334–40. And see bk. 5, PL 122, cols. 985C–990A, trans. Uhlfelder and Potter, pp. 340–41, and trans. Sheldon-Williams and O'Meara, p. 670–75.

84. Periphyseon, bk. 5, chap. 37, PL 122, cols. 987A–987D, my translation; see also trans. Sheldon-Williams and O'Meara, pp. 672–73.

85. See below n. 95.

made about the conception of resurrection he bequeathed to the twelfth century. First, his understanding of corporeal body as qualities and quantities—i.e., accidents existing in *ousia*—allowed for full acceptance of bodily change by sacrificing (as had Origen) both material continuity and continuity of external form or physiological structure as elements of identity. Second, death—the separation of soul and body and the dissolution of body into the four elements from which it came (elements that are ontologically above it)—was genuinely a step upward. The resurrection in which body returns cannot be material reassemblage, although some underlying substance survives death and according to it a spiritual body is constructed or expressed at the end of time. Third, Erigena sees that his conception implies resurrection to be fully natural (and therefore appropriately expressed in natural, cyclical images) although he pulls back from this, stating that resurrection, the greatest of miracles, is probably owing to grace as well.[86]

Finally, Erigena understands that his idea of return undercuts earthly differences of rank and gender and even religious accomplishment. It is ridiculous, he asserts, to think we rise with limbs or innards, weight or height, sex or age. How can "physical advantages" matter in heaven?[87] Yet Erigena wishes to retain some difference. The good will have joy, the evil sadness. And these good will be filled not consumed by God, as air is irradiated not dissolved by light.[88] At one point John even hints that something we might think of today as gender (in contradistinction to sex) survives eternally. Humanity was created in the image of God entirely without difference of sex, he says, but "the spiritual sexes are understood to exist in the soul—for *nous*, that is intellect, is a kind of male in the soul, while *aisthesis*, that is sense, is a kind of female."[89]

86. There is, he asserts, no miracle contrary to nature! *Periphyseon*, bk. 5, chaps. 22–23, PL 122, cols. 898–907, esp. col. 902C–D, and see trans. Uhlfelder and Potter, pp. 302–09, especially p. 306.

87. *Periphyseon*, bk. 1, trans. Sheldon-Williams, vol. 1, pp. 56–59 (PL 122, cols. 450C–451C); bk. 2, trans. Sheldon-Williams, vol. 2, pp. 21–27 (PL 122, cols. 531D–535A); *Periphyseon*, bk. 5, chaps. 13–20, PL 122, cols. 883–97; see trans. Uhlfelder and Potter, pp. 290–300.

88. *Periphyseon*, bk. 5, PL 122, cols. 944B–45 and 952–53, see trans. Uhlfelder and Potter, pp. 322–25.

89. *Periphyseon*, bk. 2, trans. Sheldon-Williams, vol. 2, pp. 29–40, especially p. 39 (PL 122, cols. 536B–542B). It is interesting to note that the passage would support the arguments of Judith Butler and Thomas Laqueur that what we call gender (i.e., socially constructed roles) is in some sense more basic than sex (biological difference). See Judith Butler, *Gender Trouble: Feminism and the Subversion of Identity* (New York: Routledge, 1990), especially pp. 66–72, and Thomas Laqueur, *Making Sex: Body and Gender from the Greeks to Freud* (Cambridge, Mass.: Harvard University Press, 1990), especially pp. 7–10.

Erigena sees that his conception denies a certain commonsense reality to evil and to matter. What is punished eternally is only the wills of the evil, which are strictly speaking no-thing. Neither heaven nor hell can be a place, because spirit cannot be localized. Thus, although avoiding the most extreme implications of his monistic position, John is aware of the extent to which he dissolves the threat of hell by dissolving difference. Indeed, he espouses explicitly the moral as well as the metaphysical vision implicit in monism. A literal heaven and hell are ludicrous not only because all accidents must be shed as spirit progresses toward God but also because those who argue that risen bodies retain their shape do so in order to imagine those bodies experiencing torment. A universe that returns to a One beyond difference is a universe whose basic rhythm is the throbbing of grace; a universe bifurcated into groups of people, forever unequal in the particularities they possessed on earth, is one dominated, says John, by "the severity of a vindictive judge."[90]

In the 1120s, toward the end of his literary career, the puzzling figure Honorius Augustodunensis summarized Erigena's *De divisione naturae* in a work called the *Clavis physicae*. As I indicated above, certain short treatises by Honorius, probably from a slightly earlier period (the *Scala coeli* and the *Quaestiones* on the descent and ascent of Christ), also take a spiritualizing stance borrowed from Erigena.[91] Yet Honorius's *Elucidarium*, written about 1100 and closely related to the teaching of Anselm of Canterbury, presented a remarkably materialist position on the resurrected body and became a major source for later materialist discussion, both in Latin and in the vernacular. Recent interpretations of Honorius as a rather pragmatic polemicist and pedagogue interested in educating the clergy and in the rights of monks to the clerical role[92] do not really explain what one scholar has politely called "the bewildering variety" of his output.[93] Why does he contradict himself so fundamentally? If his goal was to educate priests for pastoral responsibilities, the abstruse philosophy of John Scotus Erigena hardly seems appropriate.[94]

90. *Periphyseon*, bk. 5, chaps. 37–38, PL 122, cols. 984–91, see trans. Uhlfelder and Potter, pp. 340–41.

91. Endres, *Honorius*, and see n. 72 above.

92. Sanford, "Honorius, *Presbyter* and *Scholasticus*," p. 403; and Flint, *Ideas in the West*, chapter 12, who follows Sanford's interpretation.

93. Flint, *Ideas in the West*, chap. 12, p. 97. Le Goff, *Birth of Purgatory*, pp. 136–38, comments on Honorius's inconsistency.

94. It is worth noting that the other compilations of Erigena from the twelfth century seem to come from the schools. Simon of Tournai (d. ca. 1203) made use of him, and there is a florilegium of Erigenist texts in Paris Nat. lat. MS 16603; on this, see Cappuyns, *Jean Scot Érigène*, p. 246 nn. 6 and 7. Bett argues that Abelard and

Moreover—owing partly to the fact that the *Clavis physicae* has only recently been edited and partly to the continued focus of interpretation on the question of pantheism—scholars have not decided how Erigenist Honorius really was.[95]

I cannot here solve any of the mysteries surrounding Honorius. But on the specific issue of bodily resurrection, it is clear that the *Clavis physicae* simplifies but does not fundamentally alter Erigena's ideas or metaphors.[96] Honorius occasionally sidesteps articulations that suggest absorptions of self into the Godhead and sometimes elaborates metaphors in such a way as to underline the individuality of souls. For example, in chapter 53 he adds to the image of lamps joining in brightness the idea that each lamp, if removed, takes away its own, but only its own, light.[97] But Honorius clearly retains Erigena's sense that all the particularities of the body (age, sex, rank) appear as a result of sin, that Christ rose, as will we, *"non in sexu corporeo sed in homine tantum"*;[98] that "the dissolution of flesh which is called death should more reasonably be called the death of death" for it is the beginning of a growth toward spirit.[99] Erigena's metaphors of unfolding seeds and of returning spring continue, in Honorius's hands, to describe a cosmic movement that is transformation, not reassemblage.[100]

It is also clear that the *Clavis physicae* does contradict the *Elucidarium* both in its view of body and in its metaphors for salvation. Where the *Clavis physicae* spiritualizes the material, the *Elucidarium* materializes the spirit. Where the *Clavis* uses images of natural cycles and growth, the *Elucidarium* speaks of partition and reassemblage, digestion and regurgitation. Where the Erigenist treatise sees salvation as a tran-

---

Gilbert of Poitiers were influenced by him (*Johannes Scotus Erigena*, pp. 171ff.). See also O'Meara, *Eriugena*, pp. 216–17.

95. Both Endres and Sanford (cited above in n. 70) see the *Clavis physicae* as sidestepping the most extreme pantheistic statements of Erigena. Lefevre, *L'Elucidarium et les lucidaires*, p. 197, argues that the *Elucidarium* is not pantheistic.

96. Honorius knew Erigena was problematic: "In quo opere quedam minus ratione exercitatis videbuntur absona, que tamen veritatem considerantibus summa auctoritate et vera ratione constabunt subnixa," he says at the beginning of the *Clavis physicae*; see Lucentini ed., p. 3.

97. Honorius, *Clavis physicae*, ed. Lucentini, pp. 34–35.

98. Ibid., chaps. 69–80, 273–75 and 293, pp. 49–57, 221–24, and 239; and chaps. 347, 350, and 354–60 (which are Erigena, *Periphyseon*, cols. 894A–C, 896B–C, 898D–902D; see Lucentini ed., pp. 279–80). Quoted passage at *Clavis physicae*, ed. Lucentini, chap. 75, p. 52.

99. Honorius, *Clavis physicae*, ed. Lucentini, chap. 307, p. 260.

100. See, for example, ibid., chaps. 80, 212, and 273–74, pp. 57, 168, and 221–23; and chap. 354 (which is Erigena, *Periphyseon*, cols. 898D–900A).

scending of difference, the pastiche of Western texts in the *Elucidarium* stresses resurrection of the body as maintenance of rank.

In the *Elucidarium*, Honorius shares the uneasiness with natural process—especially digestion—found in other early twelfth-century texts and borrowed, in part, from Augustine's *Literal Commentary on Genesis*. Humankind needed the tree of life in paradise, he says, as a defense against aging, eating, and pain.[101] Violent, fragmenting death—especially being eaten by animals—is the paradigm of destruction; indeed death (*mors*) is named from bite (*morsus*), and sin is "burial" in the body.[102] The evil are analogized to the effluvia and excrement of the body; heretics are snot, says Honorius; and the wicked, who "burden the stomach [*ventrem*] of mother church" and are devoured by demons through "the wasting of death" [*per mortis egestionem*], are "shit for the stomach of pigs."[103]

Yet eating is the sign of humanness.[104] Christ ate after the resurrection as an indication to his disciples that he really rose in body.[105] What

101. Honorius, *L'Elucidarium et les lucidaires*, ed. Lefevre, bk. 1, qq. 69, 76, 78, pp. 373–75.

102. *L'Elucidarium*, ed. Lefevre, bk. 2, q. 96, p. 440; and bk. 3, q. 39, p. 455. Note that Caesarius of Heisterbach, writing in the early thirteenth century, gives the same etymology: *mors* named from *morsus* and also from *amaritudo*. See Caesarius of Heisterbach, *Dialogus miraculorum*, ed. Joseph Strange (Cologne: Heberle, 1851), distinctio 11, chap. 1, vol. 2, p. 266; and Carol Zaleski, *Otherworld Journeys: Accounts of Near-Death Experiences in Medieval and Modern Times* (New York: Oxford, 1987), p. 49. This etymology, or at least the reasoning and assumptions it represents, seems to lie behind the image of death in the *De disciplina claustrali*, written by the Benedictine abbot Peter of Celle (d. 1183). We also seem to hear echoes of the iconography of the harrowing of hell, in which Christ shoves the cross into death's gullet and forces it to vomit up souls; see below, chapter 4, nn. 118, 121, and 139. Peter writes:

Depict death before your eyes. . . . What tasks each of its members will fulfill in each of a person's members. Whatever strength and vigor there is in the souls and bodies of the damned, they will devour and feed on, as though they were tender sprouts. Thus the psalm declares: "Death will feed on them" [Ps. 49.14]. That the Lord may take us out of the belly of this whale, let us present ourselves . . . in confession. . . . The divinity which lay hidden in Jesus' flesh shattered the molars in death's mouth, when it rashly bit at the flesh of the Word. (Peter of Celle, *Tractatus de disciplina claustrali*, chap. 23, PL 202 [Paris, 1855], cols. 1132–33; trans. Hugh Feiss, *Peter of Celle: Selected Works* [Kalamazoo, Mich.: Cistercian Publications, 1987], pp. 112–113.)

Peter speaks further of the "jaws" of death in the same chapter; see col. 1134.

103. *L'Elucidarium*, ed. Lefevre, bk. 1, q. 179, p. 394. Footnotes 1–4, p. 394, indicate that the text of this *quaestio* is confused; I take the reading of MS B here, because Flint has argued for the B family of manuscripts as the best. See Flint, "The Original Text of the *Elucidarium* . . .," in *Ideas in the West*, chap. 8, pp. 91–94.

104. See *L'Elucidarium*, ed. Lefevre, bk. 2, q. 78, p. 435: "Fames est una de poenis peccati. . . . Indidit ergo ei Deus famem, ut hac necessitate coactus laboraret et ad aeterna hac occasione redire queat."

105. *L'Elucidarium*, bk. 1, q, 174, p. 392.

we eat in the Eucharist is so truly the flesh born of Mary that we might indeed see it bleed and be then "horrified to touch it with our lips."[106] "Just as food being eaten is turned into flesh, so whoever of the faithful eats is turned into the body of Christ by consuming this food [*per comestionem hujus cibi in corpus Christi convertitur*]."[107] Resurrection is therefore triumph over the food chain: "even if devoured by beasts or fishes or birds, member by member, all are reformed by resurrection in such a way that not a hair perishes."[108] It provides "gathering" "in the womb of the church" for those pieces cast to the winds or eaten by monsters.[109] It unites us to Christ's body, which is *integer* in heaven, however much we masticate it here on earth.[110] It restores us as the

106. Ibid., bk. 1, qq. 180–82, especially q. 181, pp. 394–95; and see pp. 135–36. The idea is found in Paschasius Radbertus.

107. Ibid., bk. 1, q. 182, p. 395; and see p. 262 for the Dominican inquisitor Nicolas Eymeric's accusation (at the end of the fourteenth century) that this idea is heretical.

108. *L'Elucidarium*, ed. Lefevre, bk. 3, q. 45, p. 456.

109. Ibid., bk. 2, q. 103, pp. 441–42: "D. Obest justis aliquid si in cimiterio ecclesiae non sepeliantur? M. Nihil prorsus. Totus namque mundus est templum Dei, quod dedicatum est sanguine Christi et sive in campo seu in silva vel in palude vel quovis loco sepeliantur vel projiciantur aut a bestis vel a belluis devorentur, semper in gremio Ecclesiae confoventur, quae per latitudinem terrae diffunditur."

110. Ibid., bk. 1, q. 183, p. 395; and see p. 136.

Guibert of Nogent makes a parallel argument. Because Christ is a literal synecdoche (says Guibert), we receive the whole Christ in each eating, but he loses no part. In his *De pignoribus* Guibert points out that if I destroy a fingernail, I claim that I, not merely a part of me, am hurt. We call friends or relatives "ourselves." How much more is all of Christ included in the *me* of *Qui manducat me* (John 6.58)? Those who eat the Eucharist eat the *totus Christus;* they eat not a part of Christ but the *universitas* of the substance (bk. 2, chap. 2, PL 156, cols. 632–34).

> Quod si particulas illas illum esse negas, partem pro toto, et totum pro parte poni posse forsitan ignoras, synecdochice nempe non solum loqui Scripturas, sed ipsos quosque illitteratos et vulgares hac figura sermonum uti, nulli non perspicuum. . . . Qui manducat me vivit propter me. . . . Est enim dicere: Qui exterius meum, carnem videlicet et sanguinem, manducat, vivit ex eo ipso quod interiorem hominem illuminando vivificat. Cum ergo fieri non possit ad litteram, ut totus ab aliquo manducetur, nisi pars pro toto accipiatur, secundum interiorem sensum indifficulter id agitur, praesertim cum fides corporis ita habeatur ut quod minutatim porrigitur, totum in suis minutiis teneatur.
>
> (Ibid., col. 632a–c)

Guibert was concerned to avoid a eucharistic theory that equates the sacrifice of the mass with the crucifixion. Hence he emphasized that the body on the altar was the body of the Resurrection; Christians should not be reminded of the dividing of Christ's body (see *De pignoribus*, bk. 2, chap. 6, col. 648; also bk. 3, chap. 2, obj. 6, col. 654). The concern may stem partly from Guibert's horrified fascination with details of bodily torture (ibid., bk. 4, chap. 1, cols. 668–69).

Such arguments seem to echo those put forth as early as the second century (by Ignatius, Irenaeus, and Tertullian) that eating Christ is an inverse cannibalism: consuming the body that cannot be consumed will make our own preeminently consumable bodies indigestible to hell and assumable to heaven.

potter restores his vase *de eadem materia* and places us in a paradise where stasis conquers change so completely that water becomes crystal and the flowers that rise from the earth never wither again.[111]

Just as was true in late antiquity, materialistic images of resurrection tend to accompany a stress on social or religious difference. A large part of book II of the *Elucidarium* is a description of the variety of statuses in society and a scathing indictment of their occupants—topics not treated at all in the *Clavis physicae*. The idea of the church as Christ's body is elaborated in such a way as to underline a hierarchy both of roles (teachers are bones; biblical commentators are teeth; peasants are feet) and of moral statuses (the obedient are ears; the discrete are the nose; heretics are snot).[112] Moreover, the heaven of the *Elucidarium* contains "a multitude of beautiful men and women," organized in the ranks of earth: "patriarchs, prophets, confessors, monks, virgins, and saints." They will appear with their "eyes and faces" and "all their interior and exterior members."[113] Luke 20.36 ("they will be . . . equal unto the angels") is quoted only to emphasize that there will be differences in glory.[114] We cannot become Peter; we can only become "like Peter." "For what one does not have in himself he will have in another," but it has not been promised that a foot can "become an eye, or a hand an ear, or a man a woman."[115] We will have full joy in heaven only when both our bodies and our friends arrive.[116]

There is no way to reconcile the divergent eschatological views found in Honorius's works nor, in the absence of any clear biographical infor-

---

111. *L'Elucidarium*, bk. 3, qq. 46, 49, 78 and 106, pp. 456, 457, 462, and 467–70. Honorius's description of the flowers and crystals of heaven parallels his descriptions of the bodies of the saints. In book 3 (q. 81, p. 464) Honorius says the different colors (signifying different virtues) in which the saints will rise will serve as their clothing; in q. 106, p. 469 (much of which is borrowed from Eadmer, *De beatitudine caelestis patriae*, PL 159, cols. 592–93), he speaks of the saints as clothed. See below, n. 113.

112. *L'Elucidarium*, pp. 405–42, and see n. 101 above.

113. Ibid., bk. 3, q. 106, pp. 467–70:

Hic est voluptas multitudinem virorum ac mulierum speciosarum videre, vestes pretiosas, . . . dulcem cantum . . . audire, thymiama et alias diversi pigmenti species odorare. . . . [Q]ui regem gloriae in decore suo cernent, omnes angelos et omnes sanctos interius et exterius conspicient, gloriam Dei, gloriam angelorum, gloriam patriarcharum, . . . gloriam virginum, gloriam omnium sanctorum videbunt, suos oculos, suas facias, omnia membra sua interius et exterius cernent, cogitationes singulorum intuebuntur. . . . Olfactio qualis. . . . qualis gustus. . . . Voluptas tactus qualis. . . . Ecce tales sunt deliciae beatorum.

For all its oddness, the passage is a striking affirmation of the survival of individual characteristics in the saints.

114. Ibid., q. 118, p. 473. Further along in the passage (p. 474), he refers to one house and many mansions (John 14.2).

115. Ibid., q. 116, p. 472.

116. Ibid., q. 27, p. 451.

mation about him, any way of understanding his motives in summarizing John Scotus. But it is worth noting that in Honorius's work metaphors of natural processes that are clearly positive—the burgeoning of a seed into flower, the return of spring, the triumph of the phoenix—are all connected with a sloughing off of what we mean, in a commonsense way, by body or matter. Not only are they about radical transformation; they are about transformation that moves away from individuality. Where resurrection is change in a Pauline sense, that which rises is spiritualized and de-particularized. In contrast, images of processes that are negative and threatening—digestion, decay, spontaneous generation from cadavers—tend to describe actual, tangible bodies. The *Elucidarium* refers repeatedly to fear of death, of putrefaction, of improper burial; it warns that even proper burial cannot save the evil from attacks by demons on their bones.[117] The resurrection imagery that accompanies these descriptions halts decay and retains difference. Thus, whether body is to be transmuted into spirit or lifted as it is into heaven, body is a locus of difference and of destruction. Understanding this does not, perhaps, help us to understand Honorius, but it does suggest some factors in the fate of his various works and of those of Erigena.

The history of Honorius's works indicates that later thinkers were very hesitant about Erigena's conceptions of self, cosmos, and salvation. Although the *Elucidarium*—in its Latin version and especially in numerous vernacular translations and adaptations—was enormously popular in the twelfth to fourteenth centuries, the *Clavis physicae* was rarely cited or copied, and the short treatises on the descent and ascent of Christ are known in only a single manuscript. Bertold of Moosburg in his commentary on Proclus cited the *Clavis*; Arno of Reichersberg, writing between 1142 and 1160, used it in his *Hexameron*; Endres has seen a reference to it in an interpolation in Heinrich of Melk's work on death.[118] But it was generally neglected. And there are hints of active disapproval as well. Gilbert of Poitiers, in a commentary on Boethius's work on Christ's natures, refers to the erroneous idea that the resurrection will bring all the elect to a state beyond humanness, where they will be godly with God; he attributes this teaching to a man "who could have been branded a heretic if he had given his name." Honorius made

117. Ibid., bk. 2, q. 105, p. 442.
118. Ibid., pp. 47–48 and 331–36; *Clavis physicae*, ed. Lucentini, pp. v–xxxii passim; Endres, *Honorius*, pp. 64–67 and 123–26; Max Manitius, *Geschichte der lateinischen Literatur des Mittelalters*, vol. 3 (Munich: Beck, 1931), p. 364; Sanford, "Honorius, *Presbyter* and *Scholasticus*"; and Flint, *Ideas in the West*. Sanford argues that Honorius puts some of the most questionable Erigenist opinions in the mouth of the "disciple" and thus avoids pantheistic heresy in a technical sense.

a point of concealing his identity and origins; Endres has argued that the man Gilbert refers to is Honorius.[119]

Even the *Elucidarium* came in for suspicion. Two twelfth-century manuscripts contain marginal notes (in one case from the twelfth century, in the other from the thirteenth) indicating that certain of its ideas are questionable. It is difficult to find the reasoning behind such comments, but their focus suggests that what was bothersome were Erigenist traces in this very non-Erigenist work. Of the eleven passages annotated in the twelfth century, eight have to do with the transcendence of the resurrected body, Christ's or ours; of the seven passages marked in a thirteenth-century hand, two are specifically about Christ's risen body.[120] By the late fourteenth century, an inquisitor found Origenist overtones even in Honorius's most materialist passages.[121] Nicolas Eymeric in his *Elucidarius elucidarii* read Honorius's citation of Augustine's metaphor of the recast vase as an argument that God makes for us *"non . . . illud sed aliud corpus"* at the resurrection.[122] He also objected to Honorius's idea that Peter will have virginity in John. Even this concession to community seemed, to Nicolas, to violate difference. "That the glory of all will be the glory of each is false and a heresy . . . if it means that the essential glory of all will be equal. . . . John 14.2 says 'In my

119. See Endres, *Honorius*, p. 125; and see ibid., n. 1 for the text of Gilbert's remark. Bett, *Erigena*, pp. 172–73, argues that Gilbert was, however, influenced by Erigena's *De divisione naturae*.

120. *L'Elucidarium*, ed. Lefevre, pp. 252–58.

121. Ibid., pp. 259–67.

It is important to note that a thirteenth-century vernacular adaptation of the *Elucidarium*, the *Lumiere as lais* of Peter of Peckham (which is actually as much an adaptation of a commentary on Peter Lombard's *Sentences* as of Honorius) retains the materialist focus of the *Elucidarium* and understands as materialist the passages that Eymeric later sees as heretical and spiritualist. See Ch.-V. Langlois, *La Vie spirituelle: Enseignements, méditations, et controverses d'après des écrits en français à l'usage des laïcs* (Paris: Librairie Hachette, 1928), pp. 66–122. For an Anglo-Norman poem that parallels this text, see Meyer "Fragment du Dialogue entre l'évêque saint Julien et son disciple"; and F. J. Tanquerey, "Originalité du Dialogue entre saint Julien et son disciple." Book 6, chapter 3, of *La Lumiere as lais* argues that we will all rise at age thirty-two years and three months; see extracts in Langlois, *La Vie spirituelle*, pp. 111–12. Book 6, chapter 4 (in ibid.) applies to the question of fingernails and hair the example of a master recasting a bronze; it asserts that he does so from "the same materials" but makes a "similar statue," as God will make a "new man." Book 6, chapter 12 (ibid., pp. 112–13) argues that all the elect will have the common joy of seeing God, but there will be special honors for special ranks; "each will have good in the other, I yours and you mine." In book 4, chapter 8 (ibid., pp. 106–7), the author takes up the question of the Eucharist and expresses doubt about Honorius's literalism; he argues that Christ's body is "our nurture," but to say it is absorbed (i.e., corrupted) by our bodies is to confuse nature and supernature.

122. *L'Elucidarium*, ed. Lefevre, p. 266; for the text of Eymeric's censure, see p. 517.

Father's house are many mansions' because there is diversity of rewards."[123]

Erigena's own text had a similar fate.[124] Excerpted and quoted by a number of figures in mid-century, it was already at that time suspect;[125] William of Malmesbury defended it as "very useful" but admitted that John was rumored "to be a heretic" because he deviated from "the well-trodden way of the Latins."[126] Pope Honorius III found it widespread in monasteries and schools in the early thirteenth century and seems almost certainly to have condemned it to be burned for "heretical perversity" in 1210. The condemnation was repeated in 1225.[127]

What disturbed authorities in the early 1200s was the appearance at Paris of a group that seemed to spiritualize or allegorize a number of Christian doctrines and to rely in part on the works of John Scotus. The exact teachings of this group—known as the Amauricians from their leader Amaury of Bene—are unknown.[128] They had Joachite ele-

123. Ibid., p. 266; for the text of Eymeric, see p. 519. Eymeric also uses 1 Corinthians 15.41 to refute Honorius and argue for diversity.

124. I leave aside here the issue, which is surely relevant, of the citation and condemnation of Erigena's eucharistic teaching; see Cappuyns, *Jean Scot Érigène*, pp. 86–91 and 242, and Johannes Huber, *Johannes Scotus Erigena: Ein Beitrag zur Geschichte der Philosophie des Mittelalters* (Munich: J. J. Lentner, 1861), p. 432ff.

125. On John's influence in the mid 1100s, see Bett, *Johannes Scotus Erigena*, pp. 171ff.; Cappuyns, *Jean Scot Érigène*, pp. 241–56; Huber, *Johannes Scotus Erigena*, pp. 432–39.

126. "Composuit etiam librum . . . propter perplexitatem quarundam quaestionum solvendam bene utilem, si tamen ignoscatur ei in quibusdam, quibus a Latinorum tramite deviavit, dum in Graecos acriter oculos intendit; quare et hereticus putatus est" (see Cappuyns, *Jean Scot Érigène*, p. 247 n. 4).

127. Cappuyns, *Jean Scot Érigène*, pp. 247–8, especially nn. 1 and 2 on p. 248; G. C. Capelle, *Autour du Décret de 1210*, 3: *Amaury de Bene: Étude sur son panthéisme formel*, Bibliothèque thomiste 16 (Paris: J. Vrin, 1932), pp. 13–15 and 89 (for the text of the condemnation); Huber, *Johannes Scotus Erigena*, p. 438; G. Théry, *Autour de Décret de 1210*, 1: *David de Dinant: Etude sur son panthéisme materialiste*, Bibliothèque thomiste 6 (Le Saulchoir, Belgium: Revue des sciences philosophiques et théologiques, 1925), p. 7; Bett, *Johannes Scotus Erigena*, pp. 174–84. M.-Th. d'Alverny does not think there was a condemnation of Erigena in 1210; see "Un fragment du procès des Amauriciens," *Archives d'histoire doctrinale et littéraire du moyen âge* 25 and 26 (1950–51): 325–36, esp. p. 335; see also H.-F. Dondaine, "L'objet et le 'medium' de la vision béatifique chez les théologiens du XIIIe siècle," *Recherches de théologie ancienne et médiévale* 19 (1952): 99.

128. The University of Paris condemned Amaury's teaching in the early thirteenth century; he appealed to Innocent III, who decided against him. Amaury died soon after, probably in 1206. Soon after his death, a group of followers appeared, who seem to have gone beyond his teaching. The synod of Paris in 1210 excommunicated him and removed his bones to unconsecrated soil, burned ten members of the sect, and imprisoned the rest for life—with the exception of a few women who were not considered responsible. See Huber, *Johannes Scotus Erigena*, pp. 434–35; and Capelle, *Autour du Décret: Amaury*, pp. 90–111. The teacher David of Dinant, who used to be thought

ments and close similarities to later Free Spirit ideas; like the later Free
Spirits, the Amauricians were seen as libertines, allowing all sorts of
license to the body because they denied its reality.[129] Charges in the
cartulary of the University of Paris and in the *Contra Amaurianos*, a
thirteenth-century tract written against them, assert that they taught
that the indwelling of the Holy Spirit *was* the resurrection.[130] They were
therefore charged with denying the resurrection of the body and with
holding that what the Parisian authorities taught about resurrection was
"a fable."[131] The fullest account we have of the doctrine of the Amauricians is that of Henry of Ostia in 1260;[132] it may be that it confuses
Amaury and Erigena.[133] But wherever the idea comes from, one element
of what Hostiensis reports as heretical is the idea that humanity will
rise with the two sexes united as they were in the first creation and as
Christ was after his resurrection.[134] Thus whether or not Hostiensis's
account of Amaury is an accurate reporting of Amaury's ideas, it is clear
that ecclesiastical authorities in 1210 condemned the position that there
is no resurrection of the material and particular body we possess on
earth.[135] The Fourth Lateran Council in 1215 required Cathars and other

an Erigenist as well, was probably influenced by very different ideas; see Théry, *Autour du Décret: David de Dinant.*

129. Thus, although their metaphysical position (which denied reality to anything
except spirit) was supposedly diametrically opposed to that of the Cathars, who saw
flesh as a second, evil reality, authorities feared the same result in both groups: a
failure to discipline the flesh and to retain its particularity as part of the person. See
below, chapter 5. For other aspects of the positions of Erigena and Amaury that worried authorities, see Dondaine, "L'objet et le 'medium' de la vision béatifique," pp.
63–75 and 98.

130. For the texts of these documents, see Capelle, *Autour du Décret: Amaury,*
pp. 89–93.

131. See the condemnation of the University of Paris in Capelle, *Autour du Décret:
Amaury,* p. 89; and *Contra Amaurianos,* especially chap. 7, in Capelle, op. cit., p. 92.

132. It is repeated by Martin of Poland; see Capelle, *Autour du Décret: Amaury,*
p. 105.

133. Huber, *Johannes Scotus Erigena,* p. 436; Capelle, *Autour du Décret: Amaury,*
pp. 27–30.

134. Huber, *Johannes Scotus Erigena,* p. 436.

135. Those who opposed the spiritualist position were clearly arguing that body
must be redeemed as body; it cannot become God because that—in their view—would
deny both divinity to God and bodiliness to body. They therefore saw the diametrically opposed spiritualist and Cathar positions as having the same consequence—i.e.,
denying bodily resurrection. *Contra Amaurianos,* chap. 9, charges the Amauricians
with teaching that God is all in all. The author of this tract against them then makes
the rather odd move of arguing that such a tenet implies that God is body; therefore,
since body is corruptible, God is corruptible. For the text, see Capelle, *Autour du
Décret: Amaury,* p. 92.

heretics to assent to the proposition that "all rise with their own individual bodies, that is, the bodies which they now wear."[136] It is also clear
that by the early thirteenth century the spiritualist and Origenist implications of Erigena's ideas were understood—and rejected—and that
one of the most threatening elements in the Erigenist position was the
claim that with the loss of materiality and integrity there would be a
blurring of the sexes at the end of time.[137]

In my fifth chapter, I shall return to the question of gender and consider—as I did in my discussion of Jerome—how far the rejection of
spiritualist interpretations of the resurrected body was a rejection of the
possibility of transcending difference, either in eternity or on earth. I
shall do so by treating with great care the specific language in which
polemicists drew the line between heterodox and orthodox belief. Such
treatment will impel me into a consideration of twelfth-century anxieties about biological processes, cadavers, and burial. Before I do so, however, I want to explore two other sorts of evidence of twelfth-century
concern with body and last things: spiritual writing and iconography.
Such evidence clearly manifests the twelfth-century emphasis on body
as physicality, but it also introduces the tendency that in the course of
the thirteenth century revolutionized eschatology by moving much of
what we mean by body into soul.

136. See Heinrich Denzinger, *Enchiridion symbolorum definitionum et declara-
tionum de rebus fidei et morum*, 31st ed., ed. Karl Rahner on basis of C. Bannwart
and J. Umberg (Freiburg: Herder, 1957), pp. 200, 216. The Second Council of Lyons
in 1274 reaffirmed this formulation.

137. It is also worth noting that on the matter of the equality of joy in the vision
of God (*par gaudium in dispari claritate*) the years around 1200 saw a shift back
toward emphasizing difference; see Wicki, *Seligkeit*, pp. 250ff.

Four

Psychosomatic Persons
and Reclothed Skeletons:
Images of Resurrection in
Spiritual Writing and Iconography

 THE COMPLICATED FATE of the writings of Erigena and of his twelfth-century disciple Honorius shows the extent to which scholastic theologians in the later twelfth and thirteenth centuries clung to materialist, literalist interpretations of resurrection. The rejection of Erigena's *De divisione naturae* and of Honorius's *Clavis physicae* was not only rejection of the idea that heaven and hell are spiritual states; it was also rejection of the notion of redemption as almost limitless transformation of self toward spirit. In other words, it represented a fear that identity cannot survive the loss of bodily structure or of physicality, that a sheaf of wheat sprouting in heaven might not be the same as the seed sown on earth. Twelfth-century devotional writing and iconography reflect, in subtle and surprising ways, the same fear.

It is true that we find images of resurrection as flowering and development in certain spiritual works by cloistered authors. But these images are not Origenist or Erigenist; they carry no implication that there will be a loss of difference in heaven. Rather than eclipsing or transcending physicality or matter, they begin to lift into soul much of the specificity and capacity to experience that was located in body by earlier thinkers. And the link between survival and material continuity does not disappear. The overriding impression left by twelfth-century eschatological discussion therefore is one of materialism and literalism. It was Jonah vomited up whole by the whale or the bones of saints reassembled at the trumpet's blast that provided the fundamental image of bodily resurrection.

Hildegard of Bingen: The Greening of Person and the Body as Dust

In twelfth-century scholastic treatises, such as Peter Lombard's *Sentences*, Hugh's *De sacramentis*, Honorius's *Elucidarium* and *Clavis physicae*, metaphors are scarce but significant. Never merely stylistic flourishes, they are sometimes a basic tool of philosophical investigation. When we turn to the spiritual and exegetical writing of cloistered authors, we find that metaphors are anything but scarce. Yet in this highly ornate prose, images and analogies are once again not mere embellishment. Because of their prominence in the Bible, metaphors themselves often provide the subject of exegetical discussion, and in the visions some cloistered authors claimed to receive, metaphors became a living text around which theological interpretation was elaborated. Thus for cloistered authors as for scholastic ones, a consideration of images takes us to the heart of basic concerns.[1]

Monastic writing was so deeply impregnated with biblical language and especially with the natural imagery of the Song of Songs, the psalms, the epistles, and the gospel parables that organic analogies were very common. Questions of grace and of sin were often spoken of in images of fertility and decay. The soul's growth toward God in this life, and after, was described as flowering or germination. Hence it is all the more

---

1. We must remember that a number of monastic writers (such as Guibert of Nogent, Otto of Freising, and Herrad of Hohenbourg) were deeply influenced by scholastic texts or training. Indeed for many of the greatest figures of the eleventh and early twelfth centuries, the monastic/scholastic distinction is misleading. For example, Honorius Augustodunensis was a monk, deeply committed to defending monastic privileges, including the right to teach and preach. He only occasionally writes in the fully scholastic *sic et non* form. Yet, as Valerie Flint has pointed out, his motives are close to those of the early twelfth-century teachers at Laon (see above, chapter 3, n. 63), and I included his works in my chapter on the schoolmen. Thus, like Anselm of Canterbury and Otto of Freising, Honorius is fully scholastic and fully monastic. Such figures illustrate how artificial is the division between monks and schoolmen that has entered into secondary literature through Jean Leclercq's great study, *The Love of Learning and the Desire for God: A Study of Monastic Culture*, 3d ed., trans. Catherine Misrahi (New York: Fordham University Press, 1982). Where Leclercq's characterization is helpful and moving is in evoking the experiential quality of devotional writing and in reminding us how stridently writers of the period themselves used the contrast of school and cloister. See also n. 75 below.

surprising to find in monastic authors as in scholastic ones a tendency to refer to the human body (both living and dead) as dust and ashes, a preference for inorganic images of the risen and glorified body, and a basic sense of bodily resurrection not as transformation but as reunion of scattered particles, which, once assembled, will shine with glory and never again undergo alteration. In the spiritual writings of Benedictines and of the so-called new monks, positive images of organic, natural transformation tend to be used to describe spiritual change; bodily change is treated in images either of rot and decay or of re-collection and reconstruction. Monastic descriptions of soul in the twelfth century tend to physicalize it and pull it toward body.[2] But monastic images for body lift toward heaven, in the second or general resurrection, exactly the physical locus of experience we inhabit on earth.

I begin my exploration of spiritual writing in the twelfth century with the polymath Hildegard of Bingen (d. 1179)—Benedictine abbess, natural philosopher, theologian, dramatist, and visionary—who might in view of her biological interests be expected to use fully developed organic images for every aspect of human experience.[3] Indeed, Hildegard has recently been celebrated (responsibly by the scholar Peter Dronke, less responsibly by creationist theologians such as Matthew Fox) for her holistic response to the cosmos and her tender concern for the human body.[4]

2. This is Carozzi's point in "Structure et fonction de la vision de Tnugdal." In his analysis of sermon 42 De diversis, Carozzi argues that Bernard's discussion of the five regions in which the elect seek God is a prolongation after death of the region of dissimilitude (ibid., pp. 223–34). To Carozzi, the continuation of the struggles, punishments, and growth of this life into the hereafter (purgatory or hell) is a physicalizing of the spiritual. But we should also note that Bernard is quite clear that what is in question in the in-between period before the Last Judgment is the soul; the body returns at the end of time. On the attribution of the sermon, see above, chapter 3, n. 65.

3. Katharina M. Wilson points out that women religious writers tend to use mechanical metaphors for their acts of writing to convey that they are instruments or conduits for God, whereas secular women writers use organic images to suggest growth of their creativity from within ("Introduction," in her Medieval Women Writers [Athens, Georgia: University of Georgia Press, 1984], pp. xx–xxi).

4. Peter Dronke, Women Writers of the Middle Ages: A Critical Study of Texts from Perpetua (+ 203) to Marguerite Porete (+ 1310) (Cambridge: Cambridge University Press, 1984), pp. 144–202; Matthew Fox, Illuminations of Hildegard of Bingen (Santa Fe: Bear and Co., 1985). Two excellent recent books on Hildegard are Barbara J. Newman, Sister of Wisdom: St. Hildegard's Theology of the Feminine (Berkeley: University of California Press, 1987) and Sabina Flanagan, Hildegard of Bingen, 1098–1179: A Visionary Life (London: Routledge, 1989). A good overview is provided by Barbara Newman in her "Introduction," to Hildegard of Bingen, Scivias, trans. Co-

Hildegard did speak frequently of the person as a garden or field, a tree that must be dug about and pruned in order to bear fruit.[5] If putrefying matter that gives birth to pus and worms is her favorite metaphor for sin,[6] Hildegard also has a strong sense that soil, seeds, and plants in fact give rise to life. To Hildegard, therefore, fertility is the other side of putrefaction, and organic growth (for example, the flowering of plants into blossoms and seeds, from whence come bread) can be an image of positive transformation. In contrast to the scholastic authors I considered in chapter 3, Hildegard—as befits someone who was a medical practitioner and gynecological theorist as well as a theologian—has a strong sense that something organic can change and still be itself, that alien substances can be incorporated without threatening identity.[7] She describes Christ as dry grain that grows like a stalk of wheat; his effect on his children is to "sow" and "water" in them the "greenness" [*viriditas*] of virtue.[8]

Indeed Hildegard says that humankind fails when it does *not* take in and give forth; it fails, for example, when it sees and smells but does not eat and digest obedience.[9] In such metaphors, the organic and bodily processes of germination and nutrition are used unambiguously to describe that which is good, and the person is presented as a psychosomatic unity.[10] Hildegard speaks of soul running through body like sap through

---

lumba Hart and Jane Bishop (New York and Mahwah, N.J.: Paulist Press, 1990), pp. 9–53.

5. See, for example, *Scivias*, bk. 1, vision 2, chap. 32, in *Hildegardis Scivias*, ed. A. Führkötter and A. Carlevaris, 2 pts., Corpus christianorum continuatio mediaevalis [hereafter CCCM] 43 and 43A (Turnhout: Brepols, 1978), pp. 34–37 (the person here is also a sheep and a pearl); bk. 2, vision 1, preface and chap. 7, pp. 110–12 and 115–16; bk. 3, vision 8, chap. 8, pp. 484–92.

6. See, for example, bk. 3, vision 8, chap. 8, p. 486–87.

7. Hildegard represents the older Benedictine tradition, in contrast to the Cistercians I discuss below. The so-called "old Benedictines," however, often agree with Cistercians in using organic imagery in positive ways. See the discussion of Peter the Venerable, below. Like the Cistercians, these "old monks" use positive images of growth primarily to describe spiritual progress from the region of dissimilitude to that of similitude.

8. *Scivias*, ed. Führkötter, bk. 3, vision 10, chap. 7, pp. 553–55. See also vision 9, chap. 20, pp. 532–33, where she says (speaking in the voice of one of the prophets voicing God's judgment) that those who seek their own wills rather than God's will be punished "quia me in hoc non quaesierunt. Et quid hoc eis prodest, quia in hoc non viriditatem sed ariditatem habent, et quoniam hoc non plantaui? Sed inutilis herba nascitur in eis absque trunco."

9. Bk. 2, vision 1, chap. 8, p. 153.

10. See, for example, her discussion of suicide. She writes, speaking with God's voice: "Sed ego de terra formaui hominem ut ab inferioribus ad superiora ascenderet

a tree—a metaphor which suggests that it is the nature of soul to invig-
orate body (book 1, vision 4, chapter 26).[11] But we must note that Hildegard's images of flowering and "greening" usually refer to the spiritual
progress of the whole human person, not to the body alone or to physiological process understood literally.

Even in Hildegard, insensate or inanimate particles—earth or mud,
dust or ashes—provide one of the basic images for the human being.
Bodily fertility is seen not primarily as a natural process but as a gift
from God. Left to itself, matter remains inert or decays.[12] It is God who
ensouls the fetus in the womb, God who gives life and fertility to the
mud or dust that is humankind: "Hear me, the Son of Man, saying to
you: Oh human, regard what you were when you were just a lump in
your mother's womb! You were mindless and powerless to bring yourself to life; but then you were given spirit and motion and sense, so that
you might . . . come to fruitful deeds."[13] Even when fertility serves as

---

et ut incipiendo et perficiendo bona opera sursum praeclaras uirtutes ad ardua aedi-
ficaret. Quapropter homo qui et corpus et animam habet, cum bona operari potest et
cum paenitere ualet, semetipsum non occidat. . . ." (Bk. 2, vision 5, chap. 60, p. 223).
There is no suggestion at all in the *Scivias* that redemption is escape from body or
that salvation could be complete without body.

For a similar view, see Peter of Celle, another Benedictine author and a contemporary of Hildegard. Peter stresses that we should see the person as a psychosomatic
unity. In his *De disciplina claustrali* he speaks with feeling of the body as the
"brother" of the soul: "O anima sine corpore ubi est modo corpus tuum? ubi est Abel
frater tuus? Ecce vermes, ecce tinea, ecce putredo quondam in ossibus tuis. Tu autem
quid? Petisne ab Abraham ut mittat Lazarum, et intinguat extremum digiti sui in
aqua, et refrigeret linguam tuam?"(chap. 23, PL 202, col. 1133C–D) And see above,
chapter 3, n. 102.

11. *Scivias*, ed. Führkötter, p. 84. In writing of baptism, Hildegard says: ". . . spirit
without the bloody material of the body is not the living person, and the bloody
material of the body without the soul is not the living person; and these two are not
strengthened unto life . . . except through the water of regeneration" (see bk. 3, vision
7, chap. 8, p. 471; trans. Hart and Bishop, *Scivias*, p. 417).

12. One of Hildegard's favorite images for sin and evil is the decayed corpse; see,
for example, bk. 2, vision 6, chap. 56, ed. Führkötter, p. 275.

13. Ibid., bk. 3, vision 10, chap. 1, p. 547; trans. Hart and Bishop, p. 473. See also
bk. 2, vision 5, chap. 46, ed. Führkötter, p. 214:

Viridem agrum in potestate mea habui. Numquid, o homo, dedi tibi illum, ut
eum germinare faceres quemcumque fructum te uelles? Et si in illum semen
seminas, num potes illud in fructum producere? Non. Nam tu nec rorem das,
nec pluuiam emittis, nec umiditatem in uiriditate tribuis, nec calorem in ar-
dore solis educis, per quae omnia competens fructus producendus est. Ita etiam
auditum hominis uerbum seminare potes, sed in cor illius quod ager meus est
nec rorem compunctionum, nec pluuiam lacrimarum, nec umorem deu-
otionum, nec calorem Spiritus sancti infundere uales, in quibus omnibus fructus sanctitatis germinare debet.

an image for spiritual growth, Hildegard often stresses that it is not natural but infused. She writes:

"As the apple tree among the trees of the woods, so is my beloved
among the children. . . ."(Song of Songs 2.3). . . . He is the most beautiful fruit of the fruitful tree; which is to say that the son of the Virgin
comes forth from virginal modesty as its fruit, giving refreshing food
to those who hunger and sweet drink to those who thirst. And thus
He excels all the trees of the woods, which is to say the human children who are conceived and live in sin, not yielding the fruit He
yielded; for He came from God bearing the fruit of the sweetness of
life, while others have no fruit or fecundity [*viriditatem*] of their own,
but only that derived from Him.[14]

Although Hildegard frequently combines organic and inorganic images
for the embodied person (we are seeds and mud, gardens and pearls, tree-
wood and stones), the body by itself is the dust and ashes of Genesis
2.7.[15] It is a tabernacle of filth in which the globe of the soul is trapped,
a vessel buried in the earth, a lump of mire surrounded with jewels
clutched to the breast of God, an unplowed field that can be made to
bear only by Christ.[16] It is threatened by incisions and breaches.[17] With-

14. Hildegard, *Scivias*, ed. Führkötter, bk. 3, vision 8, chap. 16, pp. 501–2; trans.
Hart and Bishop, pp. 439–40.
15. See, for example, *Scivias*, ed. Führkötter, bk. 3, vision 7, chap. 8, p. 472.
16. Contrast, for example, ibid., bk. 1, vision 2, chap. 32, pp. 34–37, where the
whole human being is seen as a garden (which must be cultivated by Christ), a lost
sheep, and a pearl that has slipped into the mud (thus both kinds of images are used)
with bk. 1, vision 4, pp. 61–92, where the soul is a globe that falls into the body (which
is seen as mud or a building). Even in vision 4, however, the impact of soul on body
is seen as creating a fertile and developing whole; body is like the wood of the tree to
which soul is sap (ibid., chap. 26, p. 84). In bk. 2, visions 1 and 2, pp. 110–32, the
human being is repeatedly spoken of as a clod of mud, warmed to life by God; by the
time we reach vision 2, chap. 4, p. 127, the human being formed from mud is a pearl.
In bk. 3, vision 1, we are "ut cinis cinereae putredinis et sicut pulvis instabilitatis,"
"limum nigrum et lutulentum . . . circumdatum lapidibus pretiosis atque margaritis"
(pp. 329 and 331–32). In vision 10, chaps. 6–7, pp. 551–55, we are fields, dust, and
ashes that must be plowed and sowed by God.
17. For Hildegard's distress at the idea of bodily breaches (which can nonetheless
be made fertile by God), see her complex discussion of sexual intercourse and menstruation in bk. 1, vision 2, chaps. 20–21, pp. 27–28. See also the image of the pierced
body of the church in bk. 2, vision 3, chaps. 4–6, pp. 138–39, and the discussion of
suicide in bk. 2, vision 5, chaps. 59–60, pp. 222–24 ("so one who throws himself into
bodily death, not waiting for the separation I appoint for everyone but dividing himself
without hope of mercy, will fall into perdition. . . . For one who separates from a
person what I have placed in the person incurs great guilt." [trans. Hart and Bishop,
pp. 233–34]).

out the irradiating of God's grace, it tends toward rot and fragmentation.[18] The same body is stabilized and hardened in glory; in heaven, it is gold or a pearl or a finely cut gem.[19]

Thus, despite her strong sense of process and fertility, Hildegard does not apply such imagery to the resurrection of the body.[20] Indeed she scarcely speaks of last things at all. She does mention in passing the problems concerning bodily reassemblage so dear to Peter Lombard and other scholastics; she asserts that people rise in two sexes, without deformities or mutilation or deficiencies of matter (even if they have been victims of cannibalism);[21] she speaks of glorified bodies as "light," appropriate containers for the "fiery" souls of heaven.[22] But Hildegard actually says very little about the end of time and almost nothing about paradise. It is as if her language of growth and process has no way to describe heaven, which she simply calls glorious and changeless.[23]

Nonetheless what little she does say of last things agrees exactly with Peter Lombard's scenario.[24] The earth will shake and human bones will come together from wherever they lie to be covered with flesh. The bodies that will rise are precisely the bodies we have in this life.

> And behold, all the human bones in whatever place in the earth they lay were brought together in one moment and covered with their flesh; and they all rose up with limbs and bodies intact, each in his or her gender, with the good glowing brightly and the bad manifest in blackness. . . .
> And suddenly from the East a great brilliance shone forth; and there, in a cloud, I saw the Son of Man.[25]

18. See, for example, *Scivias*, ed. Führkötter, bk. 2, vision 6, chap. 43, pp. 268–69.

19. See bk. 3, vision 8, chap. 8, pp. 489–90, where the good are seen as flowers, gems, and pruned trees, but the greatest emphasis is on the image of finely cut stones and that is the image that is explicitly related to the heavenly Jerusalem.

20. An exception is bk. 2, vision 5, chap. 31, pp. 201–2.

21. Bk. 3, vision 12, especially preface and chaps. 3, 7–8, 13–16, pp. 604–13.

22. Ibid., pp. 605, 609–10, and 612. And see bk. 2, vision 6, chap. 52, p. 273, where Hildegard says that those who take the Eucharist will appear in heaven *post resurrectionem* in the "same bodies" they have on earth (*in eodem corpore suo*) only brighter, just as their souls also are "enkindled by the fiery gift of the Holy Spirit" (*atque in anima sua igneo dono Spiritus sancti transfunduntur*).

23. See above, nn. 21 and 22.

24. See bk. 3, visions 12–13, pp. 604–36. Book 3, vision 12, calls the saints "flowers" (p. 610), but stresses jewels and fire; in vision 13, where the whole of the blessed person is described, both flowers and jewels figure prominently in the imagery. Hildegard sees the person as an impartible whole; thus I would in no way suggest that soul is flower and body jewel. Nonetheless, it seems important that her specific references to body are to jewels.

25. Bk. 3, vision 12, p. 605, and see plate 33; trans. Hart and Bishop, p. 515.

The miniature that accompanies this vision suggests, even more graphically than Hildegard's words, that scattered pieces of human beings come together when the trumpet sounds (see plate 4). Below the shining blessed (on Christ's right hand) are the bones from which they rise. Although the text describes a whirlwind that wafts to the throne of God the "blessed who are signed," the miniature shows detached heads of both saved and damned (light and dark) curling in the blasts of the four winds. The words seem to refer to whole figures, but the artist has painted body parts rolled together in preparation for rising. The resurrection depicted here is reassemblage and glorification, not transformation.

> And when the judgment was ended, the lightnings and thunders and winds and tempests ceased, and the fleeting components of the elements vanished all at once, and there came an exceedingly great calm. And then the elect became more splendid than the splendor of the sun. . . . And all the elements shone calm and resplendent, as if a black skin had been taken from them; so that fire no longer had its raging heat, or air density, or water turbulence, or earth shakiness. And the sun, moon and stars sparkled in the firmament like great ornaments, remaining fixed and not moving in orbit, so that they no longer distinguished day from night. And so there was no night, but day. And it was finished.[26]

Hildegard's confidence in organic change, in the beauty of the natural world and of the human body, is at the service of her understanding of spiritual change; her glorious images of growth and process describe the soul, or the person as psychosomatic unity. But the body tends toward decay and partition. Thus in resurrection, it must become subtle, crystalline, perfect, and impassible; its triumph is the attainment of wholeness and stability in that final moment that is "finished" and still.

Cistercian Writing: Images of First and Second Resurrection

When we turn to Bernard of Clairvaux (d. 1153) and other Cistercians, such as William of St. Thierry (d. 1148) and Guerric of Igny (d. 1157), we expect to find—even more than in Hildegard—metaphors of flowering and fertility. The Cistercians were, after all, "new monks"—reformers who retreated both to the literal wilderness of poverty and hardship and

26. *Scivias*, ed. Führkötter, bk. 3, vision 12, p. 606; trans. Hart and Bishop, pp. 515–16. And see plates 33 and 34 in Führkötter ed.

to the figurative wasteland of spiritual solitude. Not only their contemporaries but historians of our own day as well have marveled at the skill with which they made both deserts flower. Widely admired by recent scholars for their sensual prose, they have long been studied and enjoyed for their ideas about contemplation, interior journey, and spiritual self-awareness.[27] Thus we are not surprised to find in twelfth-century Cistercian writers extremely complex organic imagery. Deciphering what such imagery tells us about Cistercian concepts of the body and of resurrection is not, however, easy. Two general observations are necessary to establish the context.

First, as John Sommerfeldt has recently argued, the body is absolutely crucial in Bernard's anthropology.[28] Souls cannot receive the beatific vision until they regain their bodies at the end of time.[29] "For it is not fitting that complete beatitude [integram beatitudinem] be bestowed before the human being to whom it will be given is whole [integer]—any more than it is fitting that perfection be given to an imperfect Church [Ecclesiam imperfectam]."[30] Although Bernard occasionally asks in puzzlement why souls desire the body—"miserable flesh," "foul and fetid flesh"[31]—he answers that souls must crave body not for its

27. For the association of Cistercians with affective spirituality (now a commonplace in scholarly literature), see R. W. Southern, The Making of the Middle Ages (New Haven: Yale University Press, 1959), pp. 219–57; Leclercq, The Love of Learning; and Colin Morris, The Discovery of the Individual, 1050–1200 (1972; pbk. reprint, New York: Harper and Row, 1973). For an example of the new scholarship on Cistercians, which emphasizes the same aspects (although from a very different point of view), see Ann Astell, "The Mark of Gender in Saint Bernard's De diligendo Deo," Romance Languages Annual (forthcoming). On William of St. Thierry, who became a Cistercian only late in life, see below, n. 37.

28. John R. Sommerfeldt, "The Body in Bernard's Anthropology" (Unpublished paper). Sommerfeldt's paper is on Bernard, but his observations apply even more convincingly to other early Cistercians.

29. See Sommerfeldt, "Body in Bernard." For a different interpretation of Bernard's position, see Marc Dykmans, Les sermons de Jean XXII sur la vision béatifique (Rome: Università Gregoriana Editrice, 1973), pp. 40–43. The matter is a complex one, and Sommerfeldt may go a bit too far in making the body crucial. It is important to note that Bernard does hold that the souls of the saints are admitted to rest as soon as they leave their bodies. What they await (in waiting for their bodies) is "full glory," not admission to any sort of blessedness. The central texts are Bernard, Sermons for All Saints, especially sermons 3 and 4, in Sancti Bernardi Opera, vol. 5 (1968), pp. 349–60; and De diligendo Deo (see n. 34 below). See also chapter 8, n. 43 below. For a similar position to Bernard's, see Achard of St. Victor, sermon 12, paragr. 8, in Sermons inédits, ed. Jean Chatillon (Paris, J. Vrin, 1970), p. 129.

30. Bernard, Third Sermon for All Saints, paragr. 1; Opera, vol. 5, p. 350.

31. Ibid., paragr. 2: "Sed unde hoc tibi, o misera caro, o foeda, o foetida, unde tibi hoc? Animae sanctae, quas propria Deus insignivit imagine, quas redemit proprio sanguine, te desiderant, te exspectant, et ipsarum sine te compleri laetitia, perfici gloria, consummari beatitudo non potest." See also "On Conversion," chap. 6, paragr. 11, and chap. 8, paragr. 15, in Opera, vol. 4 (1966), pp. 84–85 and 89: "Insanus siquidem

merits but because without it they are not complete persons.[32] The desire of soul for body is a contortion, a twisting; it is the "wrinkle" of Ephesians 5.27.[33] Without body, souls can be a "glorious church, without spot" of sin, but they cannot be completely happy, for they are not free from the "wrinkle of distraction" until they are embodied again at the end of time. Bernard here draws on the same passage from Augustine that led Peter Lombard to assert that bodily resurrection brings something without which a self cannot be happy; as for Peter, this happiness is the removal of longing or discontent. But to Bernard the return of body is more than the end of disquiet; it is also an increase of joy.

> Do not be surprised if the glorified body seems to give the spirit something, for it was a real help when man was sick and mortal. How true that text is which says that all things turn to the good of those who love God (Rom. 8.28). The sick, dead and resurrected body is a help to the soul who loves God; the first for the fruits of penance, the second for repose, and the third for consummation. Truly the soul does not want to be perfected, without that from whose good services it feels it has benefited . . . in every way. . . . Listen to the bridegroom in the Canticle inviting us to this triple progress: 'Eat, friends, and drink; be inebriated, dearest ones.' He calls to those working in the body to eat; he invites those who have set aside their bodies to drink; and he impels those who have resumed their bodies to inebriate themselves, calling them his dearest ones, as if they were filled with charity. . . . It is right to call them dearest who are drunk with love.[34]

Bernard does not quite say it, but there is the suggestion here that body adds greater capacity for ecstasy to the soul.[35] Although he stresses that

---

labor pascere sterilem quae non parit . . ., omittere curam cordis et curam carnis agere in desiderio, impinguare et fovere cadaver putridum, quando paulo post vermium esca futurum nullatenus dubitatur" (p. 89). And see Bernard of Clairvaux, *Selected Works*, trans. G. Evans (New York and Mahwah, N.J.: Paulist Press, 1987), pp. 75 and 78.

32. See Bernard, "On Conversion," chap. 12, paragr. 24, *Opera*, vol. 4, p. 97, where—in a dialogue between will and the members of the body—Bernard has the body say: "I am your body; your own self. [*Tuum est corpus, tuus ego ipse.*] There is nothing to fear or to dread." See Evans trans., *Selected Works*, p. 84. See also sermon 10 on Psalm 90, paragr. 3, *Opera*, vol. 4, p. 445.

33. Third Sermon for All Saints, *Opera*, vol. 5, pp. 349–53.

34. Bernard, *De diligendo Deo*, section 11, paragrs. 30–33, in *Opera*, vol. 3 (1963), pp. 144–47; trans. Robert Walton, *The Works of Bernard of Clairvaux*, vol. 5: *Treatises*, vol. 2 (Washington, D.C.: Cistercian Publications, 1974), pp. 122–24. See also Bernard's Sermons for All Saints cited in n. 29 above and sermon 8 on Psalm 90 in *Opera*, vol. 4, pp. 426–35.

35. Bernard never does quite say that body adds to the capacity to experience in heaven although Sommerfeldt may be right to suggest that this idea is implicit in his

visio Dei brings peace and "tranquillity" to those who love God—a tranquillity indeed that spills over from soul into body in the anesthesia of glory—he also speaks of "intoxication" in the resurrection.

> Do we not think that the holy martyrs received . . . grace while they were still in their victorious bodies—at least in part? They were so moved within by the great force of their love that they were able to expose their bodies to outward torments and think nothing of them. The sensation of outward pain could do no more than whisper across the surface of their tranquillity. . . .
>
> It is not in dispute that they want their bodies back. . . . Until death is swallowed up in victory (1 Cor. 15.54) . . . so that heavenly glory gleams even in bodies, these souls cannot wholly remove themselves and transport themselves to God. . . . [They are still too much bound to their bodies]. . . . They do not wish to be complete without them.
>
> [But] . . . when our bodies are resurrected, we are intoxicated by immortal life, abounding in wonderful plenty.[36]

Nor is Bernard the only Cistercian writer with a profound sense of the person as psychosomatic unity and of the earthly body as a means to glory and ecstasy. William of St. Thierry,[37] who displayed an interest in physiology parallel to Hildegard's and who was deeply influenced by Gregory of Nyssa (read in Erigena's translation), also saw the body as an expression of, and an enhancer of, the soul. William, it is true, spoke in conventional language of soul regaining body in order that the partner who shares the labor of a life may share equally in its rewards. He repeatedly described the earthly body as a "living statue" forged by God.[38]

---

anthropology. He certainly does emphasize the tight union of soul and body as a source of spiritual advance in this life. And he does argue explicitly that the glorified body adds peace, freedom, and beauty in heaven: "So, to the thought of judgment is added that of the kingdom, in which kingdom we think on what we shall be: first on the state of the body when it will be immortal and impassible, then on its glory when it will be of ineffable beauty and splendor, as it is written: 'The just will be as resplendent as the sun' [Matt. 13.43]." See *Parabola 6: De Aethiopissa*, in *Opera*, vol. 6, pt. 2, pp. 291–92; and see Sommerfeldt at n. 94.

36. Bernard, "On Loving God," chap. 10, paragr. 29 through chap. 11, paragr. 33, in *Opera*, vol. 3, pp. 143–47, and in *Selected Works*, trans. Evans, p. 197–99.

37. William of St. Thierry (d. 1148) was a black Benedictine and abbot of his house from 1119; he became a Cistercian only in 1135, toward the end of his life. His two philosophical works, *On the Nature and Dignity of Love* and *On the Nature of Body and Soul*, were written early in his career—long before he became a Cistercian but after he had met and been influenced by Bernard of Clairvaux.

38. William of St. Thierry, *On the Nature of Body and Soul*, bk. 2, PL 180, cols. 707–26, esp. cols. 710 and 717; trans. by J.-M. Déchanet in *Oeuvres choisies de Guil-*

But occasionally William's statue not only lives; it also grows toward perfection as an expression of the morally developing soul. William's suggestion that the body would have grown perfect in paradise had not sin intervened is close to Augustine's idea of acquiring the *non posse mori* through eating from the tree of life; it is not a notion either that general resurrection is flowering or that the voyage of the separated soul is manifested in body. But there is at least a hint that soul needs body—throbbing, sensing, experiencing, growing body—as a revelation and expression of itself.[39]

A second point must be made as a context for understanding Cistercian resurrection imagery. Following Revelation 20.6, Cistercian authors, like many patristic writers, spoke of two resurrections, one of the soul and one of the body. Thus, as M.-N. Bouchard has emphasized, resurrection was often, to Cistercian authors, a process of cleansing in which asceticism played a role; life was seen as a long struggle of the soul to die to sin or to rise up from it—a process made possible by Christ's death and resurrection.[40] As Bernard put it: the soul is nobler than the body; it was the first to fall and is the first to rise. We should therefore devote ourselves to souls, which Christ came first to heal, and postpone all concern for our bodies until Christ comes again to reform them.[41] The monk Herman of Reun, who delivered a series of sermons based on Bernard between 1170 and 1180, summarized the Cistercian conception of first and second resurrections in a way that makes their different natures and temporal dimensions clear.[42] First resurrection is of soul and is now; second resurrection is of body and is future.

> Hearts and bodies rejoice together because, Christ rising, our inner man is freed from the death of sin and our exterior man is confirmed in the hope of his resurrection, of which he gives us an example. . . . Both are right to rejoice, because each co-resurrects with Christ, the inner [man] in fact and the outer [man] in hope. And we say that the

laume de Saint-Thierry (Paris: Aubier, 1943), pp. 100–1 and 120–21. There is an English translation by Bernard McGinn in *Three Treatises on Man: A Cistercian Anthropology* (Kalamazoo, Mich.: Cistercian Publications, 1977), pp. 101–52.

39. *On the Nature of Body and Soul*, bk. 2, cols. 710–12; trans. Déchanet, pp. 100–7.

40. Marie-Noël Bouchard, "La résurrection dans la spiritualité des premiers auteurs cisterciens," *Collectanea cisterciensia* 37 (1975): 114–29.

41. Bernard, Sixth Sermon for Advent, in *Opera*, vol. 4, pp. 191–95.

42. On Herman, see Edmund Mikkers, "Hermann de Reun," *Dictionnaire de spiritualité*, vol. 7, pt. 1 (1969), col. 278.

interior man rises in fact because sin, which is the death of the soul, is remitted ... and the exterior man rises in hope because, by the example of the Lord's resurrection, we are given an indubitable certification of the re-formation of the new man from the dust of the earth [*ex terrae pulvere*]; and this showing in the present makes confident our expectation of the future.[43]

From two deaths we say there are two resurrections: ... the resurrection of souls in the church through the word of God, when the revivified rise up from the death of iniquity through grace, ... and the [resurrection] of the body at the end of time.... For now [we] rise *in mente* through the word of the son of God and then [we] will rise *in carne* through the word made flesh. And the bodies of the saints will rise to glory without any defect or deformity.... [A]ll infirmity ... and corruption and poverty and want and all unsuitable things ... will be far from them, who will be equal to the angels of God in the resurrection.[44]

Although Cistercians such as Bernard, Guerric, and Herman of Reun often mentioned both resurrections in their Easter preaching, sermons on Christ's resurrection usually concentrated on first resurrection—that of the soul. To discover Cistercian attitudes toward bodily or second resurrection, we need to turn to sermons where actual holy bodies are discussed—such as those for All Saints or for the dedication of churches—or to sermons on the Ascension, which was sometimes seen as an analogue to the second resurrection. We also sometimes find extended treatment in contexts where we would not expect it—contexts where the image itself conjures up the body—as, for example, in Bernard's sermons on Psalm 90 where references to "tabernacle" and to "seeing the reward of the wicked" become occasions for an extended examination of the resurrection of the body.[45]

Like writers of the older Benedictine tradition, Cistercians do occasionally use language of flowering or growth for bodily resurrection. Gilbert of Hoyland, speaking of St. Lawrence on the griddle, makes the

43. Herman de Runa [Reun], *Sermones festivales*, ed. Edmund Mikkers et al., CCCM 64 (Turnhout: Brepols, 1986), sermon 24, p. 97.

44. Herman, sermon 25, *Sermones*, ed. Mikkers, pp. 102–3. And see Bernard (?), sermon 116, *De diversis*, PL 183 (Paris, 1854), col. 741.

45. Bernard, Eighth Sermon on Psalm 90, *Opera*, vol. 4, pp. 426–35. For another example, see Guerric of Igny, Sermon 54 for Devotion at Psalmody (below, at n. 47), which contains a long discussion of resurrection that is not referred to in any of the indices to his works. Because of the odd places where general resurrection tends to be discussed, sermon titles, rubrics, and even indices are not a good guide to discussions of eschatology in twelfth-century sermons.

griddle into a garden and says Lawrence's flesh will flower again when it becomes like Christ's body.[46] In a discussion of the psalms, Guerric of Igny elaborates a contrast between tombs and gardens, drawing on Song of Songs 8.13:

> [Tombs] are full of every filth and of dead men's bones, [gardens] are full of flowers or fruits in all their sweetness and grace. What if tombs are sometimes seen in gardens? For the Lord was buried in a garden.
>
> If there are tombs in a garden surely there are not gardens in tombs. Yet perhaps there are, but in the tombs of the just. There indeed a certain most agreeable pleasantness which belongs to gardens will flourish as in spring, the springtime, that is, of their resurrection when their flesh will blossom again. Not only the bones of the just man will sprout like grass but also the whole of the just man will spring up like a lily and bloom forever before the Lord. Not so the godless, not so. They are buried with the burial of an ass . . . subject to corruption.[47]

Thomas the Cistercian, who uses much imagery of germination in his commentary on the Song of Songs, speaks of Christ's flesh as a grain of wheat sown in the Virgin's belly and emphasizes that Mary's own body, one with Christ's body, will flower in resurrection.[48] Herman of Reun draws an analogy between Christ's flesh and Aaron's rod, saying: "the body of the Lord, truly our priest, placed in the aridness of death burst forth into the flower of resurrection."[49] Bernard sometimes speaks

46. See Bouchard, "La résurrection," p. 125.

47. Guerric of Igny, *Sermo ad excitandum devotionem in psalmodia*, in Guerric, *Sermons*, ed. John Morson and Hilary Costello, trans. Placide Deseille, Sc 166 and 202 (Paris: Éditions du Cerf, 1970 and 1973), vol. 2, pp. 516–18; *Guerric of Igny: Liturgical Sermons*, trans. Monks of Mount St. Bernard Abbey (Shannon, Ireland: Irish University Press, and Spencer, Mass.: Cistercian Publications, 1971), sermon 54, vol. 2, pp. 213–14.

48. Thomas the Cistercian, *In cantica canticorum eruditissimi commentarii*, PL 206 (Paris, 1855), cols. 698 and 369–72 respectively. For similar language, see Alan of Lille (d. 1202), who became a Cistercian at the end of his life: *Compendiosa in cantica canticorum ad laudem Deiparae Virginis Mariae Elucidatio*, PL 210 (Paris, 1855), cols. 64 and 69. And see the Augustinian canon William of Newburgh (d. ca. 1199), who speaks of Christ's body ripening in the grave, which he glosses as the flowery bed (*lectulus floridus*) of Song of Songs 1.15; John C. Gorman, ed., *William of Newburgh's Explanatio sacri Epithalamii in Matrem Sponsi: A Commentary on the Canticle of Canticles (12th-C.)* (Freiburg, Switzerland: Universitätsverlag, 1960), pp. 109–10. On Thomas the Cistercian, Alan of Lille, William of Newburgh, and the Marian interpretation of the Song of Songs generally, see Rachel Fulton, "The Virgin Mary and the Song of Songs in the High Middle Ages" (Ph.D. diss., Columbia University, in progress).

49. Herman, *Sermones*, ed. Mikkers, sermon 25, p. 102. We should note here, however, that only Christ's body flowers; what is emphasized for our bodies is their rotting in the tomb.

of flesh as a "fertile" "dungheap," urges the spirit to "sow and reap" in the flesh, or suggests that the body in this life, when disciplined, may renew and multiply like a seed rather than rotting in a granary.[50]

Such images are, however, rare. References to general resurrection, and to the resurrections of Christ and the Virgin, tend in Cistercian writing to stress triumph over change and fragmentation more than the germination of glory. Thomas the Cistercian, indeed, sees Mary as a garden, but one closed to rot as well as to sin.[51] The Virgin's triumph is that, flesh of Christ's flesh and bone of his bone, she shares in his resurrection, safe and immune from the law of corruption.[52] Since the threat was decay, images of flowering, when they occurred, expressed the victory of changelessness in heaven, attained by the identical body possessed on earth.

Moreover, the most elaborate images of flowering and fertility in connection with resurrection described the first resurrection—that of the soul. A close reading of Guerric's discussion of tombs and gardens, for example, makes it clear that—although he has second resurrection partly in mind—he is really discussing *spiritual* death and rebirth. The tombs he speaks of are the "bodies of sinners" in which their evil souls are "buried."[53] When he draws out at considerable length the idea, which goes back to Plato, that man is an inverted tree with the roots of his nervous system in his head, Guerric uses it to describe spiritual resurrection. "Even when his roots in the earth have grown old and his trunk has turned to dust, at the fragrance of the living water in the resurrec-

50. Bernard, Sermon 10 on Psalm 90, paragr. 3, *Opera*, vol. 4, p. 445: "Quomodo dicunt nobis carnales homines: 'Crudelis est vita vestra; non parcitis carni vestrae?'—'Esto, non parcimus semini. In quo ei magis parcere poteramus? Annon melius est illi renovari et multiplicari in agro, quam in horreo putrefieri? . . . Siquidem etiam nunc caro nostra requiescit in spe. . . ." And see Sermon 5 for the Ascension, paragr. 13, *Opera*, vol. 5, p. 157.

51. Thomas the Cistercian, *In cantica canticorum*, PL 206, col. 457. William of Newburgh also stresses resurrection as victory over decay: because the worm does not consume him, Christ's death is not in vain; Gorman, ed., *William of Newburgh's Explanatio*, pp. 109–10. See also ibid., pp. 130–31 and 133–34.

52. As Rachel Fulton, "The Virgin Mary and the Song of Songs," makes clear, twelfth-century discussion of the Bodily Assumption laid great emphasis on both the Virgin's and Christ's complete freedom from bodily decay. Authors repeatedly stressed the union of Mary and her son as a guarantee that neither experienced any putrefaction or bodily change in the grave.

53. "Corpora enim peccatorum quid sunt nisi sepulchra mortuorum?" See above n. 47. Guerric concludes: "[The unjust are] without any hope of a better resurrection. [T]hey are subject to corruption as a foretaste of their future fate. Concerning their tombs I had begun to say that as great as is the difference between their filth and the beauty of gardens in flower incomparably greater is the difference between the delight of spiritual men and the pleasure of carnal joys" (*Sermons*, ed. Morson and Costello, vol. 2, p. 518; trans. in *Liturgical Sermons*, vol. 2, p. 214).

tion, that is, in the renewal of the just, [the just man] will grow like the lily and will blossom forever."[54] When Guerric discusses the resurrection of a child performed by Elisha (4 Kings 4.32), he sees it as a gradual process: "first . . . [his] flesh grew warm, then he yawned seven times, and finally he opened his eyes." But "the child's flesh is the fleshly heart [i.e., the evil desires] of one who is little in Christ." The story is an analogy to spiritual rebirth: "first then there is the warmth of returning life when good works are performed; the second stage of resurrection is the extending of affections through prayer; perfection is reached when understanding is enlightened so as to contemplate."[55] Even when discussing spiritual resurrection, Guerric sometimes transmutes organic images into inorganic ones. In his second Easter sermon, for example, he speaks of "sowing" the body and draws on 1 Corinthians 15, but the full text reads:

> It is indeed profitable trading to despise the things which weaken and defile you in order to gain Christ . . . [and] to recover yourself with . . . a generous interest of immortality and glory. Who would hesitate to regard it as a profitable trade to sow a body, mortal, natural, unhonored, that it may rise immortal, spiritual, glorious.[56]

Moreover, Guerric's images for the body are often the images of garments, buildings, and jewels familiar since the early church. For example, he uses Song of Songs 5.14 to speak of Christ's "flesh of ivory" taken from Mary's "ivory womb," and comments: "We dwell to be sure in houses of clay, but what are of clay by reason of their material, come to be of ivory through the virtue of continence." Bodies are "sinks filled with dust," but if disciplined, they can become sanctuaries. "The ivory bodies of the saints are the house of Christ, they are Christ's garments, they are Christ's members, they are a temple of the Holy Spirit."[57]

54. Guerric, First sermon *In nativitate beatae mariae*, in *Sermons*, ed. Morson and Costello, vol. 2, pp. 478–85; trans. in *Liturgical Sermons*, sermon 51, vol. 2, pp. 195–97, esp. p. 197. The comparison of man to an inverted tree, embedded in a general description of the just as trees (based on Jeremiah 17.8), is also found in the second sermon *In festivitate sancti Benedicti*, chaps. 5–7, in *Sermons*, ed. Morson and Costello, vol. 2, pp. 64–73.

55. Guerric, Third Sermon for Easter, chap. 5, in *Sermons*, ed. Morson and Costello, vol. 2, p. 258; trans. in *Liturgical Sermons*, vol. 2, pp. 96–97.

56. Second Sermon for Easter, chap. 3, in *Sermons*, ed. Morson and Costello, vol. 2, pp. 236–38; trans. in *Liturgical Sermons*, vol. 2, pp. 88–89. Note that Guerric goes on then at considerable length about the evil returning to vomit, losing fertility, being barren ground, etc. (ed. Morson and Costello, pp. 238–40).

57. First Sermon for the Annunciation, chaps. 3–6, in *Sermons*, ed. Morson and Costello, vol. 2, pp. 112–25; trans. in *Liturgical Sermons*, sermon 26, vol. 2, pp. 34–38.

In general, Bernard's imagery is darker, less optimistic than Guerric's. His most elaborate use of metaphors of flowering and fertility in connection with resurrection comes in *On Loving God* and refers to the first resurrection, the flowering of virtue in the soul.[58] But even his discussions of spiritual growth make surprisingly little use of language of germination and flowering.[59] And when he applies images of organic change specifically to the body, they are usually negative images of rot and decay: the body—usually but not always in this context called the flesh—is a mass of pus, a cesspool, a heap of feces, or food for worms.[60] The glorified body we will receive at the end of time is endowed quite precisely with the gifts of imperviousness to change.[61] Bernard specifies that it will possess immortality so it does not become dust, impassibility so it does not experience suffering or disorder, lightness so it will have none of the downward pull of weight, and beauty so it will be clear and shining, with no spot of shadow or dirtiness.

Although eating and growth are sometimes positive images in his sermons, Bernard makes it quite clear that the body contains within itself no ability to flower. When he speaks of bodily resurrection in particular—and not of the general spiritual progress of the soul's rebirth—his favorite images are inanimate. The body is spoken of as a vessel, a lantern, or a treasure; it is the bed in which the palsied man of the gospel languished until told to take it up and walk (Mark 2.9–11); it is a garment (especially the white robe of Rev. 6.11) or a building (either the tabernacle of Ps. 90.10 or the temple of the Holy Ghost from 1 Cor. 6.19).[62] Most frequently of all, the body that will arise is called

58. Bernard, "On Loving God," chap. 3, paragrs. 7–10, in *Opera*, vol. 3, pp. 124–27, and in *Selected Works*, trans. Evans, pp. 179–82.

59. His Easter sermons are much less impregnated than are Guerric's, for example, with language of natural change.

60. See, for example, Bernard, "On Conversion," in *Opera*, vol. 4, pp. 69–116, esp. 75–79, 83–91, 94–95, 106–7; "On Consideration," bk. 5, chap. 4, paragr. 9, *Opera*, vol. 3, p. 473, lines 24–25; Sixth Sermon for Advent, in *Opera*, vol. 4, pp. 191–95; and Third and Fourth Sermons for All Saints (see n. 29).

61. See Sermon 4 for All Saints, *Opera*, vol. 5, pp. 354–60, and Sommerfeldt, "Body in Bernard." Bernard does not use the term *dotes*, but the idea that will later become that teaching is present in his writing, see Wicki, *Seligkeit*, pp. 202–9. See also, Herman of Reun, sermons 25 and 107, *Sermones*, ed. Mikkers, pp. 103 and 501.

62. Vessel or Lantern: Third Sermon for the Ascension, paragr. 3, in *Opera*, vol. 5, p. 132 (the reference here is to Christ's body). Treasure: Sermon on St. Malachy, ibid., vol. 5, p. 418, line 25. Bed: Sermon 4 for the Dedication of a Church, paragr. 4, ibid., vol. 5, p. 385. Garment: Sermon 10 on Psalm 90, paragr. 3, ibid., vol. 4, p. 445; sermon 34 in *De diversis*, chaps. 4–6, PL 183, cols. 632–34. Building: Sermon 10 on Ps. 90, *Opera*, vol. 4, pp. 442–47; Sermons 1, 2, and 4 for Dedication of a Church, ibid., vol. 5, pp. 370–78 and 383–88; Second Sermon for the Feast of the Assumption, ibid., vol. 3, pp. 238–44.

earth.[63] But this "earth" of the body refers neither to decaying mire or dung, pregnant only with pus or filth, nor to a garden or a sown field, fertile with life. The earth taken up at resurrection is dust. In his first sermon for All Saints, Bernard reads "blessed are the meek for they shall inherit the earth" (Matt. 5.5) as a reference to soul ("blessed"), which shall reign over the "earth" of the body; in his fourth sermon for the same day, he reads "earth" as "body" in Psalm 84.10 "that glory may dwell in our earth" and Psalm 71.19 "the whole earth may be filled with the majesty of the Lord."[64] In his sermon on the death of St. Malachy, he describes the holy man as depositing at Clairvaux "the earth of his body."[65]

To Bernard, body is not per se negative, although he (like Guerric) occasionally calls it a prison or a tomb. What is evil is sin, the responsibility for which lodges in the will (a part of the soul). But the change to which the body is subject is, to Bernard, primarily negative: of itself body is more often subject to decay than to positive transformation. This dark view of body is even more pronounced in Herman of Reun, Bernard's disciple. In a sermon for Advent Herman wrote:

> How can one who is going to die from the worm boast? . . . "Why is earth and ashes proud?" (Ecclesiasticus 10.9). . . . A child is conceived; perhaps it grows, perhaps it is aborted; nothing is certain. . . . Perhaps it is rich, perhaps poor . . . perhaps it grows sick, perhaps not; perhaps it is persecuted by the serpent, perhaps not; perhaps devoured by beasts, perhaps not . . . . With respect to every evil thing it is thus: perhaps it is so, perhaps it is not. But can you say: perhaps he dies, perhaps he does not? When we are born we begin at once to sicken. The sickness ends only with death. . . .
>
> Do you think man grows ill when he has a fever and is healthy when he is hungry? He is said to be healthy. But do you want to see how evil it can be to be hungry? Send him away without medicine. . . . If you refresh yourself too much you feel a deficit; too much drinking is worse than too little. . . . What therefore is this health, brother? Transitory, fragile, about to perish, vain.[66]

63. See, for example, Second Sermon for Christmas, paragr. 1, *Opera*, vol. 4, pp. 251–52: "Nam in primo quidem opere conditionis nostrae de limo terrae plasmavit hominem Deus. . . . Qualis artifex, qualis unitor rerum, ad cuius nutum sic conglutinantur sibi limus terrae et spiritus vitae. . . . Est tibi cum mundo corpus, sic enim decet eum qui constitutus est super universam huius creaturae corporae molem ex parte aliqua ei similari."

64. Sermon 1, paragr. 9, and sermon 4, paragr. 6, for All Saints, in *Opera*, vol. 5, pp. 334 and 359.

65. Sermon on St. Malachy, in *Opera*, vol. 5, pp. 417–23, esp. 417, line 17.

66. Herman, sermon 67, sections 4–5, in *Sermones*, ed. Mikkers, pp. 307–10.

To Herman, as to Bernard, change—even change (e.g., eating) that satisfies lack (e.g., hunger)—leads to further want. The basic model of bodily process is putrefaction; to live is to rot.[67] Glory means the absence of pain, want, putrefaction—that is, the absence of change. The body that rises is therefore described as a garment, put down at death and taken up again at the Last Judgment, uncorrupted by moth or decay. It is particles of dust, which can be joined together again into the temple they formed before. But the temple is now unchangeable, unthreatened by any organic process, any craving or want. It is in fact the same thing as the earthly body; but in its reassemblage it is purified, etherealized, beautified, and hardened into immutability.

In such images of re-collection and lightening, triumphant body conquers the decay to which matter is all too prone. Such images emphasize divine power as well; for they contain no suggestion that the body could, of itself, grow into glory. Bernard's actual use of language thus parallels scholastic rejection of the theory of resurrection as natural. His images also emphasize, as does scholastic debate, that material continuity is necessary for identity: exactly the body we have now will return. Bernard writes about St. Malachy:

> O good Jesus, that holy body is yours, put aside and entrusted to us. It is your treasure, deposited to our care. We shall keep it safe, to be returned to you in that time when you decide to demand its return. Only grant that it shall not go forth [to meet Christ] without its companions [i.e., the monks of Clairvaux], but let us have him as a leader whom we have had as a guest.[68]

---

67. See Bernard, Sermon 81 on the Song of Songs, chap. 3, paragr. 5, in *Opera*, vol. 2 (1958), p. 287: "Ego Dominus, et non mutor. Vera namque et integra immortalitas tam non recipit mutationem, quam nec finem, quod omnis mutatio quaedam mortis imitatio sit. Omne etenim quod mutatur, dum de uno ad aliud transit esse, quodammodo necesse est moriatur quod est, ut esse incipiat quod non est. Quod si tot mortes quot mutationes, ubi immortalitas?"

68. Bernard, Life of St. Malachy, chap. 31, paragr. 75, *Opera*, vol. 3, p. 378. In chap. 30, paragr. 67, *Opera*, vol. 3, p. 371, Bernard represents Malachy as saying that if he dies in Ireland, he wants to be able to rise again at the place where Patrick died; if he dies abroad, he wishes to await the resurrection at Clairvaux. After Malachy's canonization in 1191, he was buried beside Bernard.

Stephen Wilson points out that Bernard's request to be buried with the relic of St. Jude, recounted in his *vita*, was based on the hope that he would rise with the bone of the saint at the last day ("Introduction," in *Saints and Their Cults: Studies in Religious Sociology, Folklore, and History*, ed. S. Wilson [Cambridge: Cambridge University Press, 1983], p. 10).

In his description of his abbey's most precious possession, Bernard not only makes it clear that the relic is the resurrection body; he also speaks as if the relic is the saint.[69]

Bernard, moreover, goes beyond his patristic sources in stressing not just the necessity of body for personhood but also the necessity that the risen body be the material body of earth, numerically identical with it. Commenting on Psalm 90.8, he explicitly disagrees with Augustine, arguing that we will see God in the beatific vision with our bodily eyes. Without eyes, the soul cannot see fully even in heaven, and the eyes must be *these* eyes with which we see on earth.

"But thou shalt consider with thy eyes, and shall see the reward of the wicked." . . . [H]ere, in this short verse, the Prophet is manifestly proclaiming the immortality of the soul and confirming our faith in a bodily resurrection. For he clearly intimates that I shall survive to see the downfall of the demons, and shall contemplate with these eyes of flesh their final retribution. For it is not said simply, "Thou shalt consider with thy eyes," but "Thou shalt consider with thine own eyes," with those very eyes which now languish. . . . Think not that new organs of sight shall be given thee; no, but the former shall be restored . . . according to the promise of Truth itself, [that] not a single hair of our heads shall perish. . . .

. . . For at the resurrection, the eye shall be able to take in more than the ear, or even the mind takes in at present. It is, as I think, on account of the soul's most ardent desire to see what she already has heard of and believes, that another illustrious herald of the future resurrection has also made particular reference to the eyes: "I shall be clothed again with my skin, and in my flesh I shall see my God."[70]

Thus, to Hildegard, Herrad of Hohenbourg, Bernard, William of St. Thierry, Guerric, and Herman of Reun, resurrection was a lifting toward

---

69. This is not, of course, to deny that he argues in other passages that the separated soul experiences joy beyond this life and before resurrection or indeed that he sometimes speaks as if it is the saint. He speaks, for example, of Malachy going to God when he dies. And in his hymn for Malachy (*Opera*, vol. 3, p. 525), he says that "today" heavy flesh is lifted to heaven. In the later thirteenth century, Giles of Rome gave a useful explanation of both ways of speaking as synecdoche; see chapter 6, n. 116, below. For some perceptive remarks on this issue see Head, *Hagiography and the Cult of Saints*, pp. 144, 268.

70. Sermon 8 on Ps. 90, paragrs. 2–3, *Opera*, vol. 4, pp. 427–28; trans. by a Priest of Mount Melleray in *St. Bernard's Sermons for the Seasons and Principal Festivals of the Year*, (Dublin: Browne and Nolan, 1925), vol. 1, pp. 197–98 (with minor changes).

heaven of the body we possess on earth with all its specificity and religious attainment. The resurrection body was a recast vessel, a temple reconstructed from its scattered stones, a golden statue reforged from its original metal; it was flesh and bones reassembled from the particles and pieces of itself earlier dispersed by the four winds or by marauding beasts. Its resurrection and glorification at the end of time were guaranteed by divine power, which was strong enough not only to reconstitute it and reunite it with its soul when the trumpet blew but also to preserve it, during all the intervening years, from the decay or digestion that might threaten its being.

There is very little hint in the writings of Hildegard or Herrad, Bernard or William, that resurrection—either Christ's or ours—might be an open-ended transformation, a flowering of the Pauline seed into a different and glorious sheaf in heaven. Soul might flower, and its flowering might be expressed in body; indeed, soul needed body to be perfect and expressive and happy with God. But the body in which soul would reside at the end of time was the same body we possess on earth, reassembled or recast in the same shape and from the same particles.

Peter the Venerable and the Pauline Seed

The Pauline seed did not, however, vanish completely from twelfth-century spiritual writing. As we have seen, Cistercian authors sometimes used it to describe first resurrection. And as Guerric of Igny's extended metaphor of tomb as garden suggests, such descriptions of the soul's progress occasionally slip over into descriptions of the body as well. Located firmly in an ascetic context where discipline of the body is assumed and the moral attainments of earth are therefore projected into life after the grave, notions of germination and change no longer express an Erigenist implication that difference, particularity, and identity will be lost, that sheaf is different from seed. Now they are sometimes used, as they were in the second century, to describe the return at the end of time of the same body, made vastly more beautiful by the power of God. The sprouting seed, borne by a plant, gives rise to the same plant as before. We find such use of the Pauline seed metaphor, for example, in the beautiful letter written by the Cluniac abbot Peter the Venerable about the death of his mother and in Otto of Freising's vision of last things at the end of his historical work *The Two Cities*. In these works, confidence that person is really psychosomatic unity seems to win out, for a moment at least, over fears of decay and process, fears that identity and attainment will be lost. The vision is of person (soul and body) growing into grace.

It is perhaps no accident that Peter the Venerable's magnificent use of 1 Corinthians 15 occurs in a panegyric to a mother who was deeply loved and whose ascetic attainments could not be faulted.[71] Raingard had entered the monastery of Marcigny in 1117 after the death of her husband; her son Peter says her entry there was a burial. So "buried," she served as cellarer and as an example of holiness to her sisters until her death in 1135. In writing to his brothers about her ascetic accomplishments, Peter holds up her monastic (and metaphorical) burial and her final (and actual) one as inducements to hope and trust in God. He urges his brothers to see in the actual death of their mother the death of sin they languish in and therefore their need to die to the world. Your bodies cannot revivify unless they die, he says; they must putrefy so they can rise, dry (*arescere*) so they can flower. "The winter of this present life is to be tolerated and the harshness of rain and snow borne"; for the "fruitful sweetness of trees" has not yet appeared. You are not yet what you will be; your life is hidden with Christ. But "the time will come when the air will be clear and eternal spring will follow the cold." The earth, made fertile with marvelous warmth, will give forth in new flowers and fruits "the seeds of your bodies." "The corruptible will put on the incorruptible and the mortal immortality," writes Peter, "[therefore] . . . let her who was mother of your body generate your souls . . . lest you be like her in body [i.e., rotting] and dissimilar in soul." In such a passage, the literal and spiritual levels of discourse fuse, as do body and soul. Peter clearly speaks here of the woman who will rise again; her body will be transformed but identical, glorious but herself. But the Pauline seed refers also to first death and resurrection—that is, to the sin and redemption of the souls of his brothers existing still in their bodies of earth.[72]

There is one other important passage in Peter's writing that makes use of 1 Corinthians 15. In it, images of flowers and seeds appear alongside images of jewels and temples, vessels and clothes; resurrection is germination as well as reassemblage, the lability of plants as well as the hardness of crystal. But Peter's emphasis is more on stasis, continuity, and re-collection than on open-ended transformation. He is concerned about proper burial and about caring for every dispersed particle of the

71. Letter 53 in *The Letters of Peter the Venerable*, ed. Giles Constable (Cambridge, Mass.: Harvard University Press, 1967), vol. 1, pp. 153–73, and vol. 2, pp. 132–35.
72. See especially ibid., vol. 1, pp. 172–73.

dead. The passage is closer to Victricius of Rouen than to Erigena and Origen. And the context is relic cult. Peter writes to honor the relics of St. Marcellus, possibly on the anniversary of their translation to Cluny (sometime before January 6, 1109) or on the occasion of their transfer to a new reliquary.[73]

> The divine dignity divides his martyr into equal parts, so that he may retain his soul for himself among the mass of the blessed and give, with marvelous largess, the relics of his sacred body to be venerated by the faithful still living in the flesh. But suppose someone says: "what does it profit us to honor a lifeless body; what does it profit us to frequent with hymns and praise bones lacking in sense?" Let this kind of thinking be far from the hearts of the faithful. . . . God, the creator of spiritual and corporeal things, . . . established the human creature and, in an excellent operation, joined it together from rational spirit and flesh . . . , one person of man conjoined from [two] diverse substances. And glorifying the unity of the wonderful conjoining with felicity appropriate to the proper nature of each [of the diverse substances], he bestowed justice on the soul and incorruptibility on the body. . . . Therefore we know the spirits of the just will in the meanwhile live happily in the eternal life which we expect through faith, which he promises who is faithful in his words, and we anticipate for them a future resurrection in their bodies with immortality and in every sense incorruptibility. For this reason we do not debase as inanimate, despise as insensate, or trample under foot like the cadavers of dumb beasts the bodies of those who in this life cultivated justice; rather we venerate them as temples of the Lord, revere them as palaces of divinity, hoard them as pearls suitable for the crown of the eternal king, and, with the greatest devotion of which we are capable, preserve them as vessels of resurrection to be joined again to the blessed souls. . . .
>
> Behold whose bodies you venerate, brothers, in whose ashes you exalt, for whose bones you prepare golden sepulchres. They are sons

73. Giles Constable, "Petri Venerabilis Sermones Tres," *Revue bénédictine* 64 (1954), pp. 224–72, especially p. 231. Constable says that the fact that the sermon refers to *corpus* and *beata ossa* might mean it was not actually written for St. Marcellus since Cluny possessed only his head. But we should remember that John Beleth says in the twelfth century that a person was considered to be buried where his head was interred. We should also remember the tendency to use synecdoche to refer to the saints. A head might well be called "body" and "bones."

of God, equal to angels, sons of the resurrection. Hence you should receive them reverently as sons of God, extol them as equal to the angels with suitable praises, and expect that they will rise in their own flesh as sons of the resurrection. And in this hope I have confidence more certainly than in any human thing that you ought not to feel contempt for the bones of the present martyrs as if they were dry bones but should honor them now full of life as if they were in their future incorruption. . . . Flesh flowers from dryness and youth is remade from old age, and if you do not yet see this in your martyr it is supported by sacred authorities; do not despair of the future. Having therefore, dearest brothers, the author of the old law and the new grace, Jesus Christ, who promises to his servants the resurrection of the flesh and the glorification of human substance totally, first through the saints of old and afterwards through himself, and demonstrates [this resurrection] in his own body, we ought to reverence with due honor the body of this blessed martyr as about to be resurrected, as it will be clothed in immortal glory, although we see it as dead. . . .

. . . I say that the bodies of the saints live with God. . . . And that they live with God innumerable miracles everywhere on earth demonstrate, which miracles are frequently experienced by those who come to venerate their sepulchres with devout minds. . . . Isaiah says: "Your bones shall flourish [germinabunt] like an herb." Therefore because the bones of the present martyr shall flower like an herb, rising to eternal life, because the corruptible shall put on the incorruptible and the mortal the immortal, because this body of a just man snatched up to meet Christ shall always remain with him, who will not, with full affection, bring to be honored in this life what he believes will be elevated in the future glory.[74]

Peter can speak of bones germinating because he is sure those bones *are* the resurrection body. Any flesh that grows upon them will be similar to the flesh they wore here below. A "something" that continues undestroyed in the reliquary will "green" and "germinate" (*germinare*) at the end of time; even now it throbs with a potentiality that can spill over into miracles. Without body, there is no person to be redeemed, and Peter is certain that body is numerically one between earth and heaven because its hard particles lie undissolved in the earth until they

74. Peter the Venerable, "Sermo in honore sancti illius cuius reliquiae sunt in presenti," edited in Constable, "Petri Venerabilis Sermones Tres," pp. 265–72.

rise again, sprouting into fullness of structure and matter, when the trumpet sounds. First Corinthians 15 becomes, in his usage, a text that underlines material continuity and structural integrity in heaven.

Otto of Freising's Uneasy Synthesis: Resurrection "Clothed in a Double Mantle . . ."

In 1133 Otto of Freising, who had studied at Paris with Hugh of St. Victor and possibly with Abelard, suddenly joined the Cistercians.[75] Ten years later, he began to compose his great universal chronicle *The Two Cities*, which survives in his own revision of 1157. The eighth book, undertaken during Easter season (after a hiatus in which Otto was occupied with administrative duties), deals with the resurrection of the dead and the end (in both senses of the word) of history. Although Otto reports disagreements over eschatological matters and is himself far from fully consistent—manifesting as he does both literalist, millenarian ideas and a tendency to spiritualize—his eighth book is nonetheless a synthesis of scholastic and Cistercian concepts. Writing fifty years before Erigenist ideas were condemned, Otto was perhaps more comfortable than thirteenth-century thinkers would be with stressing a radical difference between spiritual and earthly bodies. Indeed so subtle, agile, and vaporous will we be in heaven that it is hard to see how we can be called material at all. But it never occurred to Otto that resurrection could mean loss of individuality or of identity: although ethereal, the risen body retained full structural integrity (no organs missing!) and full material continuity (no particles lost!). Thus the spiritual body we regain at the Last Judgment could now be spoken of (somewhat hesitantly) in metaphors of flowering and fertility; the Pauline seed and the embryological reading of Ezekiel 37 no longer seemed to imply either that bodies changed under their own impetus or that they changed so completely as to threaten survival of self. Body—earthly or spiritual—was the locus of difference (i.e., of inequality, above all, moral inequality) and of experience. Soul, which itself grew in life and beyond life in purgatory, was understood to need body to be fully itself; it needed body in order to inhabit heaven in its own particular "mansion" and in order to experience God as it deserved.

Otto's synthesis was an uneasy one. He vacillated both on how literally to take heaven and hell and on how the resurrection body was to

---

75. Otto is thus an excellent example of the combination of scholastic and monastic tendencies.

be understood. Toward the beginning of book 8, he asked what it could mean for heaven and earth to "pass away" and concluded, as had Tertullian hundreds of years before, that there could be change other than the transition "from being to nonbeing." Change could mean a "transfiguration from a present state to one far more beautiful." When Paul says (1 Cor. 7.31) that the fashion [*figura*] of the world "passes away," he means fashion, not nature, says Otto. Otto seems here to envision an earthly millennium in which the world is perfected and beautiful but not, so to speak, dematerialized.[76]

A little further along in his discussion, Otto grants that Greek theologians take such passages spiritually (that is, only "as similes").[77] But Otto asserts that it is better to take certain last things literally. Some think the valley of Jehosaphat is an allegory, he says, but it is preferable to hold that the Last Judgment occurs on earth: "It is more reasonable that bodies that were made of earth and that, because they were evil, were not changed to incorruption [i.e., the bodies of the damned], should be placed on earth for judgment than that they should be carried aloft to a rarer element with that weight."[78] Toward the end of book 8, Otto warns that heaven is not literally a place; "for what else is life eternal than purest blessedness?"[79] Elsewhere, however, Otto takes hell literally. He reports that "some" think the wicked in hell are tormented by fire and the worm; "others" take the worm of hell to mean "the sting of conscience" while the fire is understood literally; still "others" believe both tortures are spiritual. But "the more reasonable belief seems to be the view of those who say that the body is tormented by real flame, the soul by conscience."[80]

Just as Otto reports disagreement over how literally to understand heaven and hell, so he evidences inconsistency over the nature of res-

76. Otto of Freising, *Chronica sive historia de duabus civitatibus*, bk. 8, paragr. 9, pp. 403–4; *Two Cities*, trans. Mierow, p. 465. This seems to be what Otto means by: "Erit igitur non abolita substantia, sed mutata figura caelum novum, et terra nova, novo usui novo decore, novis corporibus decenter preparata omnique inequalitate ac squalore deterso ad instar paradisi Dei purificata."

77. *De duabus civitatibus*, bk. 8, paragr. 20, p. 419.

78. Ibid., paragr. 18, pp. 416–17; trans. Mierow, *Two Cities*, p. 478.

79. *De duabus civitatibus*, bk. 8, paragr. 33, p. 451; trans. Mierow, *Two Cities*, p. 509; and see above, chapter 3, nn. 68 and 74. See also *De duabus civitatibus*, bk. 8, paragr. 26, p. 436, where Otto says, about Rev. 21.18–21 ("the city is gold with twelve gates of pearl"): "If such things are beautiful and comely when they are interpreted literally, how much more are they found to be joyous and delightful far beyond compare when they are spiritually interpreted!" (trans. Mierow, *Two Cities*, p. 495)

80. *De duabus civitatibus*, bk. 8, paragr. 21, p. 424; trans. Mierow, *Two Cities*, pp. 484–85.

urrection bodies.[81] As modern scriptural exegetes still do, Otto focuses on 1 Corinthians 15.44 and 1 Corinthians 15.50 as the crucial texts.[82] He tells us that "some"—drawing on Paul—argue that the blessed will be transformed into spiritual substances; "others" argue that the saints will be bodies not spirits, but bodies of such fineness they cannot be handled or imagined. "But . . . we believe that our actual bodies shall rise in the actual substance of the flesh, after the likeness of our Lord, who said to his disciples after the resurrection, 'Handle me and see.' . . ." Thus Paul did not mean that the second Adam is without actual flesh; he meant rather that the body, which is "sown natural," will "rise spiritual" "because its defective substance is taken away, its true nature left." Although this particular gloss of Paul could be taken in an almost Origenist sense, Otto immediately again asserts that "true nature" means literal body; the saints "shall have in that City [i.e., the City of God—in this case, heaven] real bodies of the actual substance of flesh, but cleansed of all corruption."[83]

Otto makes it clear that the separated souls of the elect subsist and are purified after death; they are reembodied with spiritual bodies that will not taste or smell (although they will see).[84] These spiritual bodies have such purity and refinement and agility that they can be wherever they wish to be; indeed, says Otto (again sounding almost Origenist), we "ought not to ask *where* they are" since they are like the Lord after the resurrection, who entered through doors that were shut and *was* wherever he desired to be, in earth or in heaven.[85] Yet Otto also insists—following Augustine—that resurrection bodies have both structural integrity and material continuity. He repeats the standard catalogue of disasters and assures us that bodies return to the substances [i.e., persons] they were on earth whether "swallowed by waters, destroyed by flames, reduced to ashes in the bowels of the earth, devoured by beasts and incorporated in them, or scattered and spread abroad over various regions of the earth." He cites Augustine's accounts of disputes over

---

81. As I pointed out in chapter 3 above (at nn. 68–69), many of these accounts of disagreement are taken in toto from Augustine; such borrowing indicates that Otto and his predecessors have not made up their minds, and indeed Otto's own inconsistency indicates this as well. But such reports of ancient disputes do not necessarily mean that disputes were going on between figures in the schools although they may have been.

82. *De duabus civitatibus*, bk. 8, paragr. 27, pp. 436–37.

83. Ibid.; trans. Mierow, *Two Cities*, pp. 496–97.

84. *De duabus civitatibus*, bk. 8, paragr. 33, pp. 452–54; and see below, n. 86.

85. Ibid., paragr. 27, p. 438.

whether we rise in one sex or two and whether we rise at Christ's age or at the age of our individual deaths; in both cases, he takes Augustine's solution but without dogmatism.[86] He mentions explicitly problems of dwarves and giants, the lame and the mutilated, the fat, the thin, the blemished, hermaphrodites, monsters, Siamese twins, abortions and stillbirths, and those of "disagreeable" color.[87] He explains that death is dissolution; thus those caught up in the "twinkling of an eye" must in that instant be dissolved and recalled to life (although Otto also asserts that that verse can be given an allegorical meaning). Following Augustine, he defines beauty as "harmony of parts"; therefore, there can be no "defect or excess" in heaven. "Misshapen parts" must be corrected; lacunas must be supplied; "and that which is more than comely shall be removed, though the integrity of the matter is preserved." Thus, to Otto, the resurrection body is the same bits assembled in the same structure, however subtle, agile, and beautiful that reassemblage may be.[88]

Otto understood the implications of Augustine's discussion of "seeing" in heaven (*City of God*, book 22, chapter 29). And he went beyond Augustine, taking instead the position, implied by Bernard and William of St. Thierry, that body must add something in heaven.[89] "Some" think, he says, that God will be seen "with the heart only"; for Augustine argues that even if we close our eyes in heaven, we will see God. But Augustine "says many things in a nonauthoritative manner." Some therefore object to what he says and argue that God is seen in heaven in both ways. They argue that blessedness *is* seeing God; if therefore bodies are denied the vision, then the saints do not attain supreme blessedness. Indeed, Otto asserts, if vision of the heart alone were enough, heaven would not differ from our present condition; for "even now, when their bodies are moldering in the ground, the spirits and souls of the just behold God in heaven." To behold with both kinds of vision is to see "to the greater increase of blessedness, as though clothed in a double mantle, namely the flesh and the spirit." Such seeing is the eighth day that never ends. It has no evening. For the "rest of the saints" is "not terminated but doubled by the receiving of bodies."

---

86. Ibid., paragrs. 12–13, pp. 407–11. Augustine was himself, of course, undogmatic.

87. These latter are, he says explicitly, the Ethiopians. Ibid., p. 408.

88. Ibid., paragr. 12, pp. 407–9.

89. Ibid., paragr. 33, pp. 451–54; see above, chapter 2, p. 96, n. 135, on Augustine. Otto also goes beyond Hugh of St. Victor's *De sacramentis*, bk. 2, part 18, chap. 18, PL 176, col. 615, which says (following Augustine) that open eyes are not necessary for the vision of God.

There is, however, no equality in the heavenly rest. All receive a single shilling; all inhabit the same house, but "there are many mansions."[90] "The blessedness [will] be one . . . but there are differences in the enjoyment of that blessedness . . . even [as] in the present life, . . . in one Church we behold in the varying grades of honors one more glorious than another." "And even as when many together flock to one fountain, . . . he that is thirstier drinks more. . . . Therefore, in accordance with the diversity and capacity of individuals, the blessed glory of the saints will be varied and yet . . . one." As Gregory the Great preached in his Homilies on the Gospel, "separate individuals" will be "taken out of the elect" and lifted up higher into the "separate orders of the blessed spirits" according to their "rank of advancement."[91]

Like Peter the Venerable, Otto makes confident use of 1 Corinthians 15 to describe resurrection; he even adds to it the passage from Ezekiel 37 ("o ye dry bones . . .") so popular in the early church and in rabbinic exegesis but quite infrequent in twelfth-century texts. Ezekiel 37 is read as if it describes the formation of the embryo in the womb; the Pauline seed, the arid bones, the earth in winter, are all seen as dryness that must be freshened, watered, by God in order to sprout into life. The passage is about divine power; it is also about the appearance of incorruption from death and decay.

That the dead will rise again is not only affirmed by the Gospels and the Apostles and the teachers of the new law, but the fathers of old also foretold it. . . . In the book of Job we read: . . . I believe "that my Redeemer liveth, and on the last day I am to arise out of the earth" (Job 14.14 and 19.25). Note too the saying of Ezekiel: "O ye dry bones . . ." (Ezek. 37.7 and 12). . . . What, I ask you, what could be said more clearly and more plainly of a matter so mystical, so profound, so obscure? For he foretells that bones—and bones that are dry because they no longer have in them the power of life, but have physically lost their freshness—grow sinews, are clothed with flesh, are covered with skin, are spiritually reanimated and finally are by divine power led forth from the tombs. And yet by that argument of which Paul makes mention when he says, "that which thou . . . sowest is not quickened except it die first" (1 Cor. 15.36), we are also led to believe in the res-

90. *De duabus civitatibus*, bk. 8, paragrs. 29–32, pp. 439–48. This agrees exactly with Peter Lombard, bk. 4, distinctio 49, chap. 1, paragrs. 1 and 2, pp. 547–49.

91. *De duabus civitatibus*, bk. 8, paragrs. 29–32, pp. 439–48, esp. 440 and 448; trans. Mierow, *Two Cities*, pp. 499 and 506.

urrection, since every year we see the earth warmed by summer's heat, and after being so warmed, dried by the autumn's drought, and thus dried, dying in the winter's cold but aroused as from the dead when its freshness is revived by the kindly moisture of spring.[92]

Otto assumes that the sprouting seed, the reclothed bones, are the return of the same body, clad now in a glory and stasis that will prevent slime and rot from ever occurring again.

Otto, like Peter the Venerable, employs such language of growth and transformation in the context of discussing first as well as second resurrection. Indeed he connects the two resurrections as closely as do Guerric of Igny and Herman of Reun. Germination of a glorified body, changed to full incorruption and impassibility from the rotting body of earth, happens only for the just. John 5.28 ("the hour cometh . . .") means, says Otto, that Christ "can recall bodies that are ashes out of tombs." *All* will rise as reassembled ashes; for just and unjust alike, the identical body will return. But only the elect will be transformed. In this transformation, they will attain moral as well as physical immutability. They will be impassible as well as impartible, satiated and satisfied as well as eternal. At the heart of the glory of heaven is "incorruption." "Whosoever . . . shall have been raised in the first resurrection from the death of the soul shall in the second be changed and pass from corruptible to incorruption."[93]

Otto's images seem to reflect the same assumptions we find in his monastic and scholastic contemporaries. His basic eschatological metaphors are of triumph over decay, process, and digestion. They evoke change to a clear, subtle, crystalline version of the original body. Glorified body is an expression of the attainment of blessedness; it is also an expression of self. The sheaf, to Otto, is the return of the seed. Thus Otto's use of 1 Corinthians 15 or Ezekiel 37 is closer to the inorganic imagery of Honorius's *Elucidarium* than to the more Origenist language in the *Clavis physicae*. His plants are like the flowers in Honorius's heaven. And we do well to remember that when the *Elucidarium* says the blessed are like flowers, the analogy does not stress their difference from earth; it stresses their difference from each other. The elect have exactly the bodies they had in life, clothed over their nakedness with

92. *De duabus civitatibus*, bk. 8, paragr. 11, pp. 406–7; trans. Mierow, *Two Cities*, pp. 468–69.
93. *De duabus civitatibus*, bk. 8, intercisio and paragrs. 8–11, pp. 400–6, esp. 406; trans. Mierow, *Two Cities*, p. 469.

the colors of their virtues (the white of lilies for virgins, the red of roses for martyrs, etc.). A rose cannot be a lily even in paradise.

The Iconography of the General Resurrection: Devouring and Regurgitation of Fragments and Bones

Both scholastic and monastic writers in the twelfth century agreed that to be a "person"—that is, a "complete human being"—body is required as well as soul.[94] Although theological and devotional emphasis slowly shifted toward the experiences of an increasingly corporealized soul in the in-between period of purgation that came to be called "purgatory," resurrection could not be altogether ignored.[95] Body had to return. Scholastic writers mostly avoided organic imagery to describe this return, stressing instead the reconstruction of the body as temple or statue, the re-collection of body particles or dust. Monastic writers were more inclined to emphasize spiritual progress from time into eternity and to use, in discussing this, images of flowering or process. But when they spoke of body qua body, they often spoke of bones and bits. When verbs such as *reflorescere* or *germinare* were used of *caro* or *corpus*, "to flower" was the opposite of "to rot." What flowered was still the perduring dust or particles that had been laid in the earth. The resurrected body that was necessary for a person to be a person in heaven (or in hell) was fully continuous in both structure and matter with the body of earth. In monastic prose the metaphors used for body still saw it as bits and pieces, scattered abroad by death but re-collected at the end of time. Thus, neither monastic nor scholastic images suggested that body is anything other than physical or individual or integral in the resurrection or that there can be identity of body apart from material continuity.

Iconographic evidence reinforces our sense that the resurrection of the dead is, in the twelfth century, the regurgitation or reassemblage of exactly the body we possess on earth. From the Carolingian period to the early thirteenth century, depictions of resurrection frequently show the rising dead as bones still in their coffins or regurgitated body parts.[96] Damnation is eternal swallowing and digestion, eternal partition; the mouth of hell is a real mouth; second, final, definitive death is mastication. Redemption therefore is triumph over fragmentation, digestion, and rot—over natural process itself. In the miniatures of the *Hortus*

94. See above, chapter 3, n. 59.
95. See below, chapter 7, pp. 280–83.
96. See below, nn. 116, 117, and 134.

deliciarum (with which I began my third chapter), those who rise include skeletons still lying prone in their coffins, bodies emerging from sarcophagi entangled in shrouds, and body parts vomited up by birds, beasts, and fish in a visual setting forth of the chain consumption argument repeated so often in scholastic treatments of last things (see plates 1 and 2).[97]

By the late Middle Ages, matters were of course very different. Depictions of Christ's resurrection, such as the fifteenth-century Siennese altarpieces that show an ethereal Christ with wounds glowing like neon, present a transformed Savior.[98] The well-known Isenheim altar from the sixteenth century contrasts the hideously decaying cadaver of Christ on the predella with a pale, shining, almost wraithlike figure rising from the tomb.[99] Renaissance portrayals of the general resurrection of humanity at the end of time, such as Giotto's Arena chapel frescoes or Signorelli's San Brizio chapel at Orvieto, stress the ethereal splendor of the glorified body or the natural beauty of regenerated flesh.[100] In late medieval depictions of the resurrection, fully formed and even elegant bodies climb gracefully from the earth or from sarcophagi or receive rosy and attractive flesh as if it were growing on their bones (see plate 5). Indeed, despite the fascination with skeletons and death, bones are almost never depicted as rising, but if they are (as in Signorelli's magnificent fresco or in Jean Bellegambe's sixteenth-century panel painting of an angel reassembling parts), they are shown not naked but in the process of acquiring flesh.[101]

97. See above, chapter 3, nn. 4–9.

98. Keith Christiansen, Laurence B. Kanter, and C. B. Strehlke, eds., *Painting in Renaissance Siena: 1420–1500* (New York: The Metropolitan Museum of Art, 1988), pp. 134–35 and 142–43.

99. Ruth Mellinkoff, *The Devil at Isenheim: Reflections of Popular Belief in Grünewald's Altarpiece* (Berkeley: University of California Press, 1988), pp. 8–11.

100. For Giotto's *Last Judgment* in the Arena chapel, see Dorothy C. Shorr, "The Role of the Virgin in Giotto's *Last Judgment*," *Art Bulletin* 38 (1956): 207–14, especially plate 2. For Signorelli, see Massimo Carra, *Gli Affreschi del Signorelli ad Orvieto* (Milan: Fratelli Fabbri, and Geneva: Skira, 1965), pp. 24–29, and my *Fragmentation and Redemption*, plate 7.16, p. 292. For a list of the principal representations of the Last Judgment from the sixth to the fourteenth century, see Alison Morgan, *Dante and the Medieval Other World* (Cambridge: Cambridge University Press, 1990), pp. 199–200.

101. See above n. 100 on Signorelli. On Bellegambe, see Hans Posse, *Die Gemäldegalerie des Kaiser-Friedrich-Museums: Vollständiger beschreibender Katalog . . . ,* pt. 2: *Die Germanischen Länder* (Berlin: Julius Bared, 1911), pp. 147–48; and *Fragmentation and Redemption*, plate 7.17, p. 293. And see the sixteenth-century painting by Giorgio Ghisi, in Richard Cavendish, *Visions of Heaven and Hell* (London: Orbis, 1977), p. 60.

Twelfth-century depictions of the general resurrection, like later ones, are usually subordinated to other iconographic themes, such as the Last Judgment or the crucifixion.[102] Like later ones, they frequently show whole bodies rising from the earth in that scene conjured up by the brief scriptural accounts of resurrection.[103] But as Herrad's miniatures suggest, resurrection in twelfth-century iconography is also a scene not suggested by Scripture at all: the vomiting up of parts.

The iconography of the *Hortus deliciarum* is not original. Herrad's depiction of general resurrection is drawn from the so-called Byzantine Last Judgment, a complex iconographic program whose origins have been much disputed by art historians.[104] This program is best known in the West from the monumental eleventh-century mosaics at Torcello near Venice (see plate 6)[105] although a wall painting at Salonica from 1028 is probably the earliest example.[106]

102. Hubert Schrade, *Ikonographie der christlichen Kunst: Die Sinngehalte und Gestaltungsformen*, vol. 1: *Die Auferstehung Christi* (Berlin and Leipzig: de Gruyter, 1932); Gertrud Schiller, *Ikonographie der christlichen Kunst*, vol. 3: *Die Auferstehung und Erhöhung Christi* (Gütersloh: Mohn, 1971); and the works by Brenk cited in n. 104 below.

103. Revelation 20; Matthew 25; Mark 13. On Matthew, see Yves Christe, *La vision de Matthieu (XXIV–XXV): Origines et développement d'une image de la seconde Parousia* (Paris: Édition Klincksieck, 1973).

104. See G. Voss, *Das jüngste Gericht*; Gillen, *Ikonographische Studien zum Hortus Deliciarum*; Cames, *Allégories et symboles*; Beat Brenk, "Die Anfänge der Byzantinischen Weltgerichtsdarstellung," *Byzantinische Zeitschrift* 57 (1964): 106–26; idem, *Tradition und Neuerung*; and Selma Jónsdóttir, *An Eleventh-Century Byzantine Last Judgement in Iceland* (Reykjavík: Almenna Bókafélagið, 1959).

105. Renato Polacco, *La Cattedrale di Torcello: Il Giudizio Universale: Torcello Cathedral: The Universal Judgement* (Canova: L'Altra Riva, 1986); Wilhelm Paeseler, "Die römische Weltgerichtstafel im Vatikan (Ihre Stellung in der Geschichte des Weltgerichtsbildes und in der römischen Malerei des 13. Jahrhunderts)," *Kunstgeschichtliches Jahrbuch der Bibliotheca Hertziana* 2 (1938): 311–94, especially plates 275, 276, and 282; Jónsdóttir, *Byzantine Last Judgement in Iceland*, pp. 16–20; and Bynum, *Fragmentation and Redemption*, pp. 286–87. One of the leading experts on the Torcello mosaics, Irina Treadgold, has assured me that the portion that interests me is genuinely eleventh-century, not a restoration.

106. Brenk, "Die Anfänge," p. 119; idem, *Tradition und Neuerung*, p. 83. For other early examples, see Jónsdóttir, *Last Judgement in Iceland*; Kurt Weitzmann, "Byzantine Miniatures and Icon Painting in the Eleventh Century" (1966), reprinted in H. L. Kessler, ed., *Studies in Classical and Byzantine Manuscript Illuminations* (Chicago: University of Chicago Press, 1971), pp. 271–313, especially plates 303 and 304; John Galey, *Sinai and the Monastery of St. Catherine*, introductions by K. Weitzmann and G. Forsyth (New York: Doubleday, 1980), especially plates 104–6; André Grabar, *La Peinture religieuse en Bulgarie* (Paris: Librairie orientaliste Paul Geuthner, 1928), vol. 1, pp. 54–85; Deoclecio Redig de Campos, "Eine unbekannte Darstellung des jüngsten Gerichts aus dem elften Jahhundert," *Zeitschrift für Kunstgeschichte* 5 (1936): 124–33; Paeseler, "Die römische Weltgerichtstafel im Vatikan."

An eleventh-century Greek Gospel now in the Bibliothèque Nationale (BN Gr. 74) and the great Torcello west wall show us the various elements of the *Hortus* tracings assembled into a narrative whole.[107] The Greek Gospel illustrates Matthew 25.31–46 with a scene *not*, it is important to note, described in the text.[108] In the lowest level of hell we see body fragments. The artistic zone just above depicts fish regurgitating limbs and torsos while angels drive some of the damned toward Satan, who rides a beast just in the process of swallowing one of the unfortunate reprobate headfirst. In the next artistic zone an angel sounds the trumpet, while clothed dead rise from tombs, and beasts vomit up bodies and limbs. At the top, Christ in majesty sits with the elect, below whom to the left appear other groups of the blessed attired so as to indicate their earthly status and gender (see plate 7).

In the Torcello mosaic, the elements are arranged somewhat differently (see plate 6). Fragmented bodies appear at the very lower right, representing the most atrocious tortures of hell; just above them, Satan sits on a throne that devours sinners, and the damned, driven toward that throne by fierce angels, are depicted as decapitated heads. Halfway up the wall, beasts, birds, and fish in opposing and balanced oval spaces regurgitate parts, while four figures struggle out of their shrouds. At the top of the mosaic, poised above a Christ in majesty, an even larger Christ leads Adam out from hell, and the blessed rise whole from their tombs, clothed in the garments of glory.[109] Orthodox doctrine taught, as we have

107. For the Torcello mosaic, see n. 105 above. For BN Gr. 74 see Sirarpie der Nersessian, "Two Slavonic Parallels of the Greek Tetraevangelia: Paris 74," *The Art Bulletin* 9, no. 3 (1927): 223–74; Henri Omont, *Évangiles avec peintures byzantines du XIe siècle*, vol. 1: *Reproduction des 361 miniatures du manuscrit grec 74 de la Bibliothèque nationale* (Paris: Berthaud Frères, 1908), pp. 7, 11, 41, and 81; Brenk, *Tradition und Neuerung*, plate 24; and Gérard Cames, *Byzance et la Peinture romane de Germanie: Apports de l'art grec posticonoclaste à l'enluminure et à la fresque ottoniennes et romanes de Germanie dans les thèmes de majesté et les Évangiles* (Paris: A. and J. Picard, 1966), pp. 61, 94–98, 114–17, 158–59, and plate 204. We do not know, of course, exactly how the elements were assembled in the original from which the *Hortus* tracings were made, but it was probably closer to BN Gr. 74 than to Torcello. At some point a drawing of Satan in chains was inserted between the pages. See Walter, ed., *Hortus*, pp. 99–101 and plate 43.

108. BN Gr. 74, fol. 51v, illustrating Matthew 25.31–46, has the regurgitation of body parts, although the Matthew text does not speak of this. It is important to note that fol. 93v, which illustrates Mark 13.26–37 (a text that likewise does not mention regurgitation and reassemblage), has elements of the Byzantine Last Judgment, but does not include the body-parts motif. See Omont, *Évangiles*, vol. 1, pp. 41 and 81.

109. It is also important to note that the blessed grouped around Christ are highly individualized, clearly male and female and of different earthly roles. The decapitated heads driven toward hell are individualized as well. In the Byzantine ivory in the

seen, that all are reassembled at the Last Judgment, damned as well as saved, but this is *not* the visual message given by either the Gospel miniature or by the even more narratively coherent west wall.[110] What is illustrated is the association of wholeness with salvation, fragmentation with hell. The Torcello mosaic lifts the eyes of the viewer from decapitated heads, worm-eaten skulls, and body fragments (representing sins), through the moment of regurgitation and reassemblage,[111] up to the place where intact and incorrupt bodies rise shining into the presence of God. Salvation is the triumph of whole over part.

In addition to associating resurrection with Judgment, the *Hortus deliciarum* associates resurrection with crucifixion. The moment of death on the cross is presented not as defeat but as victory, because it is both the birth of church and the raising of the dead. Below the dying Christ, Herrad or her artist-collaborators show three coffins; from two rise those whom Christ resuscitated, in the third lies the skeleton of Adam.[112] Once again the iconography is not original. For example, in a depiction of the crucifixion from a medical text of 1132—about fifty years before the *Hortus*—the dead who rise beneath the cross, still in their shrouds,

Victoria and Albert Museum, the throne has four devouring mouths that swallow the damned in pieces; see Brenk, *Tradition und Neuerung*, plate 23; Alice Turner and Anne Stainton, "The Golden Age of Hell: A Guided Tour Through the Brilliant Inferno of the Twelfth Century," *Art and Antiques* (January 1991): 57.

110. There was disagreement, however, over whether the defects of the damned were repaired; see below chapter 6, pp. 265–66. For a discussion of the implications of this question for medieval drama, see Meg Twycross, " 'With what body shall they come?': Black and White Souls in the English Mystery Plays," *Langland, the Mystics, and the Medieval English Religious Tradition: Essays in Honour of S. S. Hussey*, ed. Helen Phillips (Cambridge: D. S. Brewer, 1990), pp. 271–86.

111. The depiction of events associated with the Pauline "twinkling of an eye"— that is, the sounding of trumpets and the rolling up of the heavens—underlines the impression that zone three depicts the moment of resurrection in the larger drama of the Last Judgment.

112. The rubrics tell us that the central grave is Adam's: "Sepulchrum Ade; Jheronimus refert quod Adam sepultus fuerit in Calvarie loco ubi crucifixus est Dominus." The other dead, now awakening, seem to be the saints referred to in Matthew 27.52, for the passage is inscribed here: "Monumenta aperta sunt et multa corpora sanctorum surrexerunt" (Herrad, *Hortus*, fol. 150, *Reconstruction*, plate 93, drawing 212, p. 174). See above chapter 3, n. 5. As Anna Kartsonis points out, the Anastasis (harrowing of hell) and the crucifixion sometimes merge in the Byzantine iconographic tradition; in such cases, the kings of the Old Testament can be shown rising beneath the cross alongside Adam and Eve. See the eleventh- or twelfth-century ivory book cover from Leningrad that depicts David and Solomon rising together with Adam and Eve (*Anastasis: The Making of an Image* [Princeton: Princeton University Press, 1986], pp. 146–50 and plate 49). See also Beat Brenk, "Auferstehung der Toten," *Lexikon der christlichen Ikonographie*, vol. 1 (Rome, Freiburg: Herder, 1968), cols. 219–22, especially col. 221.

are Lazarus, the saints referred to in Matthew 27.52 (which is inscribed here), and Adam (see plate 8).[113] In many twelfth-century crucifixions, Adam, lying below the cross, becomes simply a bone or two (see plate 9).[114] Such iconography illustrates the popular legend that Christ was executed in the very spot where Adam was buried and on the same tree that had led the first man into sin.[115] But more is involved. In Herrad's depiction, Christ's death is the reanimation of others, and the humanity under the cross is bones. We should remember that the figures who rise from sarcophagi in her Last Judgment are drawn enfleshed but labeled *ossa mortuorum*, and that the *membra olim devorata* rise *incorrupta*. What we see in the *Hortus* drawing of the crucifixion are the moments of resurrection occurring simultaneously—death, bones (or fragmentation), and restoration (or reassemblage).

Such presentations of resurrection as the various stages of reanimation of a corpse are not infrequent in earlier English, Carolingian, and Ottonian art. In an eighth-century Anglo-Saxon ivory, for example, we find bodies at various stages of resuscitation: lying, still wrapped in grave clothes; sitting or standing, entangled in shrouds; fully alive again, with their souls (shown as doves) flying in at the mouth (see plate 10). The mid-ninth-century ivory used on the cover of the Book of Pericopes of the German emperor Henry II depicts the general resurrection with the same motifs. One of the earliest artistic representations of the resurrection of Christ (the tenth-century Cross of the Scriptures at Clonmacnois in Ireland) shows the body of Jesus still shrouded and prone in the tomb with its soul entering its mouth as a dove.[116] Even in the thirteenth

113. Staatsbibliothek MS lat. qu. 198, fol. 320v, in Gerard Achten, ed., *Das christliche Gebetbuch im Mittelalter: Andachts- und Stundenbücher in Handschrift und Frühdruck*, Staatsbibliothek Preussischer Kulturbesitz: Ausstellung, 29. Mai–14. August, 1980, und Katalog (West Berlin: Staatsbibliothek, 1980), pp. 61–63.

114. For Adam as bones, see Arthur Haseloff, *Eine thüringisch-sächsische Malerschule des 13. Jahrhunderts* (Strassburg: Heitz and Muendel, 1897; Kraus Reprint, 1979), plates 87, 96, and 112; Hanns Swarzenski, *Die lateinischen illuminierten Handschriften des XIII. Jahrhunderts in den Ländern an Rhein, Main, und Donau* (Berlin: Deutscher Verein für Kunstwissenschaft, 1936), vol. 2, plate 938. For Adam rising under the cross, see idem, *Vorgotische Miniaturen: Die ersten Jahrhunderte deutscher Malerei* (Leipzig: Karl Robert Langewiesche Verlag, 1931), p. 62; Gertrud Schiller, *Iconography of Christian Art*, vol. 2: *The Passion of Jesus Christ*, trans. Janet Seligman (Greenwich, Connecticut: New York Graphic Society, 1972), pp. 113–14 and plates 365, 377, 381, 387, 409, 410.

115. See Walter, ed., *Hortus*, p. 88.

116. See *Fragmentation and Redemption*, pp. 284 and 289, plate 7.13. For the Pericopes of Henry II, see Schiller, *Iconography*, vol. 2: *Passion*, plate 365; and cf. plates 371, 373, 377. A similar example is the cover of the psalter from Aldersbach (mid-thirteenth century); Swarzenski, *Die lateinischen illuminierten Handschriften*,

century there is sometimes something skeletal (or only partially revived) about rising bodies (see plate 11).[117]

Moreover, in Herrad's depiction of the preparation for crucifixion, located in the *Hortus* just above the picture of Christ's death on the cross, an inscription describes that death as victory over the mouth and stomach of Leviathan. Using a passage borrowed from the *Speculum ecclesiae* of Honorius Augustodunensis, the artist explains that the first man was "lost in the sea of the world"; Leviathan "digested" [*absorbuit*] him. He is, however, saved when Christ pierces the monster's throat with the tip of the tree of life and forces him to "vomit up" those whom he has unjustly devoured [*evomeret quos . . . devorasset*].[118] The theme of salvation as regurgitation, found in the Last Judgment composition, thus continues here in word if not in image. The colorful and graphic depiction of hell in the *Hortus* also associates its torments with tearing, dividing, masticating, and swallowing (see plate 3). Antichrist's throne eats sinners, and decapitated heads are pressed under its claws; a demon forces money into the mouth of a greedy man; Jews are boiled in a cooking pot; a woman eats her child.

This use of eating to represent destruction is no more original than Herrad's other literary and iconographic motifs. The devouring throne on which Satan sits is a standard element of Byzantine iconography of the Last Judgment, and the depiction of hell as a mouth or a monster that swallows and is forced by Christ at the harrowing to regurgitate souls, is found in many twelfth-century manuscripts.[119] An English psal-

---

vol. 1, p. 109, and vol. 2, plate 326a (bottom panel). On the Clonmacnois High Cross, see Roger Stalley, *Irish High Crosses* (Dublin: Eason and Son, 1991), plate 25; the panel in question is the first scene above the base on the crucifixion side. Similar scenes appear on the contemporary high crosses at Kells, Durrow, and Monasterboice.

117. *Apokalypse: MS Douce 180 der Bodleian Library, Oxford* (Graz: Akademische Druck- und Verlagsanstalt, 1981), miniature accompanying Rev. 20.4, p. 86. See also the casket of St. Servatius (1170–80) on which the newly resurrected, still naked *justi* are shown being clothed by angels with the robes of immortality. An inscription reads: *Indue immortalem.* In the gilded copperwork, the torsos and arms of these *justi* appear to be depicted as rib cages and unfleshed upper-arm bones. See Suzanne Collon-Gevaert, Jean Lejeune, and Jacques Stiennon, *A Treasury of Romanesque Art: Metalwork, Illuminations, and Sculpture from the Valley of the Meuse*, trans. S. Waterston (New York: Phaidon, 1972), pp. 242–44 and plates. For another example in which the rising dead appear surprisingly cadaverous, see the Bamberg psalter in Swarzenski, *Die lateinischen illuminierten Handschriften*, vol. 2, plate 792.

118. Herrad, *Hortus*, fol. 150, *Reconstruction*, plate 93, drawing 211, p. 173. See also Caratzas, Straub, and Keller, ed., *Hortus*, p. 150.

119. On the motif of the mouth of hell and its connection with the Leviathan of Job 41, see Hughes, *Heaven and Hell in Western Art*, pp. 175–201. See also Camporesi, *The Fear of Hell*, chapters 12 and 13, and Joyce Ruth Galpern, "The Shape of Hell in

ter from mid-century, for example, shows an angel locking damned souls into a yawning mouth;[120] a contemporary miniature shows the risen Christ forcing a staff into hell's gullet in order to induce vomiting (see plates 12 and 13).[121] Apocalypse manuscripts sometimes show the same mouth for descent into and escape from hell.[122] Jonah, swallowed but not digested by the whale, was a symbol of death and resurrection throughout the Middle Ages (see plate 14). The regurgitated prophet served as symbol of the risen Christ as early as the third century;[123] the sculpture, stained glass, moralized Bibles, and *Biblia pauperum* of the twelfth to fourteenth centuries regularly associated the entombed and rising Christ with Jonah's loss overboard and his miraculous return.[124]

Anglo-Saxon England" (Ph.D. diss., University of California at Berkeley, 1977), pp. 119–54 and figures 2–4, 7, 11–13, 16–21, and 23–25.

120. Leaf from the Winchester Psalter of 1150–60, British Library MS 1846 Cott. Nero, chap. 4, fol. 39; see Turner and Stainton, "The Golden Age of Hell," pp. 46–57, especially plate on p. 47. Note that the motif of mouths repeats itself; both the corners and the center of the big mouths are little mouths. For other examples of hell's mouth and of damnation as mastication, see Shorr, "The Virgin in Giotto's *Last Judgment*," plates 7 and 9; Morgan, *Dante and the Other World*, pp. 15–16 and 23, plates 2, 3, and 6; and Hughes, *Heaven and Hell in Western Art*, pp. 175–201.

121. Harrowing of hell from English Psalter of ca. 1170–83, MS Douce 293, fol. 14r; see also Haseloff, *Eine thüringisch-sächsische Malerschule des 13. Jahrunderts*, plates 16, 42, and 109; and Swarzenski, *Die lateinischen illuminierten Handschriften*, vol. 2, plate 768. For a literary treatment that suggests the same association of images, see below n. 139. For the theme in Mannerist architecture, see Hughes, *Heaven and Hell in Western Art*, p. 199: a reproduction of the *bocca d'Inferno*, built by Pierfrancesco Orsini in the mid-sixteenth century. Stone stairs lead up to a large and fearsome mouth-entrance, inside which is a dining room.

122. See, for example, *The Dublin Apocalypse*, ed. Montague Rhodes James (Cambridge: Printed for the Roxburghe Club by the Cambridge University Press, 1932), plates 63, 69, 70, and pp. 18–19; Peter H. Brieger, *The Trinity College Apocalypse: An Introduction and Description* (London: Eugrammia Press, 1967), p. 48 and folio 25r (from 1225–50); and see Turner and Stainton, "The Golden Age of Hell," plate on p. 55.

123. *The Gold-Glass Collection of the Vatican Library with Additional Catalogues of Other Gold-Glass Collections*, ed. Guy Ferrari, Catalogo del Museo Sacro della Biblioteca apostolica vaticano, vol. 4 (Vatican City: Biblioteca apostolica vaticana, 1959), number 421 (Inv. 991), pp. 68–69.

124. The theme is common in pulpit sculptures and mosaics from the mid-eleventh to mid-thirteenth centuries; see Dorothy Glass, "Sicily and Campania: The Twelfth-Century Renaissance," *Acta*, vol. 2: *The Twelfth Century* (Binghamton: Center for Medieval and Renaissance Studies, State University of New York at Binghamton, 1975), pp. 140–42. Examples of manuscript illumination include a psalter from mid-thirteenth-century Würzburg (Munich: Bayerische Staatsbibliothek, Clm 3900, fols. 81v and 82) and a mid-thirteenth-century historiated Bible (Windsor: Eton College Library, MS 177, fol. 5v) from the English Midlands, related to lost glass paintings in the Chapter House at Worcester cathedral. In the former, the three Maries at the empty tomb face an elaborate floral design in which Christ sits triumphant above a regurgitated Jonah (see plate 14 in this volume and Swarzenski, *Die lateinischen illuminierten Handschriften*, vol. 2, plates 946–47). The latter shows Jonah vomited

In the famous Last Judgment tympanum from Conques, the association of being-devoured with hell and disorder (on the right) and of rising-whole with order (left) is obvious (see plate 15).[125] Nor should we forget the puzzling allegories of the battles of vice and virtue found on Romanesque columns and capitals (for example, the famous beast-column in the crypt of Otto's own church at Freising).[126] In such sculptures, the vices are depicted as especially threatening insofar as they actually eat the good.

The iconographic motif of resurrection as regurgitated parts and hell as a swallowing mouth finds its fullest development in the East and continues down into modern times in Greek, Bulgarian, and Russian frescoes.[127] In such depictions, the river of fire, which runs down from Christ's throne, becomes more river than fire; Jonah's whale becomes hell. In a splendid sixteenth-century example from the refectory at Lavra

---

up before Nineveh, the three Maries at the tomb, a lion resuscitating another lion with its breath, and portraits of Job and Jonah, the two prophets of resurrection. See Montague Rhodes James, *A Descriptive Catalogue of the Manuscripts in the Library of Eton College* (Cambridge: Cambridge University Press, 1895), pp. 100–1, and Neil Ripley Ker, *Medieval Manuscripts in British Libraries* (Oxford: Clarendon Press, 1969–77), vol. 2, p. 772. An early fourteenth-century *Biblia pauperum* that came to Weimar from Peterskloster in Erfurt draws a parallel between the entombment of Christ and the casting overboard of Jonah on folio 7v, and on folio 8r a parallel between the resurrection and Jonah emerging from Leviathan's mouth (Hans von der Gabelentz, ed., *Die Biblia pauperum und Apokalypse der grossherzogl. Bibliothek zu Weimar* [Strassburg: Heitz and Muendel, 1912], pp. 16, 28–29, and plates 14–15); see also p. 48 for a table listing other Bibles with the same depiction.

125. For the difficulties in dating the church and tympanum, see Jean-Claude Bonne, *L'Art roman de face et de profil: Le tympan de Conques* (Paris: Le Sycomore, 1984), pp. 313–17.

126. See Albert Elsen, "Die Bestiensäule in der Freisinger Domgruft," *Festschrift Kardinal Faulhaber zum achtzigsten Geburtstag, dargebracht vom Professorenkollegium der philosophisch-theologischen Hochschule Freising* (Munich: J. Pfeiffer, 1949), pp. 249–74; Wolfgang Stammler, "Die Freisinger Bestiensäule und Bischof Otto II," *Studien zur deutschen Philologie des Mittelalters: Friedrich Panzer zum 80. Geburtstag am 4. September 1950 dargebracht*, ed. Richard Kienast (Heidelberg: C. Winter, 1950), pp. 38–44; Franz Dietheuer, "Die Bestiensäule in der Freisinger Domkrypta," *Oberbayerisches Archiv für Vaterländische Geschichte* 101 (1976): 339–80; Anton Legner, *Deutsche Kunst der Romanik* (Munich: Hirmer, 1982), p. 155 and plate 93.

127. See Nersessian, "Two Slavonic Parallels of the Greek Tetraevangelia"; Grabar, *La Peinture religieuse en Bulgarie*, pp. 291–92, 324, 333–34; Paul A. Underwood, "Third Preliminary Report on the Restoration of the Frescoes in the Kariye Camii at Istanbul by the Byzantine Institute (1956)," *Dumbarton Oaks Papers* 12 (Cambridge, Mass.: Harvard, 1958), pp. 235–65, especially pp. 241, 243, 256, 259–60; *The Frescoes of the Church of the Savior at Nereditsa* (Leningrad: Russian State Museum, 1925), plates 73–75; and n. 128 below.

on Mount Athos, for example, the entire flood (containing within it Satan on his devouring throne) is swallowed by a huge fish's mouth; just above it, a veritable menagerie of beasts, occupying more than half of an enormous wall, are busy vomiting up parts for reassemblage (see plate 16).[128] Such motifs drop out of Western art after the early thirteenth century.[129] They are, however, found in a number of twelfth-century Western examples, which often recombine the elements of the Byzantine Last Judgment quite creatively or even utilize non-Byzantine motifs of salvation as regurgitation.

For example, a tempera painting of disputed date,[130] now in the Vatican museum, shows the head of a damned person attacked by the mouth of a snakelike monster in zone five and depicts both regurgitated parts and rising corpses in zone four. The parts, called by the Latin inscription *menbra* [sic] *vorata*, are here drawn so schematically that they appear to be bones and skulls rather than the enfleshed body fragments usual in such Last Judgments; moreover, the inscription also names the

128. See Gabriel Millet, *Monuments de l'Athos relevés avec le concours de l'Armée française d'Orient et de l'École françaises d'Athènes*, vol. 1: *Les Peintures* (Paris: Librairie Leroux, 1927), plate 149; and Charles Diehl, *Manuel d'art byzantin*, vol. 2 (2d ed., Paris: Picard, 1926), p. 854. The presence of the theme of damnation as swallowing, resurrection as regurgitation, on a refectory (!) wall is striking. In the narthex of the monastery of Docheiariou, also on Mount Athos, there is an equally detailed sixteenth-century resurrection scene in which dozens of animals, birds, and fish regurgitate parts with the heads outward, while a few skeletal yet whole figures break out from the earth. In the flood of hell, bodies are devoured headfirst (i.e., the feet are outward), and detached heads roll in the waves. See Millet, *Monuments*, vol. 1: *Les Peintures*, plate 247.

129. The thirteenth-century Greek and Latin psalter, known as the Hamilton psalter (Hamilton 119 [Beckford 511], fols. 110v and 111r, illustrating Ps. 49.4), now in Berlin, may be one of the latest examples; see Paul Wescher, ed., *Beschreibendes Verzeichnis der Miniaturen: Handschriften und Einzelblätter des Kupferstichkabinetts der Staatlichen Museen Berlin* (Leipzig: J. J. Weber, 1931), pp. 25–30. I have examined this psalter under special light and the motif of regurgitated parts is clearly visible. The fourteenth-century fresco in Santa Maria del Casale in Brindisi appears to me, from the photographs I have been able to consult, to depict enfleshed bodies swimming out of the waves, bones and skulls in a cavity in the earth, and animals rendering up parts. Other elements of the Byzantine Last Judgment are present in the iconography, and the moment is clearly resurrection, for we see angels blowing the final trump and rolling up the skies. See Alfredo Petrucci, *Cattedrali di Puglia*, 2d ed. (Rome: Carlo Bestetti, 1964), pp. 113, 115, 117, and plate 239.

130. Dates for the painting range from the late eleventh to the early thirteenth century; see De Campos, "Eine unbekannte Darstellung des jüngsten Gerichts," and Paeseler, "Die römische Weltgerichtstafel im Vatikan." Chiara Frugoni, "La femme imaginée," in *Histoire des femmes en occident* (Paris: Plon, 1991), pp. 371–75, argues that the painting was commissioned by a woman and shows a woman's sensitivity to "sins of word."

figures rising from the sarcophagi as the painters Nicolaus and Johannes and states that they rise *de pulvere terrae*.

The motif of restored body parts turns up as far afield as Iceland in a wood carving from Flatatunga, dated about 1070. In the surviving fragments, a seallike creature seems to carry a head. Two fish, one with the overshot upper jaw found in other such Last Judgments, bring a foot and a hand for restoration. As we find in some other Western examples (indeed in the *Hortus deliciarum* itself), the figure emerging from the mouth of the devouring animal-headed throne has been reversed so that it almost appears to be vomited up rather than eaten, but destruction is still suggested by the fact that teeth pierce it.[131]

The theme of reconstituted body parts shows up, divorced from the Byzantine iconographic program, in two thirteenth-century German psalters, one from Würzburg, the other from Bamberg-Eichstätt. The Bamberg-Eichstätt psalter seems to combine earlier Ottonian depictions of reviving corpses with the motif of reassemblage. In the center of the miniature, a cadaverous figure rises in a shroud, disentangles itself, and dons the garment of glory. To either side in the bottom register appear bodies with parts missing—something not found in Byzantine examples—while just above them are animals who carry exactly the bits needed for reattachment (plate 17).[132] In the little-known Würzburg example, which occurs on the other side of a folio giving prayers for the dead, two naked figures rise from a large coffin, below which appears a rather cheerful beast with a hand in its mouth. One of the men is missing his arm below the elbow and the creature obligingly offers a replacement with the cut part up for easy reassemblage. Examination of the original manuscript reveals that the artist first painted a whole arm and then reworked the little picture to show the beast offering a severed part (see plate 18).[133]

There are, moreover, two early Apocalypse manuscripts—probably dating from the early ninth and tenth century, respectively—in which the motif of reassembled fragments is depicted in a fashion that may derive from earlier models but appears unconnected to the Byzantine

131. Jónsdóttir, *Last Judgement in Iceland*.

132. Psalter from Bamberg-Eichstätt, MS 1903 (olim 1833), fol. 109v, Stiftsbibliothek, Melk (ca. 1255); Swarzenski, *Die lateinischen illuminierten Handschriften*, vol. 1, p. 163, especially n. 8, and *Fragmentation and Redemption*, pp. 284, 288, and 414.

133. Psalter and Breviary from Würzburg, MS Cim 15, fol. 204r, Universitätsbibliothek, Munich.

Last Judgment composition.[134] In the earlier, Trier Apocalypse, the parts are clearly to be understood as given up by the sea, and the presence of three hands suggests that more than one body is being reassembled.

Art historians used to trace such motifs back to early Christian models. They even suggested—despite the complete absence of an iconography of the Last Judgment before the early eleventh century—that Byzantine eschatological motifs had their origins in the writings of Ephraim, or pseudo-Ephraim, the Syriac. More recent work, however, attributes the creation of these visual themes to the posticonoclastic East and the Carolingian-Ottonian West.[135]

There were, of course, occasional depictions in ancient pre-Christian and Christian art of the dry bones of Ezekiel 37. The third-century paintings of Dura-Europos are well known.[136] Moreover, certain natural symbols on sarcophagi (for example, the cock, the egg, the tree, the eagle, the phoenix) may indeed have been symbols of resurrection, as art historians used to assert. But it is very difficult to be sure what an isolated and probably allegorical figure on a sarcophagus means. And it is clear from the work of Schrade, Dobschütz, Brenk, and others that depictions of the general resurrection of humankind begin to appear only in the eighth century and only as part of other scenes (chiefly the crucifixion and Last Judgment); the mysterious moment of the resurrection of Christ was not directly depicted in art before the twelfth cen-

---

134. Trier Apocalypse, MS 31, fol. 67r, Stadtbibliothek Trier (ninth century); see Richard Laufner and Peter Klein, eds., *Trierer Apokalypse: Vollständige Faksimile-Ausgabe im Originalformat des Codex 31 der Stadtbibliothek Trier: Kommentarband* (Graz: Akademische Druck- und Verlagsanstalt, 1975); James Snyder, "The Reconstruction of an Early Christian Cycle of Illustrations for the Book of Revelation: The Trier Apocalypse," *Vigiliae Christianae* 18 (1964): 142–62; and *Fragmentation and Redemption,* pp. 284, 289, and 415. On the closely related Cambrai Apocalypse, see Henri Omont, "Manuscrits illustrés de l'Apocalypse aux IX et X siècles," *Bulletin de la Société de Reproductions de Manuscrits à Peintures* 6 (1922): 62–64, 84–86, 93–94, and plate 31.

135. See Voss, *Das jüngste Gericht;* Gillen, *Ikonographische Studien zum Hortus deliciarum,* p. 19; Paeseler, "Die römische Weltgerichtstafel im Vatikan"; Brenk, "Die Anfänge"; and idem, *Tradition und Neuerung.* On the theme in Ephraim, see above chapter 2, nn. 59–63.

136. See Brenk, "Auferstehung der Toten," cols. 219–220; E. von Dobschütz, "Die Vision des Ezekiel (cap. 37) auf einer byzantinischen Elfenbeinplatte," *Repertorium für Kunstwissenschaft,* ed. H. Thode and H. von Tschudi (Berlin: Georg Reimer, 1903; reprint, 1968), pp. 382–88; and see the miniature of Gregory Nazianzus preaching on Ezekiel's vision of the bones in MS BN Gr. 510, fol. 438v, reproduced in Henri Omont, *Facsimiles des miniatures des plus anciens manuscrits grecs de la Bibliothèque Nationale du VIe au XIe siècle (Mss. Supplement grec 1286; Grecs 139 et 510; Coislin 79; Supplement grec 247)* (Paris: Leroux, 1902), plate 58.

tury.[137] Iconographic evidence strongly supports the sense we derive from scholastic debates and contemporary devotional and exegetical writing that the eleventh and twelfth centuries forged from earlier materials a strikingly materialist conception of the fate of humankind at the end of time.

Pictures of the devouring mouth of hell and the resurrection of eaten hands and feet, schoolroom debates over the destiny of cannibalized flesh, prayerful pleas to God to raise up the ordinary worshiper when he calls to himself the bodies of his saints—all this evidence suggests that partition, decay, and digestion were the most fearful destruction twelfth-century writers could imagine. "Death" (mors) was named from "bite" (morsus), as Honorius pointed out. The noun for place or container of burial (sarcophagus) meant "to eat" "flesh"—or so the liturgists John Beleth and Sicard of Cremona asserted.[138] Small wonder then that the defeat of death was depicted as a whale casting up its swallowed (but not digested) victim, a bird returning a stolen arm *that is still an arm* to its previous body, a victorious Son of God leading souls out from the mouth (literally the *mouth*) of hell to await clothing by their bodies when the trumpet sounds.

The scholastic, monastic, and iconographic representations of death and redemption discussed in this chapter and the previous one were in many ways very different. Schoolmen focused on issues of identity and integrity and stressed resurrection as reassemblage both of body and of person; monks and nuns focused more on affective growth and emphasized the resurrection of the spirit from sin; visual artists stressed bones and bodies and depicted revivification and judgment at the end of time. But behind these specific emphases lay a common fear—the fear of corruption, physical as well as moral. Thus the Benedictine author Peter of Celle, when he writes metaphorically of the power of prayer to defeat death, gives a description so specific and graphic it seems almost a gloss

137. Schrade, *Ikonographie*, vol. 1: *Die Auferstehung*; Brenk, "Die Anfänge"; idem, *Tradition und Neuerung*; and the works cited in n. 136 above. The panel on the Clonmacnois cross that I take to depict the moment of resurrection (see n. 116 above) is not, to my knowledge, found on the continent.

138. See chapter 3, n. 102, above, and Johannes Beleth, *Summa de ecclesiasticis officiis*, ed. H. Douteil, CCCM 41 and 41A (Turnhout: Brepols, 1976), chap. 159, vol. 2, p. 305: "Sarcophagus dicitur a sarcos, quod est caro, et phagin, quod est comedere, quia ibi consumitur caro." See below chapter 5, n. 4. The idea is repeated by Sicard in his *Mitrale*, bk. 9, chap. 50, PL 213 (Paris, 1855), col. 429. The etymology comes from Isidore of Seville, *Etymologies*, bk. 15, chap. 11, paragr. 2, ed. José Reta, *Etimologías: Edicion Bilingüe*, vol. 2 (Madrid: Biblioteca de Autores Cristianos, 1983), p. 250. For the connection between hell and digestion, especially in the early modern period, see Camporesi, *The Fear of Hell*, chapters 12 and 13.

on the iconography of the harrowing of hell. I close this chapter with Peter's words, for they sum up many of its themes:

> That the Lord may take us out of the belly of this whale, let us present ourselves . . . in confession, so that He who pierces its jaw with a ring may free us from eternal death. The divinity which lay hidden in Jesus' flesh shattered the molars in death's mouth, when it rashly bit at the flesh of the Word. Even if it bites us like a snake or a horned serpent, if we have the horns of the cross in our hands . . . then all that horrible armor described in Job will be destroyed. . . . For there are remedies which alleviate death. . . . Death is afraid of the power of the cross. . . . It remembers that true confession and penitence have forcefully extricated countless souls from its womb and hellish belly. . . . Let us ball up all [our prayers] into lumps to burst the innards of the devil, of death, and of hell, and with Daniel let us throw them into the mouth of the dragon.[139]

In such powerful language, the belly of death—metaphorical though it is—is no "mere metaphor." To be regurgitated is to be saved. The threat is sin and death, evil and putrefaction, process itself.

139. Peter of Celle, *Tractatus de disciplina claustrali,* chap. 23, PL 202 (Paris, 1855), cols. 1132–33; trans. Hugh Feiss, *Peter of Celle,* pp. 112–13. And see above, chapter 3, n. 102.

Five

Resurrection, Heresy, and
Burial *ad Sanctos:*
The Twelfth-Century Context

 IN THE late fourth and early fifth centuries when Gregory
of Nyssa, Jerome, and Augustine wrote of resurrection, ascetic notions of bodily discipline and the growing popularity of the cult of relics suggested that body expressed
self. The controlled, lightened, and hardened bodies of hermits and holy virgins were understood to move during life toward the
subtlety and impassibility they would have in paradise. Yet, after death,
they would rest in the earth until the sound of the trumpet. Purified
already and hinting therefore at the glory to come, the bodies of the
saints were a locus where divine power could be encountered and received. The resurrection body of which the Cappadocians and Augustine
spoke *was* the body of the saint, which would rise in all its individuality
because it had begun to be a relic while still alive.

The raised and glorified body of which monks, nuns, poets, and
schoolmen spoke in the twelfth century was described in words borrowed from Jerome and Augustine. As in the fifth century so in the
twelfth, the resurrection body *was* the body of the saint. What twelfth-
century theologians, artists, and spiritual writers envisioned when they
thought of selves in heaven were the reliquaries that glowed in cathedral
treasuries and the holy people whose sanctity shone through the bodies
"of ivory" they wore on earth.[1] The context of twelfth-century escha-

1. The phrase is Guerric of Igny's; see above, chapter 4 at n. 57.

tology was relic cult and asceticism, because both ascetic and relic were understood to express victory over the rot and fragmentation we live in (as Herman of Reun said) from birth to the grave, from womb to tomb.[2]

But much had changed between the fifth and the twelfth centuries. For by the twelfth century the faithful were enthusiastically fragmenting bodies for burial, confident that each jewellike part was its own victory over corruption. In the miracle stories told in the years around 1200, bodies—living and dead—began to behave on earth as if they were already glorified in heaven. Twelfth-century ideas of resurrection reflected, rejected, and answered contemporary burial and cultic practices, just as rabbinic and early Christian notions responded to and triumphed over persecution of the martyrs and violation of their bones. But by 1200 the fragmentation over which resurrection triumphed was practiced by pious Christians on their own dead.

Fragmentation and Burial Practices

The culture of ancient Rome had possessed strong taboos against violating tombs, burying close to human habitation, moving or dividing corpses—taboos that were overcome only over the course of hundreds of years. But by the twelfth century, the practice of dividing and distributing bodies in burial was widespread.[3] Although major liturgical manuals of the twelfth and thirteenth centuries insisted that it is logically impossible for one body to be buried in two places, this is exactly what happened.[4]

The bodies of the saints were divided up to provide relics.[5] Division

2. See above, chapter 4, nn. 43, 66, and 67.

3. R. Naz, "Cimetière," *Dictionnaire de droit canonique* (Paris: Letouzey et Ané, 1935–65), vol. 3A, cols. 729–41; Ariès, *Western Attitudes Toward Death*, pp. 14–18; idem, *The Hour of Our Death*, pp. 27–92.

4. See Johannes Beleth, *Summa de ecclesiasticis officiis*, ed. H. Douteil, chaps. 159–61, vol. 2, pp. 303–19 (probably written shortly after 1165), part of which is borrowed almost verbatim about 1200 by Sicard of Cremona in book 9, chapter 50, of his *Mitrale* and in the thirteenth century by William Durand in book 1 of his *Rationale*. See Sicard, *Mitrale*, bk. 9, chap. 50, PL 213 (Paris, 1855), cols. 424–30, and J. Mason Neale and Benjamin Webb, *Du Symbolisme dans les églises du moyen âge*, trans. M. V. O. and ed. J. Bourasse (Tours: Mame, 1847), pp. 352–60. These theologians insisted therefore that the person was buried where his or her head was buried; see Beleth, *Summa*, chap. 159, vol. 2, p. 304: "Religiosus dicitur secundum leges et instituta Romanorum omnis locus, in quo sepelitur corpus hominis siue caput tantum. Caput ideo dico, quia nullus homo potest habere duas sepulturas, sed ubi caput, ibi dicitur esse sepultura eius." And see Sicard, *Mitrale*, col. 428.

5. On the spread of relic cult, see P. Sejourné, "Reliques," cols. 2330–65; Hermann-Mascard, *Les Reliques des saints*; Geary, *Furta Sacra*, pp. 152–54; Petersen, *Dialogues*

of the saints resulted not merely (as it had in antiquity) from the kinds of execution martyrs suffered at the hands of their tormentors or from the natural dissolution cadavers undergo during long years in the tomb; division was now also deliberately practiced immediately after death. Holy bodies were cut up so that parts could be given to religious communities that wished to share in the saint's power and presence. Cadavers were eviscerated, then boiled to remove the flesh, so that bones were more quickly available for distribution.

The shape of the containers in which these parts were kept began to change. Most reliquaries from the early Middle Ages were gorgeous caskets, often of gold and jewels and sometimes made in the shape of churches. Such vessels both in their form and in their material divert attention from the precise nature of the broken and decaying fragments within and symbolically associate them with Christ's assembled body, the church. After 1150, however, what German historians call expressive or "speaking" reliquaries became popular—reliquaries (shaped like fingers, feet, ribs, heads, etc.) that indicate by their form the nature of the fragment. In the twelfth century, such containers were still sheaths of gold and jewels, which revealed fragmentation but masked decay (see plates 19 and 20).[6] By the thirteenth century, they began to contain windows of crystal through which shards of tibia or bits of finger could be viewed. The same period saw the emergence of *ostensoria*—containers,

---

of Gregory the Great, pp. 140–50; Elizabeth A. R. Brown, "Death and the Human Body in the Later Middle Ages: The Legislation of Boniface VIII on the Division of the Corpse," *Viator* 12 (1981): 221–70, esp. pp. 223–24; and Wilson, "Introduction," in *Saints and Their Cults*, pp. 9–11. For the argument that German attitudes toward relics differed in important ways from the Western European relic cult, see Rothkrug, "German Holiness and Western Sanctity."

6. On the reliquary from Osnabrück shown in plate 20, see Joseph Braun, *Die Reliquiare des christlichen Kultes und ihre Entwicklung* (Freiburg: Herder, 1940), plate 119, number 445, and p. 389, and Walter Boschers, *Der Osnabrücker Domschatz* (Osnabrück: Kommissionsverlag H. Th. Wenner, 1974), p. 46, plate 34. On such reliquaries generally, see Braun, *Die Reliquiare*, part 3, chap. 7, pp. 380ff., and plates 117–26, numbers 434–81; Hans Belting, *The Image and Its Public in the Middle Ages: Form and Function of Early Paintings of the Passion*, trans. M. Bartusis and R. Meyer (New Rochelle, N.Y.: Aristide D. Caratzas, 1990), pp. 203–13; Erich Meyer, "Reliquie und Reliquiar im Mittelalter," in *Eine Gabe der Freunde für Carl Georg Heise zum 28. IV. 1950*, ed. E. Meyer (Berlin: G. Mann, 1950), pp. 55–66; and Bynum, *Fragmentation and Redemption*, plates 7.2–7.4. As Stephen Wilson has pointed out, the Middle Ages saw the proliferation of ex-votos made in the shape of body parts. The relationship of these to "speaking" reliquaries needs study. It seems clear, however, that the ex-voto (the object shaped like a body part and offered to the saint who has healed it) represents both the illness and the cure. It stands for the specific part and the healed, whole person who offers the gift in thanksgiving. See Wilson, "Introduction," in *Saints and Their Cults*, pp. 21–22.

parallel to and sometimes identical with eucharistic monstrances, that were made especially for displaying bits of holy bodies or even the fluids they produced before or in death (see plate 21).[7]

Enthusiasm for bodily partition affected not just the saints. By 1200, especially north of the Alps, the bodies of prominent ecclesiastics or nobles were often eviscerated, boned, or boiled after death, and the resulting parts were buried in several places near several saints. (The practice was known as the *mos teutonicus*.) Between 1151 and 1573, the cloister of Ebrach in Oberfranken, for example, held the hearts of thirty-three deceased bishops of Würzburg while their bones rested in the church and their intestines in the castle chapel. A collegiate church in Magdeburg had a special "tripe chapel," where the bowels of the canons were buried.[8]

The anonymous, ordinary dead were also disturbed and divided. As the practice of reusing graves became more common, the charnel house or ossuary (*carnarium*) developed to provide a resting place for the bones and skulls that inevitably floated to the surface when older graves were reopened. Our first reference to a charnel house comes from the 1160s; by the thirteenth century, councils in Germany required churches to provide for ossuaries in burial grounds.[9] In the later Middle Ages, chapels were sometimes decorated with bones from the bonehouse; the walls of the so-called Golden Chamber at St. Ursula's in Cologne are covered with geometrical designs and inscriptions made from gilded tibias, fib-

7. Braun, *Die Reliquiare*, pt. 3, chap. 6, pp. 301–78, and plates 88–117, numbers 291–435; and Meyer, "Reliquie und Reliquiar," pp. 61ff.

8. On Würzburg and Magdeburg, see Johannes Schweizer, *Kirchhof und Friedhof: Eine Darstellung der beiden Haupttypen europäischer Begräbnisstätten* (Linz: Oberösterreichischer Landesverlag, 1956), p. 50.

9. In general, see Boase, *Death in the Middle Ages*, which has disappointingly little on cemeteries and the actual practice of burial; Henri Leclercq, "Cimetière," *DACL*, vol. 3 (1919), cols. 1625–65, especially 1625–30; R. C. Finucane, "Sacred Corpse, Profane Carrion: Social Ideals and Death Rituals in the Later Middle Ages," in *Mirrors of Mortality: Studies in the Social History of Death*, ed. Whaley, pp. 40–60; E. Brown, "Authority, Family, and the Dead"; eadem, "Death and the Human Body," pp. 221–70; and Schweizer, *Kirchhof und Friedhof*. Information on the development of the charnel house is surprisingly difficult to find. See Donald Bullough, "Burial, Community, and Belief in the Early Medieval West," in *Ideal and Reality in Frankish and Anglo-Saxon Society: Studies Presented to J. M. Wallace-Hadrill*, ed. P. Wormald (Oxford, 1983), pp. 177–201; Ariès, *Hour of Our Death*, pp. 40–62, which is somewhat misleading; Friedrich Zoepfl, "Beinhaus," in *Reallexikon zur deutschen Kunstgeschichte*, ed. O. Schmitt (Stuttgart: J. B. Metzler, 1937ff.), vol. 2, cols. 204–14; Camille Enlart, *Manuel d'archéologie française depuis les temps merovigiens jusqu'à la renaissance*, pt. 1, vol. 2, 3d ed. (Paris: Picard, 1929), pp. 909–17; and Warwick Rodwell, *The Archaeology of the English Church: The Study of Historic Churches and Churchyards* (London: B. T. Batsford, 1981), pp. 131–61.

ulas, and skulls. Ossuaries were sometimes located within churches in such a position that the bones could watch the liturgy being celebrated. A few late medieval paintings even depict the bones (usually said, in these cases, to represent the "poor souls" in purgatory) attending mass.[10]

Much about the development of the charnel house is obscure.[11] But it surely responded to both a new sense that bodies could be moved and a new insistence on the burial of all Christians in consecrated ground. The fact that our earliest texts for blessing or consecrating cemeteries come from the tenth century suggests that the practice is of Carolingian origins. Once consecrated ground was clearly set off as the only acceptable place for interment, pressure for reusing this very small area (some limited it to thirty feet around the church) greatly increased.[12] Donald Bullough has recently argued that the Carolingian period saw both a weakening of taboos on tomb violation and a growing tendency for ordinary folk to be buried adjacent to churches, crowded into the porch or atrium (from which the French word for cemetery—*aître*—comes).[13] By the twelfth century, it is clear that burial outside consecrated ground usually marked one as a sinner or a nonperson. Honorius in his *Elucidarium* and John Beleth in his treatise on the liturgy (probably written shortly after 1165) related moral and worldly status closely to place of burial. Beleth even suggested that when women die in childbirth, the fetuses—which had not been and could not be baptized—should be cut out of their bodies and buried outside the graveyard.[14] Christian bones therefore—even in reburial—had to be preserved in consecrated buildings. Following Augustine, Beleth and Honorius both protest that God does not really care where our remains are buried, but both mention that demons might attack unprotected (or evil) bones and scatter them far from the saints.[15]

The disturbing, dividing, and distributing of body parts practiced so enthusiastically in the twelfth century was an indication—not a de-

10. Philipp Maria Halm, "Armeseelen," *Reallexikon zur deutschen Kunstgeschichte*, vol. 1, col. 1084–88.

11. Zoepfl, "Beinhaus."

12. Beleth, *Summa*, chap. 159, ed. Douteil, vol. 2, p. 306.

13. Bullough, "Burial, Community, and Belief," pp. 177–201; Ariès, *Western Attitudes Toward Death*, pp. 18–22.

14. Beleth, *Summa*, chap. 159, vol. 2, p. 309, and Sicard, *Mitrale*, bk. 9, chap. 50, PL 213, col. 430; see also A. Bernard, *La Sépulture en droit canonique du décret de Gratien au Concile de Trent* (Paris: Domat-Montchrestien, 1933), pp. 134–35, and Finucane, "Sacred Corpse, Profane Carrion," p. 55.

15. Beleth, *Summa*, chaps. 159–61, vol. 2, pp. 303–19, especially pp. 307 and 318–19. See also Ariès, *Hour of Our Death*, p. 41–42.

nial—that body is integral to person. The heart of a king or the finger of a holy virgin made the earth where he or she resided fertile with saintly or royal power. When monks and canons squabbled over the relics of saints or the entrails of kings and cardinals, they were fighting for possession of more than the revenues associated with masses for the dead. The greater the number of parts and places in which noble or holy figures rested after death, the more far-flung their presence.[16]

But precisely because bones and entrails were integral to person, the practice of bodily partition was fraught with ambivalence, controversy, and profound inconsistency. The practice of dividing royal corpses (although accepted in Germany since the tenth century as having ritual significance) was still characterized by anxiety in twelfth-century England and France. When Henry I died in Normandy in 1135, his body was disembowelled for hygienic reasons and his viscera presented to a nunnery he had founded; chronicle accounts disapproved, however, of the act, remarking that one of his attendants died from contact with the decaying remains. The historian Roger of Wendover suggests that Richard I's grant of his entrails to the abbey of Charroux was taken as a sign of disdain rather than a benefit.[17] In the mid-thirteenth century, when Blanche of Castile directed that her body be divided, it was first buried intact; only three and a half months after her death did the abbess to whose convent she had bequeathed her heart succeed in getting it. When Louis IX's son Pierre d'Alençon decreed that his body be split up for burial, he spoke (as Elizabeth Brown has recently reminded us) of his "filthy flesh" and "evil heart."[18] Such stories suggest both that partition is acceptable and that it is offensive, that body is both a locus of putre-

16. See *Fragmentation and Redemption*, p. 270; Finucane, "Sacred Corpse, Profane Carrion"; and Boase, *Death in the Middle Ages*, p. 197 and plate 85.

17. Elizabeth M. Hallam, "Royal Burial and the Cult of Kingship in France and England, 1060–1330," *Journal of Medieval History* 8, no. 4 (1982): 359–80. A parallel Irish case is worth noting. After the assassination of Hugh de Lacy by decapitation, his body was removed in 1195 to the monastery of Bective in Meath, but his head was deposited (then or earlier) in St. Thomas's, Dublin. The two monasteries engaged in lengthy litigation (resolved in 1205 in favor of St. Thomas's) for possession of the complete remains. It is significant that two things were at stake: the possession of a reassembled cadaver rather than its partition between two houses and the fate of certain lands that had been bestowed on Bective along with the body. See A. B. Scott and F. X. Martin, notes to *Expurgatio Hibernica: The Conquest of Ireland by Gerald of Wales*, ed. Scott and Martin (Dublin: Royal Irish Academy, 1978), p. 354 n. 480; Goddard Henry Orpen, *Ireland Under the Normans, 1169–1333,* (Oxford: Clarendon Press, 1911–20), vol. 2, p. 70; *Register of the Abbey of St. Thomas, Dublin,* ed. John T. Gilbert, Rolls Series 94 (London: Eyre and Spottiswoode, 1889), pp. 348–50.

18. E. Brown, "Authority, Family, and the Dead," pp. 810–11. I am also indebted to an unpublished paper by Edward Peters, "Courtly Death" (1986).

faction and a locus of self. If disemboweling or division of important bodies is necessary—either because corpses have to be transported over long distances or because their economic, political, and religious power has to be distributed and shared—the full horror and insult of decay must be denied in rituals and texts that present bodily division as fragmentation without alteration.[19]

Even the saints sometimes opposed their own fragmentation. When fragmented, they sometimes reassembled themselves or remained incorrupt in their parts.[20] Accounts of translations and discoveries of relics from eleventh- and twelfth-century England, for example, stress the wholeness of holy cadavers. The martyred king St. Edmund (d. 870), pierced by arrows and beheaded, was first found in his coffin with no trace of the attack except for a thin red line around his neck. Audacious and unwise tests of the body during an early translation found that the head could not be pulled from the torso, although the presumptuous perpetrator of the tests was punished; later investigation of the body revealed that all the toes were still on the feet. By the late twelfth century, abbot Samson—remembering earlier events—limited his own tests to feeling the body through the shroud. A twelfth-century account of the translation of St. Etheldreda, based on Bede, stresses that the saint was incorrupt after sixteen years and that a tumor on her neck had healed; enhancing the motif of wholeness, the twelfth-century account adds that the sarcophagus itself became intact, so that no gap or seam could be found in it.[21]

19. Outside of the high aristocracy in Germany, real confidence in bodily partition did not develop until the thirteenth century; even in the fourteenth, it was not very popular in Italy; see Schweizer, *Kirchhof und Friedhof*, pp. 50–52, and below, p. 323.

20. On incorruption, see Herbert Thurston, *The Physical Phenomena of Mysticism* (Chicago: Henry Regnery, 1952), pp. 233–82, esp. pp. 246–52; Michel Bouvier, "De l'incorruptibilité des corps saints," in *Les Miracles, miroirs des corps*, ed. Jacques Gélis and Odile Redon (Paris: Presses et Publications de l'Université de Paris-VIII, 1983), pp. 193–221; and the works cited in my "Bodily Miracles," p. 89 n. 17. A related issue concerning incorruptibility is the incorruptibility of the bodies of great sinners; see Ariès, *Hour of Our Death*, p. 360, and Thomas, *Le cadavre*, pp. 39–44 and 199, who, however, underestimates the positive value given to incorruptibility in the Western Middle Ages. Thus it is to the bodies of great saints (Jesus, Mary, and John the Evangelist) and great sinners that the earth is reported to refuse the normal process of decay. A particularly good example of the ambivalence that must underlie such stories is Guibert of Nogent, who argues in the *De pignoribus* that decay is horrible and should not therefore be allowed to touch the bodies of Christ and Mary; on the other hand, it is return to "mother earth" and should not be inhibited by elaborate coffins. See especially *De pignoribus*, bk. 1, chaps. 3 and 4, PL 156 (Paris, 1853), cols. 623–30. On Guibert see also Mireux, "Guibert de Nogent et la critique du culte des reliques." And see above chapter 4, nn. 48, 51, and 52, on the Bodily Assumption.

21. For the St. Edmund story, see Abbo of Fleury, Life of St. Edmund, in *Three Lives of English Saints*, ed. Michael Winterbottom (Toronto: Pontifical Institute of

The *Dialogue on Miracles,* written in the early thirteenth century by the continental Cistercian Caesarius of Heisterbach, contains a number of stories of relics resisting division (although it recounts as well cases of bones inviting disturbance). Caesarius also reports cases of bones that sort themselves out so that false relics are eliminated.[22] Fifty years after Caesarius, the learned and saintly bishop of Lincoln Robert Grosseteste seems to have forbidden the deathbed division of his own corpse.[23] Accounts of the Flemish holy woman Mary of Oignies, a contemporary of Caesarius, show the full range of ambivalence about partition. According to her hagiographers Thomas of Cantimpré and James of Vitry (who were themselves anxious to possess pieces of her body after her death), Mary fragmented herself while alive by pulling out a large hunk of her hair to use as a device to cure the sick.[24] After her death the hairs con-

---

Mediaeval Studies, 1972), pp. 82–87; *Memorials of St. Edmund's Abbey,* ed. Thomas Arnold, Rolls Series 96 (London: Eyre and Spottiswoode, 1890–96), vol. 1, pp. 53–54 and 133–34; Jocelin of Brakelond, *The Chronicle . . . ,* ed. and trans. H. E. Butler (London: Nelson, 1951), pp. 111–15 (Jocelin's account is from about 1200); and Ronald C. Finucane, *Miracles and Pilgrims: Popular Beliefs in Medieval England* (Totowa, N.J.: Rowman and Littlefield, 1977), pp. 27–28. For Etheldreda, see *Liber Eliensis,* ed. E. O. Blake, Camden, 3d series 92 (London: Royal Historical Society, 1962), pp. 45, a mid-twelfth-century account adapted from Bede. These two examples are discussed in Monika Otter, "*Inventiones:* Spatial Metaphors and Narrative Self-Awareness in Medieval Historical Writing" (Ph.D. diss., Columbia University, 1991), pp. 88–92, which provides a complex and sensitive analysis of motifs of discovery and wholeness in such accounts. Twelfth-century *inventiones* in England still show a preference for finding whole bodies, although there were body parts and part reliquaries around. See ibid., p. 140; Otto Lehmann-Brockhaus, *Lateinische Schriftquellen zur Kunst in England, Wales, und Schottland vom Jahre 901 bis zum Jahre 1307* (Munich: Pestelverlag, 1955–60); and Denis Bethell, "The Making of a Twelfth-Century Relic Collection," *Studies in Church History* 8 (1972): 61–72. It is important to note that this stress on wholeness was not a distaste for the body per se; on the enthusiasm for touching holy bodies that could go along with fear of testing or dismantling them, see Finucane, "Sacred Corpse, Profane Carrion," p. 53.

22. Caesarius, *Dialogus,* ed. J. Strange, dist. 8, chaps. 53 and 60, vol. 2, pp. 125–26 and 133, for resisting division; ibid., dist. 8, chap. 88, vol. 2, p. 155–56, for bones sorting themselves into true and false relics; ibid., dist. 8, chaps. 85–87, vol. 2, pp. 151–55, for bones that invite disturbance. Guibert of Nogent in his *De pignoribus* tells several earlier tales (including the story of St. Edmund), which are intended to indicate that relics do not wish to be dismembered (see *De pignoribus,* bk. 1, chap. 4, PL 156, cols. 626–30). E. Brown points out that Godfrey of Fontaines, arguing in 1291 against division of bodies, admits that Edmund of Pontigny commanded his heart to be buried apart from his body ("Death and the Human Body," p. 243). But Godfrey says people were "horrified" when the monks severed the arm from the corpse and asserts that Edmund's body was miraculously preserved. For late thirteenth-century debates over bodily partition, see below, chapter 8.

23. See E. Brown, "Death and the Human Body," pp. 227 and 243.

24. Thomas of Cantimpré, *Supplementum* [to the Life of Mary of Oignies], chap. 1, paragr. 6–7, *Acta Sanctorum,* 3d ed., ed. J. Bollandus and G. Henschenius, June, vol. 5 (Paris: Palmé, 1867), pp. 574–75. On Mary, see Bynum, *Holy Feast and Holy Fast,*

tinued to effect cures, and on one occasion "came alive" for a whole hour.[25] Mary herself nonetheless castigated the prior of Oignies for "cruelly" extracting the teeth of a holy cadaver, and after her own death she supposedly clenched her teeth when the same prior tried to extract them as relics. When he humbly asked her pardon, however, she shook out a few teeth from her jaw for his use.[26]

Triumph over partition or putrefaction was sometimes understood per se as an expression of sanctity. Caesarius tells of a robber who was revered as a saint after his death simply because his body was seen in a vision as reassembled.[27] In folktales and vernacular hagiography, saints were frequently said to effect miracles of healing or of temporary resurrection of corpses, but they sometimes reassembled cadavers without bothering to reanimate them.[28] In a twelfth-century life of St. Barbara, for example, a decapitated head asks a priest for communion and is reunited with its body through the power of the saint although both parts remain lifeless.[29] The popular story of a leg transplant performed by the physician saints Cosmas and Damian changes in its medieval retelling to emphasize not only the grafting of a black leg onto a sick white man but also the attaching of the gangrenous white leg to the corpse of the Moor from whom the original graft had been taken. There are even miracle stories in which dismembered parts survive incorrupt while remaining dismembered. According to later legend, the little finger of the tenth-century saint Adalbert of Prague, which was swallowed by a fish, survived and shone like a candle in the fish's belly.[30]

---

pp. 115–24, and Laura Dushkes, "Illness and Healing in the Vitae of Mary of Oignies" (M.A. Thesis, University of Washington, 1988).

25. Thomas, *Supplementum*, chap. 1, paragr. 7, p. 575.

26. Ibid., chap. 3, paragr. 14, p. 577. For a miracle worked by Mary's finger, see ibid., chap. 3, paragrs. 15–17, pp. 577–78.

27. Caesarius, *Dialogus*, dist. 7, chap. 58, vol. 2, pp. 76–79. In the vision, five matrons appeared at night, fitted his head back on his shoulders, and laid him out whole on a sumptuous bier.

28. It is important to note that medieval authors sometimes poked fun at such "resurrections." Accounts of the resurrection of donkeys in the Miracles of Saint Faith, for example, may be tongue-in-cheek. Walter Map produced a series of what Otter calls "uncharitable and sometimes off-color" jokes, including an account of an unsuccessful miracle attempt by Bernard of Clairvaux, in which Walter points out that boys do usually "rise up" when monks lie down upon them. See Monika Otter, "Inventiones," pp. 254–57. And see n. 84 below.

29. See Brigitte Cazelles, *Le Corps de sainteté d'après Jehan Bouche d'Or, Jehan Paulus, et quelques vies des XIIe et XIIIe siècles* (Geneva: Droz, 1982), pp. 55–56.

30. Judith-Danielle Jacquet, "Le Miracle de la jambe noire," in Gélis and Redon, eds., *Les Miracles, miroirs*, pp. 23–52. For other examples of miracles of restoration, see C. Grant Loomis, *White Magic: An Introduction to the Folklore of Christian Legend* (Cambridge, Mass.: The Mediaeval Academy of America, 1948), pp. 82–86.

The intactness of fragments was a theme in art as well. The very reliquaries that announced fragmentation clothed the parts they displayed in crystal and gold. For example, the reliquary of Thomas Becket from 1175–80, which contains the blood of the saint and bears on its roof a large red stone, both manifests what it contains and in the precise nature of the manifestation hardens the fluid into crystalline permanence (see plate 22).[31] The shining stone—not a priceless ruby at all but simply glass and foil assembled to present sparkling yet frozen redness—signals the blood but in heavenly form.[32] Even the arm, rib, and head reliquaries of the thirteenth and fourteenth centuries deny putrefaction by covering the bits they contain in gold and crystal sheathing while simultaneously displaying in their shapes and transparency the body's partition. Thus artists as well as canon lawyers and theologians were concerned to guard against not the expressionism involved in relic display, or a sense of familiarity with the bodies of the saints, but rather an association of the body bits with those biological processes that signal decay or decomposition. When the Fourth Lateran Council in 1215 legislated against "naked" display of relics for money, their disapproval may have been directed against more than simply the threat of theft offered by the unprotected showing of such precious possessions.[33]

Ellert Dahl, who has written so knowledgeably about these reliquaries, emphasizes that medieval theologians were careful to see them as *memoria* of the saints, reminders of the glorified bodies we will receive in heaven.[34] Abbot Suger, for example, distinguished the "sacred bones" of the martyrs at St. Denis—covered "with the most precious metal we possibly can [find], with refined gold and a profusion of hyacinths, emeralds, and other precious stones"—from their "venerable spirits, radi-

---

Some of these miracles are stories of regurgitation of undigested parts: for example, an eye is swallowed by a bird, disgorged, and reattached (ibid., p. 84). For the finger of Adalbert, see ibid., p. 70; and *Miracula sancti Adalberti martiris*, chap. 1, PL 137 (Paris, 1853), col. 889.

31. See *English Romanesque Art, 1066–1200, Hayward Gallery, London, 5 April–8 July, 1984*, ed. George Zarnecki, Janet Holt, and Tristram Holland, Catalogue published in association with the Arts Council of Great Britain (London: Weidenfeld and Nicolson, 1984), p. 282.

32. Cf. the words of Victricius of Rouen almost 800 years before; see chapter 2, n. 178.

33. See Hermann-Mascard, *Les Reliques des saints*, pp. 212–17; Pierre Duparc, "Dilaceratio corporis," *Bulletin de la Société Nationale des Antiquaires de France 1980–1981* (Paris: Boccard, 1981), pp. 360–72; and my "Bodily Miracles," p. 81. On expressive reliquaries, see nn. 6 and 7 above.

34. Ellert Dahl, "Heavenly Images: The Statue of St. Foy of Conques and the Signification of the Medieval Cult-Image in the West," *Acta ad archaeologiam et Artium historiam pertinentia* 8 (Rome 1979): 175–92, esp. p. 186.

ant as the sun."[35] Hagiographers, however, frequently spoke as if the bodies and bones of the saints were already jewels, in life and in death as they would be in resurrection.

Walter Daniel wrote that Aelred of Rievaulx shone like a sun while still a baby in the cradle; in death his flesh was "clearer than glass, whiter than snow," shining "like a carbuncle." Peter Damian described Saint Romuald as, on earth, "a neglected pearl of heaven"; thus, in death, he "shines ineffably among the living stones of the celestial Jerusalem."[36] James of Vitry reported that after the death of Mary of Oignies, her body appeared in a dream "as if transformed into a very brilliant precious stone."[37]

To some, the association of spirit and bone was closer still. Theodore of Echternach wrote (about 1104) that "those who reign as kings in heaven should be gloriously housed on earth." He even argued that the bodies of the saints, which were dominated by the spirit already in life, were ipso facto resistant to worms and decay after death. The unity of body and soul, lost in paradise because of sin, is (says Theodore) restored in the saints by asceticism. Hence body, subject "by nature" to decay, can by grace and merit remain incorrupt and repel the attacks of rot and worm.

No substance of flesh is more noble than the flesh of the saints, for the more it is subject to the spirit the more it is free and glorious in the very resolution of corruption. It is born to labor and misery, but in death it is born to peace and glory. To glory it is born, I say, although what is conceived and engendered from the worm is eaten by worms, and dust reverts to dust. . . . [B]ut it is one thing from nature and another from grace and merit. From nature it is putrid and corruptible, but from grace and merits it remains for a long time without rot even contrary to nature, and it repels the greedy worms. . . . [F]or he who puts away from himself worms (that is, nasty thoughts) will not be sweet to the worm. . . . Sanctified flesh, through nature *clothed with rottenness* . . . (Job 12.5) . . . rises again from the dust through grace and merit. . . . And this is greatly to be marveled at, for it feeds worms

35. Dahl, "Heavenly Images," p. 184.
36. *Walteri Danielis Vita Ailredi abbatis Rievall*, trans. F. M. Powicke (New York: Oxford University Press, 1951), pp. 22–23, 50–51, 52–54, 62–63, and 71, quoted passage at pp. 62–63; cited in Dahl, p. 186. And Peter Damian, Life of St. Romuald, chap. 69, PL 144 (Paris, 1853), col. 1006C, cited in Dahl, p. 184. See also p. 338 below on Mechtild of Magdeburg's vision of John the Evangelist's body in heaven.
37. James of Vitry, Life of Mary of Oignies, bk. 2, chap. 12, paragr. 109, *Acta Sanctorum*, June, vol. 5, p. 572.

yet heals men, it is putrid yet it puts off putrefaction . . . it is crushed into ashes yet it shines among the stars of the morning.[38]

In the late eleventh-century account of the *inventio* of St. Ivo, Goscelin of St. Bertin states explicitly that the relic *is* the resurrection body. Goscelin not only associates it with Christ's resurrection and with the fertility of spring, he also connects its "resuscitation" with a new heaven and a remade earth.

His *inventio* took place in the year 1001 . . . on April 23. "*Aprilis*" or "*aperilis*" is derived from "*aperire*," "to open," when the sky opens up more brightly toward the summer sun, and the earth is enlivened with flowers and fruit. . . . Then plants break out in bloom, birds in song, and all things in joy over Christ's resurrection and the day of Easter: for it was fitting that at such a time the holy relics were discovered, which shall be resurrected to heavenly glory [*in aeternam gloriam . . . resuscitari*] with a new heaven and a new earth.[39]

Since reliquaries and texts presented the saints as perlucid and glorious, incorrupt and impassible, lifted to a new heaven, it should not really surprise us that the St. Firmin portal at Amiens, from the 1230s, depicts the *inventio* of the saint's incorrupt remains in such a way that they appear to be rising from the tomb (see plate 23).[40] Relic and resurrection body become visually the same. Nor should we be surprised to find on a reliquary bust from fourteenth-century Utrecht an inscription that announces that "I" (which presumably means both the skull and the saint) have been taken from the tomb and "renewed."[41] Such renew-

38. Theodore of Echternach, *Flores epitaphii sanctorum*, bk. 1, chap. 3, and bk. 2, chap. 1, PL 157 (Paris, 1854), cols. 324–26 and 337–41, quoted passage at cols. 324C–325A. See also Dahl, "Heavenly Images," p. 184; and Guth, *Guibert von Nogent*, pp. 110–27, esp. p. 117.

39. Goscelin, Life of Ivo, *Acta Sanctorum*, June, vol. 2, pp. 286–87; trans. Otter, "*Inventiones*," pp. 142–44. For another early example, see Rudolph's Life of Boniface, which reports that Boniface wished the bones of Lioba to rest next to his in the tomb "so that they who had served God during their lifetime with equal sincerity and zeal should await together the day of resurrection"; Elizabeth Alvida Petroff, *Medieval Women's Visionary Literature* (Oxford: Oxford University Press, 1986), p. 112; see also p. 86. And see the Life of Aethelwold cited in n. 79 below.

40. See Stephen Murray's account in *Notre Dame, Cathedral of Amiens: Creativity and the Dynamics of Change* (New York: Architectural History Foundation, forthcoming), typescript p. 47 n. 41. It is also worth noting that the contemporary text describing this *inventio* uses much imagery of flowering; *Acta Sanctorum*, September, vol. 7 (Antwerp, 1760), p. 34.

41. *Middeleeuwe kunst der noordelijke Nederlanden* (Amsterdam, 1958), p. 229. The inscription reads: "A(n)no D(omi)ni M CCC LXIII Decan(us) (et) cap(itu)l(u)m s(anc)ti Saluator(is) T(ra)i(e)ctten(sis) me ex tu(m)ba p(ro)tu(n)t i(n)nouaca ex(tra)hi (et)

ing of the bone in the reliquary foreshadows its renewing in heaven and suggests not only that the bone is the saint but also perhaps that the reliquary is the relic.[42]

The charnel house itself—although in some sense a perpetuation of the division and scattering of bones that inevitably accompanied the moving of skeletons—was also a counter to such fragmentation. It gathered the fragments together into a community of saints, safe (as Honorius said) from molestation by demons.[43] Liturgical manuals, such as those of John Beleth and Sicard of Cremona in the twelfth century and William Durandus in the thirteenth, stress place of burial as indicator of moral and worldly attainment. Not only were the evil or excommunicate to be buried outside consecrated ground; nobles and prelates were allowed closer to the altar than those of lower orders.[44] All Christians were to be buried in clothing appropriate to their rank and shod for the walk to Jerusalem; clergy were to be interred in their vestments and furnished with small wooden chalices as a sign of office.[45] Against such

---

fi(eri) feceru(n)t p(er) Elya(m) Scerpsvvert aurifabru(m)." Presumably *p(ro)tu(n)t* is a mistake for *p(ro) tu(lerun)t*. Finucane notes that a twelfth-century bishop of Paris had himself buried with the following words pinned to his body: "I believe that . . . on the last day of the world I shall be resurrected" ("Sacred Corpse, Profane Carrion," p. 44 and n. 13).

42. Not only were the bodies of the saints sometimes understood to be already the jewels of the resurrection, but the bodies of the evil could also be taken to be already in hellfire. Megan McLaughlin discusses a fascinating ninth-century text that refers to a soul *and body* condemned to the flames *before* the Last Judgment; the body is subsequently discovered to have disappeared from the tomb! See Megan McLaughlin, *Consorting with Saints: Prayer for the Dead in Early Medieval France* (Ithaca: Cornell University Press, forthcoming). As Finucane puts it: "The fate of the soul was linked to that of the corpse in all classes, not just among saints" ("Sacred Corpse, Profane Carrion," p. 60). Finucane also expresses this by speaking of the body's "function" as being a "symbol for the soul" (ibid.)—a formulation that seems to me to limit unduly the significance of such stories as these in which the body is symbol in a literally metonymic sense.

43. See Honorius, *Elucidarium*, bk. 2, questions 103–4, in ed. Lefevre, p. 164.

44. Roger E. Reynolds, "Death and Burial, in Europe," *Dictionary of the Middle Ages*, ed. J. Strayer, vol. 4, pp. 118–22, and the works cited in nn. 8 and 9 above. Sicard of Cremona, *Mitrale*, bk. 9, chap. 50, PL 213, col. 427, stresses that cadavers should be clothed *secundum statum et ordinem suum*, lay people in hairshirts and ashes for penitence, clerics in the robes of their orders. Both John Beleth (*Summa*, chap. 159, ed. Douteil, vol. 2, pp. 308–10) and Sicard hesitate to state categorically that we will be clothed after the resurrection, for it is sufficient to believe "quod in salvandis non erit infirmitas nec ulla deformitas" (Sicard, *Mitrale*, col. 427). But whereas John simply gives opposing opinions, Sicard seems to lean in the direction of concluding that we will be clothed.

45. It seems ironic that the old pagan practice of grave goods survives especially for the clergy! On the way in which the fate of the corpse reflected the fate of the soul, see Finucane, "Sacred Corpse, Profane Carrion," especially pp. 44 and 60, and

a background, second burial might seem a leveling; in the bonehouse all bones were equal, as an occasional inscription from the later Middle Ages points out.[46] Yet even in the *carnarium*, there was personal, differentiated survival. Skulls were sometimes labeled with their names— a particularly important practice in view of the insistence by contemporary theologians that a person was buried where his or her head was interred. The skulls of clergy were occasionally laid outside the common heap, preserving their special status even in second burial. Cases are recorded of cheekbones with cords attached in which knots were tied every time a prayer was said for that particular skull.[47]

Religious and social practices surrounding the bodies of both the holy and the ordinary dead thus provide a context for understanding twelfth-century discussions of resurrection. Irenaeus and Tertullian, in the early third century, had particularly in mind the body of the martyr when they wrote of peaceful and triumphant reassemblage and transfiguration in heaven. Two centuries later, Gregory of Nyssa and Jerome saw heaven as a glorious company of the ascetics and virgins of earth, marked with their virtues and attainments. When Bernard, Hugh, Peter Lombard, Hildegard, and Herrad stressed salvation as the reassembling and reanimating of dust and bones, the restoration of every organ and fingernail, the bestowing of crystalline hardness on every process, motion, or desire, they were speaking of the contents of reliquaries, entrail caskets, and charnel houses. Images of resurrection as regurgitation, reassemblage, and stasis reflect a new enthusiasm for bodily partition that was made possible by the confidence in ultimate victory over it. By the twelfth century, bodies were divided in order to bestow their power more widely, to associate them with disparate human communities; they were divided because they were crucial to, and therefore distributed, self. But because they were crucial, their partition was fraught with ambiv-

---

Schweizer, *Kirchhof und Friedhof*, pp. 53–69, 72–74, and 79–80. For a warning against concluding too much from the nature of grave goods, see Luc Buchet and Claude Lorren, "Dans quelle mesure la nécropole du haut moyen âge offre-t-elle une image fidèle de la société des vivants?" in *La Mort au moyen âge: Colloque de la Société des Historiens médiévistes de l'enseignement supérieur public, 1975* (Strasbourg: Université de Strasbourg, n.d.), pp. 27–48.

46. Schweizer, *Kirchhof und Friedhof*, p. 72: for example, "hie ligen bir all geleych ritter edel arm und reich;" "so ist's recht, da liegt der Meister bei seinem Knecht." Although the message is that all bones come to the same end, the bones are still understood to be Rich and Poor, Master and Servant, etc.

47. See Schweizer, *Kirchhof und Friedhof*, p. 72, and Johannes Beleth, *Summa*, chap. 159, ed. Douteil, vol. 2, pp. 303–10, esp. pp. 304 and 308–10, repeated by William Durand.

alence. Redemption had finally to be the fulfillment of Christ's promise that not a hair of our heads shall perish.

Hierarchy, Heresy, and Fear of Decay

I pointed out in chapter 2 that much recent work on late antiquity has seen an underlining of status (both moral and worldly) and of hierarchy (especially ecclesiastical hierarchy) in the tenets of orthodox Christianity. The same interpretation is found in the most recent work on the twelfth century. For the past forty years, historians of spirituality, such as Charles Dereine, Jean Leclercq, M.-D. Chenu, and Giles Constable, have emphasized that the period saw not only a proliferation of new forms of religious life but also an increasing determination to define their differences and stake out their respective claims.[48] Much attention has been paid to squabbles over revenues and rights among monks, canons, and wandering preachers; historians have argued that the competing claims of religious groups sharpened rhetoric, legal definitions, and even self-awareness.[49] In the past decade, scholars such as R. I. Moore and Michael Camille have seen the much vaunted intellectual flowering of the twelfth century—its new philosophical precision and sophistication, its expanding bureaucracy, the growth of its schools and libraries—as a drawing of boundaries that excluded and repressed. They have interpreted the new visibility of groups such as Jews, women, and homosexuals—and the proliferation of heresy itself—less as a flourishing of divergent and dissident values than as the construction of an "other" by an increasingly powerful clergy.[50]

48. See, among others, M.-D. Chenu, *La théologie au douzième siècle* (Paris: J. Vrin, 1957); Charles Dereine, "Chanoines," *Dictionnaire d'histoire et de géographie ecclésiastiques*, vol. 12 (Paris: Letouzey et Ané, 1953), cols. 353–405; Jean Leclercq, "La crise du monachisme aux XIe et XIIe siècles," *Bulletino dell 'Istituto storico italiano per il Medio Evo* 70 (1958): 19–41; M.-H. Vicaire, *L'Imitation des apôtres: Moines, chanoines, mendiants (IVe–XIIe siècles)* (Paris: Éditions du Cerf, 1963); Giles Constable, "Introduction," in *Libellus de diversis ordinibus et professionibus qui sunt in aecclesia*, ed. G. Constable and B. Smith (Oxford: Clarendon Press, 1972), pp. xi–xxvii; and the works I cite in *Jesus as Mother*, pp. 22–33.

49. See my "Did the Twelfth Century Discover the Individual?" in *Jesus as Mother*, pp. 82–109.

50. R. I. Moore, *The Formation of a Persecuting Society: Power and Deviance in Western Europe, 950–1250* (Oxford: Basil Blackwell, 1987); idem, "Postscript: The Peace of God and Social Revolution," in *The Peace of God: Social Violence and Religious Response in France around the Year 1000*, ed. Thomas Head and Richard Landes (Ithaca: Cornell University Press, 1992), pp. 308–26; and Michael Camille, *The Gothic Idol: Ideology and Image-Making in Medieval Art* (Cambridge: Cambridge University Press, 1989). John E. Boswell, *Christianity, Social Tolerance, and Homo-*

There is much truth in such an argument. The twelfth century was characterized by extraordinary concern with boundaries, definitions, self-definitions, and classifications. Twelfth- and thirteenth-century polemics—especially polemics against heresy—were less a quarrel with a clearly existent "other" than a process by which groups defined themselves through the creation of an "other." By 1210, as we have seen, denial of bodily resurrection was understood to be an aberration serious enough that people as well as books went to the flames for it. Some at least of those who characterized and countered the beliefs of the Amauricians saw their denial of literal resurrection as a denial of differentiated moral attainments and of gender difference. It is worth asking, first, how far the frenetic concern over Cathar (or dualist) and Waldensian (or evangelical) heresy on the part of Christian leaders around 1200 was owing to their perception (correct or not) that these groups espoused an aberrant eschatology, and second, whether denial of hierarchy and difference was perceived as central to denial of resurrection.

The evidence we have for medieval heresy comes mostly from its opponents and tells us therefore much more about what these opponents feared than about what the so-called heretics taught.[51] This evidence suggests that until the late twelfth century persecuting clergy focused little on denials of resurrection. The Waldensians were required at the Council of Lyons (1180 or 81) to accept resurrection of "this flesh and no other," but the formula was not new; what was added was the statement that the flesh in which Christ "truly ate and drank" was the flesh that ascends into heaven and the affirmation that alms, masses, and other good works are of benefit to the dead.[52] By the early thirteenth century, denial of resurrection was underlined as an element in Catharism but usually in connection with Cathar denial of marriage, of tran-

---

sexuality: Gay People in Western Europe from the Beginning of the Christian Era to the Fourteenth Century (Chicago: University of Chicago Press, 1980), points out the growth of repression in the period around 1200 but also argues for a flowering of gay culture in the twelfth century.

51. See, for example, Walter L. Wakefield and Austin P. Evans, Introduction, *Heresies of the High Middle Ages: Selected Sources Translated and Annotated*, ed. W. Wakefield and A. Evans (New York: Columbia University Press, 1969), pp. 1–67; Georg Schmitz-Valckenberg, *Grundlehren katharischer Sekten des 13. Jahrhunderts: Eine theologische Untersuchung mit besonderer Berücksichtigung von Adversus Catharos et Valdenses des Moneta von Cremona* (Munich: Ferdinand Schöningh, 1971), pp. 1–4.

52. Waldes of Lyons, Profession of Faith, in Antoine Dondaine, "Aux origines du Valdéisme: Une profession de foi de Valdes," *Archivum fratrum praedicatorum* 16 (1946): 231–32; trans. Wakefield and Evans, *Heresies*, number 32, pp. 206–8; see discussion in ibid., pp. 204–6.

substantiation, of meat eating, and of the full humanity of Christ. Dualist (and evangelical) denial of the redemption of the physical by Christ
was sometimes construed as a denial of (and revolt against) social difference. Twelfth-century chroniclers and preachers liked to accuse heretics of attracting women and those of the lower orders to their follow-
ings.[53] The authors of thirteenth-century tracts against heretics pointed
out that their teachings implied that gender difference might vanish,
either on earth (women might celebrate the sacraments!) or in heaven
(we might be unisex in our spiritual bodies!).[54] Salvo Burci in his *Liber
supra Stella*, written about 1235, emphasized that "this flesh" rises. He
accused heretics of making everyone equal by denying resurrection. But
what disturbed him was moral equality. Heretics deny that there is any
hell other than the suffering of this life, he says; therefore the difference
they remove is that between reward and punishment, good and evil.[55]

Close reading suggests that the opponents of heresy were indeed con-
structing their own interpretation of the importance of body by project-
ing onto an "other" that which they feared and opposed. But they did
not construe heretical denial of body primarily as an undercutting of
hierarchy and gender (although this was certainly an element). Precisely
because moralists, church lawyers, and chroniclers felt so comfortable
articulating misogyny and underlining status differences, we must take
seriously the fact that their polemics against heresy concentrated on
other aspects of physicality and individuality.[56] What they emphasized

53. Eleanor C. McLaughlin, "Les Femmes et l'hérésie médiévale: Un Problème
dans l'histoire de la spiritualité," *Concilium* 111 (1976): 73–90. And see Bernard of
Clairvaux, Sermon 65, paragr. 4, in *Opera*, ed. Leclercq, Talbot, and Rochais, *Sermones
super Cantica Canticorum*, vol. 1 (1957), pp. 174–75.

54. See Bernard of Fontcaude, *Adversus Waldensium sectam liber*, chap. 8, in PL
204 (Paris, 1855), cols. 825–28; Rainerius Sacconi, *Summa de Catharis et pauperibus
de Lugduno*, in Antoine Dondaine, *Un traite néo-manicheen du XIIIe siècle: Le Liber
du duobus principiis, suivi d'un fragment de rituel cathare* (Rome: Istituto storico
domenicano, 1939), pp. 64–78, especially p. 78, trans. in Wakefield and Evans, *Heresies*, number 51, chap. 28, p. 345; and Moneta of Cremona, *Adversus Catharos et
Valdenses Libri quinque* (Rome, 1743: reprint, Ridgewood, N.J.: Gregg Press, 1964),
bk. 1, chap. 2, sect. 4, p. 121, and bk. 4, chap. 7, sect. 1, p. 315.

55. Salvo Burci, *Liber supra Stella*, in P. Illarino da Milano, "Il 'Liber supra Stella'
del Piacentino Salvo Burci contro i catari e altre correnti ereticali," pt. 4: "Le dottrine
catare," *Aevum* 19, nos. 3–4 (1945): 281–341; see chaps. 17–18, fols. 85vb–91rb, ed.
Illarino da Milano, pp. 319–20. See also Ign. von Döllinger, *Beiträge zur Sektenges-
chichte des Mittelalters*, pt. 2: *Dokumente vornehmlich zur Geschichte der Valdesier
und Katharer* (Munich, 1890; reprint, New York: Burt Franklin, n.d.), pp. 52–85.

56. On medieval misogyny, see among others, Diane Bornstein, "Antifeminism,"
Dictionary of the Middle Ages, ed. J. Strayer, vol. 1 (New York: Scribner, 1982), pp.
322–35; R. Howard Bloch, *Medieval Misogyny and the Invention of Western Roman-
tic Love* (Chicago: University of Chicago Press, 1991); and pt. 1: "Les Normes du

in connection with heretical notions of eschatology was disrespect for proper burial, denial of purgatory, and disbelief in prayers for the dead.[57]

Guibert of Nogent, writing about 1114 of the heretics at Soissons, accused them of denying the difference between consecrated cemeteries and other ground. In the early 1130s Peter the Venerable said the heretic Peter of Bruys rejected prayers for the dead; Eberwin of Steinfeld in the early 1140s claimed that some of the heretics at Cologne denied purgatory, rejected prayers and offerings for the departed, and put no reliance in the cult of saints.[58] At the end of the century, the Waldensians and other evangelical groups were regularly attacked for denying purgatory and intercessions for the dead.[59] Cathars were said to tell "unheard-of fables," according to which we fall into terrestrial bodies and at death return again to bodies of ether in heaven; they were accused therefore of rejecting prayers for the deceased and differentiation of rewards in heaven. According to Salvo Burci, James Capelli, and Rainier Sacconi, all writing in the early thirteenth century, heretics held that Christ had no real body and did not die or rise; thus, the bodies of the saints remain dead, as did the rotting corpse Christ left behind; burial rites and consecrated cemeteries are therefore irrelevant or even offensive; the only resurrection is the rebirth of the soul in this life.[60]

As many historians have argued, the reasoning behind heretical positions is often unclear from the documents. Opposition to cemeteries, for example, can stem from antisacerdotalism or from dualist rejection

---

controle," in *Histoire des femmes en occident,* ed. G. Duby and M. Perrot, vol. 2: *Le moyen âge,* ed. Christiane Klapisch-Zuber (Paris: Plon, 1991), pp. 25–169. There is, of course, a deeper sense in which the abhorrence of bodily fertility, prevalent (as I explain below) in both mainstream and dualist Christian religiosity, is especially an abhorrence of female flesh and of female sexuality. For a very sophisticated study of the way in which scholastic disputes, and especially glosses on 1 Corinthians 15 (in this case 1 Cor. 15.24), could become loci for controversy over hierarchy versus equality of statuses, see Buc, *L'Ambiguité du livre,* chapter 2.

57. Despite what Christians charged, there is no evidence that heretics lacked concern and respect for the bodies of their dead. See Walter L. Wakefield, "Burial of Heretics in the Middle Ages," *Heresis* 5 (December 1985): 29–32.

58. See Wakefield and Evans, *Heresies,* pp. 102–3, 120, and 130–31.

59. For example, Bernard of Fontcaude, *Adversus Waldensium sectam,* chaps. 9–11, PL 204, cols. 828–35, trans. in Wakefield and Evans, *Heresies,* p. 213; and Ermengaud of Béziers (?), *Manifestatio haeresis Albigensium et Lugdunensium,* ed. in Antoine Dondaine, "Durand de Huesca et la polémique anti-cathare," *Archivum fratrum praedicatorum* 29 (1959): 268–71, esp. p. 270, trans. in Wakefield and Evans, *Heresies,* pp. 233–34, which accuses heretics of equating resurrection with transmigration of souls. See also Le Goff, *Birth of Purgatory,* pp. 171–73, 278–80, and other bibliography there. On later hostility to purgatory on the part of heretics, see ibid., pp. 331–33.

60. Wakefield and Evans, *Heresies,* pp. 269–74 and 301–46; Moneta of Cremona, *Adversus Catharos . . . ,* bk. 4, chap. 8, pp. 346–70; and see n. 55 above.

of matter. Opposition to purgatory can express anticlerical resistance to the cult of saints or dualist horror at the enshrining of relics; it can spring from antinomian conviction that redemption is the indwelling of the spirit. But what is clear, by the early thirteenth century, is that orthodox opponents thought heretics denied body because they saw it as rot. Salvo Burci accused Cathars of "dealing most slightingly with human bodies after death."

> You lay them secretly in pits here and there as best you can. This was not done with Christ's body, which was composed of the four elements. You say it was a spiritual body, but take note to the contrary that it was buried according to the Jewish rite. Hence you may clearly apprehend that it was a material body, for the Jews were not spiritual beings, but flesh and blood, and they performed burials in the earthly sense.[61]

Elsewhere he wrote:

> We want to show that the Apostle believed and preached the Son of God to be both God and man—that is, that he had and received human flesh. . . . But the heretics say: O blind church of Rome, put far away the conviction that the Son of God received flesh of the seed of David, of David's carnality, which flesh is full of worms and vermin; but that flesh of the Son of God was beautiful and clean—that is, it was spiritual not material flesh. . . . And what was the seed of David . . . ? [I]t was spiritual seed . . . whence the Apostle said that he came "in the likeness of sinful flesh." And note that he said "likeness" . . . I reply: O malignant heretics![62]

James Capelli said Cathars denied the Eucharist because they thought food was evil, "having its origin from earth." They held (he said) that "the devil divided the elements" and "gave fertility to the earth."[63] Rainier Sacconi wrote of one group of dualists: "All the Cathars who profess that Christ assumed a true human body deny that that body was glorified. . . . They say that Christ on the day of his ascension laid it aside in

---

61. Burci, *Liber supra Stella*, in op. cit., chap. 9, pp. 314–16; trans. Wakefield and Evans, *Heresies*, p. 274.

62. Burci, *Liber supra Stella*, in op. cit., chap. 19, fols. 93vb–94rb, pp. 320–21.

63. James Capelli, *Summa contra haereticos*, trans. in Wakefield and Evans, *Heresies*, pp. 304–5.

the shining sky and will resume it again on the Day of Judgment, and after the Judgment it will be resolved into pre-existent matter like a putrid corpse."[64] Thus, whether or not the historian M. D. Lambert is right in claiming that the heretical sense of body expressed disgust at organic process, it seems clear that orthodox opponents of Catharism understood Cathar rejection of body as an interpretation that equated body with putrefaction.[65]

Inconsistent though it may seem, the cannibalism libel that surfaces repeatedly against many varieties of heretics from the eleventh to the thirteenth centuries reflects the same perception. Heretics (say the orthodox) think the body is filth. They equate fertility with decay. They think therefore that nothing important can happen to the body; they deny that body is self. Thus they fornicate and eat the products of fornication; they cast the bodies of their dead into pits; they deny that any glory can be attained by flesh—ours or God's.

Although there is no reason to accord any credence to the cannibalism libel, it seems likely that some heretics actually held at least some of the opinions attributed to them by their orthodox opponents;[66] it is certain that the opponents abhorred the opinions. Yet there is reason to suspect that heretics articulated what the orthodox feared and believed. The art, spiritual writing, and scholastic debate I examined above suggest that orthodox discussion in the twelfth century was also dominated by a profound dis-ease with organic change, an association of nutrition and growth with decay.[67] Waldensian denial of cemeteries and prayers

64. Rainerius, *Summa de Catharis* . . . , in Dondaine, *Un traité neo-manicheen*, pp. 76–77; trans. in Wakefield and Evans, *Heresies*, number 51, chap. 25, p. 344.

65. M. D. Lambert, "The Motives of the Cathars: Some Reflections . . .," *Religious Motivation: Biographical and Sociological Problems for the Church Historian*, Studies in Church History, 15 (Oxford: Basil Blackwell for the Ecclesiastical History Society, 1978), pp. 49–59. See also Jacques Dalarun, "Regard de clercs," in *Histoire des femmes*, ed. Duby and Perrot, vol. 2: *Le moyen âge*, ed. Klapisch-Zuber, pp. 31–54, especially p. 37, which perceptively relates a feeling of disgust at the birth process and at decay to the elaboration of misogyny and situates such an elaboration particularly in the years around 1100. See also H. Crouzel, "Origène est-il la source du catharisme?" *Bulletin de littérature ecclésiastique* 80 (1979): 3–28.

66. See, for example, P. P. A. Biller, "Birth Control in the West in the Thirteenth and early Fourteenth Century," *Past and Present* 94 (February 1982): 3–26, esp. p. 10, which argues that heretics really held what Moneta of Cremona said they held.

67. See above, chapter 4, nn. 47, 66, 67, and 138. Eleanor Heningham, "An Early Latin Debate of the Body and Soul Preserved in MS Royal 7A III in the British Museum" (Ph.D. diss., New York University, 1939; printed by George Banta Publishing Company, Menasha, Wisconsin, 1939), p. 26, stresses the obsession with decay in the twelfth-century Latin Debate contained in the Royal manuscript and in the work of Anselm of Canterbury on which it draws. For a reflection of obsession with decay in the twelfth-century "Visions of Tondal," see below, chapter 7, pp. 293–94.

for the dead, Cathar denial of Christ's humanity and of literal resurrection, orthodox insistence on the reassemblage of a body impervious to change—all these positions (at least as expressed by orthodox writers) see redemption as triumph over process, digestion, and putrefaction. Heretical denial and orthodox assertion of bodily resurrection solved the same problem.

The orthodox thought heretics denied resurrection because heretics saw body as rot. These same orthodox wanted to see body as potential. They wanted to see the person as a self that expressed its selfhood in materiality; they sometimes even spoke of heaven as a flowering of flesh. But their flowers were really crystals. The bodies they envisioned in heaven were still reassembled bits. Resurrection was still, to twelfth-century theologians, proof that we are *not* what we eat nor what we generate. To rise was to return, like Rebecca West's conkers, numerically and formally and materially "the same." The fear of decay that Piero Camporesi has seen lying like a fog over early modern sensibility was never more present than in the antiheretical writing of the years around 1200.[68] Such fear of decay was also reflected in the numerous stories of miraculous victory over it.[69]

Miracles

When persecuting clergy accused heretics of denigrating the body, of identifying it with rot, of denying that it can be healed or glorified, they had powerful weapons. In addition to the Scripture they so often cited, the orthodox had (or believed they had) miracles. Moneta of Cremona, for example, argued against the Cathars that Christians have empirical proof of resurrection. They know bodies can be reassembled, healed, and raised from the dead because they see it happen.[70] The saints do not decay, in life or in death. They appear to us in visions, whole and shining; they move while yet alive toward the jewellike hardness of glory.

68. For Camporesi, see "Introduction," n. 12, and chapter 2, n. 191, above.

69. Recent important studies of miracles in this period include Finucane, *Miracles and Pilgrims*; Benedicta Ward, *Miracles and the Medieval Mind: Theory, Record, and Event, 1000–1215* (Philadelphia: University of Pennsylvania Press, 1982); Gélis and Redon, eds., *Les Miracles, miroirs*; and Pierre-André Sigal, *L'Homme et le miracle dans la France médiévale (XIe–XIIe siècle)* (Paris: Éditions du Cerf, 1985).

70. Moneta suggests that to deny Christ's bodily resurrection and ours is to deny miracles. For resurrection is only an extreme case of healing, but (he says) we see lots of healing miracles. Moneta, *Adversus Catharos . . .*, bk. 1, preface, pp. 2–7, trans. in Wakefield and Evans, *Heresies*, pp. 310–13.

Among the miracle stories that proliferated in Europe around 1200 were many that graphically expressed the idea that redemption is triumph over biological process, glory is the change to changelessness.

Prominent among twelfth- and thirteenth-century miracles were tales of living without eating (or by eating only the Eucharist) and of dying without decay. These miracles of miraculous inedia and incorrupt cadavers were especially characteristic of the bodies of saintly women, probably because both medical literature and misogynist tracts characterized the female body as more changeable than the male. Closer to decay because colder and wetter than men's bodies, the female body was also closer to being food for worms because it was in all ways closer to food. Women were seen not only as more voracious and greedy than men but also as being themselves nutrition—for fetuses in the womb and infants at the breast. Although all body was feared as teeming, labile, and friable, female body was especially so. Out of it came fluids and excrescences, and such products were seen more as putrefaction than as growth and new life. To theologians, hagiographers, and medical writers, fertility itself became decay.[71] Yet women could triumph over organic process. In desperate danger from digestion and rot, the female body could nonetheless be protected by the Eucharist from need for food; in death it could be protected from putrefaction (i.e., giving birth to worms) by the presence of its soul in paradise.[72] Thus closed to ordinary excretions, it might produce extraordinary effluvia (miraculous lactations, stigmatic bleeding, sweet oil and manna from graves) that cured diseases and assuaged pain.

Mary of Oignies, Alpaïs of Cudot, Christina the Astonishing, and Alice of Schaerbeek, for example, lived without eating. Hagiographers and chroniclers such as Thomas of Cantimpré, James of Vitry, and Roger Bacon were fascinated by the physiological details of their inedia and emphasized the beauty of what were in fact starving, gangrenous, or leprous bodies. A number of female saints were understood to be miraculously closed to ordinary female exudings, emanations, and breaches, both in life and in death.[73] The stigmatic Elisabeth of Spalbeek was de-

71. See my discussion of Herman of Reun above, chapter 4 at n. 66. Marie-Christine Pouchelle, *Corps et chirurgie à l'apogée du moyen âge: Savoir et imaginaire du corps chez Henri de Mondeville, chirurgien de Philippe le Bel* (Paris: Flammarion, 1983), discusses the medieval fear of the openings and exudings of the female body.

72. See my "The Female Body and Religious Practice," in *Fragmentation and Redemption*, pp. 181–238.

73. See my *Holy Feast and Holy Fast*, esp. pp. 88–93, 115–86, 196, and 274.

scribed by her hagiographer as giving forth "neither saliva nor sputum ... from her mouth nor any mucus or other fluid from her nostrils."[74] Lutgard of Aywières, who cured the sick with sweet oil that dripped miraculously from her fingers, did not menstruate or eat.[75] In the thirteenth century, we begin to hear tales of female bodies miraculously insensate and lightened. Douceline of Marseille levitated to astonishing heights; Beatrice of Nazareth and Lukardis of Oberweimar became rigid and impervious to any sensation when possessed by the spirit.[76] Herbert Thurston, the modern expert on somatic miracles, has shown that proponents of female canonizations in the late Middle Ages came to assume that women's cadavers would be found incorrupt.[77]

Triumph over process was not, however, limited to the female body. Spiritual writers from the early eleventh to the early thirteenth centuries told stories that emphasized the hardening and beauty all saintly bodies might achieve on earth. William of St. Thierry and the early thirteenth-century author of the *Ancrene Wisse* assumed that the bodies of ascetics would reflect the beauty, clarity, and agility of their souls.[78] The Life of Aethelwold, written by Wulfstan of Winchester about the year 1000, tells us that those present at the saint's death saw his corpse suddenly renewed with whiteness and rosiness, "in which observed change of the flesh appeared even on earth some hint of the glory of the resurrection [*in quo ... quaedam resurrectionis gloria per ostensionem mutatae carnis apparuit*]." Theodore of Echternach, in a *florilegium* from around 1104, argued that the saints are impervious to corruption after death because they are with God. Like Guibert of Nogent, Theodore recounted a number of cases of holy bodies resisting disturbance or decay, including one horrifying incident of a temple that burned when incorrupt bones were removed from it.[79] In such tales, the saints' power to resist change extends from their bones even to the buildings or tombs that house them. A century later, Caesarius of Heisterbach not only

74. Ibid., pp. 119, 120, and 122.
75. Ibid., pp. 122–23, 274.
76. Ibid., pp. 161–63 and 203–4.
77. Thurston, *Physical Phenomena*, pp. 246–52; and see *Fragmentation and Redemption*, p. 372 n. 32.
78. See above, chapter 4 at n. 39, and below, chapter 8 at n. 60.
79. Wulfstan of Winchester, *The Life of St. Aethelwold*, ed. Michael Lapidge and Michael Winterbottom (Oxford: Clarendon Press, 1991), pp. 62–63. Theodore of Echternach, *Flores epitaphii sanctorum*, bk. 1, chap. 3, bk. 2, chap. 3, and bk. 3, chap. 4, PL 157, cols. 324B–326A, 345A, and 375B. Guibert, *De pignoribus*, bk. 1, chap. 4, PL 156, cols. 626–28, and idem, *Self and Society in Medieval France*, bk. 3, chap. 20, p. 225, which repeats the story of the abbot whose hands were paralyzed because he investigated the remains of St. Edmund. See also Guth, *Guibert von Nogent*.

repeated tales of relics opposing their own fragmentation; he also told stories in which incorruption or other miraculous marks touched only part of a body. A master who had copied many books was found, when disinterred, to have his right hand undecayed although the rest of his body had crumbled into dust.[80] A pious man who said his prayers while walking returned after death in a vision with the words *Ave Maria* written on his boots; God, says Caesarius, puts "the mark of glory most of all on those members by which it is earned."[81]

The capacity to defeat change or to appear to change without truly changing was also reflected in innumerable folk motifs of food that is eaten without diminishing or that replenishes itself after consumption. As is well known, the late twelfth and early thirteenth centuries saw several adaptations of the Grail legend for religious purposes;[82] miracles of food multiplication and replenishment were common.[83] At least one twelfth-century saint's life suggests that hagiographers were conscious of the connection of such motifs with eschatology. In the life of St. Moling, a miracle is recounted in which a cat eats a bird that eats a fly, and each creature is then regurgitated unharmed. The hagiographer says explicitly: "In this [miracle] I saw the resurrection of the dead from a narrow sepulchre."[84]

The twelfth century was the high point of literalism and materialism in treatments of resurrection.[85] Images found in art, theology, and hag-

80. Caesarius, *Dialogus*, dist. 12, chap. 47, vol. 2, p. 354. As Carol Zaleski points out, the theme of bodies (including dead bodies) marked by the experience of soul is an old one in medieval literature (*Otherworld Journeys*, p. 79). See below, chapter 7, pp. 294–98.

81. Caesarius, *Dialogus*, dist. 12, chap. 50, vol. 2, pp. 355–56. See also ibid., chap. 54, p. 358. It is interesting to note that one of Caesarius's stories is, in modern terms, about a real body; the other is about a vision. To him there is little difference—so close had separated soul, body in the tomb, and person become.

82. See Etienne Gilson, "La mystique de la grace dans *La Queste del San Graal*," *Romania* 51 (1925): 321–47; M. I. Valory-Radot, "*La Queste del San Graal*: Roman cistercien," *Collectanea ordinis cisterciensium reformatorum* 18 (1956): 3–20, 199–213, 321–32; Nancy Freeman Regalado, "Le Chevalerie Celestiel: Spiritual Transformations of Secular Romance in *La Queste del Saint Graal*," in *Romance: Generic Transformations*, eds. Kevin and Marina Brownlee (Hanover: Dartmouth University Press, 1984), pp. 91–113.

83. See *Holy Feast and Holy Fast*, passim. For other miracles in which saints provide food or drink, or in general induce fertility, see Loomis, *White Magic*, pp. 37–39, 62, 78–81, 84–88, and 95.

84. Charles Plummer, *Vitae Sanctorum Hiberniae* (Oxford: Clarendon Press, 1910), vol. 2, p. 200; and see Loomis, *White Magic*, p. 63. For other examples of miracles of the restoration of animals, see ibid., p. 85. Loomis comments that in such miracles skin and bones usually serve as the basis for the restoration.

85. Brian Patrick McGuire, building on some of my work, has stressed the materialism of late medieval spirituality: see, "Spiritual Life and Material Life in the Middle Ages: A Contradiction? The Example of the Cistercians in Northern Europe,"

iography all suggest that salvation is reassemblage or regurgitation of exactly the bodies we have on earth; heaven is changelessness. Miracles of inedia and incorruption simply enact these ideas in more graphic form. Even in the twelfth century, however, we also find organic images for the redeemed self. William of St. Thierry wrote that flesh flowers when fertilized by spirit; Peter the Venerable thought the bones of his mother would grow to new life in the resurrection; Hildegard of Bingen, Guerric of Igny, and Thomas the Cistercian spoke of bodies not only as pearls but also as gardens. Thus it is not surprising to find that the years around 1200 saw new and extravagant tales of bodily process. Such miracles, like the popular miracles of stasis, expressed triumph over decay. Like the miracles of stasis, they too were recounted especially of the labile and friable bodies of women.

Some of these miracles, such as stigmata and miraculous lactation, were genuinely new; others, such as oil-exuding (from cadavers and from living ascetics), were known but infrequent before. Mary of Oignies and Gertrude of Delft wept and bled copiously in imitation of Christ; Christina the Astonishing and Lutgard of Aywières exuded healing oil and saliva; Dorothy of Montau swelled with mystical pregnancy in the presence of the Eucharist; Alice of Schaerbeek and Lidwina of Schiedam shed bits of fragrant skin as they lay paralyzed and dying. The bodies that experienced these emanations and breaches were those that were also wonderfully closed; they did not eat or waste away, excrete or menstruate, sicken or stink when death arrived.[86] Such miracles were therefore denial—and redemption—of ordinary organic process. Bodies that live without excreting or eating display death in life; corpses that exude sweet odors or flower into youthful beauty despite the assault of worms evidence life in death. What both the living (that is, the incorruptible) dead and the unchanging (that is, undecaying) living avoid is corruption.[87] Miracles of stasis and of process not only lodge in the same bodies; they express the same hope.

Twelfth-century images, whether lived in miracle or recounted in learned argument, were primarily metaphors of reassemblage and

---

Mensch und Objekt im Mittelalter und in der frühen Neuzeit: Leben—Alltag—Kultur: Internationaler Kongress Krems an der Donau 27. bis 30. September 1988 (Vienna: Verlag der österreichischen Akademie der Wissenschaften, 1990), pp. 285–313.

86. I have discussed this at much greater length in Holy Feast and Holy Fast, in "Bodily Miracles," and in Fragmentation and Redemption, pp. 181–238. See also now the article by Danielle Régnier-Bohler, "Voix littéraires, voix mystiques," in Histoire des femmes en occident, vol. 2: Le moyen âge, ed. Klapisch-Zuber, pp. 444–500.

87. For a similar point, see João de Pina-Cabral, Sons of Adam, Daughters of Eve: The Peasant World of the Alto Minho (Oxford: Clarendon Press, 1986), pp. 230–38, and Wilson, "Introduction," in Saints and Their Cults, p. 10.

changelessness. Where images of process were used, they frequently expressed the hope that God would triumph over it. The lovely language of florescence and germination suggested by the Song of Songs or by gospel parables of wheat and tares was usually applied only to spiritual progress. And even notions of spiritual growth carried no implication of open-ended transformation. The Pauline seed, as developed by Origen and Erigena and recapitulated by Honorius and (possibly) Amaury of Bene, was firmly rejected by the majority of twelfth-century writers. The sheaf in heaven would (they argued) merely reproduce the seed-body of earth. By the early decades of the thirteenth century, only heretics thought the elect would leave body behind in the ascent to salvation. Only heretics were willing to jettison the individuality body might express—in even its fingernails and its boots.

Yet the awkward materialism of theological discussion, the hesitant images of change without transformation, the odd miracles of static cadavers and bleeding but anorexic saints somehow express a sense of person as inextricably flesh and spirit. They express the conviction that, as Bernard said, we will not be happy in heaven until we are embodied again.[88] If miracles, pictures, and stories insisted that we must be vomited up by the tomb with every fingernail intact—i.e., that the ultimate threat is putrefaction, the ultimate victory changelessness—what was at stake was not finally fingernails.[89] It was self. The orthodox came closer than they suspected to agreeing with heretics that the devil creates fertility; process is threatening. But, in arguing that literal body must rise, the orthodox were assuming—as heretics did not—that body is integral to self.

When we turn to the late thirteenth century, we find a new focus on soul. Discussion is more philosophically agile; materialism abates. But, as we shall see, the conviction that self is by definition embodied had become lodged too firmly in Western Christian ideas to disappear.

88. See above, chapter 4 at n. 36. Peter Lombard and Otto of Freising agreed.
89. Thomas, in *Le Cadavre*, argues that all burial practices are an effort to mask and/or deny putrefaction. See also Camporesi, *Incorruptible Flesh*, on fear of decay.

Part Three

THE DECADES
AROUND 1300

Six

Resurrection, Hylomorphism, and *Abundantia:* Scholastic Debates in the Thirteenth Century

 IN CHRISTIAN ANTIQUITY, debates over the resurrection of the flesh were more central to efforts at self-definition than they have ever been since. Nonetheless the meaning of bodily resurrection remained an important issue in theological discussion and debate throughout the Middle Ages. Whether the body in heaven was understood to continue and sublimate or to change, reject, and reverse the body of earth, images of the afterlife were major loci in which theologians puzzled out and expressed notions of human destiny and of the self. In the acrimonious debates over Origenism in the early fifth century, as in twelfth- and thirteenth-century polemics against Cathar dualists or Erigenist antinomians, materialist conceptions of bodily resurrection were significant elements of the positions that triumphed as mainstream Christianity. Philosophical and aesthetic distaste for flux, as well as commonsense disgust with disease and putrefaction, surfaced again and again, but dead bodies remained central to religious practice, and the oxymorons "impassible body" and "incorruptible matter" were repeatedly defended as being at the heart of the Christian promise.

As we have seen, the Fourth Lateran Council in 1215 required Cathars and other heretics to assent to the proposition that "all rise with their own individual bodies, that is, the bodies which they now wear,"

and the Second Council of Lyon in 1274 reaffirmed the requirement.[1] Although standard histories of scholasticism have seen the immortality of the soul as the major issue of the 1270s,[2] it is clear that conservative theologians in the last decades of the thirteenth century were equally concerned that new Aristotelian ideas might make it impossible to conceptualize bodily resurrection.[3] Of the thirteen propositions condemned in 1270, one concerns soul (that soul, "which is the form of man according to which he is man," corrupts when body does), one concerns body (that God cannot give "immortality or incorruption" to a corruptible or mortal thing), and one the relationship between corporeal and incorporeal (that the "separated soul" after death cannot suffer from "corporeal fire").[4] By 1277 condemned propositions included not only an explicit and technically precise denial of resurrection ("that the corrupted body does not return one and the same, that is, does not rise numerically the same") but also other positions in which the issue of bodily identity is implicated: for example, "that God cannot give perpetuity to a mutable and corruptible thing," "that man, through the process of nutrition, can become another numerically and individually,"

1. See chapter 3, n. 136.

2. See, for example, Wicki, *Seligkeit*; Heinzmann, *Unsterblichkeit*; and Etienne Gilson, *History of Christian Philosophy in the Middle Ages* (New York: Random House, 1955). It is indicative that David Knowles, in his textbook on medieval intellectual history, chooses to treat the issue of the immortality of the soul as the exemplary case of thirteenth-century scholastic debate; see Knowles, *The Evolution of Medieval Thought* (London: Longmans, Green, 1962), chap. 17, pp. 206–18. For the modern, neo-Thomist position that lodges identity in soul, see Billot, *Quaestiones de Novissimis*, especially pp. 149–63.

3. A candidate's guide to examinations, composed by a Parisian Master of Arts in the 1230s, proposes that philosophy has nothing to say concerning resurrection because resurrection is a miracle not corresponding to natural laws; see Fernand Van Steenberghen, *Aristotle in the West: The Origins of Latin Aristotelianism*, trans. Leonard Johnston (Louvain: Nauwelaerts, 1955), pp. 95–99, esp. p. 99 n 1. A similar position was condemned in 1277 in Paris: see *Chartularium universitatis Parisiensis . . .*, ed. H. Denifle and A. Chatelain, vol. 1 (Paris: Delalain, 1889), proposition 18, p. 544; and Roland Hissette, *Enquête sur les 219 articles condamnés à Paris le 7 Mars 1277* (Louvain and Paris: Publications universitaires de Louvain and Vander-Oyez, 1977), p. 309. As Hissette points out, there need be nothing heretical about the assertion. It does suggest, however, that philosophical analysis is of no assistance to resurrection belief.

There is also some evidence from this period of religious doubt concerning resurrection. See, for example, the story of a dying student who wants to be persuaded of personal resurrection by rational argument: Alexander Neckham, *De naturis rerum*, bk. 2, chap. 73, *Rerum britannicarum medii aevi scriptores*, vol. 34, p. 297; John H. Mundy, *Europe in the High Middle Ages, 1150–1309* (London: Longman, 1973), pp. 523–24; and above chapter 5, n. 28.

4. *Chartularium universitatis Parisiensis . . .*, propositions 7, 13, and 8 respectively, pp. 486–87.

"that one should not take care for the burying of the dead," and "that death is the end of all terrors" (namely, that there is no eternal punishment of the damned).[5] It is true that by the early fourteenth century, the body-soul nexus (rather than the question of identity in resurrection) had become the crucial disputed issue in eschatology; nonetheless, the decades around 1300, like those around 200, 400, and 1215, were a period of Christian history in which the relationship of body to self became the place where preachers, artists, theologians, and ordinary folk explored what they meant by salvation.

The major discussions of resurrection in the later thirteenth century were highly technical philosophical and theological exercises—primarily either commentaries on the last part of book IV of Peter Lombard's *Sentences*[6] or so-called quodlibetal questions (written versions of disputations in which masters considered subjects proposed at random by members of their scholastic audience).[7] Such discussion was, of course, utterly unlike the highly rhetorical treatises in which Tertullian, Irenaeus, and Jerome attacked adversaries—pagan, heretical, or Christian—or the monastic exegesis of the twelfth century in which a pastiche of Biblical metaphors evoked the terrors of hell or the delights of heaven. But it was also quite unlike the works of Honorius, Hugh of St. Victor, and Peter Lombard, from which it often borrowed formulations, issues, and examples. The acquisition and appropriation in the early thirteenth century of key Aristotelian concepts, such as substance, meant that basic ideas of nature and human nature had to be reconsidered. For example, once Aristotle's analysis of generation and corruption was understood and adopted, no theologian would any longer hold that the much-discussed *veritas humanae naturae* can be a core of matter, handed down from Adam to his descendants, multiplied by itself into the adult body, and preserved in the grave until the end of time.[8] Biblical and patristic images of resurrection as reassemblage or return—images

5. Ibid., propositions 17, 25, 148, 155, 178, pp. 544–53, and Hissette, *Enquête sur les 219 articles condamnés*, pp. 187, 294, 307–8.

6. See Chenu, *Toward Understanding St. Thomas*, pp. 267–69, on *Sentence* commentaries. On the Lombard see above chapter 3, n. 13.

7. See ibid., pp. 28off.; Gordon Leff, *Paris and Oxford Universities in the Thirteenth and Fourteenth Centuries: An Institutional and Intellectual History* (New York: Wiley, 1968), pp. 163–74; and Palémon Glorieux, *La Littérature quodlibetique de 1260 à 1320*, Bibliothèque thomiste 5 and 21 (Le Saulchoir: Kain, 1925, and Paris: J. Vrin, 1935).

8. Aristotle's analysis did not actually solve the problem of how one molecule can change into another via digestion or reproduction; see Cadden, "Medieval Philosophy and Biology of Growth." What it did was to make it clear that when something decays, is digested, or reproduces, it does not retain a material core that accounts for identity.

borrowed with enthusiasm by the early schoolmen—had to be re-thought in the light of this new scientific vocabulary.[9] The seeds, stat-ues, and whales that had dominated discussion of resurrection for a thousand years were thus in the mid-thirteenth century either thrown out or radically redefined.[10]

Nonetheless metaphor did not entirely disappear. Even in the refined, adroit, and highly self-conscious theological discourse of the decades around 1300, images and examples crept in—examples that reveal far more than their authors intended. I begin my analysis of thirteenth-century ideas of resurrection by returning to the Pauline text with which I began this book. For 1 Corinthians 15.42–44 had a remarkable fate in scholastic discussion and exegesis. "Sown in corruption, . . . raised in incorruption; sown in dishonor, . . . raised in glory; . . . sown in weak-ness, . . . raised in power; . . . sown a natural body, . . . raised a spiritual body" was not, in the *Sentence* commentaries and quodlibetal discus-sions of the mid-thirteenth century, a description of a seed at all. Rather it was an enumeration of the "dowries" (*dotes*) given by the blessed soul to the glorified body in a process of "flowing over" (*redundantia* or *abun-dantia*) that arose from something some authors called *ordinatio* or *in-clinatio, affectus,* or even *desiderium.*

The Discourse of High Scholasticism: The Rejection of Statues and Seeds

Sometime between 1259 and 1265, the highly controversial theologian Thomas Aquinas commented on all the epistles of Paul. At the end of his life he took up again the task of Pauline commentary and probably wrote out his own exposition. He died just after reaching 1 Corinthians 10. After his death, Reginald of Piperno (who had written up the text of Aquinas's first Pauline exegesis) put together a commentary on 1 Corin-thians from what Thomas had completed, his own earlier transcript, and some supplementary material.[11] The commentary on 1 Corinthians 15

9. The rethinking was of course going on already in the later twelfth century. See above, chapter 3 at nn. 56 and 57, especially the example of William of Auxerre, who explained quite clearly that the material continuity of the bits of a broken statue or temple cannot account for identity even if they are reassembled, because they will have a new form.

10. On theories of bodily resurrection in this period generally, see Greshake and Kremer, *Resurrectio mortuorum;* Michel, "Résurrection"; Cornélis et al., *Resurrec-tion;* Emile Mersch, "Corps mystique et spiritualité," *Dictionnaire de spiritualité,* vol. 2, cols. 2378–97; and Weber, *Auferstehung.*

11. Aquinas, *In epistolam I ad Corinthios commentaria,* chap. 15, lectiones 2, and 5–9, in *Opera omnia,* vol. 21, ed. S. E. Fretté (Paris: Vivès, 1876), pp. 33–34, 41–52.

that has come down to us is thus not Thomas's own draft but rather a report of his early classroom teaching made by a close disciple.[12] The precision, clarity, and forcefulness with which Thomas marches through the text may be characteristic, but the content of his commentary is not original. Thomas uses 1 Corinthians 15 exactly as do such predecessors and contemporaries as William of Auxerre, Grosseteste, Albert the Great, and Bonaventure.[13] His clear but conventional readings can serve to introduce the issues and images characteristic of scholastic discussion in the 1250s and 1260s. Thomas takes 1 Corinthians 15 as raising two issues: that of the identity of the earthly and risen body and that of the nature of the additions to body in glory.[14] In the course of discussion, he rejects the seed image of verses 36–38 and 42–44, restricts the clothing image of verses 53–54, and introduces two images not present in the Pauline text at all—the image of gifts or dowries (*dotes*) and the image of spillover, overflow, or expression (*abundantia*).

Aquinas begins his exegesis of 1 Corinthians 15 with the admission that the seed metaphor might seem to imply that resurrection is natural—an unfolding of a preordained pattern from within the organism.[15] It might also imply that the second organism in question (the sheaf) is different from the first (the seed) not only in appearance (that is, accidental characteristics or qualities) but also as an individual or instance (that is, numerically—*numero*—as technical scholastic vocabulary put it). Making use of Aristotle in a way that goes back to the later twelfth century,[16] Aquinas comments that nature reproduces species, not number—that is, it reproduces the same kind of thing (like produces like), but it cannot produce again the same instance once that instance has

12. See James A. Weisheipl, *Friar Thomas d'Aquino: His Life, Thought, and Works* (Garden City, N.Y.: Doubleday, 1974), p. 372–73; Chenu, *Toward Understanding St. Thomas*, p. 248.

13. Wicki, *Seligkeit*; Joseph Goering, "The *De Dotibus* of Robert Grosseteste," *Mediaeval Studies* 44 (1982): 83–109; and Weber, *Auferstehung*, pp. 314–42.

14. Weber, *Auferstehung*, says these are the two central issues for thirteenth-century discussion of resurrection. See also Wilhelm Kübel, "Die Lehre von der Auferstehung der Toten nach Albertus Magnus," in *Studia Albertina: Festschrift für Bernhard Geyer zum 70. Geburtstage*, ed. Heinrich Ostlender, BGPTM, Supplementband 4 (Münster: Aschendorf, 1952), pp. 279–318.

15. The position he spells out only in order to refute is, of course, exactly the understanding of the seed on which Origen and Erigena drew to forge their very different notions of resurrection and body. The question of whether resurrection is natural, which so concerned thirteenth-century *Sentence* commentators, was first brought up in the twelfth century by Magister Martin and elaborated by William of Auxerre, using 1 Corinthians 15.52; see Kübel, "Auferstehung nach Albertus Magnus," pp. 288–92 and 302–6.

16. See nn. 9 and 15 above. Aquinas takes the standard position that resurrection is natural in its goal.

disappeared or corrupted. So the exegetical and philosophical challenge confronting Aquinas is to make the Pauline seed imply exactly what it appears at first glance not to imply. It must suggest both that resurrection is, in its cause, supernatural not natural, and that the body that returns is identical numerically (*numero*) and specifically (*in speciem*), not qualitatively.[17]

Aquinas accomplishes this ingenious reinterpretation of Paul by arguing that the apostle faced two sorts of opponents: "some" who think there can be no resurrection, because resurrection is not natural, and "some" who think that, because resurrection is natural, exactly the same body will return.[18] It is in answer to these positions that Paul raised the two questions of verse 35: how can resurrection occur? What kind of body will rise? But (says Aquinas) Paul answered the second question first. Therefore the seed metaphor of verses 36–44 is intended to illustrate the nature of the resurrection body, in its difference from the body of earth, not to indicate its cause. Resurrection is not a natural process. There is no force (no "seminal reason" or "virtue") in things that directs them toward return. Body dissolves into a dust that has no more power or fertility than any other dust. Resurrection is thus exactly the opposite from germination. Grain returns as an adult sheaf similar to the sheaf that bore the dissimilar seed; it returns by natural (internal or organic) process as a like but numerically nonidentical instance.[19] Body returns

17. It is significant that the issue of numerical identity is also central to Aquinas's commentary on one of the other major "resurrection texts": Job 19. 23–29; ". . . yet in my flesh shall I see God" means, says Thomas, that the man who sees will be *idem numero*, not merely in species. Thomas Aquinas, *Expositiones in Job*, chap. 19, lectio 2, in *Opera omnia*, vol. 18, ed. S. E. Fretté (Paris: Vives, 1876), pp. 119–20; see n. 117 below. For the same argument, see *Summa contra Gentiles*, bk. 4, chap. 81, in ibid., vol. 12, ed. Fretté (Paris: Vives, 1874) [hereafter SCG], pp. 593–96; and see *Quaestiones de anima*, q. 19, in Aquinas, *Quaestiones de anima: A Newly Established Edition of the Latin Text*, ed. James H. Rob (Toronto: Pontifical Institute of Mediaeval Studies, 1968), pp. 245–52.

18. *In I Cor.*, chap. 15, lectio 5, *Opera*, ed. Fretté, vol. 21, p. 41. We find the same argument in the *Supplementum* to the *Summa theologica* [or *theologiae*], quaestio 79, art. I, obj. I and reply to obj. I, in *Sancti Thomae Aquinatis doctoris angelici opera omnia iussu impensaque Leonis XIII p.m. edita*, vol. 12 (Rome: S. C. de Propaganda Fide, 1906) [hereafter *Sup.* (Leonine ed.)], p. 178; trans. Fathers of the English Dominican Province, *Thomas Aquinas: Summa theologica*, vol. 3 (New York: Benziger, 1948), pp. 2889–90. The *Supplementum* was put together after Aquinas's death (probably by Reginald of Piperno) from his early *Sentence* commentary.

19. *In I Cor.*, chap. 15, lectio 5, *Opera*, vol. 21, pp. 41–43. See *Sup.*, q. 79 art. 1, obj. 1 (Leonine ed.), p. 178; trans. English Dominicans, vol. 3, p. 2889: ". . . the Apostle is there [verse 37] comparing death to sowing and resurrection to fructifying. Therefore the same body that is laid aside is not resumed." And reply to obj. 1, (Leonine ed.) p. 178; trans. English Dominicans, vol. 3, p. 2890: "A comparison does not apply to every particular. . . . For in the sowing of grain, the grain sown and the grain that is born

not naturally but by divine power ("But God giveth it a body . . ."); it returns identical in number and species ("and to every seed his own body"), but it rises with the new qualities of glory.[20]

To Aquinas, the four pairs of contrasts in verses 42–44 refer not to the substance or species of the risen body but to its qualities: *claritas*, *agilitas*, *subtilitas*, and *impassibilitas*. These had been known at least since William of Auxerre as the *dotes* (dowries or gifts) of the glorified body.[21] It would be silly, argues Aquinas, to say we *are* air or light; rather we have subtlety—lightness or airiness—added to our bodies, spilled over or infused from the beatified soul.[22] The verb "to clothe" (*induere*) of verses 53–54 and of 2 Corinthians 5.2–4 does not mean that the body is a garment, donned on earth and discarded or replaced in heaven; it means rather that immortality (a quality) is added to what we are—i.e., "this soul" and "this body, repaired from the same dust into which it was dissolved."[23] In Aquinas's interpretation, verses 42–44 refer to contrast and diversity: the contrast of earthly and heavenly body, the diversity of gifts. Verse 41 ("one star differeth from another star in glory") is associated with verses 42–44 to suggest that although all rise, the dowries differ from saint to saint. There is no equality in heaven.[24]

---

thereof are neither identical, nor of the same condition . . . and the body will rise again identically the same, but of a different condition."

20. Aquinas uses Job 29.27 here; *In I Cor.*, chap. 15, lectio 5, *Opera*, vol. 21, p. 42. He makes the same argument in the *Expositio* on Job; see above, n. 16.

21. See Wicki, *Seligkeit*, pp. 202–12; they were developed from the seven qualities of the glorified body elaborated by Anselm and Eadmer in the early twelfth century.

22. *In I Cor.*, chap. 15, lectio 6, *Opera*, ed. Fretté, vol. 21, pp. 44–46. For other places where Thomas uses verses 42–44 to mean the *dotes* or "qualities" of the glorified body, see SCG, bk. 4, chaps. 79, 84 and 86, *Opera*, ed. Fretté, vol. 12, pp. 591–92, 602–3 and 604–5; and *Sup.*, qq. 82–85 (Leonine ed.) pp. 187–200.

23. *In I Cor.*, chap. 15, lectio 9, *Opera*, vol. 21, p. 51. Question 5 *De potentia Dei*, art. 10, also rejects the idea (which he here calls Platonic) of body as a garment or tool, because it implies something added on; see *Quaestiones disputatae de potentia*, in Aquinas, *Opera omnia* (Parma 1853–73 ed. with new intro. by V. J. Bourke), vol. 8 (New York: Musurgia, 1949), pp. 120–22, esp. p. 121 col. 2, and *On the Power of God* (*Quaestiones disputatae de potentia Dei*), vol. 2 (qq. 4–6), trans. the Dominican Fathers (London: Burns, Oates, and Washbourne, 1933), p. 147. In *Summa theologiae*, [hereafter ST], ed. Blackfriars (New York: McGraw-Hill, 1964–81) 3a, quaestio 25, art. 6, vol. 50, pp. 202–5, treating relics, Aquinas does use the garment image from Augustine's *City of God*; he also uses the image of body as temple or dwelling place. But it is important to note that he says (agreeing with Augustine) that body is "more important to us" than a treasured garment. We should also note that the context is discussion of the cadaver (which to Aquinas—as we shall see—is not really the body). In his commentary on Job (see n. 16 above), Aquinas uses the idea of body as garment or covering in explaining 19.23–29 but seems specifically to mean that we will receive back flesh to cover bone.

24. *In I Cor.*, chap. 15, lectio 6, *Opera*, ed. Fretté, vol. 21, pp. 43–44.

Aquinas hints at the Platonic argument from desire as a proof of resurrection: God would not leave soul forever with its desire either for immortality or for body unfulfilled.[25] Nonetheless he is quite uneasy with any notion of yearning toward completion. Several times in his exegesis he returns to refute the idea that there is a force (vis) or inclination (inclinatio) in the dust to which we decay. Dust is not seed (although Aquinas does suggest that, in order for the same body to rise, there must be some ordinatio of our particles for return). Like his contemporaries, he quotes Augustine's letters 56 and 118 to suggest that the dotes are a spilling over (abundantia) from the soul to the body, but he prefers to call them additions rather than infusions, and he never refers to redundantia as love.[26] When he uses (as did Peter Lombard and Bernard) Augustine's Literal Commentary on Genesis, book 12, chapter 35, to describe the separated soul, he says only that soul without body is imperfect and ignores the powerful image of the retardatio of desire so emphasized by some of his contemporaries.[27] Thomas explicitly rejects the sensual heaven of wives and banquets promised to "Saracens"; he takes the much disputed verse 50 ("flesh and blood cannot inherit . . .") to exclude from paradise not only flesh as sinfulness but also flesh as sensuality and striving. The goal of impassibilitas is freedom from "noxious passions, internal and external"—a stasis (quies) that includes the stilling of any yearning between soul and body or matter.[28]

In rejecting the fructifying seed as an analogy to the event of resurrection, Aquinas was accepting a fully Aristotelian analysis of natural change and, precisely because of this, rejecting eschatological metaphors of rebirth and return. Other mid-thirteenth-century theologians agreed. Bonaventure in his Sentence commentary (written a little earlier than Thomas's commentaries on the Sentences and on 1 Corinthians) argued that reconstituting the body is contra naturam; reuniting the body with

25. Aquinas prefers the more Aristotelian—and anthropological—version of the argument, which suggests that if homo is by definition soul and body, these two principles cannot be left separated for all eternity; see In I Cor., chap. 15, lectio 2, Opera, vol. 21, pp. 33–34.

26. In I Cor., chap. 15, lectio 5, pp. 42–43. See also ST 3a, qq. 14–15, esp. q. 15 art. 10, vol. 49, pp. 170–221; and Sup., q. 92, art. 2, reply obj. 6 (Leonine ed.), p. 222, on redundantia, and trans. English Dominicans, vol. 3, p. 2965. Albert the Great does not hold the dotes to be a spillover but does see them as added to the body because of the soul; Kübel, "Auferstehung nach Albertus Magnus," p. 305.

27. Sup., q. 93, art. 1 (Leonine ed.), pp. 224–25, mentions (but does not really utilize) the idea of removing the retardation of desire.

28. In I Cor., chap. 15, esp. lectiones 6 and 7, pp. 44 (the discussion of impassibilitas) and 47. See also Weber, Auferstehung, pp. 64–65, who suggests that Franciscans are more apt to see the dotes as redundantia, Dominicans to see them as additions; this is true, but both groups use both sorts of metaphors.

the soul is *secundum naturam* (because man *is* body and soul); uniting soul and body inseparably so that the incorruptible comes from the corruptible is *supra naturam*.[29] Thus Job 14.7, which compares resurrection to the germination of a tree, 1 Corinthians 15.37, which compares it to a sprouting seed, and Exodus 7, which tells of the birth of serpents from rods, certainly show the power of nature, which can produce life even from slime and decay. But they are not good analogies for resurrection.[30] Although Bonaventure goes further than most other thirteenth-century thinkers in locating yearning not only in soul but even in the particles of dust to which we decay, he does not make the fulfilling of such yearning a natural process: "such is the human body that it cannot be organized naturally unless both seed and womb [*vas suscipiens, scilicet matrix*] are present."[31] Bonaventure's analogy for yearning toward completion and incorruption is, as we shall see, not biological but psychological: the love (*amor*) of a man for a woman.[32]

Some of Thomas' contemporaries or disciples, who were more interested than he in biological change for its own sake, found additional problems with the seed metaphor. Albert the Great (d. 1280) not only pointed out (citing Aristotle's *On Generation*) that it raised the question of numerical identity; he also commented that a seed does not die but rather lives and germinates. So the fructifying seed signifies neither death ("the corruption of the life of the same individual numerically") nor resurrection ("the second rising [as Damascene says] of that which fell").[33] Giles of Rome (d. 1316), who argued that resurrection cannot be entirely natural,[34] rejected the seed metaphor even as an analogy to hu-

29. Bonaventure, Commentary on the *Sentences*, in *Opera omnia*, ed. A. C. Peltier, vol. 6 (Paris: Vives, 1866), bk. 4, dist. 43, art. 1, q. 5, pp. 459–62. And see Michael Schmaus, "Die Unsterblichkeit der Seele und die Auferstehung des Leibes nach Bonaventura," *L'Homme et son destin d'après les penseurs du moyen âge*, Actes du premier Congrès International de Philosophie Médiévale, 1958 (Louvain and Paris: Nauwelaerts, 1960), pp. 505–19, esp. p. 512.

30. *Sentence* Commentary, dist. 43, art. 1, q. 5, pp. 459–62, esp. *contra* 1 and 5.

31. Ibid., art. 1, q. 5, conclusio, p. 461. For the complexity of Bonaventure's position on yearning in matter, see Schmaus, "Unsterblichkeit nach Bonaventura," and below, pp. 249–51. See also Bonaventure, *Breviloquium*, pt. 7, chap. 5, in *Opera omnia*, ed. A. C. Peltier, vol. 7 (Paris: Vives, 1866), pp. 336–38; and in *The Works of Bonaventure*, trans. Jose de Vinck, vol. 2: *The Breviloquium* (Paris: Desclée, and Patterson, N.J.: St. Anthony Guild Press, 1963), pp. 294–98.

32. See n. 62 below, and cf. n. 56.

33. Albert, *De resurrectione*, ed. Wilhelm Kübel, in *Alberti Magni Opera omnia*, ed. Institutum Alberti Magni Coloniense, vol. 26 (Münster: Aschendorff, 1958) tractate 1, qq. 1–2, pp. 237–43, esp. reply to obj. 8, pp. 241–42.

34. Giles of Rome, *Quaestiones de resurrectione mortuorum*, ed. Kieran Nolan, in *The Immortality of the Soul and the Resurrection of the Body According to Giles of Rome: A Historical Study of a Thirteenth-Century Theological Problem* (Rome: Studium Theologicum "Augustinianum," 1967), pp. 69–75, 90–96, 105–13, 124–30,

man reproduction (both the ordinary reproduction of copulation and the extraordinary reproduction of the Garden of Eden) because wheat (unlike woman) can germinate by itself. It is for this reason, says Giles, that ants cut off the radicals when they store grain.[35]

What thirteenth-century intellectuals rejected in the seed analogy was exactly what Origen and Erigena had seen its power to be: a sense of body as an unfolding internal principle that might flower in an expression of self utterly different from the self of earth.[36] In rejecting this understanding of body, they continued the suspicion of natural analogies and open-ended process that their twelfth-century teachers had expressed in notions of reunited particles, reconstructed statues, or a perduring core or "truth" of human nature. But thirteenth-century schoolmen also rejected the images of reassemblage of which early scholastics had been fond. While they all maintained a conception of the resurrection body as integral—as retaining all aspects and elements of its earthly structure (the fingers and toes of the statue)—they all held that the analogy of body to statue must for highly technical reasons be discarded or radically revised.[37]

The more Aristotelian among the schoolmen move, as we shall see, to a formal understanding of identity and use analogies of the sort Methodius attributed to Origen. The identity of a thing depends on what it is (its form or, in some sense, structure) continuing over time. As Giles of Rome explains (borrowing the analogy from Aristotle, *On Generation and Corruption, 1.5*), liquid is taken into and poured out of a waterskin

see esp. q. 2, p. 92, lines 82–84. And see Nolan's discussion in ibid., pp. 65–141 passim. Giles thinks the Aristotelian position on identity makes it impossible for resurrection to be natural; uniting soul with body in resurrection cannot be the same as uniting soul with body in the womb.

Giles of Rome's *Sentence* commentary never reached bk. 4; the *Quaestiones* edited by Nolan are therefore his major statement on resurrection. Giles's position on identity clearly foreshadowed Durand's but did not go all the way to it; see Nolan, *Giles*, pp. 88 and 120, and Weber, *Auferstehung*, pp. 234–36.

35. M. Anthony Hewson, *Giles of Rome and the Medieval Theory of Conception: A Study of the De formatione corporis humani in utero* (London: University of London, Athlone Press, 1975), p. 73.

36. As we shall see, the notion of an internal principle (even one with a certain dynamism) was not rejected; to some Franciscan thinkers, it was crucial. What was threatening clearly was the idea that the body of heaven might not be fully integral, possessing all the details and particularities of the earthly body.

37. Albert the Great, for example, argued that the statue analogy is about integrity not matter. If it is useful, it is useful because it emphasizes that all members return. It does not mean that all matter must return and go to the same place it occupied at death. See Albert, *De resurrectione*, ed. Kübel, tractate 1, q. 6, art. 11, p. 257. And see Aquinas, *Sup.*, q. 79, art. 2, obj. 4 and reply to obj. 4 (Leonine ed.), pp. 179–80.

but the skin remains; similarly the soul and form of man remain the same although his flesh *secundum materiam* waxes and wanes (*fluit et refluit*).[38] As Aquinas says, a city remains a city even if the population turns over through birth, death, and migration;[39] a fire remains a fire if one keeps feeding it logs, even if all the logs are consumed.[40] It does not remain the same city if it is razed or the same fire if it is allowed to go out and is then relit.

Such analogies, in which internal structure or external container remains and contents change, suggest that the case of the statue is exactly backward;[41] the reforged statue is the same material but not the same structure or container.[42] Thus Aquinas says in his *Sentence* commentary that a remade statue is in a certain sense not the same even if it is recast from the same brass, because it has a second form, not the original one.[43] Fifty years later, John Quidort of Paris made use of these Aristotelian distinctions to argue:

There is no analogy between man and a statue, because an artificial thing has its being [*esse*] from its matter, but a natural thing from form, and the former is the same thing from identity of matter but the latter is the same from identity of form. And . . . with regards to Ezekiel 37, . . . it is true that the formed bones go back to their own place and their own joints. But it is not necessary that they be formed from the same matter.[44]

38. Giles, *Quaestiones*, ed. Nolan, q. 3, p. 110, lines 184–97.
39. *Sup.*, q. 80, art. 4 (Leonine ed.) pp. 182–84, esp. 183 col. 2, lines 60–75.
40. ST 1a, q. 119, a. 1, reply obj. 5, vol. 15, pp. 172–73.
41. The wineskin analogy is the cruder analogy, philosophically speaking.
42. For this argument in Albert, see Kübel, "Auferstehung nach Albertus Magnus," pp. 297–98.
43. Aquinas, *Sentence* commentary, bk. 4, dist. 44, art. 1, quaestiuncula 2, obj. 4, and quaestiuncula 3, *Opera omnia* (Parma 1852–73 ed. with intro. by Bourke), vol. 7 (New York: Musurgia, 1948), pp. 1072–75. The argument is complicated because Aquinas, here following a standard Aristotelian argument, holds that a statue (as an artificial thing) belongs to the genus of substance by reason of its matter; therefore, it is the same statue when remade if we consider it as a particular substance. But it is not identically the same (*idem numero*) because its form has been destroyed. A person is not, however, a statue; "the form of the human being, that is the soul, remains when body perishes." Indeed the human body has no substantial form *other than* the rational soul. Since that substantial form survives, the body it animates at the end of time is the same body (*idem homo numero*). Aristotle and his commentators had clearly established that "the matter of a statue ranks higher in the statue than the matter of a man does in man." Being formed from the same dust or ashes does not in any sense make something the same person.
44. See John Quidort, *Quaestio* on the *Sentences*, bk. 4, dist. 45, ed. by Weber, *Auferstehung*, pp. 376–77.

In other words, to John, both Augustine's statue and Ezekiel's dry bones are useful analogies to resurrection only if they refer to structure and integrity, not to material continuity.[45]

Franciscan thinkers such as Bonaventure, Richard of Middleton, and Peter of Trabes do not assert a formal principle of identity; they are therefore more comfortable with the image of the statue, to which they assimilate the image of the rebuilt ark (which is, in fact, Tertullian's ship). They use it, as the Lombard did, to suggest both material continuity and integrity (or continuity of structure).[46] Bonaventure comments: "If an ark dissolves and is remade from the same planks according to the same order, we do not say it is another ark but the same."[47] In the case of human death, soul and body are separated from each other, and body is "incinerated" into "dust"; but God "like a good craftsman" collects the ashes and unites them into *idem corpus—idem* because it has the same *perfectio* (that is, integrity) as before.[48]

Bonaventure clearly worries, however, that this is not a sufficient solution. If we follow his reasoning closely, we see that he proceeds to analyze the analogy out of existence. "Corruption is of two types," he argues. One is dissolution into particles; the other is destruction of form. Body appears to undergo both; its form (which, for Bonaventure, is not the soul) seems to dissolve in the grave, and new forms emerge in the decaying cadaver.

> It is certain that the form of human flesh is corrupted, and there is generated from it worms and serpents; and just as it can be corrupted into the flesh of serpents and other animals, so it can be resolved (like that of an animal) into the four elements, and these elements can be

45. Aquinas agreed. But at least in the relatively early position of his *Sentence* commentary (see n. 43 above), he assumed that we, like the statue, will in fact be made again of the same dust—although matter does not account for identity. Indeed, he even considered it probable (although not necessary) that the dust will return to the part (that is, the organ or structure) from which it came.

46. See Bonaventure, *Sentence* commentary, bk. 4, dist. 43, q. 4, conclusio, p. 457, and Weber, *Auferstehung*, p. 245. Tertullian used the ship analogy to assert integrity, not material continuity, although he assumed material continuity in other places. See above chapter 1 at n. 63.

47. Aquinas would not disagree; see above, n. 43.

48. Bonaventure, *Sentence* commentary, bk. 4, dist. 44, dub. 4, p. 475. Bonaventure asserts clearly that, "if a statue has a soul," then it is the same statue because its matter and final form are the same, if not its intermediate forms. The position comes fairly close to a formal principle of identity; Bonaventure even says here "the whole reason of personhood comes from soul." But he goes on to say that if the flesh (which is an intermediate form) must be the same, it is beyond nature to restore this; hence it is the same statue only *supra naturam*.

corrupted into others and the corrupted forms thus mixed; therefore it is necessary that it become other elements numerically and other flesh. . . . But resurrection must be the same numerically or it is not resurrection.[49]

We see here vestiges of the old fear of decay and fertility that twelfth-century thinkers such as Hugh and Peter Lombard dealt with by asserting some sort of unchanging *caro radicalis* or perduring particles of matter—by denying, that is, that human flesh truly grows and decays in life or in the tomb. Bonaventure, however, good Aristotelian that he is, accepts the reality of flux.[50] Thus he solves the problem of identity, first, by asserting divine power: the same form *can* be restored after corruption *per virtutem divinam* although not *per naturam*.[51] Second, he develops the Augustinian notion of seminal reasons to suggest that the form of the body is latent in some way in the particles. Nature cannot draw it out, for nature acts by flowing in or imparting (*influendo, impertiendo*), but God can reform—draw out of the particles—the identical form that existed before.[52]

The solution is an ingenious if incoherent one—and it bears some similarities to the way in which Origen hundreds of years earlier coped with the need to admit flux (although the internal dynamic pattern it implies is teleological and determined, not open-ended, and the role of divine action is much more carefully delineated). What is clear, however, is that Bonaventure (almost as effectively as Albert and Thomas) has undercut any notion that the resurrection body is a rebuilt ark or statue although its structure and matter may be the same. Reassembling bits of matter after destruction is no longer a useful analogy for explaining the process of resurrection. If the resurrection of the body involves bringing particles together, the particles are not, to Bonaventure, bits of inert stuff; they are dynamic—pregnant with something akin to feeling.

In general, therefore, images of the resurrection body as re-born, regurgitated, or reassembled fell out of thirteenth-century discussion. Images of body itself as a prison or house, stole or garment also became unimportant, although images of beauty or glory as a garment or gift or endowment *added to* body became, as we have seen, very common. The

49. Bonaventure, *Sentence* commentary, bk. 4, dist. 43, q. 4, conclusio, p. 457.

50. Ibid., q. 4, contra, p. 456. I accept the position of Van Steenberghen, *Aristotle in the West*, that Bonaventure made full use of Aristotelian concepts.

51. Bonaventure, *Sentence* commentary, q. 4, conclusio, p. 457.

52. Ibid., pp. 457–58.

images that emerge into new prominence, building on twelfth-century uses of Augustine, suggest however a far closer union of soul and body. Soul is said to need, to desire, to love, and to yearn for body, as a man loves a beautiful virgin.[53] Peter of Trabes glosses the "cry" of souls under the altar (Rev. 6. 9–10) as desire for the body's return [*desiderium animarum sanctarum ad corporum resumptionem*].[54] Richard of Middleton comments that the saints in heaven desire our completion as well as their own, because only when the number of the elect is filled up will the trumpet sound: "because of their natural desire to resume their own bodies, they pray more efficaciously for us."[55] Theologians such as John Quidort, who disdain erotic metaphors for technical reasons, nonetheless speak of an orientation (*ordinatio*) or aptitude toward body (if not toward the particular body possessed before, at least toward body as species). Such inclination must be answered in order that the disturbance of incompleteness can come to rest (*quies*).[56] Aquinas even suggests that body is the product of soul, its expression or unfolding: "whatever appears in the parts of the body is all contained originally and, in a way, implicitly in the soul ... so neither could man be perfect unless the

53. For the analogy in Richard Fishacre and Albert the Great, see Kübel, "Auferstehung nach Albertus Magnus," esp. pp. 300–2 and n. 153. For Giles of Rome, see Nolan, *Giles*, pp. 130–31; for Godfrey of Fontaines, see John F. Wippel, *The Metaphysical Thought of Godfrey of Fontaines: A Study in Late Thirteenth-Century Philosophy* (Washington, D.C.: Catholic University of America, 1981), p. 365; on Augustinus Triumphus, William of Ware, and Eustace of Arras, see Weber, *Auferstehung*, pp. 257–370.

54. Weber, *Auferstehung*, p. 213 n. 235.

55. Richard, *Sentence* commentary, bk. 4, dist. 43, art. 5, q. 1, cited in Weber, *Auferstehung*, p. 304 n. 197: "propter naturale desiderium resumendi corpora sua efficacius orent pro nobis."

56. On John Quidort, see *Quaestio* on the *Sentences*, bk. 4, dist. 49, ed. by Weber, *Auferstehung*, pp. 378–83; and see Weber's discussion, p. 239. John rejects the analogy to love of a woman, because he says it makes resurrection natural; he asserts explicitly:

Anima separata non habet maiorem inclinationem ad hanc materiam quam ad aliam. Anima enim non appetit corpus nisi ut perificiatur in specie humana. ... Sed aliqui dicunt, quod ante infusionem bene indifferens erat, sed per colligantiam factam iam tollitur indifferentia, sicut ponunt exemplum: Video tres mulieres. ... Sed certe si istud esset verum ... concludo necessario resurrectionem esse naturalem. ... Ita dico, quod anima ante infusionem indifferens est ad hoc et illud corpus, sed per opus divinum introducitur in isto, et iterum separetur anima, non poterit dici, quod propter hoc quod fuerit colligata cum illo corpore, naturaliter inclinetur ad illud et non ad aliud, immo ratione suae indifferentiae numquam unietur corpori pernaturam, sed solum per virtutem divinam. (Quaestio on dist. 49, in ibid., pp. 379–80.)

On whether John has any notion of material continuity, see Franz Pelster, "Ein anonymer Traktat des Johannes v. Paris O.P. über das Formenproblem in Cod. Vat. lat. 862," *Divus Thomas* 24 (1946): 26–27; and my *Fragmentation and Redemption*, p. 262.

whole that is contained enfolded in the soul be outwardly unfolded in the body."[57]

These metaphors of love, production, or unfolding thus express an ontological point. To speak of the desire of separated soul for body is another way of saying that to be a human being (*homo*) is to be embodied, that soul without body is not a person. The notion of bodily perfection as a manifestation, or spilling over (*redundantia*), of soul is a means of underlining the intrinsic necessity of every particular detail of the risen body. Henry of Ghent argued that the separated soul is "retarded" or "dragged down" not by "a natural desire for the body" but by something even deeper: its "imperfect personhood." For while separated, it subsists only *in imperfecta personalitate* and cannot be "perfectly borne by its own action to the object of fruition."[58] Aquinas wrote: "Beatitude is the perfection of man as man. And since man is man not through his body but through his soul, and the body is essential to man insofar as it is perfected by soul, it follows that man's beatitude does not consist chiefly otherwise than in an act of soul and passes from the soul on to the body by a kind of overflow."[59] "Since then at the resurrection it behooves man's body to correspond entirely to the soul . . . it follows that man also must rise again perfect."[60]

Thinkers as different in philosophical orientation as Richard Fishacre, Bonaventure, and Giles of Rome even suggest some *inclinatio* or yearning in matter.[61] Bonaventure writes:

For the rational soul, because it is soul, differs from an angel . . . and has an inclination [*inclinationem*] toward the body; because it is ra-

57. *Sup.*, q. 80, art. 1, respondeo (Leonine ed.), p. 181; and trans. English Dominicans, vol. 3, p. 2894. See also *Sup.*, q. 85, art. 1, reply obj. 4 (Leonine ed.), pp. 198–99 (where Aquinas also speaks at length of Gregory the Great's image of the glorified body as gold and crystal); *Sup.*, q. 92, art. 2, reply obj. 6 (Leonine ed.), p. 222; and SCG, bk. 4, chap. 86, *Opera*, ed. Fretté, vol. 12, pp. 604–5.

58. Henry, Quodlibet 6, q. 5, cited in Weber, *Auferstehung*, p. 206 n. 201. Godfrey of Fontaines argues slightly differently but to a similar conclusion. A part enjoys a more perfect being when it exists within its whole, he says (Quodlibet 9, q. 8). The separated soul retains an inclination or appetite for the body; it is not a full *suppositum* because this inclination is not fulfilled. Therefore, separated soul does not have full blessedness, not because it lacks body but because it lacks the personhood it cannot have without body (Quodlibet 2, q. 1). See Wippel, *Godfrey of Fontaines*, pp. 246–48.

59. *Sup.*, q. 92, art. 2, reply obj. 6 (Leonine ed.), p. 222; trans. English Dominicans, vol. 3, p. 2965; see also ibid., q. 85, art. 1 (Leonine ed.) pp. 198–99.

60. *Sup.*, q. 80, art. 1 (Leonine ed.), p. 181; trans. English Dominicans, p. 2894; see also SCG, bk. 4, chaps. 86–88, *Opera*, ed. Fretté, vol. 12, pp. 604–6.

61. See Weber, *Auferstehung*, pp. 223–25, for Henry of Ghent and Richard of Middleton, who have a sense that matter retains some kind of special potential to be a particular body.

tional [its inclination is] toward the human body . . . and it inclines toward one more than another because of the conjoining it had to it [before]. An example is this: if someone wants to marry [*contrahere*] two virgins equal in beauty and goodness and all other conditions, the choice would be indifferent. But if he is united to one—and it is through love [*ex amore*]—then he will not want another even more beautiful. . . . Thus the soul is united with love [*affectus*] to the substance of the flesh which first it vivified, because it is not completely satisfied unless it is joined to her wherever she may have been hiding. And so it appears that the soul has an orientation and desire [*orientationem et appetitum*] through which it is ordained [*ordinatur*] to this body, however much it might be conformed to others. But the body [too] has an orientation [*ordinationem*] by reason of divine providence. What however it might have through some other orientation that is of and in itself, coming from that out of which it was dissolved, I do not dare assert, because neither reason nor authority nor faith compels a position. But because this could be what God gives, I do not obstinately deny it. . . . For whether or not there is a yearning in the dust [*in pulveribus appetitus*] even if it is dissolved into the tiniest particles, something [*aliquid*] however does not perish which has respect to the resurrection. . . . But into whatever dust or ashes it is turned, . . . into the substance of whatever other bodies, or into the elements, or into whatever food, it will return, at that [last] moment of time, to the soul which animated it at first.[62]

Richard Fishacre, writing in the 1240s, speaks of body feeling an *affectio* for its elements:

The body having been dissolved in ultimate dissolution and into the purest elements, there remains however a greater disposition [*major affectio*] toward the same elements, numerically speaking [*numero*], than toward others because of the preceding union. . . . And indeed unless the same elements are united to it again its appetite [*appetitus*] is not satisfied and it remains indeed wretched [*misera*].[63]

In such discussion, not only body but also desire is fraught with re-

62. Bonaventure, *Sentence* commentary, bk. 4, dist. 43, q. 5, conclusio, p. 462. For Giles of Rome, see Nolan, *Giles*, pp. 130–36.
63. See Kübel, "Auferstehung nach Albertus Magnus," p. 302 n. 153, citing Richard Fishacre, Cod. Oxford Balliol 57, fol. 337ra.

markable ambivalence.[64] Desire is love, expression, a creative spilling over [*abundantia*] from soul into body. It is surely no accident that the word chosen for the impact of soul on body is *dos*, the marriage gift from bridegroom to bride.[65] But desire is also a *retardatio*—a downward pull— that keeps the soul from heaven.[66] Hence resurrection should bring *quies* or *satietas*—a stilling of desire that corresponds to the cessation of heavenly motion that will come with the final trumpet.

Such ambivalence rings, for example, through the short treatise on the resurrection written by Augustinus Triumphus of Ancona in the early fourteenth century.[67] There are, says Augustinus, five reasons (or arguments) for resurrection: the first is the argument from desire (that is, that our appetite and need for blessedness must be filled); the second is from Christ's merits; the third from the integrity of human nature, to which body pertains; the fourth is from punishment and reward (that is, that they are owed to body as well as soul); the fifth from divine justice, which will reward its saints. In explaining his third argument, Augustinus treats the problem of identity:

> Man cannot be identical in number unless he has body as well as soul, for these two make the integrity of human nature. For although soul separated from body may be more perfect as what it is [*quantum ad aliquod*] than when joined to body, because it can more freely carry out its intellectual operations, however, speaking simply, the soul is more perfect joined to the body than separated from it, because body is an integral part of man.

It is hard not to read these words as heavy with regret; Augustinus appears puzzled about what body could really contribute to blessedness, saddened by the need to call soul back from the "freedom" of its unencumbered rationality.

64. Part of the ambivalence stems from an ambivalence far older than these texts— one that is at the heart of the Platonic notion of desire that Augustine adopted.

65. Bonaventure, *Sentence* commentary, bk. 4, dist. 44, art. 2, q. 1, reply 3, p. 481, uses marriage (understood as a contracted relationship) as an analogy to explain the orientation of matter toward soul: "et ideo, sicut matrimonium legitime contractum cum aliqua non potest solvi, si illa contrahit de facto cum aliquo, sic nec caro potest ordinationem ad primam carnem perdere."

66. We should note that the relationship of soul to body is sometimes called administration, so that what soul is seen as missing while separated is, so to speak, someone to boss around. See Bonaventure, *Sentence* commentary, bk. 4, dist. 49, pt. 2, art. 1, sectio 1, q. 1, p. 579.

67. Augustinus Triumphus of Ancona, *Tractatus sive theoremata de resurrectione mortuorum*, ed. Weber, in *Auferstehung*, pp. 359–62.

Nonetheless, in explaining his first argument, Augustinus waxes lyrical. Aristotle tells us that everyone possesses a natural desire to be blessed; but here on earth such desire cannot be assuaged. Thus there must be another life in which "we shall be satiated and replete . . . beyond all evil, in the fruition of all good." For in this earthly life we suffer from infirmities and are weakened by ignorance; we find "no joy without sadness, no rest without motion, no sweetness without bitterness." Thus we must be freed from punishment, liberated to achieve our destiny, transferred to a life of resurrection, healed (here Augustinus quotes the *City of God*, book 22) from the illnesses of the flesh by the grace of Christ.

In these words, desire or love has become an expression of self, lifting the whole human being toward heaven. But it is worth noting that even here Augustinus almost forgets the body. Although intended as an argument for *resurrectio mortuorum*, the text in fact speaks almost exclusively of *beatitudo*. The one reference to *resurrectio* could indeed refer to first, or spiritual, resurrection. And within a few years after Augustinus's death in 1328, the papal bull *Benedictus Deus* would define such *beatitudo* as coming to the separated soul before it regains its body at the end of time.[68]

The images of reassemblage and regurgitation that were so popular in twelfth-century art and theology were replaced in thirteenth-century discussion by images of perduring structures (fire, city, or waterskin), of additions and infusions (the *dotes* of the glorified body), and of yearning for completion (the *affectus* of soul and even of matter). The change was philosophical and theological, not aesthetic. Thirteenth-century treatises on resurrection turned to new issues. From the time of Magister Martin in the late twelfth century, it came to seem increasingly important to determine whether resurrection was "natural"—implicit, that is, in human ontology—or "supernatural"—an overriding of normal organic process by the power of God.[69] Beginning with the summae of Alexander of Hales and Albert the Great, resurrection was placed much more carefully in a christological context than it had been in Peter Lombard's *Sentences*.[70] William of Auxerre, Grosseteste, and Albert established the tradition of focusing not only 1 Corinthians 15.42–44 but a major portion of *Sentence* commentary as well on the nature of the glo-

68. See below chapter 7, pp. 284–91.
69. Kübel, "Auferstehung nach Albertus Magnus," p. 289.
70. Ibid., pp. 279–306; F. M. Henquinet, "Les questions inédites de Alexandre de Hales sur les fins dernières," *Recherches de théologie ancienne et médiévale* 10 (1938): 56–57.

rified body.[71] With Albert and Thomas, the issue of identity, implicit in earlier discussion but given new urgency by the adoption of Aristotelian definitions of change, came increasingly to be the crucial philosophical question raised in quodlibetal debates.

In one sense therefore the shift in metaphor simply recapitulates the story of a shift in philosophy familiar to us all from the work of the great French and German historians of scholasticism. The new sophistication with which the Pauline seed was treated stemmed from the complexity of the debate over "nature" and from the fascination felt by thinkers such as Thomas of Cantimpré, Roger Bacon, Albert, and Giles of Rome with biological phenomena for their own sake.[72] The rejection or reformulation of Tertullian's ship and Augustine's statue arose from the struggle over definitions of identity. The new metaphors of overflow, of endowment, of *ordinatio* and desire, reflected the retention and elaboration of Augustinian understandings of self and world. It will now be necessary to treat some of these developments in greater detail, with more attention to the positions of individual thinkers. I do so, however, not merely to retell the story of thirteenth-century philosophy and theology, but also to suggest that there is a wider context for the shift in metaphors. For in another sense the story of eschatological debates and images around 1300 is not so much a story of scholasticism as of pious behavior and belief. Growing enthusiasm for the practice of fragmenting the cadaver, development of the doctrine of purgatory and the tales it spawned of otherworld journeys and visions, elaboration of a rhetoric of desire in devotional and mystical literature—these too were the background to the late thirteenth-century understanding of body and resurrection. They prepared the way for what was, from one point of view, an eclipsing of body by soul but was, from another, the emergence of an eschatology in which body and soul truly became the person.

Bonaventure and the Ambivalence of Desire

Bonaventure's major theological writing was done between 1248 and 1255 when he was a relatively young man. He was born in 1221 and entered the Franciscan order, of which he later became Minister General, in about 1238.[73] His chief statements about eschatology occur, as

71. Wicki, *Seligkeit*, pp. 202–36 and 280–96.
72. See *Fragmentation and Redemption*, pp. 224–28.
73. See generally Etienne Gilson, *The Philosophy of St. Bonaventure*, trans. I. Trethowan and F. J. Sheed (Paterson, N.J.: St. Anthony Guild Press, 1965); J. Guy Bougerol, *Introduction à l'étude de saint Bonaventure* (Strasbourg: Université de Strasbourg,

one would expect, in his lengthy commentary on book 4 of the *Sentences*, and in his short summa of theology, the *Breviloquium*. Bonaventure is often explored merely as a mid-thirteenth-century alternative to the positions of Aquinas. For example, he maintained universal hylomorphism—that is, that all substances (including angels and human souls) are composed of form and matter—whereas Thomas did not. Unlike Thomas, he accounted for self through the doctrine of the plurality of forms—that is, that every being assumes as many forms as it has different properties. On some of these issues, his position would be considerably more popular in the decade after his death (he and Thomas both died in 1274) than Aquinas's own. But what is important for my purposes is not so much his use of technical notions from Aristotelian metaphysics as his development of the Augustinian idea of desire. For his discussion—with all its power and confusion—not only influenced other thinkers well into the fourteenth century but also seems to mark the limits of what was possible, at least to a scholastic theologian, in positive conceptions of body.[74]

Desire is crucial to Bonaventure's eschatology because, as Schmaus has explained, he wants to make resurrection supernatural (that is, effected by God) but grounded ontologically and functionally in the nature of the human being. Thus he argues that soul *as what it is* has the function of quickening, administering (that is, directing and dominating), and perfecting body.[75] A complete substance composed of its own form and matter, soul nonetheless needs body for completion; longing for body (*appetitus, desiderium, inclinatio ad corpus*)[76] is thus lodged in its very being.[77]

1961); Joseph Ratzinger, *The Theology of History in St. Bonaventure*, trans. Z. Hayes (Chicago: Franciscan Herald Press, 1971); and *S. Bonaventura, 1274–1974*, vol. 4: *Theologia* (Grottaferrata: Collegio S. Bonaventura, 1974). On Bonaventure's eschatology, see E. Randolph Daniel, "St. Bonaventure: Defender of Franciscan Eschatology," in ibid., pp. 793–806, and esp. Schmaus, "Unsterblichkeit nach Bonaventura."

74. Some might argue, of course, that Thomas's conception of body is more positive (see Greshake, pt. 2, chap. 1, section 2, in Greshake and Kremer, *Resurrectio mortuorum*, pp. 216–39); it depends on whether one sees body as absorbed into soul in Thomistic metaphysics. For the continuation of Bonaventure's sense of Augustinian desire in later thinkers such as Eustace of Arras, see Weber, *Auferstehung*, pp. 220–38 and passim.

75. See Schmaus, "Unsterblichkeit nach Bonaventura"; and Gilson, *History of Christian Philosophy in the Middle Ages*, pp. 331ff.

76. Bonaventure, *Sentence* commentary, bk. 4, dist. 45, dub. 1, p. 507; ibid., dist. 49, pt. 2, art. 1, sectio 1, q. 1, p. 579; ibid., dist. 43, art. 1, q. 1, p. 451.

77. See Schmaus, "Unsterblichkeit nach Bonaventura," pp. 512–15. He comments that Bonaventure thinks there can be a desire built into nature that is not filled nat-

Several problems are, however, attendant upon this conception of desire. The first is that Bonaventure seems sometimes to assert and sometimes to deny that matter yearns also.[78] In the passage from his *Sentence* commentary quoted above, he says that matter is marked by God for the soul that loves it, but he does not dare assert that such marking is natural. Elsewhere, discussing the vexed issue of digestion and material continuity, he refuses to adopt the position of "some" who hold that there is, planted eternally in dust, an *appetitus* that will not permit it to be vivified by another immortal soul.[79] Yet in the *Breviloquium* (pt. 7, chaps. 5 and 7) he asserts: "the completion of nature requires that man be body and soul, because form and matter need and seek each other." God created body and soul in "a natural and mutual relationship" but "assigned the government of the body to the soul, willing that in the state of wayfaring the soul should incline to the body." For this reason, "soul cannot be fully happy unless body is returned to it, for the two have a natural *ordinatio* to each other." Body, intended thus for union with the blessed soul, must even on earth "bend and submit" as much as body "is able to conform to spirit."[80] These passages are especially moving because they contain one of the rare hints—in this period of individualistic spirituality—that the union of matter and form, body and soul, might also signify a gathering of community. Bonaventure says that the rising of body for union with soul is like the restoring of Christ's dead body (the church) to life and likeness with its head through grace.[81]

Nonetheless, Bonaventure remains unwilling to decide how far matter or body yearns for soul. This unwillingness is connected to an even

---

urally. See also Bonaventure's First Sermon on the Assumption, which argues that Mary's happiness would not be complete unless she were bodily assumed into heaven. "The person is not the soul; it is a composite. Thus it is established that she must be there [in heaven] as a composite, that is, of soul and body; otherwise she would not be in perfect joy" (Sermon *De assumptione B. Virginis Mariae* 1, sect. 2, in *S. Bonaventurae Opera omnia*, ed. Collegium S. Bonaventurae, vol. 9 [Quarrachi: Collegium S. Bonaventurae, 1901], p. 690).

78. Schmaus, "Unsterblichkeit nach Bonaventure," p. 515.

79. *Sentence* commentary, bk. 4, dist. 43, art. 1, q. 5, conclusio, p. 461. But see also ibid., dist. 44, pt. 1, art. 2, q. 1, conclusio, pp. 479–81, where he speaks of a *dispositio* or *ordinatio* of flesh *secundum speciem* toward the soul that vivified it before.

80. *Breviloquium*, pt. 7, chap. 5, par. 5, ed. Peltier, pp. 336–38, and trans. de Vinck, pp. 296–98; and chap. 7, par. 4, ed. Peltier, pp. 340–41, and trans. de Vinck, p. 305.

81. Ibid., pt. 7, chap. 5, par. 2, p. 295. On the unimportance of a communal element in this period, see Greshake in Greshake and Kremer, *Resurrectio mortuorum*, p. 236 n. 220. See Aquinas, *Commentary on St. Paul's Epistle to the Ephesians*, chap. 4, lectio 4, trans. Matthew Lamb (Albany, N.Y.: Magi Books, 1966), pp. 162–67, for another example.

more consequential ambivalence in his thought. Desire itself is to him both negative and positive, both a *retardatio* or need that must be removed and stilled for completeness of joy (*gaudium*) and a diffusion or expression of love (*redundantia, abundantia, influentia, delectatio*) that is joy itself.[82] Bonaventure begins his discussion of resurrection (*Sentence* commentary, d. 45, article 1, q. 1) with the classic Greek definition of happiness: *beatitudo est quies omnium desideriorum*. Therefore body must return to soul in order for soul to be perfectly blessed. When Bonaventure turns to the gifts of the glorified body (d. 49, pt 2, art. 1, sect. 1, q.1), he repeats this definition and quotes both Bernard's *On Loving God* and Augustine's *Literal Commentary on Genesis*, stressing not only that unfulfilled desire weighs down the soul but also that in resumption of body the soul is inebriated by God.[83] As he says elsewhere, "privation of love is a great affliction"; moreover, "quiet is more noble than motion."[84] "Therefore if the world after the resurrection will be in the most perfect disposition, all bodies [then] will rest in [God]." Desire is desire for completion, or, to put it another way, the goal of desire is its own cessation. As the celestial spheres will cease to rotate at the end of time, so too the soul will cease to yearn; stasis is the condition of heaven. The return of body is the end of psychological, emotional, interior motion.

> Body must rise, that it may be blessed through co-participation in [*comparticipatio*] and overflowing of [*redundantia*] blessedness. And so it is with grace, for if grace exists in the soul in the rational power it flows over into the sensible power, and the more it quiets that power through its abundance the greater the pleasure [*delectatio*], as the Psalmist says: *My soul thirsts for thee* [Ps. 62.2]. Thus when there is perfect, overflowing abundance [*abundantia*] and delight [*delectatio*] in glory, we should not marvel if it flows over [*redundat*] into body; and no one doubts this unless he has never known it.[85]

Yet, as this passage suggests, the yearning or love the soul feels toward the body is not merely a retarding or dulling of its capacity for heaven. Desire is not merely an impediment. It is also a manifestation

---

82. *Sentence* commentary, dist. 49, pt. 1, art. 1, q. 3, p. 573, and pt. 2, art. 1, sect. 1, q. 2, p. 581.

83. Ibid., pp. 451 and 579.

84. Ibid., d. 44, pt. 2, art. 3, q. 2, p. 501; d. 48, art 2, q. 2, pp. 561–62.

85. Ibid., dist. 49, pt. 1, art. 1, q. 3, p. 573.

of the soul's experience of God.[86] Bonaventure concludes his *Brevilo-quium* with words he borrowed more than once from Anselm:[87]

> My body, what do you love? My soul, what do you seek? Anything
> you love, anything you seek, is here. . . . Is it swiftness and might, and
> . . . a bodily freedom no barrier can contain? The elect will be as *angels
> of God* [Matt. 22.30] for what is *sown a natural body rises a spiritual
> body* [1 Cor. 15.44]. . . . Is it inebriation? You will be inebriated with
> the plenty of His house. Is it melody? Here the choirs of angels sing.
> . . . Is it pleasure . . . ? Thou, O God, *shalt make them drink of the
> torrents of thy pleasure* [Ps. 35.9]. Is it friendship? Here the elect shall
> love God more than they love themselves, and one another as much
> as themselves.[88]

These phrases surely suggest that blessedness is not the cessation but
the expression of desire, that love moves and seeks even in heaven, that
body can be the probe, the taster, the instrument of heavenly experience.[89]

Such assumptions about body and emotionality are reflected in the
astonishing passage of the *Breviloquium* devoted to the crucifixion.[90]
There Bonaventure suggests (and the idea is not original with him) that
the more perfect a body is, the more fully it experiences.[91] Because
Christ's body was untainted by sin, unhampered by weakness, it suffered
"in every part . . . and in every power of his soul." "As his body was in
perfect health and his senses thus to the highest degree alive, as his soul
burned with perfect love for God and supreme concern for neighbor, his
anguish in both body and soul was immeasurable." Bonaventure does
not, of course, hold that Christ's divinity suffered or that suffering is
blessedness; rising from the dead, Christ assumes "the same body he

86. The subject of blessedness is, says Bonaventure, the human being (*homo*); blessedness—joy in the good—is in the soul by inherence (*per inhaerentiam*), in the body
by overflow (*per redundantiam*). As Augustine says, blessedness is not of bodies, but
it flows over from souls into bodies. Ibid., p. 572.

87. He also uses this passage at the end of the *Soliloquium* and at the end of the
Perfection of Life; see p. 311 n. 39 of de Vinck's translation of the *Breviloquium*.

88. *Breviloquium*, pt. 7, chap. 7, par. 7, ed. Peltier, p. 342, and trans. de Vinck, pp.
308–9.

89. On the senses in heaven, see nn. 98 and 99 below.

90. *Breviloquium*, pt. 4, chap. 9, ed. Peltier, pp. 292–94, and trans. de Vinck, p. 172.

91. The idea is also found in the *Ancrene Wisse*, pts. 2 and 7; see *The Ancrene
Riwle (The Corpus MS.: Ancrene Wisse)*, trans. M. B. Salu (Notre Dame: University
of Notre Dame Press, 1956), pp. 49–51 and 173; see below, chapter 8 at n. 54.

had quickened before . . . but what was subject to pain and death rises impassible and immortal to live forever."[92] Nonetheless, the odd contradiction remains—the suggestion that Christ's capacity to experience pain more deeply than we do lay exactly in the closeness of his earthly body to glory (and not merely, as some theologians held, in a miracle that blocked the impact of glory).[93]

Bonaventure's detailed discussions (which are commonplace by the 1250s) of the dowries of *agilitas* and *subtilitas* further underline the inconsistency at the heart of his conception of both body and desire.[94] If soul expresses in the glorified body a *quies* that is the cessation of all yearning, a stasis that is the psychological reflection of the stillness of the spheres once the world of generation and corruption has ended— why is the body in heaven gifted with motion?[95] The inconsistency becomes acute and explicit when Bonaventure considers the beatific vision. This *visio Dei* can, he says, come as soon as the good soul separates from body; it need not wait—as Bernard suggested it should—until the resurrection. Yet if the separated soul in possession of the beatific vision still yearns for body, that soul has hope for something it does not possess. There cannot however, says Bonaventure, be hope (which is a recognition of incompleteness) where there is completion.[96] There cannot be any need or lack where there is possession of God. The contradiction persists.

Thus, Bonaventure is led finally to ask whether there is greater joy after the resurrection. He answers: "we must say 'yes.' " For (as Peter Lombard said, drawing on Augustine):

92. *Breviloquium*, pt. 4, chap. 10, par. 1, ed. Peltier, p. 294, and trans. de Vinck, p. 174.

93. See Aquinas, ST 3a, q. 14, art. 1, obj. 2 and reply to obj. 2, vol. 49, pp. 170–77, where he says that glory flows over into the martyrs' bodies and blocks their pain. (This idea had been around, as we have seen, since Tertullian.) See also ST 3a, q. 15, art. 5, obj. 3 and reply to obj. 3, vol. 49, pp. 204–07, and ibid., q. 54, vol. 55, pp. 18–35. Aquinas argues that in the case of Christ God blocks the blockage, in order to permit him to suffer the agony of the Passion. Otherwise Christ's body, in possession of the *visio Dei* because of his divinity, would constantly manifest both the transfiguration and the anesthesia of glory.

94. Bonaventure assumes that 1 Corinthians 15.42–44 is a "summary" of the dowries and the defects they remove. *Sentence* commentary, bk. 4, dist. 49, pt. 2, art. 2, sect. 2, q. 1, p. 583.

95. Bonaventure explains that animals and plants, which have birth from and roots in matter, are not suited for eternal life and will not be renewed. The heavens however, which are "disposed to incorruption," will be renewed in glory. *Sentence* commentary, bk. 4, dist. 48, art. 2, q. 4, pp. 564–65.

96. See Schmaus, "Unsterblichkeit nach Bonaventure," p. 512.

there is no doubt that the human mind, . . . having shed its flesh after death, is not able to see the incommutable substance, that is God, as the holy angels see it, either from some more hidden cause or because there is present in it a certain natural desire to administer the body [*appetitus corpus administrandi*], by which desire it is retarded [*retardatur*] so that it does not continue uninterruptedly to the highest heaven until that desire is stilled [*conquiescat*]. For . . . the body is . . . a burden. . . . [But] when it receives not an animal but a spiritual body . . . , it will have the perfect expression [*modum*] of its nature, . . . with such ineffable ease that what was to it a prison will be to it a glory.[97]

The Lombard's text, like Augustine's before it, is a curiously pallid, cautious, even vacuous description of glory. So is the discussion of blessedness with which Bonaventure glosses it. He concludes that the glorified body adds nothing "substantially" although it adds "extensively" (that is, a second component of person—body—now shares the experience) and "intensively" (that is, the impediment of desire for body is removed).[98] Even the *agilitas* gained in glory is a kind of stability; the body does not incline to any place determined for or by it but moves instantaneously everywhere as the soul wishes.[99] In Bonaventure's description of the glorified body, language of stasis—of gold and crystal—abounds.[100]

Nonetheless more may be implicit in the notion of a "certain *appetitus*" or even a "hidden cause" (the phrases come originally from Augustine) than Bonaventure is able to articulate. Desire is at the heart of person; it is the metaphysical cement binding body to soul (as hylo-

97. *Sentence* commentary, dist. 49, pt. 2, p. 578, *expositio* of the text of Peter Lombard, *Sentences*, bk. 4, d. 49, chap. 4, art. 3, vol. 2, p. 553, which in turn quotes Augustine, *Literal Commentary on Genesis*, bk. 12, chap. 35, PL 34, col. 483. See above chapter 3, n. 51. Bonaventure adds *id est, Deum* after *incommutabilem substantiam* in the Lombard's text.

98. *Sentence* commentary, bk. 4, dist. 49, pt. 2, art. 1, sect. 1, q. 1, p. 579. Bonaventure goes on to argue (sect. 3, qq. 1–2, pp. 584–89) that only the senses of sight and touch (and possibly hearing) will be in act in heaven. For we are sure that the media of seeing (light) and touching (the subjoined flesh) are present in heaven, but not of the other senses.

99. *Sentence* commentary, bk. 4, dist. 49, pt. 2, art. 2, sect. 4, q. 2, p. 599: "Quoniam igitur corpus gloriosum totam suae existentiae, et nobilitatis, et stabilitatis rationem trahit ab anima, ideo inclinatio ejus est ad animam, non ad aliquid extra. . . . Unde agilitas non inclinat ad aliquem locum determinatum . . . sed est promptitudo, ut corpus moveatur in omnem locum ad quem vult movere anima."

100. *Sentence* commentary, dist. 49, pt. 2, art. 2, sects. 2–4, pp. 591–99.

morphic union is for Aquinas). Thus, it is significant that Bonaventure devotes so much of his commentary on the Lombard to delineating the nature of the glorified body, so little to the beatific vision that comes before resurrection. However curious and imprecise his assertion that body adds something to blessedness, the description of body that follows is the description of a heavenly self.[101] It may be gold and crystal, but fire of many colors shines in it. "We will recognize people in the heavenly country, for they will have the countenances they had in life . . . just as a sword does not lose its color through cleaning but rather has splendor added to it . . . and a brand is more luminous in the flame."[102] What Bonaventure describes in the last folios of his *Sentence* commentary is not a soul-self to which a house or garment or tool has been unaccountably or adventitiously added, nor even a soul-self expressing that self in body. It is a body-soul-self: a particularized, experiencing, glowing, and, at least partially, sensual person, moving ever deeper into delight.

Much of what Bonaventure says in describing the risen body follows the Lombard closely. Like Peter, he is concerned with material continuity and structural integrity: every particle, every organ, will be restored, and Bonaventure is more insistent than Augustine ever was that matter will indeed return to the organ from which it came. We will be colored and luminous (like a polished sword or a burning candle) but not transparent, for if we became so subtle that we did not stop the rays of sight, an eye would be indistinguishable from a nose.[103] More clearly than for Peter Lombard, however, the resurrection body reflects for Bonaventure the moral, emotional, experiencing self. The elect will rise with all deformities corrected, but the scars of the martyrs will shine forever as "signs of merit and triumph." The damned will have mutilations repaired and excrescences removed, but other deformities will rise with them, for God will not give to the evil any beauty they lacked on earth.[104] We will rise with our own stature and shape (Ephes. 4.13), two in gender, for "*vir* in the Bible often means person and can be said of woman." Nor is Aristotle right that a woman is a defective (*occa-*

101. Bonaventure is careful to preserve the role of God in the bestowing of glory. Joy does not merely spill over from soul into body; God prepares and disposes. Indeed, Bonaventure's doctrine of the plurality of forms seems relevant here, for he holds that the *forma corporeitatis* prepares body for the flowing over of glory; ibid., art. 1, sect. 2, q. 2, pp. 580–81, and Weber, *Auferstehung*, p. 314ff.

102. *Sentence* commentary, bk. 4, dist. 49, pt. 2, art. 2, sect. 2, q. 1, p. 592.

103. Ibid.

104. Ibid., dist. 44, pt. 1, art. 3, qq. 1–2. pp. 482–85.

sionatus) man, for woman—although colder than man and closer to death—nonetheless was intended by nature. Men and women rise with their genitals—as with their humors, hairs, and intestines—"because of perfection."[105]

Thus we will rise perfect and beautiful, but particular as well. Star differs from star (1 Cor. 15.41), and God's house has many mansions (John 14.2). Because we will not rest in heaven until all the elect are gathered up, we will finally rejoice in the joy of others as much as in our own delight. But we carry with us forever our individuality and merit: Peter will not be able to rejoice in Linus's joy with Linus's capacity but only with his own.[106] The *dotes* are a locus of inequality: "the fullness of delights, the raptures of bliss, flow from God down upon the skirt of the garment, [which is] the body of man," but "different members of Christ receive these gifts in different amounts." The robes or dowries of glory come diversely to the bodies of preachers, of virgins, and of martyrs.[107] Our resurrection bodies express our individuality to each other and our merit to God; the crowns, stoles, and dowries they bear in heaven differ as much as did their suffering, service, and status on earth.[108]

105. Ibid., dist. 44, pt. 1, dub. 2, p. 473. For the same position in Richard of Middleton, see Hewson, *Giles of Rome and Conception*, p. 46. Prudence Allen sees the rise of Aristotle as a victory for sexism but argues that medieval teaching on the resurrection of the body, with its assertion that human beings rise in two sexes, undercuts the negative Aristotelian position (*The Concept of Woman: The Aristotelian Revolution, 750 B.C.–A.D. 1250* [Montreal and London: Eden Press, 1985]). As my discussion in chapter 2 above suggests, the commitment to resurrection in two sexes was established long before the thirteenth century and does not have much to do with Aristotle.

106. *Sentence* commentary, dist. 49, pt. 1, art. 1, q. 6, p. 577.

107. *Breviloquium*, pt. 7, chap. 7, par. 4, ed. Peltier, p. 341, and trans. de Vinck, p. 306. And see *Sentence* commentary, dist. 49, pt. 2, art. 1, sect. 2, q. 2, p. 584.

108. I should point out that thirteenth-century thinkers such as Bonaventure and Thomas were only beginning to make steps toward distinguishing individuality from numerical difference—i.e., distinguishing what we moderns mean by individuality (individual distinctiveness) from the fact that there is more than one instance of something. In general, medieval philosophy moved (although slowly) from a concern with individuation (what accounts for the occurrence of more than one instance of a universal?) to a concern with the individual (what is the ontological status of the distinctiveness of cases?). But neither question was explored primarily within eschatology. See Jorge J. E. Gracia, *Introduction to the Problem of Individuation in the Early Middle Ages* (Munich and Washington, D.C.: Philosophia Verlag and Catholic University of America Press, 1984), esp. pp. 255–78. It is clear, however, that by the later thirteenth century there was no "person" without body. It is also clear that some distinctive characteristics that to us moderns would be "individuality" (such as height, weight, sex, appearance, etc.) were associated with body (whether as expression of the substantial form soul, as included in *forma corporis* or *corporeitatis*, or as

Albert the Great, Thomas Aquinas, and Giles of Rome: Resurrection, Hylomorphism, and Formal Identity

As a number of Bonaventure's contemporaries recognized, there was a philosophical problem with lodging desire at the heart of anthropology. To see body as a mass of particles yearning for soul, to understand the person as a marriage of soul (bridegroom) to body (beloved virgin), maintains the importance of body that seems required by the doctrine of *resurrectio carnis*; it maintains in ontology something of our commonsense understanding of matter as tactile, unstable, fertile "stuff," constantly in flux. But it makes the person a partnership (or, depending on how far one carries the notion of plurality of forms, a committee) rather than a unity.[109]

No theologian in the mid-thirteenth century held, as Hugh of St. Victor and Robert of Melun had done in the early twelfth, that the person is a soul using a body.[110] All conceived of person as, by definition, a psychosomatic whole. Nonetheless some went considerably further than Bonaventure in using Aristotelian concepts of substance, form, and matter to account for this unity. Rejecting universal hylomorphism (that is, the theory that every subsisting entity must be understood as composed of form—structure or definition—and matter—potency), thinkers such as Albert the Great, Thomas Aquinas, and Giles of Rome denied that body is an entity composed of a form of bodiliness and the potency it activates; they also denied that soul activates its own spiritual matter or potentiality.[111] Rather, with portentous consequences for their understanding of *resurrectio carnis*, they limited hylomorphism to the ma-

accidental forms) and were thought to return in resurrection. But nothing that was understood as a defect would return in the blessed. For example, persons would rise male or female but not hermaphroditic (see below, n. 143). Medieval thinkers apparently wanted to preserve identifiability in heaven (see n. 102 above). But it is clear that they saw many fewer differentiating characteristics as ultimately worth preserving than would modern people.

109. See Daniel A. Callus, "The Problem of the Plurality of Forms in the Thirteenth Century: The Thomist Innovation," in *L'Homme et son destin*, pp. 577–85; Gilson, *History of Christian Philosophy in the Middle Ages*, pp. 416–20; and Greshake in Greshake and Kremer, *Resurrectio mortuorum*, p. 225ff.

110. See Heinzmann, *Unsterblichkeit*. See also Weber, *Auferstehung*, pp. 123ff.; Greshake in Greshake and Kremer, *Resurrectio mortuorum*, pp. 217ff.; and chapter 3, n. 59 above.

111. Giles's basic work on resurrection is the *Quaestiones* edited by Nolan; see above, n. 34. Albert treated resurrection in his *Sentence* commentary from the mid-1240s and in a treatise *De resurrectione* (composed prior to 1246), which was probably intended as a conclusion to his *Summa de creaturis*. For the complex problems of the relationship of the *De resurrectione* to the *De creaturis*, see A. Ohlmeyer, "Zwei neue

terial world and maintained that there is a single form in man.[112] Body thus became matter to the soul, its form; death became the severing of the metaphysical components of the subsisting individual *homo;* resurrection was guaranteed not by the desire of soul for its partner but by the necessity for ontological completeness. Soul was understood to be able to subsist without body (because it is a "substantial form"), but in that subsistence soul is by definition incomplete: a form should inform matter.[113] Thus body must rise in order to provide matter to form; until the resurrection "I" am not truly "I."[114] Or, to put it another way, "There is no act of man [*homo*] in which body does not take part," because soul alone is not man.[115] Giles of Rome pointed out in a quodlibetal question: "The vulgar say [that Peter is in Paradise]. We can however verify that

---

Teile der *Summa de creaturis* Alberts des Grossen," *Recherches de théologie ancienne et médiévale* 4 (1932): 392–400; O. Lottin, "Commentaire des Sentences et Somme théologique d'Albert le Grand," in *Recherches de théologie ancienne et médiévale* 8 (1936), pp. 117–53; F. M. Henquinet, "Vingt-deux Questions inédites d'Albert le Grand dans un manuscrit à l'usage de S. Thomas d'Aquin," *The New Scholasticism* 9 (1935): 283–329; and Kübel, "Auferstehung nach Albertus Magnus." On Albert generally, see *Albertus Magnus, Doctor Universalis, 1280–1980,* ed. G. Meyer and A. Zimmermann (Mainz: Matthias Grünewald, 1980).

112. Albert said: "quia error pessimus est dicere unius subiecti plures esse substantias, cum illae substantiae non possunt esse nisi formae" (Callus, "Plurality of Forms," p. 580 n. 12).

113. This, of course, implied problems for the immortality of the soul, which Aquinas solved by holding that soul is both the form of body and a subsisting immortal spirit; it is a form that has and bestows substantiality. See Greshake in Greshake and Kremer, *Resurrectio mortuorum* (p. 225) who points out that this is not a fully Aristotelian conception of form because, to Aristotle, form cannot subsist without matter. For an excellent brief statement of Aquinas's position that differs somewhat from my own in emphasis, see Brian Davies, *The Thought of Thomas Aquinas* (Oxford: Clarendon Press, 1992), pp. 207–20.

114. Aquinas, *In I Cor.,* chap. 15, lectio 2, *Opera,* vol. 21, p. 34: "anima autem, cum sit pars corporis homini, non est totus homo, et anima mea non est ego; unde, licet anima consequatur salutem in alia vita, non tamen ego vel quilibet homo." See also ST 1a, q. 75, art. 4, reply obj. 2, which argues that the soul is no more the person than a hand or foot is the person; vol. 11, pp. 20–21: "non quaelibet substantia particularis est hypostasis vel persona, sed quae habet completam naturam speciei. Unde manus vel pes non potest dici hypostasis vel persona, et similiter nec anima, cum sit pars speciei humanae." In general, see Theodor Schneider, *Die Einheit des Menschen: Die anthropologische Formel anima forma corporis im sogenannten Korrektorienstreit und bei Petrus Johannis Olivi: Ein Beitrag . . . ,* BGPTM: Texte und Untersuchungen, n.F. 8 (Münster: Aschendorff, 1973); and H. Seidl, " "Zur Leib-Seele-Einheit des Menschen bei Thomas von Aquin," *Theologie und Philosophie* 49 (1974): 548–53.

115. Aquinas, Quodlibet VII, q. 5, art. 11, ad 3, in *Quaestiones quolibeticas,* in *Opera omnia* (Parma 1852–73 ed. with intro. by Bourke), vol. 9 (New York: Musurgia, 1949), p. 561: "nec tamen est verum quod aliquis actus sit hominis in vita praesenti in quo corpus non communicet." And see Greshake in Greshake and Kremer, *Resurrectio mortuorum,* pp. 227–28.

this is said by synecdoche . . . because it is his soul that is there. And we say of any dead man that he is in the tomb; but this is also by synecdoche, because it is his body that is there."[116] Aquinas argued, in commenting on Job 19:

There are those who assert that we will rise with celestial bodies, but Job excludes this when he says: "And my skin will surround me again." . . . For in this way of speaking he gives the reason of the resurrection, that the soul not remain denuded forever of its proper clothing. And there are others who say that the soul will resume the same body it laid down but according to the same condition—that is, that it will long for food and drink and will carry out the other works of this life. But this is excluded by the words "yet in my flesh I shall see God." For it is clear that the flesh of man according to the state of the present life is corruptible, as Wisdom 9.15 says: "The corruptible body weighs down the soul." So no one living in this mortal flesh can see God. But the flesh the soul resumes in resurrection will be the same in substance and will through divine gift have no corruption, as the Apostle says in 1 Corinthians 15.53. In this condition it cannot impede soul. . . . And so Porphyry was ignorant when he said that the soul is blessed when it is in flight from all body. Because [if this were so] then it would be the soul and not the human being [homo] that would see God. But the passage says: "whom I myself shall see." It does not say "my soul"; it says "I." And "I" subsists from soul and body. . . . Because the repaired human being, the same in number [idem numero] not merely in species, is the one who sees God, [Job] adds "and no other," which means no other numerically. Thus we do not expect the kind of repairing of life Aristotle refers to in book 2 of On Generation, saying that if the substance of things is corruptible then what is repeated is the same in species not in number.

These things being said concerning cause, time and means of resurrection, and the glory and identity of the risen, [Job] adds "My hope reposes in my breast" to show that this hope is held not in words only but hidden in the heart.[117]

116. Giles, Quodlibet 4, q. 4, fol. 47va; cited in Nolan, Giles, p. 60 n. 49.
117. Aquinas, Expositiones in Job, chap. 19, lectio 2, Opera, ed. Fretté, vol. 18, pp. 119–20. The use of the metaphor of body as clothing, which is not usual with Thomas (although the dowries are fairly frequently said to be clothing), is suggested (Aquinas himself tells us) by verse 20. On this commentary, Chenu remarks (Toward Understanding St. Thomas, p. 246) that it is devoted to the literal sense and "not as carved up into subtle distinctions" as are Aquinas's other biblical commentaries. In De po-

Implicit in the concept of matter as pure potency and of soul as the single form of body is a new solution to the problem of identity—a problem that had lurked in discussions of resurrection (whether at the center or on the fringes) at least since Celsus and Origen debated the consequences of material flux for immortality. If soul is the one form of body (*unica forma corporis*) and bears the nature of *homo* (including, as it must, the nature of bodiliness, because it is man's only form), then soul guarantees self. What self is (including what body is) will be packed into soul; body will be the expression of that soul in matter.[118] As Aquinas said: "It is more correct to say that soul contains body [*continet corpus*] and makes it to be one, than the converse."[119]

A full spelling out of the consequences of such a position—known technically as formal identity (that is, the idea that a thing's form or "whatness" accounts for its being the same thing)—obviates the materialist questions of risen fingernails and foreskins popular since Tertullian. If the nature of body is carried by soul and can be expressed in any matter that soul activates (matter being pure potency), then one cannot hold that a person's body or matter waits to be reassembled after death. Once the *unica forma* has departed, the person's body or matter will not exist at all. (The cadaver that does exist is second matter—formed matter—but it is informed not by the form of the soul but by the form of the corpse.)[120] Therefore, when the human being rises the body that is matter to its form will by definition be *its* body. As Durand of St. Pourçain put it, we may not say that God can make the body of Peter out of the body of Paul, because this is, technically speaking, nonsense; if it is

---

tentia Dei Aquinas takes the criticism of Porphyry further, arguing that soul has more happiness when it repossesses body; see n. 23 above.

118. In addition to the works by Weber, Michel, and Greshake and Kremer, cited above in n. 10, see Norbert Luyten, "The Significance of the Body in a Thomistic Anthropology," *Philosophy Today* 7 (1963): 175–93; Wolfgang Kluxen, "Anima separata und Personsein bei Thomas von Aquin," in W. P. Eckert, ed., *Thomas von Aquino: Interpretation und Rezeption: Studien und Texte* (Mainz: Matthias Grünewald, 1974), pp. 96–116; Bernardo C. Bazan, "La Corporalité selon saint Thomas," *Revue philosophique de Louvain* 81, 4 ser. 49 (1983): 369–409; J. Giles Milhaven, "A Medieval Lesson on Bodily Knowing: Women's Experience and Men's Thought," *Journal of the American Academy of Religion* 57, no. 2 (1989): 341–72; and Richard Swinburne, *The Evolution of the Soul* (Oxford: Clarendon Press, 1986), pp. 299–306, esp. n. 9.

119. ST 1a, q. 76, art. 3, vol. 11, pp. 60–61 (my translation). And see Greshake in Greshake and Kremer, *Resurrectio mortuorum*, p. 227 n. 190.

120. Those who hold this position are aware how closely the living body and the cadaver resemble each other. They explain this by arguing that the two forms are indistinguishable to the eye—not a very satisfactory solution. See Wippel, *Godfrey of Fontaines*, pp. 218–24.

the body of Paul it is the body of Paul.[121] But God can make the body of
Peter out of dust that was once the body of Paul.[122]

A number of historians and theologians have recently made much of
the theory of formal identity—including Hermann Weber, whose mag-
isterial study (1973) of thirteenth-century eschatological treatises and
quodlibetal questions must be the basis for all future work, and Gisbert
Greshake, whose theological reinterpretation (1986) of the doctrine of
bodily resurrection draws heavily on Weber's conclusions. But interest
in the Thomistic solution to the identity problem goes back in this century to the work of Segarra in the 1920s.[123] Indeed, the theory has received attention ever since the work of Suarez in the seventeenth century. Suarez argued incorrectly that Durand was the first to articulate
the position, but by so arguing he paved the way for study of other figures
(such as Giles of Rome, Peter of Auvergne, John Quidort of Paris, and
James of Metz) by whom the idea was developed.

What is interesting for my purposes, however, is less the intellectual
breakthrough the theory undoubtedly represents than the nonevent it
turned out to be. Although scholars have fiercely debated how far Aquinas understood and espoused the implications of his own ideas, it is clear
that throughout his career (and not just in his early period, when he held
a kind of predisposition of matter for resurrection) he sometimes spoke
in ways that implied material continuity.[124] Moreover he worried—as

121. Durand of St. Pourçain, In Sententias theologicas Petri Lombardi commen-
tariorum libri quatuor (Lyon: Apud Gasparem, 1556), dist. 44, q. 1, fol. 340v–341r:
"Utrum ad hoc quod idem homo numero resurgat, requiratur quod formetur corpus
eius eisdem pulueribus in quos fuit resolutum." (The printed edition of the commentary is the third and last redaction, moderate in comparison to earlier ones; see Gilson,
History of Christian Philosophy in the Middle Ages, p. 774 n. 81.).

122. In answer to the question whether the soul of Peter can be in the body of Paul
(which he says is misformulated), Durand argues (In Sententias, dist. 44, q. 1, paragrs.
4 and 5, fol. 341r): ". . . quaestio implicat contradictionem: quia corpus Petri non
potest esse nisi compositum ex materia et anima Petri . . . ergo anima Petri non potest
esse in corpore Pauli nec econverso, nisi anima Petri fiat anima Pauli. . . . Restat ergo
quod alio modo formetur quaestio . . .: supposito quod anima Petri fieret in materia
quae fuit in corpore Pauli, utrum esset idem Petrus qui prius erat." He concludes
(ibid., paragr. 6, fol. 341r): "cuicumque materiae vniatur anima Petri in resurrectione,
ex quo est eadem forma secundum numerum, per consequens erit idem Petrus secundum numerum."

123. Weber, Auferstehung; Greshake in Greshake and Kremer, Resurrectio mortuorum; Francisco Segarra, De identitate corporis mortalis et corporis resurgentis:
Disputatio theologica (Madrid: "Razón y Fe," 1929). For the argument that Durand's
originality was overestimated, see Weber, Auferstehung, pp. 217–53 and 76–78, and
Michel, "Résurrection," cols. 2561–65.

124. In a famous passage of the Summa contra Gentiles, Aquinas appears to pull
back from a purely formal theory and assert the conventional position that people do
not have to receive all their previous matter in resurrection; God can make up the
difference: SCG, bk. 4, chaps. 80–81, Opera, ed. Fretté, vol. 12, pp. 593–96. Interpre-

did thinkers after him—about the theological consequences of jettisoning a more commonsense understanding of matter.[125] Indeed, the implications of the unicity of form, and the idea itself, were condemned in
the late thirteenth century before they were fully elaborated. A number
of major figures, such as Henry of Ghent and Duns Scotus, continued
to hold that some kind of form of bodiliness was necessary to explain
resurrection and glorification.[126] And even after Peter of Auvergne, John
Quidort, and Durand had articulated its philosophical attractiveness so
clearly, the theory of formal identity was not so much rejected as
ignored.[127]

It thus seems important, in looking at figures such as Aquinas who
used Aristotelian metaphysics in new ways, to concentrate not merely
on the technical philosophical solutions implicit in their work but also
on the explicit confusions and tensions. For there is much in the lengthy
treatments of resurrection by Albert, Thomas, and Giles of Rome that
is very similar to the concerns of Peter Lombard and Bonaventure, however differently the Lombard, Bonaventure, and Thomas may have conceived of body and person. Albert, Thomas, and Giles continued the
discussions of risen fingernails and embryos, of the fate of genitals and
intestines in heaven. Like Bonaventure, they were deeply concerned
about the wholeness of the resurrection body. Although they discarded
images of reassemblage and rebirth, using instead analogies (such as
those of the waterskin or fire) that imply self to be structure not matter,
they all spoke as if the body will in fact be remade from the identical
dust into which we fall (identical in the sense of spatio-temporal continuity). They all suggested some kind of *ordinatio* in matter and *abundantia* in the soul.[128] Like Bonaventure, they were fascinated and confused by the body-soul nexus, and, paralleling the ambivalence in his
notion of desire, they held body to be a drag that retards soul, an instru-

---

tation of this passage has been controversial. See Weber, *Auferstehung*, p. 229; and E.
Hugueny, "Résurrection et identité corporelle selon les philosophies de l'individuation," *Revue des sciences philosophiques et théologiques* 23 (1934): 94–106. Hugueny
argues that Thomas's thought developed away from the idea of material continuity
and toward formal identity.

125. See below at n. 138 on the body of Christ.

126. On Scotus, see Michel, "Résurrection," cols. 2559–62. On Henry of Ghent,
see Wippel, *Godfrey of Fontaines*, pp. 261–66.

127. Greshake in Greshake and Kremer, *Resurrectio mortuorum*, pp. 237–39. See
below at n. 186.

128. They all, of course, reject any idea of seminal reasons in matter; the nature
of a thing is determined by its substantial form actuating a matter that is pure potency.
But they all argue that matter, once it has been formed into body, retains some sort
of direction (not *naturaliter* but by divine gift) toward receiving that form again. On
Giles, see Hewson, *Giles of Rome and Conception*, pp. 43–46.

ment that improves its performance, and an unfolding that *is* its expression.

Although there has been an immense amount of scholarly debate over the question, it seems clear that Albert, Thomas, and Giles all adumbrate the idea of formal identity, however unclear some of their formulations. Arguing that the risen body could be constituted by God out of matter other than that which it possessed in this life, Aquinas explained: "Corporeity, however, can be taken in two ways. In one way, it can be taken as the substantial form of a body. . . . Therefore, corporeity, as the substantial form in man, cannot be other than the rational soul."[129] All three thinkers raise the problem of the *veritas humanae naturae* (Albert calls it *id quod resurget*) and embrace full natural process, procreation as well as nutrition, with real enthusiasm. They not only reject the Lombard's argument that food never becomes "of our substance" but passes through (as Matthew 15.17 says) on its way to the privy; they also deny any possibility of specific particles tagged or determined for reassemblage. All three thus argue that it must be structure or definition—that is, form—that accounts for survival through time.[130] And since all three deny the plurality of forms and therefore a form of bodiliness (Giles only after real hesitation), all imply that identity lies with rational soul.[131] Albert explains that a cut-off hand is not really a hand, nor is a dead tree a tree.[132]

Indeed all three authors devote attention to the problem of explaining death once life is understood to be full biological process.[133] If there is

129. SCG, bk. 4, chap. 81, *Opera*, ed. Fretté, vol. 12, p. 594: "Corporeitas autem dupliciter accipi potest: Uno modo secundum quod est forma substantialis corporis, prout in genere substantiae collocatur; et sic corporeitas cujuscumque corporis nihil est aliud quam forma substantialis ejus, secundum quam in genere et specie collocatur. . . . Oportet igitur quod corporeitas, prout est forma substantialis in homine, non sit aliud quam anima rationalis." See Bazan, "La Corporalité selon Thomas," pp. 407–8.

130. Aquinas ST 1a, q. 119, art. 1, vol. 15, pp. 162–73; and *Sup.*, q. 80 (Leonine ed.), pp. 180–85. Also Albert, *De resurrectione*, ed. Kübel, tractate 1, q. 6, pp. 248–57, esp. art. 9, pp. 254–57. And see also Nolan, *Giles*, pp. 115–23. There is some question whether Giles fully understands or espouses the Aristotelian argument about matter and species.

131. Giles came to unicity only slowly; he wrote his attack on plurality in 1278; see E. Hocedez, "La condemnation de Gilles de Rome," *Recherches de théologie ancienne et médiévale* 4 (1932): 34–58; Gilson, *History of Christian Philosophy in the Middle Ages*, p. 418. After the condemnation of the unicity thesis in the 1280s, Giles waffled on the question; see esp. his Fifth Quodlibet of 1290. Hewson, *Giles of Rome and Conception*, pp. 11–12.

132. Albert, *De resurrectione*, tract. 1, q. 6, art. 1, solutio, par. 3, p. 249; and Callus, "Plurality of Forms," p. 582. Thomas explains that we survive as does the fire whose logs are replaced while it burns on; Giles compares identity to the waterskin whose contents empty and fill. See above, nn. 38 and 40.

133. Giles of Rome is especially interested in this; see Nolan, *Giles*, pp. 42–46.

no core of matter that survives (and ages) while the stuff around it waxes and wanes and no *forma corporeitatis* that accounts for what body is apart from the immortal rational soul, how do we explain the fact that the body weakens and decays? If it has only one, rational form that informs potency, why does it not remain in an eternal balance of intake and excretion?[134] And why is resurrection not natural? If a single substantial form accounts for identity and any stuff is in potency to it, could not the act by which God regenerates us *idem numero* at the end of time be a fully natural actuating of matter by form just as is the ensouling of the fetus in the womb? The answers are less important than is the novelty of the questions, generated as they are by understanding matter as pure potency, identity as lodged in a single form.[135] More important still, however, is the fact that despite such sophisticated analysis all three authors continue to speak as if God does at the end of time reassemble the same bits of dust that constituted the body before.

Albert, Thomas, and Giles devote a good deal of attention (although less than Peter Lombard had) to the fate of the bits God will reassemble. All three debate the cannibalism question, detailing exactly where the matter will go if a father or mother who eats only embryos passes on to progeny material that is crucial for the constitution of the eaten person.[136] Aquinas explains carefully that a relic, although not identical to the living body of the saint "on account of its difference of form—viz., the soul, *is* the same by identity of matter, which is destined to be reunited to its form."[137] Concentration on the rational soul as self should

134. See Nolan, *Giles*, pp. 50–57, especially the notes, for extensive quotations from Giles's *Sentence* commentary, bk. 2, q. 19. See also Richard of Middleton, *De gradu formarum*, "expositio objectorum: rationes theologicae," and "responsio, in homine," in *Richard de Mediavilla et la controverse sur la pluralité des forms: Textes inédits et étude critique*, ed. Roberto Zavalloni (Louvain: Études de l'Institut Supérieur de Philosophie, 1951), pp. 61 and 90–91. Richard, who holds the plurality of forms, reports arguments against the position.

135. Indeed, in order to answer these questions, the three thinkers have to revert either to some sense of material continuity as involved in identity or to an Aristotelian understanding of form that makes the Thomistic substantial form problematic. Albert holds that matter has a potential for perfection up to age thirty, after which it—and we—pass our peak. Giles argues that our regeneration at the end of time is miraculous because it is the same act as before, whereas according to Aristotelian analysis of the formation of matter, a second act after an interval of time, even by the same form, is a second act not an identical one. See Albert, *De resurrectione*, tract. 2, q. 6, solutio, par. 4, p. 264; and Nolan, *Giles*, pp. 96–104.

136. See Michael Allyn Taylor, "Human Generation in the Thought of Thomas Aquinas: A Case Study on the Role of Biological Fact in Theological Science" (Ph.D. diss., Catholic University of America, 1982); Albert, *De resurrectione*, tract. 1, q. 6, art. 9, pp. 254–57; Nolan, *Giles*, pp. 114–23; and *Fragmentation and Redemption*, pp. 243–44.

137. ST 3a, q. 25, art. 6, vol. 50, pp. 202–5. And see q. 15, art. 10, obj. 3, vol. 49, pp. 218–19, which says the saints have souls in heaven and (dead) bodies in the tomb.

have suggested that what happens in the tomb (and the womb) is un-important, but Thomas emphasizes that Christ's body did not decay in the grave (nor did it—conceived perfect in form—undergo any development in Mary's womb other than increase in size). Moreover, every particle of it is now in heaven. Thomas argues that the blood of Christ displayed in churches comes from abused crucifixes or miraculous hosts, not from the *corpus* that hung on the cross.[138] Despite implying that identity is formal, Aquinas thus stresses that Christ and the martyrs rise materially the same.[139]

Moreover there are hints in Thomas's treatment—as in Albert's—that matter, if not marked or inclined naturally toward its own soul, is nonetheless ordained by God for resurrection. Albert assumed that our present particles carry with them something latent that ordains them to constitute our body, although he emphasized that they do not guarantee self or personhood.[140] In his *Sentence* commentary and *Supplementum* (the works by which he was best known to thinkers who followed him), Aquinas also held some sort of ordaining of matter by indeterminate dimensions—a position that not only suggested material continuity in resurrection but also some "actuality" in matter by which it individuates form.[141] Giles of Rome, like Aquinas, admitted that the desire of soul to administer matter might imply a desire in matter itself,[142] but Giles went further. Corruption (that is, change) comes be-

138. On Christ's body in the tomb: ST 3a, q, 51, art. 3, vol. 54, pp. 146–49; on Christ's body in the womb: ST 3a, q. 33, arts. 1–2, vol. 52, pp. 56–65; on Christ's blood: ST 3a, q. 54, art. 3, esp. reply obj. 3, vol. 55, pp. 26–31, esp. p. 31. Cf. the argument of Braulio of Saragossa in the seventh century; see above chapter 2, n. 179.

139. He explains his position in the case of Christ by stressing the union of Christ's body in the grave with his divinity—an argument later thinkers such as Giles, Henry of Ghent, and Godfrey of Fontaines would find inadequate. They held that philosophical interpretations of identity must be the same for our bodies and Christ's. See Wippel, *Godfrey of Fontaines*, pp. 329–30. Thomas's argument was not new.

140. Kübel, "Auferstehung nach Albertus Magnus," p. 303.

141. See Weber, *Auferstehung*, pp. 228–29. According to most interpreters, Aquinas does not go all the way toward seeing matter as potency. In his early work (chiefly the *Sentence* commentary), he holds that individuated matter in some sense subsists after soul and body are separated. It is not that this matter is individuated by determined dimensions; rather, it retains in flux a certain relation (undetermined dimensions) to the individuality it had when it was formed by the human soul. See Michel, "Résurrection," cols. 2557–58, and Weber, *Auferstehung*, pp. 220–21. On the influence of the *Sentence* commentary, see Chenu, *Toward Understanding St. Thomas*, p. 270; Le Goff, *Birth of Purgatory*, pp. 267–68, asserts the importance of the *Supplementum*, despite the fact that it was put together after Thomas's death by disciples who rigidified his early formulations.

142. Aquinas, *Sup.*, q. 78, art. 3, and q. 79, arts. 1–2 (Leonine ed.), pp. 177–80; he asserts that there is no *inclinatio* and no natural *ordinatio* but only one given by God. Nolan, *Giles*, pp. 130–33.

cause matter desires another form, he argues; therefore, the desire of matter must, like the soul's desire, be "satiated." The stilling (*quies*) that comes when the heavens cease to turn is a filling of matter so completely with form (i.e., beatified soul) that it can never change again.

The concern for the wholeness of body in the afterlife displayed by Albert, Thomas, and Giles is less a concern for the fate of material particles, however, than a concern for integrity. Whether or not the resurrection body is put together from exactly the bits it possessed on earth, it must retain every organ and fragment. Stasis—the inability to lose any particle—is the guarantee of perfection; fragmentation is evil, wholeness good. The fundamental argument is not any longer—as it had been with Hugh and Peter Lombard—that body (a partner and tool of self) comes along with bits of matter and is put back together with them. Rather the argument is that self, contained in form, is expressed in the details of body. Thus sex difference of course continues in heaven,[143] as do differences in stature and shape; the scars of the martyrs also remain, as their special glory.[144] If we all rise the same age, it is not in order to efface our particularity, but because each person reaches his or her own peak of perfection at age thirty (or thirty-three) and rises therefore in the moment at which self is most fully manifest.[145] Thomas is concerned to emphasize that there will be no loss of matter even in hell where the damned will weep dryly, with no "dissolving" into tears, and will gnash their teeth without losing any enamel.[146] Moreover he and Albert hold that all defects (not merely mutilations, as Bonaventure argued) will be repaired for damned as well as elect. The restoration comes, however,

143. See above, n. 105. Also Augustinus Triumphus, *De resurrectione*, theorema 7, quoted in Weber, *Auferstehung*, p. 258 n. 479:

> Non omnes resurgentes eundem sexum habebunt, nam masculinus sexus et femininus, quamvis non sint differentiae formales facientes differentiam in specie, sunt tamen differentiae materiales facientes differentiam in numero. Et quia in resurrectione quilibet resurget non solum quantum ad id quod est de identitate specifica, secundum habet esse in specie humana, verum etiam resurget quantum ad id, quod est de identitate numerali, secundum quam habet esse in tali individuo. Ideo oportet unumquodque cum sexu proprio et cum aliis pertinentibus ad integritatem suae individualis naturae resurgere, propter quod femina resurget cum sexu femineo et homo cum masculino, remota omni libidine et omni vitiositate naturae.

144. SCG, bk. 4, chap. 88, *Opera*, ed. Fretté, vol. 12, p. 606, and ST 3a, q. 54, art. 4, vol. 55, pp. 30–35. See also *Sup.*, q. 96, art. 10 (Leonine ed.), p. 238, on whether the scars of the martyrs are an aureole. In general, thirteenth-century theologians drew on Augustine, *City of God*, bk. 22, chap. 17 ("vitia detrahentur, natura servabitur") on this matter; see Weber, *Auferstehung*, p. 79 n. 194.

145. Albert, *De resurrectione*, tract. 2, q. 6, pp. 263–65; Aquinas, *Commentary on Ephesians*, chap. 4, lectio 4, p. 167.

146. Aquinas, *Sup.*, q. 97, art. 3 (Leonine ed.), p. 241.

not in order to conceal their past experience but because their bodily defects might be adventitious, not truly reflecting moral character. This-worldly defects such as blindness or fever have nothing to do with guilt or merit. Hence in heaven and hell, the damned and the blessed will be repaired in order to manifest the perfection of the species *human*. But the blessed will have gifts and crowns that reveal their individual achievements, and even in purgatory they will reside in receptacles appropriate to their status and merit.[147] In hell, the damned will reflect their moral disorder and blindness in bodies that are dark, heavy, and infinitely passible. Nothing in what Thomas says precludes the idea that they will suffer in ways appropriate to the nature of their crimes although he rejects any implication that in purgatory punishments are proportional to sin on earth.[148]

The concept of body implicit here is not entirely coherent or consistent. The same ambivalence we found in Bonaventure creeps in. But whereas Bonaventure's ambivalence lodges in desire (and in this, Giles of Rome follows him), Aquinas is ambivalent about body itself.[149] Body is the expression, the completion, and the retardation of soul.[150]

Aquinas is adamant that soul is capable of the vision of God as soon as it sloughs off body. "There is no reason for deferring punishments or rewards after the moment in which the soul is capable of receiving them."[151]

[The Apostle] says: . . . *Knowing that while we are in the body, we are absent from the Lord. (For we walk by faith and not by sight.) But we are confident, and have a good will to be absent rather from the body, and to be present with the Lord* [2 Cor. 5.6–8]. Now there would be

147. Albert, *De resurrectione*, tract. 3, q. 1, p. 305; Aquinas, *Sup.*, q. 93, art. 3 (Leonine ed.), pp. 225–26; and q. 96 art. 13, pp. 239–40. On the *dotes* as loci of inequality, see Wicki, *Seligkeit*, pp. 238–49; on the importance to Aquinas of preserving difference in purgatory, see below, n. 163.

148. Neither Albert, Thomas, nor Giles suggests that the torture of the damned "fits" their crimes in the sense in which otherworld visions imagined it to do. But as the three theologians all hold both that the tortures are merited and that the damned are treated differentially not equally, there is nothing in their views incompatible with the more graphic visions of the poets and mystics. On Thomas's rejection of proportionality of punishment in purgatory, see Le Goff, *Birth of Purgatory*, pp. 273–74.

149. Giles of Rome uses the conventional argument that desire to administer the body retards the separated soul from blessedness; see Nolan, *Giles*, p. 46.

150. *Sup.*, q. 80, art. 1 (Leonine ed.), p. 181; q. 92, art. 2, reply obj. 6, p. 222; q. 93, art. 1, pp. 224–25; q. 96, art. 10, p. 238; *De potentia Dei*, q. 5, art. 10 (Parma 1852–73 ed.), vol. 8, pp. 120–22.

151. SCG, bk. 4, chap. 91, paragr. 1, *Opera*, ed. Fretté, vol. 12, p. 609.

no use in our desiring *to be absent,* that is separated, *from the body,* unless we were to be at once *present with the Lord.* But we are not present, unless He is present to our sight. . . . Therefore as soon as the soul of the just man is separated from the body, it sees God; and this is final beatitude. . . . This disposes of the error of certain Greeks who deny purgatory and say that souls, before the resurrection of the bodies, neither ascend into heaven nor are cast into hell.[152]

It is thus unclear why soul might be retarded or distracted—as Augustine says it is—by the wait for body, because it is unclear what body could add to *visio Dei.*[153]

Yet Aquinas insists that it is unfitting, unnatural, and imperfect for soul to remain forever without body.[154] In his *De potentia Dei,* he argues that soul is happier when body is restored; in his *De anima* and *Sentence* commentary, he insists, although hesitantly, that body adds capacity for knowing.[155] The sensitive powers of the separated soul are restricted; they expand in resurrection. Both Albert and Thomas argue (in contrast to Bonaventure) that all five senses will be in "act" once body is restored in paradise, although they are unsure how far to allegorize such experiences as the odor of sanctity or the taste of heavenly sweetness.[156]

152. Ibid., p. 611; trans. by the English Dominican Fathers, *The Summa Contra Gentiles of St. Thomas Aquinas* (London: Burns, Oates, and Washbourne, 1929), p. 310.

153. *Sup.,* q. 93, art. 1 (Leonine ed.), pp. 224–25. Cf. ST 1a2ae, q. 4, art. 5, ad 5, vol. 16, pp. 100–7, esp. p. 101.

154. SCG, bk. 4, chaps. 79, 80 and 82, *Opera,* ed. Fretté, vol. 12, pp. 591–93 and 596–98.

155. See *Quaestiones de anima,* ed. Rob, esp. qq. 15–21, pp. 206–73; *Sup.,* q. 70, arts. 2–3 (Leonine ed.), pp. 148–51. See also ibid., q. 71, art. 11, pp. 157–58, on burial practices where he says (p. 158 col. 2, lines 40–45): ". . . quia caro est pars naturae hominis, naturaliter homo ad carnem suam afficitur."

156. Aquinas held that risen bodies will have the capacity for touch; see SCG, bk. 4, chap. 84, *Opera,* ed. Fretté, vol. 12, pp. 602–3. Risen bodies will not, however, eat: see SCG, bk. 4, chap. 83, ibid., pp. 598–602. In *Quaestiones disputatae de potentia,* q. 6, arts. 5–10 (Parma 1852–73 ed.), vol. 8, pp. 132–46, Aquinas argues that Christ willed to eat after the resurrection in order to show the reality of his body; angels cannot, however, really eat and speak (i.e., move the organs and the air or divide food and send it throughout the body). The analysis makes it quite clear that the human body-soul nexus is far closer than that suggested by any model of a spirit using a material object (as the angels do). See esp. article 8, reply to obj. 8, p. 142, where Aquinas explains why Christ's eating after the resurrection is different from the angels' eating even though in neither case can food be changed into flesh and blood. See also ST 3a, q. 55, art. 6, vol. 55, pp. 56–65. Albert the Great (*De resurrectione,* tract. 2, q. 8, art. 5, p. 278) argues that, in order to demonstrate his resurrected body, the resurrected Christ ate without the food becoming of his substance; we too could eat that way in the glorified body but have no need to, since we need not demonstrate the resurrection. See also Albert, *De sensibus corporis gloriosi,* ed. F. M. Henquinet,

When discussing epistemology, Aquinas argues that body pulls soul "toward inferior things." "When the soul is separated from the body, its vision is directed to higher things alone, and from these it receives an influx of universal intelligible species." But the separated soul will know through species "only generally and indistinctly in the manner in which things are known through universal principles." It cannot know "individually and determinately." This explanation appears to imply that resumption of body by soul in paradise would add a mode of knowing— that is, the capacity to grasp the particular as particular. It is significant, however, both that Aquinas does not ask explicitly what the resurrection body adds to soul and that he asserts:

> With respect to the knowledge the souls of the saints possess through grace, [it] is not the case [that they do not know natural things individually]. For as regards that knowledge the saints are made equal to the angels inasmuch as they, like the angels, see all things in the Word.[157]

Having espoused an epistemology that implies that resumption of body brings noetic improvement (or at least difference), Aquinas seems to all but deny the implication.[158]

The fundamental contradiction in Aquinas's thought thus rests in exactly the place where philosophers have seen his greatest creativity: his use of the Aristotelian notions of substance and hylomorphic union. For it is not finally clear whether Thomas places primary emphasis on soul as substantial form, united with God in beatific vision and spilling

---

"Une pièce inédite du commentaire d'Albert le Grand sur le IVe livre des sentences," *Recherches de théologie ancienne et médiévale* 7 (1935): 273–93. Weber shows how thirteenth-century theologians vacillated in their treatments of whether there is tasting in heaven (*Auferstehung*, pp. 259–60). Basic principles conflicted: on the one hand, vegetative functions were seen as eliminated in heaven; on the other hand, as Albert said: "Nulla potestate nobili destituentur."

157. *Quaestiones de anima*, ed. Rob, q. 18, p. 240; trans. J. P. Rowan, *Aquinas: The Soul* (London: Herder, 1951), p. 237; and see Milhaven, "Bodily Knowing."

158. See SCG, bk. 4, chap. 95, *Opera*, ed. Fretté, vol. 12, p. 613–14, where Aquinas clearly states that angels are higher than we are (even when we are separated souls) because they do not need the senses or discursive reasoning. The hierarchy of ways of knowing is clear, and bodily knowing is at the bottom. It is also significant that Aquinas maintains it took a miracle for Christ's human body to overcome the anesthesia of glory and experience the Passion whereas Bonaventure at least hints that the very perfection of Christ's body might have made it more open to sensation. See above, nn. 90–92. Aquinas also argues that the *visio Dei* flows over into the body and enables the martyrs to bear up under pain; ST 3a, q. 15, art. 5, obj. 3 and reply obj. 3, vol. 49, pp. 204–7, and ibid., q. 14, art. 1, obj. 2 and reply obj. 2, pp. 170–77.

forth its glory in an expression of self we call body, or whether he gives first importance to the substance *homo,* whose component parts are each incomplete without the other. On the one hand, Aquinas suggests that soul is a self that carries all our structure and integrity packed into it; it is thus in perfect joy when it attains *visio Dei.* The body we will achieve at the resurrection is only an expression of its glory—an expression that must indeed be kept under rather strict control by soul if it is not to slip away again into changeability or murkiness.[159] As Albert the Great says in his *Sentence* commentary, the *dotes* of the soul cause those of the body; the clarity of the risen body is an "effect of mind," a "clear glass" through which rich color (soul) shines.[160] On the other hand, Thomas argues that soul without body is a fragment. "When separated from the body, [it] is, in a way, imperfect, even as any part is when severed from its whole; [for] the soul is naturally part of human nature."[161] "Not every particular substance is a hypostasis or a person, but that which has the complete nature of its species. Hence a hand or a foot cannot be called a hypostasis or a person; nor likewise is the soul so called, since it is a part of the species human being."[162] Thus soul is a fragment, mute and limited; without body, it is blocked up. The blueprint of all we are—our shape and size, our gender and intellectual capacity, our status and merit—may be carried in soul, but it is realized in body. Without bodily expression, there is no human being (*homo*), no person, no self. Aquinas can be read both as eclipsing and as guaranteeing the ontological significance of body.

Exactly through this contradiction, Aquinas solved—as Origen had done centuries before—the problem of identity: resurrection of body was necessary because soul (form) must inform something, and possible be-

159. On this sense that body's essential lability might erupt again, see SCG, bk. 4, chap. 95, cited above in n. 158.

160. Albert the Great, *Sentence* commentary, in *Opera omnia,* ed. A. Borgnet (Paris, 1890–99), bk. 4, dist. 44, art. 30, vol. 30, p. 582; and Wicki, *Seligkeit,* p. 288 n. 32.

161. SCG, bk. 4, chap. 79, *Opera,* ed. Fretté, vol. 12, p. 592:

Adhuc, Ostensum est supra naturale hominis desiderium ad felicitatem tendere. Felicitas autem ultima est felicis perfectio. Cuicumque igitur deest aliquid ad perfectionem nondum habet felicitatem perfectam, quia nondum ejus desiderium totaliter quietatur; omne enim imperfectum perfectionem consequi naturaliter cupit. Anima autem a corpore separata est aliquo modo imperfecta, sicut omnis pars extra suum totum exsistens; anima enim naturaliter est pars humanae naturae. Non igitur homo potest ultimam felicitatem consequi, nisi anima iterato corpori conjungatur, praesertim quum ostensum sit quod homo in hac vita non potest ad felicitatem ultimam pervenire.

162. ST 1a, q. 75, art. 4, reply to obj. 2, vol. 11, pp. 20–21; and see n. 114 above.

cause a substantial soul accounts for identity through its subsistence. Moreover, by packing body into soul—that is, into a form that defined and stabilized, rather than a seminal reason that unfolded—Aquinas retained the particularity of self without threat to heavenly hierarchy and differentiated rewards.[163] What he sacrificed by understanding matter as potency (a position that tends to force matter's characteristics into form) was our commonsense experience of body as presence—labile, fertile, and therefore threatening presence—not merely lack or absence.[164] It was this sense of matter and body that later thinkers, such as Richard of Middleton, Eustace of Arras, Henry of Ghent, even Giles of Rome and John Quidort (who, as we have seen, followed Thomas on many theoretical points), tried to retain, either by arguing that there is a form of bodiliness or by lodging in matter some kind of *inclinatio* or yearning for form.[165] Indeed, Thomas himself retained something of commonsense notions when—in a theoretically incoherent move that has puzzled later philosophers—he lodged individuation in matter.[166]

Moreover, as we have seen, Aquinas sometimes spoke as if there were continuity of matter in resurrection. Indeed, where earlier thinkers, such as the seventh-century theologian Braulio of Saragossa, had admitted that not all of Christ's physical flesh need be in heaven, Aquinas spoke as urgently as had Guibert of Nogent about the necessity that every particle of his body ascend.[167] The empty tomb was an empty symbol

163. Retaining the particularity of souls even in purgatory was important to Aquinas; he argued that there were a large number of different receptacles for them, corresponding to their different statuses and merits; see Le Goff, *Birth of Purgatory*, pp. 270–72.

164. Greshake in Greshake and Kremer, *Resurrectio mortuorum*, pp. 237ff.; L. Hoedl, "Neue Nachrichten über die Pariser Verurteilungen der thomasischen Formlehre," *Scholastik* 39 (1964): 178–96; Schneider, *Die Einheit des Menschen*, pp. 127ff.; and Seidl, "Zur Leib-Seele-Einheit," pp. 548–53.

165. See *Fragmentation and Redemption*, pp. 406–7 nn. 69, 75; Wippel, *Godfrey of Fontaines*, p. 262. For efforts by Duns Scotus to retain an explanation of bodiliness see Greshake in Greshake and Kremer, *Resurrectio mortuorum*, pp. 238–39. See also Richard of Middleton, *De gradu formarum*, ed. Zavalloni, pp. 38, 59–61, 64, 74–75, 135. Much of Richard's discussion has to do with accounting for the fact that the cadaver appears similar to the living body in color, physical marks, etc. Both the cadaver and the living body decay, and our experience of this must also be accounted for, says Richard; see ibid, pp. 90–99, 139, and passim. John Quidort of Paris, in his *De unitate formae*, dealt explicitly with the objection that the unicity of form threatened the belief that Christ's body was Christ's in the *triduum*; see Pelster, "Ein anonymer Traktat des Johannes v. Paris," pp. 26–27.

166. See n. 141 above. By about 1300 James of Metz, who followed Thomas on the unicity of form and moved explicitly toward a formal identity theory, saw that treating matter as the principle of individuation does not work philosophically; see Gilson, *History of Christian Philosophy in the Middle Ages*, p. 472.

167. See above, n. 138.

unless the body that had occupied it rose to earth, and then to heaven, totally untainted by decay. Relic cult was the veneration of mere mementos unless the dust enshrined in reliquaries itself rose. Religious concerns held Aquinas to the position that there is material continuity in the bodies of heaven and hell. Later thinkers such as Godfrey of Fontaines, who saw the implications of formal identity more clearly than did Aquinas, gave explicitly theological reasons for hesitating to accept it.[168] And even before its philosophical or theological consequences were understood, a conservative reaction in the schools of Paris and Oxford questioned and condemned it.

The Condemnations of 1277 and the Materialist Reaction

The available evidence for the conservative reaction of the 1270s is hard to interpret. The doctrine of unicity of form was not condemned in 1277 at Paris when 219 propositions, including twenty taken directly from Thomas Aquinas, were condemned.[169] Roger Marston reported that the opinion was "excommunicated" in solemn assembly about 1270 with Aquinas present; what this means is not clear.[170] Giles of Lessines suggested to Albert the Great in 1278 that the condemnations of 1270 had included the thesis of the equivocality of body (the argument that—because there is a single form accounting for the person—the dead body and the living body cannot be the same numerically), but there is no evidence this was so.[171] Henry of Ghent and William of La Mare attempted to give the impression in Paris in the 1280s that unicity had been condemned in 1277, but Henry was forced to admit that it had not.[172] The investigation of Giles of Rome some time before 1279 and his forced retraction about 1285 was not (as older scholarship claimed) directed primarily at the unicity doctrine but rather at Aristotelian-Averroist notions of evil and the eternity of creation.[173]

168. Wippel, *Godfrey of Fontaines*, pp. 319–48.
169. Five of the propositions taken from Thomas had to do with the related issue of the individuation of species. The condemnation of Aquinas's positions was removed in 1325, just after his canonization, but the rest of the condemnation of 1277 lasted until the fifteenth century. See Hocedez, "La condamnation de Gilles de Rome," esp. p. 57.
170. Gilson, *History of Christian Philosophy in the Middle Ages*, p. 417.
171. Weber, *Auferstehung*, pp. 76–78, 150–51; and *Fragmentation and Redemption*, p. 407 n. 75.
172. Hocedez, "Condamnation de Gilles de Rome," p. 40; Wippel, *Godfrey of Fontaines*, p. 318 n. 89 and pp. 345–46.
173. Hocedez, "Condamnation de Gilles de Rome."

Nonetheless there is much to suggest that religious and philosophical anxiety was triggered by the theory that one substantial form accounts for the nature and thus the identity of person. Questions concerning identity (including the identity of living persons through biological change) were raised in the Parisian condemnations of 1277;[174] and proposition 17 seemed to require adherence to material continuity in resurrection. To believe that the corruptible body does not "return" and "rise" "the same numerically" was condemned as error.[175] Clearly the issue of unicity was what Gilson has called a "zone of tension" in the 1270s.[176] Its narrow escape in Paris was followed not only by its condemnation in 1277 at Oxford—a condemnation that was repeated in 1286—but also by a flood of theological writing devoted to enforcing the idea of some kind of actuality or seminal reasons in matter and some multiplicity of form, at least to the extent of a second form—that of bodiliness—to account for the human person.

The debate over unicity/plurality involved of course a number of theological and scientific issues other than eschatology. The nature of the body-soul, matter-form nexus had obvious implications for transubstantiation, the transmission of original sin, the growth of the fetus in the womb, the processes of nutrition and decay; theologians of the 1280s did not fail to explore these questions at new and great length.[177] But a crucial element of what historians have called the conservative reaction of 1277 was a concern to preserve some materiality (in a commonsense understanding of the term) in the resurrection body and, paradoxically, an insistence on the completeness of the separated soul as well. The reactions of the 1280s in favor of some actuality in matter, some material continuity in resurrection, and some form of corporeity to account for the cadaver or relic, can be seen as materialist whereas the last eschatological controversy of the Middle Ages—the debate over the beatific vision in the 1330s—seems at first glance to eliminate body from eschatological significance and lodge self squarely in soul. Both are however implicit in the anti-Thomist reaction of the 1270s.

---

174. *Chartularium universitatis Parisiensis*, vol. 1, p. 552. Hissette, *Enquête sur les 219 articles condamnés*, p. 187.

175. *Chartularium universitatis Parisiensis*, vol. 1, p. 544; see Hissette, *Enquête sur les 219 articles condamnés*, p. 308. And see above, n. 5.

176. Gilson, *History of Christian Philosophy in the Middle Ages*, pp. 416–20.

177. For new interest in embryology, see Hewson, *Giles of Rome and Conception*, p. 46 n. 21, and Richard of Middleton, *De gradu formarum*, ed. Zavalloni, pp. 70ff. and 81ff.; for Richard's interest in the cadaver, see n. 165 above.

In response to the condemnations at Paris and Oxford, several Franciscan theologians seized the opportunity to compose and circulate "corrections" of the errors of Thomas Aquinas.[178] Those drawn up by the Englishman William of La Mare sometime before 1279/80 are especially instructive in indicating what implications of Thomas's eschatological position distressed conservative theologians and seemed to them to offer a rallying point in the schools. William objects not only that Aquinas's version of hylomorphism denies the physicality of the body and the lability of matter in earthly life but also that it makes the separated soul too partial, too intellectual as it were, after death. Thomas holds, says William, that neither soul nor matter are composites; rather, matter is potency (which cannot therefore be "made" even by God without form) and soul is a single, intellective form.[179] From this, William claims, follow propositions 13 and 16 condemned by Kilwardly at Oxford in 1277: "that the living body and the dead body are body equivocally" and "that the intellective soul is united to prime matter in such a way that that which corrupts proceeds toward prime matter."[180] Several heresies follow as well: that Christ's body living and dead is "not the same in number"; that a new substantial form and also new accidental forms had to be introduced into Christ's body during the *triduum* because it had become prime matter; that Christ did not take his body, but only prime matter, from Mary; that the bread on the altar is not Christ's body; and that there is no original sin in man.[181] The fact that William returns

178. I agree with R. Zavalloni (*Richard de Mediavilla et la pluralité des formes*, preface, p. i) when he rejects earlier interpretations that saw the controversy largely as a matter of competition between orders.

179. William de la Mare, *Declarationes Magistri Guilelmi de la Mare O.F.M. de Variis Sententiis S. Thomae Aquinatis*, ed. Francis Pelster (Münster: Aschendorff, 1956), pp. 19, 22. On the date of William's Corrections, see Valens Heynck, "Zur Datierung des 'Correctorium fratris Thomae' Wilhelms de la Mare: Ein unbeachtetes Zeugnis des Petrus Johannis Olivi," *Franziskanische Studien* 49 (1967): 1–21.

180. William, *Declarationes*, p. 19; William comes back to the problem of Aquinas's view of the equivocality of body in chap. 107, p. 30, and says that Thomas claimed he retracted this position, but the retraction is nowhere to be found in his writings. He repeats that the idea follows from the unicity of form and involves several heresies. On the condemnations of 1277 at Oxford, see *Chartularium universitatis Parisiensis*, vol. 1, pp. 558–59.

181. William, *Declarationes*, pp. 20–21. The argument behind the last two is not explained; one can see what is involved in Richard of Middleton's treatise on the plurality of forms. The idea seems to be that there must be a form of bodiliness to account for the replacement of the form of bread by the form of *hoc corpus* and to convey the taint of sin from parent to offspring (since the intellective soul is not added to the fetus in the womb until weeks after conception). See Richard, *De gradu formarum*, ed. Zavalloni, pp. 100–1 and 105.

again at the end of his treatise to argue that equivocality of body follows from unicity of form and involves error concerning Christ's body in the tomb suggests that he is particularly troubled by the threat to the continuity of body between life and grave.[182] He is also troubled, however, by a suspicion that Aquinas's view of the soul as a single, substantial, intellective form limits soul's ability to know, and to suffer, and to contain (so to speak) our individuality. According to Thomas, the separated soul—like the angels and God himself—would not know particulars. Therefore it would not know Christ's passion or its own individual sins; its suffering from the "corporal fire" required by Scripture would be allegorized into mere mental impediment. The separated soul would be similar—even equal—to other souls, for it would be an intellect knowing itself and other souls as intellects.[183]

Thus William seems to object both that Thomas's theory does not explain how bodies (Christ's and ours) in the grave are crucial to self and that it does not make the separated soul able to know and suffer and experience joy as completely and "corporeally" as it will after the Last Judgment. While there is surely something inconsistent in the attack, both prongs reject the tight union of form and matter crucial to Thomas's conception of person. William assumes that both the cadaver and the separated soul are hylomorphic compositions, that physicality and lability should lodge in both. He seems to want perfect bliss (including full sensual knowledge and full individuality) guaranteed for the separated soul without body; yet he wants resurrection guaranteed for the cadaver in the grave (both by the *forma corporeitatis* and perhaps by some sort of material continuity as well). Like the majority of theologians at the end of the thirteenth century, he assumes a form for body but also packs much of bodiliness into separated soul. His concern for correct understanding of both soul and body stems explicitly from theological and devotional considerations—that is, from the implications of philosophical definitions for pious practices such as the Eucharist and the care of the dead.

Objections to equivocality of body thus seem to follow from concern about the relationship of cadaver to resurrection. To suggest this is not mere speculation on my part. Scholastic theologians seldom discuss devotional practices, but in the condemnations of 1277 and 1286 and in

182. See n. 180 above.
183. William, *Declarationes*, pp. 21, 22, 26–28. William's attack probably misrepresents Thomas; see above, n. 157. But Thomas's position was inconsistent.

dozens of quodlibetal questions from the decades around 1300, resurrection, relics, and burial practices were explicitly connected.[184] Theologians repeatedly objected to unicity and formal identity because the position implied that cadavers in the tomb and relics in reliquaries do not rise from the dead. A *forma corporeitatis* or *corporis*—even some sort of seminal reason, *inclinatio,* or yearning in the bones of *carnarium* and casket—seemed required to underscore the appropriateness of the cult of martyrs.

John Peckham, renewing in 1286 the Oxford condemnations of 1277, argued that equivocality denied that the living and dead bodies of Christ, the saints, and indeed all persons, were the same in number before they were changed by putrefaction into dust or elements.[185] Henry of Ghent explicitly rejected Thomistic unicity of form (toward which he was drawn as a philosophical solution) because it suggested that the relic is not really the saint.[186] John Quidort of Paris had to defend himself against critics who charged that formal identity removed all justification for pious cult. In his answer, John not only argued, as theologians had since Augustine, that relics are to be honored because they bring before our memories the life and suffering of the martyrs; he also held—in what almost amounts to a concession to material continuity—that the "first matter" (which does not quite mean mere potency) in relic and living holy person is the same and glorified in the body.[187]

Godfrey of Fontaines, who made repeated arguments against numerical identity in dead and living bodies for philosophical reasons, held back from espousing unicity of form. Arguing that Thomas's position and (as he analyzed it) that of Henry of Ghent made Christ's body ex-

184. Proposition 155, condemned in 1277, stated that care should not be taken for burial of the dead; *Chartularium universitatis Parisiensis,* vol. 1, p. 552. Hissette, *Enquête sur les 219 articles condamnés,* p. 294, connects the idea to denial of personal immortality and says its source has not been identified; he suggests that material continuity in resurrection provided support against the proposition and that a challenge to it was therefore perhaps also involved. He fails to note that the idea was a standard charge against heretics in this period, see chapter 5, pp. 216–19, above. And see below on scholastic discussions of burial practices, chapter 8 at n. 37.

185. *Registrum epistolarum fratris Johannis Peckham, archiepiscopi cantuariensis,* ed. C. T. Martin (London: Longman, 1882–85), vol. 3, pp. 921–23, and Wippel, *Godfrey of Fontaines,* p. 345 n. 183. Note that the argument here is for a *forma corporis* not material continuity, which was clearly becoming increasingly difficult to defend theoretically for the period after full-scale putrefaction had set in.

186. Wippel, *Godfrey of Fontaines,* pp. 320, 330; and see E. Brown, "Authority, Family, and the Dead."

187. Pelster, "Ein anonymer Traktat des Johannes v. Paris," p. 26; Gilson, *History of Christian Philosophy in the Middle Ages,* pp. 413–16; and see n. 165 above.

ceptional, Godfrey urged repeatedly that whatever solution one finds to explain continuity between living body and cadaver must apply to all bodies. Some sort of *forma corporeitatis* explains decay more satisfactorily than does a single substantial form, says Godfrey. Christ's body might have escaped putrefaction naturally by the spices used in the tomb or by the sort of miracle that, even in Godfrey's own day, preserved many saintly bodies incorrupt, but to attribute to the hypostatic union the fact that his body in the *triduum* was "his body" threatens our salvation and our personhood because it leaves no explanation for *our* material continuity in resurrection. In debate with Oliver of Tréguier in the early 1290s, Godfrey opposed the French aristocratic practice of corpse division by arguing both that whole burial is more consonant with whole resurrection (although God can, of course, unite fragments) and that it is "horrible" to mutilate a body that "still retains its form."[188] Philosophically sympathetic to lodging identity in one substantial form, Godfrey was thus drawn toward some sort of plurality by considerations arising from burial practice; he even suggested that matter retains some *inclinatio* to be informed with its own body while soul is separated from it after death.[189]

No mainstream theologian of the late Middle Ages denied the doctrine of bodily resurrection. None—not even those who held the theory of formal identity—denied that, under normal circumstances, God will reassemble and reanimate at the end of time the same material particles (*eadem in numero*) of which body was composed on earth. As we have seen, a concern for literal, material resurrection led some philosophically very astute theologians to shy away from the elegance and coherence of Thomas's theory of a single substantial form. Down into the seventeenth century, and even beyond, sermons and hymns that offered to Christians the hope of resurrection spoke of it in images of reunited fragments reminiscent of Tertullian's.[190] I shall turn in chapter 8 below to the context of such intellectual positions and pious promises in the practices of the late thirteenth century.

188. E. Brown, "Death and the Human Body," p. 243.
189. Wippel, *Godfrey of Fontaines*, chap. 8.
190. See, for example, John Donne, "Sermon No. 3. Preached at the Earl of Bridgewater's House in London at the Marriage of his daughter, the Lady Mary, November 19, 1627, on Matthew 22.30," in *The Sermons of John Donne*, vol. 8, ed. Evelyn Simpson and George Potter (Berkeley: University of California Press, 1956), pp. 94–109. The theme is a common one with the Metaphysical Poets, who use it with great subtlety.

But before I do, I must acknowledge that the story of intellectual developments does not end with the conservative reaction of the 1270s and 1280s. Whatever censure (and narrow escape from censure) the unicity doctrine saw in the decades before 1300, the formal theory of identity was not itself condemned. As I explained above, it gained ground steadily in the second and third decades of the fourteenth century.[191] Condemnation of those Thomistic notions that implied it was lifted in 1325.[192] Durand of St. Pourçain's identity theory (which spelled out clearly the implications of Thomas's) was *not* condemned when other aspects of his teaching were extracted from his *Sentence* commentary for censure.[193] Although discussion stayed in the narrow confines of the university and theologians indeed remained uncomfortable with some of its ramifications, unicity of form and formal identity became fairly widespread assumptions by 1330. For example, Dante used the notions quite correctly in the *Divine Comedy* to account for both aerial and resurrection bodies.[194]

In university circles of the early fourteenth century, attention turned increasingly to soul. The confusion that resulted from the plurality-of-forms doctrine led in 1311–1312 to condemnation of the view that the intellective soul can relate to body only through lower levels of soul. But this was not (as recent scholars have realized) a victory either for unicity or for body.[195] Nonetheless, the increasing focus on soul led some to ask whether body contributes anything to blessedness. As Dondaine has demonstrated, discussion of soul's encounter with God in *visio*—unimportant in thirteenth-century summae—played a major role, in some cases *the* major role, in quodlibetal debates around 1300.[196] The last important eschatological controversy of the Middle Ages—the controversy over the beatific vision in the early 1330s—established that full enjoyment of God might come to the separated soul before it received its body back. Although a pope himself supported the claim that vision "face to face" will be delayed until "person" is reestablished with resurrection, the claim was defeated.

191. The position remained, however, a narrowly philosophical one. See the appended texts in Weber, *Auferstehung*.

192. See above, n. 169.

193. Weber, *Auferstehung*, p. 242 n. 404.

194. See below, chapter 7, p. 302.

195. Greshake in Greshake and Kremer, *Resurrectio mortuorum*, pp. 237–38.

196. H. F. Dondaine, "L'Objet et le 'medium' de la vision béatifique chez les théologiens du XIIIe siècle."

The beatific vision controversy can thus from one point of view be seen as a rearguard and unsuccessful action by the partisans of the body. It was, however, in a deeper sense an indication of how far the separated soul had (as William of La Mare suggested) come to contain the particularity and capacity for experience earlier treatments had lodged in body. The soul that was defined in the bull *Benedictus Deus* of 1336 was not a self for which body is the completion or housing or garment, but a self of which body is the expression (*abundantia* or *refluentia*).

I therefore turn in my next chapter to the controversy over *visio Dei*, and to twelfth- and thirteenth-century notions of somatomorphic soul that provide the background to it. I turn to beatific vision not in order to shift attention to the topic of soul but in order to explore the final episode in the story of medieval concepts of the resurrection body: the point at which even separated soul becomes in some sense "embodied."

Seven

Somatomorphic Soul and Visio Dei: The Beatific Vision Controversy and Its Background

THE BEATIFIC VISION CONTROVERSY of the 1330s was an event of some importance in the history of theology. Three popes, a king, an emperor, and dozens of theologians participated.[1]

The debate concerned the experience of separated soul between death and Last Judgment. It focused on that eschatological period and place in which body is absent, still asleep in the tomb awaiting resurrection. Thus the controversy might seem, at first glance, to have nothing to do with body and therefore nothing to do with the topic of this book. But in fact the debate was really about body and resurrection. For to suggest that *visio Dei* can come to separated soul—that the final bliss of heaven might be given before the Judgment—is to suggest that body adds little if anything to blessedness. The *visio Dei* controversy was thus the final episode in medieval discussions of the ontological and soteriological importance of body.

Behind the controversy lay the idea of purgatory and the antiheretical polemic of the thirteenth century. Before I consider the events of the

---

1. On the importance of the controversy over the beatific vision and the number and status of the people involved, see Decima Douie, "John XXII and the Beatific Vision," *Dominican Studies* 3, no. 2 (1950): 154–74. For background, see X. Le Bachelet, "Benoît XII," *DTC*, vol. 2, col. 653–96, and Wicki, *Seligkeit*.

1330s, I must therefore turn briefly to changing notions of the afterlife in the preceding two hundred years.

Purgatory

Jacques Le Goff's popular and important history of purgatory has been much criticized for dating the appearance of the belief to the late twelfth century, for spatializing the concept, and for relating it closely to Dumézil's theories about threefold social structures in the Indo-European tradition (and therefore to the emergence of the bourgeoisie).[2] Nonetheless much of Le Goff's analysis is subtle, perceptive, and convincing, especially his demonstration that—between the later twelfth and fourteenth centuries—preaching as well as formal theology paid increasing attention to an "in-between" time and place for the separated soul.[3]

As Le Goff explains it, the doctrine of purgatory located an experience of suffering and expiation between personal death and general judgment. In the course of the thirteenth century this experience was both "infernalized" and "tilted toward heaven."[4] Purgatory became, that is, the location of horrid punishments, often indistinguishable from those of hell, but theorists made it clear that no change in ultimate soteriological status could be effected there. Purgation was consequent upon a prior decision that the soul was destined for heaven; it was unavailable to those destined for hell.

Thus the doctrine of purgatory rapidly came to be important both for devotional purposes and for social control. It made prayers for the dead effective—but not too effective! Some development was possible for the souls of ancestors, relatives, and even holy people after death (as long as

2. See, for example, Adrian H. Bredero, "Le moyen âge et le Purgatoire," *Revue d'histoire ecclésiastique* 78 (1983): 429–52; Aaron J. Gurevich, "Popular and Scholarly Medieval Cultural Traditions: Notes in the Margin of Jacques Le Goff's Book," *Journal of Medieval History* 9 (1983): 71–90; Alan E. Bernstein, review of Le Goff in *Speculum* 59 (1984): 179–83; Jean-Pierre Massaut, "La Vision de l'au-delà au moyen âge: A propos d'un ouvrage récent," *Le Moyen Age* 91 (1985): 75–86; Graham R. Edwards, "Purgatory: 'Birth' or Evolution?" *Journal of Ecclesiastical History* 36 (1985): 634–46. Since Le Goff has been criticized by theologians for too much attention to social setting and by students of popular culture for too much attention to formal theology, he must have done something right.

3. Purgatory was first defined as doctrine at the Second Council of Lyons in 1274; the definition was repeated with slight modification at the Council of Florence in 1439; see Denzinger, *Enchiridion* (1957 ed.), pp. 216, 252–53. The first official pontifical pronouncement on purgatory was in 1254; it actually goes beyond the Second Council of Lyons in giving a name, *purgatorium*, to the place of purgation and associating it with fire; see Le Goff, *Birth of Purgatory*, pp. 284–86.

4. Le Goff, *Birth of Purgatory*, pp. 4–7, 204–8, 310–15, 358–59, and passim.

they were destined for heaven as well as in need of cleansing).[5] But the moment of dying was determinative. It decided one's place in the afterlife. There could be neither hope nor terror that one might change beyond the borders of death into a self unrecognizable, in moral terms, as a continuation of the self of earth.[6] Purgatory reinforced rather than undercut age-old concerns with reward and punishment.

It has sometimes surprised modern scholars that the "in-between" period of purgation was imagined by poets and visionaries in such strikingly somatic terms or that theologians insisted (as did both Thomas Aquinas and William of La Mare, who accused him of denying it) that the separated soul in purgatory experienced corporeal fire.[7] They have therefore tended to resort to theories of the imagination drawn from comparative religion, psychology, or literary analysis to explain the large number of eleventh-, twelfth-, and thirteenth-century visions in which corporealized souls undergo complex journeys after death but before resurrection.[8] This is a subject to which I shall return below. What is relevant here is simply the observation that preachers, hagiographers, and schoolmen saw nothing fundamentally inconsistent in depicting the bodily tortures of disembodied spirits although they sometimes admitted it was odd.[9] Purgatory and resurrection were different (and not fully compatible) eschatological emphases, but medieval theorists did not see

5. My emphasis here is a little different from Le Goff's; he stresses purgatory as a victory for the idea of progress—growth—beyond this life and says it makes death a "bogus boundary" (Le Goff, *Birth of Purgatory*, p. 288). There is truth in this, and Le Goff is right to point to the fact that Greek theologians accused Westerners of being "Origenist" in their view. But it seems to me that the emphasis on death as decisive was fundamental.

6. See the discussion of Hadewijch at n. 39 below. See also the perceptive remarks of Jean-Claude Schmitt in "La Fabrique des saints," *Annales: Économies, sociétés, civilisations* 39 (1984): 296–97.

7. Thomas's account does tend to psychologize the experience of fire, however, suggesting that it somehow limits the soul. The proposition that the separated soul does not suffer *ab igne* was condemned in Paris in 1277; see *Chartularium universitatis Parisiensis . . . ,* proposition 19, p. 544; and Roland Hissette, *Enquête sur les 219 articles condamnés*, pp. 309–10.

8. Carol Zaleski tends to reduce somatomorphism either to a literary reaction— what she calls a "law of the imagination" that leads writers in many religious traditions to picture the soul as body—or to a psychological or even neurological reaction related to the "phantom limb" syndrome (see *Otherworld Journeys*, pp. 5 1ff., 117, and 192ff). For further discussion of this issue, see my "Faith Imagining the Self: Somatomorphic Soul and Resurrection Body in Dante's *Divine Comedy*."

9. See Le Goff, *Birth of Purgatory*, p. 6, and below, pp. 291–307. Robert W. Ackerman argues that the thirteenth-century Middle English *Debate between the Body and the Soul* reflects "popular belief" in its idea that the soul has a "material body," depicted in art as a homunculus ("The Debate of the Body and the Soul and Parochial Christianity," *Speculum* 37 [1962]: 549 and 564).

them as contradictory. As Thomas Aquinas's objection against Greek theology (quoted above, p. 267) suggests, those who polemicized against heresy or error connected denial of resurrection, denial of pious burial, and denial of purgatory.[10] Cathars, who were accused of abhorring the body and rejecting its resurrection, were thought to be equally hostile to a period of purgation in which self is soul.[11] A Latin translation of a thirteenth-century Greek work presented to pope John XXII in 1326 or 1327 associated the Greek "error" that souls will not go immediately to heaven or hell at death with the Cathar opinion that souls linger "in the air" until a final judgment.[12] Polemics against dualists and Amauricians in the first two decades of the thirteenth century, debates over eschatology in the 1230s, efforts at reconciliation with the Greek church in the 1250s, the Second Council of Lyons in 1274, and the Parisian condemnations of 1277 all maintained that both the doctrine of purgatory and the doctrine of resurrection were necessary to a theology in which death is decisive, prayers for the dead are effective, and self is a psychosomatic unity.[13]

Purgatory implied an afterlife in which significant moments might occur before the end of time.[14] It thus prepared for the view, which triumphed in 1336, that the beatific vision might come to the blessed whenever they were spiritually cleansed.[15] Resurrection and the resurrection body were not necessary in order to see God.[16]

10. See chapter 5, nn. 57–67, and chapter 6, n. 152.

11. See Le Goff, *Birth of Purgatory*, pp. 168–73, 278–80, 331–33; and Dykmans, *Sermons de Jean XXII*, pp. 12–18. Moneta of Cremona and Durand of St. Pourçain, for example, argued that Cathars deny immediate entry into paradise or hell at the moment of death. Thus Cathar denial of purgatory is seen as a denial that death is decisive and a preference for some notion of sleep until the end of time. Cathars were also, of course, held to deny resurrection.

12. Dykmans, *Sermons de Jean XXII*, p. 30.

13. See Le Goff, *Birth of Purgatory*, pp. 237–88.

14. See Le Goff, *Birth of Purgatory*, pp. 254 and 269, for Bonaventure and Thomas arguing that release from purgatory can come before the end of time.

15. Dykmans (*Sermons de Jean XXII*, pp. 17–20) cites a forged letter concerning Jerome's miracles, purportedly from Cyril of Jerusalem to Augustine, that was circulating in Europe about 1300. It asserted that Greek heretics denied not only that the beatific vision came before the end of time but also that any punishment or reward was bestowed before the body was resumed. Dykmans suggests that it could have been forged by the enemies of John XXII anxious to associate his position on the beatific vision with the denial of any personal judgment at death. The fact that denial of purgatory, of personal judgment, and of immediate beatific vision were associated suggests that making the moment of death the decisive eschatological transition was close to the heart of the issue in the early fourteenth century.

16. The idea that we do not see the divine essence in *visio Dei* but rather some sort of theophany—as Dionysius and Erigena were taken to suggest—was already

This view was, however, less a rejection of body than a subsuming of it into soul. Although separated soul was by definition, of course, without body, a good deal of the theological squabbling of the 1320s and 1330s involved the condemning of positions that implied any epistemological lack, even lack of quasi-corporeal experience, in soul. Whereas those who argued for postponed *visio Dei* spoke of body as a garment or stole added at the end of time, those who supported immediate beatific vision spoke of body as a manifestation or flowing out that appears almost timeless. It thus seems probable that the position of *Benedictus Deus* gained ground steadily in the thirteenth century and prevailed in the fourteenth, at least in part because theologians, poets, and visionaries imagined the soul that achieved beatitude as if it already in some way possessed, or expressed itself in, its body.

The Controversy Over the Beatific Vision

The controversy over the beatific vision began in the fall and early winter of 1331 when pope John XXII preached two sermons asserting that the souls of the saints now rest "under the altar" (Rev. 6.9) in contemplation of Christ's humanity but will at the general resurrection and final Judgment be raised above the altar to the perfect joy of *visio Dei*. Drawing on Augustine and Bernard as well as on gospel parables of the talents and the workers in the vineyard (Matt. 20 and 25), John argued that the separated soul is imperfect; it is therefore incapable, until reunited with its body, of attaining the goal of all desire: full vision of the divine essence "face to face." By Epiphany, 1332, John seems to have asserted (these sermons survive only in fragments and may have been censored) that final damnation of the wicked and full revelation of Christ in his divinity will be deferred until the Last Judgment.[17]

---

condemned in 1241. Thus direct encounter was important. See Dondaine, "L'Objet et le 'medium' de la vision béatifique chez les theologiens du XIIIe siècle."

17. Douie, "John XXII and Beatific Vision"; Le Bachelet, "Benoît XII"; N. Valois, "Jacques Duèse: Pape sous le nom de Jean XXII," in *Histoire littéraire de la France,* vol. 34 (Paris: Imprimerie Nationale, 1914), pp. 551–627; J. E. Weakland, "Pope John XXII and the Beatific Vision Controversy," *Annuale mediaevale* 9 (1968): 76–84; Dykmans, *Sermons de Jean XXII*; Robert of Anjou, *La Vision bienheureuse: Traité envoyé au pape Jean XXII,* ed. Marc Dykmans (Rome: Presses de l'Université Gregorienne, 1970); Marc Dykmans, *Pour et contre Jean XXII en 1333: Deux traités avignonnais sur la vision béatifique* (Città del Vaticano: Biblioteca Apostolica Vaticana, 1975); Katherine Walsh, *A Fourteenth-Century Scholar and Primate: Richard Fitzralph in Oxford, Avignon, and Armagh* (Oxford: Clarendon Press, 1981), pp. 89–107; and Lucy Freeman Sandler, "Face to Face with God: A Pictorial Image of the Beatific Vision," in *England in the Fourteenth Century: Proceedings of the 1985 Harlaxton Sympo-*

John's own position in the opening decades of the fourteenth century appears to have been the one popular since the 1240s—that is, that full beatific vision can come before the end of time.[18] Bulls of canonization he promulgated in the 1310s and 1320s (including that for Thomas Aquinas) spoke of the saints seeing God "face to face." But the issue had clearly begun to puzzle the pope in the 1320s when he made marginal notations in a copy of Gerard of Abbeville's quodlibetal questions exactly where Gerard adduced a number of skillful arguments for the position that resumption of body must add to blessedness because full beatitude is promised to the psychosomatic unit "person," not to the soul. John himself saw the matter as having devotional and pastoral implications; he defended his later notion of postponed *visio* by commenting that the Mass implies the possibility of improvement when it exhorts us to pray for the dead.[19]

Several chroniclers tell us that John's sermons of 1331–32 "scandalized many." But it was a year before opposition was articulated—by the English Dominican, Thomas Waleys, preaching at Avignon—and Waleys was soon accused of heresy and imprisoned. The pope's opinions were widely discussed in the universities of Paris and Oxford, where they met with no favor, and the French king openly sided with the Parisian theologians. The new Minister General of the Franciscans, Guiral Ot (Geraldus Odonis), then delivered a disputation at Paris in the autumn of 1333 that supported the pope but moved discussion toward a theory of three different kinds of vision, the most perfect of which (the *visio eterna*) was delayed until after the Last Judgment. When John re-

---

sium, ed. W. M. Ormrod (Woodbridge, Suffolk: Boydell Press, 1986), pp. 224–35. Much of the outrage over the pope's opinion was owing to its (Nestorian) implication that the humanity and divinity of Christ were separable and that the separated soul received a vision of the humanity without the divinity; see Walsh, *Richard FitzRalph*, p. 90.

18. In general, thirteenth-century theologians raised the question of *visio Dei* in discussing Peter Lombard, *Sentences*, bk. 4, dist. 49, q. 1, art. 4: "Whether the beatitude of the blessed is greater after the resurrection than before." The standard answer was "yes." Debate was over the nature of "greater." Aquinas, for example, gave up the notion that blessedness would increase in intensity, although he maintained that it would increase "in extension." See Dykmans, *Pour et contre Jean XXII*, p. 50. For Bonaventure's opinion, see above, chapter 6 at n. 98.

19. John's opponents also appealed to pastoral and devotional concerns. An anonymous *De visione beata* of 1333–34 (Paris BN lat. 3170, edited by Dykmans) argues that those who deny immediate beatific vision are in effect denying purgatory, profaning the martyrs, and rejecting prayers for the dead. The implication is that to postpone any aspect of heavenly reward is to postpone all postmortem experience and judgment until body is restored (Dykmans, *Pour et contre Jean XXII*, pp. 40–54).

quested an opinion from Durand of St. Pourçain and received (in 1334) a vindication of the idea of immediate vision, he submitted Durand's treatise to a tribunal of theologians, who found eleven errors. Jacques Fournier—the most renowned thinker among the cardinals and the future Benedict XII—then, however, vindicated Durand on several of his alleged errors and presented to the pope his own *De statu animarum*, which defended the idea of immediate vision but allowed for the possibility of a still more perfect and complete *visio* after the resurrection.[20] A consensus was clearly building around an intermediate opinion. John retracted his most extreme formulations on his deathbed, asserting (still with a strong hedge concerning the significance of body): "the holy souls see God and the divine essence face to face and as clearly as their condition as souls separated from their bodies allows."[21]

On January 29, 1336, Jacques Fournier, now Benedict XII, issued *Benedictus Deus*, which defined doctrine on four of the five issues that had emerged at the heart of the controversy. Pure souls (asserted the pope) see the divine essence *nude, clarte, et aperte* before the end of time; this vision is true beatitude and full repose (*requies*). Because of its presence, the theological virtues of faith and hope, which involve anticipation, cease; because it continues forever, no other *visio Dei* will come to replace it after the resurrection. Benedict did not settle the issue (on which a number of thirteenth- and fourteenth-century theologians were unclear) of whether there is increase in the intensity of the beatific vision after the Last Judgment, although his personal opinion was that there was.[22] He did use the bull to affirm both personal and general judgment: the wicked descend to hell at death (he asserted); yet they must appear again with all humankind when the trumpet sounds so that body as well as soul can receive recompense.

20. Douie, "John XXII and Beatific Vision," p. 168; Le Bachelet, "Benoît XII," col. 665; Thomas Käpelli, *Le Procès contre Thomas Waleys O.P.: Études et documents* (Rome: Istituto storico domenicano, S. Sabina, 1936); Joseph Koch, *Durandus de S. Porciano, O.P.: Forschungen zum Streit um Thomas von Aquin zu Beginn des 14. Jahrhunderts*, BGPTM 26 (Münster: Aschendorff, 1927), pp. 173–76; Anneliese Maier, "Die Pariser Disputation des Geraldus Odonis," and "Zwei Prooemien Benedikts XII," in *Ausgehendes Mittelalter: Gesammelte Aufsätze zur Geistesgeschichte des 14. Jahrhunderts*, Storia e Letteratura, 97, 105, and 138 (Rome: Edizioni di Storia e Letteratura, 1964–77), vol. 3, pp. 327–33 and 447–89; Dykmans, "A propos de Jean XXII et de Benoît XII: La libération de Thomas Waleys," *Archivum Historiae Pontificiae* 7 (1969): 115–30; and Walsh, *Richard FitzRalph*, p. 92.

21. Douie, "John XXII and Beatific Vision," p. 157; Walsh, *Richard FitzRalph*, p. 103 n. 69.

22. Le Bachelet, "Benoît XII," cols. 669–72; for the text of *Benedictus Deus*, see cols. 657–58, and Denzinger, *Enchiridion* (1957 ed.), pp. 229–30.

A number of the treatises and documents produced in the course of this controversy have recently been edited by Anneliese Maier and Marc Dykmans.[23] Much is at stake in them, as we have seen: matters of Christology, epistemology, and soteriology, of pastoral care and papal authority. For my purposes they provide a final dossier of many of the metaphors, images, and biblical phrases used by schoolmen to discuss the resurrected body. Skillful and often tendentious in their deployment of scriptural references to attack opponents, these polemicists and theologians were fully aware of the contradiction in their own ideas between the goal of repose or stasis (*requies aeterna*) and the active pull of *appetitus* or *retardatio*; they understood the ambiguity of their inherited concepts of *desiderium* and of *corpus* itself.

If we look, for example, at Gerard of Abbeville's quodlibetal question "whether beatified souls see the uncreated light more clearly when they have resumed their bodies than they did before"—a thirteenth-century work that influenced John XXII—we find Gerard fully aware of the ambivalence in Augustine's idea of a *naturalis inclinatio ad corpus* retarding the soul before resurrection.[24] Gerard points out that Hugh of St. Victor concluded from the notion of the drag of corruptibility that soul is better off without body. Nonetheless, he tries to solve the dilemma by making the *affectus* for body "natural" (and therefore positive) and by arguing that it is only the decaying body that distracts the soul by "busying" it with the need to "manage" corruption. He subsumes the removal of impediment into the satisfaction of *inclinatio* as a final act that makes the soul more perfect.

To Gerard, body, like perfection, is something added to soul. Such a conception of body appears to be at the heart of the arguments of John XXII as well. Using 2 Corinthians 5.1–10, John describes the resurrection body as resumed clothing, a rebuilt house or tabernacle, a stole put on. It would be odd, asserts John, if body added nothing, for it adds at least "the eyes of the body" for seeing. It would be similarly odd if final reward were bestowed before final Judgment. Most of all it would be perplexing if a soul at rest could incline anywhere, let alone downward. How can a soul in possession of full vision of God be distracted by anything? How,

---

23. For Dykmans' contributions, see above, n. 17. Anneliese Maier's studies and editions have been reprinted in *Ausgehendes Mittelalter*, vol. 3, pp. 319–590.

24. Gerard, a secular master at the University of Paris, died in 1272. His quodlibetal question on the separated soul and the beatific vision is edited in Dykmans, *Sermons de Jean XXII*, pp. 45–49.

in other words, can a soul so beatified even notice—in the blinding light of God's presence—that its body is missing?[25]

Those who disagreed with John disagreed, of course, with the devotional and pastoral consequences of delaying full delight for the good soul until a distant resurrection.[26] But they also seem to have disagreed with the notion that body is something added on, and with the ambiguity implicit in thirteenth-century notions of *retardatio* or *desiderium*. Thomas Waleys, preaching against the pope, used Ecclesiastes 2.23, Ecclesiasticus 34.11, and Isaiah 57.20 to argue that John's position meant there was no rest for the separated soul, which would ebb and flow, drawn by sadness, like a troubled sea.[27] Durand of St. Pourçain, replying in the summer of 1334 to John's request for an opinion, devoted much attention to the pope's metaphor of the body as garment or stole (derived from the parables, Rev. 6.11, and 2 Cor. 5) but argued that workers in the vineyard need not wait for an outer garment in order to receive their reward.

Durand's position is not, however, a rejection of body. In full philosophical accord with his espousal of formal identity, Durand (like Waleys) spoke as if glory spills forth from soul into body as soul's expression—an image that in a certain sense makes the bond between the two far tighter than the biblical metaphor of a second stole or garment added to a first.[28] Another of John's opponents, the future Benedict XII, agreed most strongly with the censuring of Durand at that point where Durand himself seemed to hold back some "bodily" experience from separated soul. Durand argued that soul before resurrection but in receipt of bea-

<hr />

25. John, Sermon 2, pars. 26–27, 29, 72–74 and 76, in Dykmans, *Sermons de Jean XXII*, pp. 114–15, 115–16, 138–39, 142–43; see also the discussion of sermon 6 on the Ascension in ibid., p. 59. It is interesting that John uses a reference to Bernard to argue that soul cannot enter the joy of the Lord without body any more than a prelate can enter without his people (sermon 1, paragr. 10, in ibid., p. 97); he thus shows some awareness of the social implications of resurrection—an aspect that was usually ignored in this period.

26. The anonymous treatise *De visione beata* even argues that the pope is the equivalent of a Waldensian heretic in his denial of purgatory; *De visione beata*, pt. 2, reason 9, ed. Dykmans, in *Pour et contre Jean XXII*, p. 49.

27. See Waleys' sermon, edited in Käpelli, *Le Procès contre . . . Waleys*, pp. 95–96.

28. Douie, "John XXII and Beatific Vision," pp. 167–69. This position also, of course, tends to remove the temporal dimension; spilling over has overtones of Neoplatonic emanation. To say this is not to suggest that Durand thought the body was resumed or expressed before resurrection; it is only to point out that once one moves to this conception of body, there is no clear reason why whatever "body" means could not be expressed or resumed before. See Greshake in Greshake and Kremer, *Resurrectio mortuorum*, pp. 237–39. See also Waleys' sermon and the charges against him; Käpelli, *Le Procès contre . . . Waleys*, pp. 93–108 and 109.

tific vision would be unable to delight in corporal things because it lacked sense organs. Benedict XII was willing, it seems, to grant it even such delight.[29]

Just after the death of John XXII and before the issuing of *Benedictus Deus*, Robert of Anjou—king of Naples and titular king of Jerusalem, brother of St. Louis bishop of Toulouse, and great-nephew of St. Louis king of France—sent to Benedict XII a treatise he had prepared to refute John's opinions. In Robert's analysis, the ambiguity of thirteenth-century concepts both of desire and of body is dealt with by moving body into soul. No longer a vessel or house reassembled from fragments and inhabited anew, no longer a resumed garment or a second stole added to glory, body becomes a flowering or expression of the soul's blessedness *(refluentia beatitudinis animae)*.

Robert argues that there cannot be any significant unrest after death for good souls. Waiting or becoming or desiring is a kind of violence; it cannot be inflicted on the blessed. The unrest of desiring the beatific vision would be far greater than that of desiring the body.[30] Such unrest must be stilled; beatific vision must come immediately after death to those who are ready and to others as soon as they can be cleansed. If any waiting for body, any becoming or change, remains possible after *visio*, it must be unimportant. Souls in beatitude are not subject to time or mutation; blessedness is stasis or *quies*. If, therefore, there is any *appetitus* or *desiderium* for body in blessedness, it is only *per accidens* not per se.[31] Robert eliminates most of the ambiguity in the Augustinian and Bernardine concept of desire by eliminating the body as object of desire; desire for body is now neither a negative retardation nor a positive love, for it is not really desire at all. True desire is for the soul's blessedness, and it will be quieted long before the end of time.

Body may add something, Robert asserts, but soul's operation is perfect without it. It is foolish to argue, as Bernard appears to do, that separated souls will see Christ "in his humanity," not his divinity. Separated souls are spiritual, as is God; how could they have a special object of blessedness that is corporeal? Separated souls have "essentially per-

29. See n. 20 above.

30. Robert, *La Vision bienheureuse*, ed. Dykmans. The position is similar to Albert the Great's; see Le Goff, *Birth of Purgatory*, p. 257–58. Albert argues that souls in purgatory desire not their bodies but God; hence deprivation of the beatific vision *is* the punishment inflicted in purgatory.

31. Robert, *La Vision bienheureuse*, ed. Dykmans, pt. 1, paragr. 12, lines 15–22, pp. 11 and 68*. Robert admits that some kind of unimportant *inclinatio* for body may remain in souls "under the altar," pt. 5, paragr. 1, p. 68 n. 2 and p. 80*.

fect" contemplation.[32] Moreover, Thomas Aquinas did not say that we must have the disposition or sensation of body in order to have essential happiness. Body is necessary on earth, for the imperfect knowing of earth; it is necessary after resurrection, for the expression of soul's glory. But "essential blessedness is principally in the soul; then by consequence it flows over [*redundat*] into the body and the senses."[33] Once body is restored, there is more glory, asserts Robert; and this glory perhaps has greater unity although it is not changed in essence. But body is merely the fullness or expression of soul.

Robert explains what this means only by metaphor. Body is to soul as a gesture is to one who prays, as alms-giving is to one who possesses the virtue of charity, as act is to someone who has the *habitus* for it.[34] These metaphors, combined with the technical concept of *habitus*, imply a greater impulsion, a greater need to express or flow out or act, than does the technical theological analysis. Body is clearly not rejected. We are in the presence, however, of the same contradiction we found lodged at the center of Thomas's use of hylomorphic union. Body is packed into soul. On the one hand, then, some impulsion of that soul-form to inform something, to express itself in act, is built into the concept itself; on the other hand, however, such expression or gesturing or flowering of soul is far away from the commonsense notion of body as matter—that which eats, sickens, decays, and therefore seems to cry out for salvation.

The majority opinion among thirteenth- and fourteenth-century theologians stressed the afterlife as stasis, blessedness as the stilling of desire, purgatory as a temporary period to which admission was granted by one's moral state at the moment of death. Although they insisted that souls were passible in purgatory, they also insisted that the beatific vision, once bestowed, spilled out from impassible souls into a gift of impassibility for body. *Visio Dei* had to come before the end of time lest souls remain tossed in a sea of longing—longing both for body and for God—until a distant resurrection.

Theologians of the high Middle Ages were curious and worried about the aerial bodies souls in purgatory might assume in order to appear on

32. Robert, *La Vision bienheureuse*, ed. Dykmans, pt. 1, paragrs. 25–26, pp. 17–18 and 69*–70*.

33. Ibid., pt. 5, paragr. 58, p. 98: "beatitudinem . . . qualis erit post resurrectionem propter refluentiam beatitudinis anime in corpore et in sensus corporeos. . . . [Q]uod beatitudo essentialis principaliter est in anime, deinde consequenter redundat in corpus et sensus."

34. Ibid., pt. 1, paragrs. 27–30, pp. 18–19, and 69*. In paragr. 29, Robert attributes to Aquinas (ST 2a2ae, q. 83, art. 12) the idea that interior devotion should express itself in the outward gestures of prayer.

35. Le Goff, *Birth of Purgatory*, p. 269.

earth.[35] Thomas Aquinas, for example, devoted an inordinate amount of attention in his quodlibetal question on miracles to stories of incubi, succubi, and ghosts.[36] But as far as possible these theologians tended to make the experience of passible souls in purgatory psychological or spiritual while suggesting both that soul might function as if it had corporeal senses once it attained the stasis of beatific vision and also that the postresurrection soul-body unit (gifted with repose and impassibility) would have all five senses. Thus *requies aeterna* displaced spiritual development, and soul gained resurrection body, or aerial body, or body-likeness, at those points where its characteristics were farthest from what common sense assumed body to be—that is, experiencing and changeable.

Visions and tales of the afterlife that had circulated widely since the eleventh century had, however, a somewhat different emphasis. In them, separated soul was more corporeal, purgatory more progressive. As Le Goff has stressed, the notion of purgation after death did introduce a hope for change in the afterlife.[37] In some miracle stories told around 1200, such as those of Caesarius of Heisterbach or the vision of the monk of Evesham, the separated souls who hope to be saved by purgation and the prayers of the living are not very precisely located; the place of torment in which they reside sounds in some cases more like hell than purgatory.[38] The thirteenth-century Flemish mystic Hadewijch was convinced that she had succeeded, by Christ's special favor toward her, in praying four souls out of hell although she knew it to be theologically incorrect even to offer such prayers let alone to believe that escape from hell is possible.[39] Doctrinal pronouncements and antiheretical polemic concerning purgatory, resurrection, the beatific vision, and prayers for the dead make it clear that all these elements were part of a theology in which ultimate reward and punishment are determined at the moment

36. Aquinas, *Quaestiones disputatae de potentia*, q. 6: "De miraculis," arts. 5–10, in Aquinas, *Opera omnia*, vol. 8, pp. 132–46; and see my *Fragmentation and Redemption*, p. 226.

37. Le Goff, *Birth of Purgatory*, rightly connects this to the growth of narrative in the twelfth century. We might also connect it to what Robert Lerner calls the growth of "progressivism"—that is, of the idea that society changes in a positive direction here on earth; see Lerner's work in progress.

38. Caesarius, *Dialogus*, distinctiones 11–12, vol. 2, pp. 266–364. The vision of the monk of Evesham (1197) is, among other things, propaganda for prayers for the dead. It leaves the impression that everyone the monk meets in the afterlife is able to work his or her way toward reward. On the early medieval notion of "provisional damnation"—that is, that souls are released from hell by the prayers of the living—see Megan McLaughlin, *Consorting with Saints*.

39. *Holy Feast and Holy Fast*, p. 235.

of death; in such a theology, the goal of separated soul is to attain as soon as possible to the *quies* of *visio Dei*. Nonetheless, mystics, visionaries, and ordinary pious folk became increasingly interested in the progress and experience of the period between death and beatific vision. Moreover, if theologians such as Albert, Thomas, Durand, and Benedict XII packed bodiliness into soul in certain careful and technical ways, preachers and visionaries gave separated soul a body with considerably greater abandon. In order to understand the concept of the resurrection body in the early fourteenth century, we must consider what Carol Zaleski has called the somatomorphic soul of visions and otherworld journeys.[40]

In so doing, we come at last—where any study of eschatology must come—to Dante, who was a brilliant theorist not only of the somatomorphic soul but of the resurrection body as well.

Otherworld Journeys and the *Divine Comedy*

Visions of heaven and hell date back to the early days of Christianity, and stories of travel to the afterlife—from which journey the soul returns penitent and armed with warnings for the living—are also very old. The earliest Apocalypses and otherworld journeys display the concern with fertility, consumption, fragmentation, and reassemblage that becomes so powerful a theme in medieval resurrection imagery down through the twelfth century. In the second-century apocalypses of Peter and Paul, to which I referred in my first chapter, heaven is a flowering garden, watered by rivers of milk and honey, although its central stronghold is surrounded by wall after wall of crystal, jewels, and gold. The punishments of hell are dismemberment and digestion: hands and feet are cut off, tongues are ripped out, flesh is devoured by beasts. The greatest horror is the corruption of fertility and nutrition themselves: milk from women's breasts hardens into vipers, which turn on them to con-

---

40. Carol Zaleski, *Otherworld Journeys.* And see Frances Foster, "Visions of the After-Life in Middle English," in *A Manual of the Writings in Middle English: 1050–1500,* by the MLA Middle English Group (based on John Edwin Wells, Manual [1916] and Supplements) vol. 2, ed. J. Burke Severs (Connecticut: Academy of Arts and Sciences, 1970), pp. 452–55; Martha Himmelfarb, *Tours of Hell: An Apocalyptic Form in Jewish and Christian Literature* (Philadelphia: University of Pennsylvania Press, 1983); Le Goff, *Birth of Purgatory,* pp. 96–132, 154–208, and passim; McDannell and Lang, *Heaven;* Eileen Gardiner, ed., *Visions of Heaven and Hell Before Dante* (New York: Italica Press, 1989); Morgan, *Dante and the Other World;* Carozzi, "Structure et fonction de la vision de Tnugdal," pp. 223–34; and Ronald C. Finucane, *Appearances of the Dead: A Cultural History of Ghosts* (London: Junction Books, 1982).

sume them. Resurrection is regurgitation: God will force the beasts that have eaten human flesh to vomit it up again.[41]

In the visions recounted by Gregory the Great and Bede, as well as in the eleventh-, twelfth-, and thirteenth-century otherworld voyages, heaven hardens and the attention of the visionary or traveler turns increasingly toward hell. Although the "Voyage of Brendan" and "Patrick's Purgatory" retain a sense of heaven as a fertile and luxurious place, where trays of delicious food are served and grapes grow to enormous size,[42] the emphasis is increasingly on golden walls and jeweled barricades, on protection and stasis. Images of growth and fertility, of odors and tastes, are relegated to the outskirts of paradise; the visions of Tondal (1149) and Thurchill (1206) place at heaven's center gem-studded and golden chapels, tents, or fortresses. In contrast, the somatomorphic soul in hell or purgatory (it is often unclear and unimportant which is in question) becomes the victim of generation and corruption. It is punished not only by dismemberment but also by perverted nutrition and fertility—horrid consumptions, digestions, impregnations, excretions, vomitings, and birthings.[43] Guibert of Nogent recounts his mother's vision of the dead "with the appearance of ghosts," their hair "seemingly eaten by worms."[44] Thurchill sees several types of sinners—soldiers, priests, proud men—whose limbs are cut off and fried before they are reassembled for further torture—as well as thieves and cheats who are forced to eat and vomit up burning money.[45] Mechtild of Magdeburg sees Satan as one who "makes himself of great size" and "swallows" devils, Jews, and heathen into his "paunch" "body and soul," "eating" Sodomites and "gnawing" the greedy.[46] She writes:

41. See above chapter 1, n. 7, and Gardiner, *Visions*, pp. 1–45.

42. The emphasis is perhaps Irish, but see chapter 1, nn. 23–26 above, for such ideas in early Christian texts.

43. See Gardiner, *Visions*, pp. 51–196, 219–35; Le Goff, *Birth of Purgatory*, pp. 177–208.

44. Le Goff, *Birth of Purgatory*, pp. 181–86; Guibert, *Self and Society in Medieval France*, p. 93.

45. Gardiner, *Visions*, pp. 219–35. The mid-twelfth-century Vision of Alberic sees hell as guarded by an enormous dragon whose fiery throat devours "countless souls" (Le Goff, *Birth of Purgatory*, p. 187). E. T. Becker, *The Medieval Visions of Heaven and Hell* (no publication place, 1899), p. 11, notes the prominence of eating and mangling imagery in Christian versions of the otherworld-journey story. For the connection of hell with digestion and some perceptive remarks on how this relates to eucharistic theology, see Camporesi, *The Fear of Hell*, chapters 12 and 13; see also chapter 4, nn. 119–121 above.

46. Mechtild of Magdeburg, *Das fliessende Licht der Gottheit*, bk. 3, chaps. 15 and 21, in *Mechtild of Magdeburg: "Das fliessende Licht der Gottheit" Nach der Einsiedler Handschrift in kritischem Vergleich mit der gesamten Überlieferung*, ed. Hans Neumann (Munich: Artemis, 1990), vol. 1, pp. 94–97 and 100–4; see also *Das flies-

What each one takes with him from earth
he must there [in hell] eat and drink!

. . . .

high up on hell is a mouth ever open,
those who enter in experience everlasting death.[47]

In the "Visions of Tondal"—by far the most popular otherworld story
before Dante and indeed a text that rivaled Dante's own in the north of
Europe throughout the fourteenth century—the carefully organized tortures of hell or purgation seem to reflect the dreaded putrefaction of the
grave, whose contents are devoured by the very worms to which they
spontaneously (so people thought) give birth.[48] Tondal—himself called
"food" for the fire because of his sins—sees the greedy eaten by a huge
beast, murderers and persistent sinners "cooked and recooked" in skil-
lets or cauldrons until they are liquid, gluttons and fornicators forced
into a mountain "like an oven where bread is baked," their genitals
chewed by worms that gush from within.[49] Other fornicators (both male
and female) are digested in the stomach of a monster, then vomited or
defecated forth pregnant with vipers.[50] These vipers, devouring the en-

---

sende Licht, trans. Margot Schmidt (Einsiedeln/Zurich: Benziger, 1955), pp. 153–62;
and *The Revelations of Mechtild of Magdeburg (1210–1297) or the Flowing Light of
the Godhead*, trans. Lucy Menzies (London: Longmans, 1953), pp. 81–88. It is unclear
why Mechtild refers here to "body and soul." By the later thirteenth century, several
mystics see visions of the whole psychosomatic unit (i.e., the person) in hell and
heaven; on the significance of this, see below pp. 334–41. In a vision of purgatory,
Mechtild sees souls "stewing and roasting" together; *Das fliessende Licht*, ed. Neumann, bk. 3, chap. 15, pp. 95–96. For a different translation of pt. 3, chap. 21, see John
Howard, "The Flowing Light . . .," in *Medieval Women Writers*, ed. Katharina M.
Wilson, pp. 173–77.

47. Mechtild, *Das fliessende Licht*, ed. Neumann, p. 104; *Revelations*, trans. Menzies, p. 88.

48. On the way in which images for the afterlife parallel and reflect the process of
putrefaction, see Thomas, *Le Cadavre*, and Hertz, "Collective Representation of
Death." The association of tomb with womb and belly is, of course, standard in medieval devotional literature; see for example the text from Peter of Celle quoted above
in chapter 3, n. 102. For other evidence of extravagant concern with decay in the
twelfth and early-thirteenth centuries, see below pp. 331–32.

On the popularity and diffusion of the "Visions of Tondal," see Becker, *Medieval
Visions*, p. 82; Roger S. Wieck, "*The Visions of Tondal* and the Visionary Tradition
in the Middle Ages," in Wieck and Kren, eds., *The Visions of Tondal from the Library
of Margaret of York* (Malibu, California: J. Paul Getty Museum, 1990), pp. 3–4; and
Carozzi, "Structure et fonction de la vision de Tnugdal."

49. *Visio Tnugdali: Lateinisch und Altdeutsch*, ed. Albrecht Wagner (Erlangen:
Deichert, 1882), p. 10, lines 6–7, and pp. 16–23, especially p. 23, line 9.

50. *Visio Tnugdali*, ed. Wagner, p. 27, line 20–p. 28, line 2: "[animas] . . . rediger-
entur ad nihilum, pariebat [bestia] eas. . . ." Gardiner, *Visions*, p. 169, interprets this
as "vomited." Madeleine McDermott and Roger Wieck, on the basis of the Old French

trails within, then pecking their way out all over the body with razor-sharp beaks, are hooked into the flesh from which they are "born" and double back upon it, consuming it "down to the nerves and bone."[51] In the deepest part of hell, Satan squeezes souls with dozens of hands, then inhales, devours, and exhales them forever, so that for all their suffering they can never achieve the release that would come from annihilation.[52]

In some of these visions, a living person descends through an opening in the earth; in others—and this form became more common—a soul voyages while its body appears asleep or gravely ill to those left behind.[53] When the hero of the voyage or recipient of the vision is a separated soul, some authors call attention to their decision to embody it.[54] Particularly in early visions, soul is sometimes depicted as a bird, a bubble or spark; both Tondal and the monk of Evesham, who usually see souls fully corporealized, occasionally describe them as sparks; Caesarius of Heisterbach reports three cases in which soul is seen as a sphere with eyes before and behind.[55] But by the thirteenth century souls almost invariably appear with highly individualized bodies in highly individualized raiment. Caesarius, for example, portrays a ghostly visitor from the afterlife with the prayers he had offered written on his boots.[56]

---

version, interpret it as "defecated"; see *Visions of Tondal*, Wieck and Kren, eds., p. 49.

51. *Visio Tnugdali*, ed. Wagner, pp. 28–29. The genitals also become vipers and double back to consume the body.

52. *Visio Tnugdali*, ed. Wagner, pp. 35–39.

53. See Zaleski, *Otherworld Journeys*, pp. 45 and 51, and Le Goff, *Birth of Purgatory*, pp. 177–208. In the stories of "St. Patrick's Purgatory" and the "Voyage of Brendan," for example, the whole person journeys or descends: in the "Visions of Tondal," the soul travels while the body sleeps.

54. Dinzelbacher, in an important recent study, has pointed to a basic change in the nature and structure of vision literature about 1200. In the early Middle Ages, visions are more apt to involve travel outside the body and personal transformation; after the mid-thirteenth century, the visionaries (now usually women) seem more passive and their visions are more frequent and less transformative. See Peter Dinzelbacher, *Vision und Visionsliteratur im Mittelalter* (Stuttgart: Hiersemann, 1981); Zaleski, *Otherworld Journeys*, p. 6; and Bynum, *Holy Feast and Holy Fast*, p. 418 n. 51.

55. Zaleski, *Otherworld Journeys*, pp. 45–55; Morgan, *Dante and the Other World*, pp. 54, 68, 73.

56. See above chapter 5, n. 81. Caesarius's story of the man with *Ave Maria* on his boots is paralleled by a story in the *Golden Legend* of an unlettered Cistercian who could learn only the *Ave Maria*; after his death his fellow monks cleared his grave to find growing from his mouth a lily on whose petals the two words of the prayer were inscribed in gold. See James of Voragine, *Legenda aurea vulgo historia lombardica dicta*, 3d ed., ed. Th. Graesse (Breslau: Koebner, 1890), p. 221, and James, *The Golden Legend*, trans. and adapted by Granger Ryan and Helmut Ripperger (New York-London: Longmans, Green, 1941; reprint, 1969), p. 207.

More is at stake in such cases than merely the visionary's (and the author's) need to express his insight in visible form. Caesarius suggests that we have to experience souls as bodies when we are in the body; once we are free of flesh, we will see them as spheres. Others suggest that souls need bodies not only to return to earth and warn the living (a theme as old as the biblical story of Dives and Lazarus) but also in order to experience torture or reward and to be fully particularized as selves. The seventh-century vision of Barontus says the separated soul is like a tiny bird; it has the five senses but cannot speak or travel until it gets a body of air.[57] Guibert of Nogent recounts his mother's vision of a spirit (her dead husband) who will not give his name; the suggestion is that without a body he lacks in some way his identity.[58] Dante plays with the close association of body with identity, or at least identifiability, in canto 33 of the *Inferno*. There Dante the pilgrim initially fails to recognize Friar Alberigo, whose body is still in the world but whose soul freezes in hell for the sin of treacherous hospitality. Although the passage certainly suggests that, without somatomorphic soul at the least, person is unrecognizable, the poet also indicates through the incident that those in the world who trust in appearances may be misled; there are in fact persons so evil that their souls have already gone before them into hell, leaving behind bodies occupied by demons.[59]

Those who return from near death are sometimes said to manifest in their resumed earthly bodies the marks of what has happened to them on their voyage beyond this life. Bede tells of a soul that returns to a body scarred on shoulder and jaw; for "what soul suffered in secret, flesh showed openly."[60] James of Voragine, drawing on an earlier miracle collection, tells of an evil judge who was tortured before the judgment seat of God by Saint Lawrence "in great wrath"; allowed to return from death for thirty days to make restitution, he found that "his arm was black and burnt, as though he had suffered this punishment in the flesh; and

57. Zaleski, *Otherworld Journeys*, 45–55. As Le Goff points out (*Birth of Purgatory*, pp. 98–99), the idea that the soul has a *similitudo corporis* that enables it to feel the fire of hell goes back to Augustine and Julian of Toledo.

58. Le Goff, *Birth of Purgatory*, pp. 182 and 185.

59. It should be pointed out that Dante also fails to recognize a number of figures who are consigned to hell after their deaths, and that Fra Alberigo, although alive, is fully in hell, his body on earth "taken from [him] by a devil who thereafter rules it." Dante, *The Divine Comedy*, trans. Charles S. Singleton, *Inferno*, I: *Text*, Bollingen Series 80 (Princeton: Princeton University Press, second printing with corrections, 1977), canto 33, lines 130–32, p. 357.

60. Zaleski, *Otherworld Journeys*, p. 78; Gardiner, *Visions*, p. 55; Le Goff, *Birth of Purgatory*, p. 113.

this mark remained upon him as long as he lived."[61] The monk of Evesham speaks of a leg that was healed in the other world; in this case (as in the healing of the tumor on St. Etheldreda's body after death) the disappearance of a mark in the earthly body provides proof of what has happened beyond.[62]

Although authors sometimes called attention to somatomorphic souls as metaphors or images, they were far more apt to use "as if" when representing souls as spheres or sparks.[63] The soul's body was increasingly treated as the conventional and obvious way of presenting its experience and individuality, its exact moral state and social status.[64] Indeed the soul's body was sometimes seen as more real (in a moral and ontological sense) than the body of earth. In the early thirteenth-century vision of Thurchill, for example, souls appeared to the voyager black, white, or spotted, depending on their degree of guilt; their color in the afterlife thus reflected their true nature far more accurately than their color on earth.[65] James of Voragine, retelling in the later thirteenth century the stories of the martyrs, reported that holy Agatha said to the persecutor Quintianus, who threatened to cut off her breasts: "Impious and cruel tyrant, who would dare to amputate in a woman that which sustained you in your own mother! But I have within my soul whole breasts [mamillas integras] from which I nourish all my senses, which I have from infancy consecrated to God."[66] Mechtild of Magdeburg told of a deceased lay brother who appeared in a vision with a blemish on his face because of his "sternness." She removed the mark with a simple sigh.[67]

61. Legenda aurea, ed. Graesse, pp. 494–95, and Golden Legend, trans. Ryan and Ripperger, p. 444, drawing on the Miracles of the Virgin. Saints' lives often emphasize the survival of scars after healing in this life; the scars provide proof that the ordinary person has been touched by the power of a saint. For example, in the Golden Legend account of St. Francis, a little "T" remains where the saint cured a diseased leg, because "with this letter Francis had been wont to sign his name"; Legenda aurea, ed. Graesse, p. 673; Golden Legend, trans. Ryan and Ripperger, p. 609. The scar is thus explicitly, in this case, the saint's signature; to cure is to write on the body of the diseased.

62. Zaleski, Otherworld Journeys, pp. 78 and 83, and see above chapter 5, n. 21. We should note that incorrupt holy bodies obey the same principle—that is, they manifest corporeally on earth the state of their souls in paradise.

63. Zaleski, Otherworld Journeys, p. 51.

64. Peter Dinzelbacher, "Klassen und Hierarchien im Jenseits," Miscellanea Medievalia 12 (1979), pp. 20–40; idem, "Reflexionen irdischer Sozialstrukturen in mittelalterlichen Jenseitsschilderungen," Archiv für Kulturgeschichte 61 (1979), pp. 16–34; and Morgan, Dante and the Other World, p. 54.

65. Le Goff, Birth of Purgatory, pp. 296–97; Morgan, Dante and the Other World, pp. 230–31.

66. Legenda aurea, ed. Graesse, p. 171 (my translation).

67. Mechtild, Revelations, trans. Menzies, p. 248.

Almost all early visions particularize souls by gender and religious status. There are very few that do not mention prelates or clerics as a separate group. But expressing rank and affiliation was a much more important concern of thirteenth- and fourteenth-century visions.[68] Paralleling the emerging theological discussion of the *in*equality of dowries and crowns, an English vernacular sermon, "Soul's Ward," from about 1200 carefully sketched the variety of moral and ecclesiastical statuses in paradise.[69] In the later thirteenth century Mechtild of Magdeburg not only saw holy women occupying the highest rung of heaven, above martyrs and apostles; she also pointed out that hell was (except for princesses) entirely peopled by powerful males, secular as well as ecclesiastical.[70] By the mid-fourteenth century, we find a Franciscan vision listing the numbers of various religious orders who make it to heaven: 20,000 hermits and monks of St. Anthony, 100,000 Benedictines, 50,000 Dominicans, and "many thousand" Poor Clares and Franciscan tertiaries as well as 100,000 Franciscan friars.[71] As Peter Dinzelbacher has pointed out, otherworldly reflections of the *ordines* of secular society go back as far as the ninth-century vision of Wetti but are unimportant until the later Middle Ages. By the fifteenth century, Francesca Romana—in an unusually detailed vision—saw the occupants of hell divided not only according to types of crimes but also according to worldly occupation.[72] The somatomorphism of medieval visions was thus some-

---

68. See above, n. 64. According to Zaleski (*Otherworld Journeys*, p. 51), the Narrative of Zosimus (third century, although the surviving versions are more recent) tells of Zosimus's visit to the Earthly Paradise where he sees souls as shapes of light, "perfect in all the body apart from the distinction of male and female."

69. McDannell and Lang, *Heaven*, p. 107. In general, of course, the issue of whether we will all be equal in heaven was for medieval thinkers a question about whether moral difference will be leveled; see Anne H. Schotter, "The Paradox of Equality and Hierarchy in *Pearl*," *Renascence* 33 (1981): 172–79, and n. 72 below.

70. Bynum, *Jesus as Mother*, p. 242. Mechtild stresses that the "merit" of each will be "ordered" in heaven "according to their works" (Mechtild, *Revelations*, trans. Menzies, p. 206; *Das fliessende Licht*, trans. Schmidt, p. 323). She includes worldly rank in her description of heaven but not, interestingly enough, strictly hierarchically. Under the first arch will be the patriarchs, Stephen and the martyrs, and married folk with their children; under the second, popes and spiritual fathers; under the third, Christ's humanity, Mary, knights and "the whole empire down to the poorest peasants," and many martyrs (*Revelations*, trans. Menzies, p. 207; *Das fliessende Licht*, trans. Schmidt, p. 325). This suggests that we will be recognizable in heaven by worldly status but not ranked according to it. Even on moral difference in heaven, Mechtild is quite subtle; she asserts that reward (according to works), merit (according to virtues), and crown (according to love) are not the same (*Revelations*, trans. Menzies, p. 153).

71. Dinzelbacher, "Reflexionen irdischer Sozialstrukturen," p. 25.

72. Ibid., pp. 16–34. Dinzelbacher points out that family ties are mostly left behind in visions, that concern for moral differentiation always outweighs concern for un-

thing more than a literary device: if souls appeared with breasts and scars, crowns and cowls, it was because they were assumed to be male or female, Franciscan or Dominican, aristocratic or rustic in heaven.

Such intense particularity characterizes the somatomorphic souls of Dante's *Divine Comedy*. Our ranks and merits differ in heaven, just as does the color of our hair (*Paradiso*, canto 32, lines 70–72). Yet so glorious and necessary is body to Dante, in all its fullness and complexity, that the aerial body is not enough. We "yearn" for the "luster" and "ripeness" of a resurrection that completes rather than overcomes fertility— and we desire it not only in order to know but also in order to love. In cantos 22 and 30 of the *Paradiso* (where, significantly, angels are "sparks" and souls are "flowers") Dante sees (before the trumpet sounds!) the resurrection body.[73]

The *Divine Comedy* was completed shortly before Dante's death in 1321, a decade before the opening of controversy over the beatific vision. It uses with consummate sophistication and subtlety many of the technical concerns of scholastic theology as well as the themes of the otherworld-journey narrative, and the two enrich each other.[74] Awareness of the implications of unicity of form and an intense self-consciousness about somatomorphic representation enable Dante to solve the identity problem and quell the ambivalence at the heart of the Augustinian notion of yearning for body.[75] He is thus able to weave, from the traditional and powerful contrast of digestion-mutilation with reassemblage-wholeness, an afterlife in which fear of fertility no longer permeates the

---

derlining secular status, and that along with the late medieval tendency to detail status differences comes a more accessible and friendly heaven and a God open to appeal from even the humblest peasant.

73. Dante, *The Divine Comedy*, trans. Singleton, *Paradiso*, I: *Text*, pp. 245–55 and 335–45. Dante also sees the blessed as spheres and as light. It is worth noting that Dante, having washed his eyes in a river of sparks, sees details more clearly after canto 30; thus perception of individual features is treated as progress in "seeing."

74. On Dante's relationship to earlier literature, see Morgan, *Dante and the Other World*, pp. 5–10.

75. A recent study of Dante's idea of the resurrection body that differs in approach from my own is Kevin Marti, "Dante's 'Baptism' and the Theology of the Body in *Purgatorio* 1–2," *Traditio* 45 (1989–90): 167–90. Marti lays great emphasis, as I do, on Pauline images of clothing and plants as important for discussion of resurrection. An older study is Etienne Gilson, "Dante's Notion of a Shade: *Purgatorio* XXV," *Mediaeval Studies* 29 (1967): 124–42. On desire in Dante, see Rachel Jacoff, "Transgression and Transcendence: Figures of Female Desire in Dante's *Commedia*," *Romanic Review* 29 (1988): 129–42; reprinted in *The New Medievalism*, ed. M. Brownlee, K. Brownlee, and S. Nichols (Baltimore: Johns Hopkins University Press, 1991), pp. 183–200.

imagery. The physicality and particularity we associate with body be-comes an expression of self. Love is desire, not stasis.[76]

Like the author of the "Visions of Tondal," Dante uses mutilation-mastication of body as a basic image for evil and its punishment. Frag-mentation becomes worse as one descends through the circles of hell. At the very bottom, the three most vicious sinners of history provide Satan's eternal dinner, Judas differentiated from Brutus and Cassius only in that he is "champed," "bitten," and "clawed" in Satan's maw head-first.[77] Cantos 32–33 of the *Inferno* associate evil and cannibalism in complex ways. Two conspirators who betrayed each other are depicted frozen together "in one hole so close that the head of the one was a hood for the other; and as bread is devoured for hunger, so the upper one set his teeth upon the other where the brain joins with the nape" (*Inferno,* canto 32, lines 125–29). In life one has starved the other to death with his sons; now they are fused together as gnawer and gnawed for all eter-nity.[78] The pathos of the dying children's cry to their father that he should eat the miserable flesh he has put upon their bones (through procreation) is not mere pathos; these figures are deep in evil, and the cannibalism the sons suggest is heinous sin, a twisting of fertility and generation, an expression of despair.

In certain ways, then, Dante continues the powerful and literal use of somatomorphic soul characteristic of the otherworld journey tradi-tion. As Rachel Jacoff has pointed out, body in the *Inferno* is often not problematized at all. It receives and expresses evil. Scars and deficiencies manifest sin; rippings and mutilations are simply painful; sinners are dark and ugly, dwelling in a darkness that contrasts to the light and lightness of heaven.[79] Yet these bodies are aerial bodies; Dante and Virgil

76. A number of fine recent studies relate the issue of body (and the physical nature of language) to Dante's understanding of his task as poet; see, for example, Guiseppe Mazzotta, *Dante, Poet of the Desert: History and Allegory in the Divine Comedy* (Princeton: Princeton University Press, 1979), John Freccero, "Manfred's Wounds and the Poetics of *Purgatorio,*" in *Dante's Poetics of Conversion,* pp. 195–208; and Joan Ferrante, "Word and Images in the *Paradiso:* Reflections of the Divine," in *Dante, Petrarch, Boccaccio: Studies in the Italian Trecento in Honor of Charles S. Singleton,* ed. Bernardo and Pellegrini (Binghamton: SUNY Press, 1983), pp. 115–32.

77. Dante, *The Divine Comedy,* trans. Singleton, *Inferno,* I: *Text,* canto 34, lines 54–60, p. 365. And see R. Durling, "Deceit and Digestion in the Belly of Hell," in *Allegory and Representation,* ed. Stephen J. Greenblatt (Baltimore: Johns Hopkins University Press, 1980), pp. 61–93.

78. *Inferno,* trans. Singleton, pp. 339–55, esp. p. 347.

79. For example, in *Inferno,* trans. Singleton, canto 32, lines 97–106, p. 345, Dante yanks out a tuft of hair from a "shade." I am drawing here on a grant proposal by Rachel Jacoff for a book to be entitled: " 'Treating Shades as Solid Things': The Dis-course of the Body in Dante's *Divine Comedy.*"

"set their feet" upon an "emptiness" that only "seems" real body (*Inferno*, canto 6, lines 34–36).[80] Even in the *Inferno*, Dante provides an elaborate comment on embodiment, making it clear that aerial body is temporary, that aerial body is *not* "real" body (that is, the physical body of earth and resurrection), and that "real" body is good.[81]

In cantos 24–25, thieves are punished by losing even the ghostly bodies that are their own: they fuse with the bodies of other humans and reptiles in a hideous parody of embryological development as well as of the phoenix's immolation and return. In cantos 9–10, the basic error of those heretics who deny immortality is to think soul *is* body; for thus repudiating both components of person, such heretics are enclosed in tombs of pain, their souls treated as if they were cadavers. But at the resurrection (says Virgil) the bodies that have been "left above" will be restored, and the whole person denied by these heretics will be shut up in the grave eternally.[82] In canto 13, the souls of suicides are not bodies but trees that must be eaten and ripped in order to speak at all. Sprouting up from the seeds (or "grains") of their souls, these plant-bodies are torn completely to pieces in punishment, then reassembled for further torture. Although all souls will resume their earthly bodies at Judgment Day, "it is not just that a man have what he robs himself of" (line 105).[83] These suicide-souls will not be reclothed with bodies but will receive them again only as skins or coverings—additions not fully integrated into self—to drag through the "mournful wood" and hang forever on the "thornbushes" of their "nocuous shades" (lines 106–108).[84] Dante the traveler may sometimes forget that those he encounters are mere shadows, but Dante the poet never lets the reader forget that these are *not* the bodies of earthly or of eternal life. Neither does he let us conclude that fertility itself is sinister, that process erases integrity or identity. Even the perverted generatings and digestings of hell do not prevent body from (perverted) wholeness and from expressing (perverted) self.

In the *Purgatorio*, it becomes much clearer that the bodies the travelers see are the ghostly bodies of the period between death and resur-

80. *Inferno*, trans. Singleton, p. 61.
81. Singleton in *Inferno*, II: *Commentary*, p. 100, says that the further down in hell souls are, the more "substantial" and "corporeal" they are; this is true. But Dante's position on embodiment is considerably more complicated than this observation implies. As I note below, he considers it worse to have a nonhuman than a human body. In the *Purgatorio* he delineates yearning for body, and the regaining of body is triumph in the heaven of the *Paradiso*.
82. *Inferno*, trans. Singleton, p. 99.
83. Ibid., p. 135.
84. Ibid.

rection. The opening and closing cantos call attention to the difference between Dante the traveler, who retains his earthly body and therefore casts a shadow (cantos 1–3 and 26), and the souls in purgatory, who are mere "shades" "treated as solid things" (canto 21, line 136). Indeed Dante the poet now draws the contrast—familiar in Christian theology at least since Augustine's *De cura pro mortuis gerenda*—between what happens to the body after death and the fate of the soul. He gives to Dante the voyager our natural human concern about the cadaver but makes such concern problematic. Manfred (canto 3) and Buonconte da Monte Feltro (canto 5) recount to the curious traveler the abuse inflicted on their dead bodies as if such information were a matter of importance. But in canto 31, Beatrice berates her lover for abandoning her once she has died, grieving for the body that went to earth and forgetting her soaring spirit.

The somatomorphic soul of purgatory thus both is and is not an advance on the psychosomatic self of earth. In canto 10, Dante sees the proud coming toward him "not . . . persons, but what it is I do not know" (lines 112–13). Virgil warns him that we are worms or larvae "born to form the angelic butterfly" that flies naked to judgment.[85] The point is clearly that the body of earth rots, releasing the butterfly of the soul; these dim figures crushed under stone do not look like men and women; in whatever aerial body they suffer, it is temporary and passible, not the body either of this life or of heaven. Toward the end of the *Purgatorio*, Virgil reassures the traveler Dante about purgation by saying he can traverse the "belly" of flame (*l'alvo di questa fiamma*) because God promises "it could not make you bald of one hair" (canto 27, lines 25–27). The traditional resurrection text (Luke 21.18) reminds us that the pilgrim is still in an earthly body, vulnerable to pain and destruction.[86] To cross the fire, he must be assimilated not to the ghostly body but to the risen one. The text thus subtly underlines how much more the two "real" bodies have to do with each other than either has to do with the aerial body of the period of transition.

Nonetheless, however imaginary (in every sense) the aerial body may be, it is an expression of the separated soul—the same soul that is grub on earth and butterfly in heaven. By the time the fleshly traveler from this world finally asks about the aerial body and receives in answer a disquisition from Statius (*Purgatorio*, canto 25), it is clear—poetically as well as philosophically—that images of fertility and change do not

85. Dante, *The Divine Comedy*, trans. Singleton, *Purgatorio*, I: *Text*, p. 197.
86. Ibid., p. 293; and see Singleton, *Purgatorio*, II: *Commentary*, p. 652.

302 THE DECADES AROUND 1300

threaten identity.[87] Why are these shades thin and hungry when they are not even bodies (asks Dante)? Virgil begins to answer with reference to reflections of self other than body (for example, the image in a mirror), but Statius immediately gives a summary of theological embryology of the sort we might find in Albert or Giles of Rome. Just as a unitary soul develops in the fetus giving it shape, so after death this one substantial soul impresses itself on air, like flame from a fire, making a shade-body with an organ for every sense.

Self in the *Divine Comedy* has thus nothing to do with survival of material particles; the bodies of Manfred and Beatrice are still dust (*Purgatorio*, cantos 3 and 31). Yet even aerial flesh reflects in some way the individuality and wholeness of earthly flesh; Dante does in most cases recognize his friends and acquaintances, and even the souls in trees and tombs are forever reassembled for continued torment. Identity and integrity are, in a fully Thomistic sense, packed into and guaranteed by soul.[88] Because of this guarantee, intensely developmental imagery can be used for the generation of a child in the womb, the expression of self in aerial body, and the resumption of body in resurrection. The Garden of Eden is imagined in canto 28 of the *Purgatorio* as possessing all the fertility of spontaneous generation; heaven itself is an enormous rose to whose petals the angels fly like a swarm of fertilizing bees (*Paradiso*, canto 31, line 7).[89]

Yet the body we will finally resume is not the shade-body of purgation but the beloved and whole body of earth, expressing the person in its every detail and sensual experience. In canto after canto, the imagery itself has suggested that it is natural for soul to express itself in body, but that shades are not enough. Despite earlier instances in the poem of shade touching shade, Statius clutches only air when he stoops to embrace Virgil.[90] It is therefore hardly surprising that Dante the poet, who foreshadowed the resurrection even in hell, should give Dante the trav-

---

87. *Purgatorio*, trans. Singleton, pp. 269–277; and see *Commentary*, pp. 591–619.

88. See also *Purgatorio*, trans. Singleton, canto 18, lines 49–54, p. 193.

89. *Paradiso*, trans. Singleton, p. 347; on the bee metaphor, see *Commentary*, pp. 512–13.

The seeds that flower in Dante's paradise are not Pauline or Origenist; they are the seeds of Thomas and Albert the Great. To Dante, the flowers (bodies) of heaven reproduce exactly the flowers of earth, but these plants are now (in that wonderful mixed metaphor of the thirteenth-century *dotes* tradition) endowed with the bridal gifts of agility, subtlety, beauty, and impassibility. On the rose as an erotic symbol in later thirteenth-century literature, especially the *Roman de la Rose* and the mystical *Zohar*, see Jeremy Cohen, *"Be Fertile,"* p. 312, and Peter Dronke, *Medieval Latin and the Rise of European Love-Lyric* (Oxford: Clarendon Press, 1965–66), vol. 1, pp. 75.

90. *Purgatorio*, trans. Singleton, p. 233. And earlier, in *Purgatorio*, canto 2, lines 76–81, pp. 17–19, Dante fails three times to embrace his friend Casella. But cf. *Pur-*

eler a glimpse of the risen and glorified body in paradise even before the end of time. Nor is it surprising that, speaking of resurrection in images of resumed clothing, ripening seeds, glowing coals, fertile wombs, and love, he puts these images in the mouths of Solomon (author of that erotic paean to heavenly marriage, the Song of Songs), Bernard (theorist of the Augustinian yearning for body), and his own Beatrice, beloved in her fleshly femaleness.[91]

In canto 14, Solomon assures us that—with flesh resumed—we will see more; and with more sight, we will gain more fervor, winning by such fervor greater radiance. Like living coals that keep their shape in the midst of flame, we will add "brightness" to the luster we now possess when we resume the flesh "which the earth still covers." Thus not only for ourselves but also for all those we love, we yearn to welcome back the body of earth (*corpi morti*), its resurrected organs stronger for heavenly joys (*ché li organi del corpo saran forti/ a tutto ciò che potrà dilettarne*).

> So sudden and eager both the one and the other chorus seemed to me in saying "Amen," that truly they showed desire for their dead bodies—perhaps not only for themselves, but also for their mothers, for their fathers, and for the others who were dear before they became eternal flames.[92]

In canto 22, Benedict assures Dante that his "high desire" to behold the blessed in their "uncovered shapes" will find final attainment there where all desires "are fulfilled," "perfect, mature, and whole." And in that last sphere alone "is every part there where it always was."[93] Explaining the resurrection in canto 7, Beatrice tells Dante that he will

---

gatorio, canto 6, line 75, p. 59, where Sordello embraces Virgil; and *Inferno*, canto 3, line 19, p. 25, where Virgil puts his hand on Dante's.

91. Two recent studies on the Song of Songs in medieval literature are E. Ann Matter, *The Voice of My Beloved: The Song of Songs in Western Medieval Christianity* (Philadelphia: University of Pennsylvania Press, 1990), and Ann W. Astell, *The Song of Songs in the Middle Ages* (Ithaca: Cornell University Press, 1990). And see Bernard McGinn, "With 'the Kisses of the Mouth': Recent Works on the Song of Songs," *The Journal of Religion* 72 (1992): 269–75. On the significance of Beatrice, see Astell, *Song*, p. 121 n. 4 and p. 141 n. 13, and Dronke, *Medieval Latin and Love-Lyric*, vol. 1, pp. 75, 87–97.

92. *Paradiso*, trans. Singleton, canto 14, lines 45–69, pp. 155–57. The relatively rare notion of heaven as a place where we share joys and the connection of this to restoration of the body is found also in Bonaventure; see above, p. 249. For a perceptive discussion of the question of the social joys of heaven, see McDannell and Lang, *Heaven*, pp. 89–100.

93. *Paradiso*, trans. Singleton, canto 22, lines 53–72, p. 249.

surely decay into the elements, but the pattern of wholeness perdures; by it we will be reformed in resurrection in a manner we can "infer" if we remember how "human flesh" was made "then when the first parents were both formed."[94] The same Beatrice later reminds the traveler that the saints are a "fair garden which blossoms beneath the rays of Christ," the Virgin a "womb which [is] the hostelry of our desire."[95]

In the final cantos of the poem, body, fertility, and desire come together. Bernard guides the gaze of Dante deep into the ranks of the heavenly rose beyond "sorrow, or thirst, or hunger"—beyond, that is, any contingency—to the place where the Virgin sits, she who is already bodily assumed into heaven.[96] There Dante finds, not the *requies aeterna*—the stasis—of the scholastic theologians, but the great wheeling motion of love. Unlike Tondal and Thurchill, whose heaven was barricaded with jewels and immobilized in crystal, Dante sees heaven as a flower. And that flower itself, like the souls who people it, spins and whirls with desire.

> Thus my mind, all rapt, was gazing, . . . ever enkindled by its gazing. . . .
> . . . [M]y own wings were not sufficient . . . , save that my mind was smitten by a flash wherein its wish came to it. Here power failed . . . but already my desire and my will were revolved, like a wheel that is evenly moved, by the Love which moves the sun and the other stars.
>
> (*Paradiso*, canto 33, lines 97–99 and 139–45)[97]

There was thus, in the early fourteenth century, more than one solution to the deep ambivalence with which a religious thinker such as Bonaventure expressed desire. Longing could be enhanced as well as

---

94. Ibid., canto 7, lines 121–48, pp. 79–81. Although not spelling out an embryological image for resurrection, the lines suggest it, particularly in light of the Statius canto (canto 25) in the *Purgatorio*.

95. *Paradiso*, trans. Singleton, canto 23, lines 71–75 and 103–5, pp. 261–63. On the problematic nature of female desire in Dante, see Jacoff, "Transgression and Transcendence."

96. Ibid., canto 32, lines 52–54, p. 363.

97. *Paradiso*, trans. Singleton, cantos 32 and 33, pp. 359–81. Dante also speaks, as did scholastic theologians, of terminating, or stilling, desire by fulfilling it, but his notion of quieting and filling clearly includes enkindling anew. See, for example, *Paradiso*, canto 31, lines 65–66, where Bernard is sent to Dante by Beatrice "*A terminar lo tuo disiro*"; canto 32, lines 61–63, where Bernard warns that no will dares desire more love or delight than there is with Christ; and canto 33, lines 46–48, where Dante, drawing near "*al fine di tutt' i disii*," finds the ardor of his longing heightened to the utmost. See below, pp. 334–41, on this idea in the mystics.

stilled. Just at the moment when theorists such as Durand, Robert of Anjou, and Benedict XII were preparing to solve the ambiguity of love by bestowing *visio Dei* on the soul before the spheres cease to turn, the author of the *Divine Comedy* prolonged yearning until the resurrection—perhaps even into eternity—and projected the motion of desire onto heaven itself.

I shall return below to the significance of Dante's conception of desire. But first I must consider a little further the theme of fragmentation and wholeness that was crucial not only to the *Divine Comedy* but also, as we saw in chapter 4 above, to the iconography and hagiography of the high Middle Ages.

The Hagiography and Iconography of Wholeness

In the imagery of the *Divine Comedy*, as in the "Visions of Tondal," the contrast between heaven and hell is still a contrast of disorder and order, fragmentation and wholeness, darkness and light. In hell, the damned are reassembled only for perpetual partition, mutilation, and mastication; in heaven, the blessed rise beautiful and whole, individualized one from the other by appearance, experience, merit, and spiritual capacity but every one jeweled and shining amidst the splendor of flowers and thrones. Dante is more comfortable than were twelfth-century artists, poets, and hagiographers with describing resurrection in images of fertility and germination exactly because he is certain that identity is guaranteed by substantial soul. His imagery no longer assimilates change to putrefaction; process per se is no longer, as it had been for the Tondal author and for twelfth-century scholastics, a challenge to identity and survival.[98] The description of souls as sparks or flowers in the *Paradiso* is not, however, a suggestion that self escapes from body in heaven or that heavenly body will grow beyond the particularity of earth. The reclothing of bones with sinews and flesh when the trumpet sounds will not obscure a single mark or characteristic of the earthly body. Even aerial body provides access to bliss or torture, but body in heaven and hell will finally be not aerial but real—identical (in a numerical sense) to the body of this life.

The shades Dante the pilgrim meets on his journey are mere adumbrations of the resurrection body, more "fictive" in the *Purgatorio* than in the *Inferno*.[99] Dante the poet comments self-consciously on the pro-

98. See above, pp. 121–37, and Bynum, "Faith Imagining the Self."
99. See above, n. 81.

cess of poetic creation by calling attention to the failure of Dante the pilgrim to understand that his whole journey occurs in the between-time of nonembodiment. The obtuseness of the traveler to the fact that the visible but nonmaterial world in which he moves is imagined by his eponymous poet-creator underlines, of course, the imagining; the reader comes to see that poetry making itself is a process of giving body.[100] At the end of canto 21 of the *Purgatorio*, it is a poet, Statius, who forgets that he and Virgil are shades; it is also a poet, Virgil, who understands.

Dante's genius aside, such self-consciousness is made possible both by the poetic tradition of the somatomorphic soul and by the nature of literary creation, which visualizes in words.[101] For painters and sculptors, however, the aerial body and indeed the whole period of purgation (which was, by definition, limited to the in-between and therefore nonembodied) offered more problems than opportunities. Thus, as recent art historians have pointed out, the first paintings influenced by the *Divine Comedy* drop purgatory entirely and add a Last Judgment (see plates 24, 25, and 26).[102] They situate in the resurrection period of embodiment the hell and heaven discovered by Dante the pilgrim in their aerial manifestations. Not so much illustrations of the *Comedy* as in-

100. See above, n. 76.

101. See Rudolf Arnheim, "Notes on the Imagery of Dante's *Purgatorio*," *Argo: Festschrift für Kurt Badt zu seinem 80. Geburtstag . . .*, ed. Martin Gosebruch and Lorenz Dittmann (Cologne: DuMont Schauberg, 1970), pp. 57–61; and Zaleski, *Otherworld Journeys*, pp. 45–55.

102. See Hans Belting and Dieter Blume, eds., *Malerei und Stadtkultur in der Dantezeit: Die Argumentation der Bilder* (Munich: Hirmer, 1989), passim and especially plates 10, 11, 13, 93, 97, 110, 111, 124; Hans Belting, "The New Role of Narrative in Public Painting of the Trecento: Historia and Allegory," *Studies in the History of Art* 16 (1986): 151–68; Morgan, *Dante and the Other World*, pp. 199–200; and Hughes, *Heaven and Hell*, p. 159. None of the northern Italian representations of heaven and hell I have been able to find from the fourteenth century includes a depiction of purgatory (whether or not the painting is supposedly influenced by Dante). All include the Last Judgment. This association with the Last Judgment makes it clear that the bodies painted are resurrection bodies (i.e. "real," or paintable, bodies) not the aerial bodies Dante describes. See Giotto's Arena chapel at Padua, painted by 1305 (plate 5, and chapter 4, n. 100 above); Buffalmacco(?)'s Campo Santo at Pisa, which recent opinion dates to about 1330 (plate 24); the Strozzi chapel of Santa Maria Novella, Florence, by Nardo di Cione(?) from about 1357, which Boccaccio says is influenced by Dante's *Comedy* (plates 25 and 26); the "Road to Heaven" by Andrea da Firenze in the Spanish chapel of Santa Maria Novella, from 1366–68; the frescoes in Santa Croce, Florence, of uncertain attribution, which Vasari says are copies of ones at Pisa; and Taddeo di Bartolo's "Hell" at San Gimignano, from about 1396. The "Bridge of Trial" in the fourteenth-century fresco in S. Maria in Piano, although it represents purgation, is not, it seems, a full-scale depiction of Purgatory; see Morgan, *Dante and the Other World*, p. 36, plate 11. Le Goff (*Birth of Purgatory*, pp. 367–68) describes what he claims are three fourteenth-century depictions of purgatory: two are French miniatures, one a Spanish fresco.

terpretations that telescope it back into earlier otherworld-journey traditions, they emphasize two elements in Dante that continue earlier resurrection iconography: the contrast of darkness and disorder with order-light-wholeness and the specificity of the bodies of the resurrected (especially of the blessed) in terms of gender, status, and personal beauty.

These elements of Dante's vision and of the early frescoes that illustrate it are striking but not unique. They are present in the great west wall at Torcello, the *Hortus deliciarum* miniature, and the Vatican panel painting I discussed in chapter 4—each of which stresses the wholeness and particularity of the blessed. What is in noticeable contrast, however, to the Byzantine iconographic tradition of Torcello and the *Hortus* manuscript is the absence of the theme of regurgitation and reassemblage.

By the early thirteenth century, the Byzantine theme of resurrection as the vomiting up of parts in a context of cosmological renovation had faded from Western art to be replaced by the tradition, created in the post-Carolingian West and spreading rapidly in the twelfth century, of resurrection as return from the grave under the watchful eye of Christ the judge.[103] The great tympana of twelfth- and thirteenth-century cathedrals—St. Faith at Conques, St. Stephen at Bourges, St. Peter at Poitiers, St. Andrew at Bordeaux—subordinate resurrection to judgment by focusing attention not on disentombment but on the division into saved or damned. They invariably depict the resuscitated dead (usually in a smaller register below a monumental Christ-Judge) emerging whole (sometimes naked, sometimes clothed) from tombs (see plate 27).[104] Only a few (albeit important) vestiges of the twelfth-century fear of mastication and digestion survive into high medieval resurrection iconography: the continued prominence (especially in manuscript illuminations) of the image of Jonah vomited up from the whale, the standard treatment of hell as a mouth that swallows the damned, and the prominence of tortures of cooking and chewing in hell (see plates 28 to 32).[105]

103. See above, chapter 4, nn. 104–106, and plates 5, 10, and 15.
104. See Willibald Sauerländer, *Gothic Sculpture in France 1140–1270*, with photographs by M. Hirmer, trans. J. Sondheimer (London: Thames and Hudson, 1972), pp. 506–8; see also ibid., pp. 504–5 and 510–11, for Bourges and Bordeaux. For Conques, see above, plate 15. See also Richard Cavendish, *Visions of Heaven and Hell* (London: Orbis, 1977); and David Bevington, et al., *Homo, Memento Finis: The Iconography of Just Judgment in Medieval Art and Drama* (Kalamazoo, Mich.: Medieval Institute Publications, 1985), plates 2–17.
105. See above, chapter 4, nn. 119–24; Hughes, *Heaven and Hell*, pp. 175–89, 196–99, and 207; Morgan, *Dante and the Other World*, p. 23; and Getty MS 30, fols. 13v and 17, in Wieck and Kren, eds., *The Visions of Tondal*, pp. 41 and 45. Note also the

With occasional exceptions, resurrection in Western art is no longer the regurgitation, or the reconstitution, or the reclothing of bones.[106] Yet the dead who rise whole from either coffin or earth are increasingly particularized by haircolor, sex, age, and (when clothed) by raiment that expresses details of worldly rank and power. Indeed, on the tympanum at Bourges where the dead rise naked, headgear—crowns, helmets, and miters—is added to indicate a variety of social statuses (see plate 33).[107]

The development of iconography thus parallels that of literature. In the thirteenth century, images of resurrection as reassemblage drop out of art, scholastic discourse, and poetry. Fragmentation continues as an image of evil and pain, and wholeness as an image of paradise. But wholeness is no longer so much a victory over partition, a patching together of dispersed bits, as a reflection of what human nature is. The *Divine Comedy* continues the association of mastication-partition with hell found in the "Visions of Tondal," but such images seem no longer to be a comment on the dangers of fertility.[108] Whereas the Tondal text removed flowers, grasses, and fountains to the outskirts of paradise and protected the saints behind wall upon wall of gold and gems, Dante's heaven is a rose. Whereas the figures Tondal meets on his travels are more particularized (and somatized) in hell, to Dante heaven is peopled not by rank upon rank of "martyrs" and "virgins" but by a Beatrice and a Bernard. The glory of wholeness is for Dante—as it is for Bonaventure

---

prominence of hell's mouth in the resurrections found in plates 2, 12–14, and 17 of Bevington et. al, *Homo, Memento Finis.*

106. See above, chapter 4, nn. 100 and 101. A fifteenth-century woodcut of the Last Judgment from Syon convent (Bodleian Library MS Rawl. D.402) is another striking exception (see Bevington et al., *Homo, Memento Finis,* plate 18). The woodcut depicts Christ the Judge above two zones, in the lowest of which appear scattered bones and a shrouded figure from whom worms crawl. These body parts would seem to signify the dead, clearly still dead and fragmented. In the zone above, two torsos (nicely rounded off at the middle) seem to represent saved and damned. They appear to be the resurrected, but they are still (at least visually) parts. It is particularly striking that Christ the Judge (who is shown with lavishly bleeding wounds) is flanked by two banners, on one of which the five wounds are depicted; hence even Christ is here divided and fragmented. The image appears to be related to Birgitta of Sweden's devotion to the Five Wounds, for it says *"Arma beate Birgitte."*

107. Sauerländer, *Gothic Sculpture,* pp. 504–5. The anatomical specificity of the resurrection bodies depicted in the Trinity College Apocalypse is also worth noting; see plate 28 above, and chapter 4, n. 122, also n. 117.

108. Even a quick glance at the Buffalmacco and Nardo di Cione paintings from mid-century (plates 24, 25, and 26) shows that the lowest rungs of hell are no longer characterized by images of body parts although tortures of devouring and being devoured continue to be prominent.

and Thomas—an expression of person. The issue is not so much the continuity of material particles as the continuity of self.

When we turn to late thirteenth-century hagiography, we find a similar tendency to assert wholeness. The theme of reassemblage is not supplanted; hagiography is a very conservative genre. But even here, in the midst of a multitude of mutilations and tortures, triumph over evil is not only the gathering of scattered bones for quiet sepulchre but also an assertion that the corruptible is incorrupt, the part *is* the whole.[109]

As many recent scholars have pointed out, both the vernacular saints' lives of the high Middle Ages and the new Latin collections of legends made for the use of mendicant preachers agreed in their archaizing tendencies.[110] Looking to distant events in Christian history and choosing heroines or heroes singularly unsuitable for pious imitation, hagiographers filled their pages with stories of torture and execution. For example, the *Golden Legend* of James of Voragine (d. 1298), by far the most popular compendium of these racy yet moral tales, seems obsessed with bodily division.[111] Of the 153 chapters devoted to saints' days, at least 75 have dismemberment as a central motif; James details 81 kinds of torture.[112] But as was true in the early martyrologies from which medi-

---

109. I have discussed this in *Fragmentation and Redemption*, pp. 285–94, and "Bodily Miracles and the Resurrection of the Body in the High Middle Ages," pp. 68–106, especially pp. 79–83.

110. Cazelles, *Le Corps de sainteté*, pp. 219–20 and passim, and G. Philippart, *Les Légendiers latins et autres manuscrits hagiographiques*, Typologie des sources du moyen âge occidental, 24–25 (Turnhout: Brepols, 1977), pp. 40, 47.

111. On the popularity of the *Golden Legend*, see Brenda Dunn-Lardeau, ed., *Legenda Aurea: Sept siècles du diffusion: Actes du colloque international . . . à l'Université du Quebec à Montréal, 11–12 mai 1983* (Montreal and Paris: Bellarmin and J. Vrin, 1986), and Konrad Kunze, "Jacobus a (de) Voragine," *Die deutsche Literatur des Mittelalters: Verfasserlexikon* (Berlin: de Gruyter, 1983), vol. 4, col. 454.
On James's interest in torture and mutilation, see Giselle Huot-Girard, "La justice immanente dans la *Légende dorée*," *Cahiers d'études médiévales* 1 (1974): 135–47; Alain Boureau, *La Légende dorée: Le systeme narratif de Jacques de Voragine (+ 1298)* (Paris: Éditions du Cerf, 1984); Sherry L. Reames, *The Legenda Aurea: A Reexamination of Its Paradoxical History* (Madison: University of Wisconsin Press, 1985); and Marie-Christine Pouchelle, "Représentations du corps dans la *Légende dorée*," *Ethnologie française* 6 (1976): 293–308. Pouchelle underlines the fear of division in James's stories; she also emphasizes the role of body as avenue to God—a point rather similar to my interpretation in *Holy Feast and Holy Fast*. André Vauchez, "Jacques de Voragine et les saints du XIIIe siècle dans la *Légende dorée*," in *Legenda Aurea: Sept siècles de diffusion*, ed. B. Dunn-Lardeau, pp. 27–56, gives an interpretation opposed to that of Boureau and Reames.

112. Of the 153 chapters (many of which tell several stories), 91 chapters treat martyrs; the majority of the martyrs discussed are not merely killed but in some way dismembered. For further discussion see my "Bodily Miracles," p. 101 n. 78, and Bou-

eval legendaries copied, the point is not the presence but the absence of suffering. There are only one or two references in all of James's hideous stories to the fact that being cut apart might hurt.[113]

When he discusses the tortures of purgatory, James underlines the pain they cause; he points out that a female saint giving birth in prison experienced all the ordinary horrors of labor.[114] In martyrdom, however, the saints receive the anesthesia of glory. As James reports blessed Agnes to say: Christ's body is already with the bodies of the saints; even during torture they rest already in the "embrace of his pure arms."[115] Indeed Thomas Aquinas, writing just as James was compiling his *Golden Legend*, explained that the martyrs bear up under pain exactly because the beatific vision flows over naturally into their bodies.[116] Contemporary artists repeatedly depicted saintly heroes and heroines as unaffected psychologically (and even physiologically) by graphic and remarkable tortures.[117]

Owing in part to the development of relic cult, the attitude of thirteenth-century hagiographers toward decay and bodily division was far more complex and ambivalent than that found in the stories of Tertullian's day or even Jerome's. James of Voragine (like Caesarius of Heisterbach earlier) tells of relics that protest division and of those that welcome it, of frantic and courageous efforts to bury the martyrs and of saints who resist honorable sepulchre, of incorruption that manifests

---

reau, *La Légende dorée*, p. 116. There is real sadism in James's accounts. He seems to enjoy detailing the mutilations suffered by the saints; see, for example, his accounts of Vincent, Juliana, and Eugenia (the latter under Saints Protus and Hyacinth); *Legenda aurea*, ed. Graesse, pp. 117–20, 177–78, 602–5; *Golden Legend*, trans. Ryan and Ripperger, pp. 114–17, 166–67, 536–39. He puts in the mouth of Dominic a masochistic speech asking for fragmentation a little at a time; *Legenda aurea*, ed. Graesse, p. 468; trans. Ryan and Ripperger, p. 415.

113. See Boureau, *La Légende dorée*, pp. 60–61 and 115–33.

114. For James's recognition of pain in purgatory, see the stories he borrows from Peter the Chanter in *Legenda aurea*, ed. Graesse, pp. 731–32; *Golden Legend*, trans. Ryan and Ripperger, pp. 650–51. For a woman's pain in labor contrasted with the absence of pain during martyrdom, see *Legenda aurea*, ed. Graesse, pp. 798–99; trans. Ryan and Ripperger, p. 736.

115. *Legenda aurea*, ed. Graesse, p. 114: "jam amplexibus ejus castis adstricta sum; jam corpus ejus corpori meo sociatum est. . . ."

116. Thomas, ST 3a, q. 15, art. 5, obj. 3 and reply to obj. 3, vol. 49, pp. 204–7; and see also ST 3a, q. 14, art. 1, obj. 2 and reply to obj. 2, pp. 170–75. Bernard of Clairvaux expresses the same opinion in *De diligendo Deo*, section 10, paragr. 29, *Tractatus et opuscula*, p. 144.

117. See Bynum, *Fragmentation and Redemption*, pp. 231–33 and plates 6.14 and 6.15. And see below, nn. 129 and 130.

the glory of body and of failure to decay naturally that signals evil, even the work of devils.[118] But whatever complicated cultural attitudes toward body and burial such stories betray, wholeness is their crucial theme, whether expressed in tales of reassemblage, in metaphors of fertility, or in miracles of metonymy. James often describes heroic efforts to gather bones for burial; he occasionally recounts—and gives unabashed religious significance to—division and scattering. But in the lat-

118. When king Clovis breaks off the arm of St. Denis, he is punished by insanity (*Legenda aurea*, ed. Graesse, p. 686; trans. Ryan and Ripperger, p. 622); a cloth relic bleeds when cut (*Legenda aurea*, ed. Graesse, p. 198; trans. Ryan and Ripperger, p. 186); Julian the Apostate's plan to scatter the body of John the Baptist is called a "second martyrdom" (*Legenda aurea*, ed. Graesse, p. 568–73, esp. p. 569; trans. Ryan and Ripperger, p. 504). Persecutors are said to be denied decent burial (*Legenda aurea*, ed. Graesse, p. 145; trans. Ryan and Ripperger, p. 167) or to suffer decay or violent fragmentation while alive (*Legenda aurea*, ed. Graesse, pp. 33, 69, 203–4; trans. Ryan and Ripperger, pp. 41, 71, and 592). But dividing up St. Augustine for relics is presented as perfectly acceptable (*Legenda aurea*, ed. Graesse, pp. 562–63; trans. Ryan and Ripperger, p. 498). The faithful are said to strive to collect the bones of John the Baptist (*Legenda aurea*, ed. Graesse, pp. 566–67, 569; trans. Ryan and Ripperger, p. 502 and 504), Denis's companions (*Legenda aurea*, ed. Graesse, p. 685; trans. Ryan and Ripperger, p. 620), Bartholomew (*Legenda aurea*, ed. Graesse, p. 543; trans. Ryan and Ripperger, p. 482), Hadrian (*Legenda aurea*, ed. Graesse, pp. 600–1; trans. Ryan and Ripperger, pp. 534–5), Boniface (*Legenda aurea*, ed. Graesse, p. 318; trans. Ryan and Ripperger, p. 286), and Petronilla's companions (*Legenda aurea*, ed. Graesse, p. 343; trans. Ryan and Ripperger, p. 300). Even when scattered, martyred flesh is said to be "untouched" by scavenger beasts or is collected by divine means for burial (*Legenda aurea*, ed. Graesse, pp. 345–46 and 602; trans. Ryan and Ripperger, pp. 304 and 536). The body of St. Paul is said to turn in its coffin, grateful to be rejoined to its skull (*Legenda aurea*, ed. Graesse, p. 385; trans. Ryan and Ripperger, p. 345). But James stresses that St. Marcellinus is so humble he does not want burial (*Legenda aurea*, ed. Graesse, p. 271; trans. Ryan and Ripperger, p. 245); Mary of Egypt asks to become dust (*Legenda aurea*, ed. Graesse, pp. 247–49; trans. Ryan and Ripperger, pp. 229–30); the Seven Sleepers of Ephesus refuse the golden coffins offered by the emperor and ask instead to lie in the earth (*Legenda aurea*, ed. Graesse, p. 438; trans. Ryan and Ripperger, p. 386): "et cum [imperator] jussisset fieri loculos aureos, in quibus mitterentur, in ipsa nocte apparuerunt imperator dicentes, ut, sicut hactenus in terra jacuerunt et ex terra resurrexerant, ita eos dimitteret, donec dominus iterum eos resuscitaret." A miracle attached to the life of Benedict even recounts that a monk who deserted the monastery and died was rejected by the earth and could not decay until his parents buried a consecrated host with him (*Legenda aurea*, ed. Graesse, p. 211; trans. Ryan and Ripperger, ibid., p. 201). Yet the bodies of Christ and Mary the Virgin are said not to decay because they are not tainted with sin (*Legenda aurea*, ed. Graesse, pp. 239 and 504–17; trans. Ryan and Ripperger, pp. 220 and 450–57). And incorruption in the grave, occasionally a sign of evil, is frequently presented as a sign of the purity of the body (*Legenda aurea*, ed. Graesse, p. 441; trans. Ryan and Ripperger, p. 389).

The attitudes behind these stories are not fully consistent, but in general violent fragmentation and disrespect for bones is evil, quiet burial and decay is good; incorruption (when it is a sign of genuine purity) is even better than gentle reception by the earth. Reassemblage is an act of piety, but where reassemblage and sepulchre are not possible, the part is treated as if the whole were present there.

ter cases he almost invariably asserts the part to *be* the whole, denying in metaphor the very partition he chronicles in fact. James's legends thus suggest—not (as we are sometimes told) that the body *is* the saint—but that saints are present wherever any fragment of them is found.[119]

So extravagant, indeed, is James's denial of fragmentation that, as several modern students of hagiography have pointed out, it is hard to say why he finally allows one among a series of lengthy tortures to dispatch his hero or heroine; in any case the actual death is often singularly anticlimactic.[120] What is underlined repeatedly is either a reassembling of body parts for burial or (particularly in the case of virgin women) the victory of intactness over division. Although sundered limb from limb, female saints are said to be "whole" because they avoid sexual violation. Despite frightful methods of execution, the bodies of both male and female martyrs triumph miraculously over disintegration.[121] For example, the story of St. Margaret, bound on the rack, beaten with sharp instruments until her bones were laid bare, burned with torches, and plunged into water, describes her body as "unscathed."[122] The beheaded martyrs Nazarius and Celsus are found "intact" [*integrum et incorruptum cum capillis et barba*] in the tomb—a description that makes a claim not for reassemblage but for incorruption![123] Burned on the pyre, St. Theodore renders up his soul, but his body is "unharmed" (*ab igne illaesum*).[124] St. Christina bleeds milk without her severed breasts and speaks without her amputated tongue.[125] Left by the emperor Diocletian to wolves and dogs, the bodies of two martyrs survive "intact" (*intacta*) until the faithful can collect them for burial.[126] James (or a later inter-

119. See my "Bodily Miracles," p. 81 and nn. 90–91.

120. Hippolyte Delehaye, *The Legends of the Saints*, trans. V. M. Crawford, Westminster Library (London and New York: Longmans, Green, 1907), pp. 97 and 130–34; René Aigrain, *L'hagiographie: Ses sources, ses méthodes, son histoire* (Paris: Bloud and Gay, 1953), p. 146; Baudouin de Gaiffier, "La Mort par le glaive dans les Passions des martyrs," in *Recherches d'hagiographie latine*, Subsidia hagiographica, 52 (Brussels: Société des Bollandistes, 1971), pp. 70–76; Cazelles, *Le corps de sainteté*, pp. 50–60; Boureau, *La Légende dorée*, pp. 126–33; Alison Goddard Elliott, *Roads to Paradise: Reading the Lives of the Early Saints* (Hanover and London: University Press of New England, 1987), pp. 14–15, and 151.

121. See my "Bodily Miracles," p. 79 and nn. 77–78.

122. *Legenda aurea*, ed. Graesse, pp. 400–3; trans. Ryan and Ripperger, pp. 351–53.

123. *Legenda aurea*, ed. Graesse, p. 441; trans. Ryan and Ripperger, p. 389.

124. *Legenda aurea*, ed. Graesse, pp. 740–41; trans. Ryan and Ripperger, p. 662. And see the similar account of St. Mark in *Legenda aurea*, ed. Graesse, p. 267; trans. Ryan and Ripperger, p. 240.

125. *Legenda aurea*, ed. Graesse, p. 421; trans. Ryan and Ripperger, p. 366.

126. *Legenda aurea*, ed. Graesse, pp. 601–2; trans. Ryan and Ripperger, pp. 535–36; see also *Legenda aurea*, ed. Graesse, pp. 345–46; trans. Ryan and Rippenberger, p. 304.

polator) describes as "unharmed" and "unhurt" Sophia's three daughters, who were fried in a skillet, had their breasts torn off, were stretched on the rack and finally beheaded. In contrast, the emperor Hadrian, who presided over the torture of the three young girls, is said to have "withered away, filled with rottenness (*totus putrefactus*)."[127]

James thus asserts that—whatever the historical events—the good are intact when divided, while the evil fragment or decay even without violence. Such assertions are mirrored in those late thirteenth-century visions in which bodies in heaven are seen as clear and perfect—not the crystalline spheres in which an Origen or a Caesarius of Heisterbach described souls but anatomically perfect bodies made translucent by light. Marguerite of Oingt saw Christ's body thus. And it was as a translucent and apparently sleeping figure, complete down to the eyebrows and eyelashes, that Mechtild of Magdeburg saw John the Evangelist, who (she believed) had been bodily assumed into heaven.[128]

Indeed, we should note in this connection that late medieval artists, when they painted the martyrs outside a narrative context, depicted these saints carrying body fragments as attributes but themselves shining and whole. When Lucy or Agatha appears in the timeless context of eternity, she is placid, restored, and beautiful while carrying her severed breasts or eyes on a platter (see plates 34 and 35).[129] Although executed

127. *Legenda aurea*, ed. Graesse, pp. 203–4; trans. Ryan and Ripperger, p. 592. It is worth noting that Sophia is said to have gathered up the remains of her daughters and buried them with the help of bystanders; she was then buried with her children. This chapter, not found in the 1283 manuscript, is probably a later interpolation but is fully in the spirit of the other chapters; see Boureau, *La Légende dorée*, pp. 27–28.

In the account of Agatha, the saint's severed breasts are restored to her by miracle before burial. But her torturer dies when horses run away with his chariot, and his body is never recovered for burial; *Legenda aurea*, ed. Graesse, pp. 170–73; trans. Ryan and Ripperger, pp. 157–60; and see n. 66 above. In the story of Juliana, fish and wild beasts eagerly devour the bodies of her persecutors; *Legenda aurea*, ed. Graesse, pp. 177–78; trans. Ryan and Ripperger, p. 167. In contrast, persecutors are unable to get rid of the dead body of St. Vincent, which is refused by the sea and the fish to whom it is given for devouring; *Legenda aurea*, ed. Graesse, pp. 119–20; trans. Ryan and Ripperger, pp. 116–17.

128. Marguerite of Oingt, *Speculum*, chap. 3, in *Les Oeuvres de Marguerite d'Oingt*, ed. Antonin Duraffour, Pierre Gardette, and Paulette Durdilly (Paris: "Belles Lettres," 1865), p. 99. Mechtild of Magdeburg, *Das fliessende Licht*, trans. Schmidt, pp. 205–6, and see below, chapter 8, pp. 334–41.

129. Plate 34, Modena, Biblioteca Estense, Lat. MS 1023, fol. 17v, depicts St. Lucy with her eyes restored and on a platter; see Domenico Fava and Mario Salmi, *I Manoscritti miniati della Biblioteca Estense di Modena*, vol. 1 (Florence: Electa Editrice, 1950), p. 35 and plate 7, no. 2. Plate 35 shows the Martyrdom of St. Agatha from Paris MS, Bibliothèque nationale, N.A.FR. 23686 f. 247v; for which see *Les manuscrits à peintures en France du XIIIe au XVIe siècle*, pref. by A. Malraux (Paris: Bibliothèque Nationale, 1955), p. 16 no. 15; and Robert Branner, "Note on the Style of the Kansas

saints sometimes carry their heads in their hands in narrative depictions, the heads often return to shoulders when the painted or sculpted
figures are associated with Judgment, resurrection, or heaven (see plate
36).[130]

Like artists and female visionaries, James of Voragine goes beyond
stories of reassemblage—either by human effort or by divine power—to
explicit assertions that body, however disfigured or divided, is perfect
and intact.[131] Such assertions are sometimes made in metaphors of food
or flowering that seem to echo, at hundreds of years remove, the sublime
paradoxes of Irenaeus and Ignatius of Antioch. When he tells the story
of St. Vincent, for example, James quotes Ambrose and Augustine:
"[Vincent] was pulverized that he might become solid, burned that he
might be refined."[132] The account of Andrew the Apostle stresses that

---

City Leaf," *The Nelson Gallery and Atkins Museum Bulletin* 5, no. 1 (1971): 31 n. 3.
Although art historians have usually spoken of such depictions as if the severed limbs
are attributes (or aids to identification), more is involved. The saint in glory is reassembled as if in resurrection, but the part or mark she bears is also an aspect of who
she is for all eternity.

This iconographic reassemblage of saints is in interesting contrast to contemporary depictions of Christ. In the later fourteenth and fifteenth centuries, Christ's body
is regularly divided into pieces in representations of the Five Wounds; see Gertrud
Schiller, *Iconography of Christian Art*, vol. 2: *The Passion of Jesus Christ*, pp. 184–
97 and plates 664–73. We also find increasing visual emphasis on Christ's suffering
in crucifixion, although depictions of the saints show them impassive and impassible
under torture; see Bynum, *Fragmentation and Redemption*, pp. 231–33, 271, and 278–
79. It is as though—at least visually—Christ, because he is God, takes on all the
culture's obsession with torture and partition, while the saints are guaranteed (by
their participation in beatific vision and blessedness) to be free of pain and fragmentation. The point is worth pursuing but would take me beyond the early fourteenth
century.

130. Plate 36 is another miniature series from Paris MS, Bibliothèque nationale,
N.A.FR. 23686 (cited above in n. 129); it shows St. Quentin both beheaded and intact.
Stephen Murray in *Notre Dame, Cathedral of Amiens* points out not only that the
relics of St. Firmin are sculpted on the St. Firmin portal at Amiens as if they were
rising from the dead but also that the column statues of the saints on the same portal
give a premonition of resurrection; see plate 23 and chapter 5 at n. 40. Two of these
saints are cephalophores but others are decapitated martyrs who have once again
received their heads.

131. Of two self-mutilations carried out by early saints, one is overcome by the
restoration of the severed hand, but in the second case (St. Mark's severed thumb) the
moral of the story is simply that mutilation does not matter; the Evangelist is ordained
without restoration of the missing part. It is significant, however, that just after the
account of Mark's self-mutilation we are given a story of how he healed a cobbler's
severely mangled hand with a paste made from dust. James, *Legenda aurea*, ed.
Graesse, pp. 367 (St. Leo) and 266 (St. Mark); trans. Ryan and Ripperger, pp. 331, 239.

132. *Legenda aurea*, ed. Graesse, p. 120: "torquetur Vincentius, ut exerceatur, fla-
gellatur, ut erudiatur, tunditur, ut subsolidetur, exuritur, ut repurgetur . . ." (my translation). And see above, n. 127.

the saint did not die when crucified, but chose rather to expire three days later when the crowd wanted to take him down from the cross. Saying "it is time for Thee [God] to give my body back to the earth, . . . which may keep it and restore it to me on the day of the resurrection of the body," he then disappeared in a cloud of light, and for years after, manna "in the form of flour" and scented oil issued from his tomb. This saint, who became food in the grave, supposedly told his persecutor: "To Almighty God I offer daily a Lamb without stain, who, after all the people have eaten Him, remains alive and whole."[133]

In James's account of Catherine, her fifty converts are thrown into the fire for their faith, and the language in which their death is described assimilates execution and resurrection. Asserting an intactness that begins long before the trumpet sounds, the hagiographer writes: "not a hair of their heads nor a shred of their garments suffered the least harm from the fire."[134] In another account that explicitly echoes not only Luke 21.18 but also 1 Corinthians 15.42–44, the martyr's words deny exactly the bodily division he suffers. St. James the Dismembered speaks to his severed toes:

> Go, third toe, to thy companions, and as the grain of wheat bears much fruit, so shalt thou rest with thy fellows unto the last day. . . . Be comforted, little toe, because great and small shall have the same resurrection. A hair of the head shall not perish, and how much less shalt thou, the least of all, be separated from thy fellows?[135]

James of Voragine repeatedly attributes fertility to the saints, not only because of their proselytizing in life but also because of a germination beyond the grave that combines making disciples by example with rising whole before God in resurrection. He describes Germanus the Bishop, in whose story resurrections play an especially prominent role, as a "sprouting seed" and derives the saint's name from "seed" [*germen*] "above" [*ana*].[136] Of the contemporary saint Peter Martyr, he says:

133. *Legenda aurea*, ed. Graesse, pp. 12–22; trans. Ryan and Ripperger, pp. 9–16.
134. *Legenda aurea*, ed. Graesse, pp. 789–97, esp. 792; trans. Ryan and Ripperger, pp. 708–15, especially p. 712.
135. *Legenda aurea*, ed. Graesse, pp. 799–803; trans. Ryan and Ripperger, p. 719.
136. *Legenda aurea*, ed. Graesse, pp. 448–51, esp. 448; trans. Ryan and Ripperger, pp. 396–99, especially p. 396. On etymologies, see Roswitha Klinck, *Die lateinische Etymologie des Mittelalters* (Munich: Wilhelm Fink, 1970), especially pp. 57–70, and Anders Winroth, "The Etymologies in the *Golden Legend* of Jacobus de Varagine" (M.A. thesis, Columbia University, 1992).

He was like a grain of wheat that falls to the ground and is picked up by the hands of unbelievers, and dying rises again in a fertile stalk. He was the grape that in the press gives forth much juice. He was the spice that, ground in the mortar by the pestle, gives forth a wondrous odor. He was the mustard seed that increases in strength when it is ground.[137]

As Guibert of Nogent had pointed out more than a hundred and fifty years earlier, the eucharistic host, fragmented by human teeth and digestive processes yet in every minute crumb the whole body of Christ, is the guarantee that wholeness (impartibility and impassibility) is God's ultimate promise to humankind.[138] During the thirteenth century, theologians devoted much attention to the doctrine of concomitance—the teaching, that is, that Christ is fully present in each species and in every particle of the Eucharist.[139] Thus it is not surprising that James's most extravagant assertion of *pars pro toto* is a eucharistic miracle. In his account of St. Gregory, a woman who doubts the Eucharist sees it as the body of Christ. But what she sees lying on the altar at the consecration is a finger! It is hard to imagine a more graphic (and to modern tastes offensive) assimilation of Eucharist to relic, of communion to cannibalism.[140] But the story is also a symbol of the bodiliness of God, the bodiliness of us all, and the hope not only of future resurrection but of present wholeness. If in Christ and in the martyrs part is whole, perhaps we too shall be—even *are*—whole in every fragment no matter how threatened by consumption, death, and decay. James draws on such ideas when he puts into St. Catherine's mouth the claim (almost blasphemous in its eucharistic overtones) "I desire to offer my flesh and blood to Christ, as He offered Himself for me," or assimilates the bodies of Andrew and John the Evangelist to the food that never diminishes by recounting that their graves filled inexhaustibly with manna.[141]

137. *Legenda aurea,* ed. Graesse, p. 282; trans. Ryan and Ripperger, p. 251.
138. See Bynum, "Bodily Miracles," pp. 77–78. Eucharistic miracles from the twelfth to the fourteenth century were characterized by an emphasis on part being whole; see Benedicta Ward, *Miracles and the Medieval Mind,* pp. 15–18.
139. Bynum, *Holy Feast and Holy Fast,* pp. 51–53 and 255; Gary Macy, *The Theologies of the Eucharist in the Early Scholastic Period: A Study of the Salvific Function of the Sacrament According to the Theologians, ca. 1080–ca. 1220* (Oxford: Oxford University Press, 1984), passim.
140. *Legenda aurea,* ed. Graesse, pp. 197–98; trans. Ryan and Ripperger, pp. 185–86.
141. *Legenda aurea,* ed. Graesse, pp. 793, 12–22, and 56–62; trans. Ryan and Ripperger, pp. 713, 9–16, 58–63. For an example from devotional literature of an emphasis on each of the parts of Christ as if it were the whole, see *Ancrene Riwle,* trans. M. B. Salu, pt. 2, pp. 49–50.

Both at the level of theological and philosophical discourse, and at the level of popular devotion, much changed between the second and the fourteenth centuries. But as James's tales suggest, deep anxieties about decay continued to lurk under the surface of theological discussion, miracle story, and preaching. Decay was sometimes redeemed (and denied) in metaphors of fertility, as it had been in second-century writing about resurrection; more often it was redeemed (and denied) in images of reunion or incorruption of parts. Such images, in keeping with the intensely graphic and somatic quality of late medieval piety, came increasingly to be enacted in matter. As I pointed out in chapter 5 above, bodies began to perform in the present life and in the tomb (or so people believed) exactly as preachers said they would in resurrection. James's text is filled with miracles at which the early Passions of the martyrs merely hinted. If anything, therefore, Western piety was both more somatic and more paradoxical in 1300 than in the days of Tertullian and Irenaeus. Although philosophical theory could account for identity of person without material continuity, body—as the locus of decay, of experience, and of encounter with the divine—was more important than ever before. It was divided and distributed in order to disperse its power; but in order to revere and protect that same power, it was declared whole even when mutilated and partitioned.

I turn in my last chapter to the context of these paradoxical beliefs and practices, first, in the new ways people treated living and dead bodies in the decades around 1300 and, second, in the emergence of a rhetoric (as powerful as it was hesitant) that made body both the location and the object of desire.

Eight

Fragmentation and Ecstasy:
The Thirteenth-Century Context

 THE RESURRECTION BODY was an important element in the controversies of the 1270s and 1280s over soul and immortality; it was centrally at issue in the debate of the 1330s over the beatific vision. At first glance, these controversies seem to indicate—as followers of Oscar Cullmann have sometimes argued—that a modified version of Greek dualism triumphed in Western Christian theology by the fourteenth century.[1] They suggest, that is, that the immortal soul became the container and guarantee of what we mean by self.[2] The elaboration of a formal theory of identity (extrapolated from the unicity of form), fol-

1. See the works cited in my introduction, nn. 2, 4, 7, and 9–11 above, especially Gooch, *Partial Knowledge,* and Greshake and Kremer, *Resurrectio mortuorum.*

2. The Middle Ages did not, of course, have a Latin word for "the self"; see John F. Benton, "Consciousness of Self and Perceptions of Individuality," in *Renaissance and Renewal,* ed. Benson and Constable, pp. 263–95, and Bynum, "Did the Twelfth Century Discover the Individual?" in *Jesus as Mother,* pp. 82–109. Theologians used "person," at least by the thirteenth century, to mean precisely *not* the soul but the psychosomatic unit that would exist after the resurrection. By this latter move they clearly meant to make resurrection philosophically as well as theologically necessary. My point here is that—as many theologians (mostly Protestant) have pointed out—it is not clear whether labeling the separated soul "not a person" is sufficient to make resumption of body at resurrection necessary for what we in the twentieth century mean by "self."

lowed by the doctrinal pronouncement that blessedness is complete with soul's reception of *visio Dei*, seems to eclipse body philosophically and theologically. Such positions assert that soul needs some matter for resurrection; indeed, in the ordinary course of events, the matter reanimated at the end of time will be the particles that had fragmented in the grave. But in an emergency, any matter will do. Body adds something to blessedness, but it is not clear what; soul has already attained the quiet of eternity.

The study of religious language I have carried out suggests, however, a different story. Images of the resurrection body in thirteenth- and fourteenth-century scholastic discourse, hagiography, poetry, and art seem to make it more crucial and integral to self than ever before. Body is a beloved bride, rewarded with gifts particular to her because of her experience and merit on earth; it is a flowering plant or the perduring container that organizes flux; body is the expression of soul, its overflow, the gesture that manifests soul's intention. In quodlibetal debates as in mystical visions and otherworld journeys, body seems anything but eclipsed. The *exempla* of preachers and the stories of hagiographers make soul unabashedly somatomorphic; tales of the in-between period of purgatory—the period in which, by definition, soul is without body— become increasingly tales of souls so labile, expressive, and particularized that they seem to have pulled their bodies either forward (so to speak) from this life or backward from the moment of resurrection. Technical theological discussion stresses the wholeness of the final person (including the restored person in hell) more than ever before. It asserts, however inconsistently, some kind of material continuity between Christ's body in the *triduum* and in heaven, elaborates the theory of Mary's Bodily Assumption, and strives to account for the shape and integrity of the cadaver before decay. Despite a certain distrust of physical pleasure, it bestows on the risen body all the organs and senses— even the scars—of earthly experience. Otherworld images and stories from the years around 1300 tend (depending on how one looks at it) either to embody the soul or to enliven the corpse. In many senses therefore metonymy replaces reassemblage. Whereas twelfth-century imagery implied that salvation was the reuniting of fragments, fourteenth-century images implied the part (whether metaphysical or physical) to be the whole. In vision, in art, and in literary metaphor, soul was sometimes self. Body was sometimes self. But finger or toe was also sometimes self.

It is time now to turn—as I did in discussing the second, fourth, and twelfth centuries—to a consideration of the social context of bodily images.

The Practice of Bodily Partition

Several aspects of the social and religious history of the thirteenth and fourteenth centuries shed light on the tendency of theologians to somatize soul or lift the body into heaven.

All descriptions of the period emphasize its greater social stratification, the emergence of finer gradations of secular and ecclesiastical hierarchy, and the manifestation of status and class differences in details of dress, ritual, and manners.[3] It is thus hardly surprising that commentators on 1 Corinthians 15 stressed verse 41 ("star differeth from star in glory"), underlining the inequality of dowries and crowns, or that visionaries saw physical characteristics and occupational roles, as well as moral qualities, stamped on somatomorphic souls in the afterlife.[4]

Accounts of the period also stress the new scientific curiosity and sophistication found in universities and among doctors and scholars outside them; we should not discount such curiosity as a motivation of theologians. Historians of science John Murdoch, Edith Sylla, and Joel Kaye have taught us that abstruse and technical theological issues (such as transubstantiation or the locomotion of angels) became in the early fourteenth century the site of scientific speculation.[5] Albert the Great

3. For an interesting discussion of this, especially as it affects women, see Diane Owen Hughes, "Les Modes," in *Histoire des femmes*, ed. Duby and Perrot, vol. 2: *Le moyen âge*, ed. Klapisch-Zuber, pp. 147–69.

4. Dinzelbacher, "Klassen und Hierarchien im Jenseits"; idem, "Reflexionen irdischer Sozialstrukturen"; Schotter, "The Paradox of Equality in *Pearl*"; Ian Bishop, "Relievers at the Court of Heaven: Contrasted Treatments of an Idea in *Piers Plowman* and *Pearl*," in Myra Stokes et al., eds., *Medieval Literature and Antiquities: Studies in Honour of Basil Cottle* (Cambridge: Brewer, 1987), pp. 111–18; and Jean Batany, "Une Image en negatif du fonctionnalisme social: Les Danses macabre," in Jane M. Taylor, ed., *Dies Illa: Death in the Middle Ages: Proceedings of the 1983 Manchester Conference* (Liverpool: Francis Cairns, 1984), pp. 15–28.

5. See the essays in *The Cultural Context of Medieval Learning*, ed. John Murdoch and Edith Sylla (Dordrecht and Boston: Reidel, 1975) and Joel Kaye, "The Impact of Money on the Development of Fourteenth-Century Scientific Thought," *Journal of Medieval History* 14 (1988): 251–70, and "Quantification of Quality: The Impact of Money and Monetization on the Development of Scientific Thought in the Fourteenth Century" (Ph.D. diss., University of Pennsylvania, 1991). Greshake in Greshake and Kremer, *Resurrectio mortuorum*, p. 237 (citing Theodor Schneider, *Die Einheit des Menschen*) suggests that one reason why the Thomistic doctrine of unicity and formal identity does not win out is its incompatibility with a commonsense understanding

and Giles of Rome discussed embryology and generation as parallel to resurrection and regeneration; Godfrey of Fontaines and Henry of Ghent struggled to account for the survival of structure in a corpse (matter) after form (soul) has departed.[6] Such investigations reflected a not entirely religious interest in human physiology from fetus to cadaver and groped slowly toward understandings of process that did not assimilate change to decay.[7] Aquinas's speculation about the resurrection of eaten embryos, for example, was inquiry into the nature of digestion and reproduction as well as of identity.[8] Fourteenth-century discussions of the Immaculate Conception and Bodily Assumption of Mary were explorations not only of the nature of sin but also of the nature of sex and the female body.[9] Moreover, an occasional theologian-physician (or theologian-alchemist) actually attempted to make money or reputation by developing techniques that offered, if not resurrection, at least preservation of the corpse until the trumpet sounds.[10]

But as in the case of earlier polemics against Gnosticism, Origenism, and Catharism, mainstream Christian discussion of the resurrection body in 1300 does not seem primarily to be a locus of scientific investigation, social control, or ideological repression. (To say this is not, of course, to argue that such investigation, control, or repression did not occur.) Discussion of the resurrection body seems to have been about body—about the horror and the glory of the physical stuff in which human beings feel, suffer, experience the world, grow and give birth, decay and die.[11] I turn now finally to consider deep shifts in pious practices,

---

of matter, and this at a time when materiality and physicality were newly important to natural philosophical investigation.

6. In addition to the discussion in chapter 6 above, see Luke Demaitre and Anthony A. Travill, "Human Embryology and Development in the Works of Albertus Magnus," in James A. Weisheipl, ed., *Albertus Magnus and the Sciences: Commemorative Essays, 1980* (Toronto: Pontifical Institute of Medieval Studies, 1980), pp. 405–40.

7. See the works cited below in nn. 17, 25, and 26, for Bacon's ideas about life prolongation and corpse preservation.

8. Taylor, "Human Generation in the Thought of Thomas Aquinas"; Nolan, *Giles*, pp. 114–23.

9. It is striking how much more speculation there was on the conception of Mary than on the conception of Christ. It seems likely that this is (at least in part) because Mary, a human being, was conceived as we are; thus, her conception provides an opportunity to speculate on sexual reproduction generally and on its moral significance. Christ's conception, although uniquely important theologically speaking, did not provide a locus for discussing sex. See *Fragmentation and Redemption*, pp. 80 and 224–28.

10. See below, n. 25.

11. See Bynum, "Bodily Miracles," and eadem, review of Michael Camille, *The Gothic Idol*, in *The Art Bulletin* 72, no. 2 (1990): 331–32.

attitudes, and emotions that underlay images of the body as living metonymy, of the body as beloved. Although we should not expect to find in 1300, anymore than at any other period, a direct inscribing of funerary practices in theology or a doctrinal dictation of religious behavior, the insistence on wholeness and on understanding part *as* whole that we notice in the telling of saints' stories, the construction of reliquaries, and the formulation of doctrine has roots in the new enthusiasm for partition of bodies living and dead. Emphasis on integrity and identity in resurrection both made it all right to divide the body in burial and underlined such division as distribution of self.

Historians have paid much attention recently to the emergence of various forms of bodily partition in the years around 1300. The first clearly recorded autopsies and postmortems were performed at Bologna in the 1280s to determine cause of death in legal cases. By the second decade of the fourteenth century, dissection for the purpose of teaching anatomy had been introduced into the medical school curriculum. Again our first evidence comes from Bologna.[12]

The same period saw increased enthusiasm for boiling and dividing holy bodies in order to produce relics for quick distribution. There is, for example, some evidence that Thomas Aquinas's body was boiled in 1303/04 when a Cistercian monk (fearing appropriation of the body by a Dominican pope) decapitated the corpse in the hope of retaining part of the remains. An (unboiled) hand given to his sister was, significantly, found later to be "incorrupt."[13] Holy bodies were also embalmed because, as witnesses testified at one canonization proceeding, "God took such pleasure in" their bodies and their hearts.[14] Out of this practice

12. Pouchelle, *Corps et chirurgie,* pp. 132–36. She claims that the earliest official dissections (in 1315) were dissections of female bodies. The dissections to which she refers were clearly not the first dissections or autopsies of any sort. Dissections arising out of embalming or for the purpose of determining the cause of death in legal cases were practiced at least from the early thirteenth century on; dissections of the human body for teaching purposes were practiced at Bologna about 1300. See Walter Artelt, *Die ältesten Nachrichten über die Sektion menschlicher Leichen im mittelalterlichen Abendland* (Berlin: Ebering, 1940), pp. 3–25; Mary Niven Alston, "The Attitude of the Church Towards Dissection Before 1500," *Bulletin of the History of Medicine* 16 (1944): 221–38; Ynez Viole O'Neill, "Innocent III and the Evolution of Anatomy," *Medical History* 20, no. 4 (1976): 429–33; Nancy G. Siraisi, "The Medical Learning of Albertus Magnus," in Weisheipl, ed., *Albertus Magnus and the Sciences,* p. 395; Jacquart and Thomasset, *Sexuality,* p. 40; and Katharine Park, "Opening the Body: Autopsy and Dissection in Prevasalian Italy" (Paper for the New England Renaissance Conference, November 2–3, 1990).

13. E. Brown, "Death and the Human Body," p. 234 n. 48.

14. Enrico Menesto and Silvestro Nessi, eds., *Il processo di canonizzazione di Chiara de Montefalco* (Scandicci, Florence: "La Nuova Italia," 1984), p. 339; Park, "Opening the Body"; Camporesi, *Incorruptible Flesh,* pp. 3–11.

came the first claims that special marks of sanctity can be found inside holy persons (e.g., the "wound of love" in the heart) as well as outside (e.g., stigmata). By the mid-fourteenth century, the bodies of putative saints were sometimes torn open after death to look for signs of sanctity in the viscera. For example, when the sisters of Clare of Montefalco decided to embalm her body a few days after her death in August, 1308, they found in her heart "a cross, or the image of the crucified Christ." Three precious stones, inscribed with pictures of the Holy Family, were found in the heart of the pathetic little blind saint, Margaret of Città di Castello.[15] By the fifteenth century inquisitors at canonization proceedings looked to autopsy evidence for proof of paramystical phenomena such as miraculous abstinence.[16]

Enthusiastic partition of nonholy bodies was practiced as well. Established in Germany in the twelfth century and known as the *mos teutonicus*, the custom of eviscerating and boiling the corpses of royalty and aristocrats and burying the resulting body parts in various localities became common north of the Alps in the later thirteenth century although it was never popular in Italy.[17] As Elizabeth A. R. Brown has recently demonstrated, the bull *Detestande feritatis*, issued by Boniface VIII in 1299 to forbid the practice, was not enforced in the early fourteenth century; by 1351 Clement VI decreed that the French rulers would no longer need any special exemption for division of the body. By the fifteenth century at least one pope had his own body embalmed. Indeed, immediately after Boniface's death, opponents charged that he was a heretic because his concern to prevent fragmenting or tampering with cadavers proved, they said, that he did not believe in resurrection.[18]

As Edward Peters has recently reminded us, the years around 1300 also saw the revival of torture as a judicial procedure.[19] And there is some

15. See n. 14 above on Clare; for Margaret, see *Holy Feast and Holy Fast*, p. 145 and p. 364 n. 212.

16. See, for example, the account of the autopsy of Columba of Rieti; *Holy Feast and Holy Fast*, p. 148.

17. E. Brown, "Death and the Human Body," pp. 221–70; Park, "Opening the Body."

18. E. Brown, "Authority, Family, and the Dead." If it is true (as Paravicini Bagliani has argued) that Boniface was influenced by the ideas of Roger Bacon about life prolongation, the charge may have meant not that Boniface denied any form of survival but that his concerns made resurrection natural, not supernatural. In other words, the old pope's obsession with preserving his body from decay obscured the dividing line between life and death and implied that, with sufficient medical or alchemical manipulation, the body might indeed live forever; a natural process would therefore be substituted for resurrection via grace. See below nn. 25 and 26.

19. Edward Peters, *Torture* (Oxford: Blackwell, 1985). The fact that torturers (who were permitted to squeeze, twist, and stretch in excruciating ways) were forbidden to

evidence, at least for England, that the use of mutilation as punishment for capital crimes increased in frequency in exactly these decades. Chronicle accounts make it clear that dismemberment was reserved for the most repulsive crimes and that the populace was expected to be able to interpret the nature of the offense from the precise way in which the criminal's body was cut apart and the pieces displayed. Drawing and quartering, or burning (that is, reduction to the smallest possible particles: ashes), were punishments reserved for treason, witchcraft, and heresy, particularly when practiced by those of lower social status or inferior gender.[20] R. I. Moore and Saul Brody have attributed the scapegoating of lepers in the same years not only to increased incidence of the disease but also to changes in its conceptualization. In the general flaring up of intolerance that many historians have seen to be characteristic of the late thirteenth century, the bodies of lepers came to be paradigms for sin because they fragmented and putrefied while alive.[21]

For all the recent study of bodily partition, historians have not agreed about its significance or about attitudes toward it. Marie-Christine Pouchelle has claimed that the writings of French surgeons display an odd combination of reverence and almost prurient curiosity about what is contained inside (that is, the "secrets" of) cadavers, especially female cadavers.[22] A number of Renaissance historians have taken the fact that the first dissections were performed on the bodies of criminals as evi-

---

effect bodily division suggests that it was highly charged. It is also worth noting that medical practice preferred to cure by adjustment of humors and fluids; physicians, who did not cut or cauterize, had higher status than surgeons, who were in certain ways assimilated to barbers, a social rank below them. See Faye Marie Getz, "The Faculty of Medicine Before 1500," in *The History of the University of Oxford*, vol. 2: *Late Medieval Oxford*, ed. J. I. Catto and R. Evans (Oxford: Clarendon Press, 1992), pp. 373–405.

20. J. G. Bellamy, *The Law of Treason in England in the Later Middle Ages* (Cambridge: Cambridge University Press, 1970), pp. 9, 13, 20–21, 26, 39, 45–47, 52, and 226–27. As Bellamy points out (ibid., p. 227), historians often know the nature of the crime only from the type of execution inflicted. We know, for example, that a homicide had been adjudged petty treason in fourteenth-century England if the male perpetrator was drawn and hung or the female perpetrator burned. See also Camporesi, *Incorruptible Flesh*, pp. 19–24, and Finucane, "Sacred Corpse, Profane Carrion," pp. 50–51 (on execution by mutilation and partition), pp. 57–58 (on burning).

21. Saul N. Brody, *The Disease of the Soul: Leprosy in Medieval Literature* (Ithaca, N.Y.: Cornell University Press, 1974), pp. 64–66, 79, 85–86. See also R. I. Moore, *The Formation of a Persecuting Society*, pp. 58–63; idem, "Heresy as Disease," in *The Concept of Heresy in the Middle Ages (11th–13th Century): Proceedings of the International Conference, Louvain, May 13–16, 1973*, ed. W. Lourdaux and D. Verhelst (Louvain: University Press, 1976), pp. 1–11; and Camporesi, *Incorruptible Flesh*, pp. 90–96.

22. Pouchelle, *Corps et chirurgie*, especially pt. 1, chap. 4.

dence that surgeons (like executioners) expressed the values of a newly effective, coercive state.[23] Medical historians such as Nancy Siraisi and Katharine Park have disagreed, arguing that early accounts of embalming, autopsy, and dissection display no squeamishness or hesitation about opening the corpse.[24] The motives of Boniface VIII in *Detestande feritatis* have been much debated; scholars have variously attributed his position to political maneuvering against the French kings and the friars, to the influence at the curia of Baconian and possibly alchemical ideas about balance and decay, and to a personal, obsessive fear of death on the part of the old pope. The expert on French funerary practice Elizabeth Brown has herself vacillated about how much horror of decay there was, emphasizing both the enthusiastic and continuing practice of the *mos teutonicus* and the profound discomfort with corpse tampering expressed in university debates of the 1280s and 1290s.[25]

What seems clear is that there were real differences among regions and within status groups, among medical practitioners, and among theologians and preachers concerning the significance of both decay and division. These differences were particularly acute around 1300. But there was deep agreement that what happened in and to the cadaver was an expression of person. Some among both clergy and laity attempted to preserve the shape and integrity of corpses (either by embalming or by consigning them to the earth in a simple wrap); others removed body parts for burial in scattered sites, opened corpses to search for secret

23. Francis Barker, *The Tremulous Private Body: Essays on Subjection* (London: Methuen, 1984), pp. 72–112. See also Jonathan Sawday, "The Fate of Marsyas: Dissecting the Renaissance Body," in Lucy Gent and Nigel Llewellyn, eds., *Renaissance Bodies: The Human Figure in English Culture, ca. 1540–1660* (London: Reaktion Books, 1990), pp. 111–35. In their conclusions Barker and Sawday seem to me to make a rather uncritical use of Foucault.

24. Park, "Opening the Body." Park's own account suggests that doctors and embalmers may have felt some fascination with the secrets inside the body, but she is certainly right that there is no reason to take cutting and dividing as punitive per se, at least for the fourteenth century.

25. Pierre Duparc, "Dilaceratio corporis," *Bulletin de la Société Nationale des Antiquaires de France 1980–1981* (Paris: Boccard, 1981), pp. 360–72; E. Brown, "Death and the Human Body"; eadem, "Authority, Family, and the Dead"; Agostino Paravicini Bagliani, "Rajeunir au moyen âge: Roger Bacon et le mythe de la prolongation de la vie," in *Revue médicale de la Suisse romande* 106 (1986): 9–23; idem, "Storia della scienza e storia della mentalità: Ruggero Bacone, Bonifacio VIII e la teoria della 'prolongatio vitae'," in *Aspetti della Letteratura latina nel secolo XIII: Atti del primo Convegno internazionale di studi dell' Associazione per il Medioevo e l'Umanesimo latini (AMUL) Perugia 3–5 ottobre 1983*, ed. C. Leonardi and G. Orlandi (Florence and Perugia: "La Nuova Italia," 1985), pp. 243–80; and Francesco Santi, "Il cadavre e Bonifacio VIII, tra Stefano Tempier e Avicenna, inforno ad un saggio di Elizabeth Brown," *Studi Medievali,* 3d ser., 28, no. 2 (1987): 861–78.

signs of holiness, or divided cadavers to signal their political or demonic treachery. No one, however, suggested that the corpse was merely a husk left behind. Nor did any ritual, *exemplum*, or liturgical formula indicate fear of corpse pollution. No practice implied—as rites often do in other cultures—that hasty destruction of the cadaver would speed the flight of self to more important climes.[26]

The assumption that the material body we occupy in this life is integral to person was reflected in legend, folktale, and even "science." Many stories that circulated in the later Middle Ages implied that the body was in some sense alive after death. Moralists told of temporary resurrections; hagiographers described dead saints who sat up momentarily to revere the crucifix or eucharistic host; medical writers spoke of cadavers that continued to move or grow while on the embalming table or in the tomb; folk wisdom held that corpses would bleed to accuse their murderers; holy cadavers, especially holy female cadavers, were sometimes said to exude oil or even milk that cured the sick.[27] Down into the seventeenth century, learned treatises were written by doctors on the *life* of the body after death—a phenomenon that seemed proved to some by the apparent growth of fingernails and hair observed in corpses.[28] The claim that all or part of a saint remained incorrupt after burial was an important miracle for proving sanctity, particularly the sanctity of women.[29] Indeed, in what appears to have some parallels to modern cryonics, alchemists and physicians in the thirteenth century experimented with ways of returning the body to its pristine state before the fall, convinced that they might thus free it, more or less indefinitely, from decay.[30]

26. Paravicini Bagliani suggests that there is a newly positive attitude toward the body implicit in the Baconian ideas; see the works cited in n. 25 above and n. 35 below.

27. Henri Platelle, "La Voix du sang: Le cadavre qui saigné en presence de son meutrier," *La Piété populaire au moyen âge*, Actes du 99e Congrès National des Sociétés Savantes, Besançon 1974 (Paris, 1977), pp. 161–79; Finucane, *Miracles and Pilgrims*, pp. 73–75; Michel Bouvier, "De l'incorruptibilité des corps saints," in *Les miracles, miroirs*, pp. 193–221; Ariès, *Hour of Our Death*, pp. 261–68 and 353ff.; Jacques Gélis, "De la mort à la vie: Les 'sanctuaires à reprit'," *Ethnologie française* 11 (1981): 211–24.

28. Ariès, *Hour of Our Death*, pp. 261–68 and 353ff. Although some people today still believe such stories, growth of hair and nails does not occur in corpses. Robert W. Ackerman, "The Debate of the Body and the Soul and Parochial Christianity," *Speculum* 37 (1962): 549, argues that the thirteenth-century Middle English Debate between the Body and the Soul reflects "popular belief" in its implication that the cadaver retains for a little while after death the "capacity and will to speak."

29. Thurston, *Physical Phenomena*, pp. 246–52; Bynum, *Fragmentation and Redemption*, p. 372 n. 32.

30. Paravicini Bagliani, "Rajeunir au moyen âge"; idem, "Ruggero Bacone, Bonifacio VIII, e la teoria della 'prolongatio vitae' "; and Getz, "Faculty of Medicine."

Partition was abhorrent to some, it is true. Torturers were forbidden to sever; quartering in execution was understood to mirror the evil of destroying the body politic; the living cadaver of the leper—insensate, corrupt, shedding fragments—became a walking symbol of sin.[31] Canonists were hesitant about private property and trafficking in holy body parts.[32] Even reliquaries that underlined the partial nature of their contents sheathed these parts with incorruptible gold and gems, and sometimes announced in inscription that they foreshadowed the integrity of heaven.[33] Some fourteenth-century French wills instructed executors that the body not be divided for burial.[34] The new emphasis of doctors on models of internal balance—especially Baconian ideas that one might achieve an almost "natural immortality" by medical means—tried to prefigure (possibly even to effect) here on earth the final wholeness and stasis theologians argued to be the gift of God only in heaven.[35] Although Boniface VIII gave no theological justification for his prohibition of embalming, boiling, and dividing—merely asserting the practice to be monstrous—he drew on a considerable body of theological discussion that agreed with him in preferring quiet sepulchre for whole cadavers.[36]

Nonetheless, the years around 1300 saw enthusiastic prying into the body—studying it, severing it, distributing and scattering it. No one objected to reburial once bones were clean of flesh, although—as we have seen—even in the charnel house there was sometimes attention to the dignity and status of skulls. Theologians never forgot that the promise of resurrection made a variety of burial practices acceptable. Oliver of Tréguier argued in 1291 that dividing the corpse would conduce to its spiritual health by garnering more prayers for it and suggested a parallel to doctors who had sometimes to bring physical health by opening or amputating the body. God will (insisted Oliver) unite the pieces in res-

31. The leper's body was a particularly useful image because its disease, and the disease of original sin, were seen as sexually transmitted; see Brody, *Leprosy*. The miracles of leper saints thus inverted decay, fragmentation, and sin. Alpaïs of Cudot, Alice of Schaerbeek, and Lutgard of Aywières offered up their leprosy for God bit by bit. Saints such as Lidwina of Schiedam, whose bodies shed fragrant pieces, were an inversion on a more profound level of what was feared in leprosy. Bynum, *Holy Feast and Holy Fast*, pp. 116, 121, 124–28, 196, 211, 234, 273.

32. Hermann-Mascard, *Les Reliques des saints*, pp. 212–17, 313–19; Duparc, "Dilaceratio corporis."

33. See above, chapter 5, pp. 202, 209, 211–12.

34. Hallam, "Royal Burial and the Cult of Kingship," pp. 359–80.

35. In addition to the works cited in n. 25 above, see Charles Webster, "Alchemical and Paracelsian Medicine," in C. Webster, ed., *Health, Medicine, and Mortality in the Sixteenth Century* (Cambridge: Cambridge University Press, 1979), p. 302, and Bynum, *Holy Feast and Holy Fast*, pp. 196 and 274, on Baconian notions of bodily equilibrium as they affected old age, food intake, and excretion.

36. E. Brown, "Authority, Family, and the Dead."

urrection. Gervase of Mont St. Eloi and Godfrey of Fontaines, who opposed the *mos teutonicus*, had to agree. Like Boniface, they might prefer a scientific and philosophical theory of the cadaver that emphasized the slow fading of its form in decay, but they were forced to admit that God would restore that identical flesh and form when the trumpet sounds.[37]

Enthusiastic recourse to bodily partition at the very heart of a religion that denied, on the ontological level, that partition occurred at all; prurient fascination with torture and division in a culture that not only articulated opposition to these practices but also found innumerable euphemisms for them; efforts to lodge the identity of person in soul while continuing to assert an *inclinatio* in matter, a *forma corporeitatis*, and even an aerial body or somatomorphic expression for separated soul— these aspects of the late thirteenth century are profoundly contradictory. None however suggests either dualistic rejection of body or the equation of self with soul.[38] If assertion of wholeness replaced hope of reassemblage in the conception of resurrection in the early fourteenth century, it was because body had become so crucial to person that the line between form and matter, death and life, earth and eternity, fragment and whole, had almost disappeared.

Yet resurrection was not merely the assertion of wholeness. It was also the object of desire. Even to those schoolmen who imagined heaven as quiet and order, body was a beloved bride. Solomon told Dante the pilgrim that we yearn for body, not only for ourselves but also for those we love, in order that *they* may enjoy both God and their friends in the flesh and that *we* may thus delight in God and in them. By the late thirteenth century some mystics seemed to lodge desire not only before the resurrection in a soul that yearns for body as well as for God but also in a psychosomatic unity whose longing will not be sated for all eternity. From a yearning for flesh that retards or distracts the spirit to a hunger that is the deepest expression of a spiritual yet embodied self, imaginings of desire themselves changed. What had been merely a hint in Augustine became a deep ambivalence in Bernard and Bonaventure, a lyrical and sensual vision in Dante and Mechtild of Magdeburg. Great religious

37. E. Brown, "Death and the Human Body"; see also eadem, "Authority, Family, and the Dead."

38. Ackerman, "Debate of Body and Soul," p. 551, sees in the vernacular literature of the thirteenth century (more than in the Latin) an "unchristian and dangerous dualism," implied in the personification of Body as "an active principle of evil." But he also gives a good deal of evidence from the same treatises of love for the body and suggests, tellingly, that the debate form is adopted because of its "dramatic possibilities." It seems to me that we do not have here real "dualism" but rather a sense of self as psychosomatic unity—a self in which part can stand for whole and in which an imbalance between parts leads to evil.

writing was no less paradoxical in 1300 than it had been in 200, but the embodied self Marguerite of Oingt or Mechtild of Magdeburg imagined before God's throne found its deepest expression not (as Tertullian and Jerome had done) in incorruptible or impartible matter but in hungry and impassible love.

The body described by scholastic theologians (however tentatively and ambivalently) as bride, as gesture, as unfolding and overflow, was the body of mystics and courtly lovers. Behind the changing images I have described is the flood of affective expression that many of the greatest medievalists of the twentieth century (André Wilmart, C. S. Lewis, R. W. Southern, Jean Leclercq) have charted. I therefore turn in closing to new imaginings of body and desire in the devotional and mystical literature of the high Middle Ages.

Devotional Literature: Body as Locus of Experience and as Friend

Desire for God throbbed in religious poetry long before the thirteenth century.[39] Even before Augustine, hunger for a God who seeks the searcher was voiced in the psalms and the Neoplatonic prayers by which Augustine's prose was so deeply influenced.[40] However much the theologians of the thirteenth century might define blessedness as the stilling of desire, spiritual writers came increasingly to treat love as a longing that cannot be satiated or filled, magnifying itself forever as each increase of joy further stimulates need.[41] In the twelfth century, Bernard, stunned with grief for his dead brother, cried out: "Since love never comes to an end, you will not forget me forever."[42] Of God's love, he

39. On the flowering of affective expression from the eleventh century on, see André Wilmart, *Auteurs spirituels et textes dévots du moyen âge latin: Études d'histoire littéraire* (Paris: Bloud and Gay, 1932). For scholarship generally on affective spirituality, see Bynum, *Jesus as Mother*, pp. 4, 83–85.

40. Peter Brown, *Augustine of Hippo*, pp. 156–57 and 168–81; on the conception of desire in Augustine (and in Origen before him), see also McGinn, *Foundations of Mysticism*, pp. 144ff. and 310ff.

41. For a fascinating explanation of how the early fourteenth-century enthusiasm for quantification led to efforts to measure desire, see Joel Kaye, "Quantification of Quality." Kaye's analysis shows that schoolmen thought qualities such as desire or love could be represented in technical, mathematical terms as infinite and infinitely expanding. They were thus, in certain technical ways, in agreement with the mystics' understanding of desire as movement, not stasis. But this development really comes after the end of the story I am telling here.

42. Bernard of Clairvaux, sermon 26, in *Opera*, ed. Leclercq, Rochais, and Talbot, *Sermones super Cantica Canticorum*, vol. 1 (1957), p. 173; trans. Kilian Walsh, *The Works of Bernard of Clairvaux: On the Song of Songs* (Kalamazoo, Mich.: Cistercian Publications, 1971–80), vol. 2, p. 63. And see Astell, *Song of Songs*, pp. 127–35, for a

said: "To those who seek and long for the presence of God, memory is in the meanwhile and for the moment sweet, but it does not satisfy; rather it makes more intense the desire for that from which satisfaction comes."[43] A century later Hadewijch, writing of the paradoxes of divine love in the metaphors and rhythms of the secular love lyric, spoke of desire as "inseparable satiety and hunger"; "new assaults of love," she wrote, "[are] new hunger so vast that new love may devour new eternity!"[44]

Such love, however, was lodged in spirit; often it was a yearning to escape from body and earth. What is significant for the study of images of resurrection is the slow emergence not only of a yearning for body, fraught though it was with ambivalence, but also of an (equally ambivalent) sense of body as the locus of yearning for God. Both are background to the final cantos of Dante's *Divine Comedy*; both are particularly associated with devotional and mystical writings for and by women;[45] both suggest an interpretation of the late Middle Ages very different from the deeply learned but misguided charges of over-

---

sensitive analysis of desire in Bernard. She comments aptly (p. 133): "What [scholars] fail to understand is the degree to which both Bernard and the *Pearl* poet affirm the necessity of longing in the salvific process." The complex discussion of desire in Bernard's sermon *De conversione*, chap. 14, paragr. 27, argues basically that we should desire God because such desire (unlike earthly desires) will by definition be fulfilled. But the passage also states that this desire is more powerful than all other desires and at least hints, by quoting Ecclesiasticus 24.21, that the filling of such desire leads to its own increase. See *De conversione*, in *Opera*, vol. 4 (1966), pp. 101–2.

43. Bernard, *De diligendo Deo*, section 4, paragr. 11, in *Opera*, vol. 3 (1963), p. 127.

44. *Hadewijch: The Complete Works*, trans. Columba Hart (New York: Paulist Press, 1980), pp. 222–23.

45. On the embodied quality of women's spirituality, see my *Fragmentation and Redemption*, pp. 181–222 and 365–85; Karen Glente, "Mystikerinnenviten aus männlicher und weiblicher Sicht: Ein Vergleich zwischen Thomas von Cantimpré und Katherina von Unterlinden," in Peter Dinzelbacher and Dieter Bauer, eds., *Religiöse Frauenbewegung und mystische Frömmigkeit im Mittelalter* (Cologne and Vienna: Böhlau, 1988), pp. 251–64; Elizabeth A. Petroff, "Women's Bodies and the Experience of God in the Middle Ages," *Vox Benedictina* 8, no. 1 (1991): 91–115; and Danielle Régnier-Bohler, "Voix littéraires, voix mystiques," in *Histoire des femmes en occident*, ed. Duby and Perrot, vol. 2: *Le moyen âge*, ed. Klapisch-Zuber, pp. 443–500. I do not want to suggest that every female mystic located desire in the body (or stressed desire for body) the way Mechtild and Marguerite did; Hadewijch and Gertrude the Great, for example, wrote almost exclusively of the soul desiring God. Most female writers did, however, employ unusually sensual prose and manifest spiritual responses somatically; see Régnier-Bohler, "Voix littéraires," pp. 461, 485–99. On the tendency of men to associate somatic phenomena and bodily desire with women, see Bynum, *Holy Feast and Holy Fast*, pp. 94–149; on the background of such assumptions in misogyny, see Régnier-Bohler, "Voix littéraires," pp. 443–51, 464–70, 472–80.

wrought emotionalism and arid allegorical virtuosity leveled by the great Dutch historian Johan Huizinga.[46]

Devotional and mystical writing in the thirteenth century continued—as did art, hagiography, and miracle story—to associate body with decay. If not the "dangerous and unchristian dualism" Robert Ackerman has seen in it, such literature did give full voice to fear of aging and putrefaction.[47] It expressed anger at the drain on joy and courage humans often experience from hunger, sexual need, disease, pain, and the terror of death. The popular debates between personifications of Body and Soul gave detailed and revolting attention to the decay of the corpse, although, as a number of scholars have pointed out, they were psychomachias—virulent and polemical debates between components of a unitary self—in which Body (especially in the Latin versions) often made telling charges against Soul.[48] The *Ancrene Wisse,* written probably in the early thirteenth century for female recluses, spoke of the flesh as a privy hole, slime and stench, clods and mud, a "prison," a "torture-chamber," a "foreign country" for the soul.[49] In such texts, desire for body is often, at best, Augustine's *retardatio*—a necessary drag that distracts both embodied and separated soul from heaven. As the author of the *Ancrene Wisse* put it:

> This is one of the greatest marvels on earth: that the thing which is highest under God, that is, man's soul, as Augustine testifies, should be so closely united to the flesh, which is mere mud and dirty earth, and that, because of this union, she should love it so much that . . .

46. Johan Huizinga, *The Waning of the Middle Ages: A Study of the Forms of Life, Thought, and Art in France and the Netherlands in the XIVth and XVth Centuries,* trans. F. Hopman (1924; reprint Garden City: Doubleday, 1956).

47. See above, n. 38, and chapter 7, n. 9.

48. Heningham, "An Early Latin Debate of the Body and Soul"; Ackerman, "Debate of Body and Soul"; Marjorie M. Malvern, "An Earnest 'Monyscyon' and 'thinge Delectabyll' Realized Verbally and Visually in 'A Disputacion Betwyx the Body and Wormes,' A Middle English Poem Inspired by Tomb Art and Northern Spirituality," *Viator* 13 (1982): 415–43; Jacques Le Goff, "Corps et idéologie dans l'Occident médiéval: La Révolution corporelle," in *L'Imaginaire médiéval: Essais* (Paris: Gallimard, 1985), pp. 123–27; Zaleski, *Otherworld Journeys,* pp. 48–49. For a general discussion of this debate literature, see Francis Lee Utley, "Dialogues, Debates, and Catechisms," in *A Manual of Writings in Middle English:* vol. 3, ed. Albert Hartung (1975), pp. 691–96.

49. *Ancrene Riwle,* trans. M. B. Salu, pt. 3, pp. 62, 75; pt. 4, pp. 122–23; pt. 6, pp. 159–61. These passages, in strongly Pauline language, stress that the same body that here below is earth, rot, and the breeder of feces and maggots, will be glorious, light, and beautiful in heaven. In heaven we put off the "old flesh" or "garment" and don the new, which will shine "sevenfold brighter than the sun."

she ... angers her Maker. ... [But God did not want the soul to fall into pride, and so He has] tied a heavy clod of earth to [it], like a man hobbling a cow or any other animal that is likely to stray.[50]

Marveling that we love it so, this author describes body as a cherished "enemy."[51]

Yet even *retardatio* often receives in such texts a warmer, more affectionate treatment. The *Ancrene Wisse* speaks approvingly of four kinds of earthly love: between friends, between man and woman, between mother and child, between body and soul.

> The soul loves the body greatly, and this is clearly seen in their parting, for dear friends are sorry when they must separate. But Our Lord willingly separated His soul from His body in order to join ours together, world without end, in the happiness of heaven.

Indeed, we should never say that we love only the soul of another, not her body. For "the soul and the body are but one person, and ask for one judgment. Will you divide into two what God has joined together? [Matt. 29.6] He forbids this."[52] Literature of spiritual advice, like scholastic textbooks, uses marriage imagery to stress that body and spirit are bound together by tenderness, even passion, into "one flesh"; person is a psychosomatic unity.

Drawing on such ideas, Middle English devotional texts (for example, the *Castel off Loue* and the *Cursor Mundi* among others) regularly include descriptions of soul loving the body so tenderly that it lingers at death until all the senses are lost.[53] Such discussion explic-

---

50. Ibid., pt. 3, p. 62. The author then goes on to read Job 28.25 ("who madest a weight for the winds") as if it refers to the body, which he calls here "the heavy flesh which pulls the soul down." See also pt. 7, pp. 172–73.

51. Ibid., pt. 3, p. 61.

52. Quoted passages at ibid., pt. 7, pp. 172–75, especially p. 175, and pt. 4, pp. 81–2.

53. Robert Grosseteste (?), *Castel off Loue*, ed. Richard F. Weymouth (London: The Philological Society, 1864), p. 57, lines 1169–80; *The Pricke of Conscience (Stimulus Conscientiae): A Northumbrian Poem* ... [formerly attributed to Richard Rolle], ed. Richard Morris (Berlin: Ascher, 1863), pp. 227–28, lines 8443–68; *Cursor Mundi*, ed. Richard Morris, Early English Text Society 59 (London: Kegan, Paul, Trench, and Trübner, 1875), vol. 2, pt. 1, pp. 974–75, lines 17009–26 (probably borrowed from the *Castel*). On these works, see Robert R. Raymo, "Works of Religious and Philosophical Instruction," in *A Manual of Writings in Middle English*, vol. 7, ed. Albert Hartung (1986), pp. 2268–9, 2276–77 and 2337–38. For a detailed elaboration of the soul's love for the body and her reluctance to depart therefrom (expressed often in nuptial imagery), see *The Departing Soul's Address to the Body: A Fragment of a Semi-Saxon Poem*, ed. and trans. Thomas Phillipps and S. W. Singer (London: Luke James Hansard, 1845).

itly includes the idea (found also in Bonaventure's *Breviloquium*) that the more perfect flesh is, the more it experiences. Thus Christ's every sense was perfectly acute on the cross, and in its acuity of experience lay our salvation. Nor did his senses fade, gradually relinquishing his soul for its journey; rather his soul *chose* to depart from the flesh it loved and in which it manifested its love for his friends. There is a suggestion here of wonder that any soul—even God's—could bear to depart from such glorious flesh, unweakened and untainted by sin.[54]

In these descriptions, a new use of synecdoche throbs with enthusiasm for body and for all that to which body gives us access. Bodily part becomes body; body and soul become each other; body manifests self. The author of the *Ancrene Wisse* exclaims that, as St. Bernard tells us, Christ wept with every part of his body, not only his eyes.[55] As "people tie knots in their belts to remind them about things," so "Our Lord . . . puts marks of piercing in both His hands, to remind Him of us."[56] Body is no longer a prison (even a loved prison) in which self is housed until it can escape. It is rather a locus of self-expression: the marks of stigmata are not the results of torture or pain but the pledge—the dwelling-place—of friendship. As the thirteenth-century saint Christina *Mirabilis* supposedly said, body is our "beloved," our "best and sweetest . . . companion in the present sadness."[57]

None of this is irrelevant to resurrection; for the body we fear, love, and discipline on earth is—as Christina said—the body we will regain in heaven.[58] The author of the *Ancrene Wisse* asserted as confidently as Tertullian that the fasting and constraint we inflict on the flesh here will appear in the flesh we receive before the throne of God. The

54. On Bonaventure, see above, pp. 251–52. See also the lines from the *Castel off Loue* and the *Cursor Mundi* cited in n. 53 above, and *Ancrene Riwle*, pt. 2, p. 49–51, and pt. 7, p. 173.

55. *Ancrene Riwle*, pt. 2, p. 49, referring to Bernard, sermon 3 for Palm Sunday, in *Opera*, vol. 5 (1968), pp. 54–55: "Ubi quidem non solis oculis, sed quasi membris omnibus flevisse videtur, ut totum corpus eius, quod est Ecclesia, totius corporis lacrimis purgaretur."

56. *Ancrene Riwle*, pt. 7, p. 175.

57. "Now, O best and sweetest body . . . you will rest in the dust and will sleep for a little and then, when the trumpet blows, you will rise again purified of all corruptibility and you will be joined in eternal happiness with the soul you have had as a companion. . . ." *Life of Christina Mirabilis*, chap. 5, number 36, paragrs. 47–48, *Acta Sanctorum*, July, vol. 5, p. 658–59; trans. Margot H. King, *The Life of Christina Mirabilis* (Saskatoon: Peregrina, 1986), pp. 27–28. Elizabeth A. Petroff discusses this passage briefly but with characteristic insight in *Medieval Women's Visionary Literature*, p. 36. For a twelfth-century reference to body as brother, see Peter of Celle, *De disciplina claustrali*, chap. 23, cited above chapter 4, n. 10.

58. See above, n. 57, and *Fragmentation and Redemption*, pp. 236–37.

recluses advised in the *Ancrene Wisse* also expect transfiguration. Like Tertullian's martyrs, they will obtain in heaven reversal of the constraints of earth.[59] Lacerated here, they will be shining and whole in heaven; aging and putrefying here, they will "flower" before God; hidden in the anchorhold or even in the grave on earth, they will be in the resurrection "brighter than the sun," "lighter than the wind," "swift as a sunbeam."[60]

With homier images, warmer and more congenial rhythms, this prose speaks in entirely correct theological language of the "marriage gifts," or dowries, of the risen body.[61] As Albert, Thomas, and Robert Grosseteste agreed, our body will be *our* body when it rises, but it will be endowed with precisely the contrasts 1 Corinthians 15.42–44 was now taken to denote.[62] It will be "the same" and not "the same." Yet the *Ancrene Wisse,* and the devotional and mystical prose of the century and a half that followed, spoke not, as the schoolmen did, of *quies,* but of passionate, unquenchable, and infinite love.

Women Mystics and the Triumph of Desire

Writing in the closing years of the thirteenth century, two women mystics deeply influenced by secular love poetry, devotional literature, and contemporary theology foreshadowed the understanding of desire that flowers in the *Divine Comedy*. When the German beguine Mechtild of Magdeburg (d. ca. 1282) and the French nun Marguerite of Oingt (d. 1310) spoke of themselves, they spoke over and over again of "soul and body," profoundly anxious for the comfort of both.[63] When they saw other selves in visions of eternity, they saw separated soul embodied in its resurrection body—a body glimpsed (just as Dante glimpsed it) partly as a crystal reliquary, partly as an agile, yearning, sensual animal "swimming and flying" in God.

59. See above, chapter 1, pp. 40–43, 45–47.
60. *Ancrene Riwle*, pt. 2, pp. 41–42; pt. 3, pp. 62–63 and 72–75; pt. 6, pp. 159–61 and 165–66; pt. 7, p. 175. For "flowering" metaphors, see especially pt. 5, p. 150.
61. See, for example, ibid., pt. 2, p. 41.
62. Clear echoes of *"de dotibus"* exegesis can be found in ibid., pt. 2, pp. 39–42; pt. 3, pp. 61–63 and 72; pt. 6, pp. 161 and 166.
63. On Marguerite, see *Les Oeuvres de Marguerite*, ed. Duraffour, Gardette, and Durdilly; *The Writings of Margaret of Oingt: Medieval Prioress and Mystic*, trans. Renate Blumenfeld-Kosinski (Newburyport, Mass.: Focus Information Group, 1990); Bynum, *Holy Feast and Holy Fast*, pp. 249, 254, 265–66, 404 n. 31. On Mechtild, see n. 72 below.

Marguerite wrote of a vision in which she saw a book "like a beautiful mirror" and in it

> appeared a delightful place, which was so large that the whole world seems only a little thing by comparison. . . .
> . . . From there came so great a sweetness and such great comfort that the angels and the souls were satisfied by it to the point that they could not desire anything else . . . such a good odor . . . such a great embrace of love.[64]

But Marguerite went on to describe this sweetness not as finite and filling but as infinite, flowing out from God in thirst-quenching and thirst-inducing rivers that forever return:

> The saints will be completely within their Creator as the fish within the sea: they will drink to satiety, without getting tired and without in any way diminishing the water. . . . [T]hey will drink and eat the great sweetness of God. And the more they eat, the more their hunger will grow. And this sweetness cannot decrease any more or less than can the water of the sea.[65]

In a later passage, which describes Christ, Marguerite returns to the theme of hunger-inducing love: "He is the sweet electuary in which are all good savours. He is so good that those who taste him will be more hungry the more they receive, and they will not dare to desire anything other than the sweetness they feel flowing from him."[66]

When Marguerite received Jesus in a vision, she saw him in his risen and glorified body, still wounded but with wounds of shimmering light. It is almost impossible to read her description without thinking of the crystal reliquaries and monstrances ubiquitous in thirteenth- and four-teenth-century chapels.[67] But for all her imagery of glass and mirrors, the body Marguerite sees is not in repose. It flies and plays, tastes and yearns. Moreover, Marguerite assimilated to Christ's transparent and glowing body the bodies of the saints, who are his "members." In this vision, even her earthly sisters seem to be endowed with the dowries of

64. Marguerite, *Speculum*, chap. 2, paragrs. 16–17, in Duraffour, Gardette, and Durdilly ed., *Les Oeuvres de Marguerite*, pp. 95–96.

65. Ibid., chap. 2, paragr. 19, pp. 96–97.

66. Ibid., chap. 3, paragr. 31, pp. 100–1.

67. One is also reminded of resurrection iconography in which Christ's wounds project gold rays; see above, chapter 4, nn. 98 and 99.

agility, clarity, subtlety, and impassibility. Speaking of herself in the third person (as is common with mystics), Marguerite writes:

> She seemed to see Jesus Christ, so glorious that no human heart could conceive of him. He was clothed in the glorious garment which he took from the noble body of Our Lady. . . . From [his] glorious wounds poured forth a clarity so bright that one was astonished by it. . . . This glorious body was so noble and so transparent that one saw very clearly the soul inside of it. This body was so noble that one could see oneself there more clearly than in a mirror, . . . so beautiful that one saw the angels and the saints, as if they were painted on it. . . .
>
> Now imagine His great beauty, so great that He has granted to all the angels and all the saints who are his members, that they may be as clear [*clars*] as the sun. . . .
>
> . . . He has given to his friends an agility [*legereta*] so great that in an instant they can go wherever they wish. . . .
>
> . . .[H]e has made them so free, subtle and immaterial [*frans et si sustiz et si trapercans*] that they can enter and depart through closed doors, without any impediment, as Jesus Christ did after the resurrection.
>
> . . . [T]hey can never be sick, nor burdened, nor suffering, neither in soul nor in body.
>
> . . . He has made his friends of such noble matter that they can no longer corrupt nor grow old [*ne se porrent ja mais corrumpre, ne no porrent enveylir*], but they will live with him forever [*perdurablement*].[68]

It is not possible to say that such a complex passage refers to heaven or to earth, to now or to then, to soul and body here, to soul after death, or to soul embodied after resurrection.[69] The reference to passing through doors or moving in an instant is taken from technical discussions of the dowries of *subtilitas* and *agilitas*. The transparent body may, as Jeffrey Hamburger has suggested, reflect acquaintance with devo-

68. *Speculum*, chap. 3, paragrs. 24–34, pp. 98–101. It is important to note that in paragr. 40, pp. 102–03, she speaks of seeing God's face when our souls leave our bodies. She does thus sometimes use the category of "separated soul," and she seems aware that it would be dangerous to claim *visio Dei* in this life.

69. Danielle Régnier-Bohler's brilliant discussion of the sense of time in the language of female mystics, "Voix littéraires," p. 499, makes it clear that when language moves beyond time into eternity, it is not possible to tell whether one is before or after resurrection. See also Michel de Certeau, *La fable mystique: XVIe–XVIIe siècles* (Paris: Gallimard, 1982), pp. 243–45.

tional objects such as the Visitation Group as well as with reliquary monstrances; it is certainly an accurate use of theological texts on the *claritas* and *impassibilitas* of the body in glory.[70] The image of hungering for God was a commonplace with female mystics and drew on older Cistercian and Franciscan themes.[71] Strands not only of influence and history but also of meaning are inextricably entangled here. A schoolman who wanted to know when the beatific vision comes, what exactly it brings, and what the resurrection adds to blessedness could, in such words, find no precise answers (although he would find no heterodoxy either). But surely there shines through these paradoxes the conviction that self is an embodied self. Desire that is satisfied and yet never ceases is lodged in a body that God frees from sorrow—here, and in heaven, and after the resurrection. Indeed resurrection is hardly necessary to Marguerite, for resurrection is now.

A far greater visionary and spiritual writer than Marguerite, Mechtild of Magdeburg developed a conception of the resurrection body as glorious as Dante's. Herself suffering disease, isolation, and suspicion of heresy, Mechtild was no advocate of pain.[72] Pain is born in hell, not heaven, she argues; body is something that "flaps its wings" and distracts us, a "post or target at which people throw stones," a "beloved prison." Body must be redeemed in resurrection. "Slime" here below, it must be "remade as a beautiful robe," "formed and tempered."[73] In keeping with

70. Jeffrey Hamburger, "The Visual and the Visionary: The Image in Late Medieval Monastic Devotions," *Viator* 20 (1989): 161–82, especially p. 168, plate 3.

71. Bynum, *Holy Feast and Holy Fast*; Régnier-Bohler, "Voix littéraires," pp. 491–93.

72. For Mechtild's understanding of pain, see *Das fliessende Licht*, bk. 4, chap. 12, ed. Neumann, pp. 123–27; *Das Licht*, trans. Schmidt, pp. 189–90; *Revelations*, trans. Menzies, pp. 107–8. On Mechtild, see Jeanne Ancelet-Hustache, *Mechtilde de Magdeburg (1207–1282): Étude de psychologie religieuse* (Paris: H. Champion, 1926); Hans Tillmann, *Studien zum Dialog bei Mechtild von Magdeburg* (Gelnhausen: F. W. Kalbfleisch, 1933); Hans Neumann, "Problemata Mechtildiana," *Zeitschrift für deutsches Altertum und deutsche Literatur* 82 (1948/50): 143–72; idem, "Beiträge zur Textgeschichte des 'Fliessenden Lichts der Gottheit' und zur Lebensgeschichte Mechtilds von Magdeburg," *Altdeutsche und Altniederländische Mystik*, ed. Kurt Ruh (Darmstadt: Wissenschaftliche Buchgesellschaft, 1964), pp. 175–239; Kurt Ruh, "Beginenmystik: Hadewijch, Mechtild von Magdeburg, Marguerite Porete," *Zeitschrift für deutsches Altertum und deutsche Literatur* 106 (1977): 265–77; James C. Franklin, *Mystical Transformations: The Imagery of Liquids in the Works of Mechtild von Magdeburg* (Rutherford, N.J.: Fairleigh Dickinson University Press, 1978); Bynum, *Jesus as Mother*, pp. 228–47. On Mechtild's death date, see Neumann, "Beiträge," p. 229, and Howard, "The German Mystic Mechtild of Magdeburg," in Wilson, ed., *Women Writers*, p. 156.

73. *Das fliessende Licht*, bk. 2, chap. 24, ed. Neumann, pp. 58–62, trans. Schmidt, pp. 114–15, trans. Menzies, p. 54; *Das Licht*, bk. 4, chap. 18, ed. Neumann, pp. 132–

the story of John the Evangelist's bodily assumption in the *Golden Legend* and with Bernard's idea (questioned in the beatific vision controversy) that separated souls see Christ's humanity but wait until the resurrection for his divine face to be revealed, Mechtild thinks even the bodies of Christ, Mary, and John (although already in heaven) will be perfected after the Judgment.[74] Christ's wounds will only then heal into scars like rose petals. In an astonishing vision, Mechtild sees John's body in heaven, whole in every detail and unchangeable, like a crystal, but apparently asleep—"buried" she says—because there is no resurrection until the end of time.[75] We see in the mirror of heaven, she asserts, that we "have been formed soul and body and remain thus forever."[76] Our resurrection bodies will be "of human form," bearing in themselves the "godly flame" of the soul, which will shine through the body "as luminous gold shines through a clear crystal." Yet we will "leap and swim and fly and climb" in heaven, "clear and godly, gay and free."[77] The

---

35, trans. Schmidt, p. 196–99, trans. Menzies, pp. 112–15; *Das Licht*, bk. 6, chap. 38, ed. Neumann, p. 248, trans. Schmidt, p. 318, trans. Menzies, p. 201; *Das Licht*, bk. 7, chap. 65, ed. Neumann, pp. 310–11, trans. Schmidt, p. 401, trans. Menzies, p. 263.

74. Honorius Augustodunensis, *L'Elucidarium*, ed. Lefevre, bk. 3, q. 42, p. 455, speaks of John's bodily assumption. For the source of the legend and texts relating to it, see ibid., p. 178 n. 4.

75. *Das Licht*, bk. 2, chap. 3, ed. Neumann, pp. 39–41, trans. Schmidt, p. 89, trans. Menzies, p. 32; *Das Licht*, bk. 4, chap. 23, ed. Neumann, pp. 139–40, trans. Schmidt, p. 205, trans. Menzies, p. 118.

76. *Das Licht*, bk. 6, chap. 41, ed. Neumann, p. 250, trans. Schmidt, p. 320, trans. Menzies, p. 202; *Das Licht*, bk. 7, chap. 1, ed. Neumann, p. 257, trans. Schmidt, p. 327, trans. Menzies, p. 208. It is worth noting that when a story is told of Mechtild going to the grave of a friend, she is said to greet him there "both soul and body." And we are told that she "was in the habit of doing this." She then is said to celebrate a "feast" for him in her soul—a kind of spiritual funerary meal! See *Das Licht*, bk. 4, chap. 22, ed. Neumann, p. 138, trans. Schmidt, p. 203. In bk. 6, chap. 15, ed. Neumann, pp. 222–25, Mechtild has a vision of the martyrdom of the friars; she then speaks of Elias put to death by Antichrist and sees his soul received by God, although Antichrist prevents his body from receiving burial in order to cause Christians to abjure their faith. But all who see the body are so moved that they pray, and "the presence of this holy body so fills them with blessedness that they forget the cruelty of death and all earthly matters." These passages, which stress the importance of even the inanimate body to the "persons" of those we love or admire, make it clear that Mechtild tends to think of the self as embodied at all times, even when it is technically a separated soul.

It is also important that Mechtild refers to herself over and over again as "body and soul." In bk. 5, chap. 35, ed. Neumann, p. 196, trans. Schmidt, p. 267, where she thanks God with her "suffering body, outcast soul, sinful heart, sorrowful senses and whole being," she pleads that, at the end, she may receive God's "body" "as food for body and soul." She expresses a similar wish, for herself and others, in bk. 6, chap. 37, ed. Neumann, pp. 245–48. Once again the physicality of God and her own physicality as a means of response are emphasized.

77. *Das Licht*, bk. 7, chap. 1, ed. Neumann, pp. 254–58, trans. Schmidt, pp. 327–28, trans. Menzies, pp. 208–9. Compare the passage cited in n. 81 below, where exactly

selves of the resurrection "can go wherever they like—a thousand miles—as quickly as a man can think, but they will never come to the end of the golden streets of heaven."[78]

Unlike Marguerite, Mechtild separates now from then. A wall, thin but tough "like the shell of an egg," stands between earth and heaven, she says; bodies cannot pass through until the Day of Judgment.[79] Yet, in another sense Mechtild too breaches the wall. The slime and ordure we inhabit here on earth is a vehicle that carries us to heaven. "If he takes my body [in ecstasy], my soul belongs to him."[80] Even now, we lie "in the arms" of God.

> . . . and in [His] Triune-ness
> Soul and body fly and play,
> They romp according to their hearts' desire more
> and more
> And drink [there] like the fish of the sea.[81]

Body is *now* the access to God. Desire is *now*. Mechtild often writes as if both body and desire rise here, before death, into the eternal present of heaven. How hard it is then to bear that soul could be even for a moment in heaven without the body in which desire resides, the body whose suffering lifts the self to heaven. "When I think of death my soul rejoices . . . and I would die with great joy to come to the time of seeing God. . . . Yet I can say: I would like to live to the Last Judgment, and my longing grows for the time of the martyrs. . . . When I see my pain and suffering, my soul soars in such sweetness that my body soars too."[82]

Thus, when Mechtild says that her soul does not want to leave her body, she speaks not of fear of death, not of senses lingering around a corpse, not of the retarding of soul by its need to manage the wits and

---

the same metaphor is used. The image is also found in Marguerite of Oingt; see above, n. 65.

78. *Das Licht*, bk. 7, chap. 1, ed. Neumann, p. 257. In bk. 6, chap. 41, ed. Neumann, p. 250, Mechtild sees a mirror in heaven before the breast of each body and soul, and the Trinity is reflected in each mirror. Dante is not, therefore, the only thinker of the period who sees resurrected and glorified bodies in paradise before the general resurrection.

79. *Das Licht*, bk. 4, chap. 23, ed. Neumann, p. 140, trans. Schmidt, pp. 205–6, trans. Menzies, pp. 118–19.

80. *Das Licht*, bk. 3, chap. 3, ed. Neumann, p. 81, trans. Schmidt, p. 133, trans. Menzies, p. 70.

81. *Das Licht*, bk. 5, chap. 25, ed. Neumann, p. 185, trans. Schmidt, p. 253, trans. Menzies, p. 151.

82. *Das Licht*, bk. 6, chap. 26, ed. Neumann, pp. 234–35, trans. Schmidt, p. 306, trans. Menzies, p. 191 (with my changes).

organs, not even of the hope that flesh and decay will be redeemed in resurrection. Mechtild desires her body because desire is its own reward and body is the locus of desire. Separated soul yearns for body because it is in body that it yearns most fully for God.

There is something quaint and amusing, of course, in Mechtild's images of frolicking crystals, crystals with earthly and individual eyebrows, crystals that drink like the fish of the sea. Such language is puzzling as well. But behind, through, and in such images we find the confident assertion that body must rise. Body must rise because without it, we are not persons; we are not *our selves*. It is not our agility, our incorruptibility, or our eyebrows, that make us who we are; it is our love. We must be bodies as well as souls, because only embodied souls can fully love. If Mechtild agreed with Augustine that we *are* our desire, she nonetheless understood this desire, this weight of the heart, in a very different way. For Mechtild felt, as Augustine apparently never did, that desire must lodge in an embodied self.[83] Christ's promise to Mechtild was not only that she would be united again, soul and body, in heaven; it was also that "longing can never die."

At the turn of the fourteenth century, therefore, the fullest affirmation of bodily resurrection comes not in the words of the schoolmen but in the halting verses of an obscure and persecuted female mystic. I close my long survey of images of resurrection—images I have studied, glossed, and situated in so many ways—by quoting without any gloss at all Mechtild's powerful words.

> The Love of God lies on me. . . . And when I think that my body will be lost in death and I shall no longer be able to suffer for Jesus or to praise him, this is so heavy to me that I long, if it were possible, to live until Judgment Day. My love forces me to this. . . .
>
> And our Lord speaks in answer: "You must die. . . ."
>
> Alas, Lord, let my longing not die
> Even if I am not able any longer to gain anything
> with my body.
>
> Then our Lord replies: "Your longing will live, for it cannot die, because it is eternal. Let it yearn on until the end of time, when soul

83. There has been much discussion of Augustine's understanding of the resurrection body and the nature of desire, but commentators seem agreed that he does not find embodiment intrinsically necessary in order to experience the joys of *visio*; see Dewart, *Death and Resurrection*, pp. 164–88, and my discussion in chapter 2 above, nn. 135, 138, and 163.

and body will unite again. Then I shall establish [you] again, and you shall praise me forever. . . . You have wished thus to carry out for me all human suffering and all human service. I say again: your Being [*Wesen*] will endure until the Last Humans shall come."[84]

Epilogue

The promise of bodily resurrection—the promise, that is, that the very stuff of change and putrefaction can be lifted to impassibility and immutability while continuing itself—remained an oxymoron through all the centuries of the Middle Ages. Neither mystics such as Mechtild nor poets such as Dante, for all their genius, could solve the contradiction, not even by lifting it into the paradox of satisfied but insatiable desire.

Yet for all its incoherence and self-contradiction, the doctrine of resurrection has been of enormous consequence in shaping assumptions we still hold concerning personhood and survival. Much about our current Western notions of the individual has taproots in medieval discussions of the ontological significance of body. If we see the individual as unique—valued yet opaque and unknowable because (in the currently fashionable term) "other"—our assumption is informed by hundreds of years of puzzlement over embodiment. We in the 1990s—like medieval theologians, poets, and mystics—find it difficult to think that any survival that really counts could entail loss of those markers the body bears: sex, race, personal appearance, and so forth.[85] We find it hard to accept any future as "our own" unless it includes those experiences, whether of suffering or delight, that body makes possible. Like Mechtild, we lo-

84. *Das Licht*, bk. 6, chap. 15, ed. Neumann, p. 222, trans. Schmidt, pp. 290–91, trans. Menzies, p. 179 (with my changes). The "Last Humans" Mechtild refers to are Enoch and Elias, who will come at the end of time.

85. In saying this, I do not wish to eclipse the fact that medieval thinkers saw as "defects" to be erased certain marks such as skin color that would to us be necessary for "our individual personhood." Medieval theorists insisted that everything necessary to the perfection of *humanitas* as species would be reconstituted in each resurrected body; unfortunate color, such as that of "the Ethiopian," was to be cured. Our notions of "person" as "individual" include much more individual difference than do medieval notions. But even we operate with something like the medieval notion of the species "human." We wish for survival (or immortality) for a healed and "perfected" self; no one dreams of a future life (here or in heaven) in which AIDS, cancer, thalidomide-induced deformities, etc., remain. And in the medieval idea that the scars of the martyrs survive in heaven (although cured into "rose petals"), we find a quite astonishing commitment to self both as bodily and as individual. It was important to theologians of the thirteenth century that a nose be distinguishable from an eye in the afterlife and that martyrs retain on their bodies what they had undergone in life. See above chapter 6, n. 108.

cate desire in a psychosomatic entity, and the personal survival we hope for is not dissimilar to her notion of a longing that "can never die." Our technical arguments about identity—whether carried out by scientists who study artificial intelligence, sociologists who consider the implications of organ transplants, or philosophers who conduct thought experiments about what I think "I" really am—have not a little in common with the abstruse speculations of medieval theologians about what exactly must be reassembled at the end of time in order to constitute a "person."

Medieval debates over bodily resurrection involved more than theology and philosophy. Mystics, poets, hagiographers, sculptors, and tellers of folktales ruminated about what body could do, wherein lay its significance, how it might be redeemed. And theologians, like storytellers, expressed their concerns and concepts in images, analogies, and examples as much as in logic. Such images came not only from a fund of images inherited from the past; they came as well from daily experience. Storytellers and theologians alike feared death, buried the dead, and died themselves.

Today also, our deepest hopes and fears are betrayed in images. Indeed we may find our obsessions mirrored more vividly in an episode of *Star Trek, Max Headroom,* or *Quantum Leap* than in the philosophical disquisitions of a Derek Parfit or Bernard Williams.[86] Recent philosophy of mind, recognizing this, sometimes uses science fiction novels and film as the stuff of its investigations.[87] The dominant images of survival found in these products of popular culture are not, of course, statues and seeds but rather robots, teletransportation, and mind transplants. Much has changed since medieval ideas about embodiment were elaborated; it would not do to overstate the continuities although it is worth thinking about the fact that modern images (like medieval ones) stress reassemblage of parts more than change and flowering. It is also worth considering how far the stubborn clinging to mechanical images of body reconstitution, characteristic of the present moment, is both a reflection of a perduring fear of fertility and the female body that our current obsession with sexual expressiveness does not obviate and a response to

86. See above, "Introduction," nn. 27–28; and my *Fragmentation and Redemption,* pp. 244–53.

87. Some philosophers debate the advisability of this; see Derek Parfit, *Reasons and Persons* (Oxford: Clarendon Press, 1984), p. 200; and *Fragmentation and Redemption,* pp. 398–400 nn. 25 and 42.

recent changes in medical and computer technology that threaten long-standing notions of death and self.[88]

In closing, however, I wish to stress, not the method I have used in exploring medieval ideas and images nor the relevance of those ideas and images to specifically modern concerns, but the notion of bodily resurrection itself. For however absurd it seems—and some of the greatest theologians of the Western tradition have grappled with that absurdity—it is a concept of sublime courage and optimism.[89] It locates redemption there where ultimate horror also resides—in pain, mutilation, death, and decay. Whether or not any of the images and answers I have surveyed in this long book carries conviction, those who articulated them faced without flinching the most negative of all the consequences of embodiment: the fragmentation, slime, and stench of the grave. It was this stench and fragmentation they saw lifted to glory in resurrection. To make body crucial to personhood is to court the possibility that (to misquote Paul) victory is swallowed up in death. But if there is resurrection, then what is redeemed includes the fragments that concerned Tertullian and Athenagoras as well as the love for which Dante and Mechtild strove. We may not find their solutions plausible, but it is hard to feel that they got the problem wrong.

88. See above, "Introduction," at n. 24, where I point out how different are current assumptions and anxieties from those of late nineteenth-century psychologists, theologians, and theosophists, who tended to imagine and explore the afterlife in terms of disembodied spirits. On the implications of modern technology for conceptions of body, see Paul Rabinow, "Severing the Ties: Fragmentation and Dignity in Late Modernity," *Knowledge and Society: The Anthropology of Science and Technology* 9 (1992): 169–87.

89. For a contemporary echo, see John Updike, "Seven Stanzas at Easter," in *Telephone Poles and Other Poems*, number 72, cited in Paul Gooch, "Resurrection," p. 664:

> Make no mistake: if He rose at all
> it was as His body;
> if the cells' dissolution did not reverse, the
> molecules reknit, the amino acids rekindle,
> the Church will fall. . . .

And see the poems, each entitled "The Resurrection of the Body," by Linda Gregerson and Eric Pankey in *Poetry* 162 (April 1993): 14–15, 26.

General Index

If an item is referred to in text and note on the same page, only the page number is given. Biblical citations are indexed under "Bible" in the order used in the Vulgate.

Index of Secondary Authors

Editors and translators are not indexed unless they are also cited as authors.

Ackerman, Robert W., 281*n*9, 326*n*28, 328*n*38, 331
Aigrain, René, 312*n*120
Allen, Prudence, 255*n*105
Alston, Mary Niven, 322*n*12
Altenburger, Margarete, 63*n*12
Amann, E., 68*nn*34 and 36, 71*n*45
Ancelet-Hustache, Jeanne, 337*n*72
Angenendt, Arnold, 107*n*178
Arens, W., 112*n*190
Ariès, Philippe, 7*n*12, 53*n*132, 56*n*143, 106*n*175, 201*n*3, 203*n*9, 204*nn*13 and 15, 206*n*20, 326*nn*27 and 28
Arnheim, Rudolf, 306*n*101
Artelt, Walter, 322*n*12
Astell, Ann W., 164*n*27, 303*n*91, 329*n*42

Barker, Francis, 325*n*23
Barnard, L. W., 28*n*17, 30*n*27, 32*n*37, 56*n*143, 59*n*1, 65*n*17
Barnes, Timothy David, 35*n*54, 61*n*6

Barton, Carlin, 44*n*93, 45*n*95, 53*n*128
Barton, G. A., 47*n*106
Bataille, Georges, 45*n*95
Batany, Jean, 320*n*4
Bauer, J., 67*n*29
Bazan, Bernardo C., 259*n*118, 262*n*129
Becker, E. T., 292*n*45, 293*n*48
Bellamy, J. G., 324*n*20
Belting, Hans, 202*n*6, 306*n*102
Benton, John F., 140*n*69, 318*n*2
Bernard, A., 204*n*14
Bernstein, Alan E., 7*n*12, 280*n*2
Bethell, Denis, 207*n*21
Bett, Henry, 142*n*75, 146*n*94, 152*n*119, 153*nn*125, 127
Bevington, David, 307*nn*104, 105
Biller, P. P. A., 219*n*66
Billot, Louis, 90*n*116, 230*n*2
Bishop, Ian, 320*n*4
Bloch, R. Howard, 216*n*56
Boase, T. S. R., 118*n*3, 203*n*9, 205*n*16
Bonnardière, A.-M., 95*n*131, 96*n*134, 98*n*144

Illustration Credits

1. Herrad of Hohenbourg, *Hortus deliciarum*, ed. Rosalie Green et al., *Reconstruction* (London and Leiden: Warburg Institute/University of London and Brill, 1979), plate 93, p. 267; from BN Facs. Fol. 8 (xi), pl. 7, Avery Architectural and Fine Arts Library, Columbia University in the City of New York.

2. Herrad of Hohenbourg, *Hortus deliciarum*, ed. Rosalie Green et al., *Reconstruction* (London and Leiden: Warburg Institute/University of London and Brill, 1979), plate 141, p. 427; from BN Cabinet des Etampes Ad. 144.a. Fol., pl. 107a, Bibliothèque nationale, Paris.

3. Herrad of Hohenbourg, *Hortus deliciarum*, ed. Rosalie Green et al., *Reconstruction* (London and Leiden: Warburg Institute/University of London and Brill, 1979), plate 146, p. 439; from BN Facs. Fol. 8 (xi), pl. 20, Avery Architectural and Fine Arts Library, Columbia University in the City of New York.

4. Photo by Brepols.

5. Alinari/Art Resources, New York.

6. Alinari/Art Resource, New York.

7. Bibliothèque nationale, Paris.

8. Staatsbibliothek zu Berlin-Preussischer Kulturbesitz.

9. Staats- und Universitätsbibliotek, Hamburg, "Carl von Ossietzky."

10. Victoria and Albert Museum, London.

11. Bodleian Library, Oxford.

12. The British Library.

13. Bodleian Library, Oxford.

14. Bayerische Staatsbibliothek, Munich.

15. Hirmer Verlag, Munich.

16. Courtesy of John J. Yiannias.

17. Stiftsbibliothek, Melk.

18. Universitätsbibliothek, Munich.

19. The Metropolitan Museum of Art, Gift of J. Pierpont Morgan, 1917 (17.50.520).

20. Foto Strenger, Osnabrück.

21. Erzbischöfliches Diözesanmuseum, Cologne.

22. The Metropolitan Museum of Art, Gift of J. Pierpont Morgan, 1917 (17.190.520).

23. Copyright 1994 ARS, New York/SPADEM, Paris.

24. Alinari/Art Resource, New York.

25/26. Alinari/Art Resource, New York.

27. Hirmer Verlag, Munich.

28. Master and Fellows of Trinity College, Cambridge University.

29. *Visions of Tondal*, Getty MS 30, fol. 13v, attributed to Simon Marmion (illuminator) and David Aubert (scribe), 1474; Collection of the J. Paul Getty Museum, Malibu, California.

30. *Visions of Tondal*, Getty MS 30, fol. 17, attributed to Simon Marmion (illuminator) and David Aubert (scribe), 1474; Collection of the J. Paul Getty Museum, Malibu, California.

31. Alinari/Art Resource, New York.

32. The Pierpont Morgan Library, New York.

33. Hirmer Verlag, Munich.

34. Biblioteca Estense, Modena.

35. Bibliothèque nationale, Paris.

36. Bibliothèque nationale, Paris.

Ornaments drawn by Lisa Force

Designer:	Teresa Bonner
Text:	Trump Medieval
Compositor:	Impressions
Printer:	Edwards Brothers
Binder:	Edwards Brothers